PARENTS & TEENAGERS

JAY KESLER

WITH RONALD A. BEERS

VICTOR BOOKS a division of SP Publications, Inc.

WHEATON, ILLINOIS 60187

Offices also in
Whitby, Ontario, Canada
Amersham-on-the-Hill, Bucks, England

Third printing, 1984

Bible quotations in this book are from: the *King James Version* (KJV); the *New American Standard Bible* (NASB), © 1960, 1962, 1963, 1968, 1971, 1972, 1973, 1975, 1977 by the Lockman Foundation; the *Holy Bible: New International Version* (NIV), © 1978 by the New York International Bible Society and used by permission of Zondervan Bible Publishers; the *New King James Version* (NKJV), © 1979, 1980, 1982 by Thomas Nelson, Inc., Publishers; *The New Testament in Modern English* (PH), © 1972 by J. B. Phillips and used by permission of the Macmillan Publishing Co. and Collins Publishers; and *The Living Bible* (TLB), © 1971 by Tyndale House Publishers, Wheaton, Illinois. Used by permission.

Recommended Dewey Decimal Classification: 155.5
Suggested Subject Heading: ADOLESCENCE

Library of Congress Catalog Card Number: 84-50234
ISBN: 0-88207-817-8

CONTENTS

CHAPTER 3 • The Risks of Raising Teenagers

CHAPTER 4 • Responsibilities of Fathers and Mothers

CHAPTER 5 • Getting Personal about Parents

SECTION 2
WHAT YOU SHOULD KNOW ABOUT TEENAGERS

CHAPTER 6 • What Makes Teens Tick?

CHAPTER 7 • Identifying Teen Needs and Behavior

CHAPTER 8 • Understanding Teens' Attitudes and Emotions

SECTION 3
UNIFYING YOUR FAMILY

CHAPTER 16 • How to Help the Church Help Your Teenager

SECTION 5
BALANCING FREEDOM AND CONTROL

CHAPTER 17 • Managing the Home with Love and Authority

SECTION 6
HEALING BROKEN RELATIONSHIPS

CHAPTER 21 • When the Family Splits Up

CHAPTER 22 • When the Family Falls Apart

CHAPTER 23 • When the Family Faces Crisis

CHAPTER 24 • When the Family Runs Into the Law

SECTION 7
HANDLING EVERYDAY CONFLICTS

CHAPTER 25 • Teenagers at Home

CHAPTER 26 • Teenagers and Temptation:
How to Evaluate Outside Influences

CHAPTER 30 • Teenagers at Work

CHAPTER 31 • Teenagers at College

CONTRIBUTORS

Larry Anderson
Executive Director
Ft. Lauderdale Youth for Christ
Ft. Lauderdale, Florida

Dr. Bruce B. Barton
Vice President, Ministry Services
Youth for Christ/USA
Wheaton, Illinois

Clayton R. Baumann
Executive Director
North Area Youth for Christ
Wheeling, Illinois

Dr. V. Gilbert Beers
Editor, *Christianity Today*
Wheaton, Illinois

Dr. B. Clayton Bell
Pastor, Highland Park Presbyterian Church
Dallas, Texas

Gary D. Bennett
Director of Social Services
Teen Ranch
Marlette, Michigan

Dr. William R. Bright
President, Campus Crusade for Christ Int'l
San Bernardino, California

Dr. D. Ross Campbell, M.D.
Child and Adult Psychiatry
D. Ross Campbell, M.D. & Associates
Signal Mountain, Tennessee

Dr. Anthony Campolo, Jr.
Professor and Chairman
Department of Sociology
Eastern College
St. Davids, Pennsylvania

Rev. Glandion Carney
Director of Urban Ministries
World Vision
Monrovia, California

Mrs. Evelyn Christenson
Evelyn Christenson Ministries
St. Paul, Minnesota

Rev. Larry Christenson
Director, Int'l Lutheran Renewal Center
St. Paul, Minnesota

Al Cocannouer
Executive Director
Greater Houston Youth for Christ
Houston, Texas

Rev. and Mrs. C. Donald Cole (Naomi)
Radio Pastor, Moody Broadcasting Network
Speaker
Lombard, Illinois

Dr. Gary R. Collins
Professor of Psychology
Trinity Evangelical Divinity School
Deerfield, Illinois

Mr. and Mrs. James Conway (Sally)
Professors, Talbot Theological Seminary
Mid-Life Dimensions
Fullerton, California

Jack Crabtree
Executive Director
Long Island Youth for Christ
Dix Hills, New York

Gary Dausey
Executive Vice President
Youth for Christ/USA
Wheaton, Illinois

David Coulson Dayton
Crisis Intervention Counselor
Long Island Youth for Christ
Dix Hills, New York

Mr. and Mrs. Arthur W. Deyo (Lois)
Executive Director
Greater Columbus Youth for Christ
Columbus, Ohio

Dr. James Dobson
Associate Clinical Professor of Pediatrics
Univ. of Southern California School of Medicine
Focus on the Family
Arcadia, California

Galen R. Dolby
Youth Guidance Director
Elkhart County Youth for Christ
Elkhart, Indiana

Byron D. Emmert
Youth for Christ Special Representative
Mountain Lake, Minnesota

Rick L. Englert
Executive Director
Greater Holland Youth for Christ
Holland, Michigan

Dr. Ted W. Engstrom
President, World Vision
Monrovia, California

Rev. Leighton Ford
Associate Evangelist
Billy Graham Evangelistic Association
Charlotte, North Carolina

Dr. James C. Galvin
National Training Director
Youth for Christ/USA
Wheaton, Illinois

Dr. Kenneth O. Gangel
Professor and Chairman
Department of Christian Education
Dallas Theological Seminary
Dallas, Texas

C. Wayne George
Executive Director
Greater Greensboro Youth for Christ
Greensboro, North Carolina

Dr. Richard C. Halverson
Chaplain, United States Senate
Washington, D.C.

Dr. Howard G. Hendricks
Professor of Christian Education
Dallas Theological Seminary
Dallas, Texas

Harvey H. Hook
Youth Guidance Director
Greater Columbus Youth for Christ
Columbus, Ohio

Rev. David Howard
General Secretary
World Evangelical Fellowship
Wheaton, Illinois

Rev. Ronald P. Hutchcraft
Executive Director
Metropolitan Youth for Christ
Wayne, New Jersey

Dr. Jay Kesler
President, Youth for Christ/USA
Wheaton, Illinois

Dr. Grace Ketterman, M.D.
Practicing Child Psychiatrist
Kansas City, Missouri

Mr. and Mrs. Larry D. Kreider (Susan)
National Director, Youth for Christ/USA
Wheaton, Illinois

Mrs. Joyce Landorf
Joyce Landorf Ministries
Solana Beach, California

D. Bruce Lockerbie
Dean of Faculty
The Stony Brook School
Stony Brook, New York

Timothy Joe Loewen
Youth Guidance Director
Mid-Valley Youth for Christ
Salem, Oregon

Rev. Gordon MacDonald
Pastor, Grace Chapel
Lexington, Massachusetts

Rev. and Mrs. David Mains (Karen)
Director, The Chapel of the Air
Wheaton, Illinois

Donald I. Mardock
Regional Field Director, Northern States Region
Youth for Christ/USA
Minneapolis, Minnesota

Josh McDowell
Josh McDowell Ministry
Campus Crusade for Christ
Richardson, Texas

Dr. David L. McKenna
President, Asbury Theological Seminary
Wilmore, Kentucky

Gordon R. McLean
Youth Guidance Director
Metro Chicago Youth for Christ
Wheaton, Illinois

Gregory A. Monaco
Youth Guidance Director
North Area Youth for Christ
Wheeling, Illinois

Thomas L. Morris
Youth Guidance Director
San Gabriel and Pomona Valley Youth for Christ
Covina, California

Harold Myra
President and Publisher
Christianity Today, Inc.
Wheaton, Illinois

LaVonne Neff
Freelance Writer and Editor
Downers Grove, Illinois

Dr. Howard Newsom
Clinical Psychologist
Professor of Christian Education
Azusa Pacific University
Azusa, California

Dr. and Mrs. Raymond Ortlund (Anne)
Renewal Ministries
Newport Beach, California

Rev. John Perkins
Founder and President Emeritus
Voice of Calvary Ministries
Pasadena, California

Thomas B. Perski
Family Counselor
North Area Youth for Christ
Wheeling, Illinois

J. Allan Petersen
President, Family Concern
Morrison, Colorado

David D. Rahn
Campus Life Director
Fort Wayne Area Youth for Christ
Fort Wayne, Indiana

Dr. Lawrence O. Richards
Christian Writer's Workshop
East Lansing, Michigan

Rev. Adrian Rogers
Pastor, Bellevue Baptist Church
Memphis, Tennessee

Dan L. Sartin
Executive Director
Greater Mid-South Youth for Christ
Memphis, Tennessee

Marshall Shelley
Associate Editor
Leadership Journal
Wheaton, Illinois

Janice R. Short
Executive Director
McLean County Youth for Christ
Bloomington, Illinois

Peter D. Sjoblom
Campus Life Director
Metro Chicago Youth for Christ
Wheaton, Illinois

Timothy J. Skrivan
Youth Guidance Director
Tacoma Area Youth for Christ
Tacoma, Washington

Dwight H. Spotts
National Youth Guidance Director
Youth for Christ/USA
Wheaton, Illinois

Dr. Barry St. Clair
Director, Reach Out Ministries
Avondale Estates, Georgia

O'Ann Steere
Assistant to the President for Public Relations
Youth for Christ/USA
Wheaton, Illinois

Christie A. Stonecipher
Youth Guidance Director
North Area Youth for Christ
Wheeling, Illinois

J. Scott Susong
Pastor, Quail Valley Community Church
Missouri City, Texas

Dr. Charles R. Swindoll
Pastor, First Evangelical Free Church
Insight for Living
Fullerton, California

David R. Veerman
Executive Director
Southeast Louisiana Youth for Christ
National Campus Life Consultant
Covington, Louisiana

John W. Whitehead
Attorney at Law
The Rutherford Institute
Manassas, Virginia

Dr. Warren W. Wiersbe
Associate Bible Teacher
Back to the Bible Broadcast
Lincoln, Nebraska

Dr. H. Norman Wright
Director, Christian Marriage Enrichment
Santa Ana, California

General Editor
Dr. Jay Kesler

Editorial Director
Ronald A. Beers

Special Editors
Greg D. Clouse
Ann Himmelberger Wald
LaVonne Neff
Marshall Shelley
Stanton D. Campbell
Pamela T. Campbell
Janet Ryker Burrell
Roy Irving
Marty Williams
Cindy Atoji
Linda Stafford
John Duckworth
Don Crawford
Daniel Pawley

Special Consultants
Pamela Barden
Bruce B. Barton
Clayton R. Baumann
James C. Galvin
Claudia Gerwin
Marty Grasley
Gordon R. McLean
Gregory A. Monaco
Peter D. Sjoblom
Linda Taylor
David R. Veerman
Neil Wilson

FOREWORD

Out of the thousands of books published each year, only a handful deserve the label "important." This is certainly one of that handful.

Young people have always had growing pains, but today the problems are often deeper, more intense, and more complex. Suddenly teenagers—and their parents—find themselves facing a host of problems that were seldom encountered a generation or so ago. Teenagers are searching for identity, meaning in life, purpose, direction. Buffeted by a host of pressures from their peers and their society, they're rewriting the scripts of their lives, headed in a multitude of directions—and often running into serious trouble in the process.

Why is this so? I am convinced the basic answer lies in the rapid and severe erosion of family life today. The family is one of the most fundamental means God uses to communicate with us and shape us. In this modern information age, we know that when communication lines are broken, confusion results. Likewise, when the family breaks down, confusion and chaos are inevitable. God's pattern for the family becomes twisted and distorted.

How can this tragic breakdown be reversed? That is the subject of this book. It deals thoroughly yet readably with the challenges that face parents and teenagers today and examines the practical steps that can be taken to meet those challenges. It is by far the most comprehensive and helpful treatment I have seen of this subject, and every mother or father who reads it will be much better equipped to be an effective and loving parent. I am confident it will become a valuable family resource that will be consulted again and again.

Why is this book such a trusted resource? One reason will be found by examining the Table of Contents. I doubt if a single topic of any significance has been omitted; virtually every question and problem that teenagers and their parents are likely to encounter is treated here. In addition, take a moment to scan the list of those men and women who have contributed to this volume. They are people who have come to be trusted for their firm convictions and godly lives. They also are people with wide experience and wisdom—psychologists, psychiatrists, youth specialists, counselors, pastors, and teachers. Most important, they are parents who believe in the priority of the family and have seen what works and what doesn't. They have dedicated their lives to helping others discover God's blueprint for the family, and in this book they share their insights with you.

It is especially fitting that Youth for Christ developed this book. As a Christian organization with decades of experience working with youth and their families, Youth for Christ has always had a knack for zeroing in on the heart of a vital issue. They know the issues that are facing teenagers today, and they know how to deal with them in practical and time-tested ways.

In this book you can find the courage to sit down with your children and talk frankly about tough problems. You can learn how to cope with crisis and how to help your teens apply their faith to everyday life. You will learn the art of discipline, the joy of healthy communication, the importance of self-esteem, and the rewards of family life.

But there is one thing this book will not do for you—it will not apply for you what you read between its covers. That only you can do, with God's help. And when you do, both you and your family will be enriched beyond measure.

Billy Graham

WHERE DO YOU BEGIN?

Checking Up on the Health of Your Family

- What do all families need to be healthy?
- How to look objectively at your family to discover its strengths and weaknesses
- What not to expect from your family

- Are the teen years really the most difficult?
- Where do parents begin in building strong family relationships?
- It's not too late to develop a plan for raising your teens

Meeting the Challenges of Adolescence

Are the Teen Years Really the Most Difficult?

RAY & ANNE ORTLUND

We parents go along for years in a comfortable parent-child relationship, the one we've always known, and then suddenly—when the kid is about twelve, about to enter junior high—everything changes. It's a crisis point, the beginning of the move into adulthood. It's a challenge we've never had before, so we ourselves have to behave differently as well as relate differently to our child.

Our children's teen years were—and are—difficult for us. We've often thought that when children are very young, parents can be young too—mentally and emotionally. But when the children are teenagers, the parents have to grow up. They are going to go into deeper waters than they have ever been in before. To be

mature enough to handle these kids, they have to ask God for new depths. We had three teenagers at once—they were each a year apart—which was a handful. We used to say to our kids, "Hey, be patient—we've never had teenagers before."

There are a lot of relational pressures when you're raising teenagers. Our son, Bud, now himself a father of four, was like a great big baby bird eager to get out of the nest. He wanted to go, but he was not quite ready, and it was a constant struggle to know when to release and when to hold back. Just because it was a struggle, though, didn't mean that the situation was unhealthy or that we could have avoided it if we'd been smarter. It's very important for the baby birds to get out of the nest, and immediately before they leave there is going to be awkwardness. If they stayed really secure and comfortable in the nest, feeling just as protected as when they were three years old, they would never get out. We'd end up with a live-in adult child unable to become independent. So these awkward times are very important to get the young adult ready to leave home.

There are also space pressures. Especially if you have more than one teen, your house is likely to be full of bodies. It usually isn't big enough to hold all of them. Suddenly your little ones have grown long arms and legs, and they spend most of their time in the kitchen. It's fun, but it does mean that the house is crowded. We know. We moved into one little parsonage when our children were three, four, and five, and left when they were ten, eleven, and twelve. It was a great little house—but we really felt the difference in space.

And time pressures are never greater. The kids begin to go their own ways. They begin to miss meals, grabbing something as they go off here and there. They go to school early and stay late for sports. It may become impossible to have regular family devotions. Ours went by the wayside. We grabbed the kids when we could for Bible reading and prayer, but we were no longer able to hold to a regular time. We still have times, more evenings than not, when we either go to our teenager Nels' bedside or he comes to ours, and we pray together briefly. If structured family devotions are no longer possible, you rely on the feeding you gave in earlier years—but you still catch them every time you can.

Another pressure of having adolescents is simply the cost of everything they need and want. They're wearing adult clothes, and those aren't cheap. Just sending a young person off on a church retreat in the wintertime costs "megabucks." Added financial pressures can put a strain on families.

The teen years are a hard time for the parents' marriage too. There is a lot of joy and fun with teenagers, yet they are

"WHY I LOVE THE TEEN YEARS"

The teenage years have by far been our favorite years. I love them! I've never had more fun than I've had with our teenagers. It's a delight. In fact, if I had my way, I'd start them out as teenagers.

I've got two kids who were really easy to raise and two who were a real challenge. The reason we had such a great time is because we learned some of the right things to do when the kids were young. Then when they grew up, those early lessons stuck with them. That's not to say we didn't have our frustrations.

When kids grow up, they can talk with you on a level that's so much better than the "goo-goo" of the toddler years. I'm amazed that more parents don't take advantage of the opportunity to just talk with their teens.

Unlike young children, teens can take responsibility. You can motivate them and they can reach achievements. You can see potential and watch it bud. That gets me jazzed out of my socks!

I'm so thrilled with the teenage years, and I want to tell all the prophets of doom who say, "Just wait until your kids are teenagers—you'll hate it": I've never hated a day of it! I'm sorry that kind of bad press gets around.

Frequently, the problem is insecure and undisciplined parents. I've yet to see a really superb teen who doesn't, somewhere behind the lines, have a grandparent or parent or uncle or pastor who's modeling the right stuff. Teens can easily pick up on a good example.

Look forward eagerly toward the time when your children are teens, and when they reach that stage, enjoy it!

Charles R. Swindoll

testing the limits and you have to make so many decisions about discipline. You won't always agree with each other. When our three older children were in their teens, it seemed as if every time Ray wanted to be tender, Anne wanted to be tough—and vice versa! Sometimes it feels like teens just suck the emotional life out of you.

Adolescents have plenty of pressures of their own. They have to cope with braces, acne, hormonal and emotional changes, and simply growing too fast. They often feel unaccepted by others. They wonder what is wrong with them.

Parental expectations can make the teen years difficult too. Ray played football, and expected our sons to play football like he did or better. Parents so often want their children to do better than they did. Our ambitions for them cause pressures that they shouldn't have to face.

The person you understood when he was a child may become incomprehensible as an adolescent. So many times teenagers seem brash, especially to their parents. They act like they think they know it all. Then it's tempting to try to reduce them to size in one smashing verbal blow. But that's the first way to cut off communication. Our son, Bud, once said, after Ray had given him one of his edicts, "The wisdom of the universe has just spoken." He said it in good humor, but Ray later recalled, "It was a slam I needed." We have to learn to listen to our teenagers.

There are ways to relate well to teenagers. A key to understanding your teens is to become interested in their world. Find out what they're thinking about in school. Discuss "hot topics" at the dinner table, but if you debate them, do it in the right way. Have fun with your discussions, letting the kids know that you're listening, that you respect their opinions, that differences of opinion do not have to be put-downs.

Another way to make the teen years

less difficult is to support the children in making their own decisions. Gideon's story in Judges 6 is a good example of a wise father. Gideon wanted to respond to the Lord, but he was afraid of what his parents might think. When he obeyed God anyway, he shocked the whole town. But verse 31 tells us that Gideon's father defended him against them all. What a wonderful thing for a father to do—to take his son seriously! And in Judges 8:18 we read that each of the children in Gideon's family had the bearing of a prince. That was probably because Gideon's father didn't keep treating his children like eight-year-olds. He began to respect them; he released them to grow up.

The teen years will be much better if we maintain a good sense of humor, not laughing at the children but with them and maybe at ourselves. It never hurts to be able to joke with their friends and have fun with them too. And it's so important to let kids come into your house.

Another way we keep the peace is to make sure that our schedules are known and that we schedule some time to be together. We're continually having to say, "OK, what's on your schedule for today?" so we don't miss each other. We don't want our son to think we don't care about him, but we have to struggle to get meals together, to find time to be together, to have fun together. After thirty-two years of pastoring, we are now traveling and speaking fifteen days out of each month—so for us, especially, fellowship at home is very precious.

Nels is our last child at home now. He's nineteen, has a full freshman load at college, works thirty hours a week, and is also learning to fly a plane, so his schedule is very full. So those fifteen days of the month when we're home, clearing time to be with Nels is a high priority. Before we leave the house each morning, we talk about when we can spend time together. "Can we see you for a bite of lunch?"—he has a lunch break at work—"or will you be home for dinner tonight?" We got him a datebook and have worked on getting him to schedule us into his day just like we want him to be a part of ours. Our appointment books have to include our teenagers. They have to know they have access to us at any time. And it's just as important for parents to let their children know where they are as for teenagers to keep their parents posted.

It's stretching to have teenagers. It helps us grow up, because we're forced to enter a world that is unfamiliar, sometimes uncomfortable. We have to begin to back off and treat them as friends. We have to let them go, knowing that we cannot follow. And we have to keep our goal in mind—to help them develop into mature, godly adults.

Yes, the teen years are difficult! But it will help us to understand that they are *necessarily* difficult, to a degree, in order to prepare parents and children for the soon-coming separation.

One of our friends who's raised terrific children said laughingly to us once, "God's timing is perfect. Just about the time you have to let them go, you come to realize your nerves are saying it's really OK after all!"

Building Family Relationships: Where Do You Begin?

RICHARD C. HALVERSON

As a young pastor I learned the hard way that relationships have priority over everything else. Every evening I went home and reported my daily events to my wife, Doris, thinking that this would make her more a part of my life. I would say, "We've been doing this," and "We're meeting with so and so." One evening my wife quietly said to me, "When you say *we,* you don't mean *us.*"

Her statement of fact hit me like a ton of bricks. I began to reflect on my life as a husband and father. I hadn't given my marital and family relationships much consideration—they were supposed to develop automatically, weren't they?

After forty years of marriage I am still learning that next to my relationship with Christ, my relationships to my wife and children are more important than my relationship to any institution. *After* my family come my fellow associates in the work to which God has called me and the unbelieving world. There's nothing more important than relationships. Everything else is secondary.

I failed a great deal as a young husband and father. As an ambitious young pastor I was concerned with being all that God wanted me to be, which resulted in devoting far too many hours to my ministry with no time off. After a number of years, I began to realize that Doris and my children were secondary in my life. Doris was running her own life; she had no connection with me except for our marriage. I justified the neglect of my family on the basis that I was serving the Lord. But I was really just busy with church work.

As I began to rebuild my family relationships, I went through a gradual readjustment in my thoughts and actions. I began to see that in neglecting my responsibilities to my wife and children I had dishonored God. I had no less right to

22

fail my family than I had my congregation.

In Ephesians 1:9-10, Paul tells us that God's plan for the fullness of time is to unite all things in Christ. In other words, reconciliation in relationships is God's agenda, His program in history. In a time when the whole world is threatened by thermonuclear war, the antithesis of that war is peace or good relationships. Self-alienation from God or alienation from others is the greatest sin. Relationships are never negotiable; we must make them work out.

Reconciliation means treating alienation as intolerable. In the Sermon on the Mount, Jesus said, "If you bring your gift to the altar, and there remember that your brother has something against you . . . first be reconciled to your brother, and then come and offer your gift" (Matt. 5:23, NKJV). In other words, Jesus is saying, "Don't substitute worship of Me for reconciliation with your brother—that comes first."

I believe there are three major keys to building strong family relationships. *First,* treat the relationship seriously by giving it priority. If I am to be involved in God's agenda or program of reconciliation, then I must assume responsibility for getting people together, not dividing them.

Second, treat alienation as intolerable. Once you realize alienation exists, deal with it as quickly as possible. Go to the person on a one-to-one basis as Jesus teaches in Matthew 18:15. Whether you are the offender or the offended, *you* must take the initiative, under orders from Christ, to heal the relationship.

One of the little principles that I live by is to never retire at night with any unresolved problems between my wife or children and me. Many times I've had to ask their forgiveness. "I'm sorry, will you forgive me?" are very hard words, but I'm not too proud to say them. I think it's extremely important for parents to acknowledge failure to children, especially in relationships.

Third, strive for an effective family altar. The family should meet on a regular basis to listen to each other. We have to remember that our children's problems, though perhaps trivial, are just as important to them as our own, and should be treated as such. Family members should report their joys and hurts, pray for each other, and work at loving reconciliation.

If I were starting my family life over again, I would give first priority to my wife and children, not to my work. I believe this is what God wants. Genesis 2:24 says, "A man shall leave his father and mother, and shall cleave to his wife" (NASB). In Ephesians 5:25, Paul goes further to say, "Husbands, love your wives, just as Christ also loved the

TWELVE WORDS THAT CHANGED OUR HOME

We tried to teach our kids twelve words, not by lecturing them, but by using them ourselves frequently and unconsciously.

Please and *thank you* were the first three. Treat family members like people, not like employees or machines.

And then, *I'm sorry.* It's hard for parents to say, but if children hear us say it often to each other and to them, they'll catch on that we're human.

Then, *I love you.* These words, when spoken honestly and sincerely, can never be overused.

And finally, *I'm praying for you.* Our children knew we prayed for them. And they prayed for us as we shared prayer requests with them. If I was going out of town and it was going to be a difficult trip, they felt a part of it.

Warren W. Wiersbe

church" (NASB). There is nothing more important than the parental relationship except the marital relationship. And that marriage is to be filled with an uncondi- tional, sacrificial, totally selfless love which is developed gradually—not automatically.

It's Time for a Checkup

Evaluating the Health of Your Family

HOWARD G. HENDRICKS

Health is not determined by the absence of sickness but by the presence of wellness. Many parents feel they have done a good job if their children have not become hooked on drugs, involved in sex, or become juvenile delinquents.

But informed parents need to have much higher goals. I want my children to make an impact on their society. I want them to determine and do the will of God for their lives. I want them to reach their maximum potential.

So when we talk about evaluating health, we're looking at the positive qualities present in our families, not merely at the negative qualities that are absent.

Unfortunately, most research focuses on the sick family rather than on the healthy one. But excellent research has also been done on the traits of a healthy family.

In sifting through this material, my wife, Jeanne, and I have come up with eight descriptive characteristics of a healthy family. Obviously no family has all eight traits. But the more a family has, the healthier it is likely to be.

First, a healthy family is a *caring* family. It is a community of concerned people who assume unlimited liability for each other, who reach out to one another and build bridges instead of walls.

This may seem an obvious characteristic, but it is easy for family members to become so involved in their own activities

that they stop caring about the rest of the family.

Second, a healthy family is a *respectful* family. Family members have high regard for each other's uniqueness, and as a result, they are free to be open and honest. Many families claim they are open but what they mean by that is that the children can say whatever they want to say *provided* the parents agree.

Third, a healthy family is a *convictional* family. The family is committed to a strong central value system. There is never any doubt on the part of family members that they stand for honesty, loyalty, and integrity. Furthermore, it is not assumed that everyone knows what to do and why. Values are presented, explained, and discussed.

Not only does a healthy family have a strong central value system, but the values are practiced consistently. If values are going to be passed on to others, they *must* be consistent.

Fourth, a healthy family is a *flexible* family. It's free to change as the demands of society impinge on it. A family is flexible when the parents are working together as a team. There is a willingness to admit mistakes, instead of taking an irrational stand and spending the rest of their parenting days trying to defend it.

Flexibility develops when there is an appropriate distribution of power in the home. Though the father emerges with ultimate responsibility, he *is not* to set

24

himself up as a dictator and he *is not* to make all the decisions.

Fifth, a healthy family is *expressive*. This is different from caring—essentially *what* I do *for* others. Expression conveys the idea of *how* I respond *to* others, which includes feelings of warmth, affection, openness, and understanding. There is less conflict, and therefore more freedom to be oneself—freedom to fail, to make mistakes, to disagree, to laugh.

Sixth, a healthy family is a *responsible* family. Family members accept responsibility, and lines of communication are kept clear. In a responsible family, parents are constantly preparing their children for the time when they leave home. Then when the children do leave, the psychological umbilical cord has already been severed. Many parents are guilty of emotional incest. They get a grip on their kids and won't let go.

Seventh, a healthy family is an *initiating* family. A high level of initiative

---

CHECKLIST FOR A HEALTHY FAMILY

A healthy family is: 1. *Caring*. Do you build bridges instead of walls? 2. *Respectful*. Are people free to express their own opinions? 3. *Convictional*. Is your family committed to a central value system? 4. *Flexible*. Are you willing to change the rules? 5. *Expressive*. Do you respond warmly to those in your family? 6. *Responsible*. Does each family member have some responsibility? 7. *Initiating*. Is your family involved in outside activities, both apart and as a family? 8. *Realistic*. Do you see your family as others do?

Howard G. Hendricks

---

and energy shows in many interests, people coming and going, travel, and a variety of constructive activity.

The family is involved in a growing, biblically oriented church, in maintaining community ties, and is meaningfully involved in the school. Many people think they have a good family when in actuality it is sick because it's turned in on itself. However, a family must be balanced to the point where family members are able to spend time together.

Family activities should be done both as a group and as individuals. Togetherness activities establish unity. Activities done separately establish individuality and distinctiveness.

Eighth, a healthy family is a *realistic* family. Realistic families see themselves as others see them. They don't have their heads in the sand, but are aware of what is going on in the world around them. They look at themselves objectively.

Biblical Standards

In addition to, and complementing these characteristics of a healthy family are what I call biblical values and standards. Scripture provides the divine yardstick. We have to trust God not only for the product, but also for the process.

I use Proverbs 3:5-6 as an example of this: "Trust in the Lord with all your heart and lean not on your own understanding; in all your ways acknowledge Him, and He will make your paths straight" (NIV). "Yes, I'm trusting God," people often say, "but look what happens." But the problem is that most of us trust God for the product but not for the process. We need to trust God to show us how to rear our children, as well as to trust Him with the end result.

We pray, "Lord, help my children turn out well." But often we don't stop to ask God to give us the wisdom day by day to accomplish that objective, so we know how to relate to our children, how to model ourselves before them, and how to participate in the process.

Parents provide examples for children —both positive and negative. The secret is to teach our children to respond to our positive examples, not our negative ones.

We all tend to rationalize by saying, "Well, that's just me. I'm not that bad; everyone has their problems." But children pick up our bad examples. While we can't be perfect, we can admit our shortcomings to our children. In fact, children can learn some of their greatest lessons from our mistakes. When, for example, a child knows one of his parents has a short fuse, and the parent admits it and asks the child to forgive him and help him overcome it, then there is no harm. At times, admission of failure and asking forgiveness may be necessary to keep the family healthy.

Targeting Your Family's Strengths and Weaknesses

HOWARD G. HENDRICKS

Sometimes our desire for simple solutions prevents us from seeing problems clearly. Parents often attempt to pour every kid into the same mold. We need to be sensitive to the individuality and uniqueness of each child. Jeanne and I have four kids, two girls and two boys, and no two of them are alike. You name it, they are different. Fortunately, with some counsel, I caught on early not to treat them alike.

Our own shortsightedness can also prevent us from seeing problems. Sometimes our partner can see our mistakes easier than we can. My father was a military man and his whole approach to discipline in the home was action, i.e., swift physical punishment. Since a parent usually learns to do what was done unto him, I repeated my father's pattern.

I can still remember the day when my wife couldn't hold back her hurt any longer and tears started rolling down her face. We went off to the bedroom and she said, "Sweetheart, do you really think striking the children is accomplishing your objective?" For the first time in my life I came to grips with my behavior and realized that I wasn't doing what I wanted. So I had to think through some alternatives.

When targeting problems, realize that what makes the Christian home different is not the absence of problems or conflict, but the presence of a problem solver within. This takes parents off the hot seat. It is all right to have problems.

If you read about the eight characteristics of a healthy family earlier in this chapter, you may have thought, "We don't have them, therefore we're dead in the water." The reality is that none of us have all of them. But we can have tremendous reassurance nevertheless because we have Christ, *the* problem solver, who can help us with the consequences of our mistakes. Besides, these characteristics are only a yardstick to know what direction to move in. If you don't know the goal, you obviously are not going to move toward it.

Open communication also facilitates uncovering problems. Everyone needs to have an opportunity to share. Everyone has the responsibility to listen. We had

26

very few rules in our family, but one was that everybody got to talk and everyone had to listen when someone else talked. Periodically we'd check and say, "OK Barb, what did Bill say?" And if she couldn't come up with it, we would ask Bill to run it by us again.

Don't ignore warning signs. For instance, if a kid is very withdrawn, or very inept socially, it may be an isolated instance. If so, discuss it with the child and pray about it. Every kid goes through that phase at one time or another, but if it becomes a pattern, parents need to explore the situation before it becomes so serious that it takes intensive therapy to get the child out of it.

Preferably, the parents should seek help early for an emotionally hurting child. Most parents wait too long to get professional help. There aren't really any *specific* warning signals, but parents can confer and when both agree that the child needs help, then they ought to seek it. It's better to err by going early rather than hoping the problem will go away.

Another way to target family problems is by reading good literature, keeping informed by attending seminars, and talking with other parents who have been down the road.

Determining Family Strengths
Your family's strengths can be discovered three ways. First is periodic evaluation by the entire family. We used to do this in a time we called family council.

Many families have a council but it is usually for something negative. As a result, they focus on what is wrong with the family. The family council needs to be slanted more toward the positive, toward what is right about the family, toward its assets.

Sometimes it can be hard to focus on the positive if you have a negative mindset. One thing you can do to overcome this negative attitude is to sit down and write the three greatest strengths of your family.

Second, choose three things you would change about your family if you could. Here you will be dealing with your family's weak points but you will be doing so in a constructive way, understanding that these drawbacks won't necessarily always be there.

Exposure to other families, both stronger and weaker, better and worse, can also help you see your strengths. A study was done where the researchers categorized families into excellent

GOOD PARENTING: IN TWO WORDS

Good parenting can be summed up in two words: unselfishness and servanthood. Unfortunately, authentic unselfishness and authentic servanthood seem to be the exception, rather than the rule.

The interesting thing is that those same two words perfectly describe Jesus Christ. He was the epitome of unselfishness and servanthood. And what an example!

It's hard to put the needs of your kids above your own needs. It's hard to serve your family. It's hard to say no to something you long to do or yes to something you'd rather not do.

But Jesus Christ made the supreme sacrifice. Our heavenly Father was willing to give everything—even His own being—for us, His children. When we focus on His example, it puts our day-to-day decisions in a different light.

Concentrate on being unselfish and having a servant's heart. Continue the heritage your heavenly Father began and pass it on to your children.

Charles R. Swindoll

families and disaster families. They discovered that the disaster families had no idea that other kinds of families existed. They assumed everybody's family was just like theirs.

This was true of me. When I went to Wheaton College, it was the first time I was exposed to kids who came from intact families. I used to watch them talk to their parents when their folks visited the campus and it would blow me away. I had never seen this before. I had always assumed that everybody's family was like mine—arguing and generally tearing each other down.

Exposure to a variety of families can be accomplished in several ways. One is by inviting other families into your home. Another is by involvement in community activities, like PTA and continuing education. Block parties also stimulate interaction and provide an eye-opening experience to see what other families are like.

What Do You Really Want from Your Teenager?

Developing Realistic Expectations

ANTHONY CAMPOLO, JR.

It's unfortunate that, to a large degree, family expectations are tied to the social setting in which the parents live. Parents had better recognize that. Your child does not exist to establish your identity with your peers. If that is your expectation, you'd better get off it right away, because your kid is more than likely going to rebel against it.

When a child does not go to college and the parents are upset, is it because the child is not getting an education or because the parents are not able to look good in the eyes of their associates? I live in a wealthy suburb of Philadelphia, mainly because our college is located there. It is intriguing to see how many parents are anxious to get their kids into the right schools so they can drop the names of those schools to their peers. The same theme is seen in athletics. Little League has become more of a status symbol for parents than for their children.

Parents using kids for their own gratification is not new. Farmers in an agrarian society once expected their children to become economically productive to help make the family wealthy.

Today children are squeezed on all sides to conform—on one side is the media establishing values, and on another, the parents' associates. The kids don't even feel they are being asked to conform to *their parents'* values, but to the values of their parents' friends and associates.

The most realistic expectation in a parent-child relationship is this: parents should expect their children to be persons who love them and persons who love others. Both parents and children receive healthy gratification from such relationships. Love relationships are the *only* reason the family exists. Families have lost their economic functions.

Unfortunately, I would say that such love relationships are a distinct minority—probably less than fifty percent—in Christian families today.

Setting the Climate

Parents are responsible for setting a climate conducive to true love relationships with their kids. One of the most important things is for parents to become tremendous listeners—not passive listeners, but the kind of intense listeners that enable kids to communicate their values to their parents. Then parents know what the kids are talking about and how their values are being formed. Such listening will earn your kids' respect and deepen their love for you.

It is important to allow the kids to *lovingly* criticize you. I'm not talking about negative "rip-down" when they pick on you as they scream down from upstairs, but healthy, loving insight.

My son is on me very heavily because of my distortions in speaking. One day he told me, "You know, Dad, in some of your sermon illustrations, you distort. You tell stories in such a grand way. But they never happen as grandly and as wonderfully as you make them happen. You've got to watch that because it really raises questions about your credibility."

Well, I had to sit back and say, "Son, you're right. I think that most preachers distort, and we need to be called to repent of that." Now that my son is traveling with me and hearing the messages I deliver, I know the ball game's up when it comes to my exaggerating.

My daughter is very conscious of the way I talk to my wife and very sensitive to feminist issues. At times I talk and act in ways that incarnate male chauvinism. Then my daughter becomes a very loving critic and calls me to responsible

---

EXPECT THE BEST—
BUT DON'T DO IT FOR THEM

When I was a wrestling coach there was one thing I always told my team, and it was this: "I don't care if every man on this team loses, as long as each one of you gives a 100 percent effort." I really meant that. If a wrestler gave his very best and still walked off the mat with a loss, it really didn't bother me. All I wanted was that 100 percent effort.

I would occasionally talk to my sons in athletic terms, comparing myself to a coach, and I would tell them exactly what I had told my wrestlers. What I expected from my teens was that they give the best they had, and always commit themselves to that goal. Then, regardless of how things worked out, we both would have the satisfaction that they had given it their all.

An approach parents can use if their teen is a Christian is to tell the teen that whatever he does, he should do it knowing that God is going to see the results. When dealing with a teen who is not a Christian, parents can at least encourage their teen to be responsible to himself by making something of his life.

I also told my teens that a coach can teach and train and show a wrestler what to do, but there comes a time when the athlete has to get out on the mat, and do the job on his own.

As a father, I can teach my children, train them, and show them what they ought to do. I can give them a game plan, so to speak. But they have to get out into life and do it on their own. Realistically, I can expect my teens to do the best they can—but I can't do it for them.

David Howard

change.

At those points of criticism by my children, I have a sense that they are saying something to me that neither my wife nor I would be conscious of otherwise.

Another way of establishing relationships is for parents to have special days—not just hours—with their kids, other than birthdays. You might say, "Bart, tomorrow is your day. What can we do that you would really enjoy doing?" Maybe it will be going to a movie, a ball game, cleaning the car, or listening to rock music. But do it with him.

We expect our kids to be available to us when we want them to do something. Let's also be available to our kids.

Do You Have a Plan for the Teen Years?

KENNETH O. GANGEL

When a child hits the teen years, it's easy for parents to push the panic button. Just remember, children are often just as nervous about becoming teenagers as parents are about raising them. Both children and parents need to *prepare* for adolescence in order for a smooth transition to take place. By developing an advance plan for parenting during the teen years, you will feel more relaxed and in control when the time comes.

As parents, we prepare our children for adolescence by the way we anticipate the teenage years. In Western cultures we are schooled to believe that being a teen is the next thing to entering the valley of the shadow of death. Our responses and attitudes to this philosophy have a direct bearing on a child's understanding of this period of time.

Be careful to avoid making a self-fulfilling prophecy of catastrophe, crisis, and problems. It's easy to believe the tales of woe, get all hyped up, and watch your blood pressure rise. Some parents, by getting set for the worst during the teen years, actually bring it on themselves.

The concept of "teenager" is not yet fifty years old. People didn't even speak of "teens" before 1941. Yet parents have read and heard and seen so much that they create a negative self-fulfilling atmosphere for their adolescent children.

It is imperative that we move into the teen years just as normally as we move into any other era. Welcome the teen years with anticipation, excitement, and a positive thrust for what lies ahead.

When a child turns thirteen, don't scare him right off the bat. Some parents begin the era by explaining all the problems. Dialogue such as, "Let's sit down and have a serious talk about drugs and sex," can scare the child as much as the parents. It's almost like saying, "You'll get into trouble in the next five years—we expect it to happen and it will."

Try, instead, to prepare the child by saying, "Hey, welcome to the teen years! We all went through it and it's a great time. You'll have some great experiences. God will greatly bless you during these years." Pray with your child, thanking the Lord for allowing him to have lived that long and for the things that will happen in the years ahead.

At the same time, be on the alert for physical, social, emotional, and psychological changes during adolescence.

These changes can tip you off to the fact that adjustments and mid-course corrections may need to be made. Deal with things as they surface, rather than creating a long list of "problems to expect." Your attitude can really make a difference.

Parents can also prepare their preteens for adolescence by beginning early on to avoid some of the common causes of problems. First, parents should decide to *avoid criticism* of their children. One of the major causes of parent-teen problems is undue criticism and harassment. So often teens rebel because parents hassle them about hair, music, friends, and many other things. This critical attitude can break a child's spirit.

Second, *guard against disrespect* from your children. This is the kind of problem that parents let build for twelve years before a child becomes a teen. Parents need to teach their children responsibility in a society of irresponsibility, a society which idolizes the free spirit. Disrespect can surface in an obvious way during the teen years. If children aren't taught to respect authority, and parents in particular, it won't be "caught" as they round the bend to adolescence.

Third, *avoid an inadequate self-concept* in your teen. Peer pressure is so great in the teen years that any self-concept problems that have been brewing are going to break out. Parents need to be alert to these problems.

I firmly believe that whatever happens during the teen years is a direct product of what parents have been doing for the twelve years prior. If a child has learned obedience and respect for authority, the teen years will offer few problems, except for greater pressure exerted on him to disrespect and test freedom and independence. Visible and verbal controls in the home will help enforce continued obedience, and can be evidenced in such areas as curfews, bedtime, and homework completion.

Another area in which parents can help a preteen prepare for adolescence is the *spiritual realm.* While a child grows from total dependence on his parents to relative independence, his walk with the Lord grows just the other way.

A fifteen-year-old, for example, is more "independently dependent" on God than he was at age nine. Parents can help encourage a child's walk with the Lord by emphasizing and adding new spiritual responsibilities.

To do this, *parents must be good models.* Trite as it may sound, I can't imagine why a fifteen-year-old son would want to be dependent on God when his forty-year-old father doesn't appear to be dependent on God. Likewise, when a mother seems to get along fine without an obvious constant dependence on God, why would her thirteen-year-old daughter care to worry about that type of thing? Modeling is essential.

Our children learn in three ways: (1) experience, (2) modeling, and (3) instruction. Experience is the normal day-by-day things that happen in a family, lending themselves to "teachable" moments. Perhaps this is the most important way that children learn.

For example, if a teen comes home and says, "Mom, I need to buy this jacket for school. Everyone has one; it's got the school emblem; and I can wear it to sporting events." Let's say it costs $25. Now in today's affluent society, Christian parents are prone to give in, feeling lucky that the teen isn't taking drugs.

But this would be a good time to say, "Why don't we ask the Lord about this? Let's ask Him to make available $25 so you can buy that jacket." The day-by-day experiences are constant opportunities to show how walking with the Lord differs from walking with the world.

I remember when our son's dog died and the enormous spiritual experience of helping my fourteen-year-old through that event.

We came home from church, and the dog had literally hung himself by jumping out of the window and hanging on a chain our son had placed around the dog's neck three hours earlier. The guilt problems for our son lasted for days.

But we used that opportunity to draw near to the reality of how much worse it would have been had one of the family members been the one to die. It may seem trite to think of the death of an animal, but when you're living in the trenches of that kind of situation, it's the most important thing in the world to a boy. A lesson in the school of experience is not soon forgotten.

The second way children learn is by modeling. Don't expect children to walk around saying, "I'm watching you, Mom or Dad." But realize that they are.

The third way children learn is by instruction. By instruction, I mean specifically sitting down with the child and saying, "Hey, we need to talk about this. There's a value choice here." For example, if a teen says he can't go to church on Sunday night because he has homework to do, the parents and teen need to evaluate priorities together.

Just as parents need to prepare teens for adolescence, parents need to prepare *themselves* for parenting during this time. To begin with, parents need to ask themselves what needs of teenagers can best be met in a family context.

Obviously, we probably won't care to teach our teens computer literacy, advanced geometry, or chemistry. Some things are best delegated to other experts during the teen years.

But there are some things for which God expects parents to be responsible, because they are best done within the climate of the family. For instance, parents need to deal with the constant changes that happen during the teen years—physical, biological, and attitudinal. These changes affect other areas of life beside the family, including school, friends, church, and job; but, essentially, change needs to be dealt with in the family.

When families don't help teens deal with changes, either the teen never deals with the issues and becomes maladjusted, or the teen turns to the wrong sources

THE RIGHT FORMULA
FOR THE FAMILY

Albert Einstein spent the last thirty years of his life in a gallant attempt to formulate a unifying theory that would explain all dimensions of physics, but he never succeeded. Likewise, I doubt if the human personality will ever be reduced to a single understanding. We are far too complex to be simplified in that way. From another perspective, however, there is one "formula" that applies to all human relationships, and of course I'm referring to the four-letter word, *love.* Conflicts seem to dissolve when people live according to 1 Corinthians 13 (avoiding boastfulness, irritability, envy, jealousy, selfishness, impatience, rudeness, etc.). The ultimate prescription for harmonious living is contained in that one chapter, and I doubt if any new "discovery" will ever improve on it.

James Dobson

From *Dr. Dobson Answers Your Questions,* by James Dobson, Tyndale House Publishers, Inc., © 1982. Used by permission.

for dealing with his problems.

Another example is the kind of authority and control that is necessary to curb rebellion and lawlessness in general. Pastors, teachers, and policemen shouldn't have to provide constant controls on teenagers. Teens from Christian homes should be learning values as children that continue on during the teen years.

Love and security needs are still enormously important to the teen. Neither schools nor peer groups can provide a genuine atmosphere of love and security. That kind of emotional therapy exists within the family.

As parents, we need to be constantly developing deeper and deeper friendships with our children. And that is based on good communication patterns. I really believe that our twenty-three-year-old son is my best friend. Our twenty-year-old daughter is my wife's best friend.

This too is a cultivated thing that must begin early in life. Parents must break through the barriers of peer pressure in order to spend time with adolescents. Make it a priority and stick to it. Make an extra effort to cultivate warm relationships with family members.

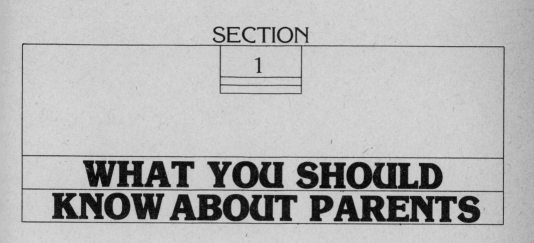

SECTION 1

WHAT YOU SHOULD KNOW ABOUT PARENTS

YOUR ROLE AS A PARENT

- What are parents really supposed to do?
- How much do parents really affect their children?
- What does God expect of me as I raise my teenager?
- Are there any rewards of being a parent?
- Just what must we sacrifice to raise our children?
- You can cherish family life
- Understanding yourself as a parent: Why do you react to your kids the way you do?

Parenting is both a process and a program. Learning to enjoy the discovery and challenge of each phase of our children's development is a continual process. Achieving our eventual goal, our children's independence, requires a well-thought-out program.

As parents, we are always working our way out of a job. We are preparing our children to stand on their own feet, no longer dependent on us. Both the process and the program of parenting present us with great psychological and personal challenges. But there is a comforting and encouraging side to being a parent—knowing that parenthood is God's idea. God does not ask us to do something we can't do.

What Can You Do for Your Children?

How to Be a Positive Influence

GORDON MacDONALD

I'm convinced that almost ninety percent of a child's character development is set before the age of eight or nine. In fact, my experience has been that parents' influence in their child's teen years is mostly by reinforcement of what has been taught before, not by establishment of new values.

The tragedy is that it's not until the teen years that most parents wake up to the fact that they haven't done an adequate job of raising their children. Suddenly they begin to realize that they're going to have to play a lot of catch-up. They find that many of the contributions, positive or negative, made in the first ten years are very hard to reverse. Like cement, they are firmly set in place.

Parents *can* have influence during the teen years, if several things are done before the boy or girl reaches puberty. The most important thing is to have good, basic communication in a nonjudgmental atmosphere. Teens need to feel free to express themselves and to know that what they say is not going to be held against them.

The teen years are more a period of experience than a time period. It's a time when young people deal with four major transitions in life. The first transition is *physiological*. Teens are moving from dealing with a child's body to an adult's body. The teen years are marked dramatically with the coming to life of certain glands and hormones, which have a very dramatic effect on the behavior, moods, and attitudes of the teenager. That must not be overlooked.

The second major transition is *social*. This is a period of time when a child moves away from the family environment and begins to develop peer relationships which may have equal or greater force than that of the family. Peer influence tends to be greater if the early childhood years have not been a good bonding period.

The third transition is *spiritual*. The young person begins to move away from the faith of his parents, and to establish an independent faith basis in terms of his own spiritual perceptions.

The fourth transition is the young person's growing awareness of *specific skills* that indicate what contributions he can make to society.

Because of these transitions, the teenager is bouncing back and forth between childhood and adulthood. On any given day, at any given moment, he is either more a child or more an adult. This creates enormous role conflict. For example, when the teenager is at home, he is likely to feel more like a child than an adult because he is around his parents. When he is away from his parents, he feels more like an adult. His whole sense of personal identity is in a shifting state for five to eight years. Parents who don't understand this have a real problem.

Physical Factors

Almost all parents have had the experience of seeing their teenager sit for an hour or two just staring out into space, doing absolutely nothing. He looks out the window, listens to music, and doesn't move an inch. Of course, the adult reaction is generally the same. "How can you waste so much time?" "The lawn needs to be cut." "Why aren't you out looking for a job?" In other words, "Do something productive!"

How a teen uses (or abuses) his time can create tremendous pressure and tension between him and his parents. But the fact that he sits there for an hour may be more of a commentary on what his hormones are doing. In puberty, the glands are very irregular. One moment those glands may be pulsating in a way

---

PREVENTIVE MEDICINE

Preventive medicine is always the best kind of medicine. The early training we give our children is so powerful. The life that parents lead at home in the early years is going to determine how that child's questioning time at age sixteen or seventeen will turn out. What parents *do,* and not what they *say,* will be vitally important as to how fast the teen comes back, or how severe the questioning is. For single parents, or parents who became Christians after their children were young, there is no need to despair. God seems to do a special work of grace.

Parents are not their children's only input. God can use a Sunday School or public school teacher, even one of your children's friends. Peer group input is very powerful. So if you blew it, acknowledge it, but don't underestimate God's ability to bring someone else into your children's lives who will have an input that you couldn't have, and perhaps turn them back to the Lord.

Joyce Landorf

that leads to dramatic amounts of energy. The next moment they may be under-secreting and causing emotional apathy. Parents find it easy to interpret this as laziness. The teenager responds, "I'm not lazy." The potential for conflict is high because the players in this little drama have two totally different interpretations as to what the behavior means.

When our son sometimes behaved this way, I tried to be careful how I handled the situation. I didn't make accusations and I didn't accuse him of wasting time *by my scale of values.* I might have kidded him a bit, but I didn't make a big deal out of it. I think this was one way we let him know that we accepted him as he was.

We saw a similar tendency in our fifteen-year-old daughter. One minute she could put on high heels, a bit of makeup, and her mother's dress; the next moment she could be with a couple of her friends and giggle for three hours, nonstop, over nothing. That silly giggling made me angry, but my wife constantly reminded me that our daughter was *both* a girl and a woman at the same time. Sometimes I had to accept her as a girl and other times as a woman. If I had insisted on one role and didn't recognize the other, I would have shut out a whole half of her life.

Parents of a younger teenager need to recognize that their child, in effect, is really two different persons. They have to constantly decode who they're relating to at that moment and treat him as such. Let me give you some examples of this in the social area.

Social Development
One of the things that we found very important was to begin to confront our preteen children with certain principles by which we intended to run the family during their adolescent years. I told both Mark and Kristi, when they were ten and twelve, "Now, look, you are going to discover rather quickly that some of your friends are going to start dating. And for us, a date is when you pair off with a member of the opposite sex for a specifically defined activity. I want you to know that I have no intention of you doing any formal dating until you are sixteen. You have a few years to go through before you get to that moment. So when kids at school ask you to do things, don't ever commit yourselves until you have checked with me. I'm not going to give in to the blackmail of 'Daddy, I already said yes and they'll laugh at me if I back down.' "

There were moments, especially for our daughter at ages thirteen and fourteen, when this was a hard principle to handle because a number of her peers were dating. Occasionally she would come home and try to get around the rule, but quickly found out that I was in no mood to compromise. However, the time came—at age 15½—when I suspended the rule and permitted her to date. Because she was more mature, she was able to really get her act together in terms of her self-esteem. She still had some good girlfriends, and established a proper concept of male relationships as well. We have never had a problem with either of our kids going through a time when they went from one member of the opposite sex to another. They really got through the dating game quite well.

And the reason *we* got through, unlike some other parents, was because we set the rules *long before* the process of socialization began. Our kids went into the period without wondering what the rules were. I think many parents fail to do that. They get well into the ball game and then realize that they are behind in terms of establishing an understanding with their kids about rules. Then they have to play catch-up. Every time they make a judgment, their kids will say, "Well, last month you let me do that." Fortunately, we never had to play catch-up at all. We set the rules for socialization.

Another rule that I set earlier in the game was that 11 P.M. was *always* curfew. I understood that there would be nights that they would be out later than that. But if there was a good reason for them to be out *past* 11, I insisted that I get a phone call *before* 11, no matter where they were. The result was that I never once wondered where my kids were. If they said they stopped at a restaurant to get something to eat, they knew that I was probably going to say OK. I've never had to pace the floor at midnight wondering where they were because we set the rule in advance and everybody knew it.

A third rule was set specifically for my daughter, Kristi. I insisted on having the right to personally meet every boy she dated before she went out with him. That has created some laughs around here because some of the boys have been absolutely petrified to meet me, but they knew that was the price they had to pay to get Kristi to go out with them. I've sensed that this has been a personal relief to Kristi as well, because she has always had that fall-back position of knowing how to turn down a guy she didn't want to go out with.

I have always told both of the kids that if they ever found themselves in a difficult situation where the peer pressure was heavy, they could feel free to make me sound like a monster. These kinds of principles, established early in the game, saved us from tensions we would have come across because we hadn't looked ahead to anticipate problems.

Skills Development and Affirmation

I've been asked, "What influence can parents have in the area of skills development?" I'm a pastor. Unlike most kids who don't see their parents at their jobs, my kids frequently see me at work. They see me preaching and they go to church where they see me in charge of things. So I make it a special point that when I go into their world, it is not as a performer or leader, but always as a spectator. There are always areas in my children's world in which *they* are the experts.

I think it's important for fathers and mothers to encourage areas of the relationship where the children know that

THE BIGGEST MISTAKE PARENTS MAKE IN AFFECTING TEENAGERS

Parents make a big mistake when they don't start affecting their teenagers in a favorable manner from Day One. But they make a bigger—perhaps the biggest—mistake when they discover their dilemma late and become overly zealous to make up for lost time.

A classic example is of two parents who attend a family life conference. On the way home they write twenty-five rules to post on the refrigerator with the corresponding punishment for any infraction of the new regime. Upon arrival, they proudly announce, "As of today we're going to. . . ."

It's no wonder that the fourteen- and sixteen-year-old teens raise an eyebrow, heave a sigh, and think, "What have we gotten ourselves into?"

Suddenly plunging in with a lot of new rules can really upset the apple cart. While a zealous attitude for reform is commendable, *how* you deliver your new policies is directly related to how well they will be received by your teens. When teens aren't so keen on the new rule system, parents often get discouraged and give up all together, not realizing that it was their manner that turned their kids off.

Charles R. Swindoll

40

they are teaching the parents. Teaching, informing, and discovering take place in both directions. For example, our son was always an excellent athlete. There was enormous pressure on a number of occasions for me to coach a Little League team. Fortunately, I never said yes. I could never serve in any way, shape, or form where I would be in control of his world as an athlete. When I went to his games, I went as a spectator and always made sure that I was asking questions about how and why the team did certain things. I let him teach *me* about the sport he was into.

The same thing was true with Kristi. Since her special area of skill is music, I asked her to teach me about music. This approach helped our children develop a healthy respect for their own capacities to be good at something, to become effective, and not to always be number two.

During the teen years, the key is affirmation. Whenever a teenager does something of value, the most important thing parents can do is to affirm him—to give him a strong sense of esteem and appreciation for his accomplishments. To cite a biblical illustration, when Jesus came out of the Jordan after being baptized by John, a voice from heaven said, "This is My beloved Son. I'm pleased with Him." What a magnificent example of affirmation. The heavenly Father was affirming the Son in the same way that parents ought to affirm their children. When a child does something of value, the parents need to say, "This is our beloved child. We're pleased." This will make the child feel good about himself. If he has been affirmed in the early days, it will develop a healthy basis for work habits later in life.

Another point: I think it is very important for parents to make sure they don't bring undue pressure on their teenager to follow in their footsteps. Sometimes parents communicate that message. Children think if they don't become a doctor like their father, they will become second-class citizens. I think many fathers expect their sons to go for great careers, but in subtle ways, they communicate to their daughters that they don't expect that kind of productivity. If anything, I worked harder to let my daughter know that I had incredible respect for her mind and that there was nothing in this world she couldn't do if she wanted to do it. I have a beautiful daughter, but I decided from the beginning that I wasn't going to affirm just her looks, but also her brain. I think we need to be careful that we give equal affirmation to both genders.

Lasting Impressions—Will They Be Good or Bad?

CHARLES R. SWINDOLL

"**T**rain up a child in the way he should go, even when he is old he will not depart from it" (Prov. 22:6, NASB).

"A righteous man who walks in his integrity—how blessed are his sons after him" (Prov. 20:7, NASB).

Parents leave a lasting impression on their children—whether it's favorable or unfavorable. Because parents are the first significant "others" to be near a child and because they fashion the child's environment, they have tremendous opportunities to mold his personality.

Today, I think the most powerful influence on a teenager's mind is his friends. More than ever before, teens are likely to listen to the counsel of their friends before that of their parents. With that in mind, I *still* believe parents *can* and *do* affect their children.

The parents' job in raising children features two important aspects that will influence their children for life. The primary job of parents is to help a child know himself fully and completely, so he can be comfortable with himself, others, and God. To have a healthy self-image, a teen must know his strengths and weaknesses, and understand how to emphasize his strengths and minimize his weaknesses. Parents must teach a child how to know and love God. People aren't born knowing how to develop themselves. Teens need to know *who* they are before they can become all God intends them to be. And they need parents who are willing to guide them through the process.

The second crucial aspect of raising teens is helping them to learn to choose good friends. The ability to discern is a skill people are not necessarily born with, yet friends are such a significant influence on a person's life.

"Do not be deceived: 'Bad company corrupts good morals' " (1 Cor. 15:33, NASB). If a teen is not taught the value of choosing suitable friends, he may be influenced negatively by them.

Parents best influence their children: (1) by their example or model, and (2) by using available, appropriate opportunities to talk with them.

"Actions speak louder than words," they say. And that is certainly true when it comes to teens and parents. Parents can be terrific examples in teaching kids about self-image or how to choose good friends. When your teen can see you modeling what you're talking about, the words have a practical meaning. Practice what you preach.

Parents can also effectively influence their teens by taking advantage of opportunities to talk with them. I don't recall too many sessions when we had a "pow-wow," and sat down and talked through every detail of growing up with our children. But as occasions naturally arose, we talked to our kids about people who encourage us and strengthen our walk, and about our personal growth. The main thing is that teaching takes place in the context of life. You can't separate your life into a "regular" part and a "Christian" part. Being a Christian permeates *all* areas of your life.

I often call these informal, natural chats "table talk." Often our talks took place at suppertime or bedtime; I tend to think a lot more counseling goes on then than at any other time of day. When the situation or moment of question happens, use the time effectively to instruct a teachable teen.

Some families try to cram all instruction into the "family altar" time. We found, however, that this didn't work well in the Swindoll home. If it works for you, that's great. But when you've got a three-year-old and a nine-year-old and a fourteen-year-old, it's rough. They're all at different places developmentally. But when I crawl in bed with my three-year-old or another of my children, it's amazing what he'll tell me. I think the thirty minutes before children go to sleep, as they're getting ready for bed, is the most remarkable time for training.

Parents *will* have an effect on their children. It is wise to pray for wisdom to know how to best influence your children for good. Knowing you will make a lasting impression, why not commit yourself to being the most godly example you can be? "Behold, children are a gift of the Lord; the fruit of the womb is a reward. Like arrows in the hand of a warrior, so are the children of one's youth" (Ps. 127:3-4, NASB).

Related Articles

PARENTS ARE CHILDREN TOO

There's an interesting story in Judges 13 of a conversation between Samson's parents and the angel of the Lord. Samson's father prays, "Teach us how to bring up the boy" (v. 8, NIV)—in other words, "Give us a course on child-raising." The angel never says one thing about child-raising. He simply describes how the parents should behave. He seems to assume that the child will turn out all right if the parents do their job.

Parents are children too—children of God. Only if they are relating rightly to God as His children, only if they have a good "Parent-child" relationship with Him, will they be able to relate rightly as parents to their own children. Then they will be able to say to their children with humility, "Look, we're not the end of the line. We're children too, God's children. As we are responsible to obey Him, you must be responsible to obey us until the time comes when you too obey only Him."

Ray & Anne Ortlund

What the Bible Expects from Parents

HOWARD G. HENDRICKS

You can tell people how to be good parents, but unless they are involved in the learning process the information will not seep down into their daily lives.

We used to go into a city for a family life seminar and tell people how to be better parents. Everyone enjoyed it, but they went home and resumed their old habits. It may have been motivational to some people and consciousness-raising, but there was no implementation because they didn't get involved in the process. From that experience I learned that the process is more important than the product.

We encourage people to study the biblical narratives of parents. We tell them to look at both good and poor examples, like Hannah, Eli, Mary, and Joseph. David was a great king, probably Israel's greatest, and yet he had a lot of limitations as a parent, especially with his son Absalom.

A second thing we encourage people to do is to ask hard questions. Samson, for example, had incredible parents and yet look at what happened to him. Or Daniel, a teenager with relatively limited exposure to his parents, and yet he enters a foreign culture and comes on like horseradish. The same is true of Joseph. Contrast him with his rascally brothers and you wonder how he could come out of the same family.

I also suggest that parents study the Book of Proverbs, the best parent training manual. The first nine chapters—ten basic sections that deal with a parent talking with his son—are especially helpful.

What God Expects of Us as We Guide Our Teens

First, God expects us to be good models, to realize that life is more caught than taught. Kids aren't looking for perfect parents, but they are looking for honest and growing ones.

For example, parents can model how to ask forgiveness. My grown kids have told me how important it was that I was willing to admit a mistake. I only wish I had learned that earlier.

God also wants us to provide instruction and input as needed. This changes a little in the adolescent years because instruction becomes indirective rather than directive. That is why it is so important to be available. You teach teens at their demand. They set the curriculum; they set the time. Instruction may be 11:30 at night when you're stretched across their bed. Yet you obviously don't say, "OK, now we are going to have a class."

We need to be careful listeners, particularly in helping our teenagers interpret what is happening within themselves. This is such an emotionally chaotic period in young people's lives, and they need somebody who can see things objectively. We also need to establish an open relationship with our teens and with their friends.

An open relationship includes letting your teen see that you are totally—not just partially—dependent on God. I believe this is why God often allows us to fail. We don't just hit bottom, but we go clean through it so that we become dependent.

Finally, God wants parents to learn to relax in the Lord and enjoy life. Psalm 127:1-2 is good advice here. You'll remember that passage begins, "Unless the Lord builds the house, its builders labor in vain" (NIV). Many parents have been saved out of some very unusual or terrible circumstances and they trust God for that. Yet they refuse to trust God for the same supernatural process in their kids.

For me, learning to relax was a process I developed. I started out very uptight and compulsive, because I was from a broken home and I was determined that my home would be different. Fortunately, I had a partner who was very relaxed and provided a counterpoint for me. I also had kids who helped me to relax. As I went on, it was really a function of my spiritual growth and maturity that enabled me to relax and trust God completely.

Basic Principles of Human Behavior in the Bible

The way to glean principles of human behavior from the Bible which apply to parenting is to identify personally with the people—to identify with their problems, situations, decisions.

In other words, crawl into their skins, think with their minds, feel with their emotions, decide with their choices. I find that when I do that, I learn more about human behavior from Scripture personalities.

Next, ask yourself three questions. What is this passage teaching me about God? What is it teaching me about myself? What is it teaching me about others? You'll discover not only the nature of God, but your own self-concept and the dynamics of personal relationships as you study.

Third, look for principles behind the cultural pattern. Often people study the Scriptures and think that they can't learn anything from Abraham because the culture was different. We need to look for universal truths that transcend culture. Obviously the Scriptures don't say anything about television, but they say a great deal about the value of using our time wisely.

Fourth, reprogram your thinking to a biblical and eternal perspective. Remember Paul's exhortation in Romans 12:2 and determine not to allow yourself to be squeezed into a mold, but to be transformed by the renewing of your mind.

Fifth, concentrate on the wisdom literature—Proverbs, Ecclesiastes, Psalms. These books are rich in insight about human behavior and the struggles and conflicts of relationships.

Related Articles

What's Your Style?

CLAYTON BAUMANN

I once asked my daughter, Kim, if she was a good kid. She responded positively. I asked her how she knew, and she said, "Because you haven't spanked me in five years." Early in my marriage and family life, my wife and I determined that our children would know the difference between discipline and nondiscipline. As a result, discipline and justice became a part of our parenting style.

There are many parenting styles and some are more effective than others, depending on the teen. Too often parents wallow in guilt because they have been ineffective in their child's life. Instead, they should admit that just as some adults excel in money investments or entertainment, others excel in raising children. In all likelihood, these situations reflect a conflict between the parental style being used and the needs of a particular teen. The parents need to adjust for the individuality of their teen.

"Rigid Disciplining" is one style of parenting. The slightest variance from what the parents and teen agree on brings discipline. Another style is that of the "Buddy-Only Approach." In this case, parents are always friends—never disciplinarians. Others include the very loose "That's OK with Me" style, the spiritualizing "What Would the Lord Have Done in That Situation?" style, and the indecisive "I Don't Know" style.

In determining what style or styles to use with a teen, I think parents must go by successes. Evaluate the teen. Is he happy? secure? making good friendships? Is there a line of open communication between the parents and the teen? Does he have the same values as his parents? Is he interested in spiritual things? Is the teen going through a stage, or are the parents really wrong? A lot of soul-searching must take place.

Parents must be objective in examining themselves and their styles of parenting. This is a difficult task. I spent a lot of time trying to be objective and found that interaction with other Christian parents was very helpful. Parents have come to me and said, "I see something in your daughter that I think you should know about." Parents need to realize that no one has all the answers, but they're all in this together.

The church can be a tremendous help in this evaluation process. One way to gain advice in parenting is by seeking out a youth pastor or other church worker who has had the opportunity to observe the teen. Teens constantly give out signals about their homes. Other ways the church can help are film series, Christian books on parenting, and parenting seminars. At my church, I am meeting with a group of fathers who are concerned about their teens. We ask all sorts of questions such as, "Do you allow your teen to see R-rated movies? Why or why not? Is your teen seeing these films regardless of your decision?" Some of the fathers get a little upset because they're not used to dealing with honesty, openness, and specifics. Yet they all believe this kind of session is helpful.

Over the years I've changed my parenting style, but those changes were not easily made. My wife and I learned to monitor each other in regard to discipline. In the past I wanted to raise my teens the exact way that I had been raised. My parents were very loving and open. At the same time they were rigid disciplinarians. I was never allowed to smoke, dance, drink, or go to movies. As a result, when my daughter first asked to go to a dance I said, "No!" However, my wife helped me see that by not allowing my daughter to go, I was creating a social outcast—most of her Christian friends didn't have a problem with dancing. So, after examining the alternatives and making some adjustments, I permitted her to go.

The high schooler today faces much more than these separation issues, with vulgarity and nudity bombarding him on cable TV channels or video recorders in the home. Many people are concerned with bars and X-rated bookstores, but what parents really need to deal with is the prevailing attitude that everything is permissible because "everyone's doing it."

Finally, though parents can fail in many ways, they can still follow a few basic rules and be successful. The first of those rules would be spending unstructured time with their teens. In my family, this time is usually during meals. Dinner becomes a time of sharing and reporting. Another thing my wife and I do is to build our recreation around our children. My teens love to water ski, so during the summer we spend a few days each week on our boat. We also make sure we bring along friends of our teens.

A second rule is to discipline the child at an early age. Maintain control of the child. Help him to understand that there are certain guidelines to life and the limitations of those guidelines.

Third, parents should look for ways to serve their teenager, such as driving him places that are out of their way. My teens more fully appreciate my actions when I take them someplace, getting to my meeting ten minutes late. I heard some feedback once from a friend who said, "Your daughter told me that you're very busy, but you've always got time for her." That was a great encouragement.

Expressing love is the fourth and final rule. A teen should see his mother and father showing love to each other, desiring to be together. Along these same lines, the climate at home should be one of fun, encouragement, and positive reinforcement.

Related Article
Chapter 7: Understanding How Teens Think

The Sacrifice of Being a Parent

BRUCE B. BARTON

You, as parents, are making sacrifices because of your choice to have children. It takes extra time as you chauffeur young people, get involved in their schedules and activities, and even as you take time to listen.

Many parents find that they must sacrifice their own personal priorities and goals due to the presence of teenagers. No longer do you have the same peace and quiet or leisure time that you enjoyed when the children were younger. Your territory is invaded. No longer is the bathroom a safe place. Someone may crash in to borrow a brush or claim the facilities. You may have a policy that your family should have an enjoyable Sunday meal together. Now teenage activities and schedules threaten that sacred time.

The best approach to take is to recognize and to acknowledge that there are costs. Don't deny it. Sink your teeth into the issue and face it squarely.

You may recall times when your parents said, "You don't know what a sacrifice this is." The feeling, "I have sacrificed," is a natural result of the extra effort and energy it takes to be parents of teenagers. Young parents begin with fresh, enthusiastic resolve, "I'm a new parent, and I'm going to do a great job." They try to do everything right and to avoid the mistakes made by their own families and friends. But after an intense period of effort, doubts set in. "Am I really going to achieve all the goals I have set?" Then doubt leads to resentment or deep feelings of inadequacy. Resentment because the results of all the effort that it takes in time, money, and personal concern are not visible. Feelings of inadequacy because the extra effort requires more than you have to give.

When you begin to experience feelings of sacrifice, you are faced with a choice: either to cease making the effort or to decide to accept the increased responsibilities. When approaching a crossroad in life—and each stage in life has one— you must choose which road to take. Some people become paralyzed with fear and anxiety. Some stop to build a monument to honor this great time of decision-making. Some build a cemetery to mourn life's unattainable dreams. As

DOES PARENTING MEAN SACRIFICE?

What does the Lord want from a mother and father? Godly offspring. That's the message of Malachi 2:15. It sets before parents a noble, sometimes overwhelming goal.

In earlier generations, parents took it for granted that they would have to sacrifice for their children, but children in those days were cherished possessions. Today, the desire for self-fulfillment means parents often see children as hindrances. Parents resent having to sacrifice any part of themselves or their lifestyles for their children.

Most parents who do sacrifice their time, money, and emotions for their children are in a sense repaying a debt to their own parents, who sacrificed for them. They're carrying on a tradition. But what about the increasing number of parents who neither cherish nor sacrifice for their children? I shudder to think what the attitude of the next generation of parents will be toward their children.

The most important thing parents can do for children is to cherish them. If they do that, the sacrifice won't seem so great. If parents recognize children as gifts of God—and this is going to mean spilled milk and heartache and inconvenience—then they also will experience the blessing of God.

My wife and I were driving home from the airport when she turned to me and said, "You know, I don't expect to do anything in all my life as important as caring for our children." That's probably true of most parents. The children they raise will be their greatest effect on the world.

When I enter into the enterprise of child-rearing, I'm going to have to sacrifice, but I'm also entering a place where God's blessing lies, and I'm fulfilling a purpose God has given.

Larry Christenson

parents, you can choose to pull back, withdraw, or stop trying *or* you can choose to grow by committing yourself to these responsibilities.

Sacrifice can settle into "self-sacrifice" or martyrdom. "I have sacrificed" becomes "I am being sacrificed." You may say, "Look how hard I've tried." "What do you expect of a parent with my limitations?" Being a parent does require acts of love and service and times of giving, often beyond what we think we can give. But a mindset of self-sacrifice focuses on yourself rather than on the needs of others, and usually degenerates into self-pity.

When teenagers are present, someone must bear the cost. If you abdicate the task of bringing them up, then the school, government, or church must pick up the slack. Ultimately, the children themselves have to bear the cost as they attempt to repair and correct their parents' unfinished job. You are in a unique position because you can choose to carry the cost yourself. In so choosing, you can regard this time of life as an investment to give children the knowledge, skills, values, and loving relationships they need. In so doing, they can become the free, independent, and maturing adults God wants them to be. You can also see your work as a contribution to the service of God. He has appointed you for this high responsibility in developing these young people. Finally, remember that efforts made before the children leave the home are more beneficial than those attempted later on in life.

Since there is a cost involved and you have committed yourself to this wonderful and terrifying responsibility, what can you do as parents?

1. *Find a significant "other" with whom you can share.* If you can talk through these feelings with your spouse, you will add a large bonus to your relationship. If both of you are involved in the struggle, you need to find another person outside the home with whom you can talk. That significant other can function as a mentor and a monitor, as you talk and receive feedback about your feelings.

2. *Join a small group.* Find a small group of parents with children of similar age, or other Christians with whom you can share your deepest feelings. The strength and bond that come from such an experience can help you face trying times.

3. *Find interests and activities outside the home.* There needs to be a focus outside the pressures of being a parent to keep you going. Without such activities, you face the possibility of experiencing burnout from unrewarded and unrefreshed effort.

4. *Set goals that have measurable results.* Since parenting is such a long-term activity, you may not see results

A TIMELY SACRIFICE

The hardest sacrifice for parents to make is often their time. Being parents gets in the way of our social lives, our work lives, our personal lives. One Friday, for example, as soon as I got off work I met my family at my son's football game. I sat through the whole game, which is not my favorite pastime. Then we had to drive all the way back to school, since it was an away game, and wait for our son to get changed back into his street clothes. That took at least an hour and a half, and when he came out, he was with a bunch of friends who wanted to go out for pizza. We took them. We got home at 2 o'clock in the morning. To me, that was a six-hour sacrifice. But that's the kind of sacrifice parents need to make so their children know how much they are loved.

Ross Campbell

until years after your children have left your care, perhaps not until they begin to raise their own children. You need to have some pastimes, hobbies, or goals that allow for immediate success or gratification. It could be a garden, a workshop, some project that's right for you. It must have a beginning and end so that you can say, "I have accomplished it."

5. *Regard your physical and mental health.* You must continue to grow as a person while you're spending time caring for your children.

6. *Develop a new source of nourishment.* In order to build yourself up, you need to find nourishing activities to sustain you. It could be taking up a new hobby, enjoying your favorite kind of music, or taking a dream trip, though the activities should be frequent and regular enough to keep up your encouragement level. Get involved with people in a new way. Do something that's fun, that makes you feel stronger, refreshed, and ready to renew yourself to face the task. These things can help to offset the tendency toward the self-sacrificing mindset so common in parents of teenagers.

Related Articles
Chapter 4: The Importance of Being Available
Chapter 10: Get Involved!
Chapter 13: Communicating Values to Our Children
Chapter 25: Parents Need Privacy Too!

The Patient Parent
The Secret of Developing Self-control

DONALD & NAOMI COLE

Was it Chaucer who said, "Patience is a virtue; get it if you can; seldom found in women and never found in man"? No matter, it isn't true. Patience is part of the fruit of the Holy Spirit, and it must grow in Christian parents, as it must in all Christians. However, its growth is neither automatic nor magical. Patience must be cultivated along with all other qualities that should characterize Christians.

Christian parents develop patience the same way as everybody else—by acknowledging its importance and working on it. The process begins at conversion and continues throughout life. Rightly handled, the special strains and stresses of parenting can contribute mightily to its growth. As the Bible says, "Tribulation worketh patience" (Rom. 5:3, KJV).

What we want, of course, is patience while we are parents—not after the children have grown up and left home. How to exercise patience at the time, that is the problem! A first step is learning what makes kids tick. Books on child-rearing can help us understand our children. If we know *why* they behave the way they do—sometimes sullen, for example, or resentful of the mildest rebuke—it is easier for us to be patient. If we know that children are more or less alike, that most children are sometimes sullen and resentful, we can more easily cope with our own children's moods. We can be patient. What is true of temptation in adults—that "no temptation has seized you except what is common to man" (1 Cor. 10:13, NIV)—is true also of children. The verse can be paraphrased: "Your child's exasperating behavior is common to all children."

We should learn to take our children's

exasperating traits less seriously than we usually do. Though we should never laugh at a child, we can chuckle to ourselves when one of our children is acting up, knowing that this stage too will pass. Learning to relax helps us keep our tempers in check. Self-control—that is, to hang loose, as young people say—is an essential element in Christian character.

Patience is impossible without a measure of discipline in the home. Proper discipline of children while they are small will prevent many serious problems later. Children also must be taught obedience and respect for their parents at a very early age. There is no substitute for this. From time to time a battle may ensue, but it *must* be won by parents. Failure here is terribly serious. How children behave in their teens is largely determined by discipline in their early years. If parents fail to establish their authority when the children are young, they will never succeed when the children are half-grown. "Discipline your son, and he will give you peace; he will bring delight to your soul" (Prov. 29:17, NIV).

Anger is not always wrong. Loss of temper is wrong, "for man's temper is never the means of achieving God's true goodness" (James 1:20, PH). But anger may be distinguished from loss of temper. Sometimes nothing else gets through to a teen. When usually self-controlled parents lose their cool, so to speak, and speak in anger, teens listen; they realize that the issue under dispute is important. It's better for parents to blow their stacks and even hand out an unfair punishment than to brood over a situation in silence while resentment builds. Brooding in resentful silence should never be confused with patience. Of course, parents must apologize if judgment or punishment was indeed hasty or ill-advised. Usually children give forgiveness when asked for it, and they hold no grudges if they perceive that an apology was sincere.

Some people find it easier to be patient than others. By nature, they are easy-going, even placid. In them, patience may be more apparent than real. Sometimes what passes for patience is merely indifference. Some parents let their children get away with murder; they just don't care what the kids do, nor do they think about character development with all that that entails.

All of us, whether mild by disposition or hot-tempered, have to cultivate genuine, biblical patience. We have to compensate for temperamental weaknesses and overcome them. If we are by nature impetuous and impatient, we must confess this as sin. When we lose our tempers, we must confess this to God *and* to our children, and we must resolve under God not to do it again. What if we fail? Humbly, we repeat the confessions and the resolution to start over again.

CONSIDER THEM BETTER

The best advice for parents of teenagers comes from the Bible. For instance, Philippians 2:3 (NIV) describes the key attitude we need to take toward our adolescent children: "In humility consider others better than yourselves." Where do they shine? What do we admire about them? What can we learn from them?

Squint your eyes. See your children as they will be in the future. Concentrate on their strengths; minimize their failures. Do you realize that attitude will spring them free to start improving? If we tell them they *always* do this, or they *never* do that, they feel that their bad habits are fixed in concrete.

That unstable, insecure teenager of yours needs your respect and affirmation. Consider him better!

Ray & Anne Ortlund

If, on the other hand, our attitude toward our children is largely uncaring, we must confess that too, never confusing our indifference with patience or love. We must ask God to give us the patience produced by the Holy Spirit—to the extent that we obey God and seek His help.

What we are at home is what we really are. If we are short-tempered or chronically irritable or impatient with our children, yet sweet-tempered and charming to everybody outside the home, our children will see the difference. They will hate the hypocrisy and injustice. As they grow older, they will turn away from us. Hence, in our own interests—and for God's sake—the exercise of patience in the home is a must.

Nobody's Perfect

HOWARD G. HENDRICKS

I went through a tremendous problem with depression because I came out of a broken home. When my son went away to college, he left a note on my desk which I found after taking him to the airport. In effect it said, "I appreciate what you've done for me and I'm sure you think you probably blew me away with your problems and depression. But I'd just like you to know that it did just the opposite. It was so thrilling to see the reality of Jesus Christ taking over in your life and changing you. It convinced me that Christianity is not just a set of ideas—it works."

It's reassuring to know that you can do a lot of things wrong as parents and still have the children turn out OK. Kids are very, very forgiving, especially if parents are honest.

If the kids go wrong, the parents think it's their problem. Well, I've worked with scores of kids who very objectively and honestly have said, "No, my parents didn't blow it. I just decided that I didn't want to go their way." This is particularly true in the spiritual realm, though kids often return to the faith later, depending on how the parents handle the situation.

You can only determine what you do as parents. You can't control what your children do. Some parents think they control their kids, but they really don't. Their control is only external and temporary.

Another reason why we can't be too hard on ourselves as parents is that there aren't any guarantees in Scripture for parenting. There are so many variables—home changes, individual changes, environmental changes. The entire parenting process is one of faith. No *direct* cause-and-effect relationship exists between what you do and what happens to the child. I've seen parents who were ideal in every respect and the kids turned out to be monsters. Then I've seen kids whose parents were less than ideal, but they still turned out fine. I'm a classic case. I have psychiatrist friends who look through my family history and my childhood environment and wonder how in the world I became what I am. But different kids react to different environments in different ways. Another child in my environment may have grown up quite differently.

Related Articles

Getting More from Your Family
The Rewards of Being a Parent

LARRY KREIDER

Not long ago, a well-known business-man in Houston was honored at a special tribute dinner for his tireless efforts and his generosity toward Youth for Christ. The program included accolades from business associates, political cronies, government officials, church leaders, and a nationally known Christian figure.

The final tribute came in the form of a letter from his daughter who was miles away and deeply disappointed that she couldn't attend the event. She said some things in that letter that she probably had never stated to her father face to face. She thanked him for being so loving, so generous, so thoughtful—for just being a great father. As the letter was read I thought, "What a reward!" How many fathers would die and go to heaven right on the spot to be so honored.

Since the majority of us parents will grow gray waiting at the mailbox for an invitation to a dinner in our honor, we must look for the kinds of rewards that quietly tap us on the shoulder and say, "Now tell me how you would have experienced that if you weren't a parent."

So let me list a few ... the kinds of rewards that I now relish and joyfully fondle as the payoff for serving in such a privileged care called parenthood.

The first reward has no equal, *learning how to survive.* When the day is over and cuts have been bandaged, broken glass swept up, dinner is burned, Johnny didn't make the basketball team, Susie did, the washer broke, a check bounced, and the neighbor's dog dug up the new shrubs, and you crawl into bed with half your sanity—then you silently laud your ability to survive.

Then your kids hit the teenage years. Broken hearts, broken fenders, sassy remarks, short-term loans, locked bathroom doors, telephone unavailable, Mom against Dad, teacher conferences, and the list goes on. Now survival is accomplished with gritting teeth, "I will make it." Survival has become its own reward.

Then there's a whole list of *skills* you never knew you had, but you'd better develop them quickly or you won't enjoy the reward of survival. The first and most essential skill reward is management. Small corporations are no greater a challenge than trying to keep a modern day household functioning. The major difference is that you can't escape the responsibilities by being fired. Unfortunately, Mom and Dad sometimes select to fire each other through the easy escape hatch of divorce.

Another skill reward necessary for survival is communication. Within the family unit you quickly learn things like nonverbal communication, or what you say is not always what you mean, or selective listening, or the meaning of inflections and tone of voice.

Communication leads to the skill reward of being a negotiator. You negotiate what will be worn to what occasion; you barter like an Arab merchant over the time to come home; you arbitrate between siblings over the use of the car; you referee squabbles, minor skirmishes, and full-scale assaults; and hopefully you enjoy the pleasurable reward of sitting at the peace table with ratified agreements in sight.

There's no skill reward quite as fulfilling as learning the demanding laws of economics. When a teenager starts driving and you get the next auto insurance statement, add up the additional gas bills, make regular payments to the orthodontist, pay for baseball registration, buy the coach a present, send the kids to summer camp, try to get prepared for college tuition, and donate to the band uniform fund, you quickly learn the art of financial juggling or plea bargaining with a loan officer.

Though there are many more skill rewards, I'll conclude with the new abilities you learn from either cross-cultural appreciation or tolerance. The foreign phrases, the latest hit album, and fashions without reason are all a part of your education process as parents. So don't fight it—there's also the reward of knowing "this too will pass."

The third reward of parenting moves us on to the more positive side of the ledger. The *fellowship* of a loving family cannot be replaced. The conversation of mutually interested parents and children is a part of this fellowship. So are the special fun times. The frivolous competition of a card game, enjoying a joke together, the

INVESTING IN OUR CHILDREN

As responsible Christians, we need to ask ourselves: When are we wasting money on our children and when are we wisely investing in them?

I once took my son with me to New Zealand during one of my speaking tours just so we could spend time together. How could I justify spending money like that rather than giving it to the poor? Because I looked at the outlay as an investment in the same way that an education is an investment, rather than as an expenditure.

Without an education your child might be able to render $200,000 worth of service to others (if service to others can be reduced to economic terms). Spending $40,000 for your child's education may result in providing him with concerns and skills that would enable him to render $1 million worth of services. Then the $40,000 spent is well worth it in terms of a return on monetary investment. Spending money on education must be an exercise in good stewardship.

Whenever you spend money wisely on a privileged child, I see it as a strong investment for the worth of the kingdom. The Bible says it beautifully—to whom much is given, much will be expected (see Luke 12:48). Make sure your child understands that.

The other justification for such expenses is that my children are the primary responsibility of my life—as your children should be of yours. Let's invest prayerfully and wisely.

Anthony Campolo, Jr.

private stories to hold over each other's head, the special times for special prayer, the reminiscing over photo albums—all of these are unique flavors beyond description for those who haven't tasted.

And then there's the delight of *receiving love*. If God isn't ashamed about His joy in receiving love from His children, then neither need we. The pat on the back, the unsolicited hug, a homemade gift, a few hand-picked flowers, a thoughtful phone call, and other loving gestures are so valuable that some people would offer every earthly treasure for such a treat.

Being parents gives us a great perspective on our relationship to our heavenly Father. Knowing what delights us as parents opens the door for us to return the same kind of love to God. The angels can only gaze with curiosity at the special relationship afforded parents and will never feel the interconnectedness of the family of mankind.

Related Articles
Chapter 1: Thanks for the Memories
Chapter 11: Developing Family Loyalty

Thanks for the Memories

How to Cherish Family Life

CHARLES R. SWINDOLL

To cherish is to hold dear, value, or admire. I think most parents cherish family life. Parents set the goal of rearing children who will look back fondly on their homes. We want our kids to have positive and pleasant memories. Those parents who simply don't care about their children are few and far between.

In understanding your role as parents, you must realize that you don't have to have a Pollyanna-type family for fond memories. Often families enjoy a deeper relationship when they have experienced injuries, disease, disagreement, feelings of brokenness and hurt, failures, financial stresses, or uncertainties together. Honors and achievements give shared joy.

I agree with Edith Schaeffer that one of the roles of the family is to be a "museum of memories." We need to build precious memories within our families.

Proverbs 24:3-4 are verses I like to quote. "By wisdom a house is built, and by understanding it is established; and by

knowledge the rooms are filled with all precious and pleasant riches" (NASB).

God can even work out the difficult experiences which are beyond our abilities to handle. And that gives children roots that they can draw from when the going gets rough.

If a fire would burn away all that we had except our family members, nothing of value would be lost. The value lies in our relationships and memories—the precious and pleasant riches that we've invested in each other's lives. Those can't be burnt to the ground. Relationships and memories are rewards of being parents.

Another reward is seeing your children model many of the things you taught them—especially when your children are older and married. It's flattering to see them uphold values that you hammered away at when they were young.

I cherish seeing the product of my children's lives. Whether they've gone through a stressful time with balance and wisdom or if they've found success, it's rewarding. I'm glad to know I had a chance to "input" into their lives.

Something else I hold dear is hearing my children's comments about their family. It means a lot to hear one of your kids express thanks for something you did. Or to overhear a child telling his friend what you did right.

It's great to hear kids relive family memories. One time our family went camping at Lake Tahoe and it was an absolutely flaky experience. It rained, was messy, got hot, we didn't catch any fish—a disaster by most people's standards. But on the way home, Cynthia made a great comment. She said, "Well, at least we have a great memory of an experience that we endured together." Well, everyone laughed, but just recently I heard my son comment on that experience, eight years past. He said even though the *experience* wasn't that great, the *memory* of it is. He remembered a specific conversation we had about the trailer hitch and my splitting headache. That's a testimony to the fact that almost anything can result in a precious memory!

It's hard to imagine parents not valuing or cherishing family life, but some tend to see family life as "boring." I challenge those parents to take a second look. They're settling for less, in my opinion.

What they might be afraid of is that family life is time-consuming and not particularly satisfying *at the moment.* Sometimes it's hard to see the value of the investment, because it is costly and takes time.

I have to limit my travel and involvements to make time for my children. Just recently my wife and I had to cancel going to an event we had looked forward to for a month and a half. But a situation in our family needed attention, and that was a priority for us. That doesn't mean the decision was made without a second thought, but it was great to be at home— because that's where we belonged at that time.

Draw on the value of putting a family together. Trust that the rewards will follow in due time. Cherishing family life is worth the effort. Don't give to *get.* But give generously to build those precious and pleasant memories.

Related Articles

GETTING READY
FOR TEENAGERS

How to Prepare for the Teenage Years

- You can be a confident parent
- Learning to accept your limitations
- What do teens need to know as they approach adolescence?
- Can parents correct their past failures?
- What happens when parents get discouraged?

Adolescence, the process of becoming an adult, runs concurrently with the teenage years. The term *adolescence* is usually used to refer to the young person's physical and psychological development, while *teenage* is more often used in connection with the young person's social development and environment.

These years between twelve and twenty can be some of the most exciting years for parents. Children of this age are no longer portable—we can no longer pick them up and set them down somewhere else; we can no longer force them to do our will. But they are now young adults, and we are able to reason and share our own experiences with them, both about coping with personal development and about living as responsible Christians in our culture.

Priorities
for Parents
Deciding Who Comes First

HAROLD MYRA

How do you get ready to parent teenagers? You have to remember what's really important. In parenting, I have two priorities, the first of which is my wife, Jeanette.

The title of one of Charlie Shedd's books says it well—*The Best Dad Is a Good Lover.* He alludes to research that shows the relationship between Mom and Dad is vital to a healthy relationship between parents and teens. So for Dad, the most important job is to show everyone in the family that Mom comes first. Mom's job is to put Dad first. Not that they don't love the kids, but the children should never feel they can pit their parents against each other. It's not inappropriate to tell them at times, "I love your mother. You kids are very important to me, but someday you'll have lives of your own. I'm going to be with your mother all my life."

A solid husband-wife relationship is not automatic. Kids can detect fissures. A firm marriage takes hard work, but hard work is required in anything you want to do well.

When the marriage is sound, when there's love between husband and wife, an energy is produced that affects the children. If that relationship is missing, all that's produced is frustration and powerlessness. When I'm mad at my wife, I can sense that I'm not much good to the kids, and I'm not much good to myself either.

How do you make sure your relationship with your spouse is top priority? Affirm it verbally. I've articulated my love to Jeanette in front of our children. And then I try to spend an occasional weekend alone with Jeanette—perhaps at a mar-

---

CLIMBING OUT OF THE RUT

A rut, simply defined, is "a groove, furrow, or track." It can also mean "a fixed, routine procedure or course of action." Often our families fall into a regular, predictable (boring), routine. We hurry through the week, each person intent on his or her schedule and agenda; and we pass each other like ships in the fog, giving signals and trying to avoid collisions.

Our rut may include our clothes, food, recreation, TV time, and family activities. The problem is that it affects the way we relate to each other. Our communication is hackneyed and laced with clichés ("When I was your age . . ."), and we learn to "read" each other without communicating. Time passes quickly, and suddenly the kids are grown, or a catastrophe forces us to reevaluate our priorities; and we grieve at our superficiality and taking each other for granted. At these moments of insight we may push for a "crash course" on family closeness; but it is artificial and hollow.

The causes for this stagnation may include poor priorities, forced "busyness," self-centeredness, tradition, or whatever; but life is too short to be lived in a rut and persons too precious to be passed quickly by!

The answer lies in *creative action*. Here are some suggestions for rocking the boat and discovering each other. Just don't try to do them all at once!

1. Talk to the children. Are they bored with "family"? What do they think and suggest? Listen!

2. Establish *short-range* experiments or goals. For example, "For one week, instead of TV, let's. . . ."

3. Try new things together (the *whole* family)—like bowling or painting or fishing or building.

4. Give family members the chance to participate in individual activities, but have a time later to share experiences.

5. Change holidays (e.g., make up one of your own and celebrate it, or combine a couple like "George Lincoln's Valentine Day Massacre" in February).

6. Explore your town, county, or state (take the train and see where it goes).

7. Let the kids plan the family vacation (or mini-vacation).

8. Surprise the family with a mystery event (meal, activity, or vacation).

In reality, climbing out of the rut is a clear statement that life is to be savored and enjoyed and that our children and spouse are valuable gifts from God. It allows us time to talk, think, listen, and discover who we really are.

YFC Editors

riage enrichment retreat or on a mini-vacation in the city.

We've made our marriage a stated priority; we consciously want to improve our relationship. Building a marriage, building romance, doesn't come naturally, especially to husbands. It must be a clear and steady goal.

The second priority for parents is establishing channels of communication with children before they ever become teenagers. And that means spending time with the kids during the thirteen years before adolescence starts creating tensions.

I know a college psychology professor in Illinois who bought a motorcycle so he and his eight-year-old son could ride together to California, where the prof was giving some summer lectures. Several weeks are involved, but he plans to do something like that every year until his son gets out of school. He's laying a tremendous base for lifelong communication.

Even if you don't go that far, one-on-one outings are valuable no matter what the age of the child. Going places with the family is great, but kids know they're special when Mom or Dad spends time alone with them individually. Just shopping, tinkering on the car, or riding bicycles can go a long way in building relationships.

I let my children see that their names are on my calendar. My son and I will go bowling or to a shopping center. I usually take my daughter to a bookstore or on a shopping trip.

To walk into a teenager's bedroom and say, "All right, now we're going to talk seriously, so please unburden yourself," is obviously doomed to failure. But when you've regularly spent time together doing things you both enjoy, communication comes naturally.

The key is not the activity but the parents' openness to talk and to listen. You must be willing to enter their world with a listening ear. It's a tone, an attitude, a spirit.

When I was a kid our dinner table was always a place where I felt my comments were taken seriously—even as a five-year-old. I'm trying to project the same atmosphere to my children. Their opinions are just as important as mine. No, I'm not saying I don't maintain my authority over my kids, but I try to use that tone of voice that receives a child's statement as worth hearing.

Respect is especially important with teenagers, who are so eager to come out of childhood and express their independence. Even when they say something stupid, the task of the parents is not to say, "Boy, was that dumb!" which shrivels their self-esteem, but to remember that children are human beings desperate to be accepted.

Next to loving my wife, that's how I can be the best dad.

Related Articles

Every Parent Has a Limit

RICHARD C. HALVERSON

I knew a pastor who lived by the principle of never admitting failure. This man's son got into some problems with the law and caused his parents much heartache. One night the pastor's son explosively said to his father, "Dad, haven't you ever been wrong? Haven't you ever made a mistake? Haven't you ever failed in your life?" Suddenly this father realized that he was frustrating his own son by never acknowledging weakness or failure.

Parents who accept their own limitations are able to treat those limitations as assets rather than liabilities. I think the only way we really learn to accept our limitations is by failing and never treating failure as final. We must see our failures as an education—as steps to becoming what we ought to be. I am becoming a different person as I discover my personal limitations.

The greatest blessing in my life is the Apostle Paul's intimate disclosure of a thorn in his flesh (2 Cor. 12:7-10). He prayed three times that this would be removed, but God said, "My grace is sufficient for you, for My power is made perfect in weakness" (v. 9, NIV). I am a very weak person and have struggled with a low self-image for many years. Based on this passage of Scripture and God's grace, I have learned to handle my low self-image, moving into situations

WHO'S RESPONSIBLE FOR THE RESULTS?

We can never hold parents totally responsible for the way their children turn out. None of us can perfectly meet our teenagers' needs, and none of us are responsible for everything that happens. We all know some kids who seem to have had marvelous parents and yet they have chosen, by their own act of will, to go against the good things of life—against God, against themselves, against everybody. Teenagers ultimately make their own choices, and parents make a mistake if they hold themselves responsible for everything.

During your children's teen years, don't try to be "all in all" to them. Stay much in prayer, but back off. Of course you're more concerned than anyone else, but look for other godly adults to play a part—surrogate parents, extended families, spiritual parents and aunts and uncles in the church congregation and in the community.

As teenagers relate to more and more adults, you can begin to fade off the scene without leaving the kids feeling insecure. And remember, your heavenly Father is more concerned about your children than anyone—even you. Lean hard on Him!

Ray & Anne Ortlund

where I feared rejection. For example, as Chaplain of the U.S. Senate, I must constantly reject such thoughts as, "I don't belong here," or "I don't have the right to be here." Instead, I thank the Lord for His grace and the opportunity to fulfill my calling to that position.

Having suffered from a poor self-image as a teenager, I tended to deal in an opposite way with my own children. Though I never discussed my low self-image with my children until they were mature adults, I had a keen awareness of my teens' need for encouragement and support. It was my responsibility to encourage them with those crazy ideas, allowing them to discover for themselves that their ideas were fallible.

Someone once said that the trouble with our culture is that we train our children for success, but we don't train them for failure. I believe that we have to condition children for failure and for frustration. Teens as well as parents must have the freedom to discover their own limitations. Many parents demand success of their children by working out their own limitations on them. The danger of this type of pattern is that the parents may prevent the child from becoming the person God created him to be.

Oswald Chambers said, "Never make a principle of your experience. Let God be as original with others as He has been with you." Parents must be careful not to impose their own experiences as standards or norms for their teens. Yet, in order for teens to have a healthy acceptance of their own limitations, parents should allow their children to see their needs, limitations, and weaknesses.

You Can't Teach Your Children Everything —But What *Can* You Teach Them?

J. ALLAN PETERSEN

The home is both a laboratory and a classroom: a place where lessons are both caught and taught. Parents are the primary shapers of their children, having far more influence than a dozen pastors, teachers, or youth leaders. And happy parents are the best teachers because people, especially children, are inclined to adopt the beliefs of those who are happy.

But parents must also be leaders, not merely pointers. They must be able to say, "Follow me," not just, "Do what I say."

What must be caught? Attitudes. They're almost never learned by being taught; they're picked up by watching other people. Thus in the home, parents must be careful what kinds of attitudes they exhibit because kids will pick them up. The right attitudes toward life, toward God, toward family members, toward problems, toward the world, toward church, toward authority, toward money—

these basic attitudes either confirm or cancel what we say verbally.

If we tell our children to be concerned for people, but we never invite anyone over for dinner or we never pray for anybody, our children will learn from our actions, not our words.

Not long ago I said to my wife, "You know, each of our three sons has a social consciousness. Where did they get that? We were never activists. We didn't do anything to raise their social awareness."

FINDING A BETTER ROLE MODEL

Many people today are imbalanced in some of their thinking about parenting. The problem may be that they aren't aware of where their priorities have been misplaced.

Most of us tend to raise our children the way we were raised. Parents who have had the misfortune of not having had a good example set by their own parents are going to have a hard time. They need to study better role models. One way to do that is to become part of a group of parents through whom you can find good role models for parenting.

We need to be made whole in the different roles in life that we are given, including that of parenting. James 5:16, in fact, could in part refer to this type of healing when it admonishes, "Confess your faults one to another and pray for one another that you might be healed" (KJV). A support group of peers committed to the Lord and to each other has real merit in healing the lopsided ways of looking at parenting that we may have inherited.

B. Clayton Bell

"What do you mean?" she said. "Every week we had someone over for dinner. We'd have widows one week, divorcees the next, and a poor family after that. What do you mean we didn't do anything?"

Besides attitudes, attributes and character traits must also be modeled: kindness, generosity, compassion, forgiveness, respect, trust, love, integrity, gratitude, courtesy, appreciation. These can't be taught without living them too.

I was in a pastor's home for four days, ate every meal with that family, and the whole time I never heard the man say please or thank you to anyone. He just barked at his family. I thought, "These children will never be thankful to God for anything because they don't see any gratitude in their father."

Finally, tastes are caught. One day I noticed my son wanted to buy some clothes, and even though he didn't have much money, he went to a very nice (and expensive!) store. I hinted that maybe he could get the same thing elsewhere, but he made the purchase anyway.

"Why did he do that?" I asked my wife. She calmly pointed out that all the time the boys were growing up, I always bought my clothes at a nice men's store. That's all they knew. They'd never seen me buy anywhere else.

So all of these—attitudes, attributes, patterns, means of expressing love, solving conflicts, facing difficulties, taking responsibility, honoring parents, handling money, having a relationship with God—all come from seeing how you yourself do it. They aren't taught so much as caught.

What is taught?

Skills.

You can demonstrate how to do something, certainly. Example is the first step, but then you have to add verbal directions. You've got to teach somebody how to drive, how to balance a checkbook, how to start a fire, how to build a house. Skills must be taught deliberately and consciously.

Traditions are also taught verbally. When we practice certain traditions in our families and explain the reasons and the significance, we pass them on to our children. And God, as we know, is great on traditions. From Passover to prayer before meals, traditions must be verbalized, reiterated, and passed from generation to generation.

Finally, truth must be taught, particularly revelational truth that comes from the Bible. There's no other place we can learn about God, Christ, the Holy Spirit, and man's nature. The basics, such as the Ten Commandments, have to be taught day after day after day.

But in addition, we need to capitalize on teachable moments when biblical truth can be applied to life. One of the best times is during meals. A survey among graduate students at the University of Chicago asked where they got their major ideas in morals and religion. The most common response: "Through conversations with our family at mealtimes." These times are precious; guard against meal conversations degenerating into clashes or critical episodes.

At times, however, special teachable moments present themselves. I read once about Robert Schuller, who's raised a great family, and what he did when his son lied to him about a date. When Schuller discovered the lie, he knew their trust had been broken.

As he stood talking with his son about it, he took a beautiful china cup and dropped it on the floor. Looking at the broken pieces, he said, "Our trust was like that cup. Now it's broken. I want you to put those pieces back together. And when you're finished, you'll understand how important it is to have trust."

His son will never forget that lesson.

Good parents combine modeling and instruction because they know that the important things in life are both caught and taught.

Related Articles

All about Models

DAVID VEERMAN

As I flipped through the pages of the mail order catalog I couldn't help noticing the models . . . beautiful people with manicured hair, streamlined physiques, and clear skin, posed in perfection. Their purpose, of course, is to draw the attention of the potential consumer and to portray what he or she could be with a particular product. These consumables cover the range from slacks and slippers to sledges and slides.

I've often thought, wouldn't it be great to see a "realistic" catalog featuring real people, worn clothes, and rusty equipment! It would certainly be more true to life, but I doubt if it would sell! In spite of our cynicism, we are affected by models— we buy and even become what we see.

This whole idea of "modeling" has been on my mind lately. I have been in youth work for over twenty years, and am painfully aware of the role of models in these young lives. Obviously I am not speaking about "paid for posing" professionals, but about the significant adults who portray what life is like "when you grow up."

You see, whether we like it or not, we are "on stage" before an audience watching our every move. It's subtle, of course; they didn't pay for admission, aren't taking notes, and probably are not even aware of it ... but it's happening. Our young people are "adults in process," and as their parents, neighbors, employers, and community 'leaders we are teaching them what life is about.

I have heard a multitude of complaints about "this generation" and what kind of leaders they will make, but what have we been teaching? Let me ask us a few hard questions.

From observing our lives, what do our children learn about values? "The best things in life are free," but we build our temporal castles and stuff them with expensive toys and status symbols. We want our kids to be kind and considerate, but they hear us shout obscenities at an encroaching driver. We believe in honesty and in love for our country, but they watch us cheat on our income tax. We preach against drugs, and then anesthetize our feelings with alcohol. Then there are the messages transmitted by marital blow-ups, littering habits, and our nation's demand for abortions and guns.

What do they learn about priorities? They watch us spend only fleeting moments with the family (the pressures of work, you know), and they notice where our money is spent.

What do they learn about morality from watching us, television, and our business, labor, and political leaders? It's frightening, isn't it!

And how about faith? Do they even know about God when they see us genuflecting before idols of money and success? I'm afraid we teach, "In us we trust."

Our government calls it a crime to "contribute to the delinquency of a minor." Jesus calls it sin. His strong rebuke is found in Matthew 18:6-7: "But if anyone causes one of these little ones who believe in Me to sin, it would be better for him to have a large millstone hung around his neck and to be drowned in the depths of the sea. Woe to the world because of the things that cause people to sin! Such things must come, but woe to the man through whom they come!" (NIV)

We have a tremendous responsibility whether we want it or not. No one lives to himself. What kind of model do our children see? God help us!

Related Articles
Chapter 2: You Can't Teach Your Children Everything—But What *Can* You Teach Them?
Chapter 13: Communicating Values to Our Children

THE MODEL PARENT

Since I'm not sure how much preaching and teaching parents can do during their children's teen years, I think their basic influence is through modeling.

Parents model their faith to a teenager by their quality of life and by their marriage. Teenagers are notorious for their ability to spot inconsistency. All parents have to do is show inconsistency in the faith process during the adolescent years and it's all over.

Probably ninety percent of the spiritual influence that parents have is from the quiet modeling that goes on day after day. I think that the verbal teaching is probably done during the first ten years of a child's life and the modeling, more than ever, is the important thing done during the next ten years.

Gordon MacDonald

Parents Need to Change Too!

EVELYN CHRISTENSON

When our first child turned eighteen, and became of legal age in Illinois, she announced at the dinner table one night that she never wanted to hear Mother's philosophy of life again. She had always been an independent child, and since she was about to enter college she decided she wanted to find out about the world for herself, to find her own way in life.

But the clincher came when she said, "Mother, do you know you actually change the tone of your voice when you give us your philosophy of life?" That really horrified me. I flew upstairs and threw myself on the bed. I sobbed and cried and prayed, "Lord, I already have promised You that I'll be the wife You want me to be. Now do I have to be the mother You want me to be too?"

The answer from God was yes. After that I went underground with the Lord, so to speak, for fourteen months. I threw myself into the Word and let God show me the mother He wanted me to be. In doing so, I applied the principle of 1 Peter 3:1-2 (a wife winning her unbelieving

---

CAN WE TAKE MODELING TOO FAR?

We hear a lot today about kids needing adult models. "We need more adult male models for boys," "We need more adult female models for girls." We now know that there's a limit to what can be taught by modeling. Modeling as a technique for communication is most effective in conveying personal *values* and *attitudes* such as honesty, punctuality, and generosity. *Skills,* however, are taught through demonstration and good practice.

There is a danger when the process and product are confused. Values cannot be demonstrated; they are modeled in everything said and done. Skills are not modeled; they are demonstrated and taught. One word of caution: You cannot choose which values to model—modeling conveys all the values you hold, both good and bad.

Values are being eroded in our society. Recently Christians have emphasized the importance of modeling because we know values must be conveyed to our young people in order for them to survive the world's temptations. Consider these questions:

- What values do you want modeled for your children?
- What values do you *not* want modeled for your children?
- What skills do you want your children to have?

Modeling can convey:	Modeling cannot convey:
The value of tithing	How to write a budget
Personal love for God	How to study the Bible
The importance of loyalty	How to select a college

Bruce B. Barton & James C. Galvin

husband by her chaste and reverent behavior) to my relationship with my daughter. I began to realize that my daughter was becoming an adult and I had to release her from my authority; I had to cut the apron strings. This hurt me more than it hurt her, but as I read the Word and prayed, I discovered that I had replaced motherhood with smotherhood and I needed to change that.

An amazing thing happened as I kept quiet with Jan. A few months after she told me she had had enough of my philosophy, I overheard her telling a friend, "Mother says this" and "Mother says that." I could hardly believe that my daughter, who hadn't wanted to hear my views on life, was now sharing them with someone else.

Had I fought with her instead of withdrawing, I think that to this day she might be trying to find herself. Fortunately, I did the changing and allowed her to discover her own character. As a result she was able to develop confidence that I wasn't going to superimpose my will on her forever. When she realized this, she came back as my friend, closer than before. And because I learned my lesson, my two other children didn't rebel in a similar fashion. They could rest assured that I didn't try to run Jan's life and I wouldn't try to run theirs either.

Principles of Change
The first step in changing my smotherhood to motherhood was to admit I needed changing. This is difficult for parents, especially because we're prone to thinking we're always right. Parents need to realize they are not God, and as a result, hardly perfect. It takes a lot of grace to be parents of a teenager, and only when parents get their wisdom, strength, and grace from God will they be able to cope.

Being changed by God does not happen overnight. It happens gradually, bit by bit, as we are transformed into the parents He wants us to be. The process begins from the time parents know the baby is on the way. From then on, being parents is a constant adjustment. Every day, parents need to pray, "Lord, change me; help me adjust and change right along with the child." After all, life is nothing but one grand, glorious adjustment.

After we admit that we, and not our children, have to change, then we need advice or wisdom on how to change. James 3:13-17 talks about four possible sources of wisdom. First, parents can receive direction from what they think— their own thoughts—but the Bible has nothing good to say about what comes out of our fleshly selves.

Then, there are sources in the world— other people, books, authorities. The third possible source James talks about is demonic. Many times Satan wants to work in either the life of the parent or the teen, and we must be very careful that our wisdom doesn't come from Satan.

The fourth source of wisdom is from God. He has given us the Bible for doctrine, reproof, correction, and instruction in righteousness. That means that I must stay daily in the Bible and get my advice from God. Even so-called good Christian literature can lead us opposite of what God's Word really says, so we must test all that we read by the Bible.

Whenever I read the Word, I search diligently for wisdom. I open myself up before I read, praying, "God, show me what needs changing; show me what You need to teach me." This isn't always negative; sometimes God shows me what He wants me to do in a positive way.

Once we know what the Bible says, we need to be willing to submit to it and let God change us. We must be submissive day-by-day to God's changing process in us and be willing to apply what God says must change in our lives.

For example, one day I was reading in God's Word about restoring a person to fellowship through a spirit of gentleness. God stopped me very emphatically and showed me that a certain person in my family needed to be restored through a spirit of gentleness. For God to tell me this meant I had to change. I couldn't ignore His command.

Of course, teens must be willing to change too. But they learn by example. If they see parents willing to let God change them, it won't be nearly so hard for teens to change. But if all teens see are stubborn, self-willed parents, they won't have much incentive to change.

Changing with Prayer

Besides being in the Word, prayer is another key to changing. I pray daily, "In this prayer of mine, in this attitude, in this thought, in this reaction, Lord, just change me. I need changing. Continuously make me holier, more like Jesus Christ." This involves being submissive to God and letting Him be my Lord.

Sometimes I wish that God would finish changing me, but of course He doesn't. As my children are now married and in grad school, I find myself praying even more, "Lord, change me today; change my attitudes; change my thinking." This is such a constant prayer for me that I don't think I get through a day without praying it at least once.

IT'S NEVER TOO LATE TO CHANGE

There's hardly a parent alive who does not have some regrets and painful memories of failures as a mother or a father. Children are infinitely complex, and we cannot be perfect parents any more than we can be perfect human beings. The pressures of living are often enormous, and we get tired and irritated; we are influenced by our physical bodies and our emotions, which sometimes prevent us from saying the right things and being the model we should. We don't always handle our children as unemotionally as we wish we had, and it's very common to look back a year or two later and see how wrong we were in the way we approached a problem.

All of us experience these failures! *No one does the job perfectly!* That's why each of us should get alone with the Creator of parents and children, saying,

"Lord, You know my inadequacies. You know my weaknesses, not only in parenting, but in every area of my life. I did the best I could, but it wasn't good enough. As You broke the fishes and the loaves to feed the 5,000, now take my meager effort and use it to bless my family. Make up for the things I did wrong. Satisfy the needs that I have not satisfied. Wrap Your great arms around my children, and draw them close to You. And be there when they stand at the great crossroads between right and wrong. All I can give is my best, and I've done that. Therefore, I submit to You my children and myself and the job I did as a parent. The outcome now belongs to You."

I know God will honor that prayer, even for parents whose job is finished. The Lord does not want you to suffer from guilt over events you can no longer influence. The past is the past. Let it die, never to be resurrected. Give the situation to God, and let Him have it. I think you'll be surprised to learn that you're no longer alone!

James Dobson

From *Dr. Dobson Answers Your Questions,* by James Dobson, Tyndale House Publishers, Inc., © 1982. Used by permission.

An extra benefit is that this philosophy has rubbed off on my children. One day my younger daughter called and told me she hadn't liked something her husband had done. "But Mom, I'm trying to pray, 'Lord, change me, not him.'" I'm thankful my children learned to follow that example.

CHANGE YOURSELF

Sometimes we recognize the need to change, but we have trouble mustering the motivation.

Recognize how damaging this part of you is. Look for the damage it is doing to the people you love the most. If I'm standing on your toe and you tell me what's hurting you, unless I'm really sadistic, I'm going to get off your toe (even though I might like where I'm standing).

Parents have protective instincts. If I *know* I'm hurting my child by something I'm doing, I will want to stop it. We must begin from the basis of how we are marking one generation after another.

Second, appeal to your own memory. One of the ways you know the damage is that you remember how it hurt you. Focus awhile on that hurt.

Third, imagine what your life could be like without that trait. Or what life could be like with the trait under control.

Take a diet, for example. No one likes to diet. Yet millions of people are motivated to diet. Why? First, they realize how they look. They think how they'll look in a bathing suit next season, and aren't happy with the vision they see. Then they muse about what they would look like *without* the trait. It's very appealing to imagine themselves looking slim and trim at poolside. This visualization can be a motivating force.

Think about the advantages for yourself and others if you choose to change. For example, if you've grown up in a family that wasn't expressive, it will be hard to express your feelings. But it would be *great* if you could get those feelings out.

The path of least resistance is to stay where you've been. But think how nice it would be, when you hurt, to be able to tell someone. Visualize what life *could* be like.

Finally, draw on your spiritual resources. Ask God to help motivate you. Look for encouragement from His Word, the Bible, and other Christians. The Gospel of Christ, coupled with real understanding, is the power to effect change.

Ronald P. Hutchcraft

Correcting Failures

Righting the Wrongs

RAY & ANNE ORTLUND

All parents have times of feeling that they have failed their children. The important thing to remember is that it's never too late. God is a God of new beginnings. He wants to pick us up and start us fresh each day. As the Apostle Paul says in 2 Corinthians 5:17, we're new creations. The old has passed away and the new is coming on. We can confidently expect God's power to work in our lives so that we're not repeating yesterday's failures.

Confession is important. We need to confess our failures to God, but also to our kids. The two of us once went to a conference about being honest and humble with your teenagers. We went home, and as soon as it was possible we took Nels out for dinner. On the way to the restaurant we went for a little ride, and we parked on a hillside overlooking the bay. We sat there thinking and talking, and we told him that we'd learned at the conference that we needed to be far more humble with him. We needed to ask his forgiveness for some things we'd been wrong about.

We've always asked our kids for forgiveness when we knew we had wronged them, but this time we said, "We know we've often made mistakes that you could feel uptight about, but we don't even know what they are. We hardly know when we've injured you or when we've been offensive or quick on the trigger when we should have been careful."

We had a wonderful time just sharing our concerns. We laughed and cried together and gave fresh love to each other, and Nels said, "It's OK, Mom and Dad. I do forgive you, and I need forgiveness myself." It was a lovely time when failures were corrected and hope given for a new start. We all knew, of course, that we would make mistakes again, but our little "summit conference" definitely put us on a new level of communication and closeness.

There are two barriers that can stand in the way of parents' humbling themselves and asking forgiveness. The two barriers are pride and fear. We're afraid to lose control or authority. We think if we don't keep the upper hand, things will go from bad to worse. But actually, it's very important for us parents of teens to begin to lose some of that authority and some of that control.

The teenager is growing up. He is more adult, usually, than the parents think. He feels like an equal now, even though he isn't. If we use one-upmanship on him, it will just increase his sense of competitiveness. If we criticize him, he'll give it right back to us. Then we have shouting matches, and a dangerous hostility develops. It's up to the parents to make the first move, to back off and deliberately lose some of our authority. Otherwise we will never effect that transformation of our children into maturity that we long for.

Our children's growth into true greatness of character will only come as they learn humility. And they will never learn humility unless they see it in their parents. So our failures need to be exposed. We need to confess them to our teenagers. Modeling humility is the only way we will ever teach our teenagers to confess, to say they're sorry, and to correct their own failures. (Anne shares more about this in her book, *Children Are Wet Cement,* Revell, 1981.)

Some parents are afraid their teenagers will take advantage of them if they humble themselves. That's a possibility, of course, but the best things in life often involve danger. Challenges always open us up to possible failure. We simply have to take the risk.

This is why we say that parents have to grow up as their children begin to grow up. You go into deeper waters than you've ever been in before. Some parents bear an enormous load of guilt over past failures. They feel as if they've been through the emotional wringer, and they're fearful of opening themselves up to the possibility of more pain. These people need to come to a deep understanding of God's forgiveness. We all need to understand God's grace if we're going to be gracious to our teenagers. We can't really forgive them, we can't show grace to them, until we have discovered how gracious our heavenly Father is to us.

And when we understand how totally He has forgiven us through the shed blood of Christ on the cross, then we can begin to forgive ourselves. We read in Psalm 103:12 that God has removed our sins from us as far as the east is from the west, in Micah 7:19 that He has cast them into the depths of the sea, in Isaiah 43:25 that He blots them out. In fact, all Scripture from Genesis to Revelation shows a God who completely forgives and forgets. Only when we truly understand what He has done with our sins of last month and last year and so on, can we accept ourselves enough to begin to function as parents.

Now, even though God forgives us as soon as we ask, correcting our failures, we must remember, may not happen overnight. Working out our relationships with our children is a process, a day-by-day humbling. But it's a walk into a beautiful new place of surrender and peace and reconciliation.

Related Articles
Chapter 2:   Becoming a Confident Parent
Chapter 2:   Parents Need to Change Too!
Chapter 3:   Dealing with Guilt

God Never Makes a Mistake

Adversity's Silver Lining

EVELYN CHRISTENSON

When I was twenty-three, God gave me Romans 8:28 and I took it as my philosophy of life. In my own words, "God is turning all things into something good for us if we love Him." Age twenty-three was a very hard time for me. I had just had my third miscarriage, my husband was just back from overseas in World War II, and his father had just died.

Through this verse, God showed me that He was not off His throne and that He was doing all this for my good. Looking back now, I know that my husband still had seven years of higher education and I had college ahead of me as well. God showed me that if we had the three babies that I wanted, we never could have gone back to school and done the things to prepare us for the paths to which God was calling.

Later, after God gave us two daughters and a son, we incorporated this verse into our family life, talking about it openly with our children. Our home was run on the principle that God never makes a mistake.

When something negative happened to the children we looked to see how God used it for good. When we couldn't see the good, we talked about how God was still working for our good and we'd understand how when we got to heaven. We taught them that somewhere along the line the situation would work for good because God promised it.

Positive through the Negative

It boils down to our faith in who God really is. He's the God who does not make a mistake and when we know that, no matter what calamity comes, we have peace. This principle works not only in big things, but in the little, daily occurrences of life. If the mailman didn't deliver something on time, then we would look to see how God was going to work it out and what good could come of it. Through the little things, our children learned that there is nothing so bad that God can't turn it into something positive.

We learned that sometimes God uses an event to discipline or train us. When our daughter was in her first semester of college she got one B because she didn't follow instructions exactly. Through that, she learned the importance of taking orders. She ended up going to medical school and became an internist. God was preparing her by teaching her a hard lesson.

It's important for this principle to become a way of life from youth. If a teen is going through a hard time and the parents say, "Well, God works everything for good for those who love Him," the teenager may rebel if this hasn't been a built-in attitude all through childhood.

When our children were young, they would occasionally come home from school very angry at the teacher or a classmate. Then we'd sit down and talk about how God was going to work this out for good and how a friendship might develop through it. Little by little, the children became less resentful when things didn't work out exactly the way they wanted. They began to look to God for the final answer.

When they became teenagers, it was a habit to look for the good in the bad. This training helped our family during the most difficult experience in one of our teenagers' lives. I can't give the details of what happened, but it was a crushing experience. The teen had been brought up in absolute faith that God was working everything for our good. When the calamity happened, it was our teen who came to us and said, "God has told me He's working this out for good." That doesn't mean it wasn't a tremendously difficult time for us, but underlying it was the assurance that God was not making a mistake. Our child had already learned complete trust in God.

On the Lookout

Sometimes lessons are very obvious and parents can say, "Of course, this is how God's going to use this." But there are times when it's more difficult to find the positive in the negative. Parents may have to search and search, only to say to the teen, "Let's think of the possibilities of how this could be used." God doesn't always show us right away; it may be two or three years later before we understand why. Other times He doesn't show us until we get to heaven.

One benefit of hard experiences is they help us help others. I told my teens many times, "Since you've learned this hard thing in your life and God has turned it into good for you, think of all the other teenagers who you'll be able to reassure, 'I know God can do this for you because He did it for me.' "

However, this principle does not apply

to someone who does not know Jesus as Saviour and Lord. It's for those who love God. Parents must be absolutely sure that their children have trusted Christ. Sometimes we forget that just because we gave birth to a child and we are Christians doesn't mean the child is a Christian too.

Parents cannot claim the promises in the New Testament unless the teen knows Jesus Christ.

Related Articles
Chapter 1: Getting More from Your Family
Chapter 2: Becoming a Confident Parent

Finding a Shoulder to Lean On

HAROLD MYRA

People need to be affirmed, and this is especially true of parents of teenagers. Just as marriage enrichment groups can help marriages, parent enrichment can help parents do a better job.

My wife, Jeanette, and I are involved in small groups at church. These aren't specifically about parenting, but they've helped us become better parents. We're with people who share our values, and we

PARENT SUPPORT GROUPS

Parenting requires a certain measure of self-confidence. Yet all the research in the world shows that classes on parenting, books on parenting, sermons on parenting don't significantly increase Mom's and Dad's self-confidence.

But the one thing that has been shown to make a significant difference is when a group of parents who are going through similar kinds of situations meet regularly and simply talk about what's happening. Such interaction goes a long way in reducing anxiety, increasing self-confidence, and finding better ways to handle children's behavior.

If parents wanted to do something that would make a real difference in the world, it would be to get together with other parents on a regular basis—every week, let's say—just to talk. This session could be totally unstructured or it could involve some background reading. Whatever the format, the emphasis should not be theoretical, but practical. For example, "Our subject tonight is discipline. Let's talk about what's been happening to us with discipline, how we feel, what our values are, what we've learned."

Group discussions enable parents to receive a lot of reinforcement from other parents as well as ideas on handling behavior.

But most of all, they help parents see that other people have the same problems they do. Knowing that other people are going through the same experiences is a great encouragement, because all parents occasionally blow it with their kids.

Larry Richards

talk informally about raising our children. Jeanette often has said how difficult it would be if our friends had a low view of marriage or didn't care about instilling values in their children. Parents need one another to keep one another strong.

Every parent can benefit from talking with other parents who share the same values. Even casually asking, "What are you learning about raising kids?" or "What are your frustrations?" can bring out helpful insights.

Of course, sensitivity and judgment must govern what you say. Teens don't appreciate being the subject of their parents' every conversation. And we must be careful not to type them—"This one's the good one; this one's the dumb one"—which can cause lasting scars. Parents must be careful not to say things that would embarrass teens if the comments got back to them.

Besides other parents, I've found support from two other sources. The first is books. There have been some marvelous things written on being a Christian parent by such authors as Charlie and Martha Shedd and James Dobson. A visit to a good church library or a Christian bookstore can unearth a lot of wisdom.

The second source of support is a Christian counselor. Our family was having some problems a few years ago with a school situation. One of our children felt attacked by his classmates. So our whole family went to the counselor and asked him to analyze exactly what we were doing and what new directions we should explore. We all learned much more about the difference between verbal and physical punches and how to handle them; we learned how to apply the insights to our family life. Good professional help meant a great deal.

Parents shouldn't feel guilty admitting they need help. Being a parent is no soft job. If resources are available from other parents, books, and professionals, it doesn't make sense to ignore them.

Becoming a Confident Parent

V. GILBERT BEERS

"**Y**ou too?" How many times parents say this when friends confide that they too have problems. It's easy to think we are all alone, that nobody else has the same problems we have. So it is a reassuring discovery to learn that our problems are not ours alone. They are shared with dozens, no hundreds, of other parents.

Perhaps this discovery came at a Bible study, a couples' retreat, or at coffee with friends. Where is not important, and how is not important. But it is extremely important for us to learn that we are not that different from hundreds of other parents, and that our teens are not that different from hundreds of other teens.

It isn't that misery loves company. Rather, it is discovering that we are not failures or that our teens are not misfits. We and they are "under construction."

The affirming knowledge that our problems are somewhat universal is a confidence-builder. We find confidence in the recognition that others have gone the same way and have survived beautifully, that teens with problems often grow up to be more conservative than we are. Confidence comes from seeing others resolve their problems and becoming role models for us, or we for them.

Confidence is a valuable by-product of affirmation. Someone needs to remind us of the good things, the right things, we are doing as parents. Husbands and wives have one another. If we are wise, we will affirm one another as parents, and not build doubts in one another.

Of course, single parents do not have a husband or wife to give affirmation. But they can seek affirming friends, those who build confidence in this important job of parenting.

This is a reminder to be an affirming husband, wife, or friend. Look for ways daily to help build your mate as a parent, and as a mate. If you are a single parent, look for other single parents who are doing a good job, alone, and affirm that friend. It is a treat to hear someone say, "You certainly do a fine job raising your son or daughter." Especially when you know that it is true.

The greatest confidence-builder of all is to hear your teen compliment you on a job well done. "I'm glad you're my mom," or "You're really a special dad." That makes you want to do twice as much. Of course, you can't ask your teen to say these things. You can't even plant something like that in your teen.

But if you are in the business of affirming your teen, you may be pleasantly surprised to hear your teen get into the business of affirming you. Of course, your affirmation must be honest, never with the intent of having it come back to you. Who wants that kind of praise?

ADVICE FOR DISCOURAGED PARENTS

When a teen rebels, it's so easy to become discouraged. But we can counteract the effects of discouragement by keeping our eyes on God, and continuing to trust Him. If a teen runs away from home, we need to keep our arms and our door open at all times.

Parents may want to kick the child out and be done with it because they are so discouraged. But I've learned never, never to give up. My brother turned his back on God when he was twenty. My mother and the rest of our family prayed for thirty years before he came back to God. That lesson in patience taught me to never give up on my children.

We need to replace our impatience over the teen's behavior with an absolute assurance that the child is going to come back. This may mean paying a costly price in disciplined prayer and letting the Lord change us. It's much easier to be disgruntled parents and just throw up our hands in defeat. But we need great strength to keep on interceding and undergirding the child in prayer.

No children do everything just the way parents want them to do. There were times when I was discouraged with my children. When that happened, I looked to God, not to the left or to the right, not to circumstances, not to myself, not to my own feelings. But I simply looked up to God and received assurance, comfort, and wisdom from Him.

In the end, no matter what the child does, we can still love him. We don't have to condone his behavior but we can continue to love the child because we want him in heaven with us. That's our ultimate goal in caring for our children.

Evelyn Christenson

Teens learn from parents who role model lifestyle. If you and your mate affirm one another, this sets an example for your teen. Somewhere, sometime, you will hear your teen begin to imitate that wonderful example. On the other hand, if your teen hears you and your mate tear one another down, or chide one another, or even make oblique references to one another, how can you expect that young person to become an affirming teen, to you, or to a future mate?

Remember, confidence in your work, even as parents, does not depend alone on how well you do. It often depends more on how well others think or say you do. Affirmation from others—mate, friends, teens—is as important in confidence-building as the quality of your parenting.

One other source of confidence-building is your own honest affirmation of yourself. No hard sell to yourself, no delusions, no pat on your own back. But if you know you're doing your best as a parent, admit it to yourself. Confidence is based on a healthy self-esteem, which is based on an honest recognition that you are doing your best with what you have.

Of course, the best source of confidence is rooted in the firm conviction that you are doing what God expects you as parents to be doing. Nobody is perfect. We all know that. But do you think God is satisfied with what you are doing? If so, that is a marvelous affirmation, the best of all. And that can give you confidence to keep on in the pursuit of excellence in the highest calling—parenting.

Related Articles

THE RISKS
OF RAISING TEENAGERS

- Can you ever stop worrying about your kids?
- Handling the pressures which affect raising children
- Involvement in the life of your teenager could get you hurt
- Dealing with the guilt of feeling like an ineffective parent
- What if husband and wife disagree over handling children?
- The effect of words spoken in anger

Arthur Miller's play *Death of a Salesman* coins the phrase, "It comes with the territory." Surely this can apply to the task of being parents. There are certain risks inherent in parenting. Young people can be hurt. They can get into deep difficulties. They can bring us heartache. But there are no rewards without risk; there are no adventures without danger.

Risk should not immobilize us and make us unable to deal with daily stress. It is stress that allows us to grow. The very process of working through difficulties is often its own reward. And nothing can compare with the joy and excitement—even though there are risks involved—of parenting teenagers.

How to Stop Worrying about Your Kids

TED W. ENGSTROM

Many parents, with furrowed brows, have asked, "Will we ever stop worrying about our kids' . . .?" Often the sentence is completed with fears for their children about driving, dating, values, or their future. Are parents destined to be worry-warts forever?

I don't think you ever quit worrying about your children. The worry level varies, of course, and you don't worry about the same things. But you'll always have a deep, deep Christian concern for the people who play a big part in your life and family. It is understandable for parents to be concerned for their children. Yet there must be a proper balance of trust and concern.

The number one way we can ease our anxiety is to *trust our children to the Lord's care*. While we agree in theory, it's a lot harder to *live* as if God is in control. Children are temporary trusts God has placed in our homes. We need to let God develop our children into the people He wants them to be.

Too many of us try to hang on to our kids too long. We have so many fears for them. Yet there is a time when we need to cut the strings on our kids. We need to gradually let those strings loosen so our children can become the kinds of individuals they were trained to be as youngsters. The teen years are too late to begin that kind of training. Start when your youngsters are preteen or before. Program ahead to let go and allow God to take over.

Somewhere along the line I think parents of a teenager need to ask, "How much do I trust my teenager?" Teens are very quick to discern this for themselves. It's important that parents not overreact or be overprotective of their teenagers. That is something I tended to have problems with, particularly with the older children. Perhaps as we gain experience in raising children, we loosen the reins a bit.

When my son was a senior in high school, he was always suspicious that I didn't trust him. I think I could have trusted him, and that deep inside I really did. But I didn't show it to him, especially when I asked dumb questions like, "Where have you been?" Fortunately, I think I was easier on the other children.

The bottom line is we need to think through the trust issue prayerfully and try to identify the areas of conduct and relationships that we feel merit trust in our children. The teenage years are a time to learn about new areas of life, such as trusting and having confidence in the Lord. Like it or not, as parents, you are role models for the young persons in your home. Help your teens see a proper balance between trust and concern.

We can turn our fears into positive action in three tangible ways. First, *establish an advocacy relationship on behalf of your young people.* If ever youngsters need someone to support them and favor them, it is during their teen years. Let them know you are on the same team; that they are part of *your* team. Unfortunately, too often teens feel as if their parents are the opponents.

Second, *help teens and preteens develop a proper value system.* All homes have certain "norms" or ways of doing things. Sometimes these norms are established by default. As Christians, we need to take active roles in establishing norms for our children.

For example, issues of how children should obey, and what their duties are in the home, need to be established. How children are to react to their parents— their attitudes—should also be decided ahead of time. A proper value system will be a firm foundation a teen can draw strength from in later years. Take advantage of the opportunity to establish this foundation in your home.

Finally, *individualized communication between parents and their kids is very important.* Show your concern for your children without being distrustful and interfering too much in their lives. It takes practice to learn to communicate your trust and concern to children in a loving manner.

As a kid, when I came home late at night, there was always a light on and I knew that one of my parents would be awake, no matter what time it was. Even though I hated it at the time, I realize, looking back, how much I appreciated that. I would have been concerned if the light hadn't been on!

Commit your children to the Lord's care, and turn your worries to trust and concern.

Related Articles

Pressures from Without and Within

Handling the Stresses of Raising Teens

GARY R. COLLINS

In addition to the day-to-day demands of raising a family, there are many pressures parents face—from both without and within—that add confusion at home.

As a psychologist, I've found ten pressures that seem fairly common. These center around situations, emotions, and peers.

1. *Time.* It's time-consuming to raise kids of all ages. But I think it's especially time-consuming to raise teenagers because parents don't have the control they had in earlier years.

With younger children, parents can hold a tighter rein. They're home all the time, you're "bigger," and the children are more likely to obey.

Teenagers, in contrast, are freer to leave the house. They have driver's licenses and more control over their lives. It takes extra time just to keep track of where they are!

2. *Unpredictability.* Teenagers don't plan ahead. They see no need to. So they decide on the spur of the moment to tell you that they're going out, they need the car, or they want help.

Sometimes you're ready to talk to them about their problems, but they're not ready to talk to *you* about what's bothering them. Yet they're ready to talk about their problems at seemingly the most awkward times. That presents problems when you're an adult trying to keep a schedule.

When teens are young and don't have a license, they're inclined to say, "Hey, I'd like to go over to so-and-so's house right now." Or, "I forgot; I have to get a notebook for school tomorrow and need to go to the store right now." That unpredictability is difficult for parents who try to keep some semblance of order in their lives.

At those times, a lot depends on our attitudes. If we're going to be parents of teenagers, we've got to realize that it's going to take time. If your teen is suddenly ready to talk, you can't be too concerned about your work or the opportunity to communicate may pass.

There have been a number of times when my wife will come to say good night to one of the teens, and that's just when one of our daughters starts jabbering. Sometimes they want to talk about very serious things; sometimes they just want to chat. Parents need to have an attitude of putting the children's needs above their own, to try to capture the *right* moment, whether in the home or out. We can even arrange special times by taking them out to breakfast or lunch, or by going other places together. But we can't let teenagers completely dominate our schedules. I think teens need to recognize that parents have schedules too, and it's up to parents to lovingly hold the line.

I have a daughter who comes hopping into my office at all hours. If I'm working intensely, sometimes I have to say, "Hey, Jan, I'll have to talk to you a little later."

Parents need to have the attitude of "Yes, I'm willing to be available and I *will* be available," but they also need to set reasonable limits.

3. *Uncertainty.* There aren't many cut and dried rules to parenting. For example, "Should I let my teens go to this meet-

ing?" "Should I let them go to this basketball game?" "Do I let them go to the local school party when I know there's going to be a lot of drugs there, even though I trust my teen?"

It's very difficult for parents to make decisions like these because they don't always have all the facts. Things have changed since they were kids, and it's difficult to know what to do.

A simple, but seldom practiced answer, is to ask God for wisdom. The Scripture records this promise: "But if any of you lacks wisdom, let him ask of God, who gives to all men generously and without reproach, and it will be given to him" (James 1:5, NASB).

As parents, we need to ask God for wisdom all the time. Sometimes He gives us wisdom and we don't even realize it. We pray, make a decision based on the best available evidence we have, and hope it works out well. It's a matter of faith and trust in God.

4. *Lack of good reasons.* It's frustrating to sense that something ought to be done or some activity ought to be stopped, but you haven't got a good, concrete reason. Intuition or guidance of the Holy Spirit is hard to explain to a teen. Yet teens in our society are trained to demand reasons.

For example, one of my teens wanted to see a particular rock group. Many of our church youth were going because apparently a lot of Christian people like this group.

We let our daughter go to the concert, and it was OK. But we felt very uneasy over that decision. We vacillated back and forth, sharing our discomforts with her. Yet we had no "good" reason. For each issue we raised, our daughter had a good response.

Sometimes parents have a gut-level feeling that things aren't right, yet they can't pinpoint what the problem is.

I have found it's best not to turn each of these situations into a power struggle. It seems to work out better when you share where you are with your teen. Say, "I feel

UNDER PRESSURE

One pressure parents face in raising teens comes when they are not at home with the kids because of work schedules or other commitments. I traveled a lot over the years and I know my absences had a major effect on each of my children. The pressure was partly guilt and partly frustration that I couldn't do the things with them that I wanted and needed to do.

Another pressure came when my wife and I could not agree on how to discipline the children. There were some areas where it was very difficult for us to come to an agreement. For example, when the children would be gone for several hours in the evening, I didn't worry about it. I would go to sleep and trust them to get home OK. My wife, however, would lie awake until they were in. If she didn't know exactly what they were doing, she was worried. I would say, "You have to trust them," and she would say, "But I've got to know what they are doing." She was probably right in this respect more often than I was, but the danger was in not seeing eye to eye.

Money can also produce pressure. We trained all of our children to look at life and finances a certain way, yet one child was always expecting more money from us. Pressure comes when a child is not really on his own, but his parents are trying to teach him how to be independent.

David Howard

like this . . . but I'll let you make the decision." Then the teen knows that you're not always out to make his or her life miserable.

Often when you really *do* feel strongly about an issue, the teen is more likely to go along with you, because you haven't made every issue a power struggle. It's worth overlooking smaller issues to be heard on the big ones.

5. *Outside influences.* Many people pressure parents, verbally and nonverbally, to make decisions.

For example, what will the neighbor think if I don't let my daughter go to the prom? What will the deacon think if I *do* let my daughter go to the prom?

Parents feel pressure from other teens' parents to conform to the popular decisions. There is also the pressure of your teenager's friends. It seems like a no-win situation because someone will be unhappy no matter what you choose.

I was told once that Billy Graham is a man who works on the assumption that it's best to decide *before God* what's right, then do it. It's important to consider what outsiders think. It's helpful to kick ideas around with other parents. But ultimately, we are responsible for our children and the decisions we've made in their regard. So sometimes I'll make a decision for my teen that's different from the decision some good friends will make for their teen who's the same age. I don't criticize my friends. I just do what I think is right and try to stick with it. Sometimes I'm wrong. But I try to do my best.

6. *Conflicting demands.* Sometimes parents find themselves with two conflicting alternatives.

For example, you want to be available to your teens, but you don't want to let them dominate you. You want to give things to your teens, but you also want to teach them the responsibility of earning money.

All parents can do is examine the two alternatives, compare the strong points and weak points of each, and make a decision on that basis. It helps when a husband and wife can agree on the decision, or at least decide to stick together when they don't agree.

7. *Mother-father disagreement.* It is important for a couple to have good communication. In our home, if I make a decision and my wife disagrees, or if my wife makes a decision and I disagree, we back each other up. Sometimes there isn't time to discuss things between the two of us before we get in a situation where the decision comes up. By backing each other up, we're not setting one parent against the other.

Our children have learned that you can't go to Mom and twist her arm. A husband and wife should support each other and act like a team.

Recently on a winter morning our sixteen-year-old wanted to drive to school. My wife was against the idea because our daughter hasn't had much experience driving on icy roads. I thought aloud, "There isn't that much ice on the road this morning." But I didn't make a big issue of it. When the children begin to see that my wife and I disagree, then they're likely to play one side against the other to get what they want. It's crucial to back each other up.

8. *Guilt.* Some parents feel guilty if they can't be available when their children need them.

If a teen wants you to come to his ball game and it's the same night as a business meeting, you feel badly. When a teen has a psychological problem, attempts suicide, or runs away from home, the parents' immediate reaction is, "It's our fault." It could be. But it might not be the parents' fault at all.

God has given teens and parents freedom. We're not robots. We need to recognize that God forgives us when we make mistakes. We need to learn from our mistakes so we don't repeat them.

It's easy for parents to whip themselves, especially if the teen has a serious problem. A mother came up to me after church one Sunday, having buried her son the day before. He had committed suicide.

I said, "I bet you feel a lot of guilt." She answered, "Oh, absolutely. There were so many things we could have done differ-ently." But I replied, "You did the best you could."

Kids can tell when parents feel guilty. When they sense it, they can use it against them. Parents need to stick together when this happens.

LIFE'S EMBARRASSING MOMENTS

"Why do my teenagers embarrass me so?" The woman leaned forward in her chair and glared at me for some answers. "I can't help it," she continued. "But some of the things they do in front of others make me so angry! My face turns beet red and I really get frustrated."

I rested my elbows on the big wooden desk. "Exactly what do your teens do that embarrass you so much?"

"Well, you know. They'll wear blue jeans to church, or they completely forget their manners when we eat at the boss' house."

"What else do they do?" I asked.

"They listen to such wild music; they don't want to kiss me good-bye when I drop them off at school; and my two sons just don't want to join any sports teams. What's the matter with them?"

I didn't know where to start so I just jumped in. After all, she did come to me for advice.

"You know, Mrs. Smith, I'd like you to look at your real reasons for being embarrassed. Are your kids really doing anything against your convictions, or are you simply reacting to their different lifestyle? Is what they're doing really *wrong?* There is more than one way to live your life without offending God and others.

"Second, are you afraid that you might look like a bad parent as a result of what your children do? Are you trying to live up to the standards of your community, or the standards of God? Distinguish between what God thinks, and what the neighbors think.

"Third, I always find it helpful to ask the question, 'Will this action by my teenager really matter ten years from now?' If what your child does *is* more serious and violates a biblical conviction, communicate with him calmly and openly with understanding. Be honest above all, and explain the reason why you are embarrassed.

"You know, Mrs. Smith, at times you may have to take some embar-rassment to allow your kids to be kids. It's only natural that their values will be somewhat different from yours. Don't take this as a sign of rejection. It is simply a sign of growing up. Give your teens time to develop a sensitivity to your feelings. The quicker you show them love and acceptance, rather than frustration and anger, the quicker they will tune in to your feelings."

As Mrs. Smith walked out the door, I didn't know if she had heard anything I'd said. Was she looking to me to affirm her feelings, or did she really care about her kids? I wondered.

YFC Editors

9. *Anger,* and its cousin, *frustration.* One thing that seems to anger or frustrate parents is trying to communicate with a teen from an adult perspective. From the teen's viewpoint, parents don't seem to be on the same wavelength.

We don't have much shouting in our house, but my daughter got angry recently and raised her voice. I said, "You don't have to talk loud." She replied, "I'm not talking loud; I'm not shouting."

Rather unwisely, I asked her sister, "Who is doing the shouting?" She agreed that it was her sister.

It's frustrating when you can't seem to communicate and when a teen seems unreasonable.

In our home, we take a little cooling down time, and then come back and try to talk about the matter. We have to continually learn more effective ways of communication.

10. *Money.* Teenagers are expensive! Any child is expensive. But teens eat a lot more and are much more concerned about designer jeans and having their hair done a certain way. Our kids are in a private school. Tuition is expensive. Graduation presents cost money. And college expenses are just over the horizon.

I have two teenage daughters, so basically we have a family of four adults now. When we go places we have to pay twice as much in adult fares as we used to. Of course, we don't have to pay baby-sitters like we used to either.

Teens can sometimes get jobs and supplement the budget, but they still are expensive.

More frustrating is that teens seem to have little or no concept of money. For example, they want to go to concerts which cost eight to fifteen dollars. That's expensive. And worrying about money matters can be a real pressure.

Parents need to set the example when it comes to teaching kids responsible money management and spending priorities. And they need to remind themselves

and their children that God will supply all their needs—not necessarily all their wants (Phil. 4:19).

Dealing Positively with Pressure

Pressures faced in raising teens can affect parents physically, emotionally, mentally/psychologically, and spiritually.

Physically, the pressures can lead to headaches or ulcers. When parents can't verbalize their feelings of frustration, they often internalize their thoughts, taking it out on their bodies.

Emotionally, parents may become discouraged and despairing. This can result in interpersonal problems with friends and family members. Often the husband-wife relationship is strained.

Because of the stress, a parent is *mentally* preoccupied and cannot think clearly.

The *spiritual* dimension is the most important. Depending on a parent's reaction, he or she will be drawn *away* from God or drawn *closer.*

As parents, you can deal with these issues by several means:

1. *Admit your frustration.* There's a healing value that comes from admitting your pressures to yourself and your spouse. Parents need to be honest enough to admit them to their children as well.

When my eldest child turned thirteen, we had a Coke and a chat together. I said, "You know, I've never been the parent of a teen, and you've obviously never been a teenager. I've heard all these stories about how terrible it's going to be. But I'm going to try to shoot straight with you. If you'll do that with me, I think we can enjoy the next few years."

My daughter is seventeen now, and we have a good relationship. We have our difficulties at times, but every family does.

2. *Read about the pressures you face as parents.* Many books are being published about the critical issues between parents and teens. Take advantage of these resources. If you check them out of a

public or church library, it won't even cost anything.

3. *Remember the spiritual resources that are available.* As Christians, I believe we can pray earnestly about these things. We can ask God to give us wisdom and strength to deal with the pressures. The Bible is full of sage advice on living together in harmony. Pray that the Holy Spirit will illumine your heart and teach you as you read.

4. *Talk with other parents of teenagers.* Who else can be so empathetic about your plight? I find real value in sharing with other parents.

My wife and I have a Bible study group, and often we'll discuss a parent-child issue. We find it very therapeutic to know what other parents are facing, and what their kids are doing. The godly counsel of other concerned Christians can really help.

5. *Get to know your teen's friends.* By becoming familiar with your teen's friends, you can better understand his

world. As pressures affect you, you'll have a greater "feel" for your teen's struggles. That should help you make more intelligent decisions.

Apparently, a lot of parents are so intimidated by teenagers that they don't talk to their *own* teens—much less their teens' friends! It seems that few adults in the church reach out to make friends with teens. Yet the teens seem to enjoy friendships with those who do.

Don't let your pressures mount to the point that you can no longer bear them. The moment you realize that things are getting to you, start taking steps to remedy the situation or your attitude. You *can* deal with your pressures effectively.

Related Articles

Involvement in Your Teenager's Life Could Get You Hurt

V. GILBERT BEERS

Parenting is a risky business. It requires a heavy investment of ourselves and our resources with no guarantee that the whole venture will pay off.

The more parents become involved, the higher the risk. It is much more than just losing the investment of time, money, and personal resources. A poor response in the child-raising business can leave us hurt and wondering. It can leave scars that never go away.

But the word *parenting* suggests we

will become involved. To talk about parenting without involvement is like talking about a business venture without investment. Involvement is part of the price and those of us who take parenting seriously pay it willingly and even happily.

Involvement suggests an investment of time, energies, money, concern, prayers, hopes, and person. It suggests that we set aside our personal interests for our teens, and instead of "doing our thing" first, we find ourselves "doing their thing" with highest priority.

Parenting suggests success more than failure. We enter into the process with the expectation that our teens will turn out right and that our investment and involvement will have been worth it all.

What causes parents to take the high risk of involvement in the lives of their teens? Why not put all that time, energy, and care into the making of money, building a business, or the pursuit of personal pleasure? Some parents do. But concerned Christian parents value their teens above these things.

When we place that higher value on the lives of our teens, we have no alternative. We *must* become involved, even with the risk that we will be hurt. Usually we don't let that risk bother us, for we assume that the more we become involved, the more likely it is that our teens will turn out right and we will not be hurt.

This will probably be true in most cases. But we must be aware of those situations where we do all we can and still get hurt. To recognize this risk is to help prevent it.

Here are some examples of hurt-producing involvement:

1. Involvement builds an "I want to share in your life" mentality in the parents. Good parents recognize an undefined boundary between sharing in a teen's life enough to provoke a warm response, and sharing in a teen's life too much, provoking a feeling in the teen that he has no privacy and that the parents are getting too nosy or domineering.

Trouble starts when the teen begins to feel "fenced in" or crowded by parental involvement. Involvement is perceived as smothering and the teen withdraws, reaching for breathing room. Things can go from bad to worse if parents think this withdrawal is a sign of an unresponsive teen and begin to step up the involvement to win the teen back. This induces a vicious cycle. Unless parents back off and give the teen some breathing room,

both can get hurt.

We must learn to keep that balance of just enough involvement to be there when needed, but not so much involvement that the teen has no room to grow up, or be his own person, or spend needed time with nonparental influences in his life.

2. The primary job of parenting is to train teens to become independent as they head into the adult years. No responsible parents want teens to remain dependent on them. But the very process of creating independence also creates distance. It invites the teen to begin "weaning himself away" from parents. That is a hurtful process, for what caring, involved parents enjoy the idea that they are contributing to the process of putting distance between themselves and their teens?

Of course, that is what we are doing. As parents, we must adjust our thinking. We become deeply involved so that we can gradually become less involved. At first glance, it doesn't make sense, but that's exactly what we must try to do. What we must do is develop a sensitivity to the art of blending these two seemingly contradictory jobs.

3. Being involved parents means we learn to give up personal pleasure, recreation, and other interests. We gladly give up these things in order to do what we should as parents.

But the hurt comes when we do this so much and so long that even when the teens have left an empty nest, we can't get back into the idea of doing something for ourselves.

Every person, even a parent, deserves some time for recreation and personal rebuilding. It's necessary for renewal and good mental health. Perhaps parents need to learn along the way that it is not a question of no recreation and personal use of time versus much recreation and personal use of time. When children are younger we may need to give up most, but not all, of this precious time. As they move toward independence, perhaps we

RISKY BUSINESS

Did you ever think of raising a family as a risky business? The many external influences and possible internal problems facing every family may require action—or change—and that's risky.

Like changing your location to get your kids out of the city. Like changing your career along with a change of location. Or reducing your standard of living along with a change in location and/or career. Like changing churches so your kids have a healthy youth group even though you're a "pillar" in your own church. Like spending extra money to put your teens in a private school.

But suppose you see your family falling apart and you know something needs to be done. The first step might be to make a list of everything you consider "not open to discussion," and then take a second look at the situation.

As you contemplate a major change, ask, "Is this change appropriate to the situation, or am I changing for the sake of change?" Don't think of a major change as a cure-all. A father may decide to make a career change to move his teen to a better area, when the real problem is that the father never spends any time with his teen. Before making a major change, get to the root of the problem.

Such external changes may be impossible for some families, so the risks may be more internal. Then what? (1) Spend more time one-on-one with your kids. (2) Explore how your church can be significant to your family and its needs. (3) Look at your church and your extended family for positive peer and role models.

Risks are of little importance when weighed against the background of salvaging (and hopefully healing) your family.   *YFC Editors*

---

need to give up less of it.

Parents who never learn to enjoy some time along the way may feel hurt and resentful when teens finally leave home. There is plenty of time now, but we've forgotten how to have fun "without the kids."

4. Involvement as a role model is perhaps one of the most significant ministries which parents can perform. Children of all ages learn most from what we do, rather than what we say. Accessible parents exemplify a God who always listens and cares. Loving, caring parents are models of a loving, caring God.

Role modeling is an expensive business. Parents must at times be more the model than they expect in their teens.

For example, many parents emphasize the dangers of too much TV. They try to tell their teens that too much time before the tube will hurt schoolwork and overshadow an involvement in athletics, reading, and other recreation.

But there is little value in preaching this unless parents are willing to practice it. Not only that, parents may need to be *more* frugal in TV watching than they expect the teen to be, realizing that the teen may not measure up to parental standards. In fact, parents may give up more than they need to give up, for they are not under some of the pressures that the teen faces.

In a sense, parents may be hurt by having to give up many things only because they will not set the example they want unless they do give them up. But that's part of the price of being involved parents, isn't it?

5. Like Hannah, we have children so that we can give them to the Lord. Unlike Hannah, we are not often called to give them up in the very early years, separating them from us as parents.

But when we cultivate in our teens a desire to serve God, we may be cultivating in them a desire to go to a mission field halfway across the world or to serve in some other way that separates them from us. We are pained to see children and grandchildren removed from our presence in order to serve God as we have so carefully taught them to do.

This too is a hurt. But it is a hurt tempered by the joy of seeing our family members please God with their lives.

Parents can look at all these possibilities for hurt and decide that it's less painful not to get involved with their teens. That, of course, can become a classic excuse. "I won't get involved because I might get hurt."

Of course, there are deeper hurts than those we have described. The deepest hurts come when we realize we have not involved ourselves in the lives of our teens and therefore they have not turned out the way we hoped.

In the end, I will gladly opt for those possible hurts that come with involvement. I would not want to face my teen and realize I had shortchanged him because I was unwilling to risk getting hurt.

When the Marriage Is Rocky

HAROLD MYRA

Even in deteriorating marriages, the relationship between husband and wife must take precedence over the relationship with the kids.

If one spouse is a Christian and the other is not, the Bible clearly tells the Christian to do everything possible to build the marriage bond.

When your spouse doesn't agree with this priority, as tough as this sounds, you still must show that person he or she comes first with you.

If you're a man, remember that there's hardly a woman in the world who won't respond to real courting within marriage. When your wife and kids gang up on you, wait for the fireworks to cool, take your wife aside, and say, "It's been a while since we went out—just the two of us. Would you like to go out for dinner tomorrow night?" Showing that you want to be in love with your wife, that you want your marriage to be special will do more than any number of lectures or confrontations.

This works for the wife too. The best strategy is a couple months of showing your husband how much you love him. Ask yourself, "What would really make my husband realize I love him?" A few unique and thoughtful expressions of love will begin to break down the barriers.

Yes, sometimes one parent doesn't

agree that the marriage is more important than the kids, and it's a dangerous situation when one spouse lines up with the children against the other spouse. If a sharp cleavage develops over how the children should be raised, you should approach your spouse and say, "We have some differences, but there's no sense having the kids watch us fight over how this should be handled. How can we work this out? Let's agree at least on how we're going to handle our disagreements."

If your partner is not a Christian, I think it's your task, then, in any situation not vital to the spiritual or physical well-being of the children, to give in to your spouse's preferences. Most nonbelieving parents want the best for their children, and things can be worked out. Even with the worst parents, an attitude of "We have a common interest in the solid growth and health of our children" is enough ground to start on.

In more difficult cases, a counselor or other third party may be helpful in bringing some objectivity into the situation.

Dealing with Guilt
Do You Feel Like an Ineffective Parent?

JOYCE LANDORF

As in every problem we have, just putting it out on the table and acknowledging it is an enormous step. There have been times I have gone to someone and asked why he was angry, and he would look at me and shoot back, "I'm not angry." So I would ask him to tell me about his life and he would come to a story and his eyes would start flashing and I'd stop him and ask, "You're not angry?" and suddenly he would realize that he was.

So first, acknowledge your guilt. Second, find someone sensitive enough to talk about it. We need so much to talk about it because it hurts so much. I cried more over my daughter, Laurie, in those four years when she was away from home than I have in nine years of pain.

I had one friend during that time who had four daughters, and I talked to her all the time about Laurie. She was an enormous comfort. She not only held me steady, but she didn't put me on a guilt trip either. She also kept up a relationship with Laurie, and talked with her whenever she could.

Be sure to acknowledge your problem within a safe context. So often Christians have gone to other Christians who are feeling their own guilt and failures. They lay an even heavier guilt trip on you by saying that their son or daughter would never do that.

We have to find the right person to share with. We can't talk it over with somebody who is going to lecture us or reject us. We need to be able to share in a free environment without judgmental attitudes and condemnation.

I remember talking to a couple whose daughter had become really wild. The wife eventually stopped going to all of her church activities because every time she got together with the church women, they would talk about their daughters and how they were marrying pastors, or going to Africa, or becoming involved in campus ministries. No one asked her about her daughter; no one cared that her daughter was going off the deep end. We

---

"WHY DOESN'T GOD HEAR?"

"I pray and pray that he'll quit mouthing off to his teachers, but nothing seems to work."

"Our home is either silent or full of tension. Why doesn't God hear my prayers? Surely He doesn't want it like this."

You pray for your kids and your home, but sometimes you feel like saying, "Why doesn't God hear? Nothing is changing."

Why doesn't God hear? Before checking up on Him, take a look at your own actions and motives. Are you praying for a better home atmosphere while you continue to be crabby and irritable? Consider *your* part in the problem. Are your prayers manipulative? By praying, you're saying you want God to handle it; so don't tell Him how to solve the problem. Maybe you think He hasn't answered because He hasn't given the answer you want.

Realize that in raising children there is a time to obey and a time to trust. Both are difficult. If your obedience seems unfruitful, you may need to rest in trusting Christ until more light is given. If your trusting seems unfruitful, ask, "Is there something *I* need to do?"

Yes, do pray about it, but not without doing your part or being willing to wait on God's timing.

YFC Editors

---

have to beware of that kind of insensitivity. We Christians know so little about bearing one another's burdens.

We can also examine the reality of the situation. We have to honestly ask ourselves if we failed, or if it was the teen's choice. Did we provide a safe, warm atmosphere where the child was free to question? If so, we can't blame ourselves.

I heard about one family with five kids and the parents would always say, "We have four kids who have come home and we've still got the light on waiting for the fifth." That was such a loving statement. It communicated their confidence that he *was* coming home.

When a child has committed suicide or overdosed on drugs and is never coming home, parents may have an even harder time with guilt. But no one knows what happened to the child in his last moments. You won't know till you get to heaven if he came home or not.

We need to remember there are no perfect parents. *Every* parent *could* have done something better. We have to watch out for the "if onlys." In my life, I know I did not do right in a number of areas, and I wish I could go back to retract the words or the deed.

But I have a choice. I can sit around and make long lists of what I should have done or said, or I can admit I didn't do those things and can no longer do anything about it. All I can do is ask God to give me the wisdom to deal with my child now and get on with business. I can't spend my entire life thinking about the "if onlys."

I can cry about the things I should have done; I can regret the bad things I did, but there is nothing I can do about it now. I can't change that. If there is something you can do now to change it or make amends, fine. But usually the past is something that is locked in.

So you have today, and you have your grandchildren. You can do with them the things you should have done with your children. I saw a bumper sticker the other day that said, "If I had known grandbabies were so much fun, I would have had them first." But there is a lot of wisdom that has gone over the dam between the kids and the grandkids.

Overcoming Guilt
What Makes Those Feelings Go Away?

DAVID HOWARD

We have four children, the three oldest of whom all followed the Lord beautifully. Then the youngest came along and at age thirteen, he turned away from the Lord. He wandered for nine long years before coming back.

I felt tremendous guilt over this, and dealing with my guilt as a parent was a difficult process. Because I had traveled a lot for my ministry over the years and had been away from home frequently, I believed my absences had a devastating effect on our son.

I don't think I was ever fully successful in overcoming my guilt. There was a difference between what I could accept mentally and what I could accept emotionally. Intellectually, I could accept that my son had the right to make his own decisions. But emotionally I couldn't accept this—I felt that it was my fault.

One way I dealt with my guilt was by turning it over honestly to the Lord. I told the Lord that I knew I had made mistakes and there was no way to recoup the things that had been done or hadn't been done because of my absences from home.

It also helped when I began to realize that this was not something to hide. When our son first began to wander, I felt ashamed and embarrassed. I didn't want anyone to know that we had a son wandering from the Lord. But as I dealt with the problem openly, I found that some of my guilt was eased.

Sharing it openly did not come naturally, but I began to recognize that what I was carrying in my heart and mind was an unduly heavy burden. I realized it wasn't right *not* to share my heartache at least with some close friends and prayer partners. So I started sharing with people I knew would support me.

From there, I began to open up a little bit in public. I do a lot of speaking at churches and for Christian groups and I felt led to share the fact that I was carrying this heavy burden. I didn't do this because I wanted them to get under the burden with me, but I wanted them to know that I was not some supersaint up on a pedestal who had no sense of failure.

I discovered as I did this that many other people were going through the same situation. Once, when I was speaking at a Christian faculty retreat, I referred to this burden as an example of unanswered prayer. I was amazed at how many faculty thanked me for sharing that because they were going through the same struggle. By sharing my problem honestly, I encouraged them.

My wife and I also openly talked with our other children about the situation. They knew the pain we were going through, and they shared it with us. They reminded us that we had raised our youngest the same way we had raised them; that he had had the same teachings, the same home atmosphere. They pointed out that he had a free will and he chose not to follow the way we had taught him. "He had a right to do that," our children said. "You can't carry guilt feelings just because he exercised his freedom of choice."

Nevertheless, I still tended to view the problem as my fault. I assumed if I had done things differently our son would have turned out differently. There's an element of truth in that, of course. But there is the other side too—that he had a free will and he was going to make his own decisions regardless of what I did. As a parent, I had to trust the Lord for the decisions my child made.

My wife's support helped see me through. She had regrets about things she wished she had done differently. But the deep feelings of guilt were much stronger on my side than hers because I was so certain that my absences had such a negative effect on the children. There were times when I got terribly depressed and she would encourage me, telling me that there was nothing I could do about my absences now.

I remember her saying to me one day when I was in the worst depression over this problem, "There are just two things that you need. You need to learn to praise and to trust. You need to praise the Lord for what we've got and just trust the Lord for what is to come."

Related Articles

Do You Feel Rejected?

*Accepting Yourself
When Your Teens Don't*

JAY KESLER

Life inevitably includes rejection of one type or another. And yet, despite its inevitability, probably none of us experience any pain greater than that of rejection. When that rejection comes from someone at home, whether a spouse or another family member, it can be devastating.

Parents often sense that their teenage children have rejected them. This rejection may be an unfavorable comparison with one of the children's heroes. The teenager has found someone—a coach, teacher, youth director, TV or movie star, or someone else's parent—who has qualities his parents don't have. Unlike his parents, his hero is not filled with life's concerns. For him, life is all fun. He always has time for sailing, climbing, jumping, running, bicycling, canoeing, sliding, and skating. The child weighs his parents against that, and they are found wanting.

These unfavorable comparisons can

NEVER TOO LATE

Is it ever too late to begin to correct our failures? It can't be, as long as we're still alive. It's easy to think it's been too long to undo some wrong, but in God's economy, lost time seldom means permanent damage. In Joel 2:25 (NIV), God says, "I will repay you for the years that the locusts have eaten."

We didn't know a lot about raising kids when we had our oldest daughter, Sherry. We were her first parents and she was our first child! Of course there was tension. She is strong-willed and very bright. We did some crazy things, and probably what we did was totally wrong for her much of the time. But now our relationship is wonderful. We've gone through reconciliation after reconciliation, as all parents have to do, and today she and her husband, Walt, are among our closest friends. No, it is never too late to begin to correct failures.

We like these hymn words by Charles Wesley: "He breaks the power of canceled sin; He sets the prisoner free." No matter how many times we've repeated a bad habit in our parenting, God is more powerful than our sin. Grace is greater, and God is always ready to break that sin's power and start His gracious correction. Isn't God wonderful?

Ray & Anne Ortlund

come in any area. Somebody else is brighter than we are, better informed, more tolerant, more willing to give time and attention to the teenager. Let's face it—sometimes we are not as good with our own kids as we are with someone else's. (Think of what someone else's kid may be telling his parents about us.)

We parents often feel rejected by our teenage children. This rejection feels even worse if it is amplified by our own inner feelings of inadequacy. Young people have a way of understanding our insecurities, and they often know how to use them against us.

I cannot imagine my father ever spending even five minutes worrying about whether or not I liked him. He was determined to do God's will, to be as honest and full of integrity as he could be, and then to let the chips fall where they may. Now I may be mistaken; he may have spent many hours in anxiety. But I don't think so.

I've concluded that we parents of today could take a lesson from him. We need to be as honest and transparent as possible;

we need to rid our lives of duplicity and deceit; and then we need to trust God that eventually we will wear down whatever rejection we feel from our kids.

On occasion, of course, we need to admit that we've done wrong. We need to sit down with our children and say, "All right, I know I haven't spent the time I should have with you. I'd like you to understand that I've had some worries on my mind, but I can't really ask you to accept that. It has felt to you like I've not been the parent I ought to be. But I want to do better, and I need your suggestions. Let's set some goals and make some decisions."

Often a frank conversation like this will start us off on fresh ground with our teenagers. But ultimately the time comes when we have to say to ourselves and to our children, "I am what God has made me, and I cannot be anything else. Therefore you're going to have to accept me as I am, and I'll try to accept you as you are. I'll be as fair as I can in my acceptance of you, and you do the same for me."

Then the waiting game begins. It often lasts well into our child's middle age. The day comes when he, having experienced rejection from his own children, comes to his parents and says, "Dad and Mom, I didn't understand then, but now I do."

The Risks of Parenting: Lessons Learned

DONALD MARDOCK

It was almost three years after my wife and I were married before our first child was born. During that time we dreamed, like all other first-time expectant parents, about how it would be to have a little boy or girl in our home. As I look back on those days, there was no way that anyone could have told us what to expect or have prepared us for the risks in parenting.

I still remember, in living color, the night we got the signal. Of course, we didn't want to appear to be novices and arrive at the hospital with a false alarm, so we took our own sweet time getting ready. Our neighbor nearly fainted when she learned how close together Glenda's pains were!

We made it; the delivery was normal, and we became a family.

Driving past an elementary school the next day, I *really* noticed little girls for the first time. I was almost overwhelmed as I watched those little beauties run around the playground. I was a parent, a brand-new parent who didn't have a clue about how to be one.

We had three repeat performances of that December night, and in almost no time, we were the parents of four beautiful daughters. Each one was different in her own special way. As soon as we thought we had parenting figured out, one of them would prove that we were still novices.

When our youngest was ten, we "placed another baby order," praying that we would have a child of another gender. Our prayer was heard and the first and only man-child joined his sisters and two novice parents.

Ten years later, and with two beautiful grandchildren in the family, my wife and I stand by proudly and watch our first two daughters and their husbands discover the risks of parenting.

Through the years we've learned many lessons, and all I can do is share with you what we have discovered, in fact, are still discovering. This will be an attempt to "skim the cream" to give the best from our bag of notes.

First, don't worry about spoiling your babies by loving them. Spoilage happens when you fail to love them enough to correct them firmly. Don't forget to let them know that it is their *behavior* you do not approve of, not they themselves.

Next, don't compare them to anyone else. Your kids are one-of-a-kind. Love them without any conditions. The risk is great when you love this way—your heart may be trampled in the process. But keep loving them unconditionally. Don't ever stop. The risk is worth it.

Laugh at yourselves when you can. So often we take ourselves far too seriously. I remember one day when our firstborn was experiencing one of the many pressure times of being seventeen. Words were flying and tears were flowing from two sets of eyes, hers and mine. Suddenly something popped into my mind. This was funny in a strange sort of way. Neither of us had ever been this way before. She had never been seventeen, and I had never had a seventeen-year-old daughter. As rank amateurs, we were each trying to impress the other that we knew what was happening. The tears slowed, then stopped. A smile began to play around the corners of her mouth, and then we were in each other's arms hugging away the frustrations and pledging to keep on working at being a teenager and a parent of one.

Be open to your children. Perhaps *vulnerable* is a better word. We know that we are not always right, so why do we try to prove that we are by shouting, ignoring, or whatever? The most difficult words to say are, "I'm sorry, I was wrong to assume that I knew what you were asking me. Please try again, and I'll really try to listen." Though they are hard to say, those "vulnerable" words are extremely important.

Don't allow a child to play one parent against the other. That is one of the most important reasons for Mom and Dad to stay close to each other. All kinds of trouble can be avoided if we establish early in their lives that when one parent speaks, he or she speaks for both.

That's tough? Right! But important. It will take work on the parents' part to stay in touch with each other, and the work will not go unnoticed by the children. The final result will be a growing sense that, "We are so important that Mom and Dad are working at the job of facing the risks of parenting with us."

As a family we have decided to follow Jesus Christ as our Lord and seek to live in obedience to Him. Recently it occurred to me that as Christians my wife is also my sister in Christ. My daughters are also my sisters. My son is more than just my son; he is my brother as well. My fellow family members are also my friends.

The Bible has much to say about husbands, wives, and children and how they relate to each other. It has a lot more to say about how brothers and sisters in the church, the body of Christ, are to love each other. When we are obeying His command to "love one another" (1 John 3:11), we are discovering that it has tremendous value in our relationships as members of a family.

I encourage you to consider asking the heavenly Father to assist you in facing the risks of parenting.

Words Spoken in Anger

JACK CRABTREE

The white station wagon blocked the road ahead. I craned my neck to see the faces of the participants in this fender-bender.

Behind the raised hood stood Lori. Her bright blond hair was unmistakable. Her appearance always made her look older than sixteen. Her friendly face was covered by a look of fright that only appears when one has an accident with her father's car.

Lori had been attending the Campus Life club that I directed. Her father was the pastor of a church in town. Lori was having the usual struggle of transferring her family's faith into her own personal faith. The fact that every guy wanted to take her out hadn't made it any easier.

The accident scene told the story. The rear bumper of the burgundy Cadillac was apparently undamaged. The white station wagon Lori had been driving had taken the blow. A blue-green lake of antifreeze continued to grow in the street under Lori's car. The policeman barked at Lori to make a decision about moving the car or he was going to call a tow truck himself.

"You should call your father," I said to Lori. "The car's radiator is ruptured, so you can't drive home. Maybe your father has someone in the church who can help get this car home without paying the tow truck."

Lori hesitated, still shaking from the shock of the collision. I put the coins in the phone and helped her dial the number. Standing in the doorway of the phone booth, I heard only one side of the conversation.

"Hello, Dad? This is Lori."

"Yes, I know that I'm late. I'm sorry, Dad."

"Dad, I had an accident and now the car won't run."

"Dad, I'm sorry. I just turned my head for a second and this car stopped right. . . ."

"I don't know what's wrong with the car. All this green stuff is dripping. . . ."

"I know it's your car, Dad. I'm sorry. I didn't do it on. . . ."

"I'm sorry, Dad. I'll get a job and pay for. . . ."

"Then I'll wait till I get my own car."

"Yes, Dad, I'm OK."

The instant that the receiver hit the hook the telephone booth was filled with tears and sobbing.

I waited. There was nothing else to do. Finally Lori looked up and answered my obvious question.

"My dad loves his car more than he loves me," she said.

That day I learned a lesson about the impact of our words on our children. I never believed for a minute that the pastor loved his car more than his daughter. But I saw that day why his daughter thought so.

His response on the phone was careless. Thoughtless words spoken in anger. Yet it gave Lori a strong message about what he valued most. His words wounded her deep inside.

Careless words are easily spoken when we are tired, irritated, or angry. We threaten our children ("I'll break your arm" or "I'll kill you"); we label them with demeaning taunts ("You're stupid!" or "You're clumsy"); or we undercut their self-worth ("I can never count on you").

These careless words slip out of our mouths too easily. We dismiss them as only words and forget them quickly. Yet these words are absorbed by our children. Unless we realize our mistaken speech and ask forgiveness, the words can take a permanent place in their minds.

Then we risk the ultimate effect—that our children believe these careless words and act accordingly.

Lori did just that. It's a long, sad story.

Related Articles

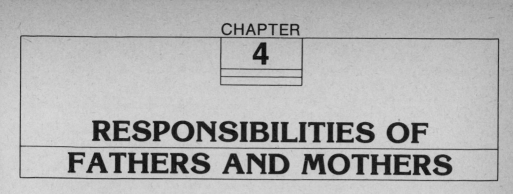

RESPONSIBILITIES OF FATHERS AND MOTHERS

- What do teens want in a father?
- What are the unique aspects of raising a daughter?
- The challenges of being a traveling father
- The real definition of success

- The challenges of being a working mother
- How to effectively manage your household
- The price of being a parent

In Genesis 1:27 we read, "God created man in His own image . . . male and female created He them" (KJV). From this passage we understand that God contains characteristics of both male and female, since mankind, made in His image, is made up of male and female. Ideally, children are raised by both father and mother, each fulfilling his or her own tasks and responsibilities.

Over the centuries, of course, these tasks and responsibilities have continually changed. Indeed, they are changing in modern society. Today fewer than half of American families adhere to the conventional model where father goes to work and mother stays home and cares for the children; over half of all mothers work at paid jobs.

This change does not have to damage families. It does, however, require a careful, intentional, and fair application of biblical principles both to the marriage and to child-rearing to bring about the greatest happiness and stability to the home.

Fathers Need to Take the Lead

BARRY ST. CLAIR

A prominent child psychologist named Urie Bronfenbrenner researched the amount of time fathers spend with their children. His test was run with a sample of fathers of one-year-olds. He first asked the fathers to estimate how much time they spent each day with their children,

and the average answer was fifteen to twenty minutes. But when he actually ran the test, he found that those fathers spent an average of thirty-seven seconds a day with their one-year-olds.

If a father spends a mere thirty-seven seconds daily with a child during the first year of the child's life, how much time can they expect to spend together by the time the child is a teenager with other friends and interests, and a car to take him wherever he wants to go? Fathers give many reasons why they spend so little time with their children, but *no amount of success outside the home will compensate for failure within the home.*

95

I think there are four success myths that need to be destroyed in order for a man to be a successful leader of his home and children:

1. *The Macho Mentality.* According to this myth, success is determined by the amount of power one can acquire.

2. *The Credentials Crunch.* The motivation behind this myth is fame and recognition.

3. *The Super-Jock Sexuality.* This myth causes a man to strive to prove his sexuality and manhood.

4. *The Financial Wizard.* Men who believe this myth spend their lives in an endless quest for wealth.

All of these myths are areas where Christian fathers feel tremendous pressure from our society. They have to come to grips with these untruths, either consciously or subconsciously, and move beyond them to discover what kind of men God wants them to be. The big problem is *how* to overcome the strong pull of the myths of society.

I think a good model for men to follow is found in Psalm 1:1-3: "Blessed is the man who does not walk in the counsel of the wicked or stand in the way of sinners or sit in the seat of mockers. But his delight is in the law of the Lord, and on His law he meditates day and night. He is like a tree planted by streams of water, which yields its fruit in season and whose leaf does not wither. Whatever he does prospers" (NIV).

The overall thrust of this passage is that when a man is who he needs to be, he will be *blessed* (happy). That happiness comes when he has real conviction in his life that is based on the Word of God. But he faces several external forces that erode that strong conviction:

• *Individualism,* the desire to "do my own thing" with no mutual sacrifice.

• *Social activities,* events outside the home that separate the father from his family.

• *Alternative authorities.* When today's young people need an answer to a question, they are likely to ask friends or teachers, or consult a book on the subject. Often their parents are the last choice for advice.

DADS SHOULDN'T BE DICTATORS

The Scriptures appoint the husband and father head of the home, but they do not make him a dictator. He is, instead, to be loving, gracious, and compassionate.

The strongest statement of this is found in Ephesians 5:25 (NASB): "Husbands, love your wives, just as Christ loved the church and gave Himself up for her." Vonette has often said that no wife will hesitate to respond to her husband's leadership if he loves her as much as Christ loved the church.

When husbands love their wives as Christ loved the church, wives respond. Every woman wants to be loved. A woman needs security more than a man does, and she finds her security in her home and husband. In fact, I have never known of an insurmountable family difficulty when the husband really loves his wife in a self-sacrificial way. You can usually trace serious family problems—conflict, separation, divorce—to the man who fails to be that kind of husband.

Sometimes the wife takes the spiritual leadership of the family, and that is wrong. But if her husband leaves the leadership to her, she has no choice. She has to take the initiative for the sake of the children. A man who does this, however, loses his family's respect and the opportunity to be a role model for his sons and daughters.

Bill Bright

• *Role confusion.* The father is often unsure as to what role he should play in the home.

• *Removal of the economic base from the home.* The father commutes each day and transfers to a new location every couple of years. Mom works. Grandma and Grandpa live back East. The children don't know their roots and some can't even tell you what their father does for a living.

• *Television.* By the time a teen graduates from high school, he will have watched an average of 15,000 hours of television. TV addiction is no less severe for many adults.

These external forces keep many men from being the kinds of fathers they should be. Yet, the forces that override the pressures of our society and bring real conviction, according to Psalm 1, are: (1) delighting in the law of the Lord, which I interpret as meaning "really enjoying a relationship with Jesus Christ," and (2) meditating on God's Word day and night, which means that Dad should not just *know* what the Bible says—he should practice it in front of his family.

A Christian father needs to spend time alone with the Lord daily. As a result, he will grow (as a tree planted by water) and he will be prosperous. I don't think he will necessarily prosper financially. He might. But I believe Psalm 1 speaks of spiritual prosperity—a proper relationship with God and success in the home with his wife and children.

A father who really wants to be a leader in his family must begin to develop the conviction described in Psalm 1. A parallel passage that gives further practical advice on *how* to foster conviction is found in Deuteronomy 6:4-9: "Hear, O Israel: The Lord our God, the Lord is one. Love the Lord your God with all your heart and with all your soul and with all your strength. These commandments that I give you today are to be on your hearts. Impress them on your children. Talk about them when you sit at home

and when you walk along the road, when you lie down and when you get up. Tie them as symbols on your hands and bind them on your foreheads. Write them on the doorframes of your houses and on your gates" (NIV).

This passage points out three areas that Christian fathers need to develop in order to be men of conviction. If they want to be good leaders in their homes and positive influences on their children, they need to evaluate how well they are doing in relation to each one.

Area #1: Priorities

1. *The priority of his relationship with Christ.* A father cannot pass along to his children something he does not possess. If he has no spiritual values, he can't "impress them on his children." But if the father has a sincere love for Jesus Christ, he won't have to tell his kids. They'll know.

2. *The priority of his love relationship with his wife.* I think the greatest need in homes today is for Dad to love Mom. More than anything else, that positive relationship will provide a secure atmosphere for kids to grow up in. Homes need both parents. God didn't provide a mom *or* dad; He created a mom *and* dad. One may teach the kids inward and sensitive qualities while the other teaches strong outward qualities. Unless there is a combination of the two, kids get out of balance. It all begins with a loving relationship between husband and wife.

3. *The priority of his love for the children.* Kids can be a blessing or they can drive you crazy, depending on the priority they have in your life. When they start getting on your nerves, maybe you should examine your life to see if it is because you are giving something else a higher priority (job, leisure time, etc.).

Area #2: Instruction

Instruction can take two forms as you communicate the reality of Christ in your home: teaching (structured) and training (unstructured). I think the passage in Deuteronomy 6 describes both methods of instruction. And I believe it is in the unstructured training where parents have the greatest opportunities to show their children how God works in everyday circumstances.

How does a father teach and train his kids? I think he must act as a "builder." Just as a construction engineer builds a house, Dad needs to build a home. He must build four things to effectively instruct his children.

1. *He must build a spiritual atmosphere*

BACK TO BASICS

When a coach sees his team begin to look sloppy and make a lot of mistakes on the field, sometimes he will decide that they need to get "back to basics." He has them focus on doing the drills that are fundamental to the game and spends less time on special plays and other extraneous activity.

Many fathers need to get back to basics with their children. They start out on the right track, but eventually come to realize that their priorities have changed, and that their children are no longer on top. I have done a lot of thinking on this subject lately, and would like to pass along what I have discovered.

The first step for a father who wants to change his priorities is to determine his purpose in life. I believe most men—even those who have to write goals and job descriptions at work—have never really thought about, "What is my real purpose in *life?*" I think the goal that all of us should strive for is to glorify God in everything we do (based on 1 Corinthians 10:31 and a number of other passages). After I reach that decision, I need to examine three areas to put me back in proper balance.

1. *The Great Commandment* (Matt. 22:34-40). I am to love God with all my heart, soul, mind, and strength. I should examine my social life, my spiritual life, my mental activity, and my physical development to see if my love for God is displayed in each one.

2. *The Great Commitment* (Matt. 19:4-6). I am to be a good husband and father. As I set goals in this area, I will start with these categories: a *priest* (to pray for my family), a *prophet* (to teach the Word of God), a *pal* (to be a friend to my family members), and a *provider* (to take care of the financial needs of my family).

3. *The Great Commission* (Matt. 28:16-20). I am to be concerned with what takes place in my ministry—my church involvement as well as my job. I am to be involved in *supplication* (praying for those on my job and in my church), *study* (learning God's Word to pass along to them), *shepherding* (discipling other people), and *supervising* (taking responsibility for a ministry to help others).

When a father decides to get back to basics, he can start with the Great Commandment (his personal life), the Great Commitment (his family life), and the Great Commission (his job and ministry). These three areas will give him biblical and practical objectives for goal-setting. As he begins to practice these basics, he will become the leader he wants to be.

Barry St. Clair

in his home. He has several options as to how to do this. A family devotional time in the morning is a good start. In our family we eat breakfast together, talk and laugh, then read a few verses from Proverbs. Each of us also has Scripture memory assignments that we recite every few days. Spending time together in the evenings, planning special events, having people in the home—all these are ways for a father to build a positive atmosphere for his family. Set aside at least one night a week for family night. Our family goes out to eat, plays ball, plays board games— all geared around what our kids want to do. It's their time and they love it.

2. *He must build quality communication with his children.* He needs to use eye contact when he talks to his kids. And there needs to be physical contact as well—hugging, kissing, wrestling. He should also focus his attention on individual children, making sure that each child gets equal consideration. Set aside time every week to take your kids out on "dates" on a rotating basis.

3. *He must build positive habits and character qualities in his children.* This one's not easy. The thing to remember is that you have to keep working with them "till they get it." You may have to tell them for 8,000 days in a row to clean their rooms, but you just keep reminding them until they learn to do it on their own. Remember, they'll model the habits and character qualities they see *in you!*

4. *He must build obedience through discipline.* Too many parents punish their children out of anger, rather than out of a desire to teach them obedience. In our house there are only two reasons for discipline: disrespect and disobedience. For example, if my son accidentally drops a dish on the floor, it might upset me but there is no need for punishment. But if he were to break the dish after I told him not to pick it up, he could expect to be disciplined for his disobedience. Punishment will teach obedience if you: (1) set limits that children understand; (2) deter-

mine whatever will constitute a violation of those limits; (3) enforce discipline when a violation occurs; and (4) are consistent.

Area #3: Time

Reread Deuteronomy 6:4-9 and look at *when* it says to instruct your children. Put simply, you should teach them to love and obey God in *all* of life's experiences. How? I think the primary method— especially for fathers—is to make time to spend with your children. You can't give your kids adequate time when you are moonlighting, bowling, and going to church four nights a week. And, like the Bronfenbrenner survey showed, you may *think* you are spending a lot more time with your children than you actually are.

My son wrote me a note a few years ago after we had spent a lot of time together. It said, "I love you, Daddy. Even when you die I'll always remember those fun times you and me had." I think his letter reflects the results of the priority, the instruction, and the time I have given him.

It's never too late for a father to start being a leader in his home. But it's never too soon, either. If you don't feel like you are the father you would like to be, set goals in each of the areas I have discussed and begin to put them into practice with your family. Don't expect results overnight. If your children have not realized that they are a priority to you by the time they are teenagers, they will be harder to reach. But if you pray for them every day, make them realize by your actions that they are a top priority in your life, instruct them by being a good role model, and begin to spend time with them, you will begin to see results. They will begin to be the children you want them to be, when you become the leader they need for you to be.

Related Articles

What Teens Want in a Father

CHARLES R. SWINDOLL

Teens want a father whom they can respect. They want someone who will not embarrass them knowingly (or unknowingly, for that matter).

I believe teens want a father who loves their mother with all his heart. There's a real sense of security in knowing that the parents love each other.

THE BIGGEST PRESSURE FATHERS FACE IN RAISING TEENS

Time is the biggest pressure fathers face in raising their teens. We all have the same number of hours in a day. Yet some men seem to make everything fit into their hours, while others always have more to do than time to do it in.

In the traditional home setting, a father is often working away from the home at least forty hours a week. When a man comes home after working all day, he is usually tired and hungry. His evening is divided by eating, talking with his wife, church and community activities, and trying to relax. Often it is hard to integrate the needs of children into the few unscheduled hours remaining. I think it takes a concerted effort to "make" time for teens. A father must make his children a priority, no matter how important his occupation is.

Often fathers tell me they feel out of touch with their teens and they don't know what the real issues are. But I wonder how much time those men spend talking with their teens, trying to discover the issues.

I think it's a great idea to get alone with your teen for a weekend when he's about thirteen or fourteen. Just talk through some things he can expect in the coming years. Pave the pathway to less pressure by opening the channels of communication early.

Too many fathers look back and regret not spending more time with their teens. The teen years only last seven years with each child; compared to your total life-span, that's not much time. I've yet to hear a parent complain about spending too much time with his teen!

Someone once said, "Time is the most valuable thing a man can spend."

Charles R. Swindoll

Vulnerability is another quality that teens hold in high esteem. When parents are vulnerable, it makes it much easier for the teen to be open and honest.

A good sense of humor is *very* important. Teens want a dad who can laugh at life and at himself. I want my kids to remember a dad who tossed their mother in the pool and lived to tell the story. I'd like them to remember me as a dad who did fun things with them—parasailing, waterskiing, and camping in the rain. I hope they remember me standing up in a football stadium, drenching wet, yelling my heart out for my son, the linebacker, when his team was getting beat 26-0.

Self-discipline in a parent is important to teens. They need a role model in order to learn self-discipline in their own lives.

One of the most important things teens want in a father is a healthy self-image, so he can admit when something is his fault. Teens have a real respect for a parent who can be honest with himself and others.

There are several things that teens do *not* want in a father. For example, I don't think teens want a dad who loses control under stress. I don't think they mind if he

IS THE FATHER'S ROLE CHANGING?

A recent surprise box office smash was a hilarious story of role-reversal. Dad is fired, Mom is hired, and Dad has to stay home and deal with the kids, the pets, and the house. Perhaps this movie was popular because so many men could identify with his plight.

Certainly, with the breakup of the family unit, an increasing number of homes with both parents working, the women's movement, and the nation's economic turmoil, the traditional parental roles are undergoing drastic changes. This, of course, leads to special identity problems and new family pressures.

Dad is especially susceptible. After all, the home is his "castle," he is the "breadwinner," and other assorted clichés. But Mom is also a valuable, contributing member of the family. Dad needs to realize this and to act accordingly. Here are some other suggestions for him.

1. On the way home, prepare for the first ten minutes after you walk through the door as though they are the most important in your day. Listen, talk to your wife and kids, and don't gripe about the "rotten day." See the first few minutes at home as a "decompression chamber" where you "come out" of the work mode and into the family.

(Wives also should protect these first ten minutes as special and not unload about the terrible kids and broken dishwasher.)

2. Make homework and child-rearing a team effort by asking, "How may I help you?" and taking the initiative in doing household tasks.

3. Realize that just because Mom's been with the children more than you doesn't mean that they don't need you, your listening ear, and loving touch.

4. Know that when you bring home the paycheck, your work is not done.

5. Constantly ask, "Am I acting in love?"

YFC Editors

is fearful—they just don't want him screaming and getting out of control. Hysteria is frightening.

I know a young man whose father is an alcoholic. He called me one night when his dad had been put in the hospital, asking me to pray for him. The father had lost control, and the son had lost respect for his father. Teens don't want a parent whom they have to apologize for to their friends.

Teens don't want a nag, a parent who continually harasses them about things that are already very clear. Once you've made your point, stop talking about it. It's usually not necessary to remind a teen when he leaves for school about something you just talked about during breakfast.

Another thing that teens don't appreciate is thoughtlessness in their parents. If you say you'll pick up a teen from school at 3:30, *be there* at 3:30. And be ready to apologize if you get there at 3:45. Often parents pull rank on a teen, rather than admit they were wrong.

Teens look up to their fathers more than they will ever admit. There's a popular opinion today that teens look up to their friends more than to their parents. When a parent complains about that, I think he deserves to have his son or daughter end up that way. He has just told his own fortune.

Too often, the deeper meaning is, "The way I'm acting around my kid, he hasn't got a lot to look up to." We have to realize that kids go through stages where they *dare* you to find one thing about them that would suggest respect. But if someone in the neighborhood talks bad about you— just watch your children defend you!

What God Expects from Fathers

RICHARD C. HALVERSON

My father was a very good man and I loved him. He was gentle and soft-spoken and he never hurt anybody. I never heard him use profanity or raise his voice. Yet he never took me fishing or played games with me. When it came time for discipline, my mother was responsible for carrying it out. As a result of that role model, I never learned to do those things with my own children.

The Bible has much to say about the role of the father. The father image is extremely important since it models the relationship between the heavenly Father and His children. When a child begins to hear about our heavenly Father the only model he has for the word *Father* is his own father. The word *father* is meaningful to a child in terms of what the parent is in the home, with his wife, children, and neighbors.

According to Scripture, the father is responsible for three main tasks. The first is that of instruction in the things of God. In Deuteronomy 6, fathers are commanded to teach God's laws to their children, while Ephesians 6:4 tells fathers to bring their children "up in the training and

102

instruction of the Lord" (NIV).

A father's second area of responsibility is that of leadership. The father is responsible for being head of the house and giving leadership to the whole family.

The third area of responsibility is discipline. The father has to be an authority figure. That doesn't mean he's a boss; he's just a father. When he says no he should mean no—otherwise consequences will follow.

Many of us fathers fail in our responsibilities. At this stage in life I long to spend time with my children. Sometimes fathers learn what to do after it's too late to do it. Then we try to compensate. Yet children are tremendously resilient; they

INSTANT REPLAY

"You big ox! How can you run so slow?" a Little League father shouts at his son who would love to be able to hide under first base. He didn't really want to play baseball in the first place, and now he can't seem to do anything to please his dad.

There's a fine line between *encouraging* our children to develop interests, get involved, and discover their abilities and *pushing* them into activities which make *us* look and feel good. Unfortunately, all too often this line is crossed as parents meet their own needs through their kids.

Some dads are frustrated "jocks," never having quite achieved their athletic goals, and their sons will be "encouraged" to be athletes. (This is also true of academic, social, and vocational goals.) Often, certain activities are "in" and parents want Junior involved. Many moms and dads are struggling with their self-concepts as they move through mid-life, and they feel fulfilled through their sons' and daughters' accomplishments. Others just enjoy basking in reflected glory. A few may even believe that this is the only way for the kids to "make it" in society.

Whatever the motive, it is certainly unchristian to use another person to meet one's needs. And parents, most of all, should protect and strengthen children's fragile egos.

All of us are guilty to a certain extent, but how can we deal with the problem? First, we must know our children, their talents, abilities, and, most important, their desires.

Second, we must communicate, quietly talking over how our teens feel and why we desire participation. It is important to find out if they are afraid of failure or of our reaction to failure. (Do we love them just as much when they fail?)

Finally, we should avoid the "big push." Here's how:

1. Know their limits.

2. Help them set their own goals and allow them to have different interests.

3. Understand that every child is different, with a unique blend of talents and desires.

4. Expend as much energy (time, money, etc.) helping them work toward their goals as we would forcing them toward ours.

5. Promote a "balanced life" (not just sports or just music, etc.).

YFC Editors

can take a terrible emotional beating and come back. Often they respond with love to a parent who hurts them.

Paul Tournier, in one of his books on grace, comments on the failures of parents: "Many parents are extremely authoritarian and many parents are extremely permissive. Most parents are in between those extremes. But whether parents are extremely authoritarian or extremely permissive or somewhere in between, if their children turn out all right, it's by the grace of God." I think that's true. As a father attempts to bring his children up in the nurture and admonition of the Lord there will be times of failure. Yet God through His grace can help that father learn through his mistakes as He has with me.

Though I've often failed in my responsibilities as a father, God has used me as an instrument of His love in my family. I am now able to spend time with my children, commuting to work or traveling. Accordingly, I try to use these precious times to encourage and express God's love to my adult children.

Related Articles

The Importance of Being Available
Making Time for Your Kids

GORDON MacDONALD

When kids enter junior high school, scheduling suddenly falls apart, and every person's world becomes dramatically different. Time frames clash. We discovered that in youth ministries, the church, and public school, almost everyone who controlled our teenager's schedule was not a parent of teenagers. Most youth pastors either have no children or their children are infants. School teachers, coaches, and youth workers are often young and have little sensitivity to what a family with teenagers is really like.

My wife and I decided early in the ball game that there was only a sixty-minute period daily when availability to our children could reasonably be guaranteed; that was suppertime. We told our kids that suppertime was a nonnegotiable item, and that ninety to ninety-five percent of the time everybody in the family was expected to be home then. We took the phone off the hook and told the kids that their friends ought not to stop by.

Over the years we found that everybody relaxed during that hour they knew they would spend at the table. It became a warm time for our family. There was a lot of laughter and sometimes very intense discussions. I credited my wife with making this family time possible.

If you talked to our kids today, I have no doubt that they would say the supper hour was the warmest memory of our family routine. We had such good times. If we had evening devotions, my wife was always ready with the Bibles. Frequently we read the Scriptures and prayed. But we didn't feel the time was a failure if devotions didn't happen. There was no pressure to perform in that area, and I think that was healthy.

Another observation on availability is that during the teen years parents are very much at the mercy of a teenager's moods. If you are watching closely and decoding the signs, you can get into some good conversations. We found that driving someplace together was a great time to talk. If you asked the right questions, you might discover some things.

Availability tends to be based on the teenager's availability. As a pastor, I was in a good position because my flexible schedule could conform to my kids' schedules.

But some parents don't have flexible schedules, and for some, there is no adequate solution. But many parents could participate more in their children's activities if they really tried. They just don't see the importance of doing it.

Regardless of your schedules, try your best to bend to your children's needs. If one parent can't be there, the other one should be. Unavailable parents is one of the growing problems of our culture. We are paying a terrible price when both parents work. I have never thought that mothers should stay home all the time, but if the mother has a full-time job, then the father should stay home. I don't think you can expect to raise really healthy kids in a home where both parents work full time.

Our kids knew that when something important was happening in their lives, one or both of their parents would be there to share it with them. I found other available times too. When my daughter goes to bed, I often slip into her room and give her a back rub for five or ten minutes. Sometimes we have some really meaningful conversations.

Do what you can to enter into your children's world in settings where they feel in charge, even to watch one of their TV programs that you might think is a bit juvenile for your tastes. That is a symbol to them that you care enough about them to spend some time in their world of interests.

Many men at about age forty wake up to what they've missed. They suddenly realize that they don't know their children or their wives. The tragedy is that they didn't make the effort and the wives and kids have learned to get along without their husbands and fathers. And when these men try to make up for lost time, the children, and sometimes the spouses, are no longer interested.

The consequences for everyone are sad. For the father it is a loss of intimacy and the satisfaction of really knowing his son or daughter. For the child whose father has been unavailable, the primary loss is generally a feeling of rejection that turns into anger. The anger gets down deep into his system and often stays there twenty years or longer. The child's self-esteem also tends to suffer.

There is another kind of unavailable parent—the emotionally absent parent. He is in sight, but he isn't there. Kids know when you're with them and when you aren't. Availability is when the parent has entered into the teenager's world, or when the parent and teenager have entered into a common world of mutual interest.

Related Articles

How Do You Spell S-U-C-C-E-S-S?

ANTHONY CAMPOLO, JR.

Describing a successful father is difficult. But to me, the most important aspect in determining a successful father is to observe how his children live their lives.

I would consider myself a successful parent if my children freely choose to live their lives in Christian service. And when I say Christian service, I do *not* necessarily mean the mission field or the pastoral ministry, but any work or vocation that renders service to other people for Christ.

I define work or vocation as an instrument through which people fulfill discipleship. I hope my children will buy into that concept, but in all reality, I'm not sure that either of my children buy into my values. It is, nevertheless, important to be constantly aware that your children will pick up many values from you.

I have endeavored to communicate values by modeling them to my children. In two major instances, I chose jobs which earned less money than others but which provided more opportunity to carry out the role of a disciple. That had a tremendous effect on the kids. I have used my teaching position and speaking engagements to promote missionary causes. That specific kind of opportunity is not available to every parent, but other opportunities are.

Successful fathering needs successful mothering as its complement. Any success I have as a father has a great deal to do with my wife. Each of us has a different emphasis and impact on the lives of our children. Mine is always programs and jobs whereas my wife's is relationships.

In a sense, my daughter is very much a reflection of my wife whereas my son's values are closer to mine. Both my children come across as ideal kids. My daughter is in her second year of law school and is probably going into corporate law. While she can use this for the kingdom, I would rather see her go into advocacy law, championing the cause of poor and oppressed people. However, I admire her commitment to define her own goals and style of service.

If you talk in terms of serving the King by living a simple lifestyle for the sake of others, I'm not sure my daughter would buy into that. But what she does buy into is also extremely Christian. She has picked up my wife's strong emphasis on visiting and reaching out to people. There is great value in visiting elderly and lonely people, making them feel "cared for." It is important to make phone calls to aunts and uncles. My wife has spent vast amounts of time doing those things, and my children, particularly my daughter, have imitated her modeling.

Much can be learned by evaluating whom you visit, who visits you, and what happens when they visit. Some families visit only people of prestige and significance in an attempt to manipulate themselves into higher status. Others make visiting a real ministry.

Who are the people you invite for dinner? Who are the people whom you visit? Do you always invite the high school principal or the minister? Or are you visiting and inviting the handicapped from your church, the person who doesn't bathe often, and those who seem boring?

I have tried to provide affirmation of my wife's model. Once my son criticized his mother for taking people out to lunch. "Why does she waste her money like that when people are starving in Asia and Haiti?"

I stopped him. "Hey, it's good to care about the starving. But do you see what your mother is really doing? Do you see the difference she's making in people's lives?"

Mistakes Fathers Make

Perhaps the most serious mistake a father can make is not modeling what he says. Our words should be backed by our actions. For example, when a father tells his children he is holding two jobs to help the family and then spends the extra money on the family, he comes across as an authentic model. The same cannot be said when he spends it selfishly on himself.

Another grave mistake is not spending time with the kids. Not just time—special time. Let me give you a concrete example. My son has taken off one semester from college just to spend time with me. This semester he's been going everywhere with me, and it's really costing us a lot of money. I spent two weeks leading a missionary conference in New Zealand and he went with me. We're together almost ten hours a day some days, talking, sharing, and exchanging. Actually, the cost is less than college tuition,

---

WHAT A FATHER SHOULD SACRIFICE FOR HIS CHILDREN

One area where a father should *not* sacrifice for his children is in his relationship with his wife. I sometimes made the mistake of not putting my wife in a more prominent place in terms of my time and interest. There's a poster that says, "The most important thing a man can do for his children is to love their mother."

I loved my wife all the time, of course, but I didn't always put her in first place, and give her priority over the children. My father, on the other hand, always gave my mother priority over us. We learned to appreciate this even though it meant sometimes we couldn't do something with him. In the long run, it was healthy and good for us.

In terms of personal sacrifice, there are things a father should give up. For me, there is one sacrifice I didn't make that I wish I had. I love to read, and I can't stand TV except for football or news. When our kids were growing up, I just despised the thought of sitting and watching TV in the evenings. I would rather read and that's what I did. My children would be downstairs in the family room watching TV and I would sit in the living room reading a book. I wish now that I had closed my book, gone down, and just watched TV with them. It would have been a sacrifice for me but it would have been good for them.

Watching TV with them would have been a simple way to let them know that I was interested in what they were interested in. I also could have monitored more closely their selection of shows. Another benefit would have been that I would have had something to talk about with them.

David Howard

and the benefits are priceless.

In today's society, a father often feels too busy to spend time with his children. To such a father, I would emphatically say—if you don't have the time, make the time! If a father does not have time for his children, he's in the wrong business, even if he's nearing a big promotion or is five years from a great retirement plan.

You have a responsibility to your children. On Judgment Day, God is not going to ask, "Did you become vice president?" He's going to ask, "Did you fulfill your responsibilities?"

Fathers have to be creative in making time—special time—for each of their children. A father can take his son out to breakfast one day and his daughter, the next. If you have to get up at 6:00 in the morning, get up at 6:00 in the morning. You'll be amazed at how enthusiastically kids respond to going out to breakfast with Dad from 6:00 to 8:30, then having Dad drop them off at school.

It seems to me that every child is entitled to a couple of hours of quality time with a parent at least weekly. If you can't provide that, then you shouldn't have become a parent. But since you are a parent, you have a primary responsibility to fulfill that job, recognizing that after twenty years the child will be gone. Don't end up saying with deep remorse, "If only I had. . . ."

Related Articles

Chapter 2:   Priorities for Parents
Chapter 2:   All about Models
Chapter 2:   Parents Need to Change Too!
Chapter 4:   Fathers Need to Take the Lead

The Challenges of a Traveling Parent

LEIGHTON FORD

My son, Kevin, and I were talking about my traveling. He said, "Dad, I understand why you did it. What helped was when you came home you really did have time for us. You coached me in basketball. You were interested in what we were doing. So I didn't feel you were just involved in your work away from home. You showed me that you cared about my life. You would also tell me about your travels, about the people you met, about what you'd seen. I learned a lot from that."

My daughter, Debbie, told me, "I remember you used to take time in the afternoons when you were home to talk with us, to take a walk with us, or play with us. You didn't make us wait until the evening when we had to do our homework, or were tired." Of course, my office was in my home, so when I was home I could do that.

I've been involved in a traveling ministry since we began working with the Billy Graham Evangelistic Association twenty-eight years ago. Roughly half my time, sometimes less, sometimes a bit more, has involved traveling.

It was very important to realize that traveling was part of God's call. The children and my wife, Jeanie, knew this wasn't merely something *I* was choosing

108

to do, but something I was responding to—that *God* had called me to do.

I didn't feel guilty about traveling except at one or two points. For instance, I had to go to Australia for four months when my daughter was just four months old. Though I had little choice, leaving Jeanie with such a young baby wasn't a very wise thing to do.

I have felt lonely though. My family is very close and being away was hard. I missed them a lot, and wanted to be with them.

Today it is difficult to find people who will take traveling assignments because of the price involved. They must be willing to sacrifice some family time as part of discipleship.

Jesus said, "He who loves father or mother more than Me is not worthy of Me" (Matt. 10:37, NASB). That element of sacrifice has recently been misplaced in our evangelical society. I don't think the sacrifice should be totally at the expense of the family; the children certainly shouldn't have to bear the brunt of it all. But it is a sacrifice to which God calls some people.

When I first began this ministry, Jeanie and I both felt strongly that if God gave us a family our children would be a priority. We knew there was no point in trying to win the whole world and lose our own family.

Priorities

When ordering our priorities, Jeanie and I often go back to Genesis 1—2 which talk about God's Creation plan. This passage teaches we are made first in His image, male and female. Then we are created to be fruitful and multiply, and finally, to be good stewards over the earth.

There are four Ps we try to remember. First, I am a *person* made in the image of God. Second, I am a *partner* if God gives me a marriage. Third, a *parent,* if He gives me children, and last, a *producer* or a *professional.* These are all important in our lives and we have to be sure that each

of them has a place. We have to be careful not to focus so strongly on one that we lose perspective on the others.

I remember when Debbie was sixteen she said, "Dad, I feel as if I don't know you anymore." I sat down and had a long talk with her. I realized she was saying, "I'm not thirteen anymore, I'm sixteen. I have new thoughts, new ideas, new struggles, and I don't think you know what is going on inside me."

So that year, I deliberately cut down on my traveling schedule. I turned down a lot of invitations in order to have more time to be with her. We would take long walks together, and if I were going to preach to young people, I'd go over my sermon with her and ask her opinion.

I once asked Debbie what she missed most. She said she missed the consistency of having me at home. I was there, and then I wasn't there. But she also said that Jeanie really made up for that, because she's been a very steady, caring, and loving mother.

Making Limited Time More Effective

I don't buy the cliché that quality time is the most important thing. Of course you have to have quality time. But if you don't have enough quantity you won't get quality. If you're away for a couple weeks, you can't return and immediately expect to pick up the dynamics of what is going on, the inner tensions. It takes time, patience, observing, and listening. You have to purposely set aside some time to be with your kids. It could be at night; it could be on the weekends, but there has to be some scheduled time.

In my case, I coached both our sons in YMCA basketball for years. I wrote it into my schedule. That gave us an activity we could do together which was fun for me as well as for them. I would also write into my schedule each year certain days when I would do things with each child.

During the summer we would go places together and have fun vacations. Before we finished any vacation, I would sit down with each of them and talk about the next school year and what they were thinking and dreaming about, what their struggles were, and we would pray

BEING DAD FROM A HOTEL ROOM

We have always tried to make it clear to our children that everything we do for the Lord, we do as a family. Our 16,000 staff members work in 151 countries, so I have lived on a plane and in hotel rooms for much of the time during the last thirty years. When I was away, Vonette wisely never communicated to the children that they were being deprived, but rather that they were a part of everything I was doing. She would take an atlas and point to the city I was in. They would talk about it, study Scripture together, and then she would say, "Let's pray for Daddy, and then we will be a part of everything he is doing."

To my knowledge, neither Zac nor Brad has ever felt deprived by my frequent absences, because they felt privileged to be a part of the work I was doing. They felt they had an investment in every person introduced to the Lord or discipled. Thanks to Vonette, they grew up feeling blessed.

And when I returned home, I always spent special time with them. They knew they were my top priority. In fact, I would say to them, "Always know that you and your mother are the most important people in the world to me. Wherever I am in the world, if you have a need, I will catch the next plane home if you wish. No matter with whom I am meeting, even if it is the President of the United States, if you want to talk to me, you don't have to wait. Just come and join the conference, or I will step out of the room and talk to you. Your father is available to you twenty-four hours a day."

They knew that was true, because sometimes they put me to the test. My older son especially would come and knock on my office door when I was in conference. I would invite him in, and he would sit quietly and listen for a while. He didn't seem to want anything except just to spend time with me.

Whenever I was home, I would go out of my way to spend time with my family. Once I had promised to take the boys to Arrowhead to play in the snow, when suddenly a famous college football coach showed up. He had come with his team to the Rose Bowl, and for a long time I had wanted to visit with him. In fact, it seemed really crucial to me that I spend time with him.

I was torn because I so much wanted to spend time with him, but I had already told the boys we were going to play in the snow. Suddenly I realized that this was a chance for them to see how important they are to me—no one can jump in and take their time. So I said a few words to the coach and excused myself, trusting he understood my explanation. Even if he didn't, I had to give the boys that assurance that my word to them was true.

I have always tried to do that, and to my knowledge they have always felt very much a part of the ministry. My older son is a minister, continuing in school. My younger son is my assistant. They both love the Lord, and both are very dear to Vonette and me. We have a warm relationship for which we thank the Lord.

Bill Bright

together about that.

When I'm in this country I try to call home fairly often. Sometimes we exchange tapes. When I was away, I tried to write regularly. Our son, Sandy, died three years ago, at the age of twenty-one. I've gone through all of his letters recently and I've come across letters that I wrote to him four or five years ago that he saved. As I read those letters I thought, "I'm so thankful I took the time to write and affirm him and sometimes urge him."

There are things you can do to compensate for absence. We had a young man attending Davidson College who came to our home almost every weekend during the four years he was there. He became like a big brother to our family. He played basketball with our sons, encouraged Deb, and was a strong spiritual influence. Not every family may be able to do that, but I think having a slightly older person like that made a difference.

Then, I remember something actor Alan Alda once said. He was talking about how important his family was. When he was on the set in California, he would fly home every weekend to New Jersey. About the time he got to Cleveland, he would deliberately try to change his mindset and forget what he had been doing all week and begin to think about his children and wife. So by the time he arrived, he had made a conscious effort to enter their world.

I think that when the working parent gets home, it is easy to still be preoccupied with business and professional life. We need to stop and make a deliberate effort to say, "Now I'm going to think about my family."

Love is a matter of the will, not just a matter of feeling. It's deliberately adjusting your communication, and making a conscious effort to think about what you're going to talk about with the family. It requires shifting gears. I need to put as much thought into my conversations with my family as I do into my work.

Related Articles

When You're Often Away from Home

J. ALLAN PETERSEN

Some fathers or mothers have jobs that force them to travel. They're away from home for days, even weeks at a time. If they're going to be effective parents, naturally they have to compensate.

Here are some guidelines for parents who must frequently travel:

First, let your children know where you are and what you're doing. A teacher of missionary children observed that children who know fairly well what their parents do have fewer problems adjusting to boarding school.

I heard a cute story about the class that was told to draw pictures of what their fathers did. One little boy made a whole bunch of circles.

"What are those?" the teacher asked.

"My dad's a doctor," the boy replied. "He makes rounds."

At least he'd heard what his father did. As much as possible, parents must share what they do with their children. It's especially important if parents must often be out of town.

Second, your wife's attitude is very important. A military study of officers' children who became delinquents revealed that in most cases the mother was unhappy and resentful toward her husband's occupation, griping that the military pushed them around, didn't respect them, and never let them know what was going to happen. The mother's resentment was passed on to the children.

A wife in this situation is key also because she must build respect for the father while he's away. Without Mom's respect for Dad, the children effectively lose the positive father figure.

Third, even while you're gone, keep in touch. Cards, or better yet, your voice over the telephone can help show the kids that absence doesn't remove your love and involvement.

It's also important to give the children certain responsibilities while you're gone— certain jobs to do, certain agreements to fulfill. And then keep in touch with them on how they're doing. This not only shows your concern for the maintenance of family life, but it gives them a way to contribute to it.

Fourth, keep your promises, especially those about spending time with family members when you return. One study in Minneapolis discovered the girls who ran away from home and got involved in prostitution almost all made similar observations about home life: "My father would not keep his promises."

Promises are an important factor in a child's development of trust and dependability. This is especially true for a parent who travels. Get your children in your date book, and then make those appointments inviolate. I know one man who travels extensively and has three young sons at home, and he arranges his schedule so he can have a private breakfast with each of them every week. Despite his busy schedule, those boys know their father is interested in them and he keeps his word.

Fifth, plan shorter, more frequent vacations instead of one longer one. You can't be gone all the time and then make up for it in one big fling. Several weekend getaways are better for catching up on family matters than two weeks in a cabin.

Finally, learn to creatively cope with your unique situation. I don't know your personality, your time frame, your emotional energy, but in our family we always planned something special when I came home, even if it meant clearing something else from the schedule.

We needed some reentry time. Sometimes, especially when children are little, you come home and expect them to jump up and receive you warmly, but they retreat; they're not ready for you. They need time to get reacquainted. So we always planned a family activity for shortly after I returned.

And the night I got back, we'd sit around the table and talk about what happened while I was gone and what I'd seen on my trip. Once when our boys were small, I mentioned that I had talked with a homosexual. "What's that?" they asked. So around the table we had a chance for training and education as well.

We discovered that I couldn't discipline the kids immediately when I got back. My wife had been doing it in my absence, and for me to come home and right away work them over would lend negative associations to Daddy coming home. So my wife would continue being the disciplinarian for the first few days I was back until I could reestablish relationships. Then I took over again.

The biggest mistake a traveling parent can make, however, isn't returning too abruptly. It's not returning emotionally at all. Some fathers get so committed to their businesses, so involved in the excitement and ego-strengthening pursuit of success, they forget to keep close touch with their children.

I'm not posing as the perfect parent here—I certainly didn't do everything right—but one thing I did do: whenever I was home, I went to every ball game, every ROTC function. I knew my sons' friends, teammates, and coaches.

Recently one of my sons went to his twentieth high school reunion and met an old classmate. The first thing this friend asked was, "How are your parents?" My son came home to ask me if I remembered this guy. "Well, he sure remembers you," my son said. "He remembered being at our house and he said he always felt so much at home."

Being a Faithful Father

DAVID HOWARD

My father was a great example to his children. Evidence of that is that all six of his children entered the Lord's service. We couldn't help but see the very strong example he lived. As I had children of my own, my father's example was a constant reminder to me that I wanted my life to show my children how to live, just as my father's life had shown me.

Part of his example was in how he dealt with his children. He never told us one thing one day and a contradictory thing the next. If he said we would be punished for misbehavior, we were. That was consistency. What he said, he meant and what he said, he did.

His personal life was also exemplary. My father made it a daily practice all his life to rise early in the morning to meet with the Lord. From the time I was little, I can remember seeing him on his knees in the early morning hours.

As a small child, I'd get up early and creep downstairs, but I never got down there before my father. He was always there. I'd find him alone in his study, often on his knees with his Bible and a prayer list spread out in front of him. As I tiptoed up behind him and looked over his shoulder, I'd see what was on his prayer list—my mother's name at the top, and then all six of his children.

I knew that he prayed at least four times every day for each of us by name—during his personal devotions, at breakfast when we had family devotions, in the evening at family devotions again, and before he went to bed at night when he and my mother prayed together.

The impact this had on me was subtle but deep. When I went away to school and had to set my own schedule, it was almost an automatic thing for me to schedule time with the Lord. My father's silent example made me realize that I also ought to begin the day with the Lord in personal Bible study and prayer.

My father never really did a lot of direct

113

teaching about having a personal quiet time, or how to have it. His own example was so consistent that it became a natural thing for me to do. His example had the same influence on my brothers and sisters too.

My father also spent time with us and, by being with us, taught us. He didn't sit us down and say, "Now we are going to learn about this." Learning was a daily occurrence. He often quoted the verse in Isaiah, "Training children is a question of 'precept upon precept, line upon line . . . here a little, and there a little' " (Isa. 28:10, KJV).

On Saturdays, he made it a point to be home with us and take us out for bird hikes or fishing or mountain climbing. Because of his example, I wanted to do these things with my children.

Of course, my father was not a perfect man. He had a strong temper, especially when we were young. I can remember temper tantrums that frightened the wits out of me. But I never remember a time when he lost his temper with us that he did not call the family together and apologize before bedtime. He believed the Apostle Paul's exhortation to the Ephesians, "Let not the sun go down on your wrath" (Eph. 4:26, KJV).

So even in his weakness he provided us with a godly example of how to deal with sin quickly and to ask forgiveness of the people you have wronged.

Related Articles

"WELL DONE"

Some years ago a doctor told me he had a theory about the need for a father to affirm his children. Throughout childhood and adolescence, there are key times when a child needs certain affirmations from his father. If a father fails to provide them at those times, a void is left that probably can never be filled any other way or by any other person. I believe the doctor was right.

If a father is not available to a child who is going through adolescence, the child often experiences increasing feelings of rejection. No matter how much the father argues that, "I'm working hard to send my kids to college" or whatever, the bottom line for the child is a strange kind of rejection that often turns into anger and loss of self-esteem.

When a child seldom or never hears his father say, "Well done," he is likely to struggle all the way from his teens to mid-life. Another bitter consequence of the failure to affirm a child is teenage hostility toward other symbols of authority. This is because of the negative experiences the teenager had with the main symbol of authority in his home.

Gordon MacDonald

Being the Child of a Successful Father

DAVID L. McKENNA

Some fathers are very visible, prominent men in their fields, deemed "successful" by the world. This can cause extra pressure on both the father and his children to come up to perceived expectations.

Studies have indicated that probably the most difficult role in the world is to be the son of a successful man. In the late '60s and early '70s, the people who became both radicals and members of a lost and wandering generation were very frequently the children—particularly the sons—of successful people. Two factors emerge from the research.

First, there seems to be an identity problem. The child of a successful man carries his father's name. So there is always the immediate expectation that the son will of course live up to his father's reputation. The expectations, therefore, are high, and it becomes hard for a son to develop his own unique identity, apart from his father.

Many of the radicals I mentioned were striving for independence apart from their successful fathers. They often chose a different career line as a way of establishing their own identity. Yet it's interesting that many of those radicals returned to the "establishment" after they acted out their rebellion.

Armand Nicolai, an evangelical Christian who heads the Counseling Center at Harvard Medical School, did a ten-year study during the '70s on Harvard students facing emotional difficulties. He found that while problems of the late '60s focused on rebellion against the home and institutions, the '70s problems dealt with a young person's excessive freedom without guidelines and standards against which to cut his own image.

The Harvard researchers went a step further to try to determine why sons had excessive freedom. The major underlying difficulty they found was the absence of the father from the home.

The second factor, then, is a fatherless home. The father's role of being prominent and successful does not allow him to stay at home. We talk about single-parent families being a problem, but the successful man who is on the move creates a single-parent setting also. For example, I know some weeks our home has been like a motel and lunch counter, because I'm out so much.

Perhaps the hardest problem for a successful father is integrating home and family life with his career in a workable fashion. The career demands often seem to clash head-on with domestic demands. Since there are pressures from both sides, it becomes crucial to set realistic priorities and keep them.

I had two different calls recently that illustrate perfectly the pressure a prominent father can have. The callers wanted me to come and speak on a Friday night, stay all day Saturday, and then preach on Sunday. I said no to both requests. I explained, "I have a fifteen-year-old son who's playing basketball Friday night and my priority is my son." Well they felt like I was defecting from the ministry. They

115

didn't understand that my family *has* to come first sometimes. Besides, when I *do* go against my better judgment, I sense the nagging guilt that I should have stayed home with the family. So I'm going to be unpopular with *someone,* either way I choose.

Another problem I think successful fathers struggle with is bringing the "executive style" home and trying (unconsciously, perhaps) to impose it on the family structure. When you're on the move and have a strong national identity you have a sense of power, whether it's speaking or knowing that people look to you for counsel. When you're in the office people jump when you say jump.

To go home and say jump to a teenager is another story. They usually *don't* jump. Perhaps the classic example in my life was with my daughter, Debi. I came home from the office tired and ready to do some painting for relaxation. I went downstairs to look for my prized paintbrush, a very expensive one. When I found it wasn't there, I began yelling, "Who's got my paintbrush?" No one would claim to be the culprit.

Finally my wife remembered that Debi and her boyfriend were talking about painting his student body president office. I asked Debi, "Did you take that paintbrush down to paint Ed's office?" She confessed.

WHAT'S WRONG WITH BEING A GENTLE-MAN?

"I fell down today, Daddy. But I didn't cry."

"That's my little man!"

From our earliest years, men are programmed to fit the macho image. "Feminine" qualities like gentleness, sensitivity, and tenderness are put down, and "tough" ones are affirmed; the heroes of television are the modern models of "real men."

In reality, real men have emotions—to deny them is to ignore a vital part of one's true identity. And the Bible is packed with real men, from David who was strong and yet expressed a wide range of emotions in the Psalms, to Jesus who threw con men out of the temple, wept over a city, and struggled in prayer.

Therefore, as a father I must ask myself, "Am I a demonstration of what a man should be or does my life perpetuate the macho myth?"

• Have my children ever seen me cry, apologize, or even compromise (or imply that these are signs of weakness)?
• Am I affectionate with my wife and children?
• Am I comfortable conversing with women (or do I stick with the guys)?
• As a father, do I spend time with my daughter(s)? (As a mother, do I spend time with my son[s]?)
• Am I willing to forgive?
• Do I display kindness, tenderness, love (and other fruits of the Spirit)?
• Do I admit my mistakes?
• Do I point my children to Jesus as their model man?

It is axiomatic that little boys grow up to be a lot like their dads and girls, like their moms. It's a tremendous privilege to be able to mold young lives—but what an awesome responsibility! God help us as we live for Him.

YFC Editors

I told her I wanted her to go get it (with the implied "now"). She said she was busy with something else and didn't have time right then. Well, I pulled executive rank on her and demanded she go get it. She ended up retreating into her room, giving me the silent treatment, and didn't even come out for dinner.

Suddenly, I realized I was wrong in demanding a response that was sure to be hostile. I was miserable and grouchy. She was wrong in not responding to my request. Yet because parents are more mature and should be stronger, *we* should be the ones to initiate asking forgiveness. I don't think there's any more difficult, yet important, lesson to learn. So I swallowed my pride, put the executive demeanor on the shelf, and asked Debi to forgive me. We bawled that night. I realized that no paintbrush was worth my relationship with my daughter. To this day, Debi and I love each other very much. Yet I could have lost her at that time by being stubborn and proud. It means a lot to any child to have a parent ask forgiveness, but *especially* when that parent is used to power and visibility and praise. I don't hesitate to ask my children's forgiveness now.

I've learned not to come home and "jump" on people. But I guess I still expect some kind of "update report" on the status of our family. If I know my son, Rob, is trying out for the basketball team, I want to know how he did when I get home. It's tempting to *demand* to know. But it seems to work better when I let him come to me on his own and tell me what happened. The other thing I try to do is leave my problems at the office. I try to go home with some kind of "bounce" that will help everyone—including myself.

Another thing that I think complicates matters is that no matter how widely recognized or successful a man is in public, he tends to be *very* human at home. In public the image seems to be grandiose and stable—you know what your role is. But the wife and children see you as husband and dad, not as "president" or "doctor." My kids have kept me humble in that regard. One of the cute things my daughter said in second grade, shortly after I became a college president, was, "Daddy, what do you want to be when you grow up?" If there was any helium in my balloon before, it rapidly leaked out a pinhole!

Successful fathers often deal with the guilt of being away from their families. It's a struggle to get the right balance of quality time and quantity time. I used to structure events or conversations artificially with my son or daughter in an attempt to "make up" for my absence.

I set up a Saturday swim time with my son, for example. We'd go and swim and afterward we'd do anything he wanted to do—bowling or whatever. One Friday I got home and announced, "Well, Rob, tomorrow is our day!" I was all excited about fulfilling my role as a good father should. He looked at me fearfully and said, "Dad, do you think I could have the day off?" I realized then, that it has to be a natural kind of relationship. When you try to structure it artificially because of your guilt about being absent, you lose the essence of the relationship.

There are pressures on the son as well. I think the syndrome between the successful man and son is represented by the expectations you place on him which are probably unfair because they are too high. High expectations are all right unless they're in the cloning mold. Teens need to have growing space to be themselves.

There's a love-hate, win-lose relationship in the sense that teens need to be free to develop their own identity, yet they take pride in their reflected glory. This pride can be good or bad, often depending on the parents' modeling. All teens need to feel good about themselves. Children of successful parents may have an advantage in getting attention. If I'm on television, Rob's friends at school may say, "I saw your dad on TV last night!"

It's important that teens don't use the prominence of a successful parent for manipulation to get on an athletic team or get an office at school. But a healthy pride is an advantage. The successful person has given a certain heritage to his children that I think is valuable. Teens know who they are and it helps with their identity formation. As Shakespeare reminded us, what's in a name is *very* important. High expectations can be motivational tools, when teens are allowed to breathe.

While there is a different kind of pressure put on successful parents and their children, the effects of that pressure are determined by how they choose to respond.

Related Articles
Chapter 4:   Fathers Need to Take the Lead
Chapter 4:   Being a Faithful Father

Dads and Daughters

GORDON MacDONALD

Because a father is the first man to whom a daughter relates, that relationship is incredibly important—more so than most men realize. Daughters need to know that their fathers accept them as women and not just as little girls.

It is important for a father to make his daughter know, in all phases of her development, that he really approves of her. Beyond his appreciation of her skills and spiritual capacities, she needs his approval of her physical appearance.

Perhaps the most important thing is that he really believes in her potentiality and expresses that to her. Many girls never hear that from their fathers because some fathers think they should leave their daughter's raising to the mothers. While mothers have their own game to play, there is no substitute for a father's affirmation.

Daughters also need physical affection from their fathers. Some fathers feel embarrassed about giving affection to their daughters. They may have to push themselves and deliberately demonstrate affection until it becomes natural.

A FATHER'S TOUCH

As kids become teenagers, parents often think of them as too big to touch. This was a struggle for me as our daughters became women. I began to feel that it was inappropriate for me as a father and man to hug my daughters. But I began to realize, with Sally's encouragement, that they needed that affection from me and I shouldn't stop just because they were teenagers.

Studies show that girls who have a lot of appropriate, affectionate touching from their parents, and especially from their fathers, do not usually get married as young as those whose fathers ignore them. Appropriate affection meets their need for physical closeness and causes them to take time to make a serious marriage choice.

Jim Conway

Fathers who are unable to express affection should take a hard look at some men around them who don't have that problem. Watch them carefully, and maybe even talk to them about it. A father may have to seek counseling to help overcome this problem.

Recently I met with a thirty-two-year-old man who is struggling in a relationship with his six-year-old daughter. He doesn't think she respects him. He said, "There is no physical affection between us." During our talk he expressed feelings of intense anger toward his own father. Of course, that anger is probably affecting his relationship with his daughter. I asked him to spend a few days writing a full description of his entire relationship with his father. I want to see if I can pick up habit patterns, hurts, and struggles he has never dealt with that may be binding him up.

Related Article
Chapter 4:   Moms and Daughters

Moms and Daughters

NAOMI COLE

A good relationship between a mother and daughter doesn't just happen. It takes a lifetime of effort, as does any other good relationship.

A mother needs to understand the different stages her daughter is likely to go through. For instance, most teenagers go through periods of mild depression. If you know that, you can let them enjoy their misery; it will pass.

Mothers tend to dominate their daughters, pressing them into their own mold, making them in their own image. They want their daughters to be like them, even if they don't like themselves.

Sometimes mothers live vicariously through their daughters. A mother who didn't date very much pushes her daughter into early dating. Or, if she didn't get a college education, she may insist on one for her daughter.

It's very important that a mother encourage her daughter to be her own person, to develop her own personality and abilities. Even when quite young, a girl should be helped to make decisions whenever possible. Her preferences in hair style, clothing, bedroom decor, etc. should be respected.

Some mothers make everything a moral issue, particularly in the area of clothing. We need to distinguish between fashion and modesty. A girl should be allowed to make her own choices when the issue is only what's "in."

I remember when girls were wearing horrible, oversized men's shirts and letting them hang out so that they reached their knees. Mothers hated them. But it wasn't worth fussing over; it was a matter of style. Mothers may well be tolerant when no moral issues are at stake, when it is only a question of fashion. Girls want to be part of *their* culture.

At the time the big shirt was popular, some girls were wearing their shirts unbuttoned almost to the waist. *That* was a moral issue, not to be tolerated. "Button up, Baby!"

Mothers and daughters need to spend

time together, lots of it. When they do, conversation is natural, not forced. Even work around the house can be pleasant and beneficial to a relationship when it is done together and in the right spirit. Painting a room, cleaning the carpeting, putting a fine meal on the table can be fun when done as a team, but are drudgery when done alone. Conversation comes easily and opportunity is given to discuss naturally things that might be serious.

I think it is good when a mother and daughter have the same hobby. My daughter, Stephanie, and I both love plants and have great fun with them. We don't compete; we offer advice to each other and share helpful tidbits of information.

A wise mother will encourage her daughter to excel in an area in which she is poor. I hate to sew. I've never become skillful in operating a sewing machine. My daughter is an expert. I'm lavish in my praise of her sewing accomplishments. It not only builds her ego, but I get free alterations!

Women naturally discuss clothes and recipes and household hints. That's OK. Some women gossip just as naturally. That's bad. "Learn to discuss ideas instead of people" has been a motto in our home. A mother and daughter can stretch each other's mind as they struggle with ideas and concepts and issues. Stephanie and I frequently discuss such things as the Sunday sermon (not the preacher, but his message), the doctrine of election, the role of women in the church, the true meaning of biblical submission, etc. On a more practical level, we talk about what it means to forgive a friend, how to handle anger in a particular situation, how to help a distressed neighbor, how best to point a certain person to Christ. This encourages us both to think and to develop our own opinions. Best of all, it helps us to develop Christian maturity.

Handling Tensions

Tensions are normal; it's what we do with our tensions that matters. When there is friction, we need to do our best not to prolong it. It is the parent's responsibility to take the initiative to straighten things out.

We need to remind ourselves that when someone offends us, it is seldom done deliberately. The problem may very well be in me, not in the other person. Mother-daughter conflicts are no different. Rarely does a daughter deliberately

---

A MOTHER'S HEART

Is a father more influential in his children's lives than a mother? I don't think so. There are as many mother images in the Bible as there are father images. In my mind, God is Father/Mother. A mother embodies God's love, His care, His character and nature as much as does a father. As Chaplain of the U.S. Senate, I hear leaders of our country talk again and again about the influence of their mothers. Perhaps even more so than that of their fathers.

One eighty-two-year-old senator talks about his mother every time he gets a chance. At Senate prayer breakfasts I hear more about mother images than father images. I think the relationship between a mother and a child is much more intimate because of the nine months of gestation within the mother. There's no way in the world that a father can have that relationship. Though the father has the responsibility for instructing his children in his faith, most mothers probably do a better job.

Richard C. Halverson

set out to irritate her mother. And vice versa. Remembering this makes coping with tensions much easier.

The best way to handle some tensions is to prevent them. Often we mothers expect too much of our daughters. We think they should be able to read our minds. They can't. We need to verbalize our thoughts and to spell out our wishes. Our perspective is different from theirs. They don't see things the way we do— certainly not a sink full of dirty dishes!

On numbers of occasions, I now know, I expected my teenage daughter to read my mind. After an evening away from the house, I'd say to her, "Oh, I thought maybe you would have cleaned up the kitchen while I was out." If I had wanted her to clean up the kitchen, I should have asked her to do it.

We also need to vocalize our approval and appreciation. I regret that for many years I didn't understand the importance of expressing praise. I appreciate it when my husband says, "That was a great dinner." I appreciate it when my daughter says, "I like the way you handled that situation." And she appreciates it when I praise her. Praise doesn't cost anything; all it takes is a little thoughtfulness.

Proverbs 3:27 says, "Do not withhold good from those to whom it is due, when it is in your power to do it" (NASB). We gyp our daughters and ourselves when we fail to encourage and praise them for a job well done. And even a job not so well done! We may think they did well, but unless we say so, they'll never know.

Discipline is an important factor in a mother-daughter relationship. Wrongdoing has its consequences. Deliberate disobedience must not be ignored. But punishment should always be fair, immediate (not postponed for the father to handle when he gets home), and short-term. Mothers need to develop sweet reasonableness. Harsh discipline and an unyielding spirit will provoke our daughters to wrath.

Letting Go

Developing a mother-daughter relationship is like loosening the string of a kite. You let the string unwind little by little until the kite soars off into the blue and then you let the string go. So it is with your daughter. At the moment of birth your eyes are on her; you watch for that first breath. Later, you watch her take her first step; you watch her leave home on her first day at school; and as you watch, you let out the string, a little at a time. She develops her own personality and lifestyle and independence. Eventually, the time comes—perhaps when she goes off to college, or on her wedding day— when you must let the string go. But unlike a kite, she comes back again. It is the beginning of a whole new relationship.

She is still your daughter but a new dimension has been added. She has become your friend. There is a special understanding between you not shared with any other person, because you have put your life into hers. She will have rejected some of your ideas, but you will be continually amazed at how much of you she has absorbed.

With the passing of years, some situations will be reversed. She'll help you, comfort you, advise you. Yet if you have not tried to run her life, she won't try to run yours. That mutual respect for each other will continue to the very end, which is, after all, only the beginning.

Related Article
Chapter 4: Dads and Daughters

How to Manage Your Household

SUSAN KREIDER

When I was first married, I determined that if I didn't get in charge of my house, I would be its slave. Notice that I said house—not home. I understand the biblical responsibilities of the husband to be the head of his home and I gladly yield to him the spiritual leadership, discipline direction, financial matters, and any other areas that should be left to his discretion.

The management of the house is my responsibility and it requires full-time attention in order for it to function with some sense of order and efficiency. Therefore, I have established three basic priorities that will hopefully help control the house. There are other priorities that relate to things like personal attitudes, manners, and growth of my children—but the purpose of this article is to focus on the functional side of life—the mechanics of control.

The first priority is that everything in my house should run smoothly, orderly, and with a sense of structure. I have seen too many women who are like a Ping-Pong ball, constantly being batted around by the events of their lives. What I observe doesn't appear to be fun, so I look at order as something good. Let me also dispel one misconception that hints that you can't enjoy family warmth, togetherness, sharing, and other personal joys if you don't drop everything to meet your family's every need immediately on request. In fact, the opposite is true. Without your house being in control, you cannot fully concentrate on your family's needs when it really is necessary.

Over the years I have come up with nine rules that have helped to keep us going, and though there are still breakdowns, I would hate to think what would happen to our family if they didn't exist.

The first rule is that there are set times for set events. For instance, supper is at 6 P.M. The kids automatically know that we sit down to the table at that time. If they are over at a friend's house and forget to come home, we don't call—we begin to eat. It doesn't take too many times of coming home to cold potatoes and a lonely table before they get the message. Of course, when you have children involved in sports, there have to be exceptions, but the key is to communicate the plan so everyone knows what to expect.

We have also instructed the children to tell their friends that they cannot receive calls during dinner or after certain hours at night. If they do receive a call during those times, we have them return it.

Since we are talking about meals, I have also set a time in the afternoon when the kids get home from school for a snack. They need something to eat and we can get the refrigerator raid over with all at once. It also saves a constant mess in the kitchen.

There are also set times for going to bed. Though they may plead for a reprieve because they are not sleepy, we suggest reading a book or something else until they are sleepy. Yes, we do give in once in a while when there is something special on TV. This latitude lets them know that rules are not arbitrary laws—they have purpose—and when there is a

122

better purpose than going to bed, so be it.

A second rule is that each of the kids has his own personal list of chores and a set day or time of day in which the work is to be done. Utilize your children's energy—you are doing both of you a favor. You save yourself a job and you are teaching them family responsibility. Once they have failed at trying to change the job list, the regular routine sets in with minimum complaints except for an occasional test to see if a hairline crack has developed in the wall of Mom's or Dad's will.

The third rule applies to myself. I have a monthly calendar placed somewhere close to the kitchen telephone. I am constantly looking it over and trying to keep one week's activities fairly fresh in my mind. Since there are always extra responsibilities or last minute crises, I try to pace myself by baking cookies or making presents well in advance. I also request—no, I insist—that the kids write their schedules on this master calendar. This makes everyone responsible for keeping up with schedules and I can't be scolded for forgetting a birthday party.

Rule number four is that I will always look for opportunities to carpool to regular events. Whether it's gymnastics, baseball practice, picking the kids up from a movie, or even orthodontic appointments—I'm eager to find another mother who would like to team up.

The fifth rule has to do with the use of the freezer. There are always times when we need a fast meal. Therefore, I try to cook 1½ to 2 times the size of servings needed for one meal and freeze the rest. This provides quite a savings from the fast trip to Burger King or Pizza Hut.

A sixth rule is that I have a set day for washing each week. The kids can't wear three different outfits in one day and complain because they have no clean clothes by the middle of the week. I also would rather save one day a week solely for washing and not have piles of folded or unfolded clothes laying around all week. Now that my children are in school all day, I also do most of my housecleaning on that day. Then I don't have to think about those jobs the rest of the week save the daily straightening up. That is very important too. It is amazing how cluttered your life seems if your surroundings are cluttered. It is very easy to get in the habit of picking up either first thing in the morning or last thing at night.

Another rule, number seven, also has to do with a set day. This time it is for shopping. This forces everyone in the family to plan ahead and write down on the shopping list the things they need. It also prevents constant trips to the store. I usually have extra household, personal, and regularly used food items on a shelf so that there is always a replacement. When one is used up—write it down. It takes awhile, but eventually everyone catches on.

The eighth rule is if I see an item on sale that would make a nice gift, I buy several and save them for the last minute birthday party or Christmas gift. My closet is full of undesignated presents. Many a time I have gone to that shelf instead of making a special trip to the store.

The ninth and final rule has to do with that old saying, "A place for everything and everything in its place." If you have your closets and drawers organized, then everyone knows where things are. This will save you a lot of time, because we all know that only mothers can find things.

Now back to the priorities. My second priority is that our family have a time each day when we can be together. Yes, I know it's not always possible, but at least we work at it.

I've already mentioned that the kids can't receive calls during dinner because that's our time for privacy and family discussions. We also have certain traditions that may not appear all that significant, but they become very important to each member of the family. For instance, Friday night is popcorn night.

Just try to slip by without making it. There are also certain meals that the kids enjoy that we plan for every week. Friday night it's pizza and Saturday night it's usually Mexican food. It's not a rut because we all enjoy doing it. Besides, it saves planning two meals a week. I've learned that if we work hard to make their personal events a priority then they will make our family events a priority.

The third priority has to do with me. I cannot function round-the-clock with only everyone else's interests in mind. There have to be times for my own privacy. So, for instance, in the summer when the kids are home all day, they have to go to their rooms for an hour after lunch. This provides a break from one another and they can quietly read, work on baseball cards, or do whatever they enjoy.

Another thing that is very important for mothers to do is to develop their own interests by taking classes, attending seminars, joining clubs, etc. You will be amazed at what that does to your attitude about yourself and your family responsibilities. Don't forget to get some exercise also, whether it be tennis, swimming, aerobics, or jogging. It will increase your energy level and you will be able to keep going almost as long as your kids.

I try to do my shopping, spend time with friends, and accomplish other away-from-home chores while the kids are at school so that I can be home when they are home. That way I've solved two problems; I've had some time to myself and can give the kids the attention they need.

I can hear you working mothers and mothers with small children still at home saying, "That won't work for me." I realize that adjustments will have to be made to accommodate each household. The purpose of this article is to get you thinking about the state of your home and to make some suggestions for smoothing off the rough edges.

From time to time I have to reevaluate everything to see what causes the most inconveniences or problems. That takes private time. Sometimes it helps if my husband takes the kids to a movie and I have an extra couple of hours to myself. Without these times to recharge, I wouldn't be much of a mother, and if I'm not much of a mother guess what that does to Dad when he gets home.

Hopefully, my children are learning to control their own time by observing our house. I don't want to re-educate them when I have grandchildren. This job is tough enough one time around.

Related Articles

Mothers and Work

LaVONNE NEFF

Shortly after we moved to Walla Walla, Washington, a charming woman named Wilma introduced herself to me. "I teach Marriage and Family Life," she said, "and I neglect my children."

She didn't, of course. In fact, she took very good care of all four of them. In addition, she kept her house open to dozens of foreign students, and most weekends she spread an enormous pot-luck in her family room and invited a crowd to share it.

Wilma fulfilled all her responsibilities well and had energy to spare. But that didn't stop some of her Christian friends from criticizing her. In their minds, mothers should not work outside the home unless they absolutely have to.

Many—perhaps most—working mothers have no choice. Either they are the only parent in the family, or their husbands are out of work, or both incomes are necessary to keep even beans on the table. These women do what they have to do, and the last thing they need is guilt feelings piled on top of the burdens they're already carrying.

But some women do have a choice. Their incomes are not essential to keeping the family above the poverty line. Their children are living at home; they may still be preschoolers. Should women in this situation ever consider going back to work?

Before my children began kindergarten, I did not work outside the home except for an occasional substitute-teaching assignment. But then I met Wilma, and I had to admit that I was not doing any more for my children than she was for hers.

There are distinct disadvantages to being a stay-at-home mother. When I was at home all day, I quickly began to doubt my competence. Home ec and driver ed were my two worst subjects in school, and now they seemed basic to everything I did. In addition, I found myself trying to use my husband as a pipeline to the outer world. I began to focus my administrative skill on telling him how to run his life. For some reason, he was not profoundly grateful. Furthermore, I began to expect too much of our children. If they looked good and behaved well, people might think I was a competent mother. Enough. Any woman who has ever stayed home with children knows the symptoms. And

the variety of part-time and temporary jobs I had taken in the seven years since my children started school didn't alleviate all of them. If Wilma could hold a full-time job and do a fine job with her family, why couldn't I be a full-time working mother too?

I started comparing my situation with Wilma's. Her mother lives across the street and loves to baby-sit; mine lives 2,000 miles away and children make her nervous. Wilma's husband and she both have flexible job schedules—some of their work can be done at home; my husband has to put in at least eight hours a day at his office. Wilma finds cooking relaxing; when I need to relax, I read a book.

It looks so obvious on paper: Wilma's lifestyle makes her full-time job an excellent idea. Mine makes working full-time outside the home difficult, if not impossible. But I envied Wilma. And I took a full-time job—one whose hours were even more demanding and inflexible than my husband's. In addition, I had to spend an hour commuting.

My daughters assured me before I took the job that they would never let me neglect them. They didn't. But my attention span after nine hours in the office, one hour on the road, and a couple of hours for supper and clean-up—even though my family pitched in and did their share of the work—was limited. My disposition ranged from depressed to irritable. I was too tired to read, to see friends, to pray. After three months of great fun at the office but great agony everywhere else, I faced up to the differences between Wilma and me. I quit my job. But I did not quit working altogether, because I had learned something on the job: I feel much better if I am doing work that I value and that the community recognizes.

The twentieth-century housewife, once her children are in school, may feel neither valuable nor recognized. Finding a challenging full-time job is one way for her to make a contribution to the community that will also restore her faith in herself. But it is not the only way.

Many women who are financially comfortable volunteer their expertise to a cause they value. They hold office in the PTA or the school board. They donate regular hours as teacher aides. They help out at a hospital, or run fund raising programs for various charities.

Other women are able to find part-time or at-home work. Ginny is a receptionist from 9 to 3. Ruth is an editor three days a week. Judy is a curriculum developer from an office between the bathroom and the baby's bedroom. And I am a writer whose word-processing computer sits in a corner of the master bedroom.

It's easy to create a false dilemma for ourselves by assuming that there are only two solutions—working full-time in an office or staying indoors all day doing domestic tasks. It is human, once we have made our own choice, to want to generalize and say everyone should be like us. But life isn't like that.

In fact, all parents have two responsibilities to fulfill. First, we must take care of our children's needs. This includes feeding, clothing, and sheltering them as well as teaching, loving, and playing with them. For some of us, this means that we must work full-time outside the home. For others, it means that we must not. Our situations are different.

Second, we all must do what God has called us to do in the wider community. Again, some of us will do this through paid work, while others will do it through volunteer work.

In short, we're all different. Our gifts are different. So are our children, our spouses, our energy levels. Why should we expect someone else's solution to fit our needs?

If you are feeling dissatisfied with your present situation—perhaps you are restless at home, or maybe you have more to do than you can handle—it's time to reexamine your family's needs, your gifts, and the various ways you could handle your responsibilities. You may decide that the time has come to take a paid job, full-time or otherwise. Or you may decide to quit or restructure your present job.

You and I are different. If we see our differences as opportunities to use our unique gifts, we can all feel good about our decisions to work or not to work, no matter which way we decide.

Related Articles
Chapter 3: Pressures from Without and Within

Chapter 4: How to Manage Your Household

Chapter 4: The Challenges of a Working Mother

The Challenges of a Working Mother

O'ANN STEERE

The "traditional American family" is about as common as the bald eagle. Over half of the women in the United States work outside the home. Sixty-seven percent of mothers of school-age children are employed. For seven out of ten of these women, working is a financial necessity (forty-three percent are the sole

126

support for themselves and their dependents and another twenty-eight percent are married to men earning less than $10,500 per year). Working mothers are an important part of our society. They have been an important part of society for generations. Even the virtuous woman described in Proverbs 31 combined being a wife and mother with buying fields and selling linen garments at the gate.

Combining these roles effectively isn't an easy matter. Solomon wondered, "Who can find a lady like that?" and he placed her value above rubies. Working mothers face some special challenges in fulfilling all of their obligations.

Some things don't change. The woman of Proverbs 31 got up while it was still dark and her lamp did not go out by night. She set about her work vigorously. The last eleven published studies on working mothers all list time as the number one challenge. There are only so many hours in a day and spending them effectively is important. The challenge of a working mother is to divide her days so that four critical needs are met.

So, "What's a mother to do?"

Take care of yourself. Examining our firstborn son, the wise pediatrician said, "He is healthy and the most important person in your world right now. But, by your next appointment, Mother will be the most important family member. If Mother is well, the family can be well cared for. If she is not well, no one else will be well for long."

On days when your self-esteem isn't sufficient to make you care for yourself just for your own benefit, it is helpful to remember that statement, "If Mother isn't well, no one else will be well for long."

How do you keep well? First, keep well physically. Eat and sleep. Your mother probably used to drum into you, "You need a good breakfast to start the day," or "Sit down and eat now!" She was right. You *do* need to eat. And to eat well. Good food helped Shadrach, Meshach, and Abednego, and it will help you too. Every day, hectic or just plain busy, supply your body with the basic energy materials it needs to function well. Fortified sludge won't cut it.

That doesn't mean gourmet fare to dazzle Julia Child. A local library can help you find some quick ways to make good nutrition very palatable. Try a recipe exchange among friends featuring meals that can be put on the table in one hour or less. Cheese, fruit, yogurt, cottage cheese, boiled eggs, and raw vegetables can all be stored in your refrigerator ready for quick pick-ups.

Sleep. How boring. But, how necessary. Maybe not eight hours a night but as many as are right for you. Discover how much sleep you need and get it. See if a twenty-minute rest/nap during the day reduces your need for night sleep, still leaving you refreshed.

Take care of your appearance. Some of us would be more spic with a little less span. Exercise can help. Watch what you wear at home. Most jobs require a specific style of dressing. Home is where you are free to dress as you please. But, the consistent choosing of sloppy clothes and the "unmade face" can leave you feeling depressed (not to mention what it does for your husband and children who have to look at you!).

Besides keeping well physically you should keep well personally. People need time to express themselves, to grow, and to be alone. Find time to do the things that you already enjoy and that are an important part of you. Take time to learn some new skills and enjoy new experiences. Make time to be alone, to think and rediscover who it is you are and how you would like to grow next (even if this time is stolen in five-minute trips to the bathroom or long bubble baths).

Read a book; take a class; do a craft project; listen to a bird or a symphony; take a quiet walk in the woods; have a tall glass of lemonade with a friend. Keep well.

Beyond keeping well physically and

personally, you need to keep well spiritually. This is so important that it is really a separate challenge.

Worship your God. God said it 2,000 years ago but the advice is still valuable. "Seek ye first the kingdom of God, and His righteousness; and all these things shall be added unto you" (Matt. 6:33, KJV).

The rush and clatter of meals to fix, shirts to mend, noses to wipe, reports to write, and even people to love can easily crowd out the desire for personal time with God. "Surely, God knows me and sees the mess I'm in. He'll understand if I skip today." Yes, fortunately He will. As working mothers, we can be liberated from any guilt about missing one day's devotions.

But Psalm 1 describes the wicked as being like chaff that the wind blows away and the man who meditates on the Word as being like a tree planted by streams of water. The demands of a busy day can make you feel pulled loose and blown about like chaff. If the picture of a beautiful tree planted by streams of water is what you want your life to be, time with God is required.

Great men of the faith like John Wesley and Hudson Taylor found that great business required more time alone with God. "I will be so busy today that I cannot have less than two hours for prayer," said Wesley.

God isn't changed by your time together. His love and character are steadfast. But you are changed. Most of us need that kind of changing.

Nurture your children. Here is where the crunch of being a working mother really comes in. No one objects to single women working to earn their own living. Almost no one objects to married women supplementing the couple's income by working. But when children enter the picture the decision gets more complicated.

We know that children are a blessing and a heritage from the Lord. That blessing can't be ignored. Or even shuffled off into some corner of our minds and time. Kids need consistent loving and that means consistent giving of time and energy. Presumably, you and your husband have come to an agreement on who will care for your children when you are not available.

What about the time that you *are* with your children? The "quality vs. quantity" rhetoric abounds today. You know the line, "It's better to spend ten minutes of quality time with your child than an hour of just being there." But quality time *demands* a quantity of time. You can't sit your child down on a chair and say, "There, you have my undivided attention for the next seven minutes. Let's have quality time."

Scripture talks about training a child when you rise up, when you go to sleep, while you are walking in the way, when you sit down. How does the working mom meet this challenge?

The answer is individual, but it must involve working out your life so that some love (beyond just clean clothes and breakfast) is demonstrated before you leave for work, some when you come home, some in the evening, and some at bedtime. Be creative. Can you have family devotions while eating breakfast? What do you talk about on the way to the sitter or school—the lousy traffic or the blessing squirming and chattering in the seat beside you? (Having child care near your work rather than near your home can redeem commuting time.) What greets your school-age children when they walk in the door—an empty room, or a note or cassette tape from Mom and a set-out snack? Is preparing meals an hour of martyrdom for you or do you allow fifteen minutes longer for cooking so that interruptions are allowable? We don't do too much "walking in the way" these days but taking one kid along alone on errands can buy you some very important quality time. Bedtime is critical. Even a teenager who seems aloof and independent needs to be loved like the little one you used to tuck in with a night-light and teddy bear. Every child every night should hear your love expressed.

Proverbs 22:6 instructs us to train up a child in the way he should go. Train up has two meanings. It is to bring into submission, like breaking a wild horse and making it a usable animal. It also referred to the action of a midwife who would dip her index finger into crushed dates and massage the inside of a new-born infant's mouth to create a sucking sensation. To create a thirst. The challenge of a working mother is to do both these types of training. Discipline cannot be overlooked in the desire to be liked by your children. In order to create a thirst for the way a child should go, you will have to understand your child well enough to know his way. Again, time and energy must be expended. The Proverbs 31 description of a virtuous woman begins with her relationship to her husband. Maybe because it is easy to let him fend for himself. "After all, he's a big boy now. . . ."

God is very clear about the priority of marriage. His standard is higher than "if it works out. . . ." It is higher than "Make it work out!" Your marriage should be an earthly model of the relationship between Christ and the church. God describes Himself in terms of a groom and a bride. You and your husband will have to make that illustration understandable to your unsaved neighbors. That will be a challenge.

A posted notice promoting a marriage enrichment seminar asked, "What do you and your spouse have in common?" Underneath a person had scrawled, "We were married on the same day." It is entirely possible to let that become a description of you. The challenge is to make time for you and your spouse to be with friends, to have time as a family, and to have time for just the two of you.

You will need to make sure that your love is an action as well as an attitude. Not just nurses at the change in shifts discussing the reports of your charges and the need to disinfect the area, but truly one flesh. You will need to work together, laugh together, and just be together.

Quite a challenge, isn't it? No wonder Solomon said that a virtuous woman was worth more than rubies! If you are going to be a wife, mother, individual, and child of God all at once you are going to be busy. You will rise up early in the morning and your candle won't go out at night. But such women do exist. Their children rise up and call them blessed. Their husbands praise them. May God help you to meet the challenge to be numbered among them.

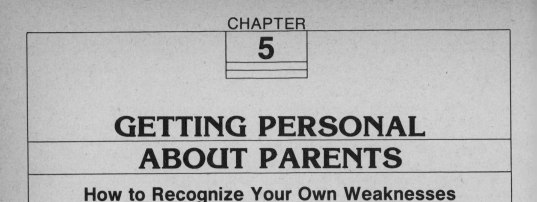

GETTING PERSONAL ABOUT PARENTS

How to Recognize Your Own Weaknesses

- What teens don't like about parents
- The side effects of an unhappy marriage
- How to avoid neglecting your children
- Where do parents go for help when their own parents were poor examples?
- The alcoholic parent—how is the family affected?

Though their complaints aren't always justified, many young people often have a right to complain about us. That's probably why the Apostle Paul wrote, "Fathers, provoke not your children to wrath" (Eph. 6:4, KJV). Indeed it is possible—even easy—to do this. We may let our own pressures weigh heavily on our children, or we may confuse them by unexpected changes. We need to repent for provoking our children, and we need to give deep thought to the ways our actions may discourage them.

Raising Kids in an Unhappy Marriage

J. ALLAN PETERSEN

Let's not confuse imperfect marriages and unhappy ones.

Every marriage is imperfect, and every couple has times of struggle, strife, disagreement, and unhappiness. But that's not an unhappy marriage.

An unhappy marriage is one dominated by constant argument, criticism, and threats. Before looking at some steps to take, let's see the side effects of this kind of home. There are several.

First, it undercuts the security of the children. Children find their security when parents love one another. They think, "Mom and Dad love each other—even when they argue, they stay together. They're not going to leave each other, or me." Children need that assurance to grow up confident, balanced, and assured.

I heard recently about a man who was sitting in the frontseat of his car, telling his wife it was all over and he was leaving her. Both of them had forgotten their two-year-old son was in the backseat. When they looked back, the boy had his fingers in his ears, his head bowed, and a look of agony on his face. He couldn't bear to hear what they were saying.

Shortly after his father left, the boy became unmanageable, emotionally disturbed. Why? Because love wasn't demonstrated in his home, and without that, young people become emotionally crippled. As they grow up, they're vulnerable to all sorts of unhappy relationships with other kids their own age.

A court judge in Denver, a man who handled over 28,000 delinquency cases, once said, "The lack of affection between father and mother is the greatest cause of delinquency I know."

It's not how you treat children as much as how you treat each other. Partnership is more important than parenthood because the partnership determines what kind of parenthood there can be.

Second, strife between parents confuses children regarding values and behavior. If parents fight over money, for instance, or their roles in marriage or how to discipline kids, the children never know what's right or wrong. They're confused about basic values, and this confusion can become a tattoo that marks them for life.

Third, children become discouraged. When all they've known is an unhappy marriage, when the two smartest people in their lives can't put their marriage together, they begin to doubt if happy marriages are possible. They back off. And if the children do get married eventually, the tendency is that they'll not take responsibility for their marriage. They don't expect to succeed.

People often ask, "Should we stay together for the sake of the kids?"

That's a tough question to answer without knowing all the details. But generally, if there is no physical violence,
if it's just a tough situation with lots of bickering, I normally suggest that parents stay together as long as possible. Why? Because the whole idea of family never leaves a person. Even an unhappy home is better than a broken one.

Better yet, however, is for mother and father to admit they have a problem and begin to seek help—perhaps a counselor, perhaps by improving their available information through books or tapes. If you don't understand why the problems are occurring, what the problems are, and if you get no more information, conditions will never improve. God works with us on the basis of information. That's why we read the Bible, go to church, and listen to other people—so God has a means to work through.

For instance, you might learn to stop giving "you" messages, pointing the finger and blaming the other person. You learn to talk about subjects on which you disagree without blasting the other person.

Or another example: eliminating the words "if only"—"If only you had done this"; "If only we hadn't had the accident"; and on and on. That language indicates you're looking in the wrong direction.

New information can help you overcome some of these bad habits and make the marriage stronger.

Related Articles

What Teens Don't Like in Parents

ROSS CAMPBELL, M.D.

At the top of my list of things teens dislike in their parents are the parents' unpleasant moods and feelings. First, teens dislike parental anger. In fact, they dread and fear it. It is probably the most devastating feeling of all.

Teens have a difficult time handling anger. They don't know what to do with it in themselves, and they don't know how to respond when it is expressed toward them. When a parent becomes angry at a teen, the teen usually responds by becoming angry at the parent. This begins a vicious cycle which is hard to break. We need to express our emotions—God didn't create us to be Mr. Spocks—but within a framework of control. It is possible to be angry without being unpleasant.

Second, teens dislike seeing pessimism and negativism in their parents. Because teens are so impressionable, they have a hard time handling pessimism. If their parents see no reason to hope, then they have no reason to hope either. Pessimistic parents produce pessimistic children.

Third, teens do not appreciate unpleasant nagging. We need to uplift our teenagers, to cheer them up, not to constantly look for their mistakes so we can point them out. Teens tend to accomplish more for people who believe in them than for people who seem to believe they will not behave properly unless they are constantly nagged to do so.

Besides disliking their unpleasant moods and feelings, teens have other complaints about their parents. They do not like their parents to behave inappropriately. We need to be good examples of the behavior we want to see in our teens. Teens don't respect us when we are inconsistent. If we expect our teens to show sexual restraint, to take responsibility, and to practice self-discipline, then we should do the same.

Teens do not want their parents acting like teenagers. Some parents may try to relate to their children by getting on their level, wearing teen clothes, listening to teen music. But parents are not teenagers, and their children know this. They wonder why their parents are not happy with being adults, and they resent their intrusion into teen territory. Parents who act like teenagers irritate their children, and they do not give them good role models to follow.

Another thing teens can't stand is

WHAT TEENS LIKE IN PARENTS

Teens like it when their parents:
• Are themselves; when they act naturally and don't try to put on a front.
• Talk to them like parents, not like buddies.
• Level with them.
• Are firm, even if it's in a way the teens don't like. Teens can't stand wishy-washiness.
• Are polite to their friends.
• Respect their privacy. When teens want their parents to have information, they will volunteer it.

Ross Campbell

parents who try to live their lives through them, by pushing them in sports or music or social conquests or other areas that are important to the parents. That's a real temptation for parents, especially if their kids have special talents. Of course we have to give our children guidance, but then we have to allow them to go along their own route. Related to pushy parents are parents whose expectations for their teens are too high. Teens don't like parents to expect more from them than they are able to give.

A major teen complaint is that their parents show favoritism among their children. This is an extremely difficult situation for parents, because some teens interpret anything their parents do as favoritism, no matter what the parents intended.

First, parents need to reason with the offended teen. Sometimes reasoning works, and sometimes it doesn't. Sometimes teens feel slighted because of something that happened years before, something that cannot be changed now. If this is the case, no amount of rational talk is going to solve their problem of feeling slighted. Parents then have to deal with the irrational issue. That is, they are going

GAMES PARENTS PLAY

Professor Leonard Bart has come up with a new list of games that parents play with their children. In the professor's experience, some of the most common games are:

• *My Kid, the Thing,* in which children are regarded as parts of the family image rather than as individuals.

• *I Get My Kicks through You,* in which children are seen as objects for fulfilling parental wishes and dreams.

• *Tune Out, Turn Off,* in which parents shut off children's efforts to share confidences, interests, and experiences if those efforts come at an inconvenient time.

• *Ma, You're All Talk and No Action,* in which Mother talks and talks to the child until the young person automatically tunes out every time she opens her mouth.

• *The Big Pay-off.* It's easier to use bribe discipline, so children are bought off with material things.

• *Threaten Today, Forget Tomorrow.* Most threats are unrealistic, made under emotional duress. Kids learn what they can get away with and like to test parents to see how far they can go.

• *Let's Be Buddies,* a ploy that relieves parents of the responsibility of setting and enforcing limits.

• *The Last Word,* in which arguments are never permitted to die but are kept alive by the unending struggle for the last word.

• *Comparisons,* the game of comparing one's child to someone else's kids. This eventually boomerangs when the child joins in the fun and uses other parents' actions as a lever against his own parents.

• *The Happy Ending,* in which parents prefer to believe that a child can solve all his problems by himself. If your child has problems, you'd better find out what's happening.

YFC Editors

to have to deal with the teen's emotions, not with the reality of the situation.

If a teen thinks a sibling got a better deal than he did, it's fruitless to argue that indeed we treated the two of them equally. The teen may be wrong in thinking we showed favoritism. But if our attempts to explain this rationally fail, we then need to deal with the child's emotions. We need to say, "I'm sorry this has happened, because I wouldn't want to slight you for anything in the world."

Many times that's the only thing we can do to make it up to him. It may look like we're being manipulated, but if the problem is more with the teen's emotions than with the actual situation, it's all right for us to handle it this way.

In fact, many teen dislikes, complaints, and hurts cannot be handled on a purely rational level. Recognizing and dealing with the teen's feelings, making him feel better about himself and assured of our love, is often what is needed.

When Parents Need an Example

RONALD P. HUTCHCRAFT

When a new baby is introduced into a family, everyone immediately tries to decide whom the child resembles. As a child continues to grow, many similarities surface. Our children are very much like us, and we are very much like our parents.

But the resemblance isn't always cute. Certain personality traits and ways of doing things that aren't very desirable are passed on from parent to child.

A biblical phrase describes this phenomenon: "the sins of the fathers"—otherwise known as family sins. The Bible says that the sins of the fathers are visited on the third and fourth generations (Ex. 20:5).

Scripture is very perceptive in making this observation. There really is such a thing as "family sins." These are family weaknesses, and generation after generation is marked by these same characteristics. They're just not called family sins today because they've been around so long.

This can be documented scripturally. Abraham, for example, opted for expedience in his life. Whether it was lying about who Sarah was or sleeping with Hagar to hasten the keeping of God's promise about a son, Abraham wanted action quickly.

Interestingly, Lot, Abraham's nephew, also committed the sin of expediency when he was in Sodom. Later, Lot's daughters, fearing they wouldn't have children, incestuously slept with their father to conceive children. In three generations, we see the sin of expediency being transmitted.

First Kings 11 records one of Solomon's great weaknesses—his love of women. What does the Bible say about Solomon's father, King David? He fell prey to temptation with Bathsheba. Family sins.

We *all* have "flawed" parents, and we all *are* "flawed" parents—no one is perfect. Of course, we don't mean to pass on these undesirable traits. But all of a sudden you're a parent. People don't go to "parent school" to learn how to be good parents. There's no training or blueprint to follow.

So most parents listen to the recorder in their mind play back ways that they were handled as children by their parents. When the pressure of parenthood hits, the only real parenting model you've had tends to surface.

Family sins can also occur when a parent goes to the other extreme from his parents. This opposite pole can be just as damaging. For example, if you grew up with an authoritarian parent, you might say, "I'll never do that to *my* daughter," and end up being extremely permissive. That child will have no boundaries in her life. By going to the opposite extreme, another family sin is created.

Another common example is of a person whose parents were alcoholics or abusive. In trying to avoid repeating that mistake with his children, the parent becomes a perfectionist. He thinks, "I grew up in such a mess of a family, my family is going to be the model all-American family." This parent may end up making demands on the spouse or children that frustrate and destroy them— not to mention the parent himself. You can't be the perfect parent that your parents weren't.

If you grew up in a family where affection was not physically demonstrated, quite likely your children will be seldom touched, and they will seldom touch their children. There will be a tremendous breakdown in feelings of love as a result.

If your family was uncommunicative and silent, the chances are good that you will have lonely and isolated children, and a frustrated spouse.

If you grew up around a parent who was impossible to please, the chances are good that your children will feel they can never be good enough for you. That can create some real seeds of rebellion.

When parents exaggerate the truth, their children have a problem with the truth. Complaining, whining parents who use guilt to manipulate children breed children who do the same thing. Family sins are not just bad habits. They are deeply ingrained, unrighteous traits. That's the bad news, but thankfully we don't end our story here.

When Jesus Christ enters a person's life at salvation, it can be likened to Him entering an old, ramshackle house that's been in the hands of a neglectful, vicious owner. The garbage has piled up; it smells; the pipes have gone bad; the roof leaks; the windows are out.

The first thing Christ does is to remove the garbage bags. All the obvious litter gets taken out and you feel like a new person. But all of us have what I call "structural damage." And that takes a lot longer to fix. In fact, it takes a lifetime to fix. The sins that have been deeply ingrained in us—family sins—are like those rusty pipes and that leaky roof. The whole structure of the house needs to be rebuilt.

The Bible says we were redeemed from an empty way of life, handed down from our fathers (1 Peter 1:18). There is a redemptive aspect to the sin spiral and a way to stop sins with our generation. Too many people waste valuable time whipping themselves or their parents, rather than determining to break the cycle of family sins and weaknesses.

Here are the steps I recommend to break this cycle:

1. Call family sins "sins." Call the weakness by its true name and identify it as a sin.

2. Let the Lord have your sin. This feels like a very risky step, spiritually. But actually it's safe. Open your hand that has been wrapped around this portion of your personality for years. Let the Lord invade what has been a "no-trespassing" zone. This will be one of the most vulnerable, scary, and deeply personal encounters you will ever have with the Lord, but it's worth the risk.

3. Let your family know that *you* know about this sin. Talk to your children and mate, saying, "There are things about me I don't like that I want to change." There is something liberating in just calling attention to this fact, for by it you've warned your children to be wary of this trait in their own lives.

Yet it's easy to be fearful that your children or mate will take advantage of you, being aware of your weakness. But the fact is, they're already aware of it.

4. Ask for your family's prayerful help and support. Say, "I'm taking a risk here by asking you to help me change." Ask them not to attack you when you're not perfect—no one can handle that.

In your walk with Christ, decide to really work on this problem. Claim the James 5 promise that confession will lead to healing. Vulnerability is always a risk—someone could abuse or misuse something you've shared with them. But Scripture seems to indicate that this is

WHY IT'S HARD TO CHANGE

Even if a parent realizes that *his* parents were poor examples, it's still hard to change and short-circuit the repetitious cycle.

Perhaps the main reason it's hard for a parent to change is because it's more "comfortable" to stay where you are.

I read about a road in northern Canada where the pavement runs out. There's a sign that reads, "Choose your rut carefully. You'll be in it for the next fifty miles." I think that illustrates the point I'm trying to make.

Family sins are "comfortable" traits. It's a rut we've been in for a long time. There's almost a sense of security in knowing that people have "always" functioned that way.

The sins may cause tension and conflict at times, but many people are willing to trade off occasional stress for the comfort of functioning on "automatic pilot."

As parents we think, "I know how to get things done this way. I know how to work with this trait because I watched my parents do it this way with me for eighteen years."

We can only break the cycle by calling a spade a spade. A family sin is a family sin. For change to occur, there must be a desire for repentance. For repentance to occur, there must be something to repent of—a sin. Holding on to our pseudonyms for sin will get us nowhere.

To change, we must trust the Lord and make ourselves vulnerable. It won't come naturally at first. When a situation arises you will have to choose which way to react: the comfortable, nonthreatening way (that is sin), or the unfamiliar, "scary" way (being obedient and trusting God for the results). But gradually you will build new habits and attitudes.

Most people are afraid of change. And changing one's personality is a very intimate and threatening thing to do. But you can't grow and mature as a Christian if you're not willing to take the risk of *really* trusting the Lord. Let Him change you and build your character. He has a plan to make you into something more. But He won't do it without your cooperation.

It *is* hard to change. But it's not impossible with God's help. And it's well worth the effort, as you grow and mature in Christ.

Ronald P. Hutchcraft

the only possible way of healing.

The undesirable alternative is to continue the disservice of leaving your family without the realization of the roots of their own personality. They need to see your weaknesses, so they can see their own weaknesses and fight them.

Recently I counseled a teenage boy who told me if he gets five A's and one C on his report card, his mother always focuses on the C. In fact, nothing he does seems to please her. He's really being emotionally dismantled by her critical spirit.

I'd not met his family, but I probed: "Is one of your grandparents a very critical person who's hard to please?" The young man looked at me as if I were clairvoyant. I then asked him if he noticed any sign in himself of being critical toward other people. He got a frightened look on his face and said, "I really do." He was becoming like his mom, just like she became like his grandmother. Someone has to stop the cycle. And the family network is needed for changing something so deeply ingrained.

We all have sin-scarred personalities. When we admit our weaknesses and ask others to pray for us, a new foundation for understanding is created. A bridge is built, because that undesirable trait has already been causing tension.

5. Draw on your mate's strengths. Very possibly you're married to someone who may have strengths in the areas where you're weak. Thank the Lord if your spouse didn't grow up in the background you did.

Jay Kesler uses the illustration that everyone has a "flat" side. If we roll down a hill alone, we'll go "ka-boom, ka-boom." But my flat side and your flat side make us roll smoothly down that hill together. When married couples put their flat sides together, their children are the beneficiaries.

If for instance, you aren't a toucher or a talker, ask your mate to teach you. Use your strengths to encourage one another.

6. Make a conscious effort to move in the other direction. John the Baptist said to people: "Bring forth fruits in keeping with repentance" (Luke 3:8, NASB). Do something the opposite of the way you've been doing it to demonstrate your commitment to change.

"Fruits in keeping with repentance" means that, if you've grown up in a family that didn't express affection very demonstratively, you will touch your family when you come home in the evening. It's not instinctive; you have to make yourself do it. You'll feel awkward at first. But you can't just *say* you want to change— you have to take a "changed" or "repentant" action.

If you're guilty of being a workaholic and your parents were overcommitted and busy all the time, you will have to be firm in precommitting family time in your date book. Schedule time.

If you're not an encourager, make a conscious commitment to find something about which to compliment each member of your family on a daily basis. As you go to sleep each night, ask yourself who you complimented that day and who you didn't. Make conscious steps to change your behavior.

If your sin is compromising the truth (i.e., lying), correct yourself after each "slip" of the tongue. Listen to yourself correcting yourself.

7. Really pray for the Lord's healing of any scars that you've put on the next generation. If we consciously try to follow Christ in these areas, God will make up the gap between our imperfections and what our children need. One of the great joys of Christian parenting is that it isn't all up to us.

These seven steps should help break your cycle of sins. It's a lifelong process. But remember that children imitate good character traits, as well as bad ones. Your effort could be multiplied to benefit many generations.

How to Avoid Neglecting Your Teenager

B. CLAYTON BELL

All of life and all our relationships involve a variety of commitments and a need for balance. When children are neglected, they sense that they are not as important to their parents as other commitments. Neglect instinctively creates within children the feeling that they deserve a greater place of importance in their parents' lives than they are getting, and in turn can greatly damage their self-image.

Neglect can be evident at both the physical and emotional levels. One parent may simply spend too much time away from his or her children. Another may be physically present, yet not pay attention to them. This spawns emotional neglect, particularly in giving children affirmation and instruction. If parents don't provide children with basic instruction about how to manage time, money, and homework, the children will either look elsewhere for help or they will feel deprived.

The balance between meeting the needs of a child and being responsible in other areas of a parent's life has to do with giving the child *undivided attention,* whether for a long period of time or for just a few minutes. If children receive concentrated, quality time and if their questions are answered reasonably with understanding and love, then they will feel that they have a place of priority in a parent's time. Children understand when a parent's professional commitments require him or her to be away. My father was a doctor; I never resented the outpatient emergency ward calling him away from home because, when he was home, I knew that I could have his undivided attention.

I've tried to work it out this way with my children too. In terms of my own commitments, though, I've told more than one pulpit committee that I refuse to sacrifice my family on the altar of the church. I've said to them that I hate night meetings. Fortunately, I've been able to choose churches where committee meetings are held at noon or in the late afternoon.

A parent who really enjoys his or her work may always have a struggle pulling away from it. My wife has always wished that I would spend more time at home. As I look at my life and the lives of other ministers I know, however, I think I have done a pretty good job of balancing my work with quality time for my children and family. Of course, no matter how much time you give them, they probably would like a little more.

Parents must decide what is most important in their lives. The father who thinks it's more important to play golf than spend time with his children will communicate to them that they are less important to him. But a father who decides to take a child with him to play golf communicates that the child is important, and he transfers a recreational skill to the child at the same time. This is not to imply, however, that parents don't have a right to do some things on their own.

You have a teenager for only six or seven years and you need to give him time. Here again, it's a balance between how much the teenager wants his parents around during leisure time, how much he needs to be included with them, and how much affirmation he needs. Finding the answer lies in communication. Plan your activities to give the children some choices. Then ask if they want to be included in your activities. We found that there were different preferences when it came to such choices, depending on the personality of each of our teenagers.

A child's life goes through stages. There are stages when a child is going to require more time than at other stages. Parents need to understand that they will have each child about eighteen to twenty years and, during that period, they should gear their social lives and professional commitments around whatever stage their child is in.

For instance, there are some things my wife and I just do not do and probably won't do until all of our children are grown. These include taking extended vacations by ourselves; we try to take them with our kids instead. There are certain kinds of movies that my wife and I probably would enjoy going to see. They would do us no harm because we would understand them. However, we're not going to go until our children are grown; we don't want them to see us going to movies that they can't see. I don't know that this is *sacrifice* as much as it is *selection* of activities.

The investment of time, attention, and energy in the lives of one's children is a great God-given privilege.

Related Articles

Look! Your Attitude Is Showing

LARRY RICHARDS

I once met a family where the teenager had been coming to the dinner table with dirty fingernails. This bothered the mother very much and each time he came to the table, she made him show her his fingernails. If they weren't clean, and they never were, the young person was sent off angrily to get them clean. Pretty soon, this became such a big issue that the mother and teenager were no longer speaking to each other.

From this example there are two lessons to learn about being critical of teens. First, parents have to be very careful about what they pick as issues. Too often, the issues are not the most significant ones in the teenager's development. They're simply things which grate on the parents' nerves, like what kind of music does the teen listen to, are the lights left on, are the fingernails clean? It's important not to pick issues on a personal bias which can create needless conflict.

The second and more important lesson is that if parents aren't careful, they can develop an expectation for failure. Parents have a habit of counting their children's sins. They tell them, "This is the seventh time this month, George, that you've failed to take out the garbage." Or "Sharon, this is the eighth time you didn't bring your clothes down to be washed." By doing this, parents are communicating the expectation that the teen is going to fail.

A Teen Is a New Creation

In 2 Corinthians 4—5, the Apostle Paul gave some very specific guidelines on how to relate to people and help them grow beyond their present level of development. First, he said in 4:18, "So we fix our eyes not on what is seen, but on what is unseen. For what is seen is temporary, but what is unseen is eternal" (NIV). If I can see a particular behavior in my teenager, if I can observe a reaction, one thing I can be sure of is that it's temporary. Because everything that is visible is in the process of changing.

Paul went on to say that we can have confidence that Christ is going to accomplish in people the purpose for which He died. That purpose is that all those who live should no longer live for themselves but for Him. To facilitate this kind of growth and development in their teens, parents need to follow the principle in 5:16-17: "So from now on, we regard no one from a worldly point of view. Though we once regarded Christ this way, we do so no longer. Therefore, if anyone is in Christ he is a new creation; the old has gone, the new has come!" (NIV)

Christian parents who develop this attitude say, "OK, I know that you've done the same thing with your homework ten times, but I know that you're going to develop into a responsible person because I know God is working in your life. I have confidence of that change even though I don't see the evidence now in your behavior. I'm looking to the unseen, and that is the basis of my hope." With that kind of attitude, parents can communicate very positive expectations

to their teenager.

I discovered this when my children were growing up. My youngest had the habit of making cutting remarks to others, and I realized I was communicating negative expectations to him. I had to change my relationship with him so I could put my arm around him and say, "Hey, I know you don't enjoy acting that way either, and I'm really glad that as you keep on growing you're going to change."

I didn't say, "Don't talk critically," but "One day I'm glad you're not going to." That took a lot of pressure off him because teenagers generally lack self-control and often act in ways they don't want to. Because of their insecurity, they don't need parents who keep giving them negative messages.

If the teen is not a believer, a parent can still say, "Hey, I have a great deal of confidence in you and I know God is going to keep working in your life." The parent can say this because 1 Corinthians 7:14 talks about how children of believers are in a unique relationship to the Gospel.

However, a parent can put a barrier between the young person and the kingdom of God with a negative, critical relationship. It's difficult for a teen to respond to the Gospel and its message of "I accept you for Jesus' sake, not because of your behavior" while the parent gives the exact opposite message: "I don't accept you because you haven't done the things that I, or theology, say you must do to be acceptable." The teen needs to experience through his parents the same kind of total acceptance that the Bible says we have with God.

Developing Positive Expectations

The first step in developing positive expectations is to examine the heart attitude. Often, the root of the problem is not the parent's relationship with the teen but the parent's relationship with himself. A parent who is filled with self-doubt, or who has a bad self-image will be unable to deal with his children in a helpful way.

That parent needs to recognize that his reaction to his teenager reflects his own personality, but that it isn't really the way things are. He has to deny himself and say, "Yes, that's exactly real in terms of how I feel and what I experience, but it's not real in terms of how God says I should perceive it." He has to abandon his own point of view and feelings and ask God to help him view his teen the way God does.

Then, the parent can ask God to give him the confidence that He is working on the teen. More than anything else in this stage of life, a teen needs parents who believe in him or her. Knowing that the teen's irritating behavior can and will change can transform a parent's attitude.

The changes might not happen overnight. People of faith have often prayed and waited for years before they saw positive results. There's not a three-step cure to get a teen to change tomorrow. But parents can start by changing their own attitudes and believing that God is working in their teen's life.

Related Articles

Who's in Control Here?

GARY D. BENNETT

Control becomes an issue when a parent's reasonable request leads to a major battle. As James Dobson describes it, "You have drawn a line in the dirt, and the child has deliberately flopped his big hairy toe across it." This confrontation is most noticeable during years one through four, and again during adolescence. If parents feel threatened and need to be in total control of their teen, problems will increase. On the other hand, if parents don't help their teen learn that "obeying does not mean losing," then the teenager will end up always getting his way and "running" the family.

Dealing with this issue of control involves two parental actions. First, parents must demonstrate to the teenager that he does not lose when he gives up control to an adult and meets reasonable demands; instead, everyone wins. Second, parents should provide as many opportunities for the child to make independent decisions and be self-sufficient as is appropriate to the child's age.

When parents have made a reasonable request and find that a major battle is brewing, they need to stop, look, and listen, quickly thinking through: Is the request reasonable? Are there extenuating circumstances that prohibit the teenager from obeying our request? What is the real issue?

If parents determine that it is a control issue, then they need to devise a strategy that allows the teen to obey the request without feeling that he has lost. Two supportive disciplinary techniques are helpful in this situation. The first is called "two good choices," and the second, "logical consequences."

As an example of "two good choices," consider the situation of the adolescent refusing to clean up his room. He is given the choice of (1) losing some "privilege" until he's ready to obey, or (2) cleaning it up immediately. Such choices must be given in a manner that implies that the parents don't have a strong need for the teen to select one choice over the other, and the choice is truly his.

Establishing rules that have "logical consequences" is another useful way to handle control issues. A family rule that says, "If you want junk food, you must first eat a good meal" is much more effective in overcoming battles about diet than one that says, "You must stay at the table until your plate is clean." In the latter case the teenager only has to wait until the next meal to "win" the battle.

If parents don't take charge when a child begins "bullying" to get his own way, the youngster will sense this and become insecure. He will continue to set up opportunities for his parents to take charge, and if they continue to be unable or unwilling to control the teenager in such situations, then the teen's inappropriate behavior will increase.

Remember, the goal is to teach your adolescent that he can influence the outcome by changing to meet your reasonable expectations. Being firm yet fair is what your teenager expects and needs.

_____

Related Articles

Confessions of an Alcoholic

COULSON DAYTON

Alcohol distorts perception; in fact, for many alcoholics, reality and fantasy run together. I can remember my old days of drinking when I ended up in a strait-jacket after being taken to the hospital. Alcohol had destroyed my nerves completely, producing a total nervous breakdown. Reality slid into fantasy, and I began to hallucinate. I saw monsters and snakes slithering around, trying to get me. There were crawling spiders with maniacal laughs reaching out to me with huge fangs and sharp claws. My world became one of distrust, lying, and stealing. I would do or say anything to get a drink and forget all about my lousy, rotten life.

This may sound like science fiction or a horror movie, but it happened to me! I went through it, and believe me, it's true.

The horrors of alcohol cannot be described with mere words. Thankfully, God has delivered me!

I remember a family with whom I was involved as a youth worker. There were three boys, a "gambl-a-holic" father, and an alcoholic mother. The father finally left and never returned to the family. The boys stayed with their mom, and, one by one, as they grew up, I worked with them, prayed with and for them, and counseled and took them to counseling.

The mother kept promising to go off the "booze," and each time she emphasized her sincerity by saying, "Mr. Dayton, this time I mean it. I'm really going on the wagon, for my kids' sakes." But, back she went again. Finally the youngest boy was alone after the others had grown up and left home to live their own lives. His mom loved him; but when she drank, it was awful. She threw carving knives, cursed, and beat him. (The beatings didn't really hurt. He was a big boy and well built, and he never hit back; he just protected himself.) He loved her, and no matter what happened, she was still his mother. Often at night he would go to her favorite bar and forcibly take her home. Sometimes other patrons would try to stop this courageous fourteen-year-old. But he would stand up to them and walk out with his mom while she cursed him, told him she hated him, and tried to go back to the bar. This scene would be repeated many times. It would break my heart to hear him say, "Coulson, my mom is off the bottle. She promised this time it was real, and she hasn't taken a drop now for four days." He would be so excited. Later he would come to me in tears, telling how she started drinking again. Many times I would hold him in my arms, and we would cry together. He was so frustrated living like this, but he wouldn't leave his mother.

Eventually, I am happy to report, this young man trusted Christ as his Saviour. Of course, the problems didn't disappear, but he learned to cling to the promises of

DRINKING PARENTS THROUGH A CHILD'S EYES

Parents are full-time examples and models. Our children are constantly making mental notes about us, and storing that data for future recall as they begin to structure their own lives. Sometimes they learn from positive experiences and sometimes from negative ones.

I recall as a young child that on several occasions I sat on the stairs going up to my room, listening to my parents who had been drinking.

My parents were loving, kind, and thoughtful people, but on occasion they would drink heavily. Suddenly, these parents whom I thought I knew, became different people altogether. They would become loud, argumentative, profane, and ugly. They would say things to each other and to others that would be hard to forget or retract in the days that followed.

As an impressionable child, I feared that the marriage would not survive the hate that I saw. I had nightmares of ending up in an orphanage because at that point I didn't think I could live with either parent.

I made a decision at that time in my life which I've maintained to this day . . . I would not drink.

My reasoning was not based on the number of highway deaths related to alcohol, or a self-imposed righteousness, or even a verse of Scripture. I hadn't become a Christian at that point in my life. But, with a child's logic, I simply knew that if alcohol would do this to a home and family, I wanted no part of it. Now, as a parent, my resolve is even firmer, for I know that in my home there are two sets of eyes who are constantly watching my wife and me and I know that even in the best of homes there are moments when communication is strained, sometimes about issues over which we have no control. The use of alcohol in my home is something I can control. I've never known it to be a positive influence in a home, but I am aware, as you are, of marriages that have failed, families that have lost a member through death, and violence to the extreme all because of the toleration of alcohol in the home.

Anonymous

143

2 Corinthians 12:9 and Romans 8:26-28. God continues to work in his life.

Usually the alcoholic parent loves his or her family. But alcoholism is a disease, and alcohol is an addictive drug. I've been there, cut off from my supply of drinks, and it's like the demons of hell attacked me with all their fury. After a night of drinking I have awakened in the gutter, unable to make it home. I remember being at my favorite bar when the bartender wouldn't sell me another drink. I had had enough, he said. He didn't want to see me get killed in an auto accident on the way home that night. I offered him all my money and even told him I would sign a note agreeing to draw all my money out of the bank the next day if he would just let me have one more glass of whiskey. I tried to get "friends" to buy a drink and sneak it to me. I was furious. I needed and wanted that drink so badly that I would have sold my soul to hell if that's what it would have taken. The tortures of the mind, the brain feeling like it will explode, the wild and hot feeling coursing through the blood, all would drive me on to complete, physical exhaustion. I know what "Toby's" mom felt and how

"Sue's" father was driven, but it was no excuse for them to put their kids through the tortures of "hell on earth."

The alcoholic will steal and hide money from the family. He or she will lie and buy whiskey, even when it means that the family must go without food. Everything is sacrificed to the god of alcohol. Finally, all decency goes down the drain, and the alcoholic can become dangerous, even murderous—anything, anything at all to get that drink, that bottle of booze. I drank shaving lotion when I couldn't get the real thing. It reduces a person to "subhuman" behavior.

Psalm 130 is an excellent passage of Scripture for those who are suffering with alcoholic parents. In some Bible versions it begins, "Out of the depths of hell. . . ." What more hell can teenagers experience than the disintegration of an alcoholic parent who has spurned them for alcohol? Praise God that He hears our prayers "out of the depths" and gives us His presence and deliverance.

Related Article

Chapter 23: Preparing Your Child for a Drinking Society

Incest: A Family Affair

RICK ENGLERT

The Parkers are a respectable middle-class family living in an affluent suburb. Mr. Parker is a successful businessman and Mrs. Parker owns a small business with several other women. They have three children and are regarded a model family in their community. Then one afternoon, Jill, their sixteen-year-old daughter, "freaked out" at school when her father stopped to pick her up. She refused to leave the school building, and told the principal her father had been

having intercourse with her for three years.

As a parent, I'm sure you've enjoyed those times snuggling under the covers on a cold morning with one of your children, or you may remember the warmth of your father's or mother's arm around your shoulder. The distinctions between loving support and lustful intrusion are disquietingly subtle. When common sense and intuition break down, troubles begin. People who live together, who depend on each other for love and support, and who have intimate daily contact with each other will tend to develop sexual relationships with each other. Children respond gladly with their whole bodies to loving contact. But in these relationships, the parents bear the entire responsibility to define and maintain appropriate limits of intimacy.

There are two common characteristics of those who sexually abuse their children. One is a lack of impulse control, and the other is a confusion of roles. Just as both discipline and sensuality are vital to the growth of children, the backlash of these qualities by abusive parents can blight a child for life.

Economics often play a factor in incest, particularly in areas of poor housing. The typical incestuous family lives in a home with no privacy, where all family members sleep in the same room or several children sleep in the same bed. When working with potential incest victims, a look into living arrangements can sometimes provide clues to the real problem.

Victims are often characterized by very low self-esteem, depression, guilt, substantial confusion, and ambivalence concerning sexuality. Many are withdrawn, socially restricted, suicidal, or burdened with heavy household or child care responsibilities in the home. Their understanding of sexuality is usually distorted and they often lack the verbal skills to express feelings and experiences. This can greatly hinder the child's efforts to seek help. Compounding the problem is the demand for secrecy. When the child begins to understand that this is not acceptable behavior, the abusive adult will often say, "Let's keep it our little secret." Sometimes the child will be coerced into silence.

The victimizers are often chemically dependent and have difficulty with impulse control. They frequently believe that they "need" sex and must have it readily available to them at all times.

Victimizers also tend toward violent behavior such as spouse or child abuse or even criminal activity.

In the vast majority of incest cases, the abuser is either the natural father, a stepfather, or some other male functioning in the role of a father. Often when the sexual behavior begins, female victims simply accept it as the love and affection of a father-figure.

There also are cases of mother-son incest, but these are much more difficult to detect. The mother's traditional role as nurturer makes incest on her part strictly taboo, and these cases are usually driven underground.

Within the family system, the sexually abusive father is typically overcontrolling and overly restrictive. Many of the fathers require their daughters to come home immediately after school and forbid their participation in normal recreational activities that would permit interaction with boys their own age. They maintain their control by means of special favors granted to the victim. The mother may perceive the victim as spoiled by the father, but his gifts actually serve as bribes to elicit sexual favors or to maintain secrecy.

One mother became suspicious when her teenage daughters began refusing to be left alone with their stepfather. The mother shared her suspicions with a YFC Youth Guidance staff member, who called one of the girls in for an interview. She admitted that her stepfather had been using her sexually for three years and said she suspected he was doing the same with her sister.

The staff member counseled with the mother and daughters together, and then confronted the father. He initially denied the behavior, and later refused to cooperate in getting help for the family. To protect the children, he had to be removed from the home. Both girls admitted they had wanted to talk to their mother before, but they were afraid they might be responsible for wrecking the marriage.

After extensive counseling, the family seems to be putting itself back together now that the father is out of the home. "This mother is simply marvelous," the Youth Guidance director says. "She has done a great job in releasing the girls from any guilt about the divorce or about the incestuous behavior itself."

In other cases, preventive measures will help to keep questionable activities from going any further. If you need help personally or know of someone else who does, contact someone you know and trust. Perhaps a teacher, social worker, minister, or a doctor in your own neighborhood could help. These people are trained to help you share your concerns, fears, and guilt. They will help you to unravel the sequence of events which have led up to the sexual relationship and encourage you so you can return to a functioning relationship free from fear and guilt.

Healing the Scars

Getting Things Straight with Our Own Parents

RONALD P. HUTCHCRAFT

Often, we as parents have scars that need to heal. Broken relationships can leave deep hurt and resentment. And those relationships can affect later ones, if we don't resolve the root conflict.

Scripture speaks about the root of bitterness in Hebrews 12:15. When it grows, it defiles all it comes in contact with. Many of us are carrying emotional cancer around inside of us in the form of an unresolved grudge. The scars must be healed.

First, we must recognize our *own* imperfection. That makes it easier to be forgiving with our parents. You are the child of a sinful parent, who was the child of a sinful parent.

It does no good to be mad at the sinful parent. Be mad at the sin, because of the damage it can do. Separate the sin from the sinner.

Second, to heal a scar you must *literally* go to the person, as Jesus recommended in His Sermon on the Mount (Matt. 5—7). Try to rebuild the relationship with your parent on a healthier basis than it was.

On occasion, I have seen people whose marriages were being destroyed because they were acting out their hostility toward a parent with their mate. They never had the courage to confront their parent. The hostility is still there, and the anger needs to be vented. So, intimidated by their parent but not by their mate, they direct the anger toward their spouse. The problem seems marital, but it is in fact parental. And it has destroyed marriages.

I've also seen people take courage, and write a letter to a parent saying, "Mom (or Dad), here's what I appreciate about our relationship. Here's why I love you. And here are some things I wish could have been different between us." It's a positive letter, but it *does* say there are things that need negotiating in the relationship.

Explain, "I see traits that are hurting people. I think we know about those traits. And I want you to know that I'm releasing you from the responsibility of those traits in me. I'm dealing with them, and I love and appreciate you."

One case in point is of a daughter whose mother would "freeze" her out when the mother didn't get her way. At

146

several points the mother made the daughter crawl on her hands and knees to her—literally.

The girl nearly went crazy because her mother would act like the daughter was nonexistent—until the girl came around, on the mother's terms. The mother could wait. She knew that eventually the daughter would give in.

That created a very defiant spirit in the girl. In her marriage relationship she was determined to never comply with what her husband wanted. He was a wonderful man—she admitted it. But she was treating her husband like she had wanted to treat her mother.

The liberation came when she wrote a letter to her mother saying, "This isn't good for either of us. You may never talk to me again, but I'm taking that risk to rebuild our relationship in a healthy way."

The mother froze her out and made the father call. But within a couple of weeks, the thaw came. The result was a healed mother-daughter relationship, and a healed marital relationship as well.

It came as a result of realizing that bridges have to be built back to our parents, where the root of problems may lie. Bridges may then be built ahead, to a spouse and children.

A third thing that helps heal scars and leads to a forgiving spirit is to try to look at the wounds behind a person's actions. Jesus was a good example of this principle. When He looked at the woman of Samaria, He saw one searching desperately for love and a sense of belonging. Others only saw a "low-life" woman. It's true that her lifestyle was dismal. But Jesus looked for the reasons behind her fallen state. He sought the hole in her heart that made her go looking in the wrong places, seeking comfort (John 4:5-42).

The right attitude is, "Father, forgive them; for they know not what they do" (Luke 23:34, KJV).

I've often said to teenagers: "If you saw your dad out on the street bleeding and broken, you wouldn't go out there and say, 'Why are you making so much noise?' You would do everything you could, mercifully, to try to deal with the wounds."

The wounds that make our parents abusive and "bad" to us are often wounds we can't see. Yet our parents are every bit as broken.

You can either look at how obnoxious they're being and hear all the noise they're making, or you can look underneath and see all the wounds, and try to become a healer of those wounds. You can hate the actions. Or you can be

A PRAYER FOR EMOTIONAL HEALING

As parents, we learn to pray many different kinds of prayers. One prayer that every parent will need at one time or another is what I call a "Prayer for Emotional Healing."

One of the great joys of Christian parenting is that it isn't all up to us. We can draw on the strength of the Holy Spirit.

When you need to be healed emotionally, pray this prayer:

"Lord, You see that I'm trying to change. I can't redeem the years I've already lived. I can't redeem the years my children have already lived. But please use my openness to change and my repentant heart to heal any scars put on the next generation. Use my strugglings and my vulnerability to help them. Help me live a changed life. And let my children and grandchildren learn to live changed lives. Help them fight the traits so deeply ingrained. I thank You, in faith, for emotional healing. Amen."

Ronald P. Hutchcraft

concerned for helping to heal wounds.

Scars can run deep. But there is no scar too deep for God to heal. Recognize your own imperfection. Confront the one who has hurt you. And develop a forgiving spirit by looking at the wounds behind a person's actions. Let God heal your scars.

Related Article

Chapter 5: When Parents Need an Example

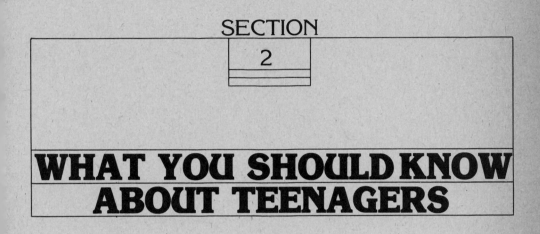

SECTION

2

WHAT YOU SHOULD KNOW ABOUT TEENAGERS

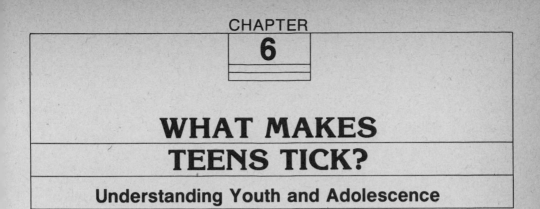

WHAT MAKES TEENS TICK?

Understanding Youth and Adolescence

- What is it really like to be a teenager? Do you remember?
- What is typical behavior for various stages of teenage life?
- How do you know if your teen is normal?
- Teens' common misconceptions about life and how to answer them
- How to prepare preteens for adolescence

There has always been a youth culture. In fact, some of our most ancient writings come from adults bewailing the irresponsibility of youth. In modern society, young people have their own subculture fueled by the profit motives of very clever people. Sophisticated marketing techniques persuade them to be consumers of the fads and ideas surrounding them. Rock music, for example, is a multimillion-dollar industry that influences many young people's clothing and hair styles, musical tastes, and purchasing patterns. We adults need to be accepted by our peers, so we should readily understand why our teenagers want to be part of their own subculture. The better we understand them, the better parents we will be.

What Is It Like to Be a Teenager?

Have Times Really Changed?

RONALD P. HUTCHCRAFT

You hear people say, "It's really tough to be a teenager today." Then they get a knowing kind of smile on their faces and add, "It's always been tough. I *know* what it's like to be a teen."

Well, I think that today's parents are raising a generation that's really facing a unique set of pressures.

First, there's a *media bombardment* that previous generations haven't had. Television, movies, and videos are media that transmit instant values that can be changed and manipulated at the whim of a few powerful people.

Second, *moral choices are being made at a much earlier age.* Every teenager has had to decide about sex, but never so soon.

Harry Reasoner did a show for CBS Reports about a year and a half ago called "Boys and Girls Together." This hour-long show on teenage sexuality revealed that sexual decisions are being made much earlier today. High school students interviewed were shocked at what twelve- and thirteen-year-olds were doing sexually. This reflects a generation gap even between seniors and freshmen in high school.

The latest research shows that one out

of five junior high age students has already had premarital sex. Yet they don't even understand what's going on in their own bodies.

Harry Reasoner's conclusion on that program was very sobering. He said, "Well, we're at that point where the documentary is to be brought to an upbeat conclusion. Frankly, we couldn't think of any." And that was the end of the show. That's a secular attitude toward teenage sexuality.

Today's teens are making moral choices about drugs, friends, liquor, and sex, before they can possibly be prepared to do it.

A third characteristic unique to this generation is the very *real possibility of no future.* Obviously, there have been wars before, and people have always died. But there has never been the capability of an entire generation being eradicated almost instantaneously.

Today's teens are almost comfortable and accustomed to the fact that "something" is going to "get" us. If a bomb doesn't, the environment or pollution will. Doomsday scenarios are commonplace.

I was with a group of teenagers not long ago, and they were discussing the future. One girl said, "You know, one of the major differences between my parents and me is that they grew up thinking a lot about their future—the house they'd have, the kids they'd have, and about their future jobs. I think the difference is that I don't think I'll have a future." That can greatly affect how a person lives. If there's no hope for tomorrow, there's no reason to hold anything off.

Teenagers today also realize that there is *no longer a moral consensus that's holding our society together.* I grew up in the '50s, in a time when there was still a Judeo-Christian consensus in our society. Not everyone was living by it, but at least they had a strong sense of right or wrong. They could *feel* it when they had violated a norm.

Today there's no sense of violating anything—because there's nothing to violate. The glue that has held our society together can be likened to a football game. You can't have a football game if you don't know where the boundaries are. (And you can't live a life without boundaries.) We knew where the boundaries were. Our kids are growing up in a society without boundaries.

Another major change has been *the difference in the structure of the home.* Incomplete families are commonplace today. There is no sense of family protection that earlier generations enjoyed. Even children of healthy marriages are asking their parents if they'll be getting a divorce. Incomplete families have become a way of life.

Unprecedented freedom has been thrust on today's generation of teens. There has never been a generation that has had so much time away from their parents' supervision, so soon. Today's teens tend to be away from home more than they're there. Teens know this. And it makes it easier to fall prey to temptation when they know no one knows what they're doing.

The availability of the automobile to teens is something that's taken for granted. Even when other generations had cars, the teens weren't so free to run around incessantly.

I also see an *emotional softness* among today's generation. By that, I am referring to their inability to cope with pain.

Other generations were not given things as easily as kids are today. Perhaps because the parents of this generation were poor and had to struggle and work hard, they wish a better life for their kids. But they are giving it to their teens easily, creating adults who don't know what to do with delay, discomfort, discouragement, and disillusionment.

So today's teens opt for desperate solutions quickly. Since they can't handle pain, they either drug themselves, run away, or kill themselves to stop the pain they can't cope with.

You can't say that today's teen generation is like all the others, when *the second greatest cause of death among teens is suicide.* When 50,000 American kids kill themselves each year, and the only age-group in our society with an increasing death rate is teenagers, this is not just another generation. The statistics say there is something uniquely wrong and difficult about today's teenage experience.

I think there are three cries that lie underneath the behavior of teens today. You can examine their behavior, or listen to the cries. When they were babies and cried, we came running to feed them, or change their diapers. Now their cries aren't as blatant. They may not even sound like cries. But they're still crying. And we still need to come running and answer their cries. Teens still need to have their needs met.

The first cry is a *cry for personal worth.* Teens are constantly pushed by their parents to improve. The focus in parenting today is not achievement, but on what needs to be improved. Because of that, teens get the feeling that they're never good enough.

The same scenario is repeated at

"WHEN I WAS YOUR AGE . . ."

Remember when your folks used to say, "When I was your age . . ." and you wanted to scream, "It's different today!" And then just the other day you found yourself parroting that phrase. Your own teen years happened such a short time ago, and you remember vividly what it was like.

Well, is it true or not? Are things really different today? The answer is an unequivocal yes *and* no.

No, things haven't changed that much. Being a teenager still means years of experimentation, discovering one's identity, and becoming independent. It is an age of pressure, especially from one's peers. (Kids still want to belong, to be accepted.) Sexual pressure continues to be a dominant force with the peak of puberty and male sex drive; and dating is still a means of discovering a mate (though many insist that it is "cruel and unusual punishment"). Moral choices have to be made today, just as they had to be made in *our* teen years.

But if these broad "categories" haven't changed, the content has. Yes, things *are* different. With the knowledge explosion and media blitz, the adult problems of yesterday have become teenage problems today. In addition, society's morality has been muddled, with many old rules and standards cast aside, and TV and movies projecting the impression that "everybody's doing it."

And there are fewer allies in the community. Teachers encourage experimentation in areas that used to be "off limits," and our neighbors are strangers. Mix in the unique problems of this generation (e.g., drug abuse, abortion, contraception, etc.), and you can see that it *is* a different world.

Obviously, the answer is that we need each other. As adults, we've made tough choices, responded to pressures, and lived to tell about it. Our kids need the insight that comes from experience. But we need to be open to them as well, realizing that it truly is a different world.

YFC Editors

school. Teens are under constant attack with their peers. At school it is "cool to be cruel." High school is a very unloving and critical place. Junior high is becoming the same way.

It's no wonder a teen cries out, "Is there *anything* right about me? What's good about me?" Even achievers feel that their achievement doesn't give them worth.

Today's teens receive many negatives in their lives and very few positives. Social research says that for every negative comment you get, you need seven positive strokes to bring you back to a zero balance. Yet the ratio today is almost reversed. Teens are getting seven criticisms for every affirmation they get—if that! It just isn't enough to balance the equation. Teens are crying out for personal worth.

Second, there's a *cry for personal intimacy.* Today's teens will do almost anything to feel "close," because of the busyness of the American family. And Christian families don't seem to be any exception. Teens see distant relationships—strangers living together as a family. The difficulty of getting close to

---

YOU NEVER WERE HIS AGE!

Not only is the phrase, "Back when I was your age . . ." a real turnoff in adult communication with kids, it also happens to be untrue.

Young people today live in a world quite unlike that in which Mom and Dad grew up. Certainly there are similarities: school, dating, a part-time job.

But the differences are significant and have a tremendous impact on a young person. Consider:

1. Young people today mature physically and mentally much earlier than previous generations. That does not mean they are wiser or have better judgment, which they may equate with that physical and mental development.

2. An older generation worried about kids drinking too much. Today, it is all manner of drugs that are rampant around a campus. And, especially in the inner city, there is violence. The *Chicago Tribune* reports, "A city kid today carries a gun as casually as a suburban kid carries a baseball glove."

3. The media explosion and invasion of the home has dramatically altered the child's information and value sources, which used to be primarily parental. Today computers, video games, television programs, and the music channel throw at the teen a world of action and excitement devoid of any moral or spiritual base. And most of it is done right in his own living room.

4. As the need for educational competence builds, young people are often kept either directly at home or dependent on their parents for a longer period of time, well up into the late teen years. The teen striking out on his own at fourteen or fifteen is not considered a potential success or individualist, but rather a national social problem. A modern-day Huck Finn would be classified as "beyond control of his parents and/or school" and detained for counseling and possible placement.

No, Mom and Dad, you never were their age, and you did not grow up in their world.

Gordon McLean

other people has created this need for "anything" that can feel "close."

People wonder how kids can get caught up in cults. It has nothing to do with their creed. Somehow, in cults young people get the "fuzzies" of being loved. Why do teens spend hours on the phone? It's a cry for personal intimacy. Teens are starved to be touched.

Ironically, they don't *seem* to be saying they need personal intimacy. When they come home, they withdraw. A teen may go straight to his room, turn on a stereo, and just sit for hours. The reason isn't because he doesn't want intimacy, but because he has despaired of getting it. If they don't receive affection, teens withdraw to an isolated world which makes them desperate for *more* intimacy.

This is probably the single greatest contributor to the sexual experimentation of teens today. I believe that many kids,. especially girls (but also guys), aren't seeking the sexual experience as much as the *feeling* that for a few minutes they belong to someone. Sex does feel like love. Unfortunately, the next morning it doesn't, if there's no love involved.

Third, there is a *cry for personal meaning.* When teens look for personal meaning, they don't want great philosophical or theological answers. They're not looking for the meaning of life but the meaning of Monday. The cry for personal meaning says, "What is there that makes a day worth getting up for?"

The psalmist's attitude, "This is the day that the Lord has made; we will rejoice and be glad in it," has been lost. Today's teenager thinks this is the day the school, his parents, and his employer have made. The concept that "This is the day the Lord has made" is gone.

This is partly frustrated, I think, because teens have watched their parents climb a mountain I call, "Mount Nowhere." They've seen their parents follow the prescribed American path to happiness: work hard, earn good money, drive a nice car, live in a nice house, and have 1.2 children. But teens aren't seeing satisfaction and happiness.

They reason, "One day I trade in my school books for a briefcase, but there's no change. I just get off one treadmill and onto another." There seems to be no meaning in it.

If you get to the top of the mountain and there's nothing there to be found, it looks hopeless. There's much more teenage suicide in the suburbs than in the city. That's because when you're at the bottom of the mountain you still have hope. The only way is up. But if you get to the top of the mountain and don't find anything, there's nowhere else to go. And that's when many kids jump.

The only purpose and meaning many teens feel they have left is trying to "feel good." They see nothing else to sacrifice for, plan for, or work for. So they try to do something to avoid the bad feelings in life. And when they can't get rid of the bad feelings, they just try to make the pain stop. That's where suicide comes in. Research on teenage suicide shows that the reason kids kill themselves is not to die, but to stop the pain. Today's teens are crying out for personal meaning.

How sad a world—to cry out and not be heard.

Related Articles

The Stages of Adolescence

LARRY RICHARDS

Adolescence is a time of transition between childhood and adulthood; between dependence—when the parents do most of the structuring of the child's time and experience—and interdependence. In the teenage years, the adolescent is beginning to move away from the parental setting and to make his own decisions. There are several things about adolescent development that can help parents understand what a teenager goes through.

These stages do not happen chronologically, as if they were assigned to years. Rather, there are five areas of critical concern where teens are forced to go through changes and take on a more significant role.

The first is developing an independent indentity. How do I become a person in my own right, distinct from Mom and Dad? A research study showed that incoming freshmen at Wheaton College still perceived themselves the way they saw the dominant parent. If they saw Dad being warm, outgoing, and hardworking, they tended to see themselves that way too. It wasn't until the junior year that a strong sense of distinct identity developed. But throughout adolescence, the young person is going through this process. He's beginning to no longer see himself as an extension of Mom and Dad.

A second area of critical concern is in interpersonal relationships. Friendship becomes very important. Teens begin to develop social skills, to learn to communicate without a sense of self-consciousness, to be part of a gang.

Third is boy-girl relationships. Teens become sexually aware and begin relating to the opposite sex. Fourth is decision-making. How do I avoid making decisions simply because the gang does it? Where do I find the courage to make decisions based on my own values? What are those values and beliefs?

Fifth, an area of ultimate concern, is God. Who is God? How relevant is He to my life? Teens begin to have serious doubts about Christianity, which before they accepted uncritically.

Working through these issues makes adolescence a painful time and often leads to clashes between parents and teenagers. This happens partly because parents are undergoing similar changes, and experiencing new struggles. They've never dealt with a teenager before.

Knowing that a teen will be developing in these areas can prevent parents from interpreting behavior incorrectly. For example, a teen comes home moping, not wanting to do anything but listen to music. Many parents will look at that behavior on the surface and become very upset. They used to have a bright and cheerful eleven-year-old and suddenly two years later, he's a totally different person. If parents don't understand some of the pressures of adolescence, like developing a separate identity, they will misinterpret the behavior.

Along with being aware of these stages, it is helpful for parents to communicate with their children so that the teens are able to talk about what they are experiencing. I drove cross-country with my youngest listening to tapes of contemporary music, which I abhor. But I listened to it because I wanted to understand what

156

he was listening to.

If we understand the five critical areas and communicate with teens, we can help their transition from childhood to adulthood to be not a traumatic passage, but a time for searching and growth.

Slowing Down Adolescence
Unfortunately, our culture forces teenagers' development too rapidly, especially boy-girl relationships. With my own teens I felt that slowing down adolescence was a positive thing and so I very consciously insulated my teens from the fast pace of growth that adolescent culture assumes.

One way I did this was by not letting them get their driver's licenses until they were out of high school. I told my oldest this when he was in eighth grade and gave him all my reasons—the differences in grades and social development, in insur-

THE MOST DIFFICULT PERIOD OF ADOLESCENCE

The thirteenth and fourteenth years commonly are the most difficult twenty-four months in life. It is during this time that self-doubt and feelings of inferiority reach an all-time high, amidst the greatest social pressures yet experienced. An adolescent's worth as a human being hangs precariously on peer group acceptance, which can be tough to garner. Thus, relatively minor evidences of rejection or ridicule are of major significance to those who already see themselves as fools and failures. It is difficult to overestimate the impact of having no one to sit with on the school-sponsored bus trip, or of not being invited to an important event, or of being laughed at by the "in" group, or of waking up in the morning to find seven shiny new pimples on your bumpy forehead, or of being slapped by the girl you thought had liked you as much as you liked her. Some boys and girls consistently face this kind of social catastrophe throughout their teen years. They will never forget the experience.

Dr. Urie Bronfenbrenner, eminent authority on child development at Cornell University, told a Senate committee that the junior high years are probably the most critical to the development of a child's mental health. It is during this period of self-doubt that the personality is often assaulted and damaged beyond repair. Consequently, said Bronfenbrenner, it is not unusual for healthy, happy children to enter junior high school, but then emerge two years later as broken, discouraged teenagers.

I couldn't agree more emphatically with Bronfenbrenner's opinion at this point. Junior high school students are typically brutal to one another, attacking and slashing a weak victim in much the same way a pack of northern wolves kill and devour a deformed carabao. Few events stir my righteous indignation more than seeing a vulnerable child—fresh from the hand of the Creator in the morning of his life—being taught to hate himself and despise his physical body and wish he had never been born.

James Dobson

From *Dr. Dobson Answers Your Questions,* by James Dobson, Tyndale House Publishers, Inc., © 1982. Used by permission.

ance costs, in accident rates. I did it ahead of time, rather than waiting until he was sixteen. That way he knew it was not personal, and not a punishment.

Another way I slowed down adolescence was by spending a lot of time with the kids in family activities and sports. I didn't cut them off from other relationships, but every day for at least an hour or two, we played a game or did something fun. This helped protect them from the fast-moving adolescent culture.

Related Articles
Chapter 6: What Is It Like to Be a Teen-ager?
Chapter 6: Why Teens Need to Establish Their Own Identity

Identity Crisis in Teenagers
BRUCE B. BARTON

As a young person enters the teenage years he or she faces a brand new task—the quest for identity. Some teenagers postpone the quest until later in life. For some, transition into adulthood is natural and easy; others experience a great deal of crisis and stress.

What is identity? *Identity* is "knowing who you are, where you're going, feeling at home in your own body, and knowing how to get approval from those who really count."

The normal process for achieving identity begins with the young person in a state of "accepting authority." Early in life decisions are controlled by parents and school authorities. Children tend to accept that authority as being all-wise and all-powerful. As adolescence approaches, children begin a period of "authority-testing" where they challenge the wisdom of their elders. As they begin authority-testing, they face two options. The first is "self-directed change" whereby they make decisions for themselves, make value choices, and establish an adult way of life. The second choice is to respond "passively and submissively" to authority. In so doing, they recycle the decisions that their parents made for them in the past and imitate the values they have experienced.

Facing these two options, children may decide not to decide anything. Teenagers can go away to college and "suspend" their beliefs about a number of personal, ethical, and theological issues. An uneasy "pause" may occur in the development of teenagers who feel that time is running out, disappointments are ahead, and disillusionments are prophesied. The pause is uneasy because adult roles are unclear. They do not know if they're going to enjoy being an adult at all. A single decision feels like it will change their whole lives; yet there is tremendous pressure to act *now*. Frozen with indecision, at that point, they may merely duplicate the values of the home, church, or community in order to receive comfort or approval. Young people sometimes cease trying to direct their lives at all because of living with what seems like a hopeless future—no job, no major in college, no marriage partner in sight.

The way through identity crisis is for teenagers to decide values and make choices about the future. This can be difficult for adults to witness. They want to alleviate some of the pain and suffering. They want to step in and give advice and make decisions rather than to be a

158

guide and a resource. Parents may seek to impose their goals and tasks on the teenager. Inadvertently, parents overly reinforce passive/submissive responses. As a result, the strength of character to make decisions may go underdeveloped in the teen.

Two characteristics adolescents exhibit when going through a normal crisis period are expansiveness and consolidation.

Expansiveness is a profound increase in emotional depth and breadth. The young person feels like "the whole world is my village" as his vision, insight, and perspective grows.

Consolidation occurs when various identities or roles are tried out, sampled, and brought together. The heroes the person regards may vary rapidly from sports figures to scientists to other family members, including Dad and Mom.

Knowing these characteristics helps parents understand the erratic behavior and mood swings that teens portray.

Since childhood the young person has taken on a series of identities and roles: student, child, and grandchild. Now, suddenly it is time to *be!* How do children sort out various identities on their pilgrimage to having their own identity? Here are four factors to consider:

1. Where do they get the information about who they are? The tendency is for teens to lock in on identity information too soon. Is the school defining their identity? Is the church? Is the home? Are negative influences shaping the young person?

2. Ways of relating within the family are coming to closure. Teens are seriously affected by all their relationships, but what their parents think about them really counts.

3. Parental directives are being reviewed and internalized. Labels and judgments are being crystallized and selected and, in some cases, rejected.

4. Norms of the society are being assimilated. These norms will give teens stability as they relate to the community. Young persons will begin to learn to accept some of the values, tools, and methods of society such as: the use of money, work demands, or community regulations.

What can go wrong during this identity crisis? If a young person avoids this process, a solid basis for self-worth that will ride out the storms of life may go unformed. If a teenager stays in a passive/submissive response to authority, he may not develop discernment or wisdom to tell truth from error. A teenager can be so confused by the quest for identity that he is unable to proceed to the next stage of development. If he does not move ahead with a settled sense of identity, he will not be able to give and receive love in the context of friendships, work, or marriage.

It is possible for parents to react negatively to the independence that their child shows and unwittingly reinforce the submissive response. The young person may not see enough adult roles to help clarify his view of what being an adult really means. If the family setting tends to worship authoritativeness, he may never develop the ability to think for himself. This is particularly difficult for us in orthodox Christian settings because we have a body of truth we are trying to portray with doctrines and theology that we support. We certainly want our children to grow up with those beliefs, but they have to go through the process of thinking them through for themselves. If beliefs are just handed down without discussion of the reasons why they are held or without enough time given to internalize them, teenagers will shed them very quickly.

How can parents help their children with identity crisis?

1. Prevent premature closure. Avoid using labels with them such as: "You're no good at math," "You're great in sports," or "You'll probably be a preacher." We have to keep reminding our

159

children that they are worth infinitely more to God than any evaluation parents or friends pin on them. Keep them from making hasty conclusions about themselves before they've had enough experience to truly know their strengths.

2. Expose them to constructive and healthy adult role models. Perhaps they can work at a summer camp or get a job with a relative. Perhaps the church youth group could invite adults to talk about their work and Christian walk.

3. Remember to show joy and pleasure in your life, your work, and in your adult sexuality. Don't allow them to believe that people die emotionally when they reach age twenty-one and no longer experience any of these feelings.

4. Help kids arrange priorities for their capabilities. Some children have more than one interest or ability. A child may like softball, biology, church work, and computers. That doesn't mean that he has to be a Christian, softball-playing, computer-biologist. It is possible to develop some abilities as hobbies, others as a vocation, and still others as occasional interests.

5. Grant recognition by giving honest approval for the things that they do well. Help them to recognize and see their strengths in skills, knowledge, and attitudes.

6. Screen your own expectations of them. Make sure that you are not prompting them toward something that is out of their depth.

7. Reassure them and yourself that late adolescence does involve some suffering.

8. Talk about your Christianity. Describe your own life experiences that have brought you to your conclusions. Use the principle of pointing rather than telling. Point them to Scripture and to the examples of other people rather than telling them what to believe. Encourage them to "look it up" for themselves, to do some research, and to talk to others in the church as they're forming ethical opinions. Give them the opportunity to challenge and disagree with you. Urge them to back up what they say. Attempt to stimulate their ability to make decisions.

Above all, make sure that during this time period you build up their identity in Christ rather than their identity based on how well they perform. So many people judge other persons on appearance or performance rather than as human beings loved and created by God. A healthy, accepting family will be the strongest support teenagers need as they face the quest for identity.

Related Articles

HELPING TEENS DEVELOP A SEPARATE IDENTITY

One of the best speeches that I have ever given is entitled "Love Means Letting Go." It's probably the toughest thing you'll ever have to do.

Successful parents, especially, have such a desire for their children to succeed. It's hard to let go and let them be themselves, especially if they choose a different vocational field.

But we have to let go and trust God for our children's futures. God knows their gifts and needs, and has a unique will for each of them. If we impose our identity on our teens, we are, in effect, thwarting God's best for them. God wants only the best for His children, just as we do. But we have only some of the facts, while God has all of them.

David L. McKenna

Why Teens Need to Establish Their Own Identity

A Theory of Adolescent Personality Development

HOWARD NEWSOM

James Marcia's concept of identity formation provides an excellent framework for understanding adolescent personality development. Marcia builds on Erik Erikson's model of human growth and development which describes the adolescent stage as "identity vs. identity confusion." Erikson believes that during adolescence a person must establish a sense of personal identity and avoid the dangers of role diffusion and identity confusion. According to Erikson, the search for an identity involves the establishment of a meaningful self-concept in which past, present, and future are brought together to form a unified whole. The individual assesses his strengths and weaknesses and determines how he wants to deal with them.

But how does one know when identity has been achieved? Is it when emotional independence from one's parents is evident? Or is it when financial independence has been accomplished? Assuming a responsible position in a community might be another indicator. Does preparation for marriage promote identity achievement? All of these factors are necessary prerequisites in our culture for a person to be considered an adult; yet they may or may not coincide with the accomplishment of identity achievement.

According to Marcia, the criteria for attaining a mature identity are based on two essential variables: crisis and commitment. "Crisis refers to times during adolescence when the individual seems to be actively involved in choosing among alternative occupations and beliefs. Commitment refers to the degree of personal investment the individual expresses in an occupation or belief" (Marcia, 1967:119).

In applying Marcia's criteria to Erikson's developmental stage "identity vs. identity confusion," four identity statuses emerge. These four statuses are not in an invariant sequence. A person does not automatically mature from identity-diffused to identity-achieved. Any one of these identity statuses could become terminal. In other words each status is not necessarily a prerequisite for the next one. Marcia, however, has not found any person in the identity-achieved status who has not experienced a moratorium status. In his original research he surveyed students regarding their occupational choices, religious convictions, and political preferences. Recent research has assessed the major cognitive, educational, adjustment, and personality correlates of identity.

The "identity-diffused" individual has no apparent personal commitment to occupation, religion, or politics and has not yet developed a consistent set of personal standards for sexual behavior. He has not experienced a crisis about this lack of commitment in these key areas. He has not gone through a time of actively exploring various alternatives. He is in a state of psychological fluidity; consequently, he is open to all kinds of influences. He is easily swayed by the latest fad or charismatic leader, with drastic fluctuations in his lifestyle as a result. This is a description of a normal developmental process especially of early adolescence but if it persists into late adolescence and adulthood, it may lead to personality disintegration.

The "foreclosure" person has made commitments in these key areas. Therefore, in everyday life, he superficially may appear very much like an identity-achieved person. However, he has not yet xperienced crises about these commit-.nents. Consequently, the commitments are not the result of personal searching and exploring; rather, they are handed, ready-made, to the individual by others, frequently parents. In my clinical experience I have observed that many Christian teenagers fit this description of identity formation. One of the adaptive aspects of this status is that it can provide a powerful buffer against negative peer influence. A young person can refuse a drink from his peers by stating, "I cannot take a drink because you know my parents; they are so. . . ." This allows the teen to save face with his peers and be protected from violating his conscience.

A maladaptive aspect of this status is the lack of an internalized value and belief system which can guide the person even when the influence of parents and church are not present. I am grateful but not overly impressed when my sixteen-year-old son follows Christian values and beliefs in my presence, but I am very pleased when he demonstrates an adherence to Christian values and beliefs when I am not present.

Many of our educational and parenting strategies foster a foreclosure type of identity development. We become uncomfortable if teens ask too many probing questions about the Christian faith and belief system. Yet that seems to be the very process by which adolescents internalize their values and beliefs. We tend to discourage the exploration of alternative lifestyles which may be countercultural but not anti-Christian per se. When parents decry an adolescent "losing his faith" in college, whose faith was lost? Was it the young person's faith or his parents' expression of the Christian faith?

Marcia's third status of identity formation is termed "moratorium." The moratorium person is in an acute state of crisis; he is exploring and actively searching for values to eventually call his own. It does not have to be a time of rebellion against or rejection of parental beliefs and values, yet the individual does actively struggle to find his identity. During this status he has not made commitments or, at best, only tentative ones. In a sense the whole decade of adolescence is treated as a moratorium in our culture during which the person gradually assumes more and more adult responsibilities and characteristics yet without being held fully accountable as an adult. In applying the concept moratorium to identity formation, Marcia implies that there are many crises and unresolved questions. The individual is in an active struggle to find an answer, explore, search, experiment, try out various roles. Students are encouraged not to specialize too early in their college studies. Graduate schools advise students to get a broad liberal arts undergraduate education and reserve the professional training for graduate studies. These practices are some of the adaptive aspects of the moratorium status.

Parents however, do not enjoy watching their children experience emotional distress and psychological pain. Parents will often actively discourage a moratorium status because they are uncomfortable with uncertainties and lack of commitments. One father exclaimed at his son's college graduation, "What do you mean you want to travel in Europe for a year to find yourself? I've already spent over $40,000 on a college education! When I graduated from college I knew what I wanted to do; what's wrong with you?"

The trauma of moratorium is not pleasant for the individual going through it either. Our tendency is to cut it off too quickly before an adequate exploration of alternatives has been accomplished. A person may marry right out of college rather than explore the possibility of singleness. Another individual may pursue a career predetermined by his parents rather than face their disapproval of exploring other options.

Some people do not successfully progress through moratorium and demonstrate a continuing inability to make commitments throughout life. While a person is actively exploring alternatives and options this maladaptive pattern may develop; yet the risk is necessary if a person is to complete the adolescent stage of identity formation.

The goal of adolescent identity formation, "identity-achieved," is the fourth status of Marcia's model. In this status the person has experienced personal crises regarding occupational choices, beliefs, and values but has resolved them on his own terms. The individual has made a commitment to an occupation, a religious belief, a personal value system, and has resolved his attitude toward sexuality. In other words, an identity has been achieved. Maturity has been attained and the person is ready to assume adult roles and responsibilities.

Ironically, it is not at all uncommon for identity-achieved persons to take positions that are fairly close to their parents' values. However, unlike the foreclosure adolescent, he has considered various other options, tried more unconventional or even more radical approaches, and finally accepted or rejected them on his own terms. Now the person has internalized his beliefs and values. Regardless of how similar they are to his parents' beliefs they will serve as guidelines for him as he moves into adulthood.

Actually one's identity is never static or permanently achieved. As a person develops through his life cycle, he will have to redefine his identity as he faces new developmental tasks. If a person successfully accomplishes an identity-achieved status during adolescence however, the likelihood is quite high that he will successfully accomplish the primary developmental tasks of each succeeding phase of the adult life cycle.

REFERENCES

Erikson, E.H. *Identity, Youth, and Crisis.* New York: W. W. Norton & Co., 1968.

Marcia, J.E. "Development and Validation of Ego-Identity Status." *Journal of Personality and Social Psychology,* 1966. 3, 551-558.

————. "Ego Identity Status: Relationship to Change in Self-esteem, 'General Maladjustment,' and Authoritarianism." *Journal of Personality,* 1967. 35,118-133.

————. "The Case History of a Construct: Ego Identity Status." In E. Vinacke, ed., *Readings in General Psychology.* New York: Van Nostrand Reinhold, 1968.

————. "Identity Six Years After: A Follow-up Study." *Journal of Youth and Adolescence,* 1976. 5,145-160(a).

————. "Identity in Adolescence." In J. Adelson, ed., *Handbook of Adolescent Psychology.* New York: John Wiley & Sons, 1980.

Related Articles

Teens' Misconceptions about Life and How Parents Can Answer Them

DAVID VEERMAN

Ecclesiastes 12:1 (TLB) says, "Don't let the excitement of being young cause you to forget about your Creator." Youth is an exciting time of life. But sometimes that youthful enthusiasm can dull the quest for God. Those of us who live with teens need to ask why.

At first glance the answer seems to be that there are so many distractions—rock music, movies, parties, drinking, and drugs to name a few. Certainly these are contributing factors. But the real answer lies at a deeper level. The fact is that there is a perspective, a world and life view, unconsciously held by young people, which impairs their vision, blinding them to many of the realities of life and to their need for Christ.

As parents, we are endeavoring to communicate to our teens a need for God and a personal relationship with Him. We agree with Solomon in Ecclesiastes that life without God is an empty, even embittering experience. We want young people to turn to God now so that they have their whole lives to live for Him. But if we're going to succeed with our young people we have to understand their thinking.

What are some of the roadblocks that keep kids from turning to God? I have listed seven of the most prominent. But this list certainly is not exhaustive.

1. *Time is on my side.* We tend to think of time as an absolute measurement of the past and future; but, in reality, time is very relative as we experience life. The last sixty seconds of an exciting basketball game pass very quickly; and yet, the final minutes of a boring class seem to last forever. In the same way, the length of a year (the most basic time-life cycle) varies as we age. The older we get the less and less a part of our life-span a year becomes, and so time passes faster and faster. The years seem to blend together, and we can even forget how old we are or how long ago certain events happened.

Conversely, to a young person, a year is a long time. Have you ever asked a three-year-old to "wait a minute"? When I was in eighth grade I remember my teacher saying, "Only ten years ago. . . ." I thought, *Only ten years ago; that's almost my whole life!* Today, ten years doesn't seem like very much at all. Many of the kids with whom I work were not even born when I started in youth ministry.

What does all this mean? First of all, young people feel like they are immortal. At seventeen years of age, thirty seems like forever. There is the idea that "Time is on my side," "I can put off getting serious," and "God is for older people." We must emphasize the benefits of living for God today.

2. *I can't wait!* The flipside to this problem with time is impatience. If adulthood is an eternity away, teenagers want their fun and privileges *now*. Adults tell them to wait until they are sixteen to

drive a car, eighteen to drink beer and to vote, twenty-one to be "old enough" for marriage and sex, and so on. Freud said that maturity was "the ability to postpone gratification." As we grow older and mature, we learn to wait; we know time will pass soon enough.

But the problem for young people is compounded by the fact that they have heard so much about their "potential" and about what lies ahead that they tend to live for the future. That is, they can hardly wait until they're in junior high or high school or college, or married. Later, as adults, they wonder what happened to those goals and promises of happiness made to them when they were young.

It becomes difficult to convince young people that they need to wait for anything. So we need to talk with them about adult responsibilities as well as adult privileges.

3. *Anyone over thirty is dead!* If ten years seems like an eternity, then older people are certainly out of touch and "over the hill." This is an attitude about adults in general. Kids tend to respond to *specific* individuals who care and spend time with them, but turn off the older generation. Thus, it is virtually impossible for young people to learn from history. After all, that happened a long time ago when things were so different. Statements like, "When I was your age . . ." or "In our high school . . ." are meaningless. Our communication, therefore, must be personal and relevant. You're never too old to communicate with your children, but you can be "out of touch" with them at any age.

4. *Pain is intolerable!* Most Americans grow up believing that pain is the exception to life and we work hard to avoid it. When tragedy strikes we cry, "Why me?" Yet we don't respond that way when something positive happens. Instead, we expect the good and sometimes feel like we deserve it. Young people are especially vulnerable to this tension avoidance. Most of them have experienced or ob-

served very little pain. Ask a group of teens sometime how many of them have *never* been to a funeral. You will be surprised at the number who raise their hands.

In reality, "*One* out of every one people dies." The older we get the more funerals we attend and the more pain we experience. When I had a kidney stone, the pain was intense. But I soon learned I did not have a corner on pain. At church the next Sunday, people came out of the woodwork to tell me about their painful experiences.

Pain is the *rule,* not the exception. Because pain is intolerable to young people, they tend to live by the "pleasure principle" and to avoid difficult situations and hard work. Perhaps this will help us understand why games and refreshments go over better than discussions or projects, and why our kids avoid thinking about the suffering, conflict, and tensions in the Christian life. But simply because they want to avoid the topics doesn't mean we should. In fact, if we help them face the tensions, we may be innoculating them against wipe-out when future crises arise.

5. *I am the center of my world (everything revolves around me!).* The story of our lives from birth until we leave home is that our needs are met by others. We are sheltered, clothed, fed, and loved; even in very bad homes there is some sense of security.

Our culture also teaches us to be self-centered. So it is no wonder kids resist commitment to Christ and His difficult teachings like, "It is better to give than to receive," "The meek shall inherit the earth," "Sell all you have; give it to the poor, and follow Me," "Bear your cross." We want teens to reach out to others but they want to grab for themselves.

6. *Love is everything!* Television, movies, and records proclaim love (and/or sex) as the salve of life. Love heals all wounds and makes life meaningful.

Young people fall for the line and believe in an idealized brand of love that is emotionally oriented and geared to "getting." Kids play the dating games, have fun with sex, and look forward to that time when they will fall for Mr. or Miss "Right" (this may or may not include marriage). We are all affected by the myth of love as a warm way of feeling, but the love spoken of in 1 Corinthians 13 and elsewhere in Scripture is a tough, giving decision to meet someone else's needs.

It is our responsibility as parents to paint an accurate picture of love and marriage, not as a solution to all a person's problems, but as a relationship that takes work and gives a different set of problems.

7. *God is a concept.* To most young people, God is something you learn in church. You can discuss Him, believe in Him or not, but He is a concept. This makes God distant and unknowable. If this is just a theological discussion, who cares? Young people want to know what difference His existence makes in day-to-day life.

It's up to us to bring the theory down to where they live. We can start by looking at God's Word to show how God through Christ became man and lived among us.

But for God to become more than just a theory, teens need to see His love enacted in the lives of parents who listen, care, give, and spend time with them in their world. When we have won the right to be heard, we can talk about involvement, sacrifice, tensions, life, and love. Most of all, we can point young people to Christ.

Reprinted from *Campus Life* magazine, *Leader's Guide Addition.* Used by permission.

Related Article
Chapter 7: Understanding How Teens Think

What to Do Before the Teen Years

ART & LOIS DEYO

In our twenty years of working with teenagers in Youth for Christ many parents have observed our own children and have asked, "What's your secret? They seem so well behaved! We can't seem to get anywhere with our teens. What can we do?"

The answer to such questions is easier the younger your children are. If they have arrived at their teenage years without much preparation for adolescence, watch out. You're probably in for a rough road.

Charles Swindoll in his book, *You and Your Child* (Bantam, 1977, p. 23), quotes the Minnesota Crime Commission, which gave the following as the partial reason for the rise in the crime rate: "Every baby starts life as a little savage. He is completely selfish and self-centered. He wants what he wants when he wants it, his bottle, his mother's attention, his playmate's toy, his uncle's watch. Deny these, and he seethes with rage and aggressiveness, which would be murderous, were he not so helpless. He is, in fact, dirty. He has no morals, no knowledge, no skills. This means that all children, not just certain children, are born delinquent. If permitted to continue in the self-centered world of his infancy, given free reign to his impulsive actions, to satisfy his wants, every child would grow up a criminal, a thief, a killer, a rapist."

The Bible says, "Behold, I was brought forth in iniquity, and in sin my mother conceived me" (Ps. 51:5, NASB). Other Scriptures also attest to our being sinners from birth (Ps. 58:3; Rom. 5:12). Therefore, we can only raise our children through the power of God, and the sooner we start the better.

The following are nine principles that we instilled in and taught to our two children, Deanna and Jeff, from a young age:

1. *Communication.* Be there to talk, even if you are busy. Discipline yourself to listen to your children, even to the unimportant, and you will later share in your child's teenage years more fully. Because Lois did not work, she faithfully met our children at the door every day after school from the second grade on. She spent fifteen minutes each day with no interruptions talking to them individually about their days. *This activity* more than any other has kept the lines of communication open to this day (Deanna is seventeen and Jeff is fourteen).

Other communication opportunities had to be planned: Art and Jeff hiking, canoeing, or camping together; Lois and Deanna shopping; or either of us driving them to school, music lessons, or athletic events. We often planned a family night, had family devotions, and talked and prayed with them every night before bed.

2. *Trust.* This is based on trust in God. Be real and show them that you hurt and have deep concerns. Cry and laugh with them. If you pretend to be perfect, they will not be willing to share themselves with you. Say you're sorry when you've wronged them and you will gain great respect.

Keep your promises. If you say you'll be there at 5 o'clock, be there. If you say you'll take them, take them. If you threaten discipline, don't forget to follow through. Force yourself to do it, even

when you don't want to. Call when you're going to be late getting home, especially at night.

Be truthful—to the penny! Take money back to the store if you were undercharged, and let your children know you did this. Jeff once allowed some friends to convince him to lie about his age to get into a smorgasbord near our home to eat at the children's price. Because we had taught him to be honest, he came home and confessed the incident. He then decided to return to the restaurant and give them the money he owed.

As we taught trust to our children, we gradually extended their privileges and boundaries of how far they could go. First it was our yard, then the neighbor's yard, then around the block, then across the street, then across the next block, then to school or to a friend's home. Because she has earned our trust, today our seventeen-year-old is sometimes allowed to go with her friends to get pizza after a ball game until midnight or after.

3. *Building relationships.* The basic principle here is to plan for time with friends and family to allow for natural interactions to take place. As a family we modeled this by Saturday pancake breakfasts and fancy dinners, taking trips together, playing games together, and Art's monthly dates with each family member.

We often allowed them to be around our friends to see us forming relationships. This helped them in forming their own friendships, for we stressed patience (knowing that they would fail each other), loyalty (keeping confidences), and listening (compassion and caring).

In all of this we have taught our children to share their faith. Sometimes they've been hurt by insensitive, uncaring friends, but they have seen several friends come to Christ.

4. *Self-discipline.* Your children should be dependable, responsible, and constant in how they use their time, their talents,

and their treasures. Parents must be an example here in such areas as quiet time, TV watching, work, time-off, spending and saving, etc. We have never allowed more than one hour of approved TV each day, and many days it is not watched at all. We divided up daily and weekly responsibilities for trash, dishes, cleaning, yard work, and laundry. We encouraged the use of their talents in the areas of flute, piano, voice, drums, writing, speaking, drawing, caring, etc. Today Deanna practices two hours per day on the flute and forty-five minutes on the piano. But this has come gradually over an eight-year period.

We have also given them an allowance ever since first grade. We required them to tithe ten percent and save twenty percent. Guidelines were placed on how they spent the remaining seventy percent.

5. *Thinking.* Children need to be taught to think logically and deeply. A person who stands for nothing will fall for anything. Mealtimes, trips, family devotions, or bedtime discussions have been important to help Deanna and Jeff formulate what they believe about evolution/Creation, abortion, mercy killing, the inspiration of Scripture, nuclear war, politics, Christian commitment, and sexual promiscuity.

Remember that we are not to tell children what they can and cannot do without training them to understand why or why not. If truly Christian, our children will be in the minority and need to have strong defenses and convictions necessary to help them stand alone against a powerful world system.

After twelve years of teaching collegians, Dr. Kenneth Gangel noticed that the ones who had the most difficulty adjusting to university life were those who got "the list" at home. Those who were given the freedom to develop their thoughts in keeping with the Scriptures while they were growing up at home were the ones who seemed to sail through with

the least number of problems (from *You and Your Child,* p. 64).

6. *Values.* This goes one step further than "thinking." We need to instill a planned set of values in our children. One value we have sought to inculcate is "experiences instead of things." We have done a great deal of traveling, camping, hiking, mountain climbing, and picnicking with our children. Once our extended family decided not to exchange gifts at Christmas but to spend the holiday together at a state park lodge.

Spiritual values have been taught by sharing together in family devotions as well as encouraging each other in individual quiet times. One year we each kept prayer notebooks.

When we moved to Columbus, Ohio a few years ago, we dedicated our house by going into each room and praying over the future activities of family members who would live there.

7. *Compassion.* This trait causes children to reach out and love their neighbors, expecting nothing in return. We have made bread and strawberry jam for new neighbors or shut-ins. When we first moved to Denver we lived next to an elderly gentleman to whom we occasionally took food. But mostly he enjoyed our company, as we would sit and talk on his porch swing. Now we live next to a retirement village and have befriended several of the residents.

We taught our children to make beds for other family members or to do cleaning or dishes for one another. Often we would come in late in the evening, take the baby-sitter home, and discover a note on our pillow. One of Deanna's read, "Dear Mom and Dad: We *love* you and hope you have a *good* sleep! We didn't get scared anymore. Hope you had a good time at the concert. We got your pajamas out and turned down the bed for you, so you could just crawl in and go nighty-night. Nighty-night! Deanna and Jeff."

Touching and hugging is a big part of living out our compassion. Here's a note we got from Jeff when he was twelve. "Dear Mom and Dad: You're special people to me! Mom, you cook so well! I think it's great! You always take such good care of me when I'm sick! Dad, I like going to all those places with you! It's so fun! You always like to help me with lots of things—homework and some different projects, etc. Whenever I'm hurt emotionally or physically you both care a lot. With lots of love, Jeff."

That kind of caring for them often is reciprocated. After we had spent two years helping Deanna through the trauma of school busing, she came home after school (fourth grade) one day to find Lois very blue because she had ruined a dress she was making professionally. Deanna promptly prayed with Lois to encourage her. It works both ways.

8. *Faith.* Unless you teach your child faith, you might as well not try the rest of these principles. Solomon wisely said, "Remember also your Creator in the days of your youth, before the evil days come and the years draw near when you will say, 'I have no delight in them' " (Ecc. 12:1, NASB).

The greatest challenge you have as parents is to lead your children to Christ at a young age. What a thrill it was when both of our children accepted Christ at age four. Though they certainly didn't grasp it all, they committed as much as they knew of themselves to as much as they knew of Christ at the time. Since then, we have helped them build on that initial relationship with Christ. Art loved to sit on their beds when they were young and answer their theological questions. That was one way they knew to legitimately extend bedtime!

Teenage peer pressure is very great, but strong faith in God will get teens through. This involves concentration and patience. Do not preach, but listen and get to know your children. Know their spiritual needs, and be prepared to meet them. Teach them to pray and have a quiet time.

The Bible says, "He who walks with wise men will be wise, but the companion of fools will suffer harm" (Prov. 13:20, NASB). Your son's or daughter's friends will either make or break them. Jeff has tried to be a witness to his peers. In fact, he has led three of them to Christ, but he has suffered persecution from some of the neighbor boys as a result. But our encouragement of Jeff and praying with him has caused this experience to strengthen his faith.

9. *Sense of humor.* "A joyful heart makes a cheerful face, but when the heart is sad, the spirit is broken" (Prov. 15:13, NASB). The other day our daughter said to Lois, "If you and I didn't have such a good sense of humor, we'd have more arguments."

When your family is together, laugh a lot. Be spontaneous! Don't make a joke out of everything, but relax and see the funny side. Don't take everything so seriously.

We have often wrestled with the kids on the floor or on the bed on Saturday morning. Art used to hide his head under a towel and chase the kids around the house. Many times our family has played "hide and seek" in the house. Board games are fun if not taken too competitively. While riding in the car we have often told funny stories by adding one sentence at a time. We have even been known to laugh while we pray. Just recently, while the two of us were kissing in the kitchen, our two teenagers were crawling back and forth between us. It put everyone in "stitches."

There are many other ingredients in child-raising, such as the balance needed between love and discipline. But if you can instill these principles in your children, you will be way ahead in what they give back to you.

Related Articles

Some Things Never Change

RONALD P. HUTCHCRAFT

Some things don't change from one generation to the next. It seems like a lot of changes are changes in degree. For example, teens have always had to decide what to do about the glands in their bodies. Though the responses may be changing, the basic problem or issue is about the same.

We seem to go in cycles in some areas. For example, we've come full circle on materialism. The only difference is that in the '50s people pursued material things because they felt it would give life meaning. In the '80s they're pursuing material things as a sedative, knowing that nothing gives life meaning. Today's materialism is more cynical.

People were basically self-centered in the '50s. The '60s and '70s brought in a world-consciousness and a desire to change things. In the late '60s and early '70s students were studying the social sciences. They were training to teach and do noble things. Today, the largest major in colleges is business. Young people are out to make money again.

These cries have been constant throughout the years, but they were either delayed or muted by a secure family and sense of future. Part of the answer of having personal meaning is that what you're doing now will pay off in the future. If you take away the sense of future, there's a futility to what a person is doing at the present time.

When there is an absense of personal faith and a moral consensus, the cries surface sooner. The more that relationships break down in our society, the more desperate the cries become, and the sooner they come.

Another thing that has changed only in degree is the action or response to the sense of futility. Today there is a greater availability of destructive ways to answer the cries. Group norms used to keep young people from suicide, premarital sex, and whatever else a person might try to answer the cries.

Unfortunately, teens are more a product of their culture than of Christianity. Only a firsthand personal faith can answer the cries effectively. But many of today's youth have a secondhand faith that looks and sounds the same. They give the right answers and attend the right meetings. There might be only a degree of difference among youth in your church.

In the American church this can be proven. For example, imagine a continuum where one represents purity and ten is debauchery. Some years ago, the world was at six and the church was at three. I maintain that the distance between the world and the church is always fairly constant, so the church can feel more "righteous" than society.

But what has happened in the last few years is that the world has moved from a six to a nine. And the church has moved from a three to a six. When the world moves, the church moves also. That's why Christians today are tolerating things in their lives that they wouldn't have even dreamed of ten years ago.

Teens today tend to compartmentalize their lives. There is little or no connection between belief and behavior.

An obscure example is when former-

President Jimmy Carter asked the American athletes to boycott the 1980 Moscow Olympics due to Soviet aggression and oppression in the world. He was trying to connect beliefs to behavior. Yet the athletes saw no connection. They said, "We're athletes." They put themselves in a compartment.

Today's church teen lives in a world that's more different from the precepts of Christ than any of us grew up in. I've been in Youth for Christ for twenty years, and I've never known less kids living for Christ. Teens aren't making the connec-

WHAT IS YOUR TEEN LIKE AWAY FROM HOME?

The "generation gap" is real. Age, interests, adolescent pressures, and the push for independence drive a large wedge between parents and teens. Suddenly those innocent boys and girls are emerging adults with ideas and lives of their own. In addition, the car makes physical separation from home so easy.

As parents, we recognize that our responsibility continues (and we love our children), but there grows a gnawing suspicion of their actions away from home. This is heightened by stories of "good kids" who get in trouble and statistical reports of teenage problems and pressures. We begin to wonder about their actions on dates, with friends, at school, and about their language and manners.

It is usually a mistake to confront the teen or to rescind freedom because of these fears. Instead of genuine concern or love, the discussion will focus on *trust*. "Mom, what did *you* do at sixteen that makes you afraid to trust *me* now?" "Don't you trust how you raised me?" "Don't you trust *me*?" These retorts sting, but they are the natural responses of someone who is assumed "guilty until proven innocent."

Instead of feeling isolated from their world (and thus filled with questions and fears), become involved. Begin by reading the newspaper (get the school paper too, if you can), and join the PTA. Make an effort to get to know your teenager's friends—open your home to them so they don't always have to go elsewhere. And don't be surprised if you seem to relate better to the friends than to your own child. You can still learn a lot from them.

Perhaps the most important ingredient in building a bridge to your teenager is the climate at home. Open it up! If you don't eavesdrop or hold against them what you hear them say on the phone, they'll be more open with you and that will enhance communication. Respect their privacy (don't read mail, notes, or diaries). Try not to be shocked, and don't let one bad event erase a whole list of good ones. And in a discussion, if they express negatives (or make really stupid-sounding statements), don't overreact. In short, use the golden rule and treat your kids as you would your friends.

Another helpful action is to take into confidence some trusted parents of your child's friends. You will be able to share, inform, and help each other (but never break a confidence).

Finally, relax and trust God—if you know you taught them correctly, don't worry.

YFC Editors

tion between Sunday morning and Monday morning at all.

The model in youth culture today is, "Fit in at all costs." Teens today do what will fit in when they're in youth group. When at a party, they adjust to fit in there. Everything is negotiable because of the cry for intimacy and belonging.

So we have teens who give all the right answers, bow their heads at the right times, and look like they're listening. They want to get along with their families and church and have a sense of belonging there.

A teen can believe in his "belief compartment" that premarital sex is wrong. But in his "behavioral compartment," he'll do it.

Too many parents are satisfied that their kids are fitting in. Parents need to challenge their teens to see if they have a firsthand faith. A secondhand faith just can't survive in the world we live in today.

Related Articles

Changing Roles
Making Adjustments as Teens Grow Older

DAVID VEERMAN

"**H**e used to be such a good boy, but now he talks back and seems to deliberately defy me."

"I thought I could trust Susie. I never thought she would lie to me."

"It is so frightening to realize that in just a few months they'll be away from us and on their own."

These comments typify parents caught in the transition years—the teenage years. In a sense, every year of a child's life involves change and movement from one stage to the next. The "terrible twos" became the "thrilling threes" and then the "fearful fours" and so on. But there's nothing quite like older adolescence. The late teen years are fraught with intense conflict, emotional upheaval, and soul-wrenching struggles as children stretch, push, and fall into adulthood.

Don't assume that these symptoms are the exclusive domain of young people. In reality, parents are often the suffering ones caught in the throes of these feelings. It's not easy watching our little boys and girls become men and women. It was just "yesterday" that we changed those diapers, and we want to hold them just a little longer.

But change must come (it is normal and inevitable), and parents must be ready! From my observation, here are the "pressure points" for the emotional drama and trauma (see chart on the next page).

These conflicts arise during the tenuous in-between years (ages fifteen to twenty-two). We want our children to grow up. It's just that we know the risks, remember our own mistakes, want to help, and still feel like being in control.

Here is what we can and must do to help:

• Understand the normalcy of this process. The rites of maturity are not unique to our teens.

172

Changing Roles for Child

Child	Adult	Conflict
1. Dependent on others (food, shelter, clothes, money, car)	1. Independent (makes own money and supports self)	1. Doesn't need parents anymore and wants to "break away" on own
2. Immature and inconsistent (emotionally up and down, unsure of self)	2. Mature, consistent, patient	2. Doesn't want to be "treated like a kid"
3. "Other" disciplined with normal irresponsibility; "now" oriented	3. Self-disciplined; can handle responsibilities and pressures; goal oriented	3. Wants to be trusted with time, money, car, authority, etc.
4. Echoes parent's ideas and values	4. Ability to think for self—own ideas, morals, and values	4. Often has differing ideas (political, moral, religious) than Mom and Dad
5. Physical changes and growth	5. Has stopped growing	5. Adult body and adult temptations, often with immature emotions
6. Preparation; learning	6. Practice, career, etc.	6. Different career than parents desired; use-of-education conflicts

- Believe that the process is *good*, albeit unpleasant and tiring.
- Recognize our changing roles and our own needs which cry to be met:
  Loneliness. A home, once full of life, becomes the "empty nest."
  Insecurity. It's back to just me and my spouse. Can the marriage take it?
  Diminishing influence. Teachers, employers, and press constantly impact our children, now more than Mom and Dad.
  Self-analysis (guilt, etc.). Did we parent well?
  Lack of control. We can no longer tell them what to do and when.
- Look for opportunities to trust them as adults, expecting them to respond as adults, and allowing them to experience the consequences of their actions.
- Communicate at a feeling level with openness to their ideas and individuality and with readiness to share our needs and doubts, and to admit our mistakes.
- Give opportunities for decision-making in curfew, car, college costs, career,

clothes, consumption. Carefully show how to think through situations.
- Grant privileges *with* understood responsibilities, including the use of money with budget and accountability.
- Relate as peers, talking across, not down. We want them to be our adult friends, not just our kids.

Obviously this process is not easy, but it can be life-changing! We must bathe our actions (and reactions) in prayer and trust God for the ultimate results. He has entrusted to us little lives to nurture and protect. As good stewards and also as good parents, we know that our goal is to watch them leave our hovering care and to live on their own as mature Christian adults. The transition may be painful, but there is no greater thrill than to see them grown and living for Christ. Probably only when they repeat the parenting process will they fully understand our love.

Related Articles
Chapter 18: Does Discipline Change As Teens Mature?
Chapter 20: Preparing to Let Them Go
Chapter 20: How to Help Your Teenagers Become Independent

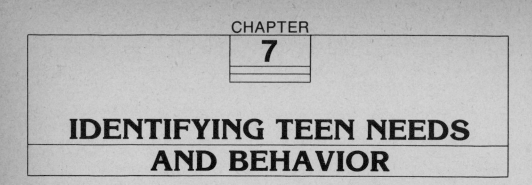

IDENTIFYING TEEN NEEDS
AND BEHAVIOR

- How to determine teen needs vs. teen wants
- Why are teens always so interested in their appearance?
- Understanding how teens think
- Is your teen a "late bloomer" in his sexual development?
- What do teens do with all their time?
- Why do teens use foul language?

Part of being an adolescent is needing to be accepted, to belong. If a boy never grows taller than five-foot-four, he is not likely to be accepted by the basketball team. If a girl is overweight and nearsighted, she may never make cheerleader. If both teenage society and parents make these children feel like failures, they may develop behavior patterns and psychological hang-ups that terrify their parents.

Parents must adjust their expectations so that they become allies of their teenagers. Are these children musical? computer whizzes? compassionate? Parents should affirm what a child is, not what he or she is not. This is the ultimate meaning of Proverbs 22:6: "Train up a child in the way he should go (or, *according to his bent*), and when he is old, he will not depart from it."

Does Your Teen Really Need It or Just Want It?

DONALD & NAOMI COLE

We had the advantage of bringing up our children in Africa where many of the people lived a subsistence existence. It was a marginal life and the possession of a shirt or two was evidence of prosperity.

When we came back to the States, what our kids needed and wanted was very different from what they needed and wanted in Africa. We need to remember that children are, in fact, a part of their culture and needs vary from one culture to another.

This problem is not limited to teenagers. How many adult American Christians have come to grips with the question of distinguishing between needs and wants and have actually solved the problem?

In Don's work in Africa, his clothing needs were extremely simple. But when we returned to the United States and Don began a ministry with Moody Bible Institute that required a certain amount of contact with the public, his clothing needs changed. He had to wrestle with, "What kind of suit do I need? Where do I buy it? What kind of home do I need?"

The answers vary from culture to culture. Because Don works in downtown Chicago, he lives more or less like an average businessman or college professor. He is indistinguishable from his peer group. Is this right or wrong? We don't think it is necessarily wrong, but we don't think all of these questions are going to be answered until we get to heaven.

One essential quality to teach is stewardship. Don recalls, "When I was thirteen, I got a job as a newsboy. I'll never forget my father's reaction when I showed him the pile of quarters and dimes I earned my first week. He looked it over and said, 'Good, how much are you going to give to God?' I hadn't thought of giving God anything. But I started."

Christmas or birthdays are times when you can meet some "wants." It's a perfect opportunity to find out and give what will really please your children. We remember one Christmas we decided not to give our kids any gifts, but to give money we would have spent on presents to those in real need. While it was certainly a noble idea, when Christmas came we felt terrible that we had neglected the children and we found something to give them.

We enjoy giving gifts. Naomi likes going out and looking for something that our daughter wants, but doesn't really need. "I enjoy trying to find something she would really like. It is a token of my love for her."

Related Articles

Body in Transition

Understanding Your Teen's Physical Development

JAY KESLER

Can a leopard change his spots? Can an Ethiopian change his color? These questions were placed in the Bible to help us deal with inevitabilities. The physical body, in many respects, is one of those inevitabilities.

Coming to terms with a changing body can be difficult for a young person. Most adults have either come to terms with their bodies or have given up on them. Eventually, most people decide to settle for what they have and quit punishing themselves and others for having been given a bad deal.

In fact, criticism of self is criticism of God, because God is our Creator. It is God "that hath made us, and not we ourselves" (Ps. 100:2, KJV). But young people struggle deeply with this issue, because they're smart enough to see that much of the youth culture is closely tied to physiological gifts, gifts that we cannot alter very much.

This is further complicated by our society's constant talk about nutrition and exercise and cosmetics and cosmetic surgery and all sorts of other ideas for physical alteration. Television commercials for spas imply that if you come, you'll look like the shapely young woman in the leotard who is doing the exercises. Of course, in most cases the young woman looked like that before she ever saw the spa, and the group of pudgy

175

women jumping around her to various kinds of Christian and secular music are never going to look like her.

I'm not denying that taking care of our physical bodies will make us healthier. It may even make us look better. But it will not necessarily make the cosmetic changes we think we need to conform to society's ideal of beauty. Our basic body structures, our facial features, the thickness of our hair—these are all genetically determined, and we are not going to drastically change them.

In my years of working with teenagers, I've discovered that beautiful girls and handsome young men seem even more concerned about their bodies than plain and ordinary young people. How many boys does the beautiful cheerleader have to conquer? How many girls does the powerful athlete have to attract? The answer?—always one more. For these attractive young people, the physical body has been their main claim to fame. They must, then, constantly test and prove their worth in this area.

The solution to this problem lies in helping young people understand that all of us are unique creations of God. God made the tall ones and the short ones, the wide ones and the narrow ones, the heavy ones and the light ones, the pale ones and the swarthy ones, the ones with pimples and the ones without, the ones with straight noses and the ones with crooked noses, the ones who can afford orthodontia and the ones who can't, the hairy ones and the balding ones.

When young people's identities are based on the fact that they are creations of God, rather than on her likeness to a centerfold or his similarity to an underwear ad, they are on solid ground. Teenagers must constantly relate their sense of who they are with their understanding of a God who knew what He was

YOUR TEENS ARE GROWING UP
FASTER THAN YOU DID

Statistical records indicate that our children are growing taller today than in the past, probably resulting from better nutrition, medicine, exercise, rest, and recreation. And this more ideal physical environment has apparently caused sexual maturity to occur at younger and younger ages. It is thought that puberty in a particular child is "turned on" when he reaches a certain level of growth; therefore, when environmental circumstances propel him upward at a faster rate, he becomes sexually mature much earlier. For example, in 1850, the average age of menarche (first menstruation) in Norwegian girls was 17.0 years of age; in 1950, it was 13.0. The average age of puberty had dropped four years in that one century. In the United States, the average age of menarche dropped from 14.2 in 1900 to 12.9 in 1950. More recent figures indicate the average has now dropped closer to 12.6 years of age! Thus, the trend toward younger dating and sexual awareness is a result, at least in part, of this physiological mechanism. I suppose we could slow it down by taking poorer care of our children ... but I doubt if that idea will gain much support.

James Dobson

From *Dr. Dobson Answers Your Questions,* by James Dobson, Tyndale House Publishers, Inc., © 1982. Used by permission.

doing when He created them. I have watched this truth absolutely transform thousands of young people over the years.

Growing up also brings other kinds of guilt and struggle related to physical development. Young men have wet dreams, nocturnal emissions, that often frighten them. They feel they must have done something ugly and awful, because their dreams often include fantasies of things they would be embarrassed to do in their conscious life.

As young women come into maturity, they too face new emotions and desires. The obvious new shape of their bodies may embarrass them, especially if it attracts male attention. Or they may feel inadequate if they develop more slowly than their peers. The onset of menstruation brings its own set of problems.

We need to comfort young men and women who are just discovering their adult sexuality. We need to let them know that their new desires and fears are normal, that all healthy men and women have such thoughts. It is important for young people to understand that their moms and dads experienced these things and still grew up all right. Mothers and daughters, fathers and sons should have frequent private, reassuring discussions throughout this period of rapid physical change.

Young people raised in an atmosphere where physical changes are not hush-hush, but are seen as a normal part of growing up, will end up as happy, well-adjusted adults. On the other hand, families that treat these things as something ugly that happens in the subterranean areas of life create phobias and fears and guilts that sometimes cannot even be dealt with clinically or professionally later in life.

A great deal of what teenagers live with and must face is tied to their changing bodies. Though they seem strong and physically capable, often they bite off more than they can chew. Many of their problems are tied to simple fatigue, the result of burning the candle at both ends and trying to get everything done at once.

Ideally, this will level out as they mature and learn the limitations of their own bodies. In the meantime, raising a teenager means raising a developing person who does not yet understand how the body works, or how the various physical, emotional, and spiritual aspects of life fit together. To raise a teenager effectively, it is important for parents to understand how one part of his life affects all others. It is also important not to take any one event too seriously.

Related Articles

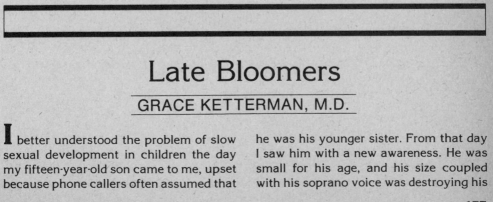

Late Bloomers

GRACE KETTERMAN, M.D.

I better understood the problem of slow sexual development in children the day my fifteen-year-old son came to me, upset because phone callers often assumed that he was his younger sister. From that day I saw him with a new awareness. He was small for his age, and his size coupled with his soprano voice was destroying his

177

self-image.

We took him for a medical checkup, which is a good first step for any child who seems to be maturing slowly. In our son's case, the doctors gave him some hormones that helped him a great deal. His voice lowered; he started to grow, and he began to see himself more as a young adult and less as a child.

But even if the doctor can't do anything to help your child physically, your teen will at least receive the emotional support of knowing you have done everything you can do. Then it becomes a matter of finding the patience to wait with your child, encouraging him until he eventually matures.

Slow sexual maturation is a kind of grief experience for young teens. They notice they aren't like other kids, and they need a lot of reassurance and understanding. Grief can be overcome faster if it is expressed and shared with someone else, so it is very important for parents to talk openly with their children.

Any young person who is bothered by his or her slow maturation should have a routine medical exam to make sure there

WHY GIRLS MATURE FASTER THAN BOYS

Sexual maturity is taking place at an earlier age for today's teens than it did for their parents' generation. Girls normally develop at a younger age than boys. It is not unusual for girls these days to begin their menstrual cycles at eleven or twelve, while boys are usually thirteen or fourteen before they begin to show signs of change.

Girls undergo more obvious changes. Their figures change as their hips fill out and they begin to develop breast tissue. Hair begins to grow under their arms and in the pubic area. And of course the first menstruation is a very dramatic experience.

The changes in boys are slower, later, and less extreme. They begin to get a little hair on their faces, but it doesn't become heavy for several years. Their voices lower, which is probably the most noticeable change and often embarrasses them. But the most alarming development that boys encounter is the nocturnal emission, better known as a wet dream. This sign is an evidence that they are beginning to develop the ability to become fathers some day, but many parents don't think to explain to their sons what is taking place.

Because wet dreams occur at night, I think more often than not boys think they have wet their beds a little and are embarrassed to talk about them. Nocturnal emissions don't leave the telltale stains that a girl's menstrual flow does, so parents don't realize they are happening. Even if parents suspect their child is going through this stage of development, many just can't bring themselves to discuss sexual issues at all.

Teens are going to mature sexually whether the parents recognize the fact or not. And they are going to have questions about what is happening to their bodies, whether or not parents give them a chance to ask them. At this confusing stage in their lives, parents need to be ready to explain to them the differences in male and female sexual development and to support and encourage their children in any way they can.

Grace Ketterman

is no physical problem. But then it's up to the parents to encourage their child to discuss what he or she feeling. It helps to tell your teen something like, "I know you're probably worried, but the same thing happened to me (or Uncle Henry, or Aunt Sally)." Then the child is assured that he or she can look forward to becoming a normal adult. Usually, the father will be more aware of what his son is going through, while mothers relate better to daughters.

Parents are often uncomfortable approaching their children about sexual problems. If so, they should talk to each other and to trusted friends until they become more at ease discussing such matters. The more they can talk about them, the more comfortable they will become. I recommend approaching a child very openly and saying, "We have some things we need to talk about. Frankly, I'm not very comfortable discussing them, but they are so important I think we should do it anyway. I want you to talk with me so I'll know what you're thinking, and so you'll feel OK about your body."

Even talking about these issues in general around the dinner table can be helpful. As a teen brings up events at school or in the neighborhood, alert parents can sometimes sense that he is really trying to tell them something else. And the teen is watching to see how his parents react. If the parents are confident and positive about their child's development, the teen will know. But if the parents look nervous or worried, the teen might assume that something is wrong with him, withdraw, refuse to communicate his true feelings, and develop a bad attitude about himself.

I think slow sexual development might even have its advantages. Unfortunately, young people are hurried to focus on sexual issues far too soon. Someone who is a little slow to develop might decide it is all right to just stay a kid a while longer. Then he is older and more mature when he begins to try to understand the changes his body is going through. Consequently, he might be able to cope more comfortably and with less anxiety.

Because my son was short, the girls didn't flock around him like they did some of the more macho boys. As a result, he didn't go through the kind of failure and rejection that many young people face when they first start dating. Instead, he maintained an interest in camping trips and "boys' stuff" for several years longer. He dated some in high school, but didn't get too serious until college. He's happily married now, so I think everything worked out all right for him.

Slow development in teens sometimes tends to be a genetic trait, but not always. My son was a late bloomer, but my youngest daughter began her menstrual cycle at age eleven. She was one of the first in her fifth-grade class, and her early development was kind of rough. Parents need to be sensitive to problems at any stage of their child's development.

I want to stress once more the importance of open communication between parent and child. Look for books or articles that can be shared or quoted. As bad as most TV programs are, once in a while you can find one that is really worth sharing and that will lead to natural discussions. Whatever it takes, make sure your child knows that you care.

Related Articles

Skin Deep

Preoccupation with Physical Appearance

DAVID VEERMAN

From dozens of anti-acne miracle drugs to designer clothes, young people seem obsessed with their appearance. Check out the ads in the teen magazines; they aim right for that ego—fragile, vulnerable, desperate to look good. Even the person whose costume seems outrageously unique obeys unwritten rules. Follow him for very long and you will discover others in similar garb. Whether "prep" or "punk," "clothes make the man" (or woman).

We shouldn't be too surprised; during adolescence the emotions are focused on identity. This is the "self-search" time of life, when teens are trying to discover "who I am" and "where I fit in." These are years of doubts and "moments of truth." Consider the girl who heard dozens of relatives remind her of how pretty she was—but now in high school, a less than average complexion has rendered her "plain." Or the boy, pushed into football to meet the needs of a frustrated father— he's fine until his pituitary refuses to cooperate. While *everyone* else adds height, weight, and muscle, Johnny becomes one of the little guys, a "has-been" at fifteen.

Besides the normal push for identity and the unrealistic expectations fostered by well-intentioned adults, the problem is exacerbated by peers. They are struggling too, with egos "on the line," and the competition becomes brutal. Peer approval means so much, but kids can be so cruel. "Where'd you get that shirt, the Good Will box?" "Are you expecting a flood?" "Your mother sure dresses you funny." "Pizza face." "You're a junior? But you're so short!"

What can we do? Here are a few suggestions.

• *Don't be surprised.* As already mentioned, it's normal to want to be accepted, to "dress up" for one's peers or that special person. In this regard, let's not judge hastily—we adults do the same thing. We follow fashion gurus religiously. Analyze your wardrobe and count how often you check your appearance in a mirror.

• *Don't condemn.* Instead, we should gently help our teenagers understand the necessity for cultivating deeper qualities —love, compassion, communication, honesty, discipline, and others. We should affirm those qualities in their lives and friends, whatever their appearance.

• *Understand the problem.* Our standards of beauty are cultural and superficial. We are all infected by society's sickness. Studies show that "beautiful people" tend to be favored in school, politics, and business. Our kids live this reality—from class officers to homecoming royalty. They need to know that we struggle as well, fearing the aging process in the midst of the youth cult.

• *Feel their hurt.* It's easy to dismiss their situation as a "stage" or "growing pains," but the pain is real.

• *Steer them into areas of affirmation.* There are many sports which don't emphasize size. Soccer, swimming, cross-country, tennis, and gymnastics actually favor smaller competitors and have gained national prominence and popularity. There's more to life than football. We can find creative alternatives—most high schools provide a smorgasbord of extracurricular activities, many of which provide excellent training for the future (e.g., debate, publications, music, and drama). Hobbies such as collecting and finishing can help, and youth clubs like Campus Life, Young Life, and Campus Crusade for Christ as well as the church youth group will offer acceptance by peers *and* caring adults.

• *Emphasize God's total acceptance and love.* To most teenagers, God is a concept, and that's tough to love or to care about. But God is a Person who created, accepts and loves them, and wants the very best for their lives. Jesus, God in the flesh, was the epitome of unconditional love. He touched lepers, prostitutes, and other outcasts. Quiet and loving reminders of these realities (not preaching) will bring understanding and healing to our young people.

• *Remind them of our love and acceptance.* It's not too "cool" to admit that they enjoy Mom's and Dad's affirmation and affection, so they probably won't admit it, but we must not stop. Inside, teens long for acceptance from their parents. Our words and actions will often make *the* difference in their lives.

• *Purge personal prejudices.* We must be sensitive to our own lives. Our actions and careless words can quickly betray prejudices and contradict all that we have tried to teach. How do we choose our friends? How do we treat the handicapped or persons of another race? Do we gossip about the neighbor's clothes, or were we scandalized by what was worn to church? Do we really believe that God loves us "no matter what"? Our lives must show it!

God has given us the opportunity to mold young lives. Let us prayerfully and carefully fulfill our responsibilities.

Related Articles

Masturbation

CLAYTON BAUMANN

Everyone who has dealt with the issue of masturbation has gotten in trouble. I'm not willing to call masturbation a gift of God since the issue of lust can't be avoided. However, I am willing to say that the Christian young person should seek total freedom.

The severe guilt that results from masturbation is my main concern. Guys, in particular, try to maintain control. Yet, if they slip, they shouldn't assume that they are dirty, or that they are going to grow fur on their hands, or become crazy.

Unfortunately, too many girls don't understand the problems that guys have. I am amazed to see how naive girls can be about their immodest dress codes. I once said to a girl, "What would happen if you were on the beach, and every guy who walked by touched you in a nice warm stroke." "I'd go bonkers in about an hour," she replied. The feeling is somewhat comparable for guys.

Many guys assume that girls are dressing a certain way to turn them on. However, the girls may only be trying to gain attention; they don't realize they are being offensive.

At camp, I was often asked to give sex talks. Once I told a group of 125 girls that they had caused some guys to lose some sleep. They quietly said they didn't understand, so I said, "You've caused some of the guys to lust and practice old habits." A positive result of that talk was that one girl publicly apologized to the guys about her choice of clothing.

On the other hand, guys have an obligation to deal with the sexual tension and pressure they are experiencing. A really outstanding Christian guy told me, "I can't take this summer. I'm afraid to date because of what I might do." "Go work out for three hours to where you have to drag yourself to the car," I replied. "And if you have no other alternative, masturbate, and then go out on a date."

Parents have a responsibility to deal with the issue of masturbation. They should try to communicate to their teen that in some stages of life, the struggle with masturbation is normal. If I had sons instead of daughters, I would try to discuss the topic with them at the beginning of puberty. I would at least categorize masturbation so that when my teens discovered the act they would respond, "Oh, that was what Dad was talking about," rather than with self-inflicted guilt and unnecessary pain.

Providing your teens with books on the topic of masturbation can be one way of opening communication. Let your son or daughter know that you've scanned the book and are willing to discuss or answer any questions he or she might have. I see tremendous freedom when a father says to a son, "I've had that problem." If they don't feel comfortable discussing masturbation with you, encourage your teens to talk to their youth pastor or some other counselor.

Again, the problem with masturbation is that it has potential to foster lust and a fantasy world. Eventually, the real world isn't meaningful or fun anymore. Some people get married and find that sex with a partner isn't as fulfilling as what they could do by themselves.

For example, a girl may have a masturbation problem. After marriage, she understands what is stimulating to her much better than her husband. As a result, there can be disappointment when she has to constantly communicate what is desirable. A real marital adjustment must take place.

In the same way, many husbands have been very disappointed in their marriages. They have allowed their minds to lust over fantasies that can never take place in the real world. They end up with problems that face them the rest of their lives.

Related Article
Chapter 7:   Body in Transition

Could Your Teen Be Hyperactive?

CLAYTON BAUMANN

When I think of the hyperactive teen, I think of a twelve-year-old who was in my home recently. He didn't understand the words, "Sit down," or "Stay here." I wanted to take a fly swatter ten feet long and whack him. He drove me crazy.

I'm not referring to the teen who needs clinical help. I'm talking about the teen who is very active. For example, my younger daughter will be bouncing on a trampoline or doing cheers or running around the house on any given evening, while my older daughter has trouble getting off a chair. The very active teen, like my younger daughter is very noticeable.

Now, they are from the same home, yet I am lost as to how to raise the younger girl. The older girl always had one close friend, and they spent most of their time in the privacy of a bedroom, quietly talking. She hardly ever used the phone; she was just a quiet child. On the other hand, my fifteen-year-old is constantly on the go and gets twenty phone calls a night.

Now is one a bad kid and one a good kid? I don't think so. What I am discovering is two totally different personalities. Therefore, my girls must be raised in totally different ways.

Some parents whose first child is hyperactive think they have a major problem when their second child is extremely reserved. The same can be true of parents whose first child is extremely reserved. Teens' styles can be diametrically opposed. This is where the parents' rigidness must flex.

I've observed rebellion in many situations where parents try to raise an active child in the same manner as they would a fairly calm teen. The teen sees the parents holding him back for no apparent reason. In this sense, parents can be the cause of hyperactivity.

In dealing with hyperactive teens, I have found the best guideline is to keep them creatively active. For example, my wife and I find all sorts of things that will keep our daughter going to the wee hours of the morning—to the point where she is about to drop. By that I mean we push her home curfew to the maximum. If she wants to sleep over at a girlfriend's house when she has just come in from a busy day, we allow her to do that. We try to push ourselves past what would be logical for an average teen. There is a real need to keep the active child "tuckered out."

We encourage participation in an active church group and physical or recreational types of activities. My daughter is out almost every night with a group of church kids. We encourage her to participate in sports such as jogging. Finally, we work hard to make personal adjustments to meet her needs. And, her primary need at this time in her life is for a great deal of activity and motion.

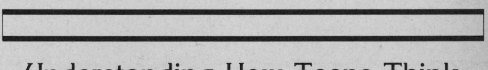

Understanding How Teens Think

JAMES C. GALVIN

A learning style is the typical way in which an individual perceives information, thinks, remembers, and solves problems. Understanding your teen's learning style will help you see how he approaches problems, how he deals with school, and will help you be more tolerant of his learning habits.

Because learning styles vary, any one learning environment will make comfortable demands on some teenagers while placing frustrating and painful burdens on others. Some will do well in a classroom and others will drop out. Some will succeed under a coach and others will quit. Some will figure out how to repair their bicycles by themselves and others will give up.

Four general categories of learning styles have been discovered by researchers. They are: (1) reflective observation, (2) concrete experience, (3) active experimentation, and (4) abstract conceptualization. All people use all four styles at different times, but tend to favor one over all the others. In order to understand which learning style is most characteristic of your teenager, these can be more easily described as learning by doing, by thinking, by watching, and by sensing.

Those who learn by sensing are characterized by their desire to derive information through direct, hands-on experience. They exhibit extraordinary development of their five senses. They appreciate order and logical sequence when learning. They like touchable, concrete materials. In a biology class, a plaster model handled by the teacher would be insufficient. They want to have the real thing to take apart and touch themselves. They prefer step-by-step directions when confronted with a learning situation. They not only look for directions, but they follow them. They like clearly ordered presentations and a quiet atmosphere.

If your teenager tends to learn by sensing, or feeling, you can help him better cope by taking him places with you or by seeing that he gets plenty of hands-on learning experiences. Those who learn by sensing prefer workbooks, manuals, demonstration teaching, programmed instruction, hands-on material, and organized field trips.

Those who learn by watching are distinguished by their attention to human behavior and their capacity to sense and interpret vibrations. They associate the medium with the message and tie a speaker's manner, delivery, and personality to the message being conveyed. In doing so, they evaluate the learning experience as a whole. They prefer to receive information in an unstructured manner and prefer freedom from rules and guidelines. They seem to gather information and organize the material through reflection to get what they want.

If your teenager learns through watching or reflecting, you can help him learn by letting him observe you or others, letting him ask questions, and having informal discussions with him. Those who learn by watching prefer activities which involve multisensory experiences and a busy environment. They enjoy movies, group discussions, short lectures accompanied by questions and answers, and television.

Those who learn by thinking are characterized by an excellent decoding ability with written, verbal, and image symbols. They have a wealth of conceptual pictures in their mind against which they match what they read, hear, or see in graphic or pictorial form. They like to

HOW TO TEACH TEENAGERS

For those who learn by SENSING Use	For those who learn by WATCHING Use	For those who learn by THINKING Use	For those who learn by DOING Use
• Demonstrations • Programmed instruction • Hands-on materials • Field trips	• Informal discussions • Movies/television • Observation • Short presentations with questions and answers	• Extensive reading assignments • Audio tapes • Substantive lectures • Analytical think sessions	• Independent study projects • Problem-solving activities • Optional reading assignments • Simulation games

read, listen, and use visual translation skills. A symbol or picture is worth a thousand words to them. These learners prefer a presentation that has substance, that is rational and sequential in nature. They are able to extract ideas from a logical presentation. They learn well from authorities and enjoy vicarious experiences.

If your teenager learns by thinking, you can help him learn by giving him books, tapes, or manuals on whatever you happen to be trying to teach at the time. A teenager who learns by thinking and who enjoys reading will often go to the library first whenever he needs to solve a problem. Those who learn by thinking feel the need for extensive reading assignments, substantive lectures, audio tapes, and analytical thinking sessions.

Those who learn by doing are characterized by an experimental attitude and accompanying behavior. They get the jist of ideas quickly and demonstrate the ability to make intuitive leaps in exploring unstructured problem-solving experiences. Sometimes they also have insights and make leaps in structured situations. Then they are criticized for jumping to conclusions. They use the trial-and-error approach in acquiring information. They do not like cut and dried procedures, and would like to find opportunities to discover answers in their own ways. They do not respond well to teacher intervention. They work well independently or in small groups.

If your teenager learns by doing, the best approach is to get out of the way and let him learn. Give him a challenging assignment or goal to accomplish and let him figure out the instructions on his own. Be prepared for mistakes and for his questions. However, this is the best way in which he is able to learn the material. Those who learn by doing prefer games and simulations, independent study projects, problem-solving activities, and optional reading assignments.

As an example of the differences between the four learning styles, consider how teenagers learn to drive a car. Those who learn by sensing enjoy the road part of the driver-education class, where they sit behind the wheel with an experienced driver at their side. They feel the bumps on the road and the sensation of pressing the accelerator and the brake. Those who learn by watching prefer to sit in the backseat and watch the other student make all the mistakes. They also watch their parents and friends when they drive and observe others on the highway from a distance. Those who learn by thinking receive more from the classroom part of driver education. They carefully study the textbook and imagine themselves driving a car. Those who learn by doing probably dislike driver-education class altogether. They would actually prefer their own car with a piece of pavement to try it out. A few mistakes here and there seem a lot less painful than sitting through the instruction.

In conclusion, your teenager may be very different from you in the way he thinks and learns. Recognize this difference when you want to teach him something. As parents, you need to value each learning style as equally important.

How to Help Teens Think

D. BRUCE LOCKERBIE

Parents have a responsibility to teach their children how to think critically—how to discern right from wrong, truth from error, genuine from fraudulent, and value from worthlessness. God created man in His own image and has given each of us the representation of His attributes. Among those attributes is the capacity for reasoning, thinking, and expressing His will.

In other words, the Lord whom we worship has given us minds and has instructed us to use them. We are told, "Love the Lord your God with all your heart and with all your soul and with all your strength and with all your mind" (Luke 10:27, NIV). One obligation of every Christian is to love God with his mind—intelligently, in a thinking way.

Obviously, this process doesn't begin at age twenty-one when we receive a college degree. Parents should begin early with their children to teach them how to think. They should encourage each child to ask questions, respect his inquiring mind, and recognize that answers will not always be easy.

As the child begins to reason, the parents-can ask: "How do you suppose that toy works?" "How do you think the milk got into the bottle?" "Can you think of a better way to do this job?"

Young children are almost never without their own endless supply of these questions. As the first child comes into the family, the parents are usually eager to work with him. But as the family grows, responsibilities increase and burdens mount. With increasing frequency, parents often begin to say, "Don't bother me. I'm too busy. Why are you always asking questions?"

Most parents love to hear their child talk (at first) and are terribly fascinated at how their little creature begins to put sentences together. But sooner or later they decide that enough is enough, and their businesslike tones of voice indicate to the child that he should not ask questions so often. When a parent's tone of voice communicates to the child that asking questions is a risky business that more often than not results in aggravating Mom or Dad, the parent is guilty of stifling inquiry and curiosity.

Some parents even say, "Ask your teacher. Why are you asking me?" Well, the teacher has thirty children asking questions. The child sees that he has much easier access to his mother or father than to his teacher, yet the parents say they have no time.

The Bible is clear about the parents' responsibility to train their children properly. "These commandments that I give you today are to be upon your hearts. Impress them on your children. Talk about them when you sit at home and when you walk along the road, when you lie down and when you get up. Tie them as symbols on your hands and bind them on your foreheads. Write them on the doorframes of your houses and on your gates" (Deut. 6:6-9, NIV).

Parents need to be accessible to answer their child's questions. They need to be sensitive to the needs of their child. They need to anticipate what their child will ask them, and to take the initiative in asking the questions themselves.

Perhaps parents fear they will be unable to answer a question asked by their child. The situation is bound to occur, but it is very difficult for some parents to admit that they are not the world's foremost experts on everything. Yet it is a wonderful opportunity to say, "You know, that is something I've always wondered about. How can we find the answer?" Admit your own ignorance and then go to the library, use an encyclopedia, or find some other way for you and your child to discover the answer together.

I am aware that everything that has been said so far applies to smaller children. But I am also well aware that if questions are not encouraged when the child is six or seven, he will not be asking questions when he is a teenager. Teens have many questions about the changes they are going through, and it is very important that they feel free to ask their parents.

For instance, questions about sexual development are common to all teens. But if a teen remembers a question about sex he asked at the age of seven or eight, only to see his parents react with embarrassment or disgust, he won't bother going back to his parents during those critical teenage years. He will find another source of advice, and it might not be a good one.

If parents realize they haven't been fostering an atmosphere for inquiry, they can't expect their teen to start asking questions all of a sudden. Parents must take the initiative. Dad might say, "I see you're studying the Civil War. In my day, they taught that it was started to free the slaves." And the teen will say, "No, the slaves weren't the major issue. It was a matter of economics." Then Dad can begin a dialogue.

My older son is doing graduate work in history at the University of North Carolina, and we recently had a conversation over a World War I incident that I knew very little about. It happened that he knew a great deal about it, so my ignorance became an anvil on which he could beat his hammer of knowledge. On the other hand, there are a few things I know a lot about, so we can keep each other sharp.

In other instances, problems might arise because of the temperament of the parents. A parent who by nature is taciturn and uncommunicative is probably not going to become garrulous and full of conversation overnight. But if he wants to regain a lost relationship with his teenager, he is going to have to take the first step to become involved again in the things his child is feeling.

That first step can help a child emotionally, socially, and spiritually—as well as intellectually—so it needs to be taken whether a parent has failed to communicate because of his basic nature or if he has just lost touch over the years. Some parents will have to make a complete about-face, but they might be surprised how their initial act of interest will make up for lost time.

Putting Old Heads on Young Bodies

DAVID L. McKENNA

Parents often assume that teens have the intellectual, emotional, and spiritual maturity that *they* have or expect them to have. So often, teens are treated as if they have "old heads" on young bodies. It is easy to forget that they *don't* have the experience that we adults do.

For example, I realize I'm putting expectations on my son, Rob, that may be a little presumptuous. He's in his sophomore year of high school, and I expect him to be targeting in on his career now. Yet I know that I wasn't doing so at his age.

It is crucial to see the relationship with your teen as developmental. Find out where your teen is, rather than imposing on him where *you* are or where *you* expect him to be.

This applies to spiritual matters as well. Parents often expect their teens to make profound spiritual judgments. When I was a teenage Christian, the closest I could come to witnessing in high school was to tell a religious joke. Yet I'm very serious about my son witnessing. I'm pleased to say he has done a far better job in high school than I did.

As parents, we need to let our teens be teens. They have teen heads on teen bodies, and our wishing they were old heads will only turn ours gray.

What Teens Don't Like about Themselves

DONALD MARDOCK

I still remember the feelings of disgust and despair as I looked into the mirror at the face that glared back at me. The hair didn't look right; the shape of the head was awful, and the pimples . . . ugh!

I wanted to be attractive to the kids at my new high school. To arrive in a new world as a sophomore was bad enough, but to look awful and feel awful was almost more than a fifteen-year-old could handle.

After a careful operation on the face, followed by a cold-water wash, and one more disdainful glance in the mirror, it was time to face whatever lay ahead.

The yellow bus crawled to a stop in front of the house, and I nonchalantly walked on board and casually took a seat. The toothpick in my mouth no doubt told all my potential enemies or friends that, "Here was a cool one."

My behavior didn't reveal that I was afraid, timid, searching, and empty. Instead I acted arrogant, proud, and totally selfish.

Another area of concern was my clothes. What others thought of the way I dressed was of great importance. As a result, I pressured my folks to provide the needed funds. Though my parents had very little money, they tried to provide what I needed. Looking back, I regret my lack of concern for *their* concerns.

After many years of working with young people from a wide variety of backgrounds, I came to recognize a pattern. (I wish I had known it at age fifteen.) Perhaps these insights will help you to help your teenagers through those baffling years.

1. Young people are so concerned about themselves that no one spends much time worrying or even thinking about another person's appearance. If I could have realized how little time was spent by others' talking or thinking about the shape of my head, it would have taken so much pressure off me.

2. Young people are very concerned about being considered intelligent. Think back about all the references to being "dumb" that circulated through the halls in your school. It was very important to be in the top part of the class. If you were not, then you played the part of the class "clown" to divert attention away from failure.

3. Young people desire to be considered socially "in." It is not *what they do* that is important. It is *with whom* they do it. The first question a teenager asks when invited to a function is, "Who is going?" If the right persons are planning to go, the answer will probably be yes.

4. Many young people are greatly concerned about their lack of goals for the future. This is especially true when they reach their senior year in high school. To have no answer to the question, "What are you going to do?" or "Where are you going to school?" can be devastating. We should be especially sensitive to seniors with whom we live and work.

Here are some suggestions to help teenagers with these worries:

1. We should help them realize that God has made no junk. Every person is important and included in the Creator's purpose. They must know that they are unique. That helps them to stop comparing their beauty, athletic ability, intelligence, and personality with that of others.

2. We must help each young person realize that he is accepted as he is. He doesn't have to imitate another person to have value. We must acknowledge teens as persons with unique abilities and talents. No two are alike, and God had each person in mind when He knit him together in his mother's womb (see Ps. 139:13, NIV).

3. We must appreciate them for what they are and for what they do. How often we criticize our kids when we think they could do better, but yet forget to tell them that we appreciate what they do well.

4. We should show our young people affection. One night in a Campus Life club meeting, I asked the group, "What would you change about your home?" One young man, without any hesitation, said, "I would have my dad tell me he loves me."

What teens dislike most about themselves is themselves. Their greatest quest is to come to a place where they feel comfortable and where people respect them for who and what they are.

They will find acceptance, acknowledgment, appreciation, and affection somewhere, from someone, or some group. If we don't help them find these vital ingredients in the setting of the home, community, church, or school, they will go elsewhere to find them, and we may not be pleased with the outcome.

We have a great privilege to help young people discover with the Psalmist David, "How precious to me are Your thoughts, O God! How vast is the sum of them! Were I to count them, they would outnumber the grains of sand" (Ps.

139:17-18, NIV).

Related Articles
Chapter 6: Identity Crisis in Teenagers
Chapter 12: Developing Self-worth in Your Teen

Your Teen Wouldn't Swear, Would He?

GREGORY MONACO

I remember the first time I used one of those "forbidden words" in my home. Mom and Dad treated me to an Ivory soap sandwich. I very rarely slipped up after that, at least around home!

But today foul language is a part of our children's daily environment. Peers, television, movies, and even teachers exercise their poetic license to "express themselves." Why?

In ten years working with delinquent teens, I have found numerous reasons for the use of foul language. The habit of using a word is often hard to break, and there is nothing like the shock value of a well-placed expletive from teen to adult. When most of their friends use certain means of expression, the peer pressure exists to follow suit, especially when emulating rock stars or sports heroes.

But by far, the *inability to express oneself* is the strongest motive I've found for the constant, repetitive use of foul language.

Take a long look at the people, especially the youths who use foul language as a part of their vocabulary. More often than not, you will find they are unable to express their emotions (usually anger) in a constructive, honest way. Perhaps they've been told all deep emotion is wrong, or they might feel that there is too much of a risk to share feelings honestly. They probably have many emotions within that they don't share with anyone.

Profanity, vulgarity, and foul language in general is a "safe" outlet for emotions stored inside. Verbal violence lets off steam, even commits symbolic acts of aggression, but does it from under cover. You can call someone a *blankity blank* and he'll never know why you're angry— just that you are.

There is another side of the inability to express oneself. We have raised and "educated" many young men and women who are unable or too lazy to express even simple thoughts and feelings. Many of the teens with whom I've worked had such low verbal skills that they substituted repetitive vulgarities for even simple concepts that they wished to communicate.

More than habit, shock value, peer pressure, or even role-model influence, the motive behind foul language today is the inability of people to express themselves. Be it deep emotions or simple concepts, foul language is being used as a smoke screen or a crutch to hide that inability to communicate. To help someone quit, help him learn how to identify his feelings and gain the emotional skills and rich vocabulary it takes to communicate clearly what he really wants to say!

PUT-DOWNS AND OTHER INSULTS

A famous comedian has made a sport of the quick put-down. No one is immune as he hurls his insults. Everyone laughs, but the habit has spilled off the stage into everyday life. Dripping with sarcasm, our clever retorts are meant to belittle, punish, or silence the nearest antagonist.

Family members are prime targets for the sharp tongue, and very often parents are the culprits. As a type of "punishment," their words are meant to hurt and to change behavior.

Perhaps the main reason for these verbal attacks is that our mouths are so "handy." It's much easier to yell or throw out a quick barb than to take time to reason quietly or to use creative discipline.

Sometimes, of course, it's a matter of thoughtless reaction. Baited and challenged by a child's remark, we reply "in kind." Whatever the reason, when we live this kind of example, we should not be surprised when our children follow suit.

It's frustrating to hear our kids let loose with a string of put-downs, but this habit may offer insight into their self-concepts. They may harbor feelings of insecurity and only assert themselves through their mouths. Or perhaps they use insults as "self-defense" and a way to gain revenge without physical fighting.

Others may be motivated by a desire to gain friends, to be accepted by a certain group, or to climb the social ladder. (A person can discover where he or she is in the "pecking order.")

Some teens may even use critical comments to maintain an image of bravado, hiding their real fears or personal pain.

The most obvious way to begin to deal with this problem is to refuse to become involved personally in a "put-down duel" with our kids. We must be good examples of *positive speech* and create an environment at home where it is good *not* to hurt others.

We can also encourage honesty, talking through the situation as a family. An analysis of biblical teachings on the tongue (e.g., James 1:26; 3:1-12; the Book of Proverbs) and judging others (Matt. 7:1) would be excellent places to start. Then we can lay down principles and ground rules of speech (e.g., "Only talk about someone who is there to defend himself."). Hopefully, the kids (and parents too) will open up about their real feelings and understand that they don't need the verbal crutch.

Our goal in this whole process, of course, is to help our children develop positive self-concepts and mature, Christian patterns of speech. It's worth the effort!

YFC Editors

The Mystery of the Missing Hours

What Do Teens Do with All Their Time?

DAVID VEERMAN

"**K**ids have so much free time and yet they have to stay up all hours doing their homework. Then they never have time for the things I want them to do. What do teens do with all their time?" This is a common question—the mystery of the missing hours.

The first part of the answer is a problem not unique to adolescents. Most people I know (of all ages) find it difficult to manage time. It's natural to put off the unpleasant jobs in deference to what's enjoyable. It should not be surprising, therefore, that homework is a low priority put off until the last possible moment. There is *no* problem, however, planning for the prom or waiting in line for concert tickets, not to mention the time wasted vegetating in front of the TV or just "goofing off."

We can offer much to help our teens in this area. Organizing one's time is an invaluable, lifetime skill. First, we should take an evening to draw up a weekly schedule together, blocking out regular commitments and hours for studying. This discipline will revolutionize homework, release time for other activities, and

---

TEENS NEED PRIVACY TOO

Teens are quite uncertain about their sexual identity. From the onset of puberty, body changes—along with chemical changes—are rapid and drastic, so mood swings are the norm. These changes and moods are very confusing, and privacy lessens the potential of being embarrassed, especially by the parent of the opposite sex.

As physical changes occur, the emotions are also developing. Thoughts of dating begin, even though the teen is not yet equipped to handle a mature, intimate relationship. Still, he begins to practice in his mind about that future girlfriend (boyfriend).

Fantasizing, dreaming, watching movie stars, or listening to pop singers are some of the ways teens use to "practice." This is healthy. Like so many stages in human development, we practice time and time again until we're fully capable of handling the task. So give your teen space—let him dream.

Last but not least, deep inside the teen is the almost frightening knowledge that "someday I'll be leaving this home and family." The push and pull of wanting to be nurtured, yet wanting to spread his wings, is in constant motion. Often a closed room for privacy offers both—a chance to experience aloneness or independence while in the safety or security of home.

Tom Perski

give freedom to enjoy them. In addition, we should teach them the technique of a practical "to do" list, a continuous record of appointments, assignments, activities, and actions. If they can learn to prioritize these items and to finish the most important ones first (not necessarily the easiest or most enjoyable), they will be miles ahead.

The second part of the answer to our engima of lost time is less obvious. It involves a phenomenon called "socialization." Teenagers have tremendous social needs. They are struggling to find out who they are and where they fit in. With fragile egos they seek affirmation from peers, and they desire their own "space." Much of their "wasted" time must be interpreted in this light. Whether monopolizing the phone, listening to records, "shopping" at the mall, eating-eating-eating, or just hanging out, they are learning about themselves.

Our response to this "problem" should be informed and benign neglect coupled with strong encouragement. In other words, within reason we should expect and allow this social use of time. This doesn't mean an unlimited lease of the telephone or a blank check for "messing around"—this freedom must be balanced with the schedule and list suggested earlier. Additionally, we should be aware and concerned about the influence of friends and the character of the "hang-outs." But we should give teens freedom to discover their *own* way through the maze of identity, independence, and ideas.

There are a couple of other factors to consider when analyzing our teens' use of time: (1) *Physical growth.* Adolescent bodies are maturing rapidly and need nourishment. It should not be surprising, then, that teenagers are perpetually hungry, and seem to eat all the time. (2) *Misconception of time.* To children, a year seems like an eternity and adulthood is a forever away. They spend a lot of their free time playing. Teenagers were children just a few short years ago; they still view time from that perspective, and pain and hard work are seen as life's exceptions. This makes it even more difficult for them to follow through and complete unpleasant and unenjoyable assignments.

UNDERSTANDING TEENS' ATTITUDES AND EMOTIONS

- How do you handle a smart aleck?
- Lighting a fire under the lazy teen
- What caused a sudden change in my teen's behavior?
- Understanding teen anger and de-
- pression
- Helping teens deal with failure and disappointment, pressure and anxiety, guilt and boredom
- Teens' concern for now

It is a bad mistake to think of teenagers as fledgling adults. Adolescence is a unique period of life. It is a mad rush of conflicting ideas, fears, attitudes, and emotions, often running wild and confusing the young person as well as the parents.

Ask a teenage daughter, "Why did you do that?" and she probably won't be able to answer. Why did she do it? Because she is halfway between childhood and adulthood, because her glands are secreting hormones she's never had to deal with before, because her body is changing so fast she hardly recognizes it, because people are misreading her signals. She tries to take responsibility, and people tell her she's too young. She acts young, and they tell her not to be a baby. She doesn't feel as if she belongs anywhere.

It is very important for parents of teenagers to understand what happens during adolescence. Many people point to their childhood as a happy time, but far fewer remember their teenage years that way.

How to Help Teens Manage Stress

GARY R. COLLINS

Before they can help their teens deal positively with stress, parents have to develop an attitude of understanding. There is no substitute for genuine empathy, and when kids see that we've really tried to understand what they're going through, they tend to open up more.

With this attitude, you might consider ten general guidelines I've found useful in helping teens cope with stress. When pressure builds, encourage teens to:

1. *Admit it.* To admit a problem exists is the first step toward reaching a solution. Admission is not a sign of weakness, but strength.

2. *Pray about it.* As a priority, the Lord's help must be sought through prayer.

3. *Analyze it.* This doesn't mean teens are to become little Freudians, but they need to ask such questions as: What is causing the stress? What am I doing to alleviate it? What skills might help me? Who can help me? Good friends are important; peer counseling is sometimes valuable in helping teens articulate the problem and help themselves.

194

4. *Look at it.* This is a time to be objective and realistic. Is the problem as severe as your teen thinks it is? What's the worst thing that could happen because of the problem? Is the situation like that of Elijah, who thought he was the only one not to bow before Baal? God came along and said there were 7,000 others who had also remained true to Him. Sometimes it helps to know we are not alone.

5. *Decide what to do about it.* List all the different alternatives on a sheet of paper, and decide which ones are viable. Which should be tried first?

6. *Avoid self-defeatist reactions.* Often teenagers will do something drastic—such as deliberately flunking out of school—to get back at their parents. But they fail to see that they are losing in the process.

7. *Back away from it.* As Jesus withdrew periodically from the crowds, parents should help teens do the same so they can get a different perspective on the stress.

8. *Talk about it.* Parents need to assure their kids that they can talk things over without being put down.

9. *Learn from it.* When the problem is solved, sit down and think about what was learned from it. If done in a nonthreatening way, parents can help their kids see how good things can actually result from a problem.

10. *Reach out from it.* There is real value in helping teens understand that though they have problems, other people have more, and they can reach out to them with help and understanding. The danger is in getting so caught up in themselves, that they fail to notice others.

Beyond these guidelines, parents need to be flexible. For instance, sometimes your kids will feel comfortable talking to a friend's parents about a problem. Try not to see this as rejection or a threat. Be thankful that there are other adults who can help your teenager.

A few years ago, my wife and I had to recognize that we were short on answers for one of our daughters who had entered a period of depression. So we talked to the school pediatrician, and she suggested we transfer our daughter to a private school. We never would have considered that, since, for one reason, we could not afford the cost. Still, that was the doctor's recommendation and we did our best to comply. It was exactly the change our daughter needed.

Don't be afraid to listen to other people who have more experience than you do. If

WHY TEENS DON'T LIKE TO BE SEEN WITH THEIR PARENTS

Teenagers are engulfed by a tremendous desire to be adults, and they resent anything which implies that they are still children. When they are seen with "Mommy and Daddy" on a Friday night, for example, their humiliation is almost unbearable. They are not really ashamed of their parents; they are embarrassed by the adult-baby role that was more appropriate in prior years. Though it is difficult for you now, you would do well to accept this healthy aspect of growing up without becoming defensive about it. Your love relationship with your child will be reestablished in a few years, though it will never be a parent-child phenomenon again. And that's the way God designed the process to work.

James Dobson

From *Dr. Dobson Answers Your Questions,* by James Dobson, Tyndale House Publishers, Inc., © 1982. Used by permission.

you have a fifteen-year-old daughter, and you've never had one before, you are not nearly as experienced as the schoolteacher, or school physician, or the mother of four teenagers. Sometimes other adults can help us to better understand our own kids.

When Your Teenager Blows Up
GRACE KETTERMAN, M.D.

I have a very dear friend with whom I went through med school. When it came time to dissect our cadaver, we found it helpful to talk all the time, so we got to know each other very well. He had recently gotten married, and was already going through a problem stage. His wife was prone to temper tantrums, and he just didn't know how to cope with her. He had never lived with an adult who had a problem controlling emotions.

If parents want their children to grow up to be well-adjusted adults, they must be prepared to guide them through the emotional and physical turbulence of their teenage years. Changes in their social relationships bring about the most vulnerable times of their lives. Academic pressure at school adds to their stress. And during this same period, their bodies are undergoing massive changes.

Because they don't understand everything they are going through, teens have a lot of personal anxiety and insecurity. Their bodies are growing very fast, and they wonder if something is wrong with them.

Girls particularly have a lot of premenstrual tension, both physiologically and psychologically. Their body hormone levels and balances are changing. They go through a period between ovulation and the menstrual cycle when they are very tense, nervous, and temperamental.

Then on top of everything else, they are trying to "grow up" and begin to become independent of their parents. Occasional emotional outbursts are a natural result of the inner tensions teenagers are feeling.

When these outbursts occur, it is essential that parents try to understand what their child is feeling. If parents unknowingly condemn the emotional expressions, the child will only feel like a "horrible sinner," guilty for his actions. But if the parents have patience, they can teach their child an absolutely marvelous lesson about how to control his emotions that will help him all his life.

I recommend a three-step process for parents to work through with their teenagers when emotional outbursts occur.

Step 1: Encourage teens to put their feelings into words. Some people don't agree, but I believe that all of our emotions are given by God and are OK in their proper context. I don't think it is wrong to be angry, worried, or sad, but I do think it is wrong to remain in one of those conditions or to express them in a destructive manner. So help your child identify his feelings, express how he feels, and recognize that it is OK for him to feel the way he does.

Step 2: Have them think through why

they feel those emotions. This step is usually not very hard. Teens almost always know why they feel the way they do. But often they don't feel free to explain their feelings.

Step 3: Help them to decide rationally what to do about the situation that has upset them. This is the hardest step, but an essential one as your children begin to grow into adolescence. When they were small, you made many decisions for them. But now that they are growing, they need to know that they have some power to choose what they will do. Still, parents need to sit down with their teens and help them make wise decisions about what to do when a friend borrows something and doesn't return it, when little sister won't quit nagging, etc.

Obviously, for these three steps to be effective, parents must not respond to the child's anger in kind. If, instead, parents can respond with calmness and understanding, they can tell the child, "Yes, we know you're mad. You wanted to do something, and you can't. But we love you enough to put up with your anger."

By not reacting emotionally, you can go beyond the surface problem and get to the hurt or anxiety that is underneath. I am convinced that beneath all anger is some kind of personal pain. Let your child express his anger, calm him down, and then resolve the conflict using the three-step process.

Even if the teen's emotional outbursts have become more frequent and intense, parents should try to resolve the problem in the same manner. In spite of the child's emotional state, parents need to avoid overreacting, outer signs of worry, anger, and (above all else) power struggles. Later, when the child is calm, parents should sit down with him and say, "Here's a list of how many times you have lost control during the past week. We're a little concerned about it, and we don't think you're very happy either. Let's discuss why you have been so upset, and what we can do to help you." Then work

out a plan that will help the child gain control, reduce his emotional outbursts, and react more maturely to his feelings.

Sometimes parents wait too long to respond to their child's outbursts, or try to suppress the anger. At the first signs of irritation or impatience, parents should encourage the child to talk about what's bothering him or to go off alone for a while. Teenagers need a lot of time alone anyway, so solitude is a constructive way to help them calm down. If they feel really angry, have them do something physical—like running around the block—until they work out their stress and get back in control. (And while they are out of the house, it gives the parents an opportunity to gain control as well.)

Teens often can't help the way they feel, but if they express their emotions in destructive ways I think they should be disciplined. I feel that spanking teenagers only creates more rebellion. But if they break things, hit someone, or act childishly, they should be sent to their room and then taught to handle their anger in more constructive ways.

As a parent of three, I used to assume after a child's emotional outburst that I had been a bad parent, or that it was somehow my fault. I'm learning a little late in life that another person's problem with anger is *his* problem, not mine. I will do everything I can to reach out to my children and help them solve their problems, but I no longer feel I have to blame myself or defend myself, either. I'm not suggesting that parents remain remote or unconcerned about their child's problems, but it is exciting to realize that Mom and Dad can be thoughtful and caring, and still in control of their own feelings.

ROLLER COASTER KIDS

It has been said that teens' behavior is like Chicago weather. If you don't like it, wait around a few minutes—it'll change. From moods to spurts of energy, adolescence can be marked by tremendous "swings." These can be most confusing to both teens and parents wondering if there is something wrong. Usually the diagnosis is a "case of the normals," but what causes this phenomenon, and how can we help?

Some have suggested that the culprit is nutrition. That is, a combination of "junk food," too much sugar, and fad diets creates a chemical imbalance which influences behavior. I'm sure that's a contributing factor, but the two greatest causes are "growth" and "perspective."

Teenagers' metabolism is very high, *and* they are growing physically at a tremendous rate. (That's why they always seem to be hungry.) I remember weighing 140 pounds at the beginning of the ninth grade, and then 170 pounds just nine months later. The glandular clocks are releasing hormones and ordering all sorts of changes. Besides the obvious effects of growth and maturation (hunger, sluggishness, awkwardness), there are subtle, unconscious ones relating to the "self-concept." Consider the girl who worries about being too tall or perhaps overweight, the high school junior who still looks like he's in grade school, or the coed engaged in the war against acne. We shouldn't be too surprised to find these teens brooding about themselves and their social situations.

Perspective means "a way of seeing" and, in this situation, refers to our teens' perception of life. Problems which seem insignificant to us may loom enormous and insurmountable to them. A poor grade, a broken relationship, "not being asked out," and athletic failure are pictured as matters of life and death. I thought the world would end when I lost my girlfriend.

As parents, our most effective response will involve patience and communication. Resisting our inclination to assume the worst and realizing that the "roller coaster" emotions are normal, we can "ride it out" and later "talk it out." We should let our teens know what's happening in their bodies, assuring them that changes are to be expected and that we understand that maturation can be painful physically and socially (but we survived and they will too). Affirm them as very special and beautiful persons.

Another positive reaction is to see a mood change as a "clue." Without forcing the issue, we can express our observations like, "You seem down today"—perhaps they will open up, and we can help. Maybe something happened at school involving homework/tests, friendships, or boyfriend/girl-friend relationships. (We can even check with their teachers if necessary). Once again, communication is vital. Lovingly and without condescension, we can share our "adult" perspective and solution.

Whatever our specific response, we must remember that the language of *feelings* (emotions) and the language of logic are different. Without violating their right to their feelings by arguing and debating, we must listen, accept, and guide.

David Veerman

Why Teens Get Angry

ROSS CAMPBELL, M.D.

One of our most difficult, yet most important, jobs as parents is to teach our children how to handle anger. It's a difficult job because most of us were never taught how to handle it ourselves. How many adults do you know who handle anger well?

I was married right after graduation from the U.S. Naval Academy, and we had our first daughter within a year of our marriage. I was still heavily indoctrinated with military discipline, and I thought discipline was discipline. Needless to say, I was a harsh father.

I'm thankful that Carey came first, because she was the kind of child who would turn out OK no matter what you did. But if David, our second child, had come first, I would have had a problem. David's temperament is not easy to handle. He wants to think for himself, and he doesn't take well to being told what to do. I have to be careful, because I could provoke a lot of anger in him simply by being an authority figure.

Teens get angry for a variety of reasons. Anger is David's reaction to authoritarianism. Other teens get angry over daily frustrations, too many pressures, minor irritations. Some teens get angry over inconsistency and hypocrisy. And of course, parents and siblings often do things—intentionally or otherwise—that result in the teen's anger.

When David was thirteen or fourteen, he used to get quite verbal about his anger. My first reaction was to get upset and say, "Shut up." But I've learned to

"YOU IRRITATE ME!"

Every teen knows exactly how to irritate his parents. After living with those parents for thirteen or fourteen years, he knows exactly which button to push.

When teens purposefully (though often unconsciously) try to upset us, they are testing our love. They are saying, "If you really love me, you'll be nice and pleasant even though I'm not. But if you overreact and get angry, you must not love me."

The key to controlling our reactions when we are confronted with irritating behavior is to understand that it's normal for teens to act this way. It also helps to realize that teens who express their anger verbally are less likely to express it behaviorally. The more anger that comes out of their mouths, the less they will feel the need to do bad things that would really hurt their parents.

As a parent, I have a choice. I can forbid my child to speak unpleasantly to me, or I can allow him to get his anger out verbally so that it doesn't pop up in undesirable behavior.

Ross Campbell

say to myself, "That's great—let it out verbally." Because if he lets it out verbally it won't come out behaviorally in antisocial or self-destructive behavior.

Verbal outbursts seldom last more than from five to fifteen seconds. Of course, it's amazing how long five seconds can seem when you're listening to it! But after those few seconds, the anger is out. Once the anger is out of a child, the parents can control him. But when the child is really angry, no one can control him except by force. So I remind myself that it's OK for him to let his anger out verbally, because once it's out, I have control again.

The key here is timing. I'm not saying that you should be permissive and let your teens get away with anything. I'm saying that you should be smart. It is unwise to deal with a child who is in a rage. Dealing with someone who is angry only makes the situation worse. So you have to learn to sit there and let him say what he is going to say.

Then, later, when things have calmed down and your relationship is on solid ground again, you can deal with the substance of the anger. That is also the time to train him to handle his anger more constructively. Parents need to pick the right time to do this. You have to have enough time to deal with it properly. Don't be in a rush.

When you and your teen sit down to talk, you can say, "I'm really glad you brought your anger to me, because I want you to let me know when you're happy, when you're unhappy, and when you're angry." Then try to focus on some of the good things he was doing as he expressed his anger. For example, say, "It's really great that when you were angry at me, you came to me with your anger. That's the way it should be. It's good that you didn't take it out on your little brother or the dog. You didn't bring up irrelevant details from the past, and you didn't get violent."

After you have pointed out the things your child did right, you want to move

The Anger Ladder

POSITIVE

1. PLEASANT • SEEKING RESOLUTION • FOCUSING ANGER ON SOURCE • HOLDING TO PRIMARY COMPLAINT • THINKING LOGICALLY
2. PLEASANT • FOCUSING ANGER ON SOURCE • HOLDING TO PRIMARY COMPLAINT • THINKING LOGICALLY

POSITIVE AND NEGATIVE

3. FOCUSING ANGER ON SOURCE • HOLDING TO PRIMARY COMPLAINT • THINKING LOGICALLY • unpleasant, loud
4. HOLDING TO PRIMARY COMPLAINT • THINKING LOGICALLY • unpleasant, loud • displacing anger to other sources
5. FOCUSING ANGER ON SOURCE • HOLDING TO PRIMARY COMPLAINT • THINKING LOGICALLY • unpleasant, loud • verbal abuse
6. HOLDING TO PRIMARY COMPLAINT • THINKING LOGICALLY • unpleasant, loud • displacing anger to other sources
7. THINKING LOGICALLY • unpleasant, loud • displacing anger to other sources • expressing unrelated complaints

PRIMARILY NEGATIVE

8. unpleasant, loud • displacing anger to other sources • expressing unrelated complaints • emotionally destructive behavior
9. unpleasant, loud • displacing anger to other sources • expressing unrelated complaints • verbal abuse • emotionally destructive behavior
10. unpleasant, loud • cursing • displacing anger to other sources • expressing unrelated complaints • verbal abuse • emotionally destructive behavior
11. FOCUSING ANGER ON SOURCE • unpleasant, loud • cursing • throwing objects • emotionally destructive behavior
12. unpleasant, loud • cursing • displacing anger to other sources • throwing objects • emotionally destructive behavior

NEGATIVE

13. unpleasant, loud • cursing • displacing anger to other sources • destroying property • verbal abuse • emotionally destructive behavior
14. FOCUSING ANGER ON SOURCE • unpleasant, loud • cursing • destroying property • verbal abuse • emotionally destructive behavior
15. unpleasant, loud • cursing • displacing anger to other sources • destroying property • verbal abuse • physical abuse • emotionally destructive behavior
16. passive=aggressive behavior

him up the Anger Ladder (see illustration). It's ridiculous to tell him, "From now on be pleasant." You can move him only a step at a time. You do that simply by asking him to do one thing differently the next time he gets angry.

Let's say the worst thing a teen does while verbally expressing his anger is cursing. A parent can say, "From now on, please don't call me names." The parent will need to keep reminding the teen after each incident, but eventually he will learn to get angry without cursing. Then he will be ready for the parent to move on to something else, like, "Please don't yell at the top of your lungs."

My wife finds this process easier than I do. She is a stable person with a mild temperament. She doesn't react to things as emotionally as I do. It was much harder for me to learn to handle my children's anger. The thing to remember is that the process takes a lot of time—time for the parents to learn to use it, and time for the teen to respond.

It can take months and years to train a child to handle anger well. It's not something that can be learned in one easy lesson. In fact, one of the hallmarks of maturity is being able to handle anger appropriately. Maturity takes time. We parents must not give up too soon.

Related Articles

Why Teens Get Depressed

ROSS CAMPBELL, M.D.

There is a big difference between the normal sadness that comes with difficult experiences, such as breaking up with a girlfriend or boyfriend, and true teen depression. But that difference may not be immediately visible.

Teen depression is extremely dangerous because it is so hard to detect. It usually develops slowly over a long period of time. Its symptoms are not the same as those of adult depression. Even professionals have a hard time diagnosing it, especially in the early stages.

The first symptom of teen depression is lack of concentration. We can detect this by comparing the teen's present ability to concentrate with his ability a few months ago. If he used to get through his homework in a certain length of time and now it takes him considerably longer, depression may be at work—especially if, in the longer time period, he is actually getting less done.

Teachers are in a good position to identify depression in students, because depressed students tend to daydream. The deeper the depression, the more time spent daydreaming. The attention span gets shorter and shorter. A teen who is having trouble concentrating often begins to blame himself for his difficulties. He may start calling himself stupid because he isn't studying as well as before. His grades are likely to drop.

As the teen moves on from light to moderate depression, the main symptom is a deep-rooted boredom. He becomes increasingly uninterested in what is going on around him. He withdraws more and more. Eventually the depression leads to physical symptoms like headaches and other pains. Eating habits may be affected—the depressed teen may eat too much or too little. These physical symptoms often lead to a lack of energy, a common complaint in depressed teens.

The teen suffering from moderate to serious depression is in a serious situation. When a person is depressed, a biochemical process is at work. The brain becomes deficient in neurotransmitter hormones. If nothing is done to reverse the process, the brain gets used to operating at a deficiency and it tends to remain in that state. Many adults are depressed because depression from their teen years, untreated, has persisted. Some effects of long-term depression can be irreversible.

It's important to keep in mind that a certain amount of depression is normal. When a boy turns fifteen or so, for example, he begins to see his mother as a sexual being. That's hard for him to handle, because it means he will have to separate himself from his mother. One common way to handle this thought is to put it away. But this may cause depression.

Though some depression is normal, no depression should be taken lightly. The key to successful treatment is to catch depression early. In its early stages, depression is relatively easy to treat. But as depression deepens within a teenager, a serious complication develops. His thought process begins to be affected. He gradually loses ability to think clearly, logically, and rationally. His judgment deteriorates as he focuses more and more on morbid details. He increasingly assumes that everything is bleak, nothing is worthwhile, and life is not worth living.

He now has a thought disturbance. As he loses his ability to think and communicate in a clear and rational way, counseling becomes less and less effective. The teenager begins to act out his depression in self-destructive ways. He may run away from home, experiment with drugs, or hurt himself. Boys may become antisocial, willing to do anything with an aura of excitement or danger. Girls may become sexually promiscuous.

If the depression becomes severe, teens may attempt suicide. Girls attempt it far more often than boys, but they don't succeed as often. Boys use more violent means, so when they attempt suicide, they have a much greater chance of killing themselves.

This is a frightening predicament. How can you help a teenager when you cannot reason with him? When the teen's depression turns into a thought disturbance, medical help is mandatory.

Depression may have several causes. One may be the basic personality structure. Some people are more prone to depression than others. About one-fourth of all people can be classified as having a compliant, passive personality. An overly compliant child is especially prone to depression. He gets depressed simply because there are problems in the world. He wants the world to be perfect, and it isn't. Depression may also be the child's way of reacting to external pressures, such as divorce, violence in the home, or pressure from parents, school, or athletics.

Whatever its cause, adolescent depression is not a phase that will run its course. Early detection and appropriate treatment are vital. Left untreated, depression tends to grow worse and worse until serious, long-lasting consequences result.

Related Articles

Failure and Disappointment: They're Not All Bad

TED W. ENGSTROM

Life is a series of successes and failures. Yet often teens focus so intently on their failures and disappointments, they feel that no one else can empathize with their situation. When teens experience these failures in life and become discouraged, we need to let them know that we've all been in the same boat at one time or another.

Just letting your teen know what you experienced in your younger life will make it a lot easier. I found that letting the kids know their dad was far from perfect and that I'd fallen so often was actually an encouragement to them. We need to have the courage to confess our failures to our teens, and to let them see that we're human. The Lord helped me to be candid and honest with my kids. That kind of encouragement means much more to teens than a pat on the back.

We can build on failure and disappointment by giving closer attention and analysis to these areas than to the successes. I think it is important to consider whether or not the youngster did the best he could under the circumstances, and discern if there are skills which were learned that can aid future growth and development.

We need to ask, "How will this disappointment affect the teenager? How will he interpret this failure?" It is important that the discouragement doesn't lead to social or emotional withdrawal.

When my son was a junior in high school, he was a very good football player. I only saw one or two of his football games, however, because I traveled a great deal as then-president of Youth for Christ. I could tell that he was very disappointed.

So the next year I called the high school and got a schedule of the home and away games. I booked them into my calendar without telling my son. I showed up at every game his senior year, and he was greatly encouraged by my involvement. It was more important for me to see one boy play football than to preach to a thousand teenagers on a Friday or Saturday night. I think that kind of modeling and interest by parents is vital.

I also think that teenagers should have a wide range of new adventures that test their abilities and skills. Parents can help set the stage for their children by encouraging an environment that is conducive to attempting new and healthy ventures. Then, if failure comes along, it's not the sole focus of the learning process.

Most teenagers feel enough pressure on themselves without adding to it unnecessarily. The home needs to provide a place for relief from peer pressures. Build acceptance and recognition of love into your home environment.

Above all, listen to your teenager. Be careful and quick to listen, and slow to speak. Keep the door of communication open. Allow your youngster to initiate discussion about why he is disappointed or why he is hurt.

We are so quick as adults and parents to give advice and try to dry the tears. Sometimes tears and disappointment are all right if we can listen and offer a soft shoulder. Most parents can improve on their listening skills if they're only willing to try.

Alone Again, Naturally?

DAVID VEERMAN

"Loneliness"—an emotion-filled word which evokes images of solitude, rejection, and fear. We were created as social beings. In Eden, God stated that "it is not good for man to live alone" (Gen. 2:18). We need relationships, family, friends, and loved ones who understand and accept us. Whenever we lose someone we love or are put down by our friends, we feel isolated, cut off, and incomplete.

Loneliness has been described as "one of the most universal sources of human suffering" (Henri J.M. Nouwen, *Reaching Out: The Three Movements of the Spiritual Life,* Doubleday, 1979) and "the most devastating malady of this age" (Paul Tournier, *Escape from Loneliness,* Westminster Press, 1976). No one is immune. Consider for a moment the great Prophet Elijah. First Kings 18 describes his tremendous victory over the false prophets. In a dramatic, day-long confrontation, he had spoken for God, built an altar, made a sacrifice, prayed, called down fire from heaven, and personally killed 450 men. As the chapter ends, however, we find Elijah alone, afraid, and running for his life. Soon we hear his plaintive prayer, "It is enough; now, O Lord, take my life; for I am not better than my fathers" (1 Kings 19:4, NASB), and, "I alone am left; and they seek my life, to take it away" (1 Kings 19:10, NASB). He was alone, and he felt overwhelming loneliness and depression.

I am sure we can all identify with Elijah—about the loneliness, not the fire from heaven. But what causes these feelings, and how can they be overcome?

First, we need to distinguish between being alone and feeling lonely. Though loneliness often strikes when we are alone, it is possible to be lonely in a crowd or to feel fine by oneself. Aloneness is an *external* fact, but loneliness is an *internal* feeling. Often, because we fear loneliness, we try never to be alone. I know people who cannot stand silence. As soon as they walk into a room, they turn on the radio or TV. But it is important to spend some time alone for reflection, meditation, or just plain relaxation. Often Jesus would withdraw from the disciples for prayer (Luke 9:18), and He faced Satan alone in the wilderness (Matt. 4:1-11).

Loneliness is caused by a break in a relationship, whether it is between us and God or someone we love. That person may be near, but if "divorce" has occurred, we will feel lonely. Conversely, we may be separated by thousands of miles and yet feel secure in our relationship.

The most basic and important of these relationships is the one with God. Jesus spoke about this in John 8:29 when He said, "He who sent Me is with Me; He has not left Me alone, for I always do the things that are pleasing to Him" (NASB). In other words, Jesus was totally secure in His relationship with God, His Father. Later (John 16:32-33, NASB) Jesus shared with His disciples how they could experience this inner security in their lives. He

204

told them, "An hour is coming . . . for you to be scattered . . . to leave Me alone; and yet I am not alone, because the Father is with Me. These things I have spoken to you, that in Me you may have peace. In the world you have tribulation, but take courage, I have overcome the world." In spite of the problems and pressures they would face, the disciples could experience peace—He would be with them.

The reason we do not experience God's love and peace is because there has been a break in our relationship with Him. We disobey or ignore Him and try to live on our own. The Bible calls this sin. The good news, however, is that Christ died for our sins. He took our place and experienced ultimate loneliness and separation from God. We hear His anguish as He cries "My God, My God, why have You forsaken Me?" (Matt. 27:46, NIV) But Jesus conquered sin and death as He arose from the grave! The good news is that when we put our faith in Him, our relationship with God can be restored.

Indeed, Jesus Christ offers the ultimate solution to our loneliness. He loves us unconditionally, died for our sins, welcomes us as God's children, becomes a friend who sticks closer than a brother, and gives us the Holy Spirit to live in us.

The Apostle Paul describes it this way: "Who then can ever keep Christ's love from us? When we have trouble or calamity, when we are hunted down or destroyed, is it because He doesn't love us anymore? And if we are hungry, or penniless, or in danger, or threatened with death, has God deserted us? . . . For I am convinced that nothing can ever separate us from His love. Death can't, and life can't. The angels won't, and all the powers of hell itself cannot keep God's love away. Our fears for today, our worries about tomorrow, or where we are—high above the sky, or in the deepest ocean—nothing will ever be able to separate us from the love of God demonstrated by our Lord Jesus Christ when He died for us" (Rom. 8:35, 38-39, TLB).

Of course this is not a *complete* answer to loneliness. Other relevant areas are self-esteem, communication, friendship-building, and coping with change. But our relationship with God is vital. I challenge your family to give your lives to Him.

Related Articles
Chapter 8: Why Teens Get Depressed
Chapter 12: Developing Self-worth in Your Teen

Lighting a Fire under the Lazy Teenager
JAY KESLER

It is said that most of the world's inventions were thought up by lazy people. That is, they were too lazy to walk so they developed something to ride on; they were too lazy to push something with runners so they invented wheels, and so on.

To some degree, this is true. People's innate laziness leads them to invent labor-saving devices. But it's also possible that people are not inherently lazy, but prefer doing meaningful activities. In the case of our teenage children, the struggle is to establish with them what is meaningful and to motivate them toward activity, especially activities that are assigned.

A young person can be a ball of fire when it's time to go swimming or run around with the kids, but when it's time to mow the lawn or help with the housework, he or she can be absolutely exhausted. Sometimes the exhaustion results from doing all those fun activities, and then the parents end up getting the tag end of the day.

From the time children are very young, parents need to establish with them the relationship between pleasure and work. Work must be finished and out of the way before the children are allowed to play. Letting a tired son leave the lawn half-mowed is no favor to him or to you. Insisting that he finish the mowing before he does things he wants to do is absolutely imperative.

How should we insist? Unfortunately, we can't do this without arousing a certain level of unhappiness around the home. I jokingly told one group of parents that the duty of parents is to nag. Young people dislike living with nagging. They learn that the way to get us off their case is to do what we've asked them to do. Then if we reward and affirm them, they feel motivated.

One day a boy told me, "I've never done anything in my life that my father found OK. If I mow the whole yard, the first thing he does when he pulls into the driveway is find some part of the yard that wasn't done right. I didn't trim those blades of grass around that tree, or

FINISHING THE JOB

"My kid never *really* completes the job. He just does the bare minimum!"

This is one of those typical teenage characteristics, and it is really a reflection of their lack of experience and misconception that "pain is the exception to life and intolerable." Doing hard work and being thorough can be painful, and so it is avoided.

The "shortcut" attitude is a reflection of our society. If it can't be done in a half hour (like television), it can't be done. And doing a task is not seen as fulfilling a responsibility.

We also should remember that young people approach jobs differently than adults, and they usually think that everything deserves remuneration or reward or it need not be done.

Here are some suggestions for helping our teens mature in this area of their lives. We can:

1. Be realistic in our standards of thoroughness (e.g., compulsive or perfectionist parents are usually too demanding).

2. Explain the job clearly with as many specifics as possible.

3. Give rewards, but withhold them until the job has been done right.

4. Let them know that the job is important.

5. Examine our motives behind the job. (Do we want the lawn done to perfection to look good to the neighbors? This is OK, but our kids can't identify with this motive.)

6. Refuse to "bail them out" by finishing the job for them.

7. As an object lesson, turn the tables (wash most of the clothes—but not all, cook half the meal, etc.)

8. When a job is done thoroughly, reward with *genuine* verbal praise, letting them know our appreciation (this can be more valuable than money).

YFC Editors

whatever. This has a way of deflating me."

Of course it does. Most people would have the wind taken out of them by that kind of treatment. Far better for the father to say, "That's a terrific job. I'm glad you got it done. It's hot today—you must have worked really hard." Then, if necessary, he could add, "Hey, when you get a minute, I notice a few blades there that need to be cut." Better yet, the father could go out when the boy's not around and cut them himself, just to avoid the spirit of criticism. Or he could even ignore them. If they get tall enough, eventually the boy is likely to spot them himself.

To teenagers, there is generally a close connection between affirmation and motivation. The young person who is commended for good activity is usually better motivated than the one who is not. Someone once said to me that sugared horses do better than whipped horses, and that's true. Love, affirmation, and encouragement tend to build up a desire to repeat the good behavior. Criticism, perfectionism, and cutting remarks will eventually destroy motivation.

Reward is also a motivator for most of us. Young people can learn that if they do task Y, they will get reward Z. If they mow the lawn, they can use the car this evening. If they don't mow the lawn, they can't. If they get their homework done, they can watch TV; if they don't get their homework done, they can't.

Sometimes doing things with young people can be a great motivator. If the young person doesn't know how to do the particular job, this enables the parent to show how it's done. Then when the teenager succeeds in doing it well, he or she feels the reward of a job well done. A hard day's work by a father with his son at his side can be, for both of them, a very rewarding experience, one they will want to repeat. It helps, of course, if the father avoids throwing cold water on the son's ideas. The job can be done the son's way sometimes; this will make him feel as if he has something to contribute.

Almost all motivation comes from reward or punishment. Sitting around waiting for our youngsters to feel like working never works. We have to set up some stimulus to make the assigned activity necessary. The most effective motivator is the reward of appreciation and affirmation. Like a dog who will walk clear across the yard for a pat on the head, most young people will go to great lengths to get words of affirmation and encouragement from their parents.

———————
Related Article
Chapter 14: What Motivates Teens?

"My Teenager Is a Smart Aleck"
GARY D. BENNETT

It doesn't take a psychiatrist to understand why teenagers sometimes behave as smart alecks. One of the main reasons is confusion: the teenager is finding himself and discovering who he is. Attempting to show his maturity, he tests his parents and other adults while portraying a superior and confident attitude (which we as adults see as being cocky and smart alecky).

What is meant by the term "teenage smart aleck"? If you are living with one, you need no definition; however, the following is a summary of attitudes and actions usually displayed by a "smart aleck":

1. Swearing, lack of respect, poor manners, sassiness, mouthing off
2. Always contradicting, arguing, displaying an attitude of willful disobedience
3. Ignoring, sulking, pouting, defying, etc.
4. Knowing it all, with an opinion on anything and acting as an expert on everything
5. Challenging your decisions
6. Always expecting explanations and justifications, etc.

What are some other possible reasons why we see these attitudes and actions from a teenager?

1. Testing parental feelings and limits
2. Questioning adult standards
3. Needing to assert independence, and to establish himself as a separate entity
4. Needing to demonstrate wit, prowess, and exercising new-found adolescent humor
5. Shifting from dependency to independence
6. Needing to be like his peer group

Why is such behavior a problem?

1. Parents are embarrassed.
2. Parents lose control, or at least feel out of control.
3. Parents are "turned off," disappointed in their teenager.
4. Other children in the family begin to copy the behavior.
5. Parents feel like failures.
6. Teens should respect adults, therefore parents feel pressure to teach appro-

HOW TO HANDLE A SMART ALECK TEENAGER

If your teenager is a smart aleck, it is probably because: (1) The teen is going through a phase that he will grow out of, or (2) the teen has low self-esteem, and smarts off to build himself up a little. So what can parents do if their child has a problem in this area?

One thing that has worked for me is to be honest about how much I am hurt when my child talks back. I say, "When you talk like that it really hurts my feelings because I feel put down and ridiculed. I love you, and I think you love me, and I don't want us to have this kind of relationship. What can we do to overcome this? If I tell you when I hurt, can you think of a better way to tell me what you are trying to say?"

You don't have to use this approach, but I think it will help you discover whether the child is acting that way on purpose, or to cover his insecurity. If you find out that his actions are a result of a lack of confidence on his part, you can deal with that problem directly.

In that case, you should do whatever you can to make your teenager feel important. Few things work as powerfully as honest, positive affirmation. Assign him some responsibilities to show that the family really needs him. Take pride in his achievements in sports or academics. Praise his smile, or some other characteristic that you admire.

As parents we try to appear controlled and brave, and sometimes we don't let our kids know we have real human feelings. But if we begin to go beyond parent-to-child relationships and develop friend-to-friend relationships with our teenagers, their "smart aleck" tendencies should soon disappear.

Grace Ketterman

priate behavior in readiness for adult life.

7. Such behavior may become detrimental to the teenager; i.e., getting expelled from school, losing a job, losing funds, etc.

How can you deal with this problem?

1. Ignore behavior which has little significance. If there is little reaction, the teenager may lose some of the enjoyable benefits. Above all, never allow the behavior to sidetrack the main issue.

2. Model respectful, polite behavior. Don't get caught in the same behavior as your teenager. Demonstrate appropriate ways to express anger, and do your best to express your own feelings without downgrading the teen's opinions and feelings.

3. Point out the natural consequences of rude behavior. Be affectionately firm. Teenagers want some absolutes and guidelines. Be ready to explain when you think they are wrong, but speak with the tone of voice with which you would want to be addressed.

4. Explore when the behavior is most likely to occur. Is this an indication of some underlying need in the teenager? Are there certain situations which trigger this behavior? What is the teenager trying to express?

5. Keep your communication flowing by becoming a good listener. Listening is one of the highest compliments we can pay to any person, even in the face of "smart mouthing" from our teens. Show an intense and genuine interest in their frustrations, problems, and needs without giving them the impression that you're being nosy or meddling.

6. Finally, remind yourself often that this behavior is a temporary and typical part of growing up. It will probably take care of itself as your teenager moves into his next phase of maturation. In the meantime, do your best to establish a parental image of which he can be proud and which he may set as a goal for himself.

_____

Related Articles

"I Want It Now!"

DAVID RAHN

The symptoms of a consuming, now-oriented society are not hard to find. Ride a short distance in the car with a young person and you may find an irritating and frequent change of radio stations. Kids have discovered their own way to ensure "commercial-free" music. Dead air is forbidden.

This preoccupation with the immediate is not solely the young person's domain. Technology has made "wait" a bad word for all of us. When hunger hits, satisfaction need not be far away—somewhere between the golden arches and a microwave oven. The credit card industry is doing very fine, thank you, helping us all to buy *now* and pay later. Indeed, our current technology provides a now-climate where postponement of self-gratification is not easy. Self-denial is rare indeed, and when desire is granted its every wish, sin flourishes.

The exterior (i.e., culture) and the interior (i.e., sin) drive and speak with the same voice, producing a powerful influence, especially on teens who measure their own self-worth by the swift responses of others. The now-gratification that comes from being with the crowd doing *anything* (attending rock concerts, drinking, dancing) says to a young person, "Now you are really somebody, like all of these other somebodies." Parental restrictions become particularly unbearable when "everyone else is doing it."

In this teen frame of mind, everything in life, all of the little moments—what to wear, how so-and-so looked at them as they passed in the hall, who sat next to whom at lunch—take on an exaggerated importance. All of the current signals are filtered through that critical teen grid of self-image, each leaving its imprint.

Young persons who let the Gospel message take root and frame their self-value may experience a true freedom from the oppressive "now." As they come to believe in their own worth, the word "wait" need no longer strike terror at the foundation of their selfhood.

Related Articles

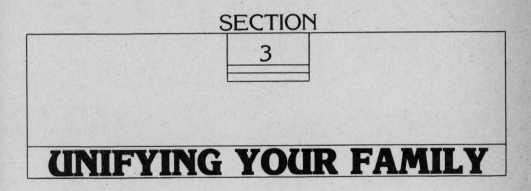

SECTION

3

UNIFYING YOUR FAMILY

HOW TO
COMMUNICATE EFFECTIVELY

- Eleven things guaranteed to ruin any conversation
- How do you read your teen's feelings?
- The art of listening
- When are the best opportunities for communication?
- Learning the secret of talking to teens
- How to answer teens' tough questions
- How do you talk to your kids without making them feel like you're prying into their business?
- What if your teen just won't talk to you?

"Do you know what I am?" a teenager once asked. "I'm a comma."

"What do you mean?" the listener replied.

He said, "Whenever I talk to my dad, he stops talking and makes a comma. Then when I stop talking, he starts right up again as if I didn't say anything. I'm just a comma in the middle of his speeches."

Many young people have never had a real conversation with an adult, especially of the parent variety. Too often we parents see our young people bottoms-up; that is, we still think of them as if they wore diapers, and we talk down to them. But good communication involves both a listener and a talker.

The rules that guide good adult communication also apply to communication between adults and teenagers, with the possible exception that teenagers may be more frightened and insecure and thus more easily scared off from sharing their real opinions. No one wants to risk ridicule or rejection. And no young person wants to play king-of-the-hill with an adult who's going to win every argument.

The Art of Communication

Communicating with Teenagers

JOSH McDOWELL

Rules without relationships lead to rebellion.

I've seen it happen over and over again. A child does something morally wrong, and the parents say, "How could this happen? We've clearly taught her what the Bible teaches about that kind of behavior." You can have all the rules you want in a family, but if you don't have relationships with your children you are going to have rebellion instead of response.

Good relationships are built on mutual respect. If you respect your children's rights, they will respect yours. Respect begins with listening. If you feel that someone is listening to you, you feel respected. Shakespeare said in *Hamlet*,

"Give every man your ear but seal your tongue." James said in the New Testament, "Be quick to listen, slow to speak" (1:19, NIV). An Irish proverb says, "God gave us two ears and one mouth, so we ought to listen twice as much as we speak."

We parents tend to treat our children's problems too lightly. "Oh, you'll get over it," we'll say. I've found that children take their problems just as seriously as you or I take ours. Their problems may not go as deep as ours, but they don't have as much experience as we do either. So that means that emotionally, we're at the same place when we face problems.

We need to be careful that we in no way make light of our children's problems. When they are facing difficulties, we have a unique opportunity to influence them. We can hug them, encourage them, share from our own experience, or walk through the problem with them. Often we don't need to say anything at all. It is tempting to step in and start giving sermonettes, but listening is usually more important. The children often just want a sympathetic ear, a sounding board.

An important part of communicating is to hear the children out. This is where I fall short. I always want to interrupt, not to wait for the whole story. But kids want to give you the whole situation, and if they feel you are not going to hear them out, they will clam up. You might get a few facts, but you won't get their feelings.

We parents seem to feel we need to give advice, to quote the Bible to our children, when often we just need to listen. A teenager said to me recently, "You know, I try to share something with my parents and as soon as I open my mouth, they start quoting the Bible. I don't want the Bible quoted; I just want them to listen to me."

Concentration on what our children are saying can be difficult. For every 100 words spoken, we can hear and understand 500, so it's easy for the mind to wander. I keep saying to myself, "Can you repeat back to your child what he or she is saying?" If I keep that thought running through my mind, it helps me concentrate.

Part of good communication is listening with the eyes as well as with the ears. Look for physical and nonverbal communication—the way your children use their eyes, the gestures they make. If you don't watch for nonverbal cues, you're missing part of their communication.

Some parents are quite ready to listen, but their teenage children won't talk. How can they encourage the kids to open up?

First, parents need to enter the children's world enough so that they are speaking the same language. They need to get their children's perspective. I'm forty-four years old, and it's hard for me to get back to junior high and know exactly what I was going through. Still, I'm constantly trying to see my children's viewpoints. I want to know their world, and I must know it if I am going to communicate with them. I need to listen to their music, read what they read, know their friends, understand their frustrations, laugh at their jokes. I also need to consider how what I say will affect them. They may not take things the same way an adult would, so I need to look at my statements to them from their perspective. Communication takes a lot of work!

Communicating with my children is easier if we are involved together in something they enjoy—surfing, soccer, basketball, jogging, cooking. We had two acres of ground that we weren't using, so we built a soccer field on it. I set up and poured a basketball court behind the garage. I have a friend who took a class with three of his kids every Thursday night for a term. It became the central topic of household discussion. They did their homework together, and Thursday mornings they would go out to breakfast together to discuss what they studied. I thought that was fantastic.

Then, parents who want to encourage their teens to talk must obey certain ground rules. With teenagers, especially, it's important to be able to keep secrets. If I go out and tell others a secret my teens have shared with me, I'm going to destroy their confidence in me.

It's also important to be open about one's faults. My children may not remember all the times I've been kind to people, but they will remember the times I lost my temper. If I try to cover up my failures, I won't fool my children. I'll just teach them to keep their tracks covered too. Instead of hiding my faults, I should confess them and use them as lessons for both myself and my children.

When things are going right with my children, I sometimes share negative things out of my childhood, like frustrations I had with my father and how we worked them through. God's Holy Spirit plants those things in their minds, and then when they go through similar frustrations, they remember them without feeling like I'm preaching to them.

Kids really respond to praise and encouragement. I try to praise my kids at least twenty-five times a day. I'm constantly going out of my way looking for ways to praise my children. I tell them what a good job they did, or how nice they look. If I use criticism and sarcasm, I get a reaction, but if I give praise and encouragement, I get a response. Touching and hugging is another key to reaching children, even after they become teenagers. Hug them when they hurt, hug them when joyful, hug them for the fun of it.

With teenagers, as with anyone else, one way to get communication going is to ask questions. If I don't plan ahead and ask questions, I usually talk only about things that interest me. But if I ask specific questions, the children end up talking about their own concerns. When they come home from school, I ask, "Did you do anything special? What didn't you like today?" I try to bring out feelings as well as facts. "How did you feel when your friend told you he'd cheated?"

Something that has really helped me communicate with my kids is to ask their opinions. Not only do I get a lot of good information that way, but I also communicate to them that they are important to me and that what they have to say is important. Several years ago when I was preparing some talks on forgiveness, I got my children and a friend's children together at breakfast and asked their help. The children made a list of reasons that some people are unwilling to confess their sins to God and receive forgiveness. They gave me good ideas, and they also became a part of my ministry. They still talk about that experience today.

My wife, an exceptional woman with tremendous ability to listen and communicate, is a barometer for me. She'll say, "Honey, you need to spend a little more time with Sean, listening to him." Or, "You know, Kelly wanted to say something to you this afternoon, and you didn't really listen to her. I think maybe you need to go into her room." If I don't know quite how to respond to one of the children, sometimes I'll say, "Let's ask Mother to come in here. Let's see what she has to say." My wife plays a major role in maintaining good communication in our family. Much of what I've learned, I've learned from her.

Fathers as well as mothers need to take communication with their children seriously. I once did a week-long conference at a large evangelical church. Apart from my speaking, I had forty-two personal appointments with junior high and high school students who wanted counseling. I asked each one of these kids, "Can you talk with your father?" Only one said yes. The number one question I kept getting from these students was this: "Josh, what can I do about my dad? He never talks to me; he never takes me anywhere; he never does anything with me."

If we parents make talking with our

children a number one priority, it will rub off on them and they will make a priority of talking with us. I've found that I need to plan ahead if I'm going to have a good discussion with my family. My wife and I sometimes plan discussion topics for the dinner table. Other good times for communication include riding to school—an excellent time to discuss their likes and dislikes, their feelings, what they are going to be doing that day—and riding to church.

I like to take a child with me when I make a trip into town. Recently I had to drive to Ramona, a little over twenty miles from our home, so I took my three-and-a-half-year-old daughter along for the ride. Ahead of time, I thought through five or six questions to discuss with her. If I hadn't planned, we wouldn't have had that discussion. The time would have just slipped by.

Some of the most intimate times between parents and children can take place in their rooms or in the master bedroom. There is a different feeling if you are in their territory or they are in yours. And bedtime, of course, is an excellent time to communicate. But once again, I find that if I don't think ahead about what I'm going to say, I don't say anything.

It's easy to let the day's pressures crowd out precious time for communicating with our children. One day I was under tremendous pressure to finish a book that I'd promised the publisher. I had stayed up all night working on it. Then my son came in and wanted to talk. I knew he had been upset by a visit to the doctor, who had commented about his small stature, but I would not have chosen that moment to discuss it.

"Josh," I said to myself, "you're going to have pressure deadlines the rest of your life. You're always going to have work to do, but you're not always going to have a hurting child to talk to. Take advantage of the opportunity." So I just pushed my stuff aside and spent the next half hour talking with him about his shortness, the fact that he's unique and that God made him that way, and the advantages and disadvantages of being short.

Sometimes, of course, I just can't talk to the child when he wants my attention. Too often I used to say, "Honey, I can't talk right now," and then when I was free it was too late to help. I've found that it's best to say, "You know, Son, I want to discuss this with you, but I can't right now. If you will come back at such and such a time, then I'll be free and I'll give you my full attention." I've found that my children have a whole different attitude when I do that. They don't feel that they are being shoved aside, that I'm not interested in them.

If we parents show an interest in our children when they're young, they will show an interest in us later. Good communication with teenagers requires a lot of time and thought, but it is the foundation of a lifelong family relationship.

_____

Related Articles

The Art of Listening

NORMAN WRIGHT

As a counselor, I see it all the time. We all do it—throwing up roadblocks to listening. We tune out certain topics, expressions, or tones of voice, for example. Sometimes we're so eager to say our part that we interrupt and bypass what the other person is saying. Or we make the mistake of thinking we can listen only with our ears, forgetting that our eyes are just as important, picking up nonverbal language.

We act as if we are mind readers, predicting what the other person is going to say, what the "real" message is going to be—even what the motive is. Instead of listening, we mentally rehearse what we're going to say. We filter out facts and feelings we just don't want to hear.

Some roadblocks are especially common between parents and teens. One of the "biggies" is judging. "Well, he's just a kid," we think, and discount what he says. Or we think we're the Great Advice Giver; no matter what the teen says, we think, "I have to give an answer again." We're so busy formulating a response that we may not be answering what the young person is asking.

The roadblocks can come down. But if you're really going to listen to your kids,

THE ART OF HELPING YOUR TEEN LISTEN

There are several ways parents can help their teen really listen and hear what he is saying.

First, try to make the familiar things you say sound "fresh." Acknowledge the individuality of your teen. The way you convey something to your teen can make him receptive and interested, or bored and rebellious. Stop for a moment to think of how you would want the information conveyed if you were the listener.

Second, and perhaps even more important, is your willingness to invest in the relationship with your teen. Spend time with your teen going places and talking about things he likes, as well as going places and talking about things you like. If this rapport and interest has been established, it's more difficult for a teen to hear you griping, "Do what I want you to" instead of your intended message.

Make a conscious effort to be interested in your teenager and his concerns. Try to relate to him and dialogue with him. These efforts and positive communication experiences will outweigh the negative ones, if they are consistently pursued. The result will be a teen with open ears who really hears what you are saying. And the teenager will have some basis to make the right decision, based on the parents' counsel and interest.

Glandion Carney

you'll have to put aside what you're doing and *look* at them. That's because most communication happens through tone of voice and body language. We need to hear what the adolescent cannot put into words.

Try noticing the expression on your teenager's face when he or she talks to you. Is he fidgeting? Calm? Reflect his mood by saying something like, "It looks like you're kind of uptight about this," or, "You really look like you had a happy day." Sometimes that opens up a conversation.

But be sure to "document" your observation. If your son comes home and you take a look at him and say, "Boy, I know you're tired," you're going to get an adverse reaction. Instead, try something like, "I'm wondering what's going on, because you're not moving as fast as you usually do. You're looking sort of downcast; your eyes are kind of sad. I'm wondering if something happened today at school." That's an invitation to talk because you're saying you're willing to listen.

We also need to tune into the young person's tone of voice. The tone—whether cheerful, down, or harsh—says so much more than the actual words.

Learn to reflect your teen's verbal cues too. Instead of leaping in with commentary, make sure you understand what's been said. Say something like, "If I really understand what you're saying. . ." or, "You know, from what you're saying, it sounds like this is really bothering you."

Draw the young person out. Let your teen know that you're listening, that you're encouraging him to talk more. Amplify what he's saying. Showing that you're paying attention is a big part of listening.

You can practice such "reflecting" with your spouse. Give him or her two minutes to talk; then summarize what you've heard. Next, do that for three minutes, then five. You'll begin to perfect your listening skills. We do this a lot in our marriage seminars, and people are amazed at how much they can remember.

But what if, after you've reflected your teen's actions or words, the conversation goes nowhere because he or she doesn't want to talk? You've got *one* choice: to accept it. Say something like, "That's fine. If there's a time when you'd like to share, I'd be willing to listen. But it's up to you." Then back off and pray for patience!

Reflecting may not be easy, but avoiding our tendency to judge teens is downright difficult. We want to step in and crack down, even in the middle of a conversation. The good listener, however,

FINDING TIME TO LISTEN

"This is not a good time," we may tell our kids when they want to talk. "I'm fixing dinner. I'm tired. Come back another time."

But maybe we adults have more control over our time than our teens have over theirs. With school, extracurricular activities, part-time jobs, and dating, our kids may not have much time left. Maybe we parents need to break out of our time structures and be available when our teens are.

That's not easy. We get so tied up in our own frustrations that we may think, "Nobody listens to *me* around here. I'm not going to listen to *them*." But for parents who realize the importance of listening, the question becomes, "What am I doing with my time, and why am I doing it? Is it really more important than having time with my son or daughter?"

Norman Wright

takes it in and accepts what the other person is saying.

That doesn't mean we always agree with what our kids say. It does mean our kids can think, "I can come to you and unload, and know I'm accepted—even if what I'm saying isn't all that acceptable."

If your judgment fuse is short, try a "delay." That means telling yourself in advance, "I'm not going to respond right away. I'm going to ask at least three clarifying questions before I try to answer." By doing that, you'll gain a great deal of information instead of interrupting and frustrating your teenager. You'll probably surprise him or her too, since so often we simply react out of defensiveness, anger, or fear that we're losing control.

Effective listening doesn't start when the child is a teenager, of course. We gain a hearing as the child is growing up. If you haven't done that, you may need to go to your son or daughter and say honestly, "In the past I guess I've tuned you out. I haven't listened to you as I should have, and I'd like to apologize for that. I really do want to listen to you. If there is a time when you feel I'm not listening, I'd appreciate it if you would let me know. And I won't get upset at you for telling me."

Learning the art of listening takes time. Too often as our families grow, we get used to communicating on the run. Pretty soon we say, "What's the use?" But if we learn to listen to ourselves, our spouses, and to the Lord in prayer, we can apply those lessons to truly hearing our teens.

Related Articles

The "Grunt" Stage
What to Do When Teens Won't Talk

ROSS CAMPBELL, M.D.

When I ask someone a question, I rather expect him to say something in response. But most teenagers, at some point in their development, seem to find responding to parents impossible. No matter what the question—"Did you have a good day at school?" "Did you remember to shovel the walks?" "Would you like to go to a movie?"—the only answer forthcoming is a grunt.

The "grunt stage" is a normal part of teen development. It's an automatic process that is out of his control, a process of putting distance between himself and his parents from time to time.

When their teens reach the grunt stage, parents need to realize that the kids are very much like two-year-olds. You can't force a two-year-old to do what you want. Parents who don't know that are going to be very bewildered.

It's the same with the grunt stage. Parents who try to batter down the barrier, for example with questions, do not understand normal teen behavior. It can be damaging to force the teen to open up. He needs the space, the distance, for a while. It is a time for the parents to be as patient as possible.

During this stage, physical and eye contact become very important. They can be ways of loving the child, even without his open consent. Sometimes only physical contact is possible, because the teen avoids eye contact.

Fortunately, during this grunt stage teens aren't acutely aware of what is going on around them. So while they are reading or watching TV or daydreaming, you can just touch them lightly and briefly on the shoulders or the back. My favorite trick is either to use them as a crutch when I get up from a chair, or to lightly touch them on the back as they watch TV. I make a game of it by seeing how many times I can touch them before they notice.

It's OK if they don't notice, because the touch still registers. In fact, I prefer that they not notice. If they do notice and jerk away from me, that doesn't hurt anything. But they usually don't.

Another way parents can communicate with a teen in the grunt stage is by doing things to help him feel better. If it's a terribly hot day and you know he'd like a glass of something cold to drink, get him one. You don't have to do it so often that you look like a servant. It should look natural. You fixed a drink for yourself, so you fixed one for him too.

Parents can also arrange to spend time with teens so that they don't feel pressured to do or say anything. Different kids like different situations. With my daughter, Carey, I would take her out to eat in a place where the line was sure to be long. I absolutely abhor standing in line, but it was a way to be with her. It put her under no obligation to say anything.

With my son, David, taking him to football practice, going to a movie, or going anywhere by car are all effective. I don't have to say anything, and neither does he. He is under no pressure.

It takes time for teens to open up even in nonpressure situations. Carey required at least half an hour standing in line waiting to be served before she would begin to talk. She would start to talk about superficial matters. Then she

would go deeper and deeper until finally she would say what was really on her heart.

Teens have such a stake in what they are saying that they have to ease into it. They have to set the stage. They can't feel cornered, unable to get away from their parents. They can't have the fear of being interrupted.

Then, often, before telling their parents anything important, they put up a smoke screen. They have to be sure it is safe to open up. They will say something carefully designed to upset their parents, but this is only a test. If the parents pass the test, teens will start to share what is really bothering them. Sometimes I passed the test, and sometimes I didn't.

Another way teens communicate is by picking the worst possible moment to test you to see if you really want to listen to them. They are masters of timing. For instance, if I'm late for a meeting, they will wait until I'm putting my arm in the sleeve of my coat to say, "Hey, Dad, have you got a minute?"

Sometimes a teen who has had good communication will suddenly stop talking. He may be depressed, or he may be acting out anger. If the grunt stage goes on for days and weeks with no letup, then we know there are serious problems that we have to deal with.

Normally the grunt stage is intermittent—teens go in and out of it. We can't afford to select the times to communicate with them, because if they come out of it and we're not there, we've lost our chance. We can't be there all the time, of course, but if we're there enough, we're doing our job.

Related Articles

The Silent Treatment

JIM & SALLY CONWAY

Perhaps we should not ask why our teen doesn't want to talk, but why *should* our teen talk? What have we, as parents, done to stimulate talk or friendship or excitement? Do we have the attitude of the song, "You Light Up My Life"? Does your teen say, "I like being home sometimes. I enjoy being with my parents"? Or is coming home something your child dreads?

There are times, of course, when a child shuts down on communication because he is wrestling with some issue. Sensitive parents will detect that and won't try to pry. But they will let the teen know they are available.

If a young person is wrestling with a problem and he needs a few hours or a couple of days to just reflect alone, that is fine. Parents can do some initiating by saying, "You know I really love you and I've noticed that you've been more quiet than usual. It seems like you're worried about something. I care about you and I am praying for you. Is there anything you want to bounce off me?" If the teen says no, the parents shouldn't try to force communication but continue to be available.

There were times when one would just hang around the kids, not being nosy or pesty, but available. We would chat and she would sense an easy, open atmosphere, then begin to open up about whatever was bothering her.

Once, one of our daughters was accosted by a friend of the family in a sexual way. Nothing actually happened but the very fact he was trying to force himself on her frightened her. It had made her angry that a friend of the family would do that. She was unusually grumpy and touchy for a few days until she finally shared what had happened. We had to be sensitive to when she was ready to talk about it and be her friend as she worked through her anger and fear.

Sometimes kids quit communicating when they think we're not going to be their friend or that we're going to take the opposite side of an issue.

Even adults who are close friends sometimes don't want to talk to each other. If it is OK for adults, it should be OK for teens. Of course, it isn't good to let this go on for a long time. Parents should be searching their own attitudes for possible barriers they have erected. They should check the atmosphere they have set up in the home.

A negative example of communication happened when one of our girls confided in Sally about how she felt about a certain boy. Then she overheard Sally repeating that to a friend on the phone. That violation of trust devastated her because she had shared it in confidence. Our daughter resolved never to tell her mother how she felt about anyone. It took a while for Sally to reestablish our daughter's trust.

A great help to open up communication is when parents can admit they have been wrong. We were visiting a relative's home when the girls were young and Sally scolded them out of proportion to what they had done. She realized she had been crabby and apologized to them.

This relative later told Sally never to apologize to kids because that was a sign of weakness and showed them we were imperfect. Well, the reality is that we *are* imperfect. Our kids see that before they are very old. Kids don't respect us less if we apologize when we are wrong; they respect us for our honesty. And honesty opens up communication channels.

"I'M LISTENING, LORD"

Today's teenagers don't feel the freedom to express their opinions and questions that teens of the '60s and '70s felt. Communication has become a means for one teen to evaluate another. What they say, or the question they ask, or the emotions they show could lead to rejection by the rest of their peers.

As adults, we're more secure and open. We'll share our opinions. Our self-image is intact. We've learned that rejection of one of our ideas doesn't mean rejection of us. But, it's different with today's teenagers. We sometimes want to wave our hands in front of their eyes to see if anyone is home!

The absence of feedback—positive *or* negative—makes communication almost impossible. After all, communication is an exchange of information. It's the establishment of common ground.

As parents or grandparents of a teenager, or as adults who care about teens, you've probably experienced the frustration of communication at least once. But, how often have you and I sat like solid rock when our heavenly Father tried to communicate with us?

We think to ourselves, "God has given us wisdom and knowledge. Discussing our problems with Him means we're dumping *our* responsibility on the Lord." So we disconnect the line of communication, as it were, and set out to show God just how capable we are!

Strange, isn't it? Aren't we just like the teen who won't ask questions and won't show emotions? As adults, we often shout at our children, hoping that loudness will penetrate when logic hasn't. And sometimes, God has to "shout" at us, placing us in a situation where only His strength, His love, and His wisdom suffice.

The challenge of communication—we've all experienced it. We know the right words, and we say the right things. But, finally, we have to commit our words to the Lord, knowing the Holy Spirit is working, and the God-given truths presented are finding a listener.

Let's work together to communicate God's love. At the same time, let's strive not to frustrate God's communication to us. After all, it's God's communication to us and through us that takes us beyond our limitations of time, talent, and energy.

"Speak, Lord, for Your servant *is* listening."

YFC Editors

The Debriefing Session

A Key to Communication

DAVID & KAREN MAINS

Much has been said about the lack of parent-teen communication. But we've found a sure way of keeping the communication channels open. We call it the debriefing session, individual times with our kids when we can talk about what's going on in their world.

How parents structure this will differ. We are very active people and both travel quite a bit, yet we want to spend quality time with our children. So we try to arrange our schedules so that we're free during our kids' best talking times. For some kids that means right after school; for others, it's just before bed.

Karen usually has her debriefing times when the kids come home from school. She's pretty regular at it, though she sometimes misses when she's out of town.

Dave uses Saturday morning breakfast. He'll take one of the kids out to breakfast and catch up on what's going on in his life. The kids like this so much that when Randy came home from college he was a little miffed because Dave didn't take him out to breakfast. When Dave found out how much it meant to Randy, he quickly reinstated the practice.

No matter what time we do it, we both use the debriefing time for the same purpose—to find out what's going on in the lives of our children and to inform them about what's going on in our lives.

Debriefing basically begins with the question, "How was your day?" *But we really want to know.* If the answer is, "Oh, OK," we'll say something like, "What was good and what was bad about it?" This encourages more communication.

This time has become so valuable in terms of us being able to catch up on the children's days that we've started to debrief every day one of us is away. For instance, when Dave came back from a three-week trip to India, he told us about everything that happened to him. And we, in turn, told him about everything that happened to us while he was gone.

This is so important to us that sometimes we keep lists. That way we don't forget to share things that we really want the other family members to know about.

The process gives us a sense of emotional and psychological closure. It's necessary and healthy after any of the events in our lives to state to someone what happened and to know that that person is really listening to us.

Debriefing doesn't have to take a lot of time. It can just be ten minutes at the end of a child's school day. But, if we give our kids those minutes, they know they have communicated with us and that we are aware of what is happening in their lives.

These debriefing sessions give us the freedom to discuss just about anything. In fact, the older children regularly say to us, "Dad and Mother, thank you. We feel we can talk about anything with you, whether it is homosexuality in the world, or a negative attitude we're struggling with, or something we blew in our lives."

A variation of debriefing is something we do in a relaxed family setting, for example traveling in the car. It's a game called, "What's bad about the person and what's good?" It usually starts with "What's bad and what's good about

Dad?" The kids can be a little brutal, but they soften up because they know that eventually it's going to get around to what's bad and good about them.

This isn't a destructive process. In fact, when we say what's bad about a person, we might end with, "What can I do to help?" Or, we might realize that we haven't really encouraged the person to deal with the problem.

And we try to keep it in balance. For instance, if Mom has a pet peeve about Junior, Sis might share an entirely different point of view about how she's noticed

THE BIBLE ON COMMUNICATION

We all know the power of words. They can build us up with feelings of warmth and love or they can bring on the worst feelings of anger, hate, and isolation. And this power of communication proves never so dramatic as when it takes place within your family. The power of the tongue, compared to the rudder of a ship or fire that destroys forests, is well described in the Bible. So are the problems and solutions of communication. See for yourself what the Bible says about communication with God and your family.

Did you know that communication is not the ability to be audible, but the ability to be understood? In other words, just because you said it doesn't mean someone *heard* or *understood* you.

I. Time-tested ways to communicate with God
   1. Study God's Word—2 Timothy 2:15
   2. Pray. Prayer demonstrates trust in God and obedience.
      • Matthew 6:5-7—How to pray
      • Matthew 26:41—Why pray?
      • Luke 11:9-10—Results of prayer
II. Communicating with teenagers—three steps. One of the major responsibilities of being parents is to lead the child from dependence to independence. Good communication—establishing common ground—helps teens develop as independent, mature, *Christlike* adults.
   Key steps:
   1. Observe
   2. Listen
   3. Ask
      • Ask more questions than you try to answer—not yes/no questions
      • When you disagree, say why—dialogue
      • Allow other opinions (but still set guidelines for actions)
      • Don't show contempt—show love!
         Helpful verses to study: Ephesians 6:4; Ephesians 4:25-26; Ephesians 2:20; Psalm 37:7; 1 Corinthians 13:1-13.
III. Talking about your faith—words *and* actions go together
   • Romans 1:16—"I am not ashamed!"
   • Matthew 5:13-16—Communication through actions
   • Matthew 28:18-20—Communication through words
   • Ephesians 6:19-20—Pray for boldness in proclaiming

YFC Editors

her brother really working on that area. That puts the problem in a more realistic perspective.

There are barriers to this process. One of them is timing. Most Christians choose to confront when they are extremely angry. That's the worst possible time. Confrontation should be done in a relaxed, loving atmosphere. If we tried to discuss what's bad and good about Sis while she was experiencing an extreme emotional crisis, that would be ill-advised. But during a relaxed time she can grow from the experience and not be threatened by constructive criticism.

When a family wishes to start debriefing sessions, the parents themselves need to be vulnerable. In that way, the process can begin with them. Perhaps at a family dinner, parents can let their kids say what is bad and good about each of them. If the parents show they can take advice in stride, the kids will be open when the process turns to them.

Some kids may not be too eager to share in debriefing. But because we started doing this when the kids were young, they are used to it. They also know that we will never put them down or close them off with remarks like, "That's dumb," "That's stupid," or "You idiot." Instead, we respond, "Oh, that's interesting," or "Tell me what you're thinking."

When it's appropriate, we let the person make his own decision about what he shares with us. For instance, right now our son Joel is in swing choir, which is basically a dance group. When he came home and talked about it with us, we gulped and thought to ourselves, "Oh my goodness, that's very different from the way we were raised." But after talking the matter through, we let him make his own choice. The choice might not have been what we would have decided, but we were pleased that he had come and discussed it with us. In fact, we've decided to let all our kids exercise their adult levels of decision-making, whatever that level is.

Of course, that is done with our supervision and guidance. But by letting them make decisions, they know that we believe they are special people, that we respect them, and that we know they have used their ability to think critically about the decisions they have made.

There are levels of maturity. At different ages kids can make different decisions. Yet, as parents, we must also make some decisions for our kids. For instance, when Joel was a certain age, he thought he was old enough to date. But we didn't let him. He was miffed about it, but we talked it through and he respected our choice. We don't make decisions for our kids in an authoritarian fashion. We explain the reasons behind our choices so that the kids know why we make the rules we do.

This has been a growing experience. We make mistakes. But we're doing a better job with the younger children than with the older ones. And when we blow it, we admit it and say we're sorry about taking that approach. We try to figure out how we could do better or, at least, how we can grow from the situation.

Related Articles

Communication Killers

GARY DAUSEY

In all probability, you are reading this book because at some point in your life God gave you a child. We marvel at the creation of God as seen in a baby. The tiny fingers and toes, the alertness we sense, and the occasional smile all remind us of the miracle that has taken place.

In time, the child begins to speak and with a little more time, words are formed into sentences expressing the child's thoughts. It isn't long before the child begins to test the response to the words, "I won't!" or "No!" He or she may also test the same words on both parents, older brother or sister, or even Grandma and Grandpa, just to see if the response is the same.

As the child grows older, the issues become more complex, and the testing of the wills intensifies as parents seek to guide that child from total dependence to responsible independence.

During this growth process, it is absolutely essential that communication between parents and child flows without obstruction. We seek to communicate with each other through words, yet so often those words seem like such inadequate vehicles for our expression.

There was a study conducted at Michigan State University on communication between teenagers and their parents. Conducted by Dr. Gordon Sabine, it measured the responses of 3,000 teenagers and their parents. The bottom line of the research said that seventy-nine percent of the parents interviewed thought that they were communicating with their teenagers, but eighty-one percent of the teenagers said that their parents were not communicating with them.

During the teenage years, friends, money, dress, schoolwork, perceived laziness, and lifestyle all become focal points for the straining of relationships between parents and child. Often, though we really don't want to, we shut off the communication that is critical to the young person's development. Because this communication is so important, we must be aware of what we do that makes it break down.

What follows are what I consider to be some of the most deadly communication killers in the home:

• *Classic putdown.* Sometimes this may take the form of cheap humor at the young person's expense, but most often it can be found in phrases like, "You can't do anything right," or "You don't know anything about that."

What normally happens is that the teenager will withdraw from future conversation. Most teenagers have enough insecurities that they won't risk gaining a new one if they think they can avoid it by not talking to their parents.

• *Higher volume solution.* Most verbal arguments increase in volume at measured intervals. As one arguing person seeks to make his point stronger, he increases the volume; the other person must then counter with even higher volume until both parties end up screaming at each other. Very little can be accomplished under such circumstances.

Screaming at each other tends to be a fairly normal human response when we are fully frustrated and can't seem to convince the other person that we are right and he is wrong. I have a friend who has developed an ability to lower his voice in the midst of a debate. The impact is remarkable—as he lowers his voice, the other person tends to do the same. Have you ever attempted to carry on a full-scale argument when you are whispering to the other person? Surely not all of us can develop that skill, but we can all be aware that escalating the volume in a conversation very seldom aids us in our ability to convince the other party of anything.

• *Verbal overkill.* Many parents make a statement to their teenager and then restate their position over and over again. This tends to do little more than escalate the level of communication frustration.

It's fairly safe to start with the assumption that the young person actually heard you the first time. Most teenagers can hear fairly well. You only have to talk about something that you didn't intend for them to hear to discover that fact, even though they may have been down the hall or in their room with the radio turned on.

Perhaps the reason that they didn't respond to you the first time was because they have learned that you'll say it again. I believe our communication will be most successful if we make a clear statement once, make sure that the young person understands it and whatever negative consequence will follow if he fails to respond as expected. The key then, is in the manner in which we follow up. If our response is inconsistent with what we previously said, the young person will soon learn not to take our statements seriously.

• *Argument shift.* Sometimes a conflict will develop over a very specific issue but will degenerate into generalities. You know you've done this as soon as you start using phrases like "you never . . ." or "you always. . . ." When this happens, there is very little chance that any positive thought or action change will take place. Generally, both parties will just continue to get more and more

STEERING CLEAR OF GUNPOWDER WORDS

Even when you strongly disagree with what your teen is saying, be careful not to use what I call "gunpowder words." For example, avoid saying something like, "It really sounds like you hate that person." Judgmental or intense words like "hate" can set off an explosion. Try gently saying, "Could you tell me a bit more about that?" Or, "It sounds like you're really frustrated over that."

Eventually you can move to, "What do you suggest be done to try to solve this?" Let the young person come up with some suggestions first. Chances are he or she will be more open because you've done something surprising. You've upended the teen's assumption that "Mom isn't going to like this. She'll probably tell me to be quiet. I'm not going to get anywhere."

When a parent does something unexpected, the young person starts dropping the defenses. Then the two can really communicate.

Of course, sometimes we disagree so strongly with our kids that we get really uptight. We know that if we continue to talk, the gunpowder words will start flying. When that happens, say, "Well, I really appreciate your letting me know how you feel. I guess I need a little time to think about this. Why don't we get together in a couple of hours and talk about it then?"

Norman Wright

frustrated with each other.

• *Tarnished model.* We all tend to respond most favorably to those whom we respect. When a child loses respect for a parent for any reason, communication will be very strained. Our children are looking for models who are less confused than themselves. If they hear us say something, but know that our own lifestyles don't confirm it, all the words we use are worthless.

• *Silent language.* Anyone who has worked alongside someone whose hearing is impaired knows that words are not necessary for active communication. He or she has learned to respond to visual signals. Visual signals, however, are not the sole domain of the hearing-impaired. We all give such signals and we all learn to interpret these signals. A shrug of the shoulder, a tilted head, crossed arms, a stern face all enhance or take away from the words we use. We must decide if the body language we are using is helping or hindering our communication.

• *Fortune teller.* When you get to know someone really well, you learn to anticipate his next words. Sometimes you may be right and sometimes you may be wrong. You may have drawn certain conclusions from partial data whereas the other person with all of the data may come to another conclusion. It's imperative for good communication that you let the other person give you all of the facts before you draw your own conclusions and shut your mind off to the balance of the conversation. By all means, do not finish statements for the other person either verbally or in your mind.

• *Stone ears.* God has given to most of us the wonderful gift of hearing. It's nothing short of amazing how vibrations from another person can be captured in our ears and are then translated into electrical impulses that travel through our nerves to our brain and we, in turn, can understand the thoughts, as expressed in words, of the other person. Though we have this tremendous gift, so many of us act as though our ears were made of stone.

I was in a home some time ago where I watched as a young boy was attempting to explain something, which was of great importance to him, to his father. In the midst of this rather long and animated monologue, the father reached down, picked up a pair of stereo headphones, placed them on his head, and effectively shut out his son.

An entire chapter of this book is dedicated to the art of listening so I won't go into detail here, but I want to remind us that we can't seek to have open communication with our children if we aren't listening to what they're saying.

• *News network.* Many teenagers find themselves in a complex web of emotions and questions about life. They need someone to talk to, but they must feel secure that the person whom they choose will respect the confidential nature of their questions. As soon as that young person finds out or senses that you have shared this information with someone else, communication will cease. Though this young person may be crying out for help on the inside, he may never express it on the outside because his need for perceived external wholeness is so great.

• *Environmental context.* Have you ever watched a fly buzz around in a moving car and wondered if it must fly at fifty-five miles per hour to stand still if that's how fast the car is traveling? Have you ever asked yourself why attire worn by very conservative Christians at a beach would not be acceptable in the environment of a local church? The root of the answer in both cases is the same. It is the relationship between what is happening and its specific environmental context. Communication between parents and children fall prey to the same facts of life. The environment in which communication takes place may often be as important as the words themselves. Does the young person sense that the basis of your

228

communication is love? Admittedly, that may be difficult to sense in the midst of a heated argument, but there is a sizable difference in the outcome if the young person feels that the words he hears come from a context of hate and disdain rather than love.

• *Foreign culture.* If you've ever traveled to another country where you could not speak or understand the language, you know something of the frustration of not being able to communicate. In addition to language difficulties, there are often cultural differences that may be as difficult to interpret as the language.

Generally, most children and their parents speak the same national language. Occasionally, your son or daughter may need to update you on the current slang. There's very little more embarrassing for a teenager than to hear his parents use a current buzz word in the wrong context.

Strangely enough, though we are all living in the same house, the cultures of a teenager and his parents may be worlds apart. That is, what is important to the parents may not be at all important to the teenager. This may be even more true from teenager to parents.

It's not necessary that we change our culture to fit theirs, but it is important that we attempt to think through the words we use in light of what is important to them. Their identity is so closely tied to their teenage subculture that when, through words, we seek to separate them from their subculture it can often force a difficult choice for them. Often it will shut off communication with the parents.

There are many things which can kill good communication between parents and children. These are just a few. Rather than leave this on a negative note, however, let me suggest some things which may help the communication in your home:

• Consider the relative importance of the issue being discussed. It's very easy to treat all arguments as though they were of equal importance. A messy closet should not be treated the same as "doing drugs" or sexual promiscuity.

• Try to think through the long-term effect of your decision rather than just the immediate desired response. To gain the desired long-term effect, occasionally some compromise on the immediate issue may be in order. Your task as Christian parents is to move your children toward responsible independence in the context of Christian principles and standards. We walk a thin line with our children and we don't want to lose them. Rigidity in unimportant issues may push some teenagers over the line. Flexibility, when it doesn't compromise spiritual, moral, or ethical principles, may be the best policy.

• Let your humanity show. Be vulnerable with your teenagers when appropriate. Let them know the struggle you have over various issues. Admit that you're wrong when you are. They probably already know it. To deny it diminishes your credibility with them.

• Be consistent when disciplining your children. If they believe that they all are equals, communication will flow easier.

• Create opportunities to demonstrate trust to your children; don't be afraid to say to your children, no matter how old, that you love them. Communication functions best in an atmosphere of love and trust.

• Provide for informal opportunities for communication. Do things with your children where they feel comfortable opening up. It may be cooking together or fixing a car together or camping together. Sometimes it should be mother and daughter or father and daughter or mother and son or father and son.

• Be alert to physical and emotional problems which can affect your communication. Sometimes stresses in families over school grades may be related to laziness or lack of discipline. If that is the case, these matters must be addressed head-on. Sometimes, however, the school problems may be related to visual or hearing problems. Sometimes there may be learning disabilities related to time perception. This can occur with the most brilliant child. The way of dealing with the latter, however, is totally different than the former. If you are unsure of the nature of the problem, seek professional help.

There is very little more rewarding than to see families that work well together, families where love is evident. Such families rarely just happen. It takes a great deal of effort and patience on the part of all parties.

The family was God's idea and I find it reassuring to know that my wife and I are not alone in the desire for our family to be successful. The very God of Creation wants our family to be successful too. It's been my experience that. those whose families are working well are those who realize that human resourcefulness alone is not sufficient. It takes daily prayer and a firm commitment of your family to the Lord to provide the environment for a healthy home.

Related Articles

Talking to Teens

Learning How to Ask the Right Questions

GLANDION CARNEY

In learning the art of conversing with teens, parents can break through to their kids by asking the right questions that keep them from feeling defensive.

Understanding how to ask questions is the first step in learning to ask the right questions. Recognize the various kinds of questions you can ask. For example: "Did your day go well?" Or, "How was your day today?" Or, "What was unusual about your day today?" Or, "What was the most unique thing that happened to you today?" Each of these questions calls for a different level of response.

Two types of questions are close-ended questions and open-ended questions. Closed-ended questions, such as "Did your day go well?" call for a simple yes or no. Most teenagers seem to enjoy closed-ended questions because they don't have to commit themselves to converse or give any other information.

Open-ended questions, such as "What was the most unique thing that happened to you today?" cannot be answered with an easy yes or no. Teens are expected to converse beyond that level. And that means increased vulnerability—letting you into their world.

When parents ask questions is also important. For the most part, your day is filled with eight hours of work, the drive home, and a meal with the family around the table. While everyone talks about their day to a degree, often parents use this time to ask teens questions related to responsibility. When teens are not conversed with on a normal day-to-day level, inquisitions, such as "Did you do your homework?" or "Did you mow the lawn?" often fall on defensive ears. Teens also need to know that you are interested in *their* activities and in them as people.

Since questions are used to gain information, consider what kind of information you are trying to gain from your teenager. If you are seeking information about how the teenager's day went, what his interests and hobbies are, or what his goals are, open-ended questions will lead to more stimulating dialogue.

Often parents get caught up with asking closed-ended questions because the questions they are asking don't relate to personal issues, such as how the teen's day went or what his goals are. For example, "Did you do this?" or, "Will you do this by such and such a time?" Often questions are couched in the form of advice, such as, "If I were you, I would. . . ." For example, "If I were you, I would definitely go back to that teacher and talk about that math assignment!"

TUNE IN

Unless your teen learns to listen, you'll have a lot of one-way conversations. But saying, "Here's what you should do to be an effective listener," probably won't be greeted with enthusiasm.

Try holding out the "bait" and backing off. Model the principles of good listening. Then ask, "How do you feel about picking up what your friends say? Do you catch it all? Can you really tune into them?"

When your teen answers, "No, I don't really hear all they say," suppress your instinct to blurt out the principles. Just say, "Well, I have three or four ideas that might help. If you ever want to hear them, just let me know."

Then wait. Most likely it will only be a matter of time before your young person says, "Hey, what are those four ideas? I want to know them."

Norman Wright

It's not really a true question. And it's not really a true command. And it can lead to defensiveness.

Teenagers like to assume that parents aren't interested in their world. For that reason, especially, you need to ask questions. Then your teenager can't come back and say "You're not interested in my world." Even though he may say he doesn't care if you are interested or not, he at least wants you to be interested to the degree that you know what is happening in his life.

An indication of this happened recently in our family. My wife and I were about to leave for Jamaica. All week long my daughter wanted to go to a football game. Yet two minutes before we got ready to go out the door she asked, "Can I go to a football game on Friday?" I said, "No you can't. You asked at the last minute; we don't know who's supervising; who's going to pick you up; and what the plans are."

That, to me, was an example of how teens want parents in their world because we have to make decisions. They are under the authority of the parents, and that is why they need to reveal at least a *little* to us.

Once parents seem to show too much interest in a teen's world—especially between the ages of fifteen and seventeen—the teen begins to feel uncomfortable because his turf is being invaded. Yet teens frequently "test" their parents to see if they are really interested in their world and activities.

When teens feel threatened by questions, parents often begin to feel threatened too and maybe a bit suspicious. Rather than casually sitting back and trying to evaluate the issue at hand, the questioning becomes panicky.

Granted, some teenagers have beautiful, open relationships with their parents, where they simply tell them everything. But that is something that the parents and teens have cultivated over the years, not something that begins at age fifteen.

Each child is different. Some are very secretive, closed, and into their own world. Others are very open, direct, and willing to let you know what is happening. Unfortunately, parents often make the mistake of establishing a principle for one child, and then use it as *the law* for their other children.

Not only must parents learn to ask the right questions, they must learn the art of conversing on the teen's level. I think it is very easy to have an open-ended conversation if the environment is nonthreatening, and the parents and teen both feel comfortable about the dialogue. Decide that you won't be defensive in all of your conversations. Talk about sports or shopping or activities or planning a vacation. Cultivate a relaxed, free-flowing posture that invites open discussion.

If a parent is under a great deal of stress and the dialogue seems stilted and formal, a teen is quick to pick up on it. Beware when the conversation becomes a confrontation.

If you find yourself becoming defensive, withdraw from the conversation. It would be helpful, in that instance, to put yourself in your teen's situation. Rethink the questions you want to ask and the points you want to make. Talk with your spouse, thinking through the responses to the answers you might have. This will help you feel less defensive when you speak with your teen. Learn how to pose the right questions to get the information you need from your teen, so he won't feel defensive either.

Teenagers will naturally feel defensive as they are growing up. All their lives they've been told what to do and have been greatly influenced by parents, teachers, and others. Suddenly they realize they have a desire to be independent and make some of their own decisions. The teen years are a time when kids sense themselves really developing, and their interests are growing in different areas.

Parents have a way of seeing their teens as children. As teens sense this, they struggle more intensely for the freedom to make some of their own decisions. Because these are first attempts at independence, teens may make irresponsible decisions. Parents then tend to become more defensive when dealing with them.

Developing a means of communication just takes time. Work patiently toward the goal of developing an open, nurturing communication style that avoids defensiveness.

Related Articles

Catch the Feeling

Teens Communicate with More Than Just Words

NORMAN WRIGHT

One of the problems in our society is that too few people take the time to listen to and understand others. Maybe the greatest gift parents can give a teen is undivided attention and time, finding out how the adolescent feels and caring about it.

Understanding your teen's feelings is vital because it's the gateway to true communication. And the young person whose mom or dad takes the time to understand knows he's loved.

But it's hard to tell others about your feelings—especially family members. That's because we're afraid of being judged, afraid the information might be used against us later, afraid of the strong reactions and open displays of anger or ridicule that typify some families.

Creating an atmosphere of trust and nonretaliation is crucial. That starts not with the teenager, but with the parents. Can you express your own emotions? Do you understand how your spouse feels? If not, start to remedy the situation by picking up a thesaurus and spotting synonyms that describe how you feel. Then find another adult with whom to practice expressing your emotions—it's better than trying to smooth off the rough spots with a volatile son or daughter.

Next let your practice partner express his or her feelings—including some you may find threatening. Rather than letting those feelings bother you, stay in a listening mode. Remember that the object is to discover the other person's feelings, not to censure them.

As you practice, and as you "graduate" to talking with your teen,

---

LEARNING YOUR TEEN'S LANGUAGE

Whenever a husband and wife come to me for counseling, one of the first things I try to do is to learn their language. I don't mean English or Spanish—I mean the way they think. Persons perceive the world differently—through what is seen, through what is heard, or through feelings. Only when I understand them can I truly "speak their language," and maybe even teach them a new one.

It's the same way with parents and adolescents. Parents need to discover how their teen takes the world in. Is it through the eyes? If the young person often says things like, "I see what you mean," or, "Do you get the picture?" you're probably dealing with a visual person. Similar statements about sounds or feelings can tag an emotionally or auditory-oriented person.

Once you've discovered how your teen tends to think, try to communicate at that level—appealing to the senses he or she uses most often.

Norman Wright

keep the following guidelines in mind:

• *Develop a feeling vocabulary.* Learn to speak on an emotional level. This is probably easier for mothers and daughters than for fathers and sons, since in our culture the male's emotions are stunted and blunted. An adolescent boy may fear his feelings, especially anger, and balk at discussing them. By word and example you can affirm that it's OK to have feelings, to talk about them, to cry.

• *Remember that emotions are often symptoms.* Depression, for example, is a signal that something else is going wrong in our lives. Anger doesn't start as anger; it grows from hurt, fear, or frustration. So when your teen rants and raves and blows off steam, go to the cause of the problem. Say something like, "Boy, I can tell that something has really frustrated you. Maybe you feel hurt or rejected." You'll bypass the explosion that might have occurred if you'd merely reacted to the anger. And you may be amazed at how your teen will open up and talk about what's really bothering him or her.

• *Watch the body language.* When you talk with someone face-to-face, your words make up only about seven percent of the message. Your tone of voice counts for about thirty-eight percent, and your body language (posture, expression, gestures) for a whopping fifty-five. So if your teenager says, "Oh, I'm fine," but the tone is downcast and the body slumps, you'd better believe the nonverbal message. Body language may not be as easily interpreted as words—for instance, a shrug can mean "I don't know" or "Don't bother me"—but a combination of all the clues should be pretty clear. Reflect the adolescent's mood with a statement like, "You're telling me you're fine, but the way you're dragging around today makes me wonder whether something else is going on."

• *Keep your teen's feelings confidential.* Say your teenage son gets upset one evening and feels free enough to cry in front of you. A month later he has some friends over, and you let it slip that he cried. Embarrassing a young person in that way could be the last straw if the relationship is fragile. At the least, it's inappropriate.

Even if you practice and follow these guidelines, of course, it's no guarantee that your young person will be more communicative. Adolescents are unpredictable, and they experience tremendous mood swings. But the chances are that your teens will be more open about their feelings if they see you and your spouse (or you and another adult if you're a single parent) talking honestly about emotions.

Related Articles

Answer Teens' Questions

BARRY ST. CLAIR

Parents have a tremendous responsibility to create an atmosphere where teens can ask questions and receive answers. I base this on Ephesians 6:4: "Fathers, do not exasperate your children; instead, bring them up in the training and instruction of the Lord" (NIV).

Unfortunately, it seems as though we've raised a generation of nonthinkers. Most evangelicals today are unwilling to answer questions, especially about sensitive areas such as marraige and the church. This mentality is carried over to their teens. When their children ask, "Why?" many parents reply, "Because I told you so. Don't ask me that question again."

We need to consider Jesus' life and ministry. His primary way of teaching was to ask and answer questions. Asking and answering questions can be great learning tools as a parent responds to a teen's curiosity.

Sometimes young people ask guarded, smoke-screen questions. Then parents must analyze and determine the real issue. A question like, "What's wrong with drinking?" could easily be the deeper questions, "Am I OK? Do you really love me?"

I believe there are six major reasons why parents need to answer their teens' questions. First, teenagers want to be treated like adults. They may act like a nine-year-old one day, and then turn around and act like an adult the next. But the more you treat them like adults, the more mature they will become.

Second, when parents answer questions, they are showing a sensitivity to their teens' needs. Third, and closely related to this is the fact that parents can provide a needed sense of security when they take time to listen and give advice. Teens need to know they are not "off the wall" when they ask questions.

A fourth reason parents need to answer questions is that it builds wisdom into the lives of teens. Proverbs 4:3-4 says, "When I was a boy in my father's house, still tender, and an only child of my mother, he taught me" (NIV). In these verses, the father is building wisdom into his son's life by asking and answering questions.

A final reason for asking and answering questions is that it helps teens learn to

THE POWER OF A LETTER

Over and over again I've seen families transformed by a rather simple idea. Here's how it works: A family member makes a conscious decision to take the time to sit down and write a letter to another member of the family. He may even drop it in the mail and have the postman deliver it. This is often a great way to open up communication that has been blocked for some time, because instead of trying to say what's on your mind, the letter will get the job done more effectively.

In the letter you can express your love, your appreciation for kindness, your hopes, your frustrations, and your forgiveness—if that's needed. Always try to be candid, but in a framework of love and affirmation for the other person.

Usually a letter is better-said, better-heard, and better-remembered. You'll say things better in a letter because you won't be diverting your loved ones in conversation. The people you love will hear a letter better because they won't be preoccupied with having to think up an immediate response. And they'll remember a letter better because they'll be able to read a letter over and over again.

Learn to write letters to people you love.

Ronald P. Hutchcraft

make their own decisions. Sometimes parents need to refrain from answering their teens' questions and ask questions of their teens instead.

Parents need to ask three kinds of questions: observation, interpretation, and application. Observation questions are concerned primarily with information—"Did you do that?" or "Have you noticed this?" Interpretative questions are concerned with feelings and convictions—"How do you feel about that?" Application questions such as, "What do you think you ought to do?" relate more to decision-making.

Following are two diagrams showing methods that parents sometimes use as they interact with their teenagers. Notice that these methods of interaction do nothing to help teens make good decisions.

Diagram 1: Interaction with teenagers is almost totally on a *restrictive/unloved* basis. These teens feel unloved and overdisciplined and often respond by rebelling or getting involved in crime.

```
                    Loved
Restrictive ─────────┼───────── Autonomous
    Teenager         │
                  Unloved
```

Diagram 2: Interaction with teenagers is almost totally on an *autonomous/unloved* basis. These teens feel unloved and undisciplined and often enter adulthood with no goals or direction in life.

```
                    Loved
Restrictive ─────────┼───────── Autonomous
                     │      Teenager
                  Unloved
```

The following diagram shows the way parents should properly interact with their children. The result of this type of interaction is that teenagers become capable of making good decisions.

Diagram 3: This is a *progression* from a restrictive/love relationship as a child, to a more autonomous/love relationship as a teenager to a totally autonomous/love relationship as an adult. These teens feel loved, properly disciplined, and capable of making good decisions as adults.

```
                    Loved
Child ──────────▶ Teenager ──────────▶ Adult
Restrictive ─────────┼───────── Autonomous
                  Unloved
```

Unfortunately, many teens move into adolescence with parents who have kept the "lid on." This causes tremendous problems. Adolescence is not a disease, but a time when teens are seeking out their own identity. By asking and answering questions in love, parents can help their child find himself, his relationship to the world around him, and an intensely personal and creative walk with the Lord Jesus Christ.

Related Articles

Chapter 6: Teen's Misconceptions about Life and How Parents Can Answer Them

Chapter 9: The Art of Communication

Time for Togetherness
ADRIAN ROGERS

I've learned that simply being in my children's presence is not necessarily spending quality time with them. Many families spend time together, but their attention is focused on the television set or a sporting event or something else, not on one another. So even though the family is in the same room, they are not spending quality time together.

In our family's experience, our best quality time is often unstructured. But unstructured time can be hard to come by. Not only do we have to plan time and take time, we also have to make time. That is, we have to set some time aside as priority time, and then we have to be careful not to think of that time as wasted even though it is unstructured.

I have observed that when our family spends unstructured time together, God brings wonderful things to pass. He draws the family together and reveals His love for us and our love for one another.

We've often laughed at ourselves when we've been trying to have a good time. You can't make good times happen— they are little serendipities. But when a family spends unstructured time together, suddenly there's a revelation of a great truth or a great need, and God moves in. I've seen this happen time and time again in our own home.

I've found that the very best Bible teaching I've done with my children has not been when I put them in a chair and said, "Now you sit still while I preach a little sermon." The best Bible teaching has come in the course of life.

One day I took our family to the zoo on an unstructured day. We were really looking forward to spending a tremendous time together. But no sooner had we gotten to the zoo than it began to rain, one of those rains that fills your shoes up to the tops. We had to scoot for the car. It looked like everything we'd planned had gone wrong.

We sat there in the car, soaking wet, and somehow began talking about the love and providence of the God who "sendeth rain on the just and unjust" (Matt. 5:45), who tells us that "all things work together for good" (Rom. 8:28). There we sat, like ducks covered with water, discussing the love of God. As I look back on it, that time in the car was better than time in the zoo would have been. Our family still talks about it. Now,

we couldn't have made that happen, but God gave us that unstructured time and we used it to teach our children.

For times like that to happen, parents have to be the catalysts. Most parents have probably had far more opportunities for times like that than they realize, but they haven't optimized them. They haven't taken advantage of the time, and they haven't prepared themselves with the Word of God so that it can overflow into the child's life.

On another occasion our family, again spending unstructured time together, was going to Pirates' World in Fort Lauderdale. When I got to the gate, I realized I didn't have enough money for all of us and it was not the kind of place where they cash checks. One of the children had turned twelve several days before this. Children under twelve were admitted at a discounted rate which would have allowed us to get In with the money on hand. We could have gotten in if we had said he was eleven, but he hadn't been eleven for almost a week.

I suppose most people would have said, "Well, a few days won't make any difference." But I refused to be dishonest. We explained to the children that God says we must be honest in all things. We looked up a friend who was willing to cash a check for us, so we were able to get in and have a good day together after all.

I think our sons grew up to be honest men because they saw their mom and dad being honest, not only in the big things but also in the very little things that to many people don't make much difference. But to us they made a big difference. And because of the unstructured time we spent together, our children saw our principles in action.

Joyce and I think it is important to include friends in our unstructured family time. Our children have always been free to bring their friends home, whether or not they plan ahead. If we're going out, we're happy for them to bring friends along.

Since ours is the pastor's home of a large church, we frequently have guests. We have tried, when we have friends in the home, to include our children in the conversation. Something very beautiful has resulted: our children's friends are our friends, and our friends have become our children's friends. When our children join us and our friends, they are able to absorb their wisdom and to see what genuine Christian friendship is. When we join them and their friends, we can observe who they're seeing and what their values are. Since our children enjoy our friends and we enjoy theirs, we have not had any great difficulty with their keeping bad company or being in places unknown to us.

Spending unstructured time together does not have to be expensive. We've found that the best vacations do not necessarily cost the most. The best ones are the ones the whole family plans together. If the girls help with the cooking or the boys help with getting together the camping or fishing equipment, the family interacts. Nobody is just a spectator, like a museum-goer or a movie-watcher.

Planning and sharing unstructured time together forces interaction between parents and teens. This interaction, if the parents are alert to the possibilities, can be the best kind of quality time. It can serve to teach lessons and build relationships like nothing else can.

Related Articles

The Importance of Admitting Mistakes

BRUCE B. BARTON

Believe it or not, apologies improve communication. Yet many parents try to be 100 percent right, to be the "answer man" in every situation, to have the final word. They believe that they must be strong, never give in, never convey any shortcomings or personal weaknesses.

It's very painful to acknowledge your inadequacies, to admit that you're wrong. Younger children tend to put their parents on a pedestal and parents enjoy this elevated position. They like to be admired and appreciated. They may like the power and control. Frankly, they may not want to come down. Parents' egos can become so involved that they are unable to think clearly and do what's right for the children.

There are many benefits of saying, "I made a mistake," "I failed," or "I have a problem." Here are some of them:

• Admitting mistakes removes barriers and promotes sharing. Teenagers are very aware of their own shortcomings and mistakes. If they feel that it's OK to make a mistake, then they can more easily relate to their parents.

• Admitting mistakes clears the channels for real communication. When both parents and teenagers honestly admit to having problems, they are standing on the same level. Neither one is looking up or

238

down on the other person.
• Apologies create warmth. A feeling of camaraderie sets in as parents and teens recognize they are growing as co-members of the family, fellow sufferers, fellow soldiers, and fellow pilgrims on the path of life.
• Admitting failures limits unrestrained idealism. If children go too long observing unreal parents who never have any problems or flaws, the shock of seeing parents fail can be very destructive. More importantly, children need to see the way parents face life's problems to learn to deal with their own problems.
• Admitting mistakes opens the way to adult-to-adult problem-solving. If children are treated like adults, then they can respond as adults and face problems in the same way. They are better prepared to be parents themselves.

Related Articles

"I WAS WRONG"

In conversing with teens, it is especially important for parents to admit their own mistakes and problems to facilitate better communication. When parents model the behavior they desire from their children, it is learned, and not just heard.

For example, if parents have an argument and the argument involves the children or if they overhear it, the parent at fault needs to admit this to the kids. Say, "You know, Mom (or Dad) and I had an argument, and I want to apologize to you children. We teach you children not to argue, but we've argued. It's important to understand that we make mistakes too and we're sorry. Please forgive us." I think that is the means of creating the kind of relationship that will foster healthy communication.

When children see your openness to be honest with them, they will be more willing to admit their wrongs. Teens soon learn that *everyone* makes mistakes on occasion. Being prideful and not admitting your failures often makes you seem less truthful or respectful in their eyes. As someone has aptly said, "What you're doing speaks so loudly I can't hear what you're saying." We have a responsibility to model the behavior we expect from our teens.

The blow can be damaging when a child wakes up one day to learn that his parents have fallen off their self-imposed pedestal. Honesty breeds closer family relationships.

When you make a wrong judgment call and accuse one of your kids of doing something that you later find out he didn't do at all, go immediately and apologize. Let your teens see that you are real. Share the successes and failures in your own life. They can't help but be attracted by your vulnerability.

Glandion Carney

What to Do When Your Teen Doesn't Want Advice

DAVID HOWARD

When it came time for our youngest son to choose a college, I stayed pretty much in the background. He was being recruited by a number of schools for his wrestling ability but he decided not to accept any wrestling scholarships. Instead, he wanted to go to school on his own, so he would be free.

Communication was limited between us at that time and I thought he didn't want any of my advice. So I backed off, respected his decision, and didn't pressure him.

In hindsight, I wish that I had urged him to consider more seriously an athletic scholarship. Because he didn't go out for college wrestling, he didn't exercise the discipline that athletics builds into a person involved in a structured program. As a result, his academic work suffered.

Our son's lack of discipline was related to his spiritual life. Personal discipline is hard enough for any of us under the best of circumstances, but when one's spiritual goals are unclear it is even harder. Thankfully, his academic problem at college made him realize that he couldn't make it on his own and was one of the reasons why he came back to the Lord. But he also said he wished someone had told him more about the consequences of his decision and given him more guidance when he was choosing a college.

Looking back, I see that I should have said, "Son, I'm going to take you to some of the colleges that are interested in you." Instead, I stayed too far out of the decision-making process.

Parents need sensitivity from the Lord as to when to put pressure on a teen and when to back off. When to give advice to a teen who doesn't feel he needs it is difficult to decide and there are no easy answers.

Related Articles

"Give Me Another Chance"
Reopening the Doors to Communication

CHARLES R. SWINDOLL

Sometimes the light dawns late. Parents suddenly realize that they haven't been assuming the appropriate role, and now they've got a teenager on their hands. This can be a rude awakening, and the parents are lost for advice.

When this is the case, I put a high priority on what I call open-ended conversation. It's easy to give a lecture or lose your temper and spout, "Get this straight because I'm not going to tell you again!"

But if you find yourself realizing that you've got a challenging kind of situation in front of you, sit down with your teen and open a conversation by discussing some of the things you've been observing.

For example, "You know, Bob, I've suddenly begun to feel some fear or uncertainty about. . . ." Begin by unzipping your emotions.

Admit some negligence on your part. Say, "I'm supposed to be the father in this family and I realize that I haven't been much of a dad. I've been buried in my job. Your mom said she's noticed that you're running around with a group that concerns her."

Then admit that you're not sure what to do. Say, "I'm not sure what the best thing to do is, and I'd like to talk with you about that." Open up and tell your teen the way you wish things were and express your desire to do something to help the family move in that direction. Be willing to meet your teen more than halfway. Ask him how you can help him and tell him you want to talk about ways he can help you.

This approach is quite different from the easy "hit-and-run" method of saying, "You're running around with a bunch of hippies and drug pushers and if I catch you with them one more time, it's no more wheels!" That method usually results in a teen's rebellion—the teen ends up running with the crowd you disdain.

Making yourself vulnerable and being humble takes guts. It takes a real commitment on the parents' part to work toward a viable solution. But it's the better way.

An opposite extreme, perhaps, of the parents who suddenly learn they have been too lenient with their children are the parents who suddenly realize that they have been too strict. When parents have set up inviolable, overbearing household rules in an attempt to control the child, they must again begin by conversing with the teen. If the standard the rule is based on is a good one, keep it. But lessen or change the associated rule. Pray for wisdom in making the rules more flexible.

Try to stress the fact that you want to maintain the administration of the home, but that you're ready to do it under a new philosophy. If you are open and honest and willing to take responsibility, the teenager will probably be excited about the change.

It's never too late to work on your relationship with your children. It's easier to work with children when they're younger and have more teachable hearts, but anytime is the right time to do what's right.

"Therefore, to one who knows the right thing to do, and does not do it, to him it is sin" (James 4:17, NASB). Don't ever let pride rob you of the joy of affecting your children for good. You can still have a powerful effect on teens.

_____

Related Articles

HOW TO DEVELOP
LASTING RELATIONSHIPS

- How to really love your teenager
- Is forgiveness always necessary?
- How to become involved in the lives of your children
- Who really gets no respect: parents or teens?

- Can parents make up for their lack of love and discipline in the early years?
- Is honesty always the best policy with teenagers?

Toward the end of a well-known play, two boys are standing on the back porch after their father's funeral. Their father was a salesman who spent all his time traveling and working, always trying to make the big sale. But as the boys look at the cement step that they and their dad built together one Saturday—he had gotten a wheelbarrow and a pile of sand and a shovel and cement, and they had mixed the cement and poured it—they say, "There's more of Dad on this back stoop than in all the sales he ever made."

This story, one of the saddest in modern literature, sums up our society's value structure that makes it easy for us to miss developing relationships. But our most treasured moments come from human relationships, not from worldly success. A boy raised on beans with his father is better off than a boy raised on steak without him.

How to Really Love Your Teenager
ROSS CAMPBELL, M.D.

Unconditional love is the basic foundation for a solid relationship with your teenager, for only unconditional love can prevent problems such as resentment, guilt, fear, or the insecurity of feeling unwanted.

Without unconditional love, parenting is a confusing and frustrating burden. The love acts as a guiding light, showing you where you are with your teenager and what to do next. When you begin with unconditional love, you can then build your knowledge and expertise in guiding your teenager and filling his needs on a daily basis.

Unconditional love means loving a teenager, no matter what he looks like, no matter what his assets and liabilities are, no matter how he acts. This does not mean you always like his behavior. Unconditional love means you love him even when you detest his behavior.

Unconditional love is an ideal. You can't love a teenager—or anyone else—100 percent of the time. But the closer you come to this goal, the more satisfied and confident you will feel, and the more pleasant your teenager will be.

It helps to constantly keep in mind that

teenagers are children, that they will tend to act like teenagers, and that much teenage behavior is unpleasant. If you convey love to them only when they please you (conditional love), they will not feel genuinely loved. But if you do your part as parents and love them despite their unpleasant behavior, they will be able to mature and give up their unpleasant ways. Children who are loved unconditionally feel good about themselves. They learn to control their behavior as they grow into adulthood.

Do you know what is the most important question on your teenager's mind? Without realizing it, he is continually asking, "Do you love me?" It is absolutely the most important question in his life. And he asks it primarily through his behavior rather than with words.

Having a warm feeling of love in your heart for your teenager is wonderful, but it's not enough. Saying "I love you" to a teenager is great and should be done, but it's not enough. For your teenager to know and feel that you love him, you must also love him behaviorally because he is still primarily behaviorally oriented. He sees your love for him by what you say and do, but what you do carries more weight. He is far more affected by your actions than by your words.

It is important to remember that your teenager has an emotional tank. He has

---

THE LOVE GIFT

Teens get a sense of security by seeing a stable relationship between their parents. Though they like to tease parents about their closeness, they appreciate the stability.

My wife and I are affectionate and when our kids catch us in an embrace in the kitchen, we get it! "There they go again. Mom and Dad are making out." But they love it.

One of the greatest gifts you can give your children is to love your spouse. Children learn the value of that.

Be affectionate toward your children. But respect their desires in public. It's not unusual for a junior higher to act as if you have leprosy when you let him out of the car at school.

I've seen mothers force their kids to kiss them good-bye in the parking lot. That signals an insecure parent. It's a doting and smothering kind of love—not an adult love.

My thirteen- and sixteen-year-olds still ask me to walk up the stairway to tuck them in at night. Recently, I was watching a game on television and my son said, "Dad, I know the game's not over, but can you tuck me in?"

I went upstairs, tucked him in, and he asked me if I wanted to pray. Now this is a thirteen-year-old who would never publicly admit that he and his dad pray together at night. But he brings it up.

Sometimes I crawl in right beside him in bed, and we just talk and share what's on our hearts.

Those are precious moments.

Love your spouse. Love your children. And don't be afraid to show it. Just don't force it.

Charles R. Swindoll

certain emotional needs, and whether these needs are met (through love, understanding, discipline, and so on) helps determine how he feels—whether he is content, angry, depressed, or joyful. It also strongly affects his behavior—whether he is obedient, disobedient, whiny, perky, playful, or withdrawn. Naturally, the fuller the tank, the more positive the feelings and the better the behavior. Only if the emotional tank is full can a teenager be expected to be his best and do his best. It is your responsibility as parents to do all you can to keep the emotional tank full.

A teenager will strive for independence in typical adolescent ways—doing things by himself, going places without family, testing parental rules. But he will eventually run out of emotional gasoline and come back to his parents for emotional maintenance—for a refill. This is what we want, as parents of teenagers. We want our adolescents to be able to come to us for emotional maintenance when they need it.

There are several reasons this refilling is so important. Teenagers need much emotional nurture to function at their best and to grow to be their best. They desperately need full emotional tanks in order to feel the security and self-confidence they must have to cope with peer pressure and other demands of adolescent society. Without this confidence, they tend to succumb to peer pressure and experience difficulty upholding wholesome, ethical values. Emotional refilling is crucial because, while it is taking place, it is possible to keep open lines of communication between parents and teenagers. When a teenager's tank is empty and he seeks parental love, communication is so much easier.

Most parents do not realize how important it is for their teenagers to be able to come to them to have their emotional tanks refilled. During times when a teenager is striving for independence, he may upset his parents to such an extent that they overreact emotionally, usually with anger. This emotional overreaction, if too excessive or frequent, makes it extremely difficult and perhaps impossible for the teenager to return to his parents for emotional refills.

Then, if parent-child communication is broken, a teenager may turn to his peers for emotional nurture. What a dangerous and frequently disastrous situation this is! For the teenager will then be easily susceptible to peer pressure, to influences of religious cults, and to unscrupulous persons who use young people.

When your teenager tests you by striving through inappropriate behavior to be independent, you must be careful not to overreact emotionally. Regardless of how your teenager expresses his drive for independence, you must keep open the avenues by which he returns to you to have his emotional tank refilled. This is crucial if he is to enter adulthood as a whole person.

Related Articles

244

Get Involved!

The Family Can't Grow without You

B. CLAYTON BELL

There are a wide variety of positive experiences that parents should provide their teenagers. They run the gamut from the way families eat their meals together to taking vacations together. Parents who love their children and really try to enjoy them—talking together at meals about dates, programs, or problems (in a positive way rather than by nagging and complaining)—provide something very helpful.

In looking back on my own childhood, I remember my parents playing a lot of games with us children. We enjoyed sitting together and playing Rook, Scrabble, and other games. That was fun! As a parent, I've tried to provide similar activities for our children. My wife isn't particularly a game player, but I've taught our children gin rummy and other games.

I think television can be a great deterrent to family togetherness. Some television programs are worth watching together, but some are just time-wasters. Parents have to decide if watching a television program is a positive family experience or merely an escape from one another. We have been pretty selective in what the children watch and have tried to pick shows to watch together.

We often tried to provide some alternative experiences. For instance, in our home, as long as we had at least one child in high school, Friday night was high school football night. We did not accept other commitments on those nights. Even if I had a wedding rehearsal, I made sure it was over in time to get to the football game with my daughter and her friends. We sometimes got a van and took a bunch of kids together.

We also tried to plan our vacations so that the whole family could be involved. I love the mountains, so I would have preferred to go to Colorado. But all the kids liked the beach better so we went to the beach. When the kids were younger, we took some cross-country trips that were great experiences. Now my wife and I are planning on guiding some tours, on which we hope one or more of our children will go.

Again, it's a matter of priority. Is it important to get away from the kids, or is it important to provide activities that include them?

"YOU ARE IMPORTANT TO ME"

Children need to hear, through our words and actions, "I love you. I care for you. I want you to become God's maximum young man or young woman. And I am committed to you, for as long as you wish, to help you to be the best that God wants you to be. I will be praying for you. I will be here to counsel. I am prepared to make sacrifices if necessary to help you. You are important to me."

Bill Bright

Love Is Action

RONALD P. HUTCHCRAFT

Sure, you love your teenager. But does he *feel* loved? If he's not getting your message, it's like a radio station transmitting a signal that's not received—the two of you are on different wavelengths.

"Of course he knows I love him," you protest. "I bought him a nice stereo; he's got a nice room—what more could a kid ask for?" But teens today take these things for granted. They never knew what it was like to grow up in a poor family without a house, car, or job, so these materialistic goods aren't important to them.

What *is* important is what they were deprived of when they were growing up: their parents' time. So while you were working hard to earn money to show your kids you loved them, they were wishing you would stay home and spend time with them instead.

It may be easier to buy your teenager a TV than to sit down and talk to him, but shortcuts to loving won't work. You have to love your kids in ways that make them feel loved. Show them you care by loving them during the *the tough times, the talk times, the touch times, and the together times.*

Loving your children in *the tough times* is the acid test of real love. How do you feel when your kids have embarrassed, hurt, or disappointed you? This is when they need your love the most. Love should not be rewarded or withdrawn based on how your child performs.

Loving your child when he fails is like watching a football game. Your kid is carrying the ball and making yardage, but then he drops the ball on the one-yard line. Everybody in the stands stops cheering and leaves, disappointed. But your child needs to know that there are still two people up there rooting him on: Mom and Dad. He needs to know that you support him, even when he's a loser.

Everybody loves a winner. It's the unlovable, low times when teens can find out how much they're really loved. Bad grades, troublemaking friends, or wrong decisions are all opportunities to love, not condemn, your teenager.

You also need to love your teens during *the talk times.* They need to feel that you think they're worth communicating with. The best talk times occur in the spontaneous, unstructured settings of life: when you're taking a walk with them or putting them to bed at night. These are times when you can share God's principles with your kids: "Impress them on your children. Talk about them when you sit at home and when you walk along the road, when you lie down and when you get up" (Deut. 6:7, NIV).

Make it a point to give each family member your undivided attention at least once a day. You don't have to spend a lot

246

of time with them—just be sure you're consistently devoted to doing it. Sometimes, it needs to be for an hour, other times, only a couple minutes; but you should be undistracted and not preoccupied or on your way to something else. We've got to earn our wings every day in this love business.

But talking is not enough. Teens need to be loved during *the touch times* too. Everybody needs to be touched—touching is so crucial that babies who are not fondled will die.

When babies grow up to be teenagers,

HOME AND HUMOR

The other day I overheard my daughter tell a friend that her daddy was "funny." At first I thought she meant "peculiar," but then I realized that she was referring to my sense of humor. It was a great compliment (and helped me feel better about my parenting efforts).

Too often, I think, we as parents take ourselves too seriously, and every problem and situation at home becomes a matter of "life and death." If continued, this attitude will cast a pall, rendering the family thoroughly unenjoyable.

I'm not sure why this occurs. Perhaps Mom and Dad are struggling with so many pressures and problems that it is difficult to relax. Maybe they're insecure, always feeling that they are on trial and every confrontation is a "power struggle," so they are unable to laugh at themselves. Or perhaps they think it's wrong to laugh. Whatever the reason, home is not a fun place to be. (Note: If you're unsure whether this applies to you, ask yourself: "Can the kids tell the difference between when I'm kidding and when I'm serious?")

Whatever the reason(s), if your home fits the description, here are some suggestions for loosening things up and having fun at home.

1. Tell the children about your childhood, not to teach a lesson, but just to let them catch a glimpse of the real you.

2. Go through old scrapbooks, wedding pictures, photo albums, and yearbooks. Nothing can be quite as funny as seeing Mom and Dad in those funny clothes and haircuts. (Take a lot of pictures of the family and periodically check out these "blasts from the past.")

3. Initiate a "memory box" which can be reviewed together annually.

4. See a funny movie together—read comics, etc.

5. Play with your kids—games that *they* want to play. Don't be ashamed to play softball even if you can't hit the ball!

6. Plan a week of humor, without jokes.

7. Have family activities away from distractions and interruptions. Camping vacations are ideal for this.

8. Be vulnerable to your kids—talk about the silly things you've done.

9. Realize that different things are funny to different people. Learn to laugh at yourself.

In a capsule, learn to enjoy your kids as people. Your home should be *fun,* and it ought to be a ball to live there.

David Veerman

though, they get harder to touch. But there are ways to touch a teenager that are different from the way you cuddled him when he was little. For example, you shouldn't leap out of your car when you drop him off at school and give him a big kiss—he'll act like Lucy when Snoopy tries to lick her and give her "dog germs." But you can put your arm around him, rough up his hair, or tap him on his rear like a football coach. And even though it's harder to be affectionate when they're older, they need it now more than ever.

Touch reinforces a parent's message of love. Kids often feel so unlovable all day at school, and a hug from Mom or Dad can erase that bad feeling. Don't assume your children know that you love them ("I love you until I tell you otherwise; if I ever stop, I'll let you know")—tell them you love them with a touch.

Teens can also tell that parents love them during *the together times.* This is when you schedule quality time to be together with your kids. Often it entails a personal sacrifice to be with them, doing things that interest them: You enter their world instead of them coming to you.

Gordon MacDonald tells a story about James Boswell, the famous British author, in his book, *The Effective Father.* One of Boswell's best boyhood memories was of a day when his dad set everything aside and took little James fishing. James never forgot that day. Mr. Boswell Senior died, and the diary he kept recorded that fishing excursion.

It simply said, "Another day wasted: took James fishing." But little did James' father realize that the day was not wasted—James grew up remembering that day forever.

You too can create lasting childhood memories by working on a car with your kids, going shopping or camping, making pizza, or just booking a motel for a crazy weekend with pillow fights. They'll value the time spent with you more than trinket love; love that says, "I can't be with you, but I'll buy you something."

But most of all, teens feel that their parents love them when they love one another. Too many families today are caught in triangular love, where the relationship between Mom and Dad has split apart and the point of the triangle is love for the kids. Since they don't love each other very much, the parents end up loving the children instead, and kids can sense that. They feel insecure and unloved, because children were meant to be caught in the overflow of Mom and Dad loving each other. Their security should be based on knowing that the love from which they came is still going strong. So love in action is not just time spent loving teens, but time invested in loving each other too.

_____
Related Articles

Honesty Is the Only Policy

CHARLES R. SWINDOLL

Honesty is an important ingredient in any lasting relationship. When you're honest and authentic with your teens, it's easier for them to be vulnerable with you. *Honesty,* defined, is "fairness and straightforwardness of conduct."

One time I wanted to go to the store alone. I wasn't in the mood for little children playing with the gumball machines and magazines. I just wanted to go quickly and get it over with.

But as I approached the door, my kids heard the keys jingling and began, "Daddy, you promised I could sit in the front seat the next time we went. . . ."

So I said OK, but boy was I mad! I was steaming as I was driving. All of a sudden I realized how angry I was. I also realized that my kids had no idea why.

I pulled over to the side of the road and I decided I'd be very honest with them. I told them honestly about my day. And they listened and listened—like a paid consultant would listen to me—and they were only about six and eight years old at the time!

After explaining my bad mood, I said, "You know, I think it might just be basic selfishness. I just wanted a quiet trip to the store to get a few things and come home."

I'll never forget Chuck saying, "Well, Dad, if you want to be selfish, you can just drive us home and go to the store alone. That's fine."

Well, I stopped being angry. And the children felt close to me. All because I chose to honestly explain the situation.

More often than not, kids can handle adult reasons. Now I don't believe you need to negotiate with a child who's run into the street in front of an oncoming truck. Sometimes you've got to snatch a child out of harm's way.

But it's honest to say, "Here are the reasons I don't want you to do that." It has a much nicer sound than, "Because I said so."

Honesty needs to be tempered with discretion, of course. Proper timing and procedure are both marks of wisdom. "He who keeps a royal command experiences no trouble, for a wise heart knows the proper time and procedure" (Ecc. 8:5, NASB).

If you operate with wisdom, you'll have much less trouble because you'll know the proper time and procedure. I think that verse describes the techniques of good parenting.

My wife, Cynthia, and I believe that our children have "teachable" moments, when they are more receptive to what we have to say. On occasion we talk about choosing the right time to approach one of our kids, not just on sex and college and career, but also to bring to his attention a rebellious spirit we're catching from conversation or bad attitudes

WHAT HONESTY USED TO MEAN

The Jew of Bible times did not think of morality in philosophical terms. He did not speak about honesty as something hard to understand. Honesty meant if you sold a man a basket of corn, you made sure it was filled to the top; if you sold him meat, you kept your thumb off the scale.

Jay Kesler

toward responsibilities.

Timing is so important. If we sense that a child is under pressure at school—it's exam time perhaps—we let it go until the exams are over.

This is a good principle for husbands and wives too. I know there are times I don't want Cynthia to tell me the three things I did wrong in a conversation. She'll wait until the right time, and I'm very open to it.

The *manner* in which we teach is important also. We try not to correct our children around others. Sometimes we'll have to pull a child aside and say, "I've noticed your abrasive spirit in the car today and several times recently when I've asked you to do something around the house. I want to talk to you about when that behavior has come up and how we can turn it around because your attitude is really taking a toll on the family."

Parents must use discretion in knowing how much and when to dump out the filth of their pasts. I use the illustration of emptying my garbage can in the back yard. My can is clean, but my child has to pick up the garbage and do something with it. I'm fine, because I've known it all along. But it could devastate my child. If I dump it out, I need to take the time to roll up my sleeves and prepare my child to take it from my hand and put it neatly into *his* garbage can.

Another aspect of honest and open communication is respecting the privacy of our children. I'm not the kind of parent that looks through keyholes.

As Charlie Shedd teaches, I try my best to help establish a self-governing mentality in the minds of our children as early as possible. Once kids realize they are doing their own governing, they also realize they've got to live with their own fallout.

We can face each other eyeball to eyeball. I don't nag by putting little notes

LET TEENS KNOW YOU'RE HUMAN

One of the mistakes I made as a parent was that I never let our children know when I was hurting because I didn't think they ought to know. If I was failing in something, I didn't tell them. As a result, they never saw failure in me.

For example, I had been a wrestler in college and had done moderately well. When our boys began to wrestle they did far better than I ever did, and I was thrilled. But I discovered that the boys thought I was the greatest wrestler that had ever come along.

The extent of my plain old-fashioned pride was made clear to me when a friend told me something one of our sons had told him. He had said, "My father is the most successful man on the face of this earth. Everything he ever put his hand on has been successful." When my friend shared this with me I thought, *what a tragedy*—obviously it wasn't true. Somehow, I had allowed my son to get this idea by only telling him of my victories in sports or my successes in Christian work.

I realized, as I reflected on this, that I had wanted the children to think this. I had only told them stories about my spectacular wins in wrestling. I never told them about my defeats, which I could still remember in painful detail.

Now I know that being vulnerable and sharing our failures as well as our successes is necessary. We can give our teens tremendous support when they experience failure by sharing with them times when we did not win or do the right thing either.

David Howard

250

in the drawers telling them what to do. Nor do I sit perched, waiting to point my finger and say, "I told you so!" We have to honestly respect the privacy of our teens.

Finally, parents need to be honest about their fears and uncertainties. When teenagers witness Dad and Mom under pressure, they are less likely to be shocked when they step into adult life. They will know that these things exist and that they can be honestly dealt with.

Forgiveness: It's Give and Take
LEIGHTON FORD

There have been times when I've exploded at my children and really lost my temper. Maybe something else was bothering me or I had punished them or blamed them for something when I didn't have all the facts. I've had to go back then and say, "I'm sorry; I was wrong," particularly if I felt I had hurt them.

Forgiveness is the key to communication in any human relationship among sinners. It's important for parents not only to forgive but to be forgiven. If we want forgiveness to be real, then we need not only to learn to give forgiveness but we have to learn to receive it.

I remember one time we asked our

FORGIVE AND FORGET

"I can forgive, but I cannot forget," is only another way of saying, "I will not forgive." A forgiveness ought to be like a canceled note, torn in two and burned up, so that it can never be shown against the person. There is an ugly kind of forgiveness in this world—a kind of hedgehog forgiveness, shot out like quills.

The Biblical Treasury

kids, "What is sin?" and one of them said, "That's what children do."

Then we asked, "Do grown-ups ever sin?"

"Oh no," was the answer.

Kids need to realize that sin isn't just bad things people do, but that sin is something that breaks our relationship with God and with other people. Forgiveness isn't just forgiving the wrong; it's reestablishing that broken relationship. We parents need to forgive as God has forgiven us. Children need to see that.

When we realize that we've done wrong and it's been our fault, we have to ask God for forgiveness and then accept that forgiveness. Corrie ten Boom once said that God puts our sin in the depths of the sea and puts up a sign that says, "No fishing."

But there are scars and we need to distinguish between facts and feelings in our Christian lives. The fact is that I am forgiven. Yet my feelings may be scarred very deeply due to my sin or the sins of others.

When parents have deep scars, they may need to talk to a pastor or counselor to understand why. Sometimes, we just have to live with them and learn that time will help. Perhaps those scars can remind us of our need of the grace of God, if we can't totally forget. But we can *be* forgiven even when we don't *feel* forgiven.

I think one of the most important things for us as Christians is not to try to atone for our own sins. That has already been done by Christ. When I've received His forgiveness and asked for the forgiveness of others, and have done everything I can to put it right, then I have to go on as a forgiven sinner. I am still a sinner, but I am forgiven.

When you are seeking forgiveness from a teen, the direct approach is best. Go to him directly; sit down alone with him, and say "I'm sorry." We shouldn't try to justify ourselves, but we can try to explain why we did what we did and say, "I'm sorry, will you forgive me?"

You have to choose a time that is good. Sometimes, you need time to cool off, and it is better to wait an hour or so. Sometimes, it's not so much a matter of forgiveness as it is sensitivity enough to know whether or not we're getting into a confrontation. Just stop talking. I think many times if we would just keep silent, we wouldn't need to ask forgiveness.

My son, Kevin, once came home from school upset because he had had a confrontation over a certain school club that he was involved in. As a result, he had resigned from the club. He asked me if he had done the right thing and I started giving him a little lecture, telling him I wished he had waited longer.

He finally got up and said, "I've got to leave." He went out for an hour and did something. After he had cooled off, he came to me and said, "Dad, I was having problems with someone else, not you. I

IT'S TOUGH TO FORGIVE— BUT YOU'VE GOT TO

Jesus said that if you don't forgive, your heavenly Father won't forgive you. I think what He meant by that was that if I do not forgive someone, then it shows I don't see my need for forgiveness. If I know of my own need of forgiveness and have experienced that, I will forgive. If I don't forgive, I haven't experienced my need.

That's why a lack of forgiveness short-circuits God's grace in our lives. It makes us live in guilt, in fear of God. It also blocks out communication in the home. Our children need to feel comfortable talking about anything with their parents. They need to know their parents are shock-resistant—that there is nothing they can say that will make us despise them or cut them off.

We may be deeply disturbed, and we may not approve or condone what they do, but they need to feel that whatever happens, they have somebody who loves them unconditionally. Nothing can make parents stop loving their child.

I remember someone saying that some people are so full of grace they have no room for truth, and some people are so full of truth that they have no room for grace. Jesus was full of grace and truth.

We need love and discipline, or love and strength; we need to be loving enough to forgive and strong enough to say no. We can be one or the other in the flesh—some people are more loving and some people are stronger and tougher. It takes the Spirit of Jesus to have both the love and the discipline, the grace and the truth.

Leighton Ford

just had to get out before I got angry at you too."

We ought to learn to withdraw for a while instead of pushing things. But when we have blown it, we need to ask forgiveness as quickly as we can and not let it fester. We can come right back and be honest. Don't make a big production of it either. Teenagers don't like big productions.

When a teen keeps making the same mistake or sin over and over again, you always forgive him. But you don't always tolerate his actions. There is a difference between toleration and forgiveness. You always forgive the person, but I don't think you always have to put up with the destructive action.

There are times when a teen has to be grounded; there are times when you have to say no. That doesn't mean you are not forgiving the person. God's love is a love that confronts; He doesn't ignore.

To ignore doesn't communicate forgiveness. I know a woman who had a child when she was a teenager. Her father never spoke to her once about having that child. As a result, she never felt forgiven by him.

I think sometimes as parents we need to recognize that when our children do something wrong, often our concern is not over what it does to them, but what it does to us. We're afraid we are going to be embarrassed or scandalized or shamed in the eyes of our Christian friends. We have such great expectations and we project them on to our children.

I remember a situation where a young man did something which jeopardized his future schooling. His mother seemed more concerned about how her son's actions would affect his schooling than in handling the situation in a way that would help him face his wrongdoing and find forgiveness. I pointed out that what he learned about handling mistakes was more important than what went on his record. It was hard for her to see this—perhaps because she felt that her reputation as a mother was at stake.

Related Articles

Sharing Begins with Parents

TED W. ENGSTROM

Sharing yourself with others is one of the key ingredients to building strong relationships in the family. Honest communication is especially important with teens. Sooner or later children discover that parents are not infallible— and they might as well learn it from us. Fortunately, we are moving away from the model of the strong, silent, uncommunicating parent in our culture.

Our relationship with the Lord Himself is not based primarily on His authority as God, but on His love for us. The same thing is true in our relationship with a youngster. We know that we have authority as parents and the children also know who is boss, but love should be the primary building block in the home.

A loving relationship is the oil which makes that authority tolerable and even welcomed in the family. When the teenager recognizes that his parents are really human beings and have flaws just like everybody else, he can relax and feel affirmed in that. If we are open and share this with our children, it helps a great deal.

Of course, the most important relationship in the home is that between the husband and wife, followed by that between parents and children. The kids should never become more important than the spouse! As parents, we need to model a loving relationship of husband and wife. Even when the kids know they are second to that wife or husband, they respect this. When they marry someday, they will remember their parents' relationship and use it as a model for their own lives.

Sharing also needs to begin with the parents, since they are the role models and set the example for the family. When teens see this willingness to share and be vulnerable, they are more likely to follow suit and begin to share. Try to open the channels of loving communication in your home.

Too often, parents seem to be more frightened of their children than the kids are of their parents. The kids realize this, and use it as a whip for torture. That's wrong.

I don't believe that we should treat children as peers when they are in their mid-teens, but the older they get, the more they should recognize that we see and enjoy them as friends, as well as

SHARING TENDER MOMENTS

To move into each other's lives by sharing our feelings is one of the first steps for creating an environment of love. Parents can begin to communicate that they are serious about making up for a lack of love by weeping before their children. This may sound naive and manipulative, but the most significant times with my kids have been the times we have wept together, not just in sadness but also in joy.

John Perkins

children. Of course, there are some intimate and confidential things parents should not share with their children, but most matters can be shared with the entire family.

A practical way I found to begin opening up and sharing with my children was to have dates with them. Have a private meeting or get a hamburger together. Ask them what's happening and where they're at in their lives. (If I were doing things over, I would spend a lot more time with my children on a one-to-one basis. We did profitable things as a family, but I didn't have as good a one-to-one relationship as I wish I would have had.)

Schedule these special dates on your calendar. Be sure to listen intently to what your children's needs are. Unfortunately, I set the agenda and it was *my* meeting. I am a strong person and I think I tended to overpower my kids.

Whenever possible, I think parents can work on communicating fresh interest in the things the kids want to talk about. Let them know that if it is important to them, you are interested in hearing it.

I remember back when if what my kids had to say didn't interest me too much, I would open a book and read. I would barely listen to them. If it was interesting, I would drop the book and they knew that I was really interested.

When we are interested, we listen closely. Be careful not to communicate to your children that you are bored. The listening ear is really important for kids. Why should they be vulnerable and risk opening up to someone who doesn't seem interested?

Too often, kids get the impression that they are second-class citizens. Parents tend to give much more attention to the guests in their home than to their own children. In some way we must let them know that they are the most important people in our lives. They will never forget that.

One example of something I shared

with my teens that made a real difference in their lives was when we decided to move from the Midwest to California twenty years ago. My decision to change careers and to bring them to an entirely different environment was a family decision. We let the kids help us decide whether or not to move, and I think being part of the decision-making process meant a great deal to them. They knew they were a direct influence on the family decision and shared in the responsibility.

Start good communication patterns in your home by being vulnerable and by modeling a sharing attitude. Watch how teens reciprocate.

Related Articles

Chapter 9:   The Silent Treatment
Chapter 9:   The Art of Communication

Communication: Relationships Rely on It

JIM & SALLY CONWAY

When one of our girls was in seventh grade, we could tell as we spent time together at bedtime that she was uneasy about something. This went on for two or three nights. Finally she shared that she was being pressured to go steady with a boy at school. Then, a night or two later she explained that the boy had given her a ring to wear and she had taken it, but now she wanted to give it back to him.

It would have been so easy just to tell her what to do. But instead of giving her our direct advice about how to handle the situation, we wrestled through it together so that when she made the decision, it would be hers. That kind of communication—open, friendly, honest—is what helped us develop good relationships with our children.

Bedtime was a time when our girls would open up. Small kids are willing to talk then because they will do anything to keep from going to sleep. We took advantage of that. The girls learned that that was their special time with the parents alone.

Each girl was put to bed separately. We prayed together and chatted about what-ever was on her mind. We assumed it would quit when the girls got into high school, but the tradition continued. They went off to college and when they came home to visit, they still expected us to spend time with them when they went off to bed.

We also found mealtimes to be a good time to talk. In some families, meals are just for eating—"Stop talking and eat your peas." It should be, "Stop eating your peas and talk." The purpose of our meals was not primarily to eat but to enjoy each other—to share our lives. As a family we tried as much as possible to eat all our meals together.

Sometimes that meant waiting for each other. When our kids got very busy in high school with a lot of extra activities or jobs, we would try to agree on when we were going to eat. We wanted to be together as a family. Sometimes the house becomes a residential McDonald's for picking up a sandwich and running.

Listening is important in communication. Often kids don't get to explain their side of an issue. Our three girls say that it really helped to know they had a voice in what was happening. The decision didn't necessarily go their way but they at least got to present their side.

As parents, we had to admit that many times our original viewpoint was not always the best. When we would give the girls a chance to explain the issue from their viewpoints, our decision was often changed. Rather than relying only on our partial knowledge or limited perspective, we were able to make better decisions. What our girls thought and felt was important to us.

Teens also need their privacy. They don't have to tell all to their parents. If you have built a good relationship with them, they will want to share what is important and ask you for your help when they need it.

We tried to be ahead of our girls in teaching life development, but sometimes we found that we were behind. We remember getting a note saying our oldest daughter, then in sixth grade, would enter a sex education class in school. We had to hurry up and tell her the night before so she would hear it from us first. We had thought that we had plenty of time to bring up the subject.

Parents constantly need to remind themselves that their kids' world is moving faster than they think. One way to keep up is to keep in close communication.

Related Articles
Chapter 9: The Art of Communication
Chapter 9: Communication Killers
Chapter 10: Sharing Begins with Parents

TABLE TALK

It's important to include our teenagers in our conversations. At some homes, we've noticed, kids have no part in dinner-table conversation. They aren't referred to in any way, and they make no effort to join in. They just sit there and shut up. That's such a shame. Even if their comments are off the wall, we need to respect them and their attitudes and what they are learning.

Sometimes we talk to our son, Nels, about the things we need to do with our house. Some of his ideas strike us as ridiculous, but some are very good. If we can refer to his good ideas when we're at the table with other adults, if we can let others know that we think our son's ideas are important, if we can invite Nels into the adult conversation, then he's going to feel good about talking with us.

Teenagers live in a very competitive world. They know they have to be aggressive and attract attention, or they risk being wallflowers. What relief if, at home, they are listened to, their opinions are valued, and they are treated with respect!

Ray & Anne Ortlund

Respectfully Yours

Developing Family Respect

TED W. ENGSTROM

Parents need to respect their teens, just as they expect their teens to respect them. Yet there seems to be much confusion about what is involved in respecting teenagers.

I suppose a young person in our society—especially if he's a student—is not respected as a responsible or important contributing individual until he reaches age twenty-one. As parents, we have an important responsibility to give our kids the support and missing status that is being denied them in their teens. Often during these neglected years our teens are under tremendous pressure.

A major adjustment is the ever-changing demands and opinions of his peers, which is the most important group in a teenager's life. A teenager's peers are more important to him than his parents. That's why he will try a cigarette, or stay out all night.

I think the teenage years ought to be an adventurous time of self-discovery. However, when I was a teenager I was very unhappy. I had a terrible self-image. I was part of a very self-righteous, narrow-minded environment. I wasn't a Christian and I was really trying to live up to the pressures that were put on me by the gang I was hanging around with. I determined as a young man that I would not reproduce that strict environment for my children.

To protect my kids from peer pressure, I told them about my background and all the strings I had on me. Though I let them make a lot of decisions, I warned them ahead of time about how I had been hurt by some of my choices. I stressed that it would hurt to see them make the same mistakes, but that I would not intentionally interfere.

Parents can show their teenagers respect in communication, conflict, and expressing independence.

Parents can begin to show respect in communication by talking on an even level, rather than "down" at teens. It is very important that youngsters have access to parents at a level that is not mainly derogatory. This is an art that has to be cultivated.

When going through a conflict, a teenager has to know that his parents have a God-given responsibility to give guidance and direction. Parents need to take the responsibility and express to the teenager that their authority is not self-imposed.

It is often difficult for parents to assert their authority and maintain respect for their teen when he is doing something that they really disagree with. The parents must be firm, and the teenager needs to know that punishment is certainly in order. Yet punishment has to be such that the child knows that it is done lovingly. As parents, we tend to be too lenient, rather than too strict. The ground rules need to be established and understood before the fact. Far too often, the ground rules are established too late.

To establish the ground rules lovingly, keep a reasonable balance in your punishment. Use whatever is effective with your teenager.

My daughter will tell you that I never spanked her. I didn't realize that until she was an adult and she told me. Yet I spanked my boys plenty of times. I think that when the kids are little, a good spanking is very appropriate.

As my children got older, instead of spanking them, I withdrew privileges from them. For example, when they were over sixteen, I wouldn't let them have the car for one or two weeks. The car was very important to the boys. I found that taking their keys to the car was the thing that got to them the most. I grounded them long enough so they would hurt over it, but not so long that they couldn't see the light at the end of the tunnel.

Parents can show respect as their teens begin to express independence by allowing them to be the unique individuals God made them to be. Different personalities and temperaments of teenagers require individual treatment. As parents you need to be willing to extend them this freedom.

Perhaps the most difficult tension in respecting your teens for who they are and what they are trying to do comes in knowing that what they are doing will lead to trouble. While warning them hardly seems adequate, there are times when the most effective lesson is one born of experience. Just be willing to be there if they should fall. At times, of course, it will be necessary to step in and discipline. Be sure your children know that while you may not approve of what they're doing, you love them for who they are, unconditionally.

Mutual respect is developed between parents and teens as a bond of trust is developed. When parents respect a teen, the teen learns to respect the parents. Respect is a two-way street.

Too often parents may have love, but not necessarily respect, for their teen. It is easy to set our ambitions too high for our children. We are easily disappointed if they don't go to college or if they don't enter a professional career. That puts a heavy burden on youngsters.

When parents feel hurt, or disappointed, they should find the reason for their hurt. Ask, "Am I hurt because I'm left out, because I've been lied to, or because I'm afraid of what other people will say?" In time, that hurt begins to heal. Then go back and look at your choices again.

If you have become angry with your child or have tried to put him in a box and control him, it won't do any good anyway. Eventually, you come to the place where you realize that perhaps your teen is going to choose another lifestyle regardless of what you do or say or believe.

LOVE AND RESPECT GO HAND IN HAND

Where love is expressed, respect is generated. You can't divorce the two.

While love is more of an attitude, respect is a standard we set up for ourselves. If certain conditions are met, then we respect an individual.

Yet love is to be unconditional. Parents must love their children without conditions. No matter what happens, a child needs love.

Respect can be lost in the midst of love. I can remember when some of my kids would do something and I would not respect them for it at all. I would be very upset and they would know it. Yet my love for them could not be lessened.

At times parents will say, "I have been hurt." Or, "I have been disappointed." Yet we need to add, "But I'm still with you, even though I don't agree with what you're doing."

Ted W. Engstrom

Sometimes you have to learn to accept it. That doesn't mean that you have to agree with it though. It is your son's or daughter's choice and you need to be assured that you have done everything you could have.

For example, what if a teen goes out and gets four speeding tickets, has three minor accidents, and then says, "Let me use the car"? If you say no, he'll say that you don't trust him. He's right. In that area he shouldn't be trusted. It's hard to trust him with the car when he's already had several chances. Yet emphasize that you trust him in other areas.

Parents and teens can disagree without losing mutual respect. Learn to affirm each other as persons. Communicate respectfully, fight fairly, and prayerfully allow the Holy Spirit to control your attitudes.

When you respect your teenager, he will learn to respect you.

Related Articles

"If I Could Do It Over Again"

Making Up for Lost Love and Discipline

JOHN PERKINS

I am the father of eight children. I was able to give the first four quite a bit of attention. But I was unable to give the last four as much attention because I allowed my ministry to get ahead of my family.

I had an advantage over most ministers because I created my ministry around my family. It developed out of our involvement with the community, and my children were able to be involved right alongside me. That turned out to be both an asset and liability.

It was an asset because my children are all committed to the ministry. But it was a liability many times when it crowded out their concerns. It was easy for them to get lost in the shuffle.

At the holidays one year, my daughter Priscilla and I were cleaning up the kitchen. She began to tell me she felt we had put the ministry ahead of the children and how she didn't know us. There was a lot of truth in what she was saying and I began to weep. She put her hands on me

and said, "But, Daddy, you still have the chance to make it up. You still have us."

That was a turning point in my life. She freed me so that I could begin that process. I recently received a letter from one of my sons in which he wrote how I have made up for some of the lost time.

Parents can make up for some of their lack of love and discipline, but a lot depends on the parents' and child's attitudes. Parents need to create an environment in which children can share. The child needs to have the freedom to come to you and tell you that you have blown it.

Part of that secure attitude is based on the child's knowing that his father and mother care for his highest and deepest interests. Our kids always tell us that they know we care for them and their needs.

When my daughter and I were talking about those weaknesses in my life, it was in the kind of environment where she

259

could pour out her heart to me. I could acknowledge those weaknesses and I could respond to her in a very emotional way. But I had created an environment where I could hear her. That's a difficult thing for parents to do.

Even without an environment where people are free to share, parents can make up for their lack of love. I didn't grow up with my mother or father. Fortunately, my grandmother gave me a lot of love. But she had her own family, plus the grandkids.

I was four years old when I first remember seeing my father. I responded to him in love and he responded to me the same way. But he had to leave and go back to the city where he lived.

Though I felt rejected, I knew my father loved me and there was always the chance for him to make it up. In my heart, the door was always open. The love a child has for a father or a mother is a very deep love. Even in spite of tremendous hurt, there is a longing within him for his parents to make things right.

The first step for making up for a lack of love is to acknowledge that there has been a lack. That display of honesty is the most difficult task for parents. We have such a strong tendency to cover up our faults.

Then, parents can ask their child to share his deepest need. You have to watch for the opportunity to discover the place in the child's life where he feels he really needs you. Parents can then do something for the child that is very significant.

My wife comes from a broken family but she too had a great deep affection for her father. Once a year he used to do things for her that were very special. Revivals were a very significant time in the life of her family, and her father purchased the clothes for those events. That meant a lot to her and it was a concrete way her father could show that he loved her.

_____

Related Articles

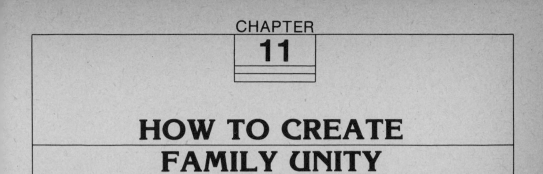

HOW TO CREATE FAMILY UNITY

- What every family needs to stay together
- Quality time vs. quantity time: which is really more important?
- How to build family memories and traditions
- Can you prevent your teens from fighting?
- TV and family: can they ever mix?
- Should teens be required to attend family activities?

"The family that prays together stays together." This old saying is very true, both because religious values are important to family unity and because strong families do things *together*. Spending time together is an important family function. You often hear nowadays that "it's not the quantity but the quality of time together that matters." This can easily be turned into a rationalization by busy people. You have to have a certain amount of quantity in order to have quality.

People who film documentaries eventually learn that you can't do one without spending hours and hours of what seems like unproductive time filming ordinary circumstances. But in the midst of the ordinariness, in a totally unpredictable fashion, every once in a while a beautiful moment occurs. The same thing happens in family life. Spending time together in quantity allows quality to break through.

What Holds a Family Together?

JIM & SALLY CONWAY

Once our girls were talking with some of their friends about how neat it is to have a family. Their list of favorite things included the following:

They liked having family times and vacations; they liked knowing that certain times of the day were special, such as meals and bedtime; they liked knowing they could say whatever they wanted and still be accepted. The fact that their parents listened and valued their opinions was also important.

Family unity is not created overnight—it takes time. Anytime you are building a relationship, you need time to be together and time to share. Statistics show that the average father spends thirty-seven seconds a day in focused attention per child. Needless to say, building a relationship takes more than thirty-seven seconds a day.

Some families plan two or three hours together a week, but it may be too structured and no one will want to be there. Or they may sit lifelessly in front of the TV, each in his own world. They are with each other, but they are not communicating. We need to share what is going on—our joys, our sadnesses, our goals.

We should not stop spending time with our family when our children become teens. They will certainly be very busy, but a family, like any relationship, needs continual care. It is not impossible to find time to be together but it does take special effort.

In our family we would rearrange our own personal schedules so that we could have breakfast together. We also made

sure we ate dinner together at least five nights a week. That was not easy, but it was worth the sacrifice.

The teens have to bend sometimes too. If they have a job or are involved in sports or music, it may not always be possible to eat together. That's OK. But if they habitually hang out with the gang instead of being home for dinner, that is a different story.

The home needs to be a pleasant place so that teens want to be there. Picking on each other, having an perfectionistic attitude, being rigid with rules, or being cross with each other are behaviors that drive a teen away.

Families can work to set up their own traditions. For us, the Sunday meal was a special time to be together. Vacations and holidays were also special family times.

The family becomes a unit of coopera-tion by working together. When children are small, they watch how their parents react to each other and to the world. They notice how we pitched in to help them and how we let them know we need help. Those little experiences of pitching in and helping each other with a chore, even if it was someone else's job, make an impres-sion and bind a family together.

We found vacation times helped to teach and reinforce cooperation. On our camping trips, everybody had a task to do. Everyone helped with cooking and cleanup so we'd have more time to go swimming or boating.

Build a history of sharing and you'll build a unified family.

DEVOTIONS AND TIGHT SCHEDULES

We have to face the fact that many Christian parents, fathers and mothers both, have to work. These parents must keep in mind that their first priority is not to make a lot of money, but to be sure their children are properly instructed in the ways of the Lord. They cannot just depend on the Sunday sermon to help them spiritually.

If possible, families should have daily devotions together. If their schedules will not allow that, then they should plan to set aside a special time at least once a week for the spiritual growth of their chil-dren. At that time, parents and children can discuss anything that is important to them. They can work out every possible problem they are facing. They can read and discuss the Word of God, and they can pray together. But such times will not just happen in families with busy schedules. They have to be planned.

Bill Bright

Does Quality Time Really Exist?

BRUCE B. BARTON

For years speakers have been emphasizing the philosophy of spending *quality* time with children. Parents picked up on this approach. They say, "I don't have to spend a lot of time with my teens because our times are quality." Are they really? Who says so? Some parents rationalize spending no time at all or as little as possible by calling any contact "quality." We may need to rethink the effectiveness of quality time. It may be that *quantity time* is an essential condition for quality time.

We know that communication happens best on a static-free channel. We need to remember that it may take time to clear the channel to get ready to communicate. I remember coming home one time with good intentions of spending quality time with my kids. As I walked through the front door, one child was playing; one was reading; one was watching TV. I said, "Hey kids, I'm home!" They looked at me like I was from outer space. They were not in a mindset to spend any time at all with me—quality or quantity. They were busy doing what they wanted to do. Most young people can't just drop what they're doing to spend time with you when *you're* ready.

Most would agree that to spend no time at all with young people is wrong. On one hand, relationships can't flourish and be nourished unless time is spent. On the other hand, spending large quantities of time in each other's presence without talking would also be a grave injustice. Togetherness without personal contact is not enough. Togetherness may mean: "We are in the same room," "We are in the same car," "We are in the same sports arena." This kind of "being together" doesn't necessarily ensure interaction.

Today we're finding that *quality* times do not emerge unless *quantity* time has been invested first. It's true that you can, on a moment's notice, focus in with rapt attention, listen intently, and share vulnerably without a large investment of time. It is also true that you are using the principle of preparation. You are preparing the atmosphere and climate for quality time. But in every case, being

BALANCED CHRISTIANITY

When the Christian family comes together, they should not just read the Bible and pray. That is essential, of course, but not enough. They need to talk about many things. They need to have a balanced life and bring Christ into all aspects of it.

I think it is important, beginning in the children's early years, for families to develop a family time to bring Christ into all parts of life. During this time they can talk about current events, politics, recreation, entertainment, jobs—in short, everything they do, because their best friend is Jesus.

Families need to view Him as Someone who is with them every minute, not just during the Sunday morning church service.

Bill Bright

prepared yourself may not be enough. Your teenager may need time to prepare also.

Here are some tremendous advantages to investing quantity time first:

1. The teenager can warm up and tune in to a more intense level of communication.

2. Parents show regard for the agenda, needs, and timetable of the teen.

MAKING THE MOST OF MEALS

The story is told of a poor, city woman who lived in the projects. One day she became a Christian. The first thing she did was to take her meager "savings" to buy an old wooden table for the family to eat around. This reborn mother had understood the importance of being together as a family.

A meal is perhaps the most natural opportunity for family togetherness and fellowship. There's a common need and the necessity for cooperation and serving each other. Too often, however, meals degenerate into fast-food counters where family members eat and run to the next activity. In our fast-paced, complex society, this can happen without our even realizing it. There are sports and music practices, plays, research papers, youth group, and other activities; and the situation is compounded when both parents work. It is no wonder that the average American father is said to spend about thirty-seven seconds a day in one-on-one conversations with his kids. (Think of how a twenty-minute dinnertime conversation would change that figure.)

A common meal is vital to your family life. Without this relaxed time together (twenty minutes isn't too long for anyone), you could pass and never really communicate or see one another. It's really not that difficult to eat together—just make it a priority and a necessary part of everyone's schedule. Remember, it doesn't have to be dinnertime. Breakfast will be fine if that fits everyone's schedule better.

Make the family meal a fun experience (not torture). Allow the kids to invite their friends—it's a great time to get to know them; make them feel welcome (they will also see your family's values). Eliminate distractions by keeping the TV off and holding all phone calls. Either unplug the phone or just explain politely that you're eating and will call back.

Plan ahead what to eat. It doesn't have to be fancy. Allow the kids to help plan, and occasionally get the whole family to prepare the meal together. (It's a great opportunity to teach nutrition and how to cook.) At other times you can order out for international or other unique foods.

Allow everyone to have input during the meal (even the youngest). A possible starter could be "What's the most interesting thing you did today?" or, if you're meeting at breakfast, "What do you want to accomplish today?" Dad can tell about his job, but the five-year-old should feel like she's important too.

From time to time, have a family activity. Push back the dishes and play a game or have devotions.

Remember, this is supposed to be an enjoyable family time, so be relaxed. Make it minutes of good fun and wholesome conversation.

YFC Editors

---

3. The teen can choose freely to relate, thereby increasing the strength of the communication.

4. Both parents and teen have time to clear the channel of distraction and static.

5. Spontaneous talking, mutual learning, and personal sharing occur more often in an unrushed atmosphere.

6. Most people need time to formulate what they really feel and really want to say. Quantity time allows a time for teenagers to assure themselves they'll be heard and understood.

7. All people have cycles when they want to talk or want to be alone. By spending more time together, you increase the odds of matching up your desires to talk.

Unfortunately, parents sometimes avoid spending quantity time with their children because they're afraid they won't have enough energy to keep up with them. In reality, spending time in relationships is self-renewing and self-energizing. You probably have more energy than you think.

Some parents avoid spending time with their children because they have different interests. Your teen may like soccer. You feel you don't have the ability, interest, or energy to get out and play soccer with him. But try to get involved anyway, for your teen's sake. You could go to soccer matches together. You could read about soccer. Parents could even take turns watching or participating if the activity is not naturally interesting. Parents should also explore relating in ways that don't follow typical sexual roles. If Mom wants to watch football practice, let her do that. If Dad's interested in some type of handcrafts, let him do that.

Warning! Here are some actions that will wreck the quality of any time spent with your teen:

1. Keeping your eye on the clock conveys, "I don't really want to be here."

2. Getting uptight conveys, "I'm not getting what I wish I could or feel I should from this experience."

3. Controlling the conversation conveys, "I don't want to listen or put up with talk that seems boring."

4. Taking yourself too seriously in sports and play conveys, "I'm afraid to have fun."

5. Jumping into quiet times conveys, "I'm afraid of what I feel when we're silent."

Find some ways to spend and to extend your time with your children. Travel together; take them along with you if you've got errands to do; find some project that you can work on together such as refinishing the basement or making Christmas presents. Find ways to sandwich play between work sessions. Challenge the family to spend an entire night without television. Try some board games or a puzzle. See what happens.

Sometimes it's difficult to reverse the trends. But begin now in smaller doses. You may not have been spending enough time with your children in the past. Try it. You may find it unexpectedly rewarding.

Related Articles

Building Memories: It's More Important Than You Think

V. GILBERT BEERS

Ask your teen or older child about his most vivid and wonderful memory. You may be surprised at the answer. If you have been involved parents, that memory will likely focus on something *you* did with him. It will also likely be something you did unhurried, with no outside pressures. And it will likely be one of "the little things of life" rather than a five-star production.

I tried this recently with some of my children. Several memories came to focus. As you might expect, Christmas and Thanksgiving were high on the list. Next on our list were the annual family outings to Turkey Run State Park in Indiana. After that came the dozens of trips that we have taken as a family.

I was surprised when we talked about a trip to Banff and Lake Louise. The Canadian Rockies are among the most magnificent mountains in the world. But the memories that jumped out first were: tiger ice-cream cones we bought in a little shop (black and orange ice-cream swirled into a "tiger" pattern), a glass ball which reflected the mountains and lake, and a hike together along Lake Louise. They finally got around to the mountains as memories, but the mountains and scenery were upstaged by tiger ice-cream cones, a family hike, and an interesting glass ball.

We have been gently reminded many times in our family that the little things make big memories. We have been reminded also that the best memory-builders involve us as parents, giving up ourselves for the delightful experience of doing things together. And we have been reminded that memory-building need not cost a fortune. It requires a determination to do things that build good memories, giving up things we might rather do at the moment (but we realize later were far less important), and putting our priorities in order with children, and mate, at the top.

Our "Turkey Run" experience is probably at the top of all memory-builders. Let me say first what it isn't. It is not expensive, a fixed agenda, a five-star production, a highly planned program, or any kind of big deal. Now, let me try to say what it is, though it may not sound like much to you. It is one weekend each fall when our entire family is committed (for as far in the future as we can see the future) to be together. That's the most important part of the whole experience. We each *want* to be there together and are willing to put all other things aside for that one weekend retreat each year.

Of course, we enjoy the hiking together along Turkey Run State Park trails, the visits to the Covered Bridge Festival, drives together through antique covered bridges, eating sausageburgers and crullers together on the courthouse lawn, browsing in flea markets and antique shops together, and walking through reconstructed Billy Creek Village together.

But the real memory-building is not the sum total of these things, or any one by itself, but experiencing these things *together*. Autumn in Indiana is beautiful, and our Turkey Run experience is at the peak of color, when evening hayrides, full

266

moon, and a fire in the lodge fireplace are warm fuzzy feelings. But we have discovered that the warmest, most wonderful part of all is experiencing these things together as a family.

Part, if not the most important part, of memory-building is anticipation and reflection. To merely do certain things together is important. But how much more important to anticipate these experiences, talk about them, dream of them, and perhaps plan a little. Of course, when they are over, it is a highlight of a winter evening to look at pictures together, and around a Sunday dinner table, when we're all together, to talk about the fun things we all did as a family.

Holidays and seasons are times for memory-building. We keep seasonal pictures in big envelopes. As the seasons and holidays come and go, so do the pictures and decorations. We have found that these highlight special times and build good memories.

Birthdays in our house are special times. The birthday person is king or queen for the day. For those still at home,

this begins with a choice of menu for the day—breakfast, lunch, and dinner. The breakfast table holds the gifts, and gift-opening is a time for picture-taking and undivided attention.

For those not at home, the day begins with a telephone call and a not-too-professional singing of "Happy Birthday to You." The whole family comes together for the evening dinner, with traditional birthday cake and candles, singing "Happy Birthday" again, and letting the birthday person know that he or she is king or queen. Of course, the birthday person is always excused from washing dishes.

Ask yourself what memories fill your mind. Aren't they the times you spent with those you love, doing the little things, having fun with family, and putting everything else aside for that moment?

Why is it that we look back on these precious moments with such delight, and yet find that they were so few? If you're starting now with teenagers, you're late, but not too late. You're never too late to

WHAT REALLY LASTS?

Experiences are the photo album of the mind. Our children will rehash those experiences and call on the results the rest of their lives as they face critical choices and value judgments. Clothes will be worn out, or simply go out of style within the year. Experiences will not.

My daughter, Lisa, recently completed a twenty-one-day bike trip through five countries in Europe with seventy other young men and women. For nineteen of the twenty-one days it poured rain. The resulting water caused many detours, wet sleeping quarters, and slow time. On returning to America (and home), Lisa was asked what the highlight of the trip was for her. Her response was "the day we rode into Koblenz, Germany ready to catch the boat for the ride to Cologne and camp. On arriving we learned that because of the rain the river had swelled to the point that the boat could not get under the bridge to reach us and we would have to ride an additional rain-soaked eighteen miles by a specific time or we would miss the boat completely. It was beautiful to watch us pull together as a team under adverse conditions, and I learned a valuable lesson that will remain with me the rest of my life."

Larry Anderson

start. But it is ideal to start at birth, and build these memories as part of the growing-up process. We have found that you never outgrow them, and that even the spouses of our children have entered into the spirit of these delightful times and have claimed them for themselves too.

Memories are among our most prized possessions. Happy indeed is the person rich in good memories, especially memories of family delight in childhood and through the teen years. Memories form the glue that binds us together as families. That's why we should be generous in building them.

Related Articles
Chapter 1: Thanks for the Memories
Chapter 11: What Holds a Family Together?

Can Anything Good Come Out of TV?

DAVID VEERMAN

The "great American wasteland" ... the "boob tube" ... the "one-eyed monster" ... these have become contemporary descriptions of television. A modern invention with tremendous potential for good, TV has become the purveyor of a continual stream of mindless "comedies," mediocre acting, violent scenes, and morals-twisting dialogue. It's no wonder that parents worry as they watch their children absorb hundreds of hours. How to control this "invader" becomes of paramount concern.

There are no easy answers, of course, but some have reacted by burning their sets. The opposite response is to do nothing, just hoping that everything will turn out all right. I believe that both of these extremes are impractical, and I would like to suggest ways to use television to our advantage, turning TV time into meaningful family activity.

First of all, it is important to analyze the current situation. To which programs are your teenagers attracted? Maybe the kids' viewing habits will tell you about the youth culture or about some of their unconscious needs. And what about *your* favorite programs—what do the kids learn from your example? Are you addicted to the soaps? To a steady diet of violence? Does a football loss ruin your day? Perhaps adjustments should be made on both sides of the generation gap.

Now for the suggestions:
• Talk over the situation together. How much time does each person spend watching TV and which shows? How does everyone feel about that? Are there any changes that should be made in viewing habits (look at all the options in the TV guide) or in use of time (what else could you do instead of watching TV)? Come to an understanding of the relation of TV time to homework, maximum hours of viewing per night, and other rules.
• Usually each person has special programs. What happens when programs conflict? Do you insist on yours, or give in grudgingly and then toss a barrage of snide remarks? Instead, look for ways to compromise. Give up one of yours to watch theirs with them, understanding that the next time it can go the other way.
• When one of the most desirable shows is of questionable character, watch

together and then discuss it. Explain your reservations and concerns for them, and listen and accept their comments. Analyze the reasons for the show's popularity. Advertisements also provide a springboard for discussion, especially values (e.g., drinking, sex, money, the myth of youngness) and what sells products.

• Encourage the family to watch news specials, including presidential conferences and speeches and reports from world hot-spots. Once again, discuss these in light of sin, God's plan, and the Christian response. (Shows required by teachers and educational programs would also fit into this category.)

• Play games together. Take turns quizzing each other on trivia from the previous show, or devise a "scavenger hunt" looking for such items as a bouquet of flowers, a gun, a cleaning woman, a shampoo advertisement, etc. (use your creativity). The person to spot the item first gets the points.

There is one final consideration—cable TV and home video games. Of course, for many people these may not be options because of finances. Don't break your budget for toys. Many have found that home video games can provide enjoyable family use of the TV, though I would advise against games featuring violence. Some respond to cable television with, "I get enough TV as it is." Others, however, point out that cable gives you more shows from which to choose. This thought has a lot of merit. There are Christian, news, children's, and a host of other channels that provide variety and educational programming. If you subscribe to cable, avoid movie channels.

Whatever your particular situation, remember that it is important to work out a solution to the family TV problem *together*. Creative options are limitless—it just takes your commitment to make them work.

Related Articles
Chapter 26: Making Faith Work in a Media World
Chapter 26: How the Media Affects the Family

Handling Sibling Rivalry

BRUCE B. BARTON

In handling rivalry between children in the family, parents are teaching basic Christian theology. It is in the nursery and in the neighborhood that we begin to show that God created all people in His own image. Yet brothers and sisters will be brothers and sisters: territory is invaded; cries of "Unfair!" are sounded; arguments begin. So here are some guidelines to follow when family feuds erupt:

1. *Avoid labeling.* Don't allow brothers or sisters to label one another. Make sure that you don't do it either.

2. *Insist on basic courtesy.* Don't allow put-downs, cuts, or belittling language. Don't allow brothers and sisters to call each other names.

3. *Eliminate physical abuse.* Don't allow hitting, physical cruelty, or bullying to occur between children.

4. *Don't compare children to one another.* Avoid saying, "Why can't you be like your brother?" or "Your sister always did it this way." Don't allow children to compare themselves to their brothers and sisters, saying, "Why can't I do what Jane did?"

5. *Don't ignore the behavior.* Some parents wait to let kids learn to solve it the hard way. The school of hard knocks may produce "hard kids."

6. *Don't use bribery.* If you say, "Cut the quarreling and I'll order a pizza," you're discounting both the behavior and the situation.

7. *Don't threaten.* If you threaten your children, you are signaling that you have

---

ENJOYING TEENAGERS?

"I really don't enjoy my kids. Frankly, they drive me crazy—they push, push, and push me to the limit!"

More than one parent has echoed that refrain. Sometimes it's real work being with teenage children (they used to be so cute when they were younger). The problem is that we love our kids and want to enjoy them—it's just not happening.

Of course, there is no magic, sure-fire formula that will eliminate all family tension. Every home is made up of fallible human beings, and there are bound to be rough edges. In addition, teens are trying to grow up, so they will test us at every turn. In any case, we can *act* to change the situation and begin to enjoy our kids again (even as teenagers).

1. We can treat our teens like adults, sharing adult problems with them and letting them in on family problems and goals. We can pray together, and they may be able to offer practical solutions.

2. We should treat their friends like they're special to us. We can even bring them on family vacations and outings. (It's difficult to keep a teen's attention on a long trip, so let him bring a friend.)

3. We can concentrate on serving our kids, not always expecting them to fit into *our* schedules. By giving of ourselves and our time (not just money or gifts), we will let them know that we want to be with them.

4. We can "conspire" with other family members to do something special for an individual.

5. We should remember that when we choose "adult" activities that teens don't enjoy, the family won't have a good time. If, however, we choose an activity that teens enjoy, but adults don't, we should stick it out. At least we will enjoy being with the kids. (It's worth it.)

We should find out what the whole family likes. Instead of waiting until "we have enough," we can spend our money while they're home. These expenditures should benefit everyone.

6. We must forget our "hidden agendas" when we talk to our kids, and we shouldn't "needle" them all the time. (We couldn't get away with that with our friends.) We should be as normal and polite with our teens as we are with others.

7. We can try to treat our teens as "peers," talking "across" to them instead of "down."

Actions speak much louder than speeches galore. As we *act* in love toward our children, barriers will collapse, and we will actually learn to respect, appreciate, and enjoy each other.

YFC Editors

---

lost control.

8. *Stick to the problem.* Distracting them works, but it doesn't teach them anything.

9. *Don't blame your spouse or the school.* This abdicates you of responsibility and teaches them to blame others for their actions.

10. *Don't defend the victim and ignore the aggressor.* You could be teaching the one needing comfort to pursue a martyr's life. Ignoring the aggressor forfeits the opportunity to teach basic justice.

In every situation where rivalry occurs in the home between brothers and sisters, there is a bright side. Each of these situations offers the opportunity for parents to teach their children important skills, knowledge, and attitudes.

Special skills can be taught such as social turn-taking. Turn-taking is superior to sharing in that sharing means, to most people, dividing equally among all the people present. Therefore, sharing the bathroom would mean tearing it apart and giving each person a piece. Turn-taking is a more easily understood term. First, Jim uses the bathroom and then, after a period of time, passes on his turn to the next person.

Rivalry offers the opportunity to teach negotiating skills. In these moments of conflict, children can learn to determine what will appeal to the other person as a motive for working together. For example, "I'll do this for you if you, in turn, will do this for me." Learning to negotiate also teaches children to accept defeat and rejection gracefully, using a normal, matter-of-fact tone of voice rather than a whining or angry tone of voice. Verbal skills can be taught such as how to be more assertive and firm in speaking about private feelings. They can learn to say, "I don't like to be pushed," or "Please don't use my clothes without asking."

Sibling rivalry offers the parents opportunities to teach areas of knowledge. Certain social insights can be taught. When disappointment hits or arguments occur, teenagers can learn it's not the end of the world. Parents can teach a family teamwork that protects the younger and weaker children, that stands up for a brother or a sister if there's a neighborhood quarrel. You can teach the basic lessons of justice. When you say, "It's time for you to give up this book and next time I'll back you when you need it," or when you say, "I don't want you to hit your brother nor do I want him to hit you," you're teaching basic Christian attitudes. You can stress the importance of the person over the property. If there is an argument over the car, clothing, or use of a tool, you can show that people are more important than the possession of things.

You can also teach basic attitudes. When you say, "I know you've been waiting a long time to watch the TV show you wanted; I know how tough that feels," it enables you to teach empathy to otherwise insensitive teenagers. You can even teach charity to otherwise uncharitable teenagers. For example, you say, "Why don't you help Mark finish his chores? Perhaps next time he'll be willing to give you a hand."

The biggest challenge you have as parents is to decide when you should intervene and when you shouldn't. There may be a time when it's good for the argument to take its course. There may be a time when you need to step in to make sure that rules of fair play are being followed. You may find that some creative use of the facilities or space may go a long way. If two are in the bathroom at the same time and it creates a fight, work out a deal where first one uses the bathroom while the other gets dressed. Then they can switch. If two children sitting together at the dinner table always quarrel, sit between them to see if that helps. Experiment with rearranging the bedroom which two children are sharing to see if a arrangement more conducive can be found.

Here are some positive suggestions you

as a family can do to diminish sibling rivalry:

1. Have a "Mutual Appreciation Week" (or day). During this time, no one is allowed to say anything negative about anyone else in the family.

2. During a month of the calendar year, celebrate everybody's birthday all over again, but do it without presents. Instead, have a special meal when members of the family give to that person an "I appreciate you" statement. Post these statements on the refrigerator door to see the real meaning of "giving."

3. Plan a vacation together each year, one that isn't spent entirely in a hotel room. Go to a camp together; take a canoe trip; travel to some historical landmark; find some trip that will facilitate communication and working together.

Related Articles

Developing Family Loyalty

JOHN PERKINS

When my son, Philip, was in college he was not living a life that was a testimony to Christ. My son, Derrick, went to Phil one night to confront him with his sin. Derrick said, "Philip, you are not acting like my brother." Philip started to weep because he had such a strong desire not to do anything to hurt the family. To me, that illustrates the power of family loyalty.

A lot of family loyalty comes naturally. We played ball with our children; we went camping with our kids; we did things together. Those shared experiences produced loyalty.

Having meals together also produces family loyalty. Six days a week, every day but Saturday, our family had a meal together. When our kids started to play football and became involved outside the home, that wasn't feasible, so we began to make Sunday dinners regular family time. Even the kids away at college would come home to eat dinner with the family on Sunday.

The father's conversation at the meal table can play an important role in the development of family loyalty. It should include consistent teaching of what he expects of the children as they grow, not just in terms of success, but in terms of values.

We would talk about values and standards at the dinner table. For example, I would tell the children I would be disappointed if they were ever a part of a church where the Word of God was not proclaimed clearly. Conversations like that created standards within them.

We also camped together. We would have one night at camp when we would share our ambitions and goals in life. As we shared our dreams with each other, we became closer.

There has to be the desire to have a heritage. The family needs to see itself as creating a heritage, to believe that the family members are responsible for carrying on a legend. My wife especially had the desire to pass on a heritage to our kids. Out of that heritage a sense of loyalty has developed.

A certain amount of family loyalty is the natural outgrowth of a large family. It is harder to foster family loyalty when the family is small, less than three kids. But if

272

that's the case, first cousins can be just as vital in creating a sense of heritage and loyalty. It is possible to love first cousins like brothers and sisters. I know that because I grew up with a lot of first cousins.

But now the word *cousin* is almost disappearing from our vocabulary. We still have aunts and uncles, but cousins are often not very important in the life of a family. Our mobile society makes it difficult to forge deep bonds with cousins. One set will live in California, another set in Alabama.

God created the family as the first phase of morality and stability. The family is responsible for teaching all of the great virtues like courage, identity, love, and compassion. We have made a mistake in shifting those responsibilities to day-care centers, to the schools, and even to the church.

We expect those virtues to be instilled at the institutional level. But if the family is abdicating its role in passing on values, it is also going to abdicate its heritage.

"DO WE *HAVE* TO GO TO AUNT MATILDA'S?"

Perhaps it's a family reunion, or the family vacation, or just a visit to Aunt Matilda's, but the teenage members of the family don't want to go. Should they be required to attend family activities? Which ones should be required (if any)?

Actually, the problem isn't so much the activity itself as it is the principle of "independence" versus what Mom and Dad want. Teenagers are becoming adults, and they want to choose their own activities. Parents, on the other hand, foresee the day when their teens will move out, and the family will change; so they want to have as many family events as possible.

Unfortunately, these parents have discovered "family" too late. Now that they have realized its importance, instead of clinging, they should begin to help their teens break away. After all, the ultimate goal of parenting is to produce responsible, independent adults. When kids are older and have other alternatives, it is unrealistic to force them suddenly into a "new idea" (that family is all-important). If they haven't been reared that way, and their parents have never modeled the priority of family, it will be almost impossible to begin at this juncture.

It takes time to learn "family-ness" if it hasn't been a priority. The secret is to work into it and not to try to change everything overnight. (Sometimes parents attend a family seminar and feel they must start a whole new lifestyle right away.)

Kids should be allowed to make choices concerning family outings. As the children get older, parents can allow a certain amount of activities that the kids can decide for or against. The options of bringing a friend along and/or having an afternoon to go off on their own might be worthwhile incentives and keep the entire family happy.

YFC Editors

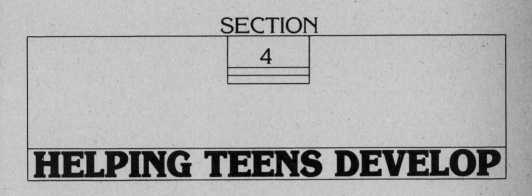

SECTION

4

HELPING TEENS DEVELOP

DEVELOPING SELF-ESTEEM

- The dangers of low self-esteem
- How do parents build their own self-image?
- Ways to develop self-worth in your children
- Helping teens discover their strengths and talents
- How to accept your kids for who they are
- Helping teens handle the sting of ridicule and teasing

Scripture encourages us to love our neighbor as ourselves. If we do not love ourselves, our neighbor is in real trouble: we will tend to telegraph our own insecurities, animosities, self-hatreds, and fears as we relate to him. Only people with healthy self-esteem can have healthy relationships with other people.

Some feel that self-love disagrees with Scripture, that we are supposed to do away with the self. But the Bible tells us not to do away with ego, but to fight egotism; not to destroy the self, but to root out selfishness. Jesus died and gave His whole redemptive plan for selves, for individuals. He *affirms* us and *encourages* us, vital parts of the self-esteem process. When Simon was still a vacillating, jello-like person, Jesus called him Peter, the rock. Simon Peter could never forget that, and eventually a rock is what he became.

Why Self-esteem Is So Important

GORDON MacDONALD

The world is filled with many mid-life people who suffer the consequences of a lack of self-esteem. Self-esteem is liking yourself and accepting your lot in life, despite your circumstances. It's realizing that as a Christian you are a child of God and thus very special to Him.

It is very important for teenagers to feel good about themselves. People need to be aware that the teen years are a time when everything is up for grabs. During those years, the teen doesn't know if he is a child or an adult. At home, teens are treated like children; at their jobs, they're treated like adults; at school, like adolescents. They are playing roles and are constantly exposed to different sets of expectations. It's a wonder they do as well as they do, because parents don't understand who teens are, and teens don't understand themselves.

Self-esteem is a very important thing because somewhere in the middle of all this confusion, there needs to be a sanctuary of sanity to which one can return and find the world right side up.

Self-esteem helps teens know who they are. Plus, they need to know that their parents love and accept them, no matter what. Certain principles will then be unchangeable and teens can count on that stability at home.

Chances are, when children venture outside the home, somebody is ready and waiting to ridicule them or to put them down. But when they come home, they don't have to look over their shoulders any longer. That's what home is for. That's what creates a sense of safety and security. I think self-esteem comes from knowing you have a significant position in the family and that you have skills and gifts that are unique to you. You have something special to contribute.

When Parents Lack Self-esteem

If we don't feel good about ourselves, often we don't want anyone else to feel good either. We tend to prevent people around us from rising higher than the level where we see ourselves.

Some parents wake up to the fact that they have a poor self-image. At that point, they must find ways to work through their own problem so they won't impose their limitations on their children. It is a great, loving, selfless act, and it needs to be done. I have seen that happen in some families in our church where parents are determined that their children are not going to grow up with the self-limitations they as parents experienced.

I know of a family where the father had

HOW TO PRAISE YOUR KIDS

A teenager's self-image sets the boundaries for his psychological and spiritual growth. The healthier the self-image, generally the more he'll achieve. And how able, gifted, and confident a teen feels is usually the result of what the parents have mirrored.

A teen realizes, though he might not admit it, that parents know him best, and if they feel good about him, then he develops self-worth, self-esteem.

The elements of self-esteem are belonging, worth, and confidence. Belonging comes from our relationships at home; worth comes from what we are intrinsically—made in the image of God. Confidence comes from what we can do. You recognize and affirm a child for who he is and praise him for what he does.

You don't praise him for who he is—he had nothing to do with that. That's God and biology. But you affirm him—point out his uniqueness and enjoy it. Appreciate his particular personality.

You praise a kid for what he does, for the efforts he makes to improve the abilities God has given, to make the most of what he's received. Any effort a child makes in the right direction should be rewarded with praise and encouragement.

Can you praise too much? Absolutely not. Not if the praise is legitimate and sincere, not flattery or manipulation. If you're praising for something the kid has done, not something he is, it isn't possible to praise too much.

Studies have shown that for every negative thing you say to a child, you must say four positive things just to keep the balance. When you realize how quick parents are to nitpick, to criticize, and how slow we are to praise, you realize overpraising is hardly a danger.

J. Allan Petersen

to win every contest with his son and had to be right in every discussion—no matter what the topic was. His son grew up expecting to lose or to be "wrong" in any given situation.

The good that came out of that bad situation was that when the boy became a leader in his adult life he was able to think twice before intimidating or inhibiting others. Now his tendency is to assume that others are right until he hears evidence that persuades him to the contrary. And believe me, that's a refreshing wrinkle in human relationships. This "I'll assume you're right till persuaded otherwise" approach has been a valuable safety valve for that Christian leader.

I determined that my children were never going to be put in the situation where Dad was always right or always had to win. Early I encouraged my son to disagree with me. If I said, "That Chevrolet is a fabulous automobile," he might say, "Yeah, but if you look at the Fords. . . ." Then I would try to respond,

"Now that's interesting! Tell me what brought you to the conclusion that a Ford is a better car." Our relationship is helped enormously when I am able to encourage independent thinking. And that builds self-esteem quickly.

Sometimes when parents lack self-esteem they try to live vicariously through their children's successes, thus boosting their own self-images. Sometimes parents overaccelerate their children's development and put too much pressure on them. A father may push his son to succeed as an athlete or pressure his daughter to make straight A's.

These are some of the negative sides of self-esteem we need to be aware of and avoid.

Related Articles

Developing Self-worth in Your Teen

RAY & ANNE ORTLUND

More than anyone else, parents play a major role in influencing their children's self-image. When we are genuinely proud of them, they catch it. And when we are constantly noticing the ways they are obnoxious and emphasizing those, they catch that too. Even if we bite our tongue and say nothing, the vibes are still there. Our children sense so quickly if we are despising them, or merely tolerating them, and this has a powerful effect on their deep-down view of themselves. Affirmation of our children's good quali-

ties is an absolute must if we are going to give our children a sense of self-worth.

We need to become aggressive in affirming every little wonderful thing we see about our children. Anne recalls, " I can remember when I was a little girl, my daddy showed me the odometer on our car and said, 'Look, Anne, 6006—it's symmetrical.' I said, 'No, Daddy, to be symmetrical one of the sixes would have to be backward.' Well, my daddy acted as if that were the most profound thing anyone had ever said! He bragged about it to his friends in front of me. I never forgot it."

If we start looking, we will find lots of things to affirm. The great need is for a sense of perspective—to think future, to think of what our children will be, not just what they are at the moment. If we do that, we can affirm them by saying in faith what they will be like, by God's grace.

Jesus told Peter, "You're Simon now, but you will be called Peter." He was saying, "I have great hopes for you; My plans for you lead to glory!" We need to give our children a great sense of optimism, under God; to let them know that His great principle is that the best wine is last. We need to emphasize that Proverbs 4:18 will be true in spite of every obstacle, "The path of the just is as the shining light, that shineth more and more unto the perfect day" (KJV). We need to plant great hope and big dreams in our children from the time they're tiny, so they believe they're on their way to significance.

One way we've done this is by asking our children for advice, by encouraging them to tell us how they feel about issues that are important to them, and then by saying, "That's good, I really appreciate that."

Even when our children were little, we deliberately asked their opinion to make them feel worthy and important. Ray would say, "You're such a good hopper; teach me how to hop the way you do." Or Anne would ask, "What should I do next, make the bed or put away the laundry?" Or, "Do you think I talk too much?" Or, "Are you proud of me as a parent?" Or, "I want to make you happy—how am I doing?"

Teenagers also need specific affirmations like, "That was a wise decision," or "That took courage," or "You seemed relaxed at dinner tonight." Some of our affirmations can encourage them to continue in the right direction: "You're beginning to finish more things that you start." "You're much more organized

now." Others will point them to a future goal: "You're going to pick a husband or wife carefully." "You're going to be a wonderful parent." "You're going to have a wonderful effect on the world for God."

When Nels was thirteen or fourteen, we began saying, "Nels, you're going to be such a good driver. We can just see how careful and courteous you're going to be. It will be so much fun just to sit in the backseat and relax and let you drive." He had that image of himself years before he got his learner's permit. Today he's a good driver.

This kind of affirmation-in-advance is a powerful tool. It makes the goal more real

WHAT DOES GOD LOOK LIKE?

Many people have image problems with themselves because they have a faulty image of God. The better we know God, the better we will know and like ourselves. The need, then, is not to work on polishing up our self-image; the need is to work on understanding the Lord, how wonderful He is, and how much He loves us.

He created you with great care; you are enormously valuable to Him. When you have Jesus as your Saviour, you are a child of God, a son, a priest. You are a choice person; you can hold your head up. This isn't pride, because it all depends on who Jesus is.

We have gone astray in trying to work on self-image apart from our image of God. It's a hopeless road. But once you see who God is and what He has done for you, you will be lifted high, because the high and lofty One has lifted you up!

Ray & Anne Ortlund

than the child's present inadequacy, which he already knows well. But if he can begin to visualize what he might become through Christ's power, he may want to move in that direction.

This technique has a profound theological foundation. When we affirm our child ahead of time, we're doing what our heavenly Father does with us. God proclaims to us His children that we are perfect. He says that right now, long before our experience tells us it's true. He looks at us through Christ-colored glasses and gives us hope that we can grow up to what He has already decreed is true. If our heavenly Father does that with us, His children, certainly we need to do the same with ours.

Of course, the first step will be to lead them to initial salvation in Christ, so that these wonderful processes can begin to work in their lives.

That doesn't mean we will face no problems. There will be plenty of sins and faults along the way, just as God has plenty of hassles with us along the road to perfection. Nels had an accident with the car a while back, not a big thing but he said he'd been reckless. Ray said, "Well, we've had accidents too—I had one not long ago that was all my fault—and I still think I'm a pretty good driver. You'll have to work and pay for it, but you're still a good driver."

There are also a thousand ways to affirm children without using any words at all: going to ball games they're playing in, or school's open house, or teachers' conferences; giving them birthday celebrations and sending little notes; seeing that there are lots of pats, hugs, and arms around the shoulders. We can say volumes without saying a word.

Of course, your affirmations have to be honest; the kids will know if you don't mean it.

So let the inner process begin with you. Ask God to give you perspective, to give you confidence in His Holy Spirit's work in your children, to give you patience and love and wisdom through the daily irritations, to give you a large dose of hope! And there has to be lots of affection. If kids don't get affection at home, they will get it elsewhere, and it may not be as healthy! They need to sense our genuine love for them. If we have a problem of being turned off by them, we need to ask God for love. He'll give it. Romans 5:5 says He pours His love into our hearts by the Holy Spirit. We can always expect that God will generously give us all the love we need for our kids. Then once we have received God's love in our hearts, we must show it with our body language, our words, and our lifestyles from day to day.

Our Margie started out life very insecure. Who can say why? Because she was the middle of three? When our undersized, frail little four-year-old had to have her tonsils and adenoids out, she was so full of fears that she went on a hunger strike afterward which lasted more or less for months.

But everybody loved our darling Margie. Even Sherry, just a year older, was her champion and defender! Everybody rooted for her. Everybody cuddled her. The two of us repeated over and over, "Margie, you're just lovin' size."

Words, hugs, hugs, words. By the time she started first grade she was putting on weight. By third grade she had roses in her cheeks. She sailed through school with good grades and many friends. She married the boy she adored. And at thirty-five she is as beautiful and secure and others-centered a pastor's wife and mother of three as we know. The power of visible, audible love!

But during the teen years children can be so insecure, can't they? It's important for us to give ten affirmations for every one correction. When our children offend us—and they will; when they need punishment and correction; let the punishment and correction come quickly. Get it over with and immediately return to the normal lifestyle of affirming. Affirmation should be the first way of dealing with our children.

It's interesting that 2 Corinthians 1:20 says that God is a God of "yes" and "amen"! So many human parents are "no-no" parents, but our heavenly Father isn't that way; He is first of all "yes." We think that's a great insight into proper parenting.

Finally, let's remember that God promises to do nothing but reinforce our children's sense of self-worth: " 'For I know the plans I have for you,' declares the Lord, 'plans to prosper you and not to harm you, plans to give you hope and a future' " (Jer. 29:11, NIV).

Related Articles

Helping Kids Discover Their Strengths

EVELYN CHRISTENSON

Our middle child, Nancy, had a rough time growing up because she was five years younger than her older sister. Nancy thought Jan was prettier, smarter, more popular, because Jan was always five years ahead of her.

That forced me to concentrate on encouraging Nancy in all the gifts that were hers. It took a lot of work, and it was years before Nancy realized that she had gifts from God that were just as important, and looks that were also God-given.

Encouraging her took many forms. We talked and prayed. We showed her examples of when she used her gifts, and encouraged her in those areas. We praised her when she accomplished something, or did something good. This didn't come naturally to me either. I had to work at making it an active attitude in my mind.

But I worked at it because I believe that as a parent I am the steward of my children. Children are a heritage from the Lord and they are entrusted to us by God.

Parents have the responsibility to discover and encourage those talents and gifts that God has given to their children. We must be good stewards not only of our gifts, but also the gifts of our children.

God will hold us accountable for what we do with the gifts of our children, whether we thwart or encourage them. The problem occurs when parents want their will for their children's lives, not God's will. Then, they see gifts that aren't there. Perhaps the child wants to be a farmer and the parents want him to be a doctor. Those parents may say, "We don't care if God has gifted our child to be a farmer; we want him to live our way."

It can be difficult for parents to accept their kids for what they are. The first step is not to blame God. God doesn't make mistakes—He withholds gifts and talents just as deliberately as He gives them. God knows what He wants that child to be.

It is for the child to find God's perfect will, which means submission by the parents to God's will. The bottom line is to let God make of that child what He wants, rather than what we selfishly want him to be. We can do this by praying, "Lord, Your will for this child, not mine."

But is it possible for parents to guide their teen without controlling his future? Yes, through prayer. We're still going through this with our youngest. When he took his test to get into a doctoral program, I prayed, "Lord, none of us, including Kurt, know if this is the direction you want for his life. So let him get the test score that is Your will for his future." Kurt ended up passing and we took this as a sign that he should go into the doctoral program. This doesn't mean he'll stay in this field forever. Perhaps God wants Kurt as a missionary and he needs the qualification of a physicist. Who knows?

In the midst of the uncertainty over Kurt's future, we don't have to stand by helplessly. We pray with him and for him continuously. We talk with him about God's will in our lives and share with him how we found it.

In all of this, we have to release the child to God and take our hands off. This doesn't happen overnight; it's an attitude we must develop. We have to continually pray, "Forgive me for my pride, Lord, because I want my child to make me look better." We can't forget that pride in the Bible is always spelled s-i-n.

Related Articles
Introduction: What Do You Really Want from Your Teenager?
Chapter 12: Developing Self-worth in Your Teen
Chapter 20: What's Right for You May Not Be Right for Your Teen

THE DANGER OF SELF-CRITICISM

One of the most obvious characteristics of a person who feels inferior is that he talks about his deficiencies to anyone who will listen. An overweight person feels compelled to apologize to his companions for ordering a hot fudge sundae. He echoes what he imagines they're thinking: "I'm already fat enough without eating this," he says, scooping up the cherry and syrup with his spoon. Likewise, a woman who thinks she's unintelligent will admit freely, "I am really bad at math; I can hardly add two and two." This kind of self-denigration is not as uncommon as one might think.

While there is no virtue in becoming an image-conscious phony, trying to be something we're not, I believe it is also a mistake to go to the other extreme. While the person is blabbing about all of his ridiculous inadequacies, the listener is formulating a lasting impression of him.

So, I do recommend that you teach a "no-knock" policy to your children. They should learn that constant self-criticism can become a bad habit, and it accomplishes nothing. There is a big difference between accepting blame when it is valid and simply chattering about one's inferiority. Your children should know that their friends are probably thinking about their *own* flaws, anyway.

James Dobson

Handling the Sting of Ridicule and Teasing

JAY KESLER

Many teenagers are deathly afraid of being teased. For them, just getting up, getting dressed, and facing school can be a major task. Fortunately this fear is usually intermittent—it doesn't hit most young people every day of the week, every week of the year. But all young people have to face a certain amount of teasing and ridicule.

It may be for something they can't control, such as the shape of their bodies, their physical coordination, the color of their hair. Or perhaps it is for something they have some control over. They may have failed to catch a ball. They may have been spectacularly clumsy in a gym routine. They may have incorrectly answered a question in the classroom. Sometimes teens are even ridiculed for doing right. Perhaps they took an unpopular moral stand. They may be unwilling to participate in drug use or drinking or sexual experimentation or foul language.

One of the greatest things parents can do for a young person is to help him or her to establish a personal identity separate from the crowd, to encourage individualistic behavior. Now individualism can sometimes be a bit of a problem to parents, because most parents secretly wish their young people would not stick out too much. A truly nonconformist son or daughter can be a real challenge. But when young people are able to stand on their own two feet, to do their own thing, to march to the beat of a different drummer when necessary, this can be a real source of strength.

Often when parents tell me they have a child who is different from other teens, I tell them to rejoice because such children can stand against pressures to conform. After all, most ridicule and teasing at school has to do with failure to conform to a particular standard or norm. If the usual practice at school is for girls to engage in casual sex, and if your daughter doesn't want to do that, she will be ridiculed by the others in order to drag her down to their level. The same thing may happen to a boy who doesn't want to drink or get involved in vandalism.

Ridicule, then, is usually aimed at producing conformity, and this conformity is often tied to destructive behaviors. Parents must constantly work with their teenagers to help them see that being their own person is a good thing, a behavior we reward. This means that occasionally we will let them do something that goes against our better judgment, because we know that letting them be their own person will increase their strength to stand against ridicule.

I've found that clear thinking often breaks down the effects of ridicule. When a young person has been hurt by teasing, it is helpful to sit down with him or her and ask, "Is this really true? Is what they're saying fair, or are they just trying to make you do something they want you to do?" As you think it through together, you almost always find that the ridicule is a tool to make your child conform to some norm that the other kids have set up, rather than a reasonable reaction to a grave deficiency on the part of your child.

"Is it the most important thing in the world to bounce a ball? I doubt it. If you don't like bouncing balls, then you don't have to do it. If you feel that bouncing balls would make you a better person, then let's practice bouncing balls together. But let's understand that life does not depend on performance in this particular area, nor does it depend on this person's affirming you or even liking you. Life is larger than this particular kid and his or her affirmation."

Often our assurance that we like our teenagers as they are is helpful. Christian youth groups, if they are indeed practicing Christianity, can be one of the strongest helps to young people who face a hostile teenage environment. Youth workers should constantly work for an atmosphere of acceptance and inclusion as opposed to one of exclusiveness and rejection. The ability to handle individual differences, to accept people with idiosyncrasies, is an important part of Christian conduct. And while this may not always be achieved in a non-Christian environment, this kind of tolerance and acceptance should be practiced within the church youth group or Christian organization at school.

Often the best thing parents can do is to encourage the young person to take more part in Christian activities and to give less importance to school activities. Increasingly in schools filled with drugs, alcohol, free sex, and academic mediocrity, kids turn to parachurch and church groups to meet their social needs. The norm in some schools is so low that the kids cannot conscientiously be involved. It's important for parents to understand this and not insist that the teenager find all his or her affirmation from school-related activities.

Parents need to emphasize the positive —to confirm the things the kid does well and, for the most part, ignore the things he does poorly. It is far better to put the accent on the positive rather than to bandage up the negative. Ridicule always hurts, but a young person who is affirmed at home is in a good position to learn how to handle it.

Related Articles

Making Home a Comfort Zone

BILL BRIGHT

Every teen needs a "comfort zone"—a place where he knows he is loved and accepted and appreciated unconditionally, not based on "because" or "if" or "when."

Teens need a comfort zone because they are going through formative years. They are finding their identities; they are deciding where they are going in life. Dr. Henrietta Mears used to say, "Nobody understands the teenager." Teens do not even understand themselves. Tremendous turmoil rages within the hearts of young men and women who are going through the dramatic physical, spiritual, and emotional changes of the teen years.

The home is the best comfort zone because it is the one place where the teenager is really loved. Ideally he can work out his questions in the place that has nurtured him all his life, that has taught him about love and God. The home is the place of security.

A comfort zone is above all a loving place. First Corinthians 13 should be memorized by both parents and children and emblazoned in neon lights where parents of teenagers can't help reading it, because without a loving, gracious spirit, there's no possible way for parents to relate to their children during those desperate, traumatic teenage years. No matter what I do for my children, if I do it without love, it is of no value whatever.

Parents can create a comfort zone in many ways. They can express love verbally. They can show their love by doing little things that matter to their children, by touching and embracing them. One way or another, they can say to their children, "You are important to our family."

Many parents never take the time to say that, or much of anything else, to their children. Statistics indicate that during the course of a day, the average parent talks to the child only a few minutes at most. That has to change, if home is going to be a comfort zone. I have asked students by the thousands, "Have your parents told you they love you?" Most have not. It is sad that so many parents who undoubtedly demonstrate their love by their actions are reluctant to express it in words. A child needs to be told over and over, "I love you."

I tell our sons "I love you" almost every time I see them. One day I said to myself, "Maybe they get tired of hearing me say that." So I asked them, and they both said, "Oh, no." I don't think anyone gets tired of hearing "I love you" if it is genuine.

The comfort zone is enhanced by a strong devotional life within the family. Throughout our thirty-four years of marriage, Vonette and I have gotten on our knees together every morning when we get up, and we pray together again at night. Our two sons learned at an early age that our dependence is on the Lord. I have said to the boys, "We are never going to own anything in the world, not even a house or car, so you are not going to inherit anything big from us. But we are going to be available to you as long as we live, to help you be God's maximum men."

Freedom from pressure is part of the comfort zone. Sometimes parents expect their children to perform. They as much as tell them, "If you do such-and-such, then we will love you, but if you don't, we are going to ignore you." It is important that we inspire our children to excel in whatever they are doing, but it is wrong to put them under pressure to perform just for our ego's sake. We have told each of our sons, "We don't care whether or not you are a college president or a pastor or a missionary or the President of the United States. All we really want of you is that you be a man of God, that you love and serve Him with all your heart, whether you are a professional person or not. We are not putting you under any pressure to perform for us."

Even the best parents cannot provide for all of the child's emotional needs. It is important for children to be taught the Scriptures so that from early youth they learn to trust God. We need to encourage them to read the Scriptures, meditate on them, memorize them. The child who has learned at an early age to love and trust God has found the true comfort zone. Then, no matter what happens to father and mother—even if they die prematurely or desert their children—the child will have a place to turn.

It is impossible for anyone to have a trusting relationship with God apart from a real understanding of Scripture. The

A.S.K.

Have you ever heard a parent say, "My kid needs to develop character—he just doesn't have it"? Maybe you've said it of your own child.

We all have strengths and weaknesses. Character strengths include a combination of a person's attitudes, skills, and knowledge. *Attitude* strengths are such things as punctuality, generosity, patience, kindness, and self-control; *skills* include reading, figuring, repairing, teaching, and entertaining, things individuals enjoy and do well; *knowledge* strengths are content areas like math and English, or know-how areas like tuning a car, sewing, or programming computers.

Every person is developing individual attitudes, skills, and knowledge and is, therefore, developing character. This is especially true in the experimental teen years. So parents, it is false to say, "My child has no character," because what you may actually be saying is, "My child is not developing the attitudes, skills, and knowledge *I* think should be developed." Examine your motives—are you trying to relive your successes through your kids or make them fix your failures?

Ask about the "A.S.K.s" in your family. What are the *A*ttitudes, *S*kills, and *K*nowledge held by your grandparents, you yourself, and your children? The accompanying chart may help.

Who?	Attitude What character traits do they display?	Skills What skills can they do well and enjoy doing?	Knowledge What do they know or know how to do?
Grand-parents			
Parents			
Child			

Teens must be allowed to discover their own character. Realize that teens can be good people without being "just like their parents."

YFC Editors

most important thing parents can do, in my opinion, is to instill within their children a tremendous appreciation for the Word of God. From the Scriptures, we need to teach them that God will love them no matter what they do. We also need to teach them that God is not just a big, loving grandfather—He is a just God, and we will reap what we sow (Gal. 6:7). We must emphasize God's love, and we must also emphasize that He disciplines us when we are disobedient. We read in Hebrews 12:6 that "the Lord disciplines those He loves."

Parents need to model faith, love, and obedience before their children. The most important thing children can observe is that father and mother love each other. If they do not get along, the children feel insecure. When they begin to argue and shout, and even to resort to physical violence, the home is no longer the comfort zone.

To a teenager, not having a comfort zone is devastating. If children do not find one in the family, they have to look elsewhere. And inevitably, they find it in people who are just as insecure as themselves.

I was talking recently with a well-known Christian leader whose sixteen-year-old daughter got pregnant. Dad was a pillar of the church, and daughter was queen of the high school campus. She was reared in the church, but she didn't know herself. Because she was so popular, she began to run with the wrong crowd. She started drinking and taking drugs. And then one day a young boy she did not even care for propositioned her, and now they were in trouble.

What could the parents do? They were not happy, of course, with what had happened, but their only alternatives were to reject and destroy her or to embrace her and say, "We love you. You have done a terrible thing, but we have all sinned. God loves you and has forgiven you, and we are with you too." They resolved at once to accept her.

Her parents realized from the beginning that their daughter's mistake was not their fault. They could have felt guilty. They could have continually asked themselves, "Where did we fail?" But this would not have helped their daughter. Instead they said, "Obviously we are not perfect parents, but we love our daughter. We have given her a warm family life, and she has been active in the church. As far as we know, we have done everything we should do. Now that this has happened, we are not going to punish ourselves. We are going to trust God to work triumph out of tragedy, and heartache and sorrow will turn to joy and rejoicing."

As a result of their warm acceptance, she came out of her rebellion. She gave the baby to a Christian family for adoption. Now she is continuing her education, and this time she has a purpose in life. Though she will bear the scars from her mistake to her life's end, she at least had the comfort zone of parents who reached out to her in love and care, not critical, not condemning, but saying, "We are in this together."

This is the kind of comfort zone that helps teenagers come through their teen years victoriously.

Kids Aren't Carbon Copies

Allowing Children to Be Themselves

LARRY CHRISTENSON

Anyone who has more than one child knows that no two are alike. Each affects the family differently. In fact, each time a child comes into the family, the relationships completely change—it's a whole new family.

Don't expect a child to be a duplicate. Some parents try to live out their unfulfilled ambitions through their children; others expect them to live up to what older brothers or sisters have done or been.

I remember my mother once visiting the school superintendent to see why my sister wasn't doing well in class. He said, "Maybe you're expecting her to be like her brothers." That was a new insight for Mom. She admitted she had unconsciously been expecting my sister to perform like her brothers.

So the key is to recognize each child's different gifts. And discovering each one's particularities is a real adventure.

In our family, for instance, our oldest son was always verbal. He talked early and developed an excellent vocabulary. Our second son was much quieter. He wasn't repressed or anything; he just didn't care to speak. And he disliked the school routine.

One day when I was at their school, a teacher casually mentioned that our second son obviously had the highest IQ in the family. We were shocked! His independent streak and reluctance to talk made it seem he wasn't performing up to his ability, but he had outstanding intelligence scores.

As he grew up, we began recognizing his gifts. He earned an M.B.A. from a business school in France, worked more than a year at a bank in Germany, took off a year to learn Spanish in Colombia, and now is a corporate consultant in Munich. He speaks four languages. All these things have been rather unorthodox, and he didn't take normal routes to get where he is. We just had to learn he is an individual.

As our children were growing up, we tried to respect their individual styles. We especially delighted in seeing them move into areas of responsibility. We ran a fairly tight ship at home, but once they got to college they were virtually on their own. We might have let them go too suddenly, but the fact they had lots of structure at home seemed to carry them through college.

A key to that home structure was our morning devotions. It was something we struggled with for the first ten years of our marriage. But about the time the kids were in early grade school, it caught on. We started reading Bible stories together every morning. I think that gave all our lives some structure and a sense of where the center was.

If I could give one word of advice to parents trying to accept their teens, it would be *pray*. Deeper attitudes cannot be coerced out of ourselves. We are limited in directly influencing our fears, concerns, and emotions. The best thing we can do is turn them over to God. He will begin helping us see our teens as individuals in need of both His love and ours.

"I'm a Failure"

Parents with Poor Self-esteem

GARY R. COLLINS

Poor self-esteem is a common problem in our achievement-oriented society. People evaluate their self-worth by how much they accomplish. If you don't succeed in your job, you think you're a failure; if you make mistakes raising your kids, you feel you're inadequate. Your whole self-concept depends on the type of house you have, how the kids turn out, and your position at work.

Kids can aggravate the problem. "Why can't we have a nicer house or bigger car like my friends?" they ask. They complain because they don't have nice clothes like everyone else. Somehow, they have sensed the insecurity in their parents and it becomes reflected in the way they think too. And when parents see this, it's like a stab in the back. No one likes to pass inferiority feelings on to their kids.

Though poor self-esteem is a common —and contagious—hang-up, it's not incurable. We need not sit around whining, "I'm no good, and I'll never be able to change"; tackle the problem with some positive action.

One thing you can try is self-talk. Psychologists say that people go through life talking to themselves. And much of what we tell ourselves is self-degrading. *I'm a lousy parent and my kids are going to turn out rotten,* you may think, and sure enough, that's what happens: a

self-fulfilling prophecy. You've geared yourself to thinking negatively, and so you act negatively.

It doesn't have to be this way. You can use self-talk to encourage yourself. Instead of thinking you're a poor parent, say to yourself: *I'm not perfect, but I'll do the best job possible raising my kids with God's help. My whole value as a person is not wrapped up in how my children turn out.* If you use self-talk to reassure yourself, it can help you break the habit of thinking that you're no good.

Talking with other parents in church or school can also be valuable. We need dialogue and support to help maintain positive internal thoughts. It helps to know that other people are having the same struggles you are facing. If you're worried that your daughter will start fooling around with sex and get pregnant, you can talk out your fears with other parents.

One youth pastor said that many parents are so uptight about being parents that they cause the things they fear most. But if they can share their concerns, their anxieties are eased. In my church, for example, we have about sixty families involved in a teenage prayer chain. This support network helps many parents through crises.

It also helps to examine our personal theology. Often a poor self-esteem stems from equating sin with failure. We know "there is no one righteous, not even one" (Rom. 3:10), so we wallow in our badness.

But we forget that God created us in His divine image. Even though we sinned, God sent His Son to die for us and forgive us. Because God loves and cares for us, we don't need to condemn ourselves—or condemn other people. It is important to forgive ourselves when we fail just as God forgives us. I once talked with a woman who blamed herself for the suicide death of her son. God did not hold her guilty, but she needed to be reminded that she should forgive herself too.

Along with our theology, we need to look at our expectations. If we have unrealistic expectations—"I must be a perfect parent," "My kids should never fail"—then we set ourselves up for failure. That doesn't mean we should have sloppy or low standards for parent-ing, but it does mean we should balance hopes and reality.

But all of these techniques for boosting poor self-esteem—lowering high expectations, examining personal theology, seeking social support, and using self-talk—won't work overnight miracles. An adult with a negative self-image is often haunted by past defeats: thirty-five years of people (including your parents) telling you that you're no good. It's not easy to remove such deeply ingrained messages. You may need constant encouragement from your spouse to turn off the incriminating memories.

When I was growing up, for example, people told me I was a terrible carpenter who couldn't hammer a nail straight on a board. For years afterward, I dreaded doing any carpentry. Then my wife helped me realize that I didn't need to be the world's best carpenter to build a bookcase—I just had to try to do the best I could. Her support helped me regain confidence in my carpentry skills.

You *can* escape problems of poor self-esteem. Begin today by challenging self-defeating attitudes and accepting yourself as a worthwhile person. After all, wouldn't you rather have your self-worth come from God and from within rather than from the size of your house or the dollars in your bank account?

MIRROR, MIRROR

There is a very close relationship between the sense of self-worth of parents and their ability to develop a sense of self-worth in their children. If parents don't know who they are, if they are always concerned about themselves, the children can feel this. Those parents are going to create children just like themselves.

Ray & Anne Ortlund

Related Articles

Self-esteem, in the Long Run

RONALD P. HUTCHCRAFT

If there's an emotional crisis plaguing youth today, it is in the area of self-worth. Parents need to realize that most of a child's behavior is simply his acting out how he feels about himself.

While this seems fundamental to us, it's not necessarily known. Often, we tend to try to change a teen's behavior without getting at the *root* of the behavior.

The greatest gift parents can give to their son or daughter, apart from a knowledge of Christ, is a sense of the child's own uniqueness and specialness. A child's behavior will reflect how well that has been established.

We don't always realize why positive self-esteem is so important. Low self-esteem creates some of the following characteristics:

1. *It creates chameleons.* The lizard that changes colors with its surroundings is cute. But that characteristic is not very becoming to a person—especially a Christian. And it can be really dangerous for teens, with the land mines lurking in the world.

For example, if a teen doesn't feel like he's important, he won't stand up to a group of people who say, "Do this, if you want us to like you." The only way a teen can have backbone and learn to stand alone is if he has a healthy self-worth. Then he can say, "I can't do that, because I'm me. And a person like me wouldn't do that."

2. *Teens become wishy-washy.* The ability to make solid decisions is based on self-worth. A person has to have confidence in himself to feel that when he makes decisions, he makes good ones. If a person doesn't think he's worth much, he'll be afraid of any decision he makes— therefore, to be safe, he won't make any. I heard about a guy who was asked if he had a hard time making decisions. He answered, "Well, yes and no."

The Bible says, "Let your yes be yes and your no, no" (James 5:12, NIV). Yet the person with low self-worth is not decisive, because decisions proceed from personal confidence.

3. *A person with low self-worth becomes rejected.* The reason, I think, is because of what I term the "dirty window syndrome." When we look out a dirty window, everything outside looks dirty. When we look out a clean window, everything looks clean.

Many people, because they look down on themselves, are looking at the way other people treat them through a dirty window. Their thinking goes, "Nobody's going to like me. Nobody treats me right. Nobody thinks I'm very worthwhile, and they probably won't want me around anyway." These persons act on what they believe, and it becomes a self-fulfilling prophecy. The person who's down on himself makes other people down on him, because he expects it from them.

This pattern can continue into adult life, making the person a paralyzed spouse, an ineffective parent, and jealous of almost everyone. For example, in a marriage situation, the person with low self-esteem is constantly trying to get his spouse to prop him up. Questions like, "Do you like me?" surface often. In the process, he becomes so possessive that he drags the other person down, driving a wedge between them. He is expecting something from his mate that the mate just can't give.

This rejected person often becomes very jealous. He's easily threatened and tends to make unfounded accusations. He almost strangles others by holding on so tight, because he's afraid of losing them.

A person of low self-worth finds it hard to give in a marriage because he has to take so much. If parents aren't careful to build self-esteem in their children, they can be sowing the seeds of marital unhappiness. A person who goes into marriage with such awesome needs for reassurance, that no man or woman on earth could meet, becomes a paralyzed partner.

Another thing that happens down the road to a person with low self-esteem is that he becomes an ineffective parent. This happens because he needs too much from his kids. When a parent needs a child too much, he tends to live his life through the child. This is characteristic of what I call the "Little League parent." When you observe these kids' leagues, the parents are animals. You wonder who is playing the game! Another example is of the mother who vicariously goes on every date with her daughter.

The problem is that a parent who needs the child too much will destroy the child. The Scriptures teach that the ultimate destiny of a man and woman is to leave father and mother (Gen. 2:24). Parents have the job of preparing their children to leave the nest. That's a hard thing to do. If the parent doesn't have his own identity, he'll try to make his children be his identity. Unfortunately, it may ruin the children in the process.

4. *Low self-esteem can make people into emotional cripples.* Some of the most self-centered people in the world are people who have a low view of themselves. It's ironic, but the person who is down on himself is always thinking about himself. He's constantly saying, "I wonder what others are thinking of me."

In the process, he's emotionally crippled because everything is focused on himself. That preoccupation with self makes a person incapable of either giving or receiving love, and that lack of love further cripples.

5. *Squandered potential is another result of low self-worth.* The poet John Greenleaf Whittier said, "For all sad words of tongue or pen, the saddest are these: 'It might have been!' " When a person feels "little," he makes little choices about his life. He sets little goals, settles for little jobs, and makes friends with little people. He reasons, "Because I'm little, this is all I deserve."

6. *Teens with low self-worth are usually moral pushovers.* A case in point is of a girl who was overweight, hardly ever dated, and suffered from low self-esteem. In our society, a girl without a boyfriend has "no worth."

Though the girl was growing as a new Christian, she fell for a guy on a white horse who came riding by with the magic words, "I love you." She'd never had a guy make her feel important before.

She had been a virgin up to this point, but he began to make demands on her, saying, "If you love me, have sex with me." She told him, "No, I don't believe in that." Then she came to me for counseling. She knew what I would say, but there was no stopping her. She thought, *The only time I've felt special in my life is with this guy, and if I lose him, there goes my special feeling.* So she went along with his desires. He got what he wanted and left. She compromised morally because of her low self-esteem.

Now imagine how she feels. If she had low self-esteem going into the relationship, it's nonexistent now. She gave up something she can never get back. She really devalued herself in order to get value. Yet she didn't get what she paid for. To a large extent, morality is based on self-worth.

So many by-products can come as a result of a poor self-image. Build an atmosphere conducive to a healthy self-image for your teens. What you see your teens doing (or not doing) reflects how they really feel about themselves.

13

DEVELOPING
FAMILY VALUES

- How do you develop value standards which will stand up outside the home?
- How do parents maintain their own values and standards?
- Can parents and teens disagree and still have similar values?

- What do you say when teens question your values?
- What should you do when your teen lies to you?
- "But everyone's doing it!" How do parents answer that one?

In a world that's no friend of grace, and even in our own beloved country with all of its high ideals, we must realize that culture is often directly contrary to the Word of God. To be Christian is to be counterculture.

A Christian family must make an intentional commitment to develop its lifestyle around biblical principles rather than around worldly standards. Unless we have made such a commitment, our children do not have a chance of growing up with Christian roots. Society—the media, the schools, peer pressure—is simply too pervasive and strong; the enemy of our souls is too clever. "Greater is He that is in you, than he that is in the world" (1 John 4:4, KJV), but we must make His standards intentional, and we must be constantly aware that we are counterculture and distinct. We can communicate this distinctiveness as a strength rather than a repressive set of do's and don'ts. Our children can understand that the lifestyle Christ offers us is indeed a better way.

Communicating Values to Our Children

Do We Practice What We Preach?

HOWARD G. HENDRICKS

Genesis 39, where Joseph dealt with the sexual advances of Potiphar's wife, is one of the classic illustrations of how a person's value system makes a differ-ence. Here was a young man willing to forfeit his freedom rather than compromise his convictions.

Three statements in the chapter indicate Joseph's values, and they stand out like neon signs: "My master trusts me," "How can I do such a wicked thing?" and "It would be a great sin against God."

In the first statement Joseph said he would be unfaithful to his master. In the second, he said he would be unfaithful to himself. In the third, he said he would be unfaithful to his God. Those three values —loyalty to his master, himself, and his

God—kept him from committing adultery.

A value is a principle which a person cherishes or prizes highly enough that he practices it in his life. Most people talk about values as something that they *should* do. But they don't think it is imperative to *practice* what they say they value.

Potiphar knew Joseph valued loyalty to his master because of what he did, not what he said. There are plenty of kids who know all the right answers about premarital sex, stealing, and drugs, but their lives do not reflect that knowledge.

Personal values contain two ingredients—the what and the why. We tend to focus too much on the what and not enough on the why. We fail when it comes to giving the reasons for having the value. We know how we stand but we're not always sure how we got there. But a young person isn't interested in the product. He is more interested in the process of how we obtained those values in the first place.

When we communicate our values, we need to watch out for the passive teen.

We are devastated by the rebellious, hostile teen. But we think the kid who keeps his mouth shut and withdraws is great. The truth of the matter is that the rebellious kid often comes out on top as an adult because he has fought through his values for himself.

The kid who never peeps may not be internalizing values. Consequently, when he becomes an adult, he may quickly drop his parents' convictions.

How to Communicate Values

As parents, we can best communicate our values in these five ways:

1. *A network of quality relationships.* The greatest relay of truth is through interpersonal relationships because they provide minimal distortion with maximum interaction. I tell my students that you can impress a person from a distance but you can only impact them up close. We communicate our values by what we are, not by what we say. Nowhere do you see that more than in the intimate relationships of a family.

2. *Firsthand involvement in the process.* Involvement is more important

OF REAL VALUE

Someone once asked me if I had only one characteristic developed in my child what would it be? I said, "Honesty." Show me a teen who is honest with God, honest with himself, honest with other people, and I'll show you someone who has a great future. Honesty is important because we get dishonest so easily. It is so easy to play games with ourselves.

Along with honesty is the value of people. Our teens need to learn that people are more important than possessions.

Then, there is the value of industry. My father taught me a lot about that. My greatest memory of him in his unsaved days was his waking up and saying, "Son, just think of it. Another day in which to work." He gave me an exhilaration for accomplishing something. We have to be careful not to become workaholics, but we can't underestimate the value of work.

Integrity is another value. What you do should match what you say. My father used to say he was going to send flowers to my funeral if I told him I would be at a certain place at 2:00 and was not there.

Howard G. Hendricks

than agreement. We get so anxious about the product that we are oblivious to the process.

If a child says, "I don't buy that," the first thing we usually say is, "O Johnny, you're a believer; the Bible says it." By doing that, we don't allow him the luxury to express his disagreement and we don't find out *why* he is disagreeing. We should say, "Let's see if we can find an answer to that." That way he will learn the why behind the what.

The whole key in adolescence is internalization. There has to be an internal motivation in the teen to behave a certain way. Otherwise, he will just be conforming on the outside.

If a teen practices a value without inner conviction, the parents are sitting on a lid rather than building inner fortifications. You can pile bricks on the lid, but someday you've got to take your hand off. The harder you hold that lid down, the higher it's going to blow when you take your hand off.

3. *A personal concern or responsibility for serving others.* I find that when a kid is involved in the process of serving other people, he develops a sense of value. It's great for a kid to work to make some money, to save it, to learn the value of a buck. But every child in a Christian home should at some time work for nothing— perhaps mowing somebody's lawn who can't afford it, or working as a volunteer at the local hospital, or cleaning the church because the janitor is sick. That's where a teen picks up values.

It creates values because reality comes to the surface in the process of serving. He begins to realize that people are more important than things. He can talk about it, but until he has the experience, it is just a bunch of words.

4. *Allowing young people to learn from the consequences of their behavior.* When parents cannot operate at a level of trust, they invariably substitute structure. They put all kinds of restrictions on the teen—"You've got to do this," "Don't forget to do that," "Come in at this time"—because they can't trust him. The result is that the kid can't trust himself, and his values are not tested.

If we don't trust our teens, they won't be able to trust themselves. We need to trust them to the point of letting them learn from what they do, or fail to do. Flunking a major test may be the way a teen learns the value of studying.

5. *Modeling what we are seeking to develop in our teens.* If you're not committed to a set of values yourself, it's pretty hard to communicate them. If we want our teens to value honesty, we must be honest. We can't tell them not to cheat on exams and then turn around and cheat at tax time. What we say and what we do have to match.

Related Articles

Instilling Values That Will Last a Lifetime

JIM & SALLY CONWAY

Developing value standards begins before children become teenagers. Beginning at birth, parents should use every situation that comes along to teach their children how to live life. You need to give them increasing amounts of responsibility and freedom to exercise choice.

Don't say to your child, "Do this because I say you should," or "I'm bigger than you," or "As long as you live in this house, you will do this." As soon as you use that method, you have a child who's functioning on the basis of parental values, not on the basis of his own values.

Children and teens need guidance and insight from their parents in order to form their values. Think about ways you can implement the following in your family:

1. From the beginning you need to talk about *why* you do things—why you keep your room clean, why you participate in family chores, why you don't lie, why you don't cheat. Simply saying, "Our family doesn't do that" is not good enough.

When the children become teenagers and go off to high school, their friends might say, "Let's go get drunk." At that point, saying "Our family doesn't do that" is not a good enough reason. A teen needs to be able to explain not only why his family doesn't drink, but also why he personally doesn't. An unprepared teen will be caught trying to stand up for family values that are not his own and will most likely end up giving in to peer pressure.

2. Before the teen years, help your

children develop a reflective approach to life. They need to ask, "What is life about?" "Why am I doing this?" "Why don't I do this?" "Why do I think this way?" "What do I want to accomplish with my life?"

It helps to talk about an issue ahead of time. If you want them to think through whether or not they will ever drink, begin at an age when it isn't a problem. If the issue is whether or not they will have premarital sex, discuss it *before* they become emotionally involved with someone.

This kind of communication should take place during informal times. You don't have to have a special session to discuss the birds and the bees, especially when kids are exposed to so much so early on TV.

Perhaps an unmarried girl your children know has gotten pregnant. Parents can use that example, even with grade-school children, to teach why premarital sex is wrong. Do so in a way that does not condemn the person involved, yet lovingly explain why to avoid such a situation.

Most parents are so busy with daily survival that they forget the long-range goal of developing this individual to be a whole person as he steps into his teen years and adulthood.

3. Of course, as children grow and move along in school, aging helps to develop some degree of maturity. Life's experiences will automatically give them insight.

But along with life's experiences they need cognitive information. They need parents to provide some of that knowledge. In developing values, teens need a variety of ideas to work with. If they are working only with their own resources or those of their friends, they have very limited material.

Get them started reading early in life. *The Living Bible* and *Campus Life* magazine would be good resources for teens.

4. Parents can also provide *experiences* that will broaden their children's cognitive information. There's nothing quite like a week away at camp, where leaders will stimulate kids' minds to think through issues. They can wrestle with what to do about sex and how to relate to their parents.

5. Then, teens need opportunities to think and reflect by themselves. They need time to meditate, to sit out in the sun, under a tree, or in their rooms—just to think about life. It is important that teens are not always busy and "on the go" or wasting time watching TV. Parents can encourage teens to have reflection times.

When our family went camping, we would take a canoe into the middle of the lake so that everyone could quietly look at the stars. That is one way to encourage reflectiveness. Another way is to teach teens how to have a quiet time. As a family, read a section of Scripture and spend time reflecting on it, asking what it means for each person's life.

6. Teenagers also need a peer group for interaction. In a group they can throw ideas around, learning what others think. By sharing thoughts and getting feedback, they are forming values.

7. Stress often helps develop values. Parents often look at the teen years, which are high stress times, as bad times. But without stress there is little value development. Teens need to experience occasional pressures and difficulties. We're not doing our teens a favor by taking all the problems out of their lives. Remember, stress times are teachable times.

When life is coasting along, there is no pressure. There is little thinking either. Some parents try to shelter their children from ever having to face a decision or temptation. But a teen's values are strengthened through wrestling with issues and problems. The stresses of life provide opportunities for new learning and new development.

8. Parents should give their kids the freedom to fail. A teen can learn as much from failure as from success. Teens need to know that their parents are going to stand with them and not abandon them when they fail—not *if* they fail, but *when* they fail.

"SHOW ME"

Teens fall into two categories. About thirty percent can be characterized as the pro-authority group. They want approval and desire to please people in authority. Their needs for security, authority, and structure are naturally met by the promises of Christianity, and thus they are generally quite receptive to the Gospel.

Seventy percent of teenagers are anti-authority. They want to think for themselves, and seek to please themselves, not those in authority. They have a "show-me" attitude. They are not receptive spiritually, and don't respond to pressure tactics. For these teens we need to be good examples. They are waiting to be shown the validity of our values. If they respect us and see our faith in action over a long period of time, they will gradually become receptive to Christianity.

Ross Campbell

Of course, parents should not knowingly let the their teens make moves that are going to alter their lives permanently. But a lot of Christian parents go overboard the other way, trying to protect their kids from ever making crucial decisions on their own.

Sometimes parents send their children to a Christian school, thinking they are going to protect them from the world's problems. There are good reasons for sending your children to a Christian school, but if your reason is to keep them away from the stresses of life, you are not helping them.

In fact, Christian schools should program stress and controversy so there is an opportunity for growth. Teens need to talk about issues and have their values deliberately questioned instead of just being told what to do.

9. Parents can help their teens recognize the difference between Christian standards and non-Christian standards. But you need to be realistic so your teens are not expecting to find evil behind every bush.

You also need to coach them that life is not all black and white. If teens are told that a movie is *totally* bad, they may see it and like parts of it. Then they begin to question their parents who told them it was awful. Parents need to show children that God has created people with a great deal of diversity. All things that are not Christian are not 100 percent evil.

10. Teach your teens to look at the world through Jesus' eyes, aware of the wrong but loving toward people. Virginia Satir, a noted family therapist, found that happy, secure, successful families have an open attitude to circles other than their own, and families in trouble tend to be suspicious and shut off from the world.

When our girls were in high school they were friends with kids that we could never have had contact with because they weren't "our kind." Yet our daughters could be friendly with them and have an influence on them, even though they didn't participate in their drinking parties.

As a result, we have later met kids who made a decision for Christ based on the friendship they had with our daughters in high school. One boy told us he would drink at his locker during breaks between classes. Brenda's locker was near his. Her friendliness and accepting attitude of him as a person impressed him. When he got out of high school he accepted the Lord. He told us Brenda's life had greatly influenced that decision.

Parents need to realize that they won't always be around to help their teens stay straight. They can't ride in the backseat of the car while the teen is on a date. They can't be at parties, making all the decisions for the teen like they did when he was two years old.

11. The best thing you can do for your teens is to be a friend and be available if they want another opinion or just want to talk. Say, "We know that you're going to be strongly influenced by your friends, but we'd like to give you another perspective from another generation if you would like to talk about it."

If you as parents haven't helped your teenagers to set values before adolescence, you need to admit that you have blown it. Explain, "We tried to *tell* you what to do instead of encouraging you to develop your own values." Then get started on helping them form values for themselves. It's late, but never too late. "One thing I do: Forgetting what is behind and straining toward what is ahead, I press on toward the goal to win the prize for which God has called me heavenward in Christ Jesus (Phil. 3:13-14, NIV).

Maintaining Integrity As a Parent

Your Kids Are Watching You

CHARLES R. SWINDOLL

Integrity is adherence to a moral or ethical principle or virtue. Maintaining integrity as parents assumes that, first of all, you *have* integrity. You don't build into someone else something that you don't have.

For parents to maintain integrity and have integrity, they must know themselves and like themselves. If you don't, you might try to live out your frustrations through your children. If you're secure, you can come to terms with things that are important to you. It's easy to get caught in the backwash of public opinion when you can be easily swayed by peers.

Children can *see* integrity or the lack of it in their parents. Even small youngsters are aware of parents' honesty. When parents admit being wrong or ask forgiveness, it makes a deep impression.

One time I embarrassed one of our children at a birthday party. I came home in a foul mood to balloons, cookie crumbs, ice cream smears, and a patio full of busy and ungrateful (it seemed to me) kids.

I'm ashamed to share it, but I dressed my daughter down—in front of the kids. About three hours later, my wife had a quiet talk with me about what she had observed and overheard. She pointed out things I'd said in anger that I didn't even realize I'd said.

I slipped into our daughter's bedroom and said, "You know, Honey, this afternoon Daddy came in preoccupied with a dozen things. I really hit the fan." She said, "Yes, you did."

I told her I realized that I'd embarrassed her and I was ashamed of that, and it hurt me terribly to think about it. I thanked her for not arguing back and for cleaning up.

Then I told her I couldn't imagine how painful it must be to have to face her friends at school the next day. I admitted that I was responsible for the incident. I promised with all the strength that was in me, and with the help of God, to never embarrass her publicly again. I didn't just *think* the promise—I *told* her. To my knowledge, I haven't broken that promise.

That is integrity. My child learned the principle of seeking the forgiveness of others when wrong. She learned by seeing a parent *model* that behavior. It would have been easier to forget the incident and keep my pride. But the harder way was the most profitable.

Any situation like that involves a choice. At that moment, we choose to act with integrity or to squeak out of the opportunity.

Another example in our family was when my wife and I were faced with a very difficult situation tax-wise. We discovered that some things hadn't been reported that should have been. We were faced with a decision: to do what was right, or to hope and pray no one would discover it. Well, we chose to do what was right. And that penalty cost us an arm and a leg. It almost wiped us out financially.

But our children walked through that with us. We didn't do it to impress our kids—it hurt too much for that! But they learned an unforgettable lesson—first, about taxes, and second, about integrity.

"Honesty is the best policy." Hypocrisy and dishonesty will get you nowhere. Children learn the integrity they see. You can develop morals and values in your teenager by modeling those values today.

Related Articles
Chapter 2: All about Models
Chapter 10: Honesty Is the Only Policy
Chapter 13: Communicating Values to Our Children
Chapter 13: Stable Values in a Changing World

Stable Values in a Changing World
Which Anchor to Hold on To

LEIGHTON FORD

I was talking with a local Young Life director a few years ago. He told me what frightened him most was that teens used to rebel over what they saw as their parents' hypocrisy. But now he just sees them weary and sad, as if they are saying, "Well, we didn't expect anything different." They are disillusioned with their parents and have given up expecting their parents to have strong values.

Young people today have more choices—more foods, more styles, more radio stations, more types of music, more kinds of movies—than ever before. These choices are available to parents too, but it is different for young people. They have grown up in a bewildering world where they not only have so many choices but must make them without the help of any absolute standard.

It's no wonder that a lot of teenagers today are so confused, with so many decisions to make and no guide by which to make them. Hans Selye, the famous Montreal doctor, who popularized the concept of stress, said that teenagers have always faced the stresses that we face today, with one exception: the stress of so many choices.

Years ago, a girl would do what her mother did; a son would do what his father did. But now we're faced with the smorgasbord effect. There are so many different options that commitment to one in particular becomes less and less important.

I walked through a shopping mall recently which featured every kind of shop imaginable. I walked through one store for thirty seconds, another one for two minutes, and I suddenly thought, "This is how many people treat life today. Two minutes for God, one minute for football, thirty seconds for morality."

I think if teens don't see a firm commitment on the part of parents, then they will look to other adult role models. They are desperate for guidance. They need to know that our values are based on something beyond what we were brought up to do, or just what we feel is right, or what society says.

One girl told me, "My father doesn't have sex with other women, but every ad he puts out has a sexy girl in it." Kids are very quick to pick up on that. If a parent comes home and has to have two or three martinis before dinner, and then talks about the dangers of marijuana or of the keg party, kids will see the discrepancy.

We have to reexamine our own standards as parents and ask if our lifestyles and values are founded simply on personal feelings and desires, handed down through social traditions, or squarely based on the standards of a God whose nature doesn't change.

The time we spend in the Bible is important. Do our teens see us reading it as well as obeying it? George Gallup says, "The fact is, despite the best efforts of our churches, our homes, and the religious media, we are producing today a nation of spiritually undernourished and religiously illiterate youth." One-fourth of all teens never read the Bible, fifteen percent can't name one of the Ten Commandments.

We have to have some rules. I remember asking our kids what would help them to develop their own character. Immediately our son, Kevin, replied, "Having some rules. I don't always like them, but I know I need them."

The Anchor of God's Word

Studying the Scriptures can help us discern the difference between what is cultural and what is from God. But it is even more helpful to study with a group of people because we tend to read our prejudices into the Bible. We also tend to want to change nothing or to go all the way and change everything. But we need a balance. Being part of a body of believers can help us look at ourselves honestly.

Learning to differentiate between our own prejudices and God's absolutes isn't always easy. Ruth Graham says that we have kept saying no a long time after God stopped. God gave us His commandments, but we keep adding new ones. If we try to teach our own particular values,

---

LIES

You taught her from when she could first talk that lying is wrong. But there it is and you can hardly believe it—a lie and you *know* it's a lie. Now what?

Probably blow up.

Well, that may not be so bad—lying makes you angry. Try to direct that natural reaction at the act of lying and not at the person (If you can think that fast).

Then, discuss it openly and take ownership of your feelings. Explain how you feel. *Allow* discussion—don't let your anger make it impossible for her to tell you the truth. She needs to express what happened and hear the lie clearly in her own words.

Talk about final consequences of lies—it is true that the truth always finds you out.

Finally, don't leave the matter hanging. Follow up. She may need punishment, but be sure she knows that you love her and won't reject her.

After it's all over, ask yourself about your example. If your kids see you cheating on your income tax or making lying excuses over the phone—what *can* you expect from them?

YFC Editors

but can't give reasons for obeying them and can't ground them in the Word of God, then our teens aren't going to listen to us.

Someone once said, "You can't become a Christian without admitting you're wrong," but conversion is the last time a lot of Christians make such an admission. Being a Christian is to realize that we need constant repentance, to realize that God is ever reshaping our minds and our thoughts. God's Word is not wrong, but we may be wrong and may have to change.

Christ had all the answers and the Scriptures provide *the* authoritative guide, but we don't have all the answers just because we're Christians. That's humility. It is a willingness to be taught, to learn even from our kids. We need to be willing to look at new ideas, and not be afraid of changing the map of reality that we grew up with.

What Kids Want from Their Parents
I was very impressed with something I read written by teens in a Canadian correctional institution. They advised parents: "Keep cool; don't lose your temper when things get rough. Kids need the reassurance that comes from controlled responses. Don't reach for the crutches of liquor and pills. We lose respect for parents who tell us to behave one way and then behave another. Be strict and consistent with discipline; keep the dignity of parenthood; we need someone to look up to. Finally, light a candle. Show us the way; tell us God is not dead or sleeping or on vacation. We need to believe in something bigger and stronger than ourselves."

Related Articles

Disagreeing without Being Disagreeable

LARRY CHRISTENSON

It's hard to disagree gracefully. Especially with your kids. And especially when you both have strong opinions about a variety of subjects.

I was helped in this area by psychologist Harry Goldsmith, who said, "I don't ask that my kids agree with me, but I do ask that they obey me." Outward behavior must conform to family standards, but teens need the freedom to dissent.

One helpful approach is to tell them you respect their different opinions, but as parents, you are responsible to God for your family's well-being, and sometimes you'll have to make unpopular decisions.

Say, for instance, your kids ask, "Why do we have to be in by 11 P.M. when other kids stay out all night?" The best approach is to tell them you'll think and pray about it. Then the next day, after you've sorted out the issues before the Lord, sit down and explain that you're accountable to God for your family, and here's your decision and why.

If the kids still object, say, "When you have a family of your own, you're going to be responsible for it, and maybe you'll be more lenient. But I can't be. I'm under a moral law that overrides my opinion. And you're under a standard that overrides your opinion. You're free to think what you like, but family policy is still my responsibility."

Another approach is to project them into the roles they'll eventually be facing. Ask them, hopefully in calmer situations, "What kind of parents are you going to be?" Point out that parenting isn't based on whim but on accountability and good judgment. Discuss how they would handle things. Sometimes they're more legalistic than you are!

I once had a boy in confirmation class who said, "I don't think children should be forced to go to church; they should be able to stay home if they want." I ignored the comment and asked the class, "Suppose you're grown-up and have a couple of kids, and you know God expects you to raise them right. What if one of your kids told you he didn't want to go to church?"

The same boy said, "I'd make him go . . ." and stopped in midsentence. He convicted himself.

The key was getting him to think of the issue from another perspective.

Related Articles

Dealing with Value Conflicts

When Others Don't Value What You Believe

LARRY KREIDER

One Friday evening my wife, fifteen-year-old son, eleven-year-old daughter, and I sat around the kitchen table enjoying pizza and soft drinks.

My daughter, Erica, had been invited to a non-Christian friend's house for a combined birthday/slumber party that night. Halfway between excited and hyper about the fun she anticipated, she was going over the agenda of events planned for the party. We were sharing her enthusiasm until she told us the name of the movie that had been rented to be shown on the friend's video recorder.

When she announced the title her brother, Brett, choked on his mouthful of pizza and half-restrained laugh. He hadn't seen it, but knew that it was R-rated.

So now we had a dilemma. Since our kids aren't allowed to see such movies, what were the options? Erica's excitement turned to tears as she envisioned one great evening rapidly going down the drain.

I had a speaking engagement that evening but before I had to leave, my wife and I tried to give her some creative ways of handling the problem. I told her that we would leave the decision up to her but when I picked her up the next morning, I would be anxious to hear how she handled the situation.

Before I tell you how this little episode turned out, I want to share the options Erica had to consider as a conscientious Christian trying to function in a non-Christian environment.

The first choice could have been to *isolate* herself from the problem. She could call her friend and explain that since our family doesn't watch R-rated movies she had decided not to attend the party.

This approach solves value conflict problems by withdrawing from them. Often 2 Corinthians 6:14-18 is quoted in defense of the withdrawal approach. Aren't we warned "not to be bound with unbelievers" but to "come out from their midst and be separate"?

This approach solves one problem but creates others. How does a person fulfill the Great Commission (Mark 16:15) if he doesn't have contact with non-Christians? Such isolation can lead to an in-house, cliché-filled language called Christianese, which is just as foreign to an unbeliever as Chinese.

A Christian also has trouble being the "salt of the earth" (Matt. 5:13) when contact with the world is avoided.

John R. Stott once called these individuals "rabbit-hole Christians." They huddle together in their own private holes and only dash across the world when they are on their way to another Christian gathering.

Consequently, the nonbeliever's view of Christians is of people who are blurred (out of focus because of the speed in

WHY TEENS QUESTION YOUR VALUES

A small child is told what to think during his formative years. He is subjected to all the attitudes, biases, and beliefs of his parents, which is right and proper. They are fulfilling their God-given responsibility to guide and train him. However, there must come a moment when all of these concepts and ideas are examined by the individual, and either adopted as true or rejected as false. If that personal evaluation never comes, then the adolescent fails to span the gap between "What I've been told" and "What I believe." This is one of the most important bridges leading from childhood to adulthood.

It is common, then, for a teenager to question the veracity of the indoctrination he has received. He may ask himself, "Is there really a God? Does He know me? Do I believe in the values my parents have taught? Do I want what they want for my life? Have they misled me in any way? Does my experience contradict what I've been taught?" For a period of years beginning during adolescence and continuing into the twenties, this intensive self-examination is conducted.

This process is especially distressing to parents who must sit on the sidelines and watch everything they have taught being scrutinized and questioned. It will be less painful, however, if both generations realize that the soul-searching is a normal, necessary part of growing up.

James Dobson

From *Dr. Dobson Answers Your Questions,* by James Dobson, Tyndale House Publishers, Inc., © 1982. Used by permission.

which they zip by) and who speak a foreign language.

A second choice could have been to completely *identify* with the values of those at the party. It's tough making friends and being accepted, so let's not create any problems by letting a ninety-minute movie ruin an evening.

Erica wouldn't be taking the Bible seriously if she had made this choice. Our minds are to dwell on things "true, honorable, right, pure, and lovely" (Phil. 4:8). That which blatantly violates our values or beliefs does not allow the "renewing of our minds" (Rom. 12:2), a condition for those serious about knowing God's will.

Another condition resulting from this approach is a diluted witness. It's difficult to share Christ and the values of His kingdom if we adopt lifestyles that are no different from non-Christians. Taking a stand for our beliefs is part of the package for being a Christian. The unwillingness to do so should be determined prior to making a commitment to Christ.

A third choice available could be called a *dual standard* approach. This assumes that there is a higher moral standard for people who are in places of spiritual responsibility. Since Erica is just a student, then it's all right for her to see the movie, but I should avoid such appearances of evil since I am in "full-time" Christian work.

Though spiritual leaders are admonished to set good examples and to understand they will be judged more strictly for their actions, there is no separate ethic for the laity than for the clergy. This approach also creates a selective obedience concept where a person is faithful to Christian values only when it is easy, unchallenged, convenient, or something that he wants to do.

A fourth choice could have been a *transformation* approach, one that many Christians choose. Erica could have tried either to convince her friends that it is wrong to be showing such a film to young girls, or to convince them they need Christ and a whole new value system.

There are many Christians who feel it is their duty to force the rest of the world to live by their standards. Though they are genuinely concerned for the welfare of society, and often genuinely concerned for those who are without Christ, they come across as perpetual scolders with their index finger waving rebuke on ungodly practices.

Other problems created by this approach include the discouragement that results from the backlash of ridicule, being ignored, and simply not seeing much progress in turning the world around.

A fifth and final option could be called the *tension* strategy. Erica could have stated her personal objection to what was being shown and then come up with a creative alternative for what to do with her time during the movie.

This approach establishes the issue with non-Christians without rejecting them as people or haranguing them about their lifestyles. The problem is, this option is often rejected by Christians because of their attitude toward the idea of tension. We are told by advertisements on TV and in magazines that tension is something to be avoided or eliminated through drugs. Yet Jesus' short ministry was one of continual tension. Every time He challenged the masses, the disciples, the various religious groups, or the Roman government, He put Himself in an adversarial role creating tension. It is important to notice, however, He didn't confront and run. He wasn't belligerent, caustic, or aloof. He would often let some spiritual truth or correction hang in animation without response while He continued walking, working, and associating with the people of that village or region.

So Erica had a variety of choices, and I was eagerly looking forward to see which one was selected. I drove up in front of her friend's home and honked the horn. She came bouncing out the door, down the sidewalk, and into the car. "Guess what, Dad," she started with excitement, "they decided not to show the movie."

I thought, "Well, there was one more option I hadn't discussed—*no choice required.*" But in reality that wasn't the case at all. Erica had selected the tension approach. She called and told her friend that she didn't want to watch the movie but she would take a game and play it in another room until it was over. Having heard this, her friend's mother decided that it would be best to find another movie. Erica was fortunate. This situation turned out to be positive for all. Some who make the right choice will be rewarded with a more painful response. The choice has to be made, however, not knowing how people will react. This fact makes it another act of faith.

Related Articles
Chapter 13: Disagreeing without Being Dis-
    agreeable
Chapter 13: Staying Friends When Your Val-
    ues Collide
Chapter 26: When Your Teen Has Permissive
    Friends

Staying Friends When Your Values Collide

JIM & SALLY CONWAY

First, we need to examine why teens should value what their parents value. That may sound odd, but it is up to the person who sets the values to explain to the other person why the values are worthwhile. We run into problems if we never bother to question why we do what we do.

Besides knowing why we value what we value, we must treat our teens as friends. When our children become teen-agers, they don't need as much parental guidance as they once did. We have to keep in mind that we are relating to persons who are nearly adults.

It helps to think about how we would interact with an adult friend. Suppose a friend is visiting and asks to use the bathroom. We don't say, "Now be sure to put the lid down when you leave, wash your hands, and leave the towel straight."

Or suppose we are talking to a friend and say, "That is a dumb way of think-ing." She asks why and we say, "Because I said so." No one talks like that to a friend. But we expect to impose our values on our teens because we think of them as kids rather than nearly adults.

Of course, teens aren't fully adults but neither are they just kids. They need to be treated about five years older than we *think* they are. It is up to parents to explain, on an adult level, why an action is valuable, how we have found it to be good in our own life experience, and how it will make their lives more effective.

If teens seem to be going in a direction opposite of what we feel is right, we still need to keep loving them for the persons they are. We must love them uncondition-ally and stay friendly.

There were times, as our girls grew, when we were concerned about a choice they might make. Maybe they were dating someone who we were beginning to feel uncomfortable about, or we saw a relationship becoming too serious for

308

their ages. We didn't let that shut us off from friendships with our daughters. We kept loving them and being natural and open about the situation.

At the same time, we were really praying for God to work in them, in the other persons, and in us. It is amazing what God does inside other people without our interference. When parents take matters too greatly into their own hands, it usually builds a wall between them and the child. Ann Mow's book, *You and Your Teenager,* gives graphic illustrations of how parents loved their children unconditionally, even when they seemed to be turning out wrong.

When our daughters were very young, Sally was watching a friend relate to her seventeen-year-old. They had such an open friendship, and Sally told her she hoped when our girls were teenagers that they could have that kind of relationship. Her advice to Sally was, "Be sure you stay friends at every stage of life." Through the years Sally remembered that advice when one of the girls didn't feel like talking, and she did her part to keep the communication lines open.

Proverbs 22:6 (KJV) says, "Train up a child in the way he should go: and when he is old, he will not depart from it." The word *train* actually carries with it the meaning of "whetting a child's appetite," not forcing him. The verse also means that the parents are to help the child develop in his or her own unique "way" or life direction, according to the gifting of God. This means that we are to create a desire in our children to go in the particular way *God* has for them.

Related Articles

"Everyone's Doing It"

DAVID VEERMAN

"**B**ut everybody's doing it!"

How often have parents heard this response by their teenagers answering or reacting to a restriction? Drinking, curfew, clothes, hairstyle, cheating, dating—all are fair game.

How should we as parents respond to this line of reasoning, considered almost "irrefutable"? First, it is important to ask *why* the argument is used—why it is so important to teens. One word helps our understanding—*security*. Adolescence is the age of identity, discovering "who I am and where I fit in." It is very threatening to be alone, to stand out from the crowd. The group and its morés mean everything.

Second, we must be honest about our own lifestyles. I'm afraid that adults are quite susceptible to group pressure. Tastes in clothes, cars, and even politics are fashioned by society. (Has anyone discovered a use for the necktie?) How often do *we* act on principles regardless of what people think? Confession is "good for the soul" and also good for relationships. It will be helpful, therefore, to "fess-up" to our tendencies.

Understanding the feelings behind the phrase and confessing our own failings, let us consider our possible answers.

It would be easy to counter with a quick retort or a dogmatic "No, because I said so!" But such a response is usually

309

counterproductive. We may win the battle and lose the war. Instead, our answers should lead to deeper communication and teaching opportunities. In that light then, here are some suggestions that are formed as questions to lead to further discussion with our teenagers.

- Why is that argument important to you?
- Is everyone *really* "doing it"? Who isn't? Why?
- When is "everyone" wrong? (Truth is often in the minority. Look at Christ.)
- What is more important, doing what is *right* or doing what everybody does?
- Are there groups of "everybodies" that you should avoid . . . or leave?
- Is "everybody" doing "it" because "everybody's doing it" or are there other reasons?
- Is it wrong to be different?
- How do *you* treat people who are different?
- Whose opinion is *most* important to you . . . that of your boyfriend/girlfriend, peers, Mom and Dad, teachers, neighbors, church people, adults, God? Whose opinion is most important to you emotionally? intellectually?
- Can *you* swim against the tide? Can you change what "everybody" is doing?

As we lead the discussion with gentleness and honesty, we help our young people develop their own values and the courage to do what is right regardless of what "everybody" is saying or doing.

Related Articles

DEVELOPING
CHARACTER

- How do you motivate teenagers?
- When do you let children fall on their faces when making mistakes? When do you step in to help?
- Can you teach teens to make right decisions?
- Helping teens to establish priorities and goals
- Helping teens reach their potential
- Giving teens room to grow

We live in a world of cause and effect, and most of life's lessons are learned as a result of natural consequences. But it is often hard for us parents to allow our children to experience the scrapes and bruises of cause and effect, especially if the stakes are high. We want to jump in and stop the experience before any damage is done. Yet most success is made of failures. Thomas Edison failed thousands of times before he came up with the incandescent light bulb, and we and our children will make many mistakes too. We must allow this process to take place.

We do not need to fear total disaster: God has promised that He "will not suffer you to be tempted above that you are able; but will with the temptation also make a way to escape" (1 Cor. 10:13, KJV). We need to have faith in the stuff of which our kids are made and in the lessons they learned in childhood. We need to allow them to make mistakes, to rid ourselves forever of the idea of the 100-percenter who is a failure if he misses one or two small points. After all, one has to bat only .300 to be a star in the major leagues.

What Motivates Teens?
JAY KESLER

Two things lead the pack in producing motivation in young people. One is showing personal interest in them and their projects and activities. The other is showing motivation in some area ourselves.

First, it means a lot to teenagers when their parents are interested in their activities. It is very hard for young people to feel that what they are doing is important if adults are showing no interest in it. Regardless of what the teenager gets involved in—stamp collecting, model airplanes, soccer, or music—parental interest helps motivate him or her to continue in it and do well. It also gives the parents an opportunity to help the young person grow by collecting information, making observations, and so on. Parents can often motivate teenagers to excellence by providing a mature adult perspective on their projects.

Second, adults who are strongly motivated in their own activities often inspire teenagers to get interested in them too.

MOTIVATING FROM THE INSIDE OUT

Parents can affect teens by motivating them to develop themselves and become all God intends for them to be. Unfortunately, parents often force extrinsic motivation on their children. And more often than not, it doesn't work.

By extrinsic motivation, I mean using an external pressure to motivate the teen. For example, if a teen is getting C's in school and the parents want him to get A's, they might make a rule of no television, and three hours of study a night. Chances are, the teenager will not be motivated to do much studying. If they're lucky, the teen will "put up with" the rule. But a heart change on the teen's part is unlikely, when extrinsic motivation is forced on him.

Intrinsic motivation is innate, already existing in a person. If parents can be sensitive and watch for a spark in their child, they can fan it into a flame, and it can change a child's life.

If you let your kids watch television, talk with them about the programs. Talk about what they want to do with their lives and how they plan to get there. Watch for things that relate to their goals. Sometimes even a simple question can get teens to think. Look for opportunities to motivate your children, by picking up on the motivation that is already there—buried inside of them.

Intrinsic motivation will have a much greater effect on your children than extrinsic. Pray that God will open your eyes and sensitize you to the motivation He has given your child. Fan the flame and watch it grow!

Charles R. Swindoll

Many young people enjoy having a share in the things that interest their parents. When they see their parents excited about something, they want to do it too, especially if they can do it together.

It is strong motivation to allow a son to share in his father's joys and a daughter to share in her mother's. Such sharing puts flesh on the word *example*. John Dewey revolutionized the educational world with the phrase, "We learn by doing." We could add that we grow by doing *together*.

There is nothing so destructive to motivation as being ignored by one's family. Many young people have never had their parents see them perform in a concert, a ball game, or even the school Christmas program. No wonder, then, that they turn to a peer group who notices them, even if the price for their acceptance is doing things they believe to be wrong.

All of us need to be noticed. And as we're noticed and affirmed in what we're doing, we become motivated to do more of it. We can predict which direction a young person will go by noticing the path where the crumbs of interest and affirmation, reward and encouragement are strewn.

Related Articles

GUIDING VS. CONTROLLING

"Youth is wasted on the young"—this familiar quote hits the mark for most parents as they observe their teenagers with unlimited energy, enthusiasm, and idealistic perspectives rush headlong into life. Painfully aware of the needless mistakes of their own youth, Mom and Dad offer advice and guidance hoping that history will not be repeated.

The temptation, of course, is to control, to tell him or her what path to take (what college to choose, which career to prepare for, when to marry); but heavy pressure usually produces the "equal and opposite" effect.

The most frustrating situation is when we *know* that they are heading in a direction that will result in disaster. The dilemma is knowing how to *guide* without trying to control their futures. There is no money-back guarantee, but here are a few suggestions:

1. *Pray!* Continually we should commit our children to God's care. This involves our attitudes and actions too.

2. *Agree!* Both parents must be in agreement on how the kids will be reared and how to handle crises. Careful and honest communication is a necessity.

3. *Look!* . . . for lines of communication that we have broken, and repair them.

4. *Check!* . . . with professionals who are in touch with your kids. Teachers, coaches, school counselors, youth ministers, and others will offer valuable insight and counsel.

5. *Swallow pride!* We must not stand in the way of what might help, professional or otherwise. Our kids' well-being is more important than "saving face."

6. *Control reactions!* We shouldn't overreact and come down too hard. This will usually cause *their* overreaction. For example, if the problem involves a habit, our goal could be to reduce the frequency—not to eliminate it completely.

YFC Editors

Helping Teens Reach Their Potential

LEIGHTON FORD

When my son, Kevin, was about eleven, he asked me, "What is my spiritual gift, Dad?" I said, "I really don't know what your spiritual gift is, but I know you have the gift of humor and the gift of speaking, plus a calm and bright spirit. These may be the gifts of the Spirit in you."

Now that Kevin has grown older, I can begin to see his gifts more specifically. An attitude of affirmation has helped me to see these in him. A genuine thank you, a hug, a word of encouragement, a little note that says he did a great job.

Not everyone is a leader, but everyone is a servant with a gift to use. One gift is leadership, but there are many other gifts: creativity, mental prowess, mercy, mathematical ability, mechanical ability, all of these things are gifts. We need to develop the attitude of servanthood in our teens and then affirm any gift they may have.

I heard once that humility is not saying, "I don't have a gift," but knowing that what I have comes *through* me and not *from* me. It's important to affirm teens and let them know they have a gift. It's equally important to say it didn't come from them, but through them from God.

To draw out your teens' abilities, you must first know your children. You have to be a student of them and of human nature. Note where they do well and what comes easily for them.

The difficulty in studying our children is that we tend to read ourselves into them. But our children are made in God's image, not our image. They may have some genetic qualities from us that tend to make them like us, or unlike us. They may have some physical qualities from us, but they are unique.

When I was fourteen, we began holding Youth for Christ rallies in my little town in Canada. My mother helped me with those, encouraged me, and even raised a little money so we could bring speakers in. She encouraged me to speak too.

Fulfillment comes when kids are trained and encouraged, and then let go to use their spiritual gifts. That is how leadership is developed, not just by talking about it, but by recognizing the gifts in your children and trusting them

HOW TO STRUCTURE YOUR LIFE

Our son had a very active temper and we finally had to work out a code for times when things were getting too far out of hand. Using the code helped us to avoid embarrassing him in front of others. I'd say, "Well, it's time to clean your room," which translated meant, "You have to get out of this situation and go off by yourself and get control." That structure really helped him.

Young people need help with structuring. When my kids were very young we always tried to help them structure certain time frames. We'd say, "How much time do you want to get ready for breakfast? How much time to get ready for school? Here's when school starts; here's when you need to get up. OK, let's see, ten hours from here is when you need to be asleep. Now there are some things we want to do at bedtime—make sure there is time for our bedtime ritual of reading with the family. So here's when you need to get started for bed."

Essentially they picked the time and worked out the schedule according to their priorities within the framework.

But one thing parents need to recognize is that it's going to cost them. Parents can't structure the kids without structuring themselves. If parents say the kids need a bedtime ritual, then Dad and Mom had better not go off and watch their favorite TV show. They need to spend that time with their kids. Bringing up children means that parents have to be disciplined too.

Larry Richards

even when they make mistakes.

I think we might do too much for our teenagers in churches today. Instead of helping them to develop their spiritual responsibility and gifts, we have youth directors and programs and sponsors. I am not against those things, but sometimes I think we are robbing our kids of an opportunity to carry out the ministry.

Teaching Teens How to Make Right Decisions

JIM & SALLY CONWAY

Teens need to think through the outcomes of their decisions. By doing this, they become reflective people. It can begin with little things like choosing clothes or deciding whether or not to go to the football game. Then, when it comes to big decisions, they've had some practice using their judgment.

The kids we see who can't make good decisions by the time they reach their teenage years have been sheltered from thinking about every side of an issue. They've been told what their opinions should be. They have never thought through the consequences or been allowed to experience them.

One way to encourage children to make right decisions is to have them decorate their rooms. By this experience, they get practice in making decisions and learn how to live with the consequences. If they've painted their room purple with red stripes, they will have to live with it a while. They may change the colors eventually, but they've made the choice and have to put up with it.

If you have been building a good friendship with your children all along, you have a good foundation for sharing with each other when the time comes to make a major decision. There were times in each of our daughters' lives when it looked like they would become engaged to guys that we didn't feel comfortable with.

Instead of saying, "You can't marry him," we had a good enough relationship so that we could talk about our misgivings together. We'd discuss the fellow's good and bad points, and our daughters were free to say, "I really like him for this, but I have a problem with that."

One time, one of our daughters became rather defensive about a particular guy. She was really pushing us to accept him, and even though we didn't feel comfortable, we prayed that God would change us if this was the man for her. Then we began to accept him as much as we honestly could.

As soon as our daughter felt we were no longer resistant, she backed off and took a realistic look at him for herself. When she did, the relationship crumbled. If we had said at the beginning, "You have to quit seeing him; he isn't good for you," she would have worked all the harder to make him appear presentable.

There really are very few times when you have to step in and forbid something if you have a longstanding friendship and open communication with your teens. In a good relationship, you are sensitive to

each other and are working together instead of taking sides.

It's time to shift roles from that of parent to friend when teens go off to college or begin to live outside the home. It becomes more complicated, however, if they are living at home while they work or go to school. Then you need to discuss the new relationship.

If your young adult children choose to stay at home for four or five years after high school, they may have to abide by some limits because they are using their parents' home. But parents also have the responsibility to realize that they have another adult in the house and should be careful not to interfere in their son's or daughter's decisions. Now is the time to enjoy each other as good friends.

TAKE HEART

Suppose my watch was not working well. Would it do any good for me to travel to the town clock, and reset the hands of my watch to match those of the city clock? You know this would do no good, for the hands of my watch would soon be as far wrong as ever. I must send my watch to the watchmaker, that he may put its *heart* right, and then the hands will go right too. So it is with ourselves and our children. We must first get our *hearts* right, and then our hands will go right, and our feet, and all else.

The Biblical Treasury

How to Help Your Teen Choose Good Friends

CHARLES R. SWINDOLL

One of the major contributions parents can make to a child is helping him learn to choose good friends.

We began when our children were very young and teachable. We pointed out the good qualities of our friends. And our children learned by seeing us interact with our friends how important they were to us.

We tried to get them to think about the type of people they wanted to spend their time with—people who would strengthen

them morally, people with good self-esteem. We stressed the advantage of finding friends with good parents and homes with high ideals.

I remember when one of our daughters chose a friend who wasn't good for her. She's a sensitive girl and was easily swayed in her early years. We sat her down one day and just talked about her friend—what her home life was like, and what the characteristics of her family seemed to be. Then we asked our daughter what things she liked in our home and what was important to her. I asked her to think about the parallels between her life and the life she wanted, and that of her new friend. As I suspected, she couldn't think of too many. By realizing that there was such a marked contrast between her life and ideals and those of her new friend, my daughter began to see things in a new light.

As I mentioned before, begin in the early years, when your child is very teachable—when he's listening and sensitive. When we let our daughter think through her new choice, she was sensitive and open to our counsel.

My daughter realized that the characteristics of her friend's home could very easily carry over into her own life. Unfortunately, when the neighbor child grew into the teen years, she mirrored the negative characteristics of her environment. One night at the dinner table, my daughter said, "Remember our talk way back about so-and-so? I'm so glad that I chose against making her a close friend."

A second point is that we've got to be careful that we don't overkill. Sometimes when parents make the decision *for* their teen, giving him no option, the teen is provoked to rebel and become an intimate companion of the person the parents disapprove of. If teens feel that they can be friends with only three people that the whole family agrees on, they can be pushed to this extreme.

A related problem in Christian homes is helping teens see the distinction between avoiding friendships with backsliders and not becoming judgmental of non-Christians. The latter portion of 1 Corinthians 5 speaks about our associations with others. As parents, we must be careful not to instill a pious "holier-than-thou" attitude with our teens. Christ was compassionate with unbelievers. Our teens need to know how to be compassionate without lowering their standards.

Friends are a very tricky, but very important area in which parents need to instruct teens. Start as soon as possible and be a role model by wisely choosing your own friends.

Do You Have to Be Friends with *Her?*
DAVID VEERMAN

"**I** don't want you hanging around with those kids anymore!"

"But they're my friends!"

"I don't care. You know the things they do. They're a bad influence."

"You don't understand anything. . . ."

Your teenager stomps out and slams the door.

Very often this familiar family scenario polarizes parents and children. The young person resents the interference and defends her friends. Mom and Dad, however, know how destructive peer pressure can be and worry about questionable relationships.

Both sides have validity, which makes

317

the problem even more difficult to resolve. Any solution must deal with the feelings of the high school person as an emerging adult while, at the same time, respecting the indispensable responsibility and love of the mother and father.

The Bible emphasizes our parental duties for guidance and discipline *and* tells us not to provoke our children to anger (Eph. 6:1-3).

As parents, we need to decide the *real* issue. This means an honest evaluation of our motives and a careful analysis of the problem. Jesus' clear instruction is to first remove our eye's log before attempting to take care of another's speck (Matt. 7:1-5). Love is never blind.

Am I truly interested in my son's well-being, or just afraid to face the fact that he is growing up?

Am I concerned for my daughter's reputation—or for my own?

Do I know that much about those kids anyway? Maybe they're really nice, but just don't look like it.

And then there is the question of *why* your child chose "those friends."

Perhaps Bill Gothard's "compatibility of rebellion" theory is true here. That is, perhaps the young person is already involved in wrong activities, and these associates offer support and acceptance. If so, the real problem is much deeper than their friends, and we would be wise to refocus our attention.

Or maybe our son or daughter is attracted to people with desperate needs and forms friendships to reach out and help them. If this is the case, then these relationships are positive signs and marks of maturity. After all, Christian students are encouraged to exemplify Christlike love and to witness to their classmates.

After honest introspection comes action. Instead of allowing the problem to degenerate into a shouting match, we should take the initiative and look for opportunities to build relationships with our young people. We must constantly ask, "How can I act with discerning love in this situation?"

We might gently ask about their

GET TO KNOW YOUR TEEN'S FRIENDS

Friends are invaluable. We need them to listen, to care, to understand, or to just be there. They influence us with their advice, ideas, tastes, and example. But they also reflect. We tend to be drawn to those who are similar to us in values and lifestyle.

Our teens' situation is similar. That's why it's important to know their friends. They exert great influence (especially during this age of peer pressure), and they also reflect our kids' motives and desires.

To begin this process, our attitude is most important. We must express the desire to know them. It will also help build our relationships with our children if they know that we welcome their friends.

Perhaps the easiest way to meet and get to know their friends is to open our homes. If possible, we can have a room where kids can be natural (even throw popcorn if they want). We should be willing to stay away and let them have that turf.

Another "sure-fire" way to attract kids is to serve food. Teens have insatiable appetites and they will flock to refreshments.

We can also look for opportunities to involve the friends in family activities: outings, vacations, special occasions.

YFC Editors

friends' needs—family situation, school activities, personal struggles, and then ask God to show us how *we* can help them.

A second response would be to open our homes to those friends. Instead of projecting an attitude that they are "undesirable" or "untouchable," this would demonstrate our respect for our children and our openness to their relationships.

Suggest that their friends come for dinner or even join the family on an outing. This will not imply tacit approval or their habits, but it may expose them to a Christian home and Jesus' love.

Finally, we should suggest alternate activities for our young people and their friends. We need to do some brainstorming with our spouse, so instead of saying no, we can offer creative alternatives.

At times, a firm rejection of an evening's agenda is appropriate. But when we offer other suggestions, this puts the judgment on the activity, not on the person.

Our children should know that we love and accept them (and their friends) unconditionally, even if we don't approve of everything they do.

In all of this, of course, our goal should be to move our sons and daughters toward Christian maturity. This highly volatile area can be a most productive opportunity for demonstrating and teaching the Christian life.

Adapted from an article first published in *Moody Monthly* magazine.

Related Article

Chapter 25: "I Don't Like His Choice of Friends!"

Giving Teens Room to Grow

HAROLD MYRA

The year our daughter was fourteen, she wanted to play on the school volleyball team. She was already taking piano lessons, and she planned on being a cheerleader for a second year. In addition, she was involved at church and with two or three other activities.

When she asked me about volleyball, I said, "It's up to you, but you might want to cut back on some of these other things. You love to read, and you need to relax sometime. Make sure you don't take on too much."

I made sure I did *not* say, "It'll kill you. Knock it off. You're doing too much." I knew that harping would only create tension and wouldn't allow her to grow, but at the same time, she needed guidance. So I tried to show I had confidence in her ability to handle things,

and still let her know how I felt. Since there was no major moral issue involved, I left the final decision with her.

She wound up making some mature choices—pursuing some things, cutting back on some other things. It was a good experience in learning to make important decisions."

This was something I learned from my parents—teens need good counsel, but they also need to make some of their own choices. In my case, whether good or not (I'm still not sure), my parents had told me throughout my childhood, "When you're fourteen, you start making your own decisions."

I grew up looking forward to that day I remember the first time I made a choice against my parents' wishes—going to see a 3-D movie called *Fort Ti.* My mother said, "You know how we stand on movies. (They were against them.) But you're fourteen now, and this is a choice you need to make."

I'm not saying every parent should turn kids loose at fourteen, but gradually you do need to stop making every decision and assume a role of loving counselor. That way the teens have practice making choices, and you're still around to discuss the options, the consequences, and to console and correct when the decisions turn sour.

The most important thing, though, is to maintain the relationship with your kids. With hugs and encouragement, let them know they are totally loved by their parents. When kids feel loved and know their parents support them and expect a growing maturity, there's usually an inner motor that begins driving teenagers. They may still go through a rebellious period; their behavior may still seem bizarre. But if parents keep the supply of love and wisdom constant, the kids will know when they're doing wrong, and when they get into bad situations, they'll be more likely to seek their parents' help.

Being patient with teens is tough. When they tell you they're sick of you, your patience is tried. The kids don't know what you're feeling inside, but you can't blow up. I'm not saying you have to mask your feelings, but neither should you show your disgust every time you feel it. Project love and acceptance even when you don't feel like it.

Yes, it's tough. But if you're a parent, you've gone through tough stages before—from diapers to squalling to childhood diseases. Teenage years do bring problems, but don't expect nothing but foolish, immature behavior. Be ready for deeply pleasing times too as you give teens room to grow and see them develop into maturity.

Related Articles

THE TWO CASTLES

A poor, but worthy man living in Paris once went to his pastor with a dejected spirit and a heart almost overwhelmed. "Pastor," he said, with the most profound humility, "I am a sinner, I feel that I am a sinner, but I really don't want to be. Every hour I ask for light, and humbly pray for faith, but still I am overwhelmed with doubts. God must surely despise me, for if He truly loved me He would not let all these struggles come my way."

The kindly pastor smiled at the poor man and then told him this story: "The king of France has two castles in different locations, and sends a commander to each of them. The castle of Montleberry stands in a place remote from danger, far inland; but the castle of La Rochelle is on the coast, where it is open to continuous siege. Now which of the commanders do you think stands highest in the estimation of the king—the commander of La Rochelle or the commander of Montleberry?"

"Doubtless," said the poor man, "the king values him the most who has the hardest task, and braves the greatest dangers."

"You are right," replied the pastor. "And now apply this case to your life and mine. For my heart is like the castle of Montleberry, and yours like that of La Rochelle."

The Biblical Treasury

MATURITY

"Maturity" is a magic wand for teenagers because it supposedly unlocks the door to adult privileges. For parents, maturity means children acting responsibly.

In reality, maturity is a process of growth, and maturity levels vary among individuals depending on age, sex, social environment, and other factors (personal and otherwise).

Our teenagers are on a maturity roller coaster. As "adults-in-process," their bodies and emotions are undergoing tremendous changes while they push toward independence. Therefore, our observed maturity in them will vary, from one day to the next and from one category to another.

As we watch our kids "act their age," we should avoid using "immaturity" as a sort of swear word to vent our frustration over behavior we don't like. One parent said, "My biggest problem with my sixteen-year-old is that she acts like a teenager."

We can help our teens "grow up" by accepting them as they are while we reward mature responses. At the same time we should not shelter them, but allow them to experience the natural consequences of immature behavior.

In the midst of this we should broaden their perspectives so they will *see* beyond themselves, understanding that their actions affect others too.

It has been said that "maturity is the ability to postpone gratification." This we can teach, but it will be better "caught." The challenge for us is to be models of mature adults, not overgrown children demanding sophisticated toys and immediate satisfaction. Maturity begins at home.

YFC Editors

INFLUENCING
SPIRITUAL DEVELOPMENT

- How do we talk to our kids about God?
- What is the difference between a religious home and a Christian one?
- How do we help our teens apply their faith to everyday life?
- Do prayers have any effect on our children?

- How important is our spiritual example?
- What should teens know about the Bible?
- How do we answer teens' common misconceptions about God?
- Family devotions—are they worth all the effort?

A wise person once said, "More is caught than taught." Though surely we want to emphasize the importance of teaching our children about God, we must recognize that spiritual life is mostly caught. What we see in others determines our behavior more than does our knowledge and our resolve.

Almost all adults can find behavior patterns in their own lives that were unconsciously developed through observing their parents. And even if they've spent a lifetime trying to change those patterns, chances are they're still there. As we live Christ before our young people, we influence them greatly. If we want them to achieve certain spiritual goals, we must be what we want them to become.

On the Beltway north of Washington, D.C. is a building called the Bureau of Standards. In it is kept the real foot, the real meter, the real pound, the real gram. We compare all others to them. One way or another, parents are the Bureau of Standards to their young people. They are the way young people determine what is a real Christian, a real lover, a real forgiver, a real witness.

Where Are My Teens Spiritually?

JAY KESLER

The first step in finding out where anyone is in any area is to choose the form of measurement. We have to decide how we measure accomplishment.

If you ask, "What does it mean to be spiritual?" you are likely to hear all kinds of discussion. I remember when kids were put in front of groups and gave testimonies more or less like this: "Now that I've become a Christian, I am no longer involved in athletics, or the school band, or whatever; I now spend all my time going to church and church activities." The adults would applaud, and the young person would feel affirmed for having pulled away from school activities to get involved in religious activities. By the standard evident in these meetings, a person's spirituality is measured by the extent of his or her participation in religious programs.

I frankly feel that a much better measurement has to do with the fruit of the Spirit. "The fruit of the Spirit is love, joy, peace, long-suffering, gentleness, goodness, faith, meekness, temperance" (Gal. 5:22-23). As we see a young person growing in these areas, we begin to realize he or she is making spiritual progress.

We can almost predict that at some stage in their spiritual development, young people will reject institutional Christianity. They will see all kinds of problems in the institution itself. This reached a high point in the 1960s when kids said, "Christ yes, Christianity no," and anti-institutionalism still persists. We parents tend to panic when this happens, and yet the institution is not what we're trying to get across. We want our children to follow Christ Himself.

Young people almost always admire Jesus when they know about Him. The more a person knows about Jesus, the more he or she likes Him. Therefore, holding up Christ to young people is much more important than holding up institutional Christianity or a list of do's and don'ts. In fact, it's the most important thing parents and youth workers can do.

The best measure of a young person's spirituality is the extent to which he or she imitates Christ. Of course, when we are measuring young people's spirituality, we have to take into account the fact that they are teenagers. Teenagers act like teenage Christians, just like adults ought to act like adult Christians. The fact that some of the "teenage-ness" spills over onto the Christian side is to be expected.

For instance, if a group of teens goes away to a Christian camp and has a pillow fight and breaks windows, it shouldn't be made into a federal case. It doesn't mean the kids are backslidden and the group is

THE GREATEST GIFT

I believe *the* most valuable contribution a parent can make to his child is to instill in him a genuine faith in God. What greater ego satisfaction could there be than knowing that the Creator of the universe is acquainted with me, personally? That He values me more than the possessions of the entire world; that He understands my fears and my anxieties; that He reaches out to me in immeasurable love when no one else cares; that His only Son, Jesus, actually gave His life for me; that He can turn my liabilities into assets and my emptiness into fullness; that a better life follows this one, where the present handicaps and inadequacies will all be eliminated—where earthly pain and suffering will be no more than a dim memory! What a beautiful philosophy with which to "clothe" your child. What a fantastic message of hope and encouragement for the broken teenager who has been crushed by life's circumstances. This is self-esteem at its richest, not dependent on the whims of birth or social judgment or the cult of the superchild, but on divine decree.

James Dobson

From *Dr. Dobson Answers Your Questions,* by James Dobson, Tyndale House Publishers, Inc., © 1982. Used by permission.

no good. Fifteen-year-olds act like fifteen-year-olds. Now if they're forty-five and still having pillow fights and breaking windows, they probably need to think it over a little bit. But young people will act like young people.

Sometimes parents find Christ later in life and feel like they have to do a lot of making up for lost time. They get super-serious about their spirituality, running back and forth to Bible studies and church meetings, reading Christian books, listening to Christian radio. And then they say, "How come my fifteen-year-old son or my sixteen-year-old daughter doesn't want to get involved in a lot of Christian activities like I do? There must be something wrong with him or her." Not necessarily. He may still be trying to figure out what happened to his parents. Is this a phase that Mom and Dad are going through, or is it real and lasting?

Teenage spirituality, then, must be measured by teenage standards, keeping a great deal of charity and tolerance in one's definition. Yes, they will act like kids. Yes, they will be anti-institutional. But yes, they will be very much attracted to the person of Christ. So don't treat their spirituality as if it has to be full-blown. Realize that it's in process, like their physical bodies. Both are somewhere between birth and adulthood.

Day-to-day growth, both physical and spiritual, is almost imperceptible. It can only be measured on a monthly, semiannual, or yearly basis. Sometimes, the growth seems to stop or, in the spiritual case, even go backward. But looking back, we can see progress. This is all we can ask.

A SPIRITUAL PHYSICAL

It's important to know where your children are spiritually. Faithfulness at quiet time and church and Sunday School do not tell the whole story. They can become routine, and children can fake interest in them. Here are some other ways to check your children's spiritual health. (1) Watch how they treat others. You can see if what you have taught them is really getting home. (2) Listen carefully to what they like to talk about to find out if spiritual things are important to them. (3) Look at their priorities. What choices are they making? How do they respond to the freedom you give them? (4) Notice how they respond to you when you bring up spiritual things. If they constantly have negative spiritual attitudes, you'd better beware. (5) Pray with them.

Josh McDowell

Religious Homes vs. Christian Homes

What's the Difference?

RICHARD C. HALVERSON

I grew up in North Dakota with some preconceived ideas about the church and its influence in the home. Though my mother had met the Lord in a Billy Sunday evangelistic meeting and attended church regularly, she never told me that God loved me and Christ died for me. She did as much as a mother could to bring us up in church, but my father never attended. My grandfather had no respect for preachers either, so I grew up believing that preachers were failures and only women and children went to church. Later, in my teenage years, I got the feeling that to be religious, I had to refrain from smoking, drinking, going to shows, dancing, and playing cards.

In evaluating my youth, I believe I was brought up in a religious home rather than a Christian home. This kind of legalistic environment is less than biblical. In fact, I would venture to say that the primary difference between a religious home and a Christian home lies in the extent of legalism versus genuine intimacy and communication of God's love.

Many teenagers have been turned off to Christianity as a result of religious training in the home. In my own home, I tried to express my faith without forcing it on my teens. My children have memories of opening the door to my study and finding me on my knees in prayer. Though I never knew it until much later, the impact of this sight left them thinking of me as a man of prayer.

I tried to make sure that my children grew up in an open environment, not a legalistic one. My wife and I never allowed our children to think they had to be different or live differently than their peers because their father was a pastor.

I believe there are two major tasks for the parents who want to make their home truly Christian. The first is to show affection and love toward every member of the family. In fact, when I do premarital counseling, I always ask the following questions: "Do you think your father and mother loved each other? How did they show that love?" In my forty years as a pastor, I've discovered that some adults have never seen their own parents express affection to each other; nor have they experienced affection from either or both parents.

The father needs to show love to the mother and children, especially to daughters. If daughters don't get affection from their fathers, they grow up not knowing how to handle intimacy. One of the explanations for young girls getting involved in sex at a very early age is that they long for intimacy. Sexual involvement becomes a substitute for intimacy with their father.

The second task for parents who want to make their home truly Christian is to create a time for family devotions in a nonlegalistic atmosphere. Insisting on participation can alienate a teenager, yet every family should try to meet the Lord sometime each day.

Parents Set the Spiritual Pace

V. GILBERT BEERS

There is something in parenting that is more than principles. You may buy every book about parenting, catalog every principle, memorize the list, and even do your best to put these principles into your teen's life. But there is something lost in translation unless principles become flesh and blood, heart and mind, and live themselves out in your life. To put it bluntly, parenting cannot be reduced to a list of principles.

From childhood, we learn best from role models. Principles mean little to a child. Example means everything. "Do as I say, not as I do" is more than a joke. It is an oft-repeated tragedy in homes where parents believe their admonitions will be sufficient for their children. But children are perceptive, often more perceptive than adults, so words are easily canceled by conduct. We say, "God listens with concern to every prayer." But if we as parents are too busy to listen to our children, how then can they understand a God who hears?

"God is a loving Father," we say. But if we fathers are less than loving to our children, how then can our children relate to their Father in heaven as a loving Person?

"The Bible is the most important book in the world," we say. But if our children never see or hear us read it, how then can they relate what we say and what we do?

"The fruit of the Spirit is . . ." and we name them all. But if our children look in vain for love, joy, peace, and the other fruit in our lives, how then shall they understand our words?

"Christ changes our lives, and we become new people," we say. But if our children watch us "cut corners" and compromise integrity in little ways, how shall they know that we will not do the same in things that matter most, those that relate to the life-changing Christ?

Words are extensions of life, not vice versa. We do not seek to fulfill what we have spoken, but rather speak what we have become because we believe it so completely. If we do not fully believe what we say, our children will quickly detect that. If we do not practice what we say, they will quickly detect that also. Thus, unless belief, words, and conduct are unified, one cancels out the others.

Never think that teens won't observe inconsistencies among belief, words, and conduct. They will probably know something is wrong before we know it.

As parents, we seek to live consistent Christian lives, not merely to set a good example for our children, but because we believe this pleases our Lord. Not only that, it must surely please a Christian wife or husband. Consistent Christian living will make you and me happier, more balanced persons, for our belief and words and conduct will be in harmony.

When all of that is happening, we will catch the attention of our teens and focus it on the living Christ. An ounce of loving role modeling is worth a pound of parental pressure.

Related Articles

KEYS TO A CHRISTIAN HOME

Lots of people think that the key to a spiritual atmosphere in the home is having spiritual exercises, a family altar.

Well, I do believe having some sort of time when you read and pray together is important. In our home it wasn't rigid. We had a regular time around the table, but if something came up—a ball game or something—we didn't force it. We said, "Go ahead and play. We'll catch it tomorrow night." It was part of the family, no question about that, but it was also flexible, so it didn't have negative connotations. But as far as creating a Christian home, two other things are even more important.

One is developing a strong sense of commitment between mother and father. Children seem to know that these people are committed to each other. That's where they get their security. Of course, Mom and Dad will have disagreements; they may even scrap once in a while, but they love each other, and they're going to stay together. That demonstrates what genuine Christian love is: a commitment that weathers storms.

The second key is that within the commitment, mother and father love one another, and demonstrate that love. Love can't be a secret, passive, inside thing. It must be expressed. That's absolutely crucial for children to see.

Martin Luther once said, "I have difficulty praying the Lord's Prayer because whenever I say 'Our Father,' I think of my own father, who was hard, unyielding, and relentless. I cannot help but think of God that way."

On the other hand, I recently read a story that illustrates what a powerful force parents can be in living out God's love.

A small boy had been consistently late in coming home from school. His parents warned him one day that he must be home on time that afternoon, but nevertheless he arrived later than ever. His mother met him at the door and said nothing. His father met him in the living room and said nothing.

At dinner that night, the boy looked at his plate. There was a slice of bread and a glass of water. He looked at his father's full plate and then at his father, but his father remained silent. The boy was crushed.

Suddenly, the father took the boy's plate and placed it in front of himself. Then he took his own plate of meat and potatoes, put it in front of the boy, and smiled at his son.

When that boy grew to be a man, he said, "All my life I've known what God is like by what my father did that night."

J. Allan Petersen

327

What Kind of Spiritual Example Are You Setting?

ADRIAN ROGERS

A juvenile delinquent is usually nothing but a child who's trying to act like his parents. Society's dropouts are not primarily the children, but the parents who have failed to be the kind of example they should have been.

Adam and Eve, the first parents, were not the best examples to Cain and Abel. Eve, for example, had a wrong set of values. I see many mothers today with the same values Eve had in the Garden of Eden. First, she valued physical gratification. She "saw that the tree was good for food." Second, she valued aesthetic stimulation. She saw that "it was pleasant to the eyes." Third, she valued intellectual investigation. It was "a tree to be desired to make one wise" (Gen. 3:6, KJV).

I think the same values are prominent today. There's nothing wrong with physical gratification, with caring for the body; but we are living in a day when parents are pampering the body while strangling the soul. Aesthetic stimulation is not bad in itself, but I know parents who would give up going to church before they would give up their new color television. When they do go to church, their primary interests are in the flower arrangements, the art, the lawn, the fashion, the furniture, and so on.

Likewise, intellectual investigation is good unless it becomes the motivating factor. So many people today are worldly wise but spiritually ignorant. Eve sold her soul to satisfy her curiosity, and her values filtered down to Cain and Abel.

Not only did those boys have a mother with the wrong set of values, they also had a father with no backbone. Adam was intended to be the head of the house, but he left his rightful place. Eve was to be his help-mate, but Adam let her lead him.

I've been a pastor for many years, and I have yet to see a home where the wife and children did not follow the man if he, from the beginning of the marriage, loved and served God. As a general rule, if the home is wrong it's because the man is wrong, because he has abdicated his place of leadership. I am convinced that if a home is wrong, God holds the man responsible.

So Eve's values were wrong, Adam had no backbone, and Cain and Abel were just left to chance. One boy went right, and one boy went wrong. Inconsistent living brings inconsistent results.

How should parents set good examples? One of our major duties is to start early. I have observed that many parents start sixteen years and 175 pounds too late. The Bible says in Proverbs 19:18 that we're to chasten our son while there's hope. Sometimes we're going to find ourselves in a hopeless situation if we don't start early enough. Proverbs 22:6 (KJV), "Train up a child in the way he should go: and when he is old, he will not depart from it," implies that we're to give him the training when he's young. The earlier we start, the better.

Then, if we are going to be good examples, we have to have strong values. Because of the world's humanistic philosophy, teenagers need definite values. They need a code to live by; they need to learn what is right and what is wrong in concrete terms. This is right and that is wrong because God says so. You see Mom and Dad living this way because the Bible teaches that this is the way we're to live.

Even games are no fun without boundaries. So many young people today don't know where the boundaries are. They have no distinct guidelines. These young people need a code to live by, a creed to believe in, something that's not just sentimentality but that is explainable and spiritually authenticated in their hearts and lives. They need to say, "The Bible is the Word of God; Christ is the Son of God; and there is indeed victory in Christ."

Not only do they need a code to live by and a creed to believe in, they also need a cause to serve. So many young people are "at sea" today because they don't have a cause. Young people today are looking for involvement. If we as parents have a soft religion, we're not going to offer any challenge.

We parents need to start early; we need to build strong values; and we need to show love. Teenagers more than anybody else on the face of the earth need love. I think they're more interested in love than anything else, and parents need to show love by touching them appropriately and often. Not only do parents need to show love to their teenagers, they also need to demonstrate it to each other. We've all heard the saying that the best thing a father can do for his teenager is to love that teenager's mother.

We also need to use discipline. The Bible says in Proverbs 13:24 that if we spare the rod, we hate our son. So often the parents will say, "I don't discipline him because I love him so much." But in truth, we don't love him if we don't discipline him; we love ourselves and don't want the problem of discipline. We don't want to risk the child's displeasure.

Fathers need to be careful that they don't try to be just another brother. Teenagers don't need more buddies; they

BE WHAT YOU BELIEVE

Not all children raised in Christian homes are on fire for the Lord. Some parents, wishing to avoid conflict, tend to back off from religious topics as their children get older. I think this is unwise. But some ways are more effective than others for reaching our older children for the Lord.

We have to model what we believe. If we want our children to be soul-winners, they need to see it in our lives. We can also expose them to other people who are good models, people who are not only living attractive, radiant lives, but who are also witnessing for Christ. We can do more through teaching than through preaching, more through example than through demands.

It is also helpful to take them to a good church for worship and praise meetings where there is excitement and enthusiasm for the Lord expressed in good taste. Look for a place where God is truly loved and worshiped and adored, where there is a lot of singing and where there are a lot of testimonies of how Christ is answering prayer and changing lives. I am a strong believer in testimonies, especially if they are given by people our children respect.

We need to expose our children to aggressive, vital, dynamic Christianity and continue to pray for them. Prayer accomplishes more than anything else.

Bill Bright

have plenty already. They don't need leaders; they develop their own. The one thing they really do need is parents who are examples, who will live the Gospel in front of them.

Yet not everything can be taught by example. We need to teach empirical truths and biblical facts. Jesus, the master Teacher, practiced what He preached and preached what He practiced; that's what made Him such a great Teacher. One without the other is not enough.

Young people need consistency. To be consistent doesn't mean to be perfect. Rather, it means holding firm to your goals, your standards, your aspirations. Then, when you fail, you confess and go right back to trying to live by your standards. I've failed many times. I've lost my temper with my children; I've been rude to their mother. I've done things that are un-Christlike and unworthy of the Lord I serve. But by God's grace, I have been enabled to confess not only to the Lord, but also to my family. And the wonderful thing is that my confession does not lessen their respect for me. To the contrary, it increases it.

I don't have to pretend to be perfect; they already know I'm not. But if they see that my confession is honest, then they know that at least I'm real. I'm not a hypocrite. That's how I can be consistent without being perfect, and how I can keep my children's and my wife's respect.

Related Articles

How Do You Talk to Your Kids about God?

BARRY ST. CLAIR

Have you ever wondered why some parents can be completely at ease as they discuss spiritual matters with their teens, while others can't seem to put two sentences together without stammering or clearing their throat? I think that's because talking to teens about God involves much more than just *talking*. Before parents can freely discuss spiritual concepts with their teens, they must first make an active commitment to *discipling* their children.

The first step toward effectively disciplining children is that *parents need to have a growing relationship with Jesus Christ.* If the parents aren't putting Christ first in their own lives, they won't be at ease as they talk to their children—knowing that children are usually quick to notice inconsistencies between "what I say" and "what I do."

The second step toward effectively discipling children is that *parents should never bore their kids with the Gospel.* What do you think goes through a child's mind when he is doing something with his parents that he enjoys, and suddenly they become serious and say, "Why don't we talk about God for a while?" The child is likely to say, "Hey, this is no fun." So the key is to connect "discipling" with "having fun." Believe it or not, it *can* be done.

Deuteronomy 6:4-9 is a passage full of good ideas for keeping discipleship fun for your children. It describes several ways to instruct them—some structured and others unstructured. Below are several suggestions to help you get started:

STRUCTURED TRAINING

1. Set aside a time for discipling each week. Build it into your schedule and don't miss it.

2. Make plans together. Decide how you want to spend your time. Share your ideas and set some goals.

3. Make sure to "build in" fun. Go out for ice cream, go shopping, play ball, etc.

4. Work on a project together. My son and I are memorizing 1 John. I'm preparing my daughter as she plans to join our church. Decide on something you can both participate in.

5. Pray together each time you meet.

6. Talk on a feeling level. Go beyond questions like, "How was school?" Say, "How do you feel about...?" Really get to know how your children think and feel.

7. Help them reach their goals. Talk about your goals. Have them write down their own goals. Make sure these goals are attainable. Keep checking back to see how they are doing.

8. Minister together. During your time together, think, "What can we do for someone else?"

9. Let your children know that during the time you set aside for them, there is nothing you would rather be doing.

UNSTRUCTURED TRAINING

1. Set the pace. Let your life be an example to your children. If you want them to memorize Scripture, *you* had better memorize Scripture.

2. Get into your children's world. If your son hurts, hurt with him. If he's having fun, have fun with him (Rom. 12:15).

3. Be positive. Emphasize your children's strengths, not their weaknesses.

4. Weigh decisions and judgments carefully. Don't make snap decisions. Wait until emotions cool down.

5. Develop an attitude of openness and forgiveness. Be a listener.

6. Don't just say *what* to do; show *how* to do it. This is true whether you are studying the Bible or fixing a bike.

7. Plan special events that will build memories—vacations, trips, local outings.

8. Help your children develop their own convictions. Today peer pressure is greater than ever. How are you going to teach your children to stand up for Jesus Christ in the midst of it? That's tough. But start by being open about your own convictions and modeling them before your family.

9. Make life an adventure. Make it fun to be a follower of Jesus.

Use these ideas as a starting point. Begin to practice them as soon as each of your children is old enough to understand what he is doing. These suggestions will work for very small children and will increase in effectiveness as the children grow. If you learn to make discipleship fun, you'll soon have the freedom to discuss *anything* with your children— spiritual or otherwise. Isn't that worth the effort?

Related Articles
Chapter 15: Helping Teens Live Their Faith
Chapter 15: Is Your Faith Rubbing Off on Your Kids?
Chapter 15: Leading Your Teenager to Christ
Chapter 15: Helping Teens Share Their Faith

Helping Teens Live Their Faith

WARREN W. WIERSBE

Helping teens apply their faith to everyday life is a balance of teaching and modeling. It's an outgrowth of your own walk with God, and it needs to begin long before children reach their teens.

In our home, my wife and I had daily devotions individually, and we also had family devotions so the kids could see how it was done.

Less overtly but perhaps more importantly, we tried to show how the Word of God applied in daily life and how we should obey regardless of the circumstances. We didn't always succeed—sometimes we lost our patience—but we tried to see every experience as an opportunity to learn from the Lord and teach our children.

For example, whenever we've made a move, we've included the children in the praying and planning. Another instance was when I was hospitalized after a car accident. My wife is the hero here—she did a wonderful job comforting the children when it was uncertain whether I would live or die. With calm and poise, she took care of details and let the children know that God was in control.

In these and other situations, we tried to instill two principles:

First, *faith is not feeling nor is it intellectual assent*. Faith is obeying God in spite of feelings, circumstances, or consequences. There's too much fuzzy "faith in faith" around today—the kind of stuff you hear about in the song, "I believe for every drop of rain that falls a flower grows." Nonsense. If that were true, we'd be up to our armpits in flowers.

Or there's a commercial faith—"God, I'll believe *if* You do this for me." That's not faith at all, and we've tried to steer clear of that.

We've tried to teach our kids the kind of faith the three young Hebrew men had in Daniel 3—"The God we serve is able to save us . . . but even if He does not . . . we will not serve your gods or worship the image of gold you have set up" (vv. 17-18, NIV). That faith means obeying God no matter what.

Second, *we don't live by explanations but by promises.* Everyone loves to speculate why God does this and why God allows that. When those questions come up, I've consistently told my kids, "I don't know." But I try to point them to a promise in Scripture.

Explanations may actually produce opposite results than intended. Some of the toughest faith problems happen in Bible colleges and seminaries where the Bible becomes a textbook, and Scripture loses its aura and mystery.

Faith is a relationship to God, not a complete understanding. I can have a great relationship with my surgeon and not know a scalpel from a screwdriver. There's a temptation these days, with all the study Bibles and Christian books, to live on explanations. You can't! The deeper you get in the Christian life, the less you can explain. I can't explain prayer—I really can't. But I pray now more than ever.

So we've tried to raise our children on promises rather than attempts to explain God's actions.

How do you make Scripture alive for teens, or for anyone? Martin Luther said it comes through study, prayer, and suffering. He pointed to Psalm 119, where over and over again the writer experiences those very things. Every third or fourth verse mentions some trial he's going through.

Families that want their teens to grow in faith can expect trouble. Don't run from it. Use it. Faith that can't be tested can't be trusted. Going through the furnace is the challenge and the opportunity.

But the key is using your own walk with God to demonstrate what the Christian life is. I really don't know any other

---

HOW GOD SOLVES OUR PROBLEMS

We need to teach teens how God solves problems. It's not usually by providing a convenient miracle. No, instead, this is the way He normally works.

He gives us:
- The courage to face our problems honestly.
- The wisdom to understand what's happening.
- The strength to do what we must.
- The faith to trust Him to do what we cannot.

This is how we taught our children that God solves problems. Where does the Word of God come in? It's woven into each step.

- Through the promises of the Word, we get the courage to face problems without running away or blaming someone else.
- Through the principles of the Word, we get the wisdom to understand, perhaps not everything we'd like to know, but the insight we need.
- Through the power of the Word, we get the strength to do what we must.
- Through persistence in the Word, we grow in faith. We tried to teach our kids not to use the Bible as a crisis tool. If you're in the Word day after day and a crisis comes, you don't need to panic. You'll be ready for it.

Warren W. Wiersbe

way to do it.

MORE THAN A BOOK OF RULES?

I often take my children downtown for breakfast. We live out in the woods, and it's about a ten-minute drive. While we're in the car, I teach them about God, the Holy Spirit, Christ, and Satan; or we review what we have learned previously by asking each other questions. When we get to the restaurant, we discuss school or read a Bible storybook together or do value determination.

Value determination, unlike value clarification, assumes that there is such a thing as right or wrong. I set up certain moral or ethical situations to see how the children would respond, and then I share with them how I think one ought to respond. For example, in a situation where lying would be easy, we talk about why it is wrong to lie. Most parents say, "Because the Bible says, 'Thou shalt not lie.' " I don't think that's a healthy response, because it gives the children regulations without a relationship. In all their values, I want them to respond to a person rather than a book of rules. So I say, "Why does the Bible say, 'Thou shalt not lie'?" Then I take it right back to the person of God.

"The Bible is an expression of the very character and nature of God," I say. "Since God is truth, anything that is nontruth is contrary to His nature. Therefore lying is sinful and unhealthy for His children."

Josh McDowell

Identifying the Supernatural in the Everyday

DAVID & KAREN MAINS

Parents can help their children see God at work in their everyday lives in many creative ways. A way we've helped our children do this is by a variation of the childhood game, "I Spy." Each of us has a notebook in which we record ways we see God working in our world. It might be an obvious answer to prayer. Or, it might be unexpected evidences of God's care. Or, it might be a combination of the two. It could also be any special timing or linkage when things just fit together to the second. Or, any special help to do God's work in the world.

One day our son, Jeremy, came home from school with a great "I Spy." It was a new school year, and up until then, he'd never had a Christian friend in his class. But in the sixth grade, they switched the kids around and Jeremy made a new friend. He brought this new friend home, and when the boy's mother came to pick him up, it turned out to be someone Karen knew in high school. And Karen knew that this lady was a Christian and that Jeremy's new friend was being raised in a Christian home.

Another time, we all went to visit our oldest son, Randy, who is living in DeKalb, Illinois. It was right before Dave was leaving for India, and he wanted to get together with Randy. But it turned out to be an extra special time because the one night when we could get together was the exact night that the Wheaton College soccer team was playing the team from Northern Illinois University. Randy had played on the Wheaton team when he was in college, so we not only got to have a meal with him but to see a great game and visit with some of the kids he knew. Only God could have worked out the timing.

About the same time, Karen became upset because Dave had scheduled a weekend series of talks at a nearby church. But it turned out to be an "I Spy" because if we hadn't scheduled the talks, we would have gone to a church retreat that would have kept us busy the whole weekend. Originally, it looked like the talks would take up the whole weekend too. But the church decided to cancel all the meetings on Saturday. Thus, we had some time to spend together before Dave left for India.

Another time, Dave was a bit upset because his parents were leaving for Florida soon and he hadn't had much time to spend with them. But, by "chance," Dave and his dad both went to the same restaurant for lunch the day before Dave's father was to leave. They had forty-five minutes just to share with each other what was going on in their lives. And Dave had a great "I Spy" to write in his notebook.

Sometimes, when we are all together, we share our "I Spys" at the dinner table. That way we have the added benefit of seeing how God is working in the lives of each member of our family. And, of

HOW GOD ANSWERS PRAYER

An example of how God answers prayer happened when our youngest child, Kurt, took his SAT college entrance tests. He asked me to call the prayer chain, and I told him that I already had, and we would be praying for God's will to be done. He replied, "Oh boy, it's just my luck that it will be God's will that I flunk."

I gently reminded him that God both opens *and* closes doors. If college was for him, then we wanted God to help him get the test scores that he needed. God did answer and Kurt got the test scores he needed not only to get into college but to erase the discouragement he had felt in math.

We tend to view God's answers simplistically. To us, it's a positive answer if our teen passes the test and a negative answer if he fails it. But that's not how God sees it. I explained to Kurt that God's closed doors are probably more important than His open doors. There are thousands of open doors, and so it's important that God close all of those which are not His will, so you can find the one that is His will. The seemingly negative answers and closed doors are, in actuality, positive. They are God's way of keeping us from going in the wrong directions.

Evelyn Christenson

course, we get a bigger picture of God at work in the "ordinary" circumstances of life.

There are other ways of helping kids become aware of God's work in their lives. We've found that when children are very small, Christian parents have to help point out God's work. It's as if you were playing hide-and-seek with tots who are too young to figure out where everyone is hiding. So, you help them by whispering where someone is hiding. Then they go and catch that person. In the same way, you whisper what God's doing in answering their prayers and soon they are able to see for themselves God's hand in their lives.

What we've seen in doing this is that kids have a spiritual sensitivity that many grown-ups have lost. They are closer to the supernatural and the unseen because they are not yet caught up in the material world in which adults live.

We're also helping our children develop prayer notebooks. If we just pray, our prayers seem to evaporate. We don't sense God's answers. But, if we keep prayer notebooks, we discipline ourselves to pray and to look for results. It's also a beautiful tool for God to use in our lives.

We saw that when Dave went to Fort Wayne, Indiana for a meeting. He was so tired after driving there, that he didn't feel much like praying. But when he looked in his prayer notebook, he saw that he had already prayed for twenty-five things in regard to the session. So, since he'd already committed the matter to God, he was free to get some sleep. He knew that God was already at work in the situation.

Keeping prayer notebooks has encouraged our kids to do the same. Randy and Melissa both keep notebooks and share with us when they have seen answers to prayers.

Our whispered hints of God at work, the prayer journals, and the "I Spy" notebooks all give our kids an assurance that God is at work in their lives.

***

Related Articles

Is Your Faith Rubbing Off on Your Kids?

DAN SARTIN

George Gallup's poll, "Religion in America," concludes with a startling thought. It states "that never in the history of America has the Gospel made such inroads into our society while having such little effect on the way people live their lives."

The indictment which this survey makes on the Christian community is one of grave importance to us as parents. Jesus commanded us to share our faith, not only with our friends, but with our own family! But therein lies the problem. Parents want their children to take the right direction in life, but all too often they expect others to do the work for them.

Faith is not transferred by programs; it's transferred by relationships. Values are not taught to your children; they are caught.

Our two-year-old son, Matthew, has picked up my love for motorcycles. He races to the window each time one passes. He has even developed the skill of imitating a motor. Both were traits from my childhood. But I never tried to teach him these things. Somehow, he just picked them up.

There's no better example of what we are facing in America today than the song written a number of years ago by the late Harry Chapin, called "Cats in the Cradle." The entire song talks about a father and a son who saw very little of each other, and were never able to develop a solid relationship. As the boy grew up, he desperately wanted his dad to be a friend. But Dad was always too busy. Before long that little boy had grown to be a man with a family of his own. One day, Dad was startled to find how quickly the time had gone and how little time he had spent cultivating a relationship with his son. So he picked up the phone and tried to start over. But it was too late. His son had become just like him.

If we would thoroughly examine our lives, we would find the things that are being transferred to our children. But, very often it is not our faith. Instead, it is a bad habit. So how can parents transfer their faith to their children? How can they infect their children's lives with faith in Jesus Christ?

One day I ran across a Scripture passage that infected my own life, and caused me to rethink how I live in front of my own children. "And these words, which I am commanding you today, shall be on your heart; and you shall teach them diligently to your sons and shall talk of them when you sit in your house and when you walk away and when you lie down and when you rise up. And you shall bind them as a sign on your hand and they shall be as frontals on your forehead. And you shall write them on the doorpost of your house and on your gates" (Deut. 6:6-9, NASB).

What this passage tells us is that parents are responsible to pass on to their children what they have been taught, what they have learned, and what they have discovered from their lives with God.

Not only does Moses tell the people to teach their children, but he also gives the method by which this type of education should take place. Parents are told to talk of their faith at any time of the day. The keys here are a willingness to share, plus

THE PRAYER CHAIR

We observe a little custom in our family the night before the first day of school in September. And it illustrates one way for a family to enjoy a positive spiritual experience together.

Since every new school year brings new challenges, new temptations, and new fears, the anxiety level begins to build. So we designate one of the chairs in our living room as a "prayer chair" and the rest of us gather around each of our kids, in turn, and place our hands on that child as an expression of our love and support for him for the new year. We pray for him and for any needs he cares to share with us.

We've even expanded this custom. Now each time a family member faces a crisis or special decision, or when I'm going on a trip, the person sits in the prayer chair and receives this special prayer and affirmation from the rest of the family. We've found that this tradition has done a great deal to bond us in a special way to one another and to the Lord.

Ronald P. Hutchcraft

the mental readiness to share when the time is right. We should be doing things in our lives that cause our children to ask, "Why?"

Ashley, our four-year-old daughter, saw a crowd of people near the duck pond as we passed. Actually it was a cemetery. She asked, "Daddy, what are they doing?"

"They are burying a friend," I said.

"Why?"

"Well, their friend has died and we bury people when they die."

"Is he with Jesus?" she said softly.

"I hope so, Honey."

Later we returned with bread for the ducks, and spent over an hour walking through the cemetery. All it took was having her with me, and questions came naturally. I was able to make an impact on my daughter by relating this visual life experience to the things I had learned about God.

There is a second method of communication presented in verses 8 and 9. The Israelites are told to bind these words to their hands and foreheads, and to place them on their doorpost and gates. In other words, these actions were to serve as a symbol of what the people believed.

The same is true for us today. There should be something in the lives of parents that compels children to believe. Authority should be won by the parents' integrity and consistent obedience to the truth. Parents' deeds and accomplishments should be governed by Scripture.

The major points in this Scripture are these: You transfer your faith to your children by your example. You should be sensitive and seek the right to be heard by your children. And you should come from a position of authority that is gained by respect as well as inheritance.

This is the same as being salt. One function of salt is to make one thirsty for water. You should make your children thirsty for Jesus Christ by the way you live your life. Your solid example is the best tool for transferring your faith.

Related Articles

Leading Your Teenager to Christ
BILL BRIGHT

How can parents lead their teenagers to Christ?

First, the parents need to be models. If children see that their parents really love the Lord Jesus and demonstrate this love in their lifestyles, Christ becomes attractive to them. But if they see inconsistency and hypocrisy, a profession of faith without practice in daily life, then they are bound to be turned off.

I have met many young people on college campuses who were totally turned off to Christianity by their legalistic parents. These parents were outwardly pious, but their children knew about the conflicts at home. They saw the inconsistency and hypocrisy of their parents' way of life, and they could hardly wait to reject Christianity because they had never been exposed to the real thing.

It is a tragedy for parents to profess something they do not live, because their children can only conclude that Christianity is just another religion, a game, a crutch needed by weak people. These children do not feel the need of such a crutch themselves, and they have no intention of being hypocrites. They are going to be honest and say to their parents, "Look, I don't believe in God, and I'm not going to kid you by playing games. Your Christianity hasn't done anything for you. Why should I be interested in it?"

I have not done any research on this, but I would say, on the basis of superficial contacts around the world, that most people in government, the media, education, and the liberal churches who are militantly antagonistic to conservative Christianity were born into very fundamentalist Christian homes. And they have rejected this kind of Christianity.

I am a fundamentalist in terms of doctrine and commitment to the basic truths of Christianity, but unless fundamentalism is embraced by and enveloped in and permeated with the love described in 1 Corinthians 13, its effect can be devastating. Legalism is a curse. It is a heresy. It has turned so many people away from the Gospel! This is why I believe effective modeling of Christian principles is really crucial on the part of fathers and mothers.

Second, the parents need to bring other vital Christians into their homes to serve as secondary models for their children. In our work, we were able to introduce our children to college students, professional athletes, and successful business people. I recommend inviting to your home college students or adults who are on fire for the Lord. Have dinner with them and listen to their testimonies. Take your children to meetings where they will be exposed to vital Christianity.

Mr. and Mrs. Arthur S. De Moss were models for me in this regard. While their seven children were growing up, the De Mosses led thousands of people to Christ in their home. They would bring in the best speakers they could find and then

---

WHO IS ON THE THRONE?

From our sons' early childhood we taught them that having Christ on the throne is much better than having self on the throne. One morning, Vonette prepared a special breakfast that we had never tasted before—a big piece of French toast with a poached egg in a hole in the middle. Brad, who was five or six at the time, said, "I don't like it. I won't eat it." He began to cry.

"Wait a minute, Brad," I said. "Who is on the throne this morning?"

"The devil and me," he answered through his tears.

"Whom do you want on the throne?"

"Jesus."

So I said, "Let's pray to Jesus." And he did. "Jesus, forgive me for being disobedient," he said. "Help me to like this egg." Then he ate it all, with delight.

Bill Bright

---

have as many as 750 people over for dinner on the lawn. Hundreds of people would come to the Lord in a single evening. Their children were exposed to parents who talked about the Lord everywhere they went, and it became a way of life to them.

Most people cannot invite hundreds of people to their home for dinner, but anybody can invite a few people, play a tape or record, and then say, "What do you think? Does it make sense? Would you like to receive Christ?"

That kind of approach helps the people you bring home, and it also helps your children. They observe you inviting the neighbors to come to Christ. They are exposed to aggressive, vital Christianity. They know their parents are genuine because they are talking about Christ all the time, and because they are also living a Christlike, loving life.

If we want our children to understand Christianity, we need to demonstrate that Jesus Christ is the most important Person in our individual lives and in our home. Vonette and I wanted our sons to grow up seeing that we love Jesus, that we depend on Him for everything. Jesus is our living Saviour. He is not someone who is far off, but Someone who indwells us, making our bodies the temple of God. He is the basis of our lifestyle, the way we think, our recreation, our times of study, our times of fellowship—Jesus is at the center of everything.

Our children have grown up seeing Jesus not as a killjoy, but as the One who makes life rich and meaningful, filled with challenge and adventure. We parents should make Christianity attractive to our children. We should create within them a hunger and thirst for God. If we expect our children to want what we have, we have to make it attractive, as indeed it is. Jesus said, "I came that they might have life, and might have it abundantly (John 10:10, NASB).

Related Articles
Chapter 15: How Do You Talk to Your Kids about God?
Chapter 15: Helping Teens Share Their Faith
Chapter 15: Resources That Help Teenagers Grow Spiritually

HOME IS WHERE YOUR FAITH IS

The most important way parents can help their child become a Christian is to pray for him. My oldest daughter has a new baby, and she said, "Mother, how can I be absolutely sure Jennifer will know Jesus as Saviour and Lord?" I said, "You can't because God gave each human a free will, but you can pray for Jennifer and present her to Jesus at every stage of development." As parents do that, they should explain as much of the Gospel as the child can understand. Then, they can gently show him he needs Jesus as Saviour and Lord.

As parents, we don't have to be fearful to admit we are sinners and need to come to Jesus and repent. We need to expose our children to the whole Christian doctrine, not just that God is love and wants to be your friend. We start there, but we go on to expose them to the doctrine of sin.

Along with praying, and telling our children about God, we need to live Jesus in front of them all the time. As we live Jesus before them, they see in action what we have told them about God's unconditional love and forgiveness.

Evelyn Christenson

Jesus, the Alternative

BILL BRIGHT

During their teen years, many children raised in Christian homes question everything they have been taught. They will not accept easy answers. They want clear thinking and strong arguments. That is why all parents should do a special study on the person of Jesus. They should study Jesus biblically and historically, evaluating the impact that His life has made on the world.

Someone has said, "History is *His* story." No one can study the life of Christ without realizing that He is without peer. After two thousand years He is still incomparable. No one can even touch the hem of His garment.

When I am sharing Christ with someone, I like to go back to the Old Testament and consider some of the prophecies concerning the promised Messiah. I show how they are fulfilled in the life of Jesus. Then I take the person through Christ's ministry, His miracles, His sinless life, His death on the cross for our sin in fulfillment of prophecy, and His resurrection. This systematic approach is a good one to use with our teenage children.

Often people doubt the Resurrection—I did myself during my agnostic years. I show them that there is no other explanation for the empty tomb. The disciples, after being with the Lord for three and a half years, ran away and even denied Him at the cross, but when they saw Him raised from the dead, they went out and died as martyrs for preaching the Resurrection. They had already demonstrated their cowardice; they certainly wouldn't have gone out to preach the Resurrection if they did not actually believe Jesus was alive. Back when I denied the supernatural, that was a powerful argument to convince me to become a believer.

As parents, we want our children to really understand who Jesus is. He is not just a figment of someone's imagination. He is an historical figure. To this day even atheists and agnostics recognize Him as the greatest person who ever lived.

One day I was talking to a very famous leader of the student revolution of the 1960s. He is a Jew by birth, a card-carrying Communist, and an atheist. I asked him, "Who is the greatest person that every lived? Who has done more good for mankind than anyone else?" And, though it was not easy for him to say it, after a while he answered, "I guess I would have to say Jesus of Nazareth." Anyone who knows the facts, whether Muslim, Hindu, Jew, atheist, or Communist, has to give that answer.

The only people who seem to doubt that are Christian children. They are raised to be believers, but they have never had to defend their faith. And so when they learn about other religions and philosophies of men, they say, "Well, maybe I've just been exposed to one truth. Maybe Christianity is not *the* truth."

We need to be able to show our children that faith in Christ is valid. It is the intellectual foundation on which Christianity is built. Josh McDowell has made a good case for this position in his book, *Evidence That Demands a Verdict*.

Our children need to be convinced in their minds while they are still at home in their formative years. We are not worshiping a God who is just a figment of our imaginations. We are not following a Jesus who never lived or who, if He did live, was nothing like the Jesus we know and the Bible proclaims.

The Christian faith is built on a solid foundation. If we understand that ourselves, and if we explain it to our children from history and Scripture, they will see Jesus as the only logical alternative to the world.

What Teens Should Know about the Bible

WARREN W. WIERSBE

Many teenagers have a negative attitude toward the Bible. One reason is that they see it as an oppressive rule book. That's largely because they haven't been taught that rules are merely one level of growing in the Word of God.

There are many levels of Bible content. We begin with stories that teach *lessons.* Little children should learn, for instance, that Moses lost his temper and he suffered for it. And this leads to *rules.* We shouldn't lose our temper. We shouldn't lie. And so on.

But rules embody *principles* that help us decide how to live in the complex situations we face. And these principles exist because God has a certain kind of *character.*

And the character of God leads us to His *promises.* This is a step that many people miss. Promises involve certain conditions, and meeting those conditions builds our character.

So teens need to see that the Bible is more than rules. It's a book full of principles and promises too, which help us mature and develop character.

A second reason for teens' negative attitudes toward the Bible is that they think it's irrelevant. Cain killed Abel. Peter lied about Jesus. So what? Besides pointing out character and principles, we must show them that the Bible—though completely factual—is a book of metaphor and symbols, which also fill teenage music. (That's one reason adults often can't understand it.)

From the very beginning of Scripture, we hit metaphor—light and darkness. The Bible pictures the Word as food, as a sword to defend us, as water to cleanse us. When teens begin to see the Bible not merely as a storybook but as food for the soul—that truth is to the spirit what food is for the body—then they begin to appreciate Scripture and learn from it.

These are the broad strokes necessary for teens. A few specifics should also be mentioned. First, they should know how the Bible is put together; it's fundamental to learn the books of the Bible.

Second, they should begin memorizing portions of Scripture. During our children's formative years, we were fortunate to be in a church with a marvelous Sunday School that emphasized memorization, and they got a lot of excellent foundational material.

Finally, they should see their parents (as well as the church) using the Bible

CREATING A DESIRE FOR GOD'S WORD

Excitement is caught, not taught. That's true of football, baseball, shrimp, tacos, or God's Word. Our attitudes are often shaped by the people around us.

Many churches have killed excitement for God's Word because they treat it like a dull book. We create excitement by being genuinely excited ourselves.

Beyond that general principle, however, let me suggest three specifics:

First, surround kids from an early age with good books. Not preachy books, but fun books that have some scriptural content. When they're young, read to them. Talk about what you're reading. Let them see *you* reading.

Second, share what you're learning. One simple way we did this was pointing out things we were thankful for. We often did this while driving together. Just spontaneous praise.

Third, consistently show your appreciation for God's Word. We tried to take 1 Thessalonians 2:13 to heart—treating Scripture not like the word of man but as the Word of God. Our children saw that this Book was important to their parents. I'm sure there were times when they respected the Bible more for our sake than from their own hearts, but they learned this Book was special.

Warren W. Wiersbe

creatively. Not just as any other book to read. Nor as a magical, mystical book of incantations to ward off bad things. But a genuine, creative approach where the Word of God enters our lives, changes us, and God through us changes our circumstances.

Bringing the Word to Life

ADRIAN ROGERS

In Deuteronomy 6:6-9 is a tremendous statement in favor of using the Bible as the key to education. "And these words, which I command thee this day, shall be in thine heart: and thou shalt teach them diligently unto thy children, and shalt talk of them when thou sit in thine house, and when thou walk by the way, and when thou lie down, and when thou rise up. And thou shalt bind them for a sign upon thine hand, and they shall be as frontlets between thine eyes. And thou shalt write them upon the posts of thy house, and on thy gates" (KJV).

God is saying here that the Bible is to be taught *creatively.* There are many creative ways to teach the Bible in the home. We can use Bible reading, Bible stories, Bible games, Bible memory, Christian books, Christian magazines, Christian albums, Christian tapes.

This verse also says that the Bible should be taught *consistently*. This is a day-by-day, year-after-year experience of teaching the Bible. Some families try to make their teenagers sit down and listen to a "Bible study" that lasts several hours. They're trying to make up for lost time. Well, that's not the idea here. In this passage the Word of God is taught all through the day in the very course of life.

The Bible should also be taught *compellingly*. Verses 20-21 of this same chapter say, "And when thy son asks thee in time to come, saying, 'What mean the testimonies, and the statutes, and the judgments, which the Lord our God hath commanded you?' Then thou shalt say unto thy son. . . ." The son, because he has been taught creatively and consistently, now is interested in being taught compellingly.

We shouldn't ram the Bible down our children's throats; we should create an interest. Bible study doesn't have to be dull. It ought to be thrilling. What we give our children should whet their appetites for more. Too many families have something called "family altar" that's like cod liver oil: a dose a day keeps the devil away. I'm not against having a family altar if we keep it brief, but more important is our creative, consistent, and compelling day-by-day use of the Bible.

The Lord ought to be preeminent in our conversations. Moses told the people to put the Word of God on their hands and on their foreheads and on their doorposts. He was saying that every act, every thought, and the entire atmosphere of our homes are to be subject to the Word of God.

I think a home ought to be visibly Christian. If you were to visit our home,

you would see on one side of our door the scriptural motto, "The joy of the Lord is my strength." On the other side you would see, "Christ is the head of this house." As you walked into the living room you would see a family Bible, open in beautiful display. In another place you would see a crown of thorns, and somewhere else some scriptural mottoes with the names of our children and the meanings of those names.

You would also see Bibles and Christian albums and Christian tracts in our home. We don't want to make it look like a Bible museum, but I believe that visual Christianity is one way to teach the Bible creatively and consistently and compellingly in the home.

We very seldom sit down and have a Bible lecture or discussion or study that lasts more than ten minutes on a regular basis. And yet we may spend as much as three or four hours together when we get into a deep Bible discussion. The children will say, "Dad, I want to know about thus and such—what does this mean?" And I say, "Go get your Bibles and a Bible dictionary, and let's dig into it. What do you think it means?" To me, that kind of teaching is the most exciting.

I can't conceive of a child who doesn't think the Bible applies to his life if his mom and dad love the Lord with all their heart, soul, and mind. Today's dropouts aren't the kids; they're the parents. You can't teach what you don't know any more than you can come from where you haven't been. If we aren't living Christianity in front of our children, we don't have any right to ask them to believe it. But if we are living the Spirit-filled life, they're going to want to know what makes us tick.

Related Articles

Family Devotions—to Have Them or Not?

LARRY RICHARDS

Family devotions are often very uncomfortable for teens. I found this out when my teenage son came and told me he had a bad attitude toward devotions. He said he felt as if I were always aiming at him, and he thought we shouldn't have a family time anymore because he wouldn't profit from it with such a bad attitude.

Paul was reacting to one of the biggest problems with family devotions. Too often, they are structured within the framework of the Old Testament priesthood. Mom or Dad sits down, reads something from the Bible, and then asks the kids some questions. Because the parents know more than the kids, the parents end up telling the kids. It's a one-way communication pattern with the kids receiving knowledge from the parents. Family devotions turn into a time of hitting the kids over the head with a Bible baseball bat.

After my son came to me, I realized that I had built my pattern on the Old Testament concept instead of the New Testament concept of priesthood, which says we are all priests. I decided to change our family experience to a two-way communication pattern, so that everyone was functioning as a believer/priest rather than a recipient of my word as lord.

We started by reading a chapter of Proverbs. I said, "As you read this chapter, try to find something in it that you think Dad needs to hear." Suddenly the Bible bullets were flying in the other direction. Each person was being treated as someone through whom God could speak and minister.

Or we would say, "Can you see something in here that might encourage Mom?" or "What in this passage makes you feel good about Paul because it describes what he is doing?" By taking little questions like that and asking them with the passage we were reading that day, every person began to function in a ministering way. It was no longer the hierarchical concept with Dad on top.

Within this New Testament framework, it's crucial for the parents to keep the questions related to the people involved. A question like, "Can we find something in this passage that reflects our Baptist heritage, or our Presbyterian view of sovereignty?" is not helpful. The purpose of family Bible study is not to define doctrines but to help the family live in a way that pleases God. It's focusing on what God is saying to each family member as a person.

In most cases, using this approach, teens will want to participate. After all, what teen wouldn't like to dig open the Word and say, "Let's find something Dad really needs to hear"? But if he doesn't want to participate, the parents don't have to make an issue of it. They can just go ahead and have family devotions without the teen. He might run off to be with his friends. But chances are he'll stick around once in a while and eventually get sold on the idea.

Beyond Devotions
There are other ways to grow in faith as a family besides family devotions. One is to

use holiday times for family rituals. For us, Christmas was always a special time. During the week before Christmas we sang carols and reenacted the Nativity scene. We did similar things at Easter, each year doing something a little different.

Parents can also use reading aloud as part of the family nurture. Even when my youngest reached high school age, I read to him every night. We read everything from theological books on Revelation when he was interested in prophecy to Johnny Cash's *Man in Black*. That tradi-

MAKE DAILY DEVOTIONS A HABIT

We started our children early in the daily devotions habit. My wife and I had our devotions individually each day, but we also had a time of family devotions together, which showed the children what to do.

Then we made it clear that they were expected to have devotions too. We never said, "If you don't, you'll get hit by a train" or anything like that, but they realized they had to do it.

When they were young, we'd get each of them the Scripture Union material, which has good, simple stories. Later they used material from Bible Memory Association. These basic tools helped get them started. Then, at a certain point, we gave each of them a good Bible. They went through the same problem nearly everyone does—they started at Genesis, trying to read straight through, and got stuck in Exodus. I told them to skip some of that for the time being.

The place for teens to start is to read straight through the New Testament, beginning with Matthew. Tell them when they come to a list of names to skip over it. But they should also read the Psalms. Why? Because they're poetry, reflecting emotion, and teens can identify with the feelings in Psalms. You need narrative and history, but you also need the emotional side too. So my recommendation is to start in Psalm 1 and Matthew 1 and alternate.

How much to read? I'd tell them to read until God begins talking, then stop and listen. It usually doesn't take long before you see something that applies to your life.

When you get to something you just don't understand, don't get bogged down. Keep going. Come back to the problem later. I still come across passages I don't understand.

The best way to instill the daily devotions habit, however, is to let the children see that *you* do it daily. I learned something from my wife here. Since our house wasn't conducive to crawling off into a corner for Bible reading, I'd usually go into my study and shut the door. My wife, however, would pray and read in the living room.

Recently when our family gathered for Christmas, our daughter, Carolyn, now grown and working as a nurse, said, "One of my indelible memories of childhood is coming downstairs and seeing Mom kneeling at the living room chair."

That convicted me. Now I see how important it is that your children *see* your example.

Warren W. Wiersbe

tion of reading and talking at bedtime was well-established and provided some great opportunities for learning and discussion.

Dusting Off the Family Altar

DAVID VEERMAN

Imagine this. It is Sunday morning and your pastor has just asked for a show of hands of those parents who have a regular "family altar." How do you feel? A common response would be embarrassment and frustration, but mostly guilt.

Christian parents want to have a regular time of devotions, but most attempts end in failure or are met with a yawn. This is especially the case where teenagers are involved. Generally "underwhelmed" by the idea, they reluctantly participate, and that's only when they are home. School, church, and friends keep the social calendar full. Unfortunately, in many homes, the most consistent family togetherness occurs in front of the TV set. And, to be honest, there are times that parents just do not feel like mustering the energy it takes to prepare and motivate the family.

But family devotions are important. These experiences can be unifying, building the home on Christ. Children who grow in an atmosphere where Bible study and prayer play vital roles will see Christ as an integral part of their lives, and they will be inclined to build their homes on Him as well.

Teaching can also occur as parents take the lead in discovering scriptural truths instead of relying exclusively on Sunday School lessons and the pastor's sermons. As conscientious parents, we have a responsibility to plant our children in the faith (Prov. 22:6) and to nurture them (Matt. 19:13-15). It would be irresponsible to expect others to care for our children's total spiritual growth.

The home is the crucible of the Christian life. Sibling conflicts, growing pains, and other normal family tensions provide real tests of faith. In fact, John implies that the home is the ultimate test. If a person hates his brother whom he has seen, how can he possibly love God whom he has not seen? (1 John 4:19-21) Families are falling apart all around us—we need the glue of God's presence to keep ours together. It may be difficult to have a family altar, but it is worth the effort.

Though most of us are convinced of the validity of the family altar, it is the "how to" which causes problems. However, it can be done! First, we must realize that "just trying" speaks volumes about us. Regardless of our success, the fact that we want to have family devotions illustrates our priorities. I can remember numerous attempts by my parents to have a consistent family altar. I don't recall which materials they used or much of the content they covered, but I know they tried. As Christian parents, they were convinced of the necessity of regular Bible study and prayer. They probably questioned many times whether

347

their fidgety, nonattentive son heard very much, but I saw—and learned.

Second, we should be consistent. There is no formula for the frequency of family devotions. Many parents strive for a daily commitment, while for others, once a week is fine. Too often the attempts are intense and sporadic. Dad will insist on devotions every day at dinnertime; but because of schedule conflicts and interruptions, this effort lasts about a week. Instead, we should decide in advance which days (and time of day) are best suited. Then we must follow through with few exceptions and insist that everyone is present. Consistency will produce expectancy and habit, and will reinforce the importance of the study.

Preparation is the third emphasis. If we believe in a family altar and want the teaching to be effective, "winging it" will not do. Also, it is a cop-out to say we are relying on the "Spirit's leading" as an excuse for our lack of preparation. Teenagers especially will see that we are

---

STEPS TO STARTING A FAMILY WORSHIP TIME

The spiritual training of children should begin in the home. If you and your children never worship together at home, you are missing one of the most rewarding experiences in life. Let me encourage you to develop a time of family worship every day. The following steps will get you started.

1. Begin when your children are young. If you haven't yet begun and your children are no longer young, begin now.

2. Select a specific time when you can meet consistently every day (first thing in the morning, at supper, right before bed, etc.).

3. Meet with your spouse ahead of time to plan and decide what to do during family worship time.

4. Have fun. Your children should worship because they *want* to—not because they *have* to.

5. Keep it short. The length of time will depend on the ages and spiritual maturity of the children involved, but fifteen minutes is usually plenty.

6. Use a good resource. "Walk Thru the Bible" has a daily devotional book called *Family Walk*. Other organizations also have quality products in this area.

7. Apply what you discuss to everyday life. After each meeting, ask, "What can you do today to practice what we just learned?" Then the next time you meet, follow up by asking, "How did your plan work out?"

8. Let your children share in leading the worship. High school teens should have regular leadership responsibilities, but even younger children can take part in smaller ways.

9. As your children get older, have them add a daily time with the Lord on their own. Then during family worship, they can begin to share what God is doing in their lives on an individual basis.

These suggestions are only guidelines. You know your family better than anyone else does. Base your planning on what you think is best for them. Challenge each other to become not only the people God wants you to be in the world, but also to be the family He wants you to be at home.

Barry St. Clair

---

only going through the motions. Adequate preparation includes choosing the appropriate topics and materials, thinking through the process, and praying for God's guidance. Paul instructs us to pray about everything (Phil. 4:6)—we will not experience success depending on our strength alone. The content for our studies could include an inductive study of a book of the Bible, the scriptural teaching about a specific subject, biographies of biblical characters, or the writings of Christian authors, scholars, and theologians. Christian bookstores have a multitude of resources available: Sunday School quarterlies, collections of personal devotions, fascinating authors from C. S. Lewis to Joni Eareckson Tada, and more. Our ministers will give guidance here, perhaps even a preview of the sermon topics so that Friday's devotion will relate to Sunday's message. Whatever materials are chosen, they should be Bible-centered.

As we ponder the actual process of our devotions, let us remember *creativity*. The family altar is not a show to be programmed, but creative planning will heighten interest and facilitate learning. We can use illustrations, ask questions, tell a story (parable), or sing a song. Perhaps the whole family could draw a picture or assemble a puzzle. And what about the leader? Why not give our children opportunities to teach us? As they teach, we should be open to their lessons, accepting what is said, and thanking them for their help.

Prayer should be a key ingredient in our devotions (not just punctuation at the beginning and end). We should allow time for each person to share requests. When we pray, we can vary the pattern—sometimes praying around the table, at other times using conversational prayer,

and so on. Our vulnerability is vital for the prayertime. We should request and share real needs. (Compiling a list is helpful.) When God answers, the family can rejoice together. When my father took a job in another city, we prayed as a family about finding a house and a new church home. When God answered our prayers, I was excited and impressed. At five years old, I learned a valuable lesson.

The length of each devotional experience may vary, depending on the subject and leader. Bible study is the head, and prayer is the heart of the family altar. Both are necessary and should be included every time. This is important to remember when we plan.

Finally, we should emphasize personal application, each time discovering what changes we should make in our lives. These practical challenges are for everyone, parents included. We need to allow God to speak to us through His Word by continuing to look for His applications. This is not an opportunity to preach at our kids—we learn *together*. We should also remember that this is an individual and personal process: each family member seeking God's Word for his or her life.

The family altar will take time, commitment, creativity, and vulnerability. The results, however, can be invaluable—learning from God's Word, sharing ourselves with our children, building the home on Christ, and being eyewitnesses to God's work in the lives of those we love dearly.

_____

Related Articles

Helping Teens Share Their Faith

A Good Defense Is a Good Offense

LEIGHTON FORD

In preparing our teens to defend their faith, an honest attitude is important. Parents must allow their children to question, as Jesus did. We must allow them to express their doubts. We don't encourage unbelief, but we have to realize the difference between doubt and unbelief. (Doubt is when I have questions; unbelief says, "I won't believe, no matter what.") Then, we need to be prepared to hear our children's doubts without making them feel they are losing their faith because they have them.

Parents themselves need to let their teens know they have questions. I don't know why my son, Sandy, died; I don't know why God allowed it to happen. I have found intercessory prayer difficult since he's been gone. In our family we have talked very freely about this problem. Even now, when I speak to a university audience about Sandy's death and share with them my doubts, people come up to me afterward and say, "I thought you had it all together. It helps me to know you can have questions and be a Christian." Our teens need to know that as well.

Along with a questioning atmosphere, positive teaching about the Scriptures is extremely important so teens know what they believe. We can accomplish this in the home by encouraging our teens to read. Kids also need to see their parents reading books of substance, books which raise questions about our faith. Paul Little's book, *How to Give Away Your Faith,* or my book, *Good News Is for Sharing,* will help familiarize parents with common questions about Christianity.

Parents aren't going to be very good teachers for their teens if they don't have a firm foundation themselves.

We should also share with our children some of the basic ways of presenting the Gospel. Parents can say, "Let's go through this so if one of your friends asks you about Jesus Christ, you will know how to present the Gospel." It's important to stress that evangelism isn't buttonholing people; it is making friendships for God. The Apostle Paul says God has changed us from enemies to friends and has given us the task of making others His friends too. The friendships come from a genuine concern and love for other people, taking the time to get to know them and care for them.

But we don't just leave it at making friends. Afterward, we present the Gospel to them. That attitude of wanting to reach out, along with knowing how to present the Gospel and believing in the power of the Holy Spirit and prayer, will help our kids share their faith.

Getting Teens to Reach Out to Their Non-Christian Friends

Parents need to believe that evangelism really matters. That is conveyed by our involvement with the Lord in every area of our lives. We say that evangelism is important; we talk about missions. My mother did that with me. She would tell me about evangelism and read stories to me about missionaries, and that started me thinking at a very young age.

Do our children see us involved in evangelism? We can't expect them to do what we don't do. Parents need to model evangelism. Teens need to see us trying to build bridges to non-Christians, or to see us participating in evangelistic events in our church or community.

We also have to recognize that there are differences in our children. Some children are naturally gregarious. They make friends easily. That gives them an advantage in talking to their friends about the Lord.

But if children are very shy and don't make friends easily, it can make them feel guilty if we say, "You ought to be going and telling everybody about the Lord." Maybe they need help in making friends first, and once they make friends, they can learn in their own quiet way how to share the Lord.

Our children have to be very secure in themselves in order to share their faith. It is the rare child of junior high age who is able to make a strong verbal presentation of the Gospel to his friends. Yet all kids can make a start by bringing non-Christian friends home or getting them involved in church youth group activities.

Children brought up in Christian homes sometimes feel that just because they are so familiar with the Gospel, other people are not interested in it. That's why it's good to involve children in activities where they can see that people are really open to our Christian message.

Related Articles

Knowing God's Will

BILL BRIGHT

Many years ago, a young man at Wheaton College came to me for counsel: "I just don't know what God wants me to do. I could be a coach, a teacher, a missionary, a preacher. I could do all kinds of things. But what does God want?"

"Take some paper," I told him, "and write down all the things you could do for the Lord. Put each possibility on a separate sheet of paper, and then under each one, list all of its pros and cons. What are the negatives and what are the positives of serving the Lord in this way? When you have done that for each option, total the good points and bad points of each. Then you will have a concrete basis for a scriptural decision."

Paul said to Timothy, "God hath not given us the spirit of fear; but of power, and of love, and of a sound mind" (2 Tim. 1:7, KJV). Do not wait for an emotional impression to help you make an important decision. Rather, on the basis of the good mind God has given you, do what you think would allow you to do your best; go where you would feel comfortable and where you would enjoy serving the Lord. In the process, always be sure that your will is surrendered to the Lord, or you will not be able to know God's will. Be sure you are filled with the Holy Spirit by faith and that no sin is unconfessed. You cannot know God's will if you are disobedient.

In fact, if you have surrendered your will to the Lord and are filled with the Spirit, you are in God's will. Know that "the steps of a good man are ordered by the Lord" (Ps. 37:23, KJV); if you are walking in the Spirit, God will direct you, so it is safe to do what comes naturally. Philippians 2:13 says, "It is God which worketh in you both to will and to do of His good pleasure" (KJV). So if you are walking in faith, God will give you the desire to do what He wants you to do.

Many times in my life, God has said to me, "Now do this." It has never been audible, but the commands and instructions have been so clear, it has been almost like God saying to Noah, "I want you to build Me an ark." Noah would have been stupid to build an ark on dry ground where it had never rained to preserve his children who had not yet been born, if God had not clearly said, "This is what I want you to do."

I do not depend on these emotional experiences, however. I obey them when they come, but most of my decisions are made according to the "sound mind" principle. We are to love God with all of our hearts, all of our souls, all of our minds (Matt. 22:37). He did not give us our minds just to be put in cold storage.

So I encourage people to seek God's will first by knowing that they have no unconfessed sins, then by being filled with the Spirit and living according to the Scriptures, and finally by using their minds to determine the way they should go.

The young man from Wheaton College came back to me in a few minutes, papers in hand. I asked, "What did God say to you?"

"Well, He not only told me what I was to do with my life, but also showed me the organization in which I am to serve Him." That all happened within half an hour, and the question had been troubling him for years. Today he is one of the most outstanding young men I know on the mission field.

This young man could have done any number of things, but God used him as a missionary to touch the lives of multitudes. He found the direction for his life by following the sound-mind principle.

Many Christians make the sad mistake of saying, "Here I am, Lord. If You have something to say to me, I'm listening. If You speak to me and tell me what to do, I may do it." That is not the way to know God's will.

You can help your teen apply this principle by actually preparing the paper for him, drawing columns under each of his possibilities. Of each option you ask, "How can you best use your time, talents, natural gifts and abilities, and training in that area?" Then, after you have listed the positive aspects, ask, "What are the liabilities?" After you have gone over all the areas together, you total the pluses and minuses and do what seems reasonable.

Now if the child says, "I still don't feel secure about that," do not worry. We have to teach the child to trust God. "You don't really have to figure out what to do with your life," we can tell him. "If God is sovereign, if the steps of a good man are ordered by the Lord, all you really have to do for the rest of your life is just be sure every day that you are doing what He wants you to do that day. Do not worry about marriage or your profession. Simply say, 'Lord, I want to do what You want.' Then it is up to Him to work in you to will and to do."

The verse that has helped me most throughout my life is Psalm 37:4: "Delight yourself in the Lord; and He will give you the desires of your heart" (NASB). When you relate that to Philippians 2:13, you discover who puts the desires in your heart in the first place.

Christianity is not difficult. It is simply a matter of delighting ourselves in the Lord and abiding in Him and letting His Word abide in us. If He lives within us in all of His resurrection power, then it is His responsibility to take our minds to think His thoughts, our hearts to love with His love, our lips to speak His words. When we understand this, we can relax and delight ourselves in the Lord.

Letting God Be Your Guide

ADRIAN ROGERS

The starting place for teenagers who want to find God's will is the parents, not the teenagers themselves. That is, the parents must be willing for their teens to be in the will of God. So often we are not willing to give them to the Lord. We try to succeed through them. We want God's will for them only if God wills them to be famous or wealthy.

Each of our children has been given to the Lord for whatever God wants him or her to be. The Bible says in Psalm 127:4, "As arrows are in the hand of a mighty man; so are children of the youth" (KJV). We've thought of our children as arrows to be polished, pointed, and then shot forth. We've given our children to God to go where we cannot go and to do what we cannot do. We've been willing to let them go, but we've found that God gives us the responsibility to aim them and pull back the bowstring.

The three greatest decisions our children will make are, of course, their salvation decision, their marriage decision, and their life's work decision—master, mate, and mission. Joyce and I have prayed constantly for our children that, in these areas especially, they would know the will of God.

We must saturate our children in prayer. We've been praying, for example, for the ones our children will marry before they've even met them. We've figured they must be alive somewhere. "We don't know their names," we say, "but Lord, keep them safe, keep them pure, and guide them to our children, because we believe You have chosen them for each other."

It's highly important for parents to teach their children that God does indeed have a will for everyone's life. Many young people go through life without this awareness. When I was saved as a teenager, someone told me that God had a specific will for my life. It was a great revelation to me. I doubt seriously if I would have looked for His will for my life had I not learned this truth.

We've tried to show our kids that finding God's will is not like going on an Easter egg hunt, with God hiding it somewhere and you trying to discover it. It is not our job to find God's will. It is God's job to reveal it, and our job to be receptive and ready.

Romans 12:1-2 is a helpful passage. "I beseech you therefore, brethren, by the mercies of God, that ye present your bodies a living sacrifice, holy, acceptable unto God, which is your reasonable service. And be not conformed to this world: but be ye transformed by the renewing of your mind, that ye may prove what is that good, and acceptable, and perfect, will of God" (KJV).

Three things stand out in that verse. First is the word *present*. This is the key for anybody who wants to know God's will: we must present our bodies a living sacrifice, totally, wholly, completely. It's only reasonable that we do this. We're not our own; we're bought with a price. So to know God's will is first of all a matter of presenting ourselves.

Then comes the word *transformed*. Paul says, "Be ye transformed by the renewing of your mind." When I present my body, the transformation results. It's nothing I do. God does it in me when I present myself to Him. The word used for *transformed* is the root of the word *metamorphosis*. A metamorphosis takes place when the inner nature comes to the surface. What was Christ's inner nature? It was glory. So when He was trans- formed—transfigured—His glory was manifested. What is the inner nature of a Christian? It is Christ. And when I present myself to Him, then that inner nature comes to the surface. Rather than being squeezed in by the world, I am trans- formed, and the inner nature, the Christ in me, is made manifest.

So the formula is this: presentation plus transformation equals realization. For, as the Bible says, then we will know the acceptable will of God. When I give myself to the Lord, He begins to change

PRINCIPLES FOR DISCOVERING GOD'S WILL

How do we determine God's will with regard to our children's college educations?

First, we have to be sure of our priorities. We must know that we are not motivated by temporal values, that we do not want them to go to college, for instance, for any reason other than to know God's will and to be equipped to do it.

Then we have to use our renewed minds. God tells us not to be conformed to this world, but to be transformed by the renewing of our minds (Rom. 12:1-2). And when God renews my mind, He expects me to use it.

James said, "If any of you lack wisdom, let him ask of God, that giveth to all men liberally, and upbraideth not; and it shall be given him" (1:5, KJV). Wisdom is not being warm around the heart or wet around the lashes; it implies judicious thinking with a new set of values. Wisdom is seeing life from God's point of view. So when I need wisdom, I can pray and expect God to give it to me.

I'm not going to find any Scripture that says, "Go to ABC College or XYZ College." So the next thing my mind tells me to do is to gather the facts, investigate them, and pray about them. Then I make a decision very much like anyone in the world would make a decision. The only difference is that I am thinking with a renewed mind. My set of values is different. So my decision may be different.

I don't come to a decision and then tell my teenager autocratically, "This is where you are going to school." But on the other hand, I don't stay out of it either, because this is such an important decision. We have to do this together.

I was talking to a businessman one day, and he told me, "Raising children is a lot like building a business executive. We grow executives by allowing them to make mistakes, but we don't allow them to make any big mistakes." The only way our teenagers are going to learn is through mistakes, and though we have to allow them to make them, we never stop guiding them.

Adrian Rogers

me. He renews my mind. I now have the mind of Christ. And with the mind of Christ, I know the will of God.

The will of God is not static. It's not like a road map. It's something that God writes afresh every day. And so daily I'm to present myself to Him, daily I'm to be transformed, daily I'm to realize His will. I don't always see His will out in front of me, but I see it behind me. And I say, "Hitherto hath the Lord helped us" (1 Sam. 7:12, KJV). Many of us would prefer a road map, but life would be dull if God did it that way.

We've tried to teach our children that they don't surrender to the ministry; they don't surrender to missions—they surrender to Jesus. They just say, "Here I am, Lord, reporting for duty." But it's hard to steer a ship that's not moving, so they must do God's will as they see it in the little things. Then God makes His will known to them in the big things. They do

things day-by-day, and they learn God's will for their lives.

To help our children know God's will, we've tried to give them opportunities. For example, some of our children are musical. We've made music lessons available to them. Some love to read. We've tried to have proper literature in our home, to give them a good education. We've sent our children on mission trips. We've allowed them to travel. By providing opportunities for them to hear the Lord and develop their gifts, we've tried to give them an environment through which God could speak to them.

Related Articles

Goals for Spiritual Growth

LARRY CHRISTENSON

Spiritual growth, unlike physical growth, won't happen unless there's a conscious effort. Parents play a key role in helping teens grow spiritually.

The most important thing parents can do is to provide an atmosphere where growth can occur. The example of your personal life is the greatest influence. They need to see you seeking God's direction in things great and small. If you're going to take a vacation, pray as a family about it. Let your kids see your whole orientation is to be in the center of God's will.

This isn't a prepackaged formula—Ten Steps to Mature Faith—or anything like that. Teens don't need a legalistic system,

but parents who openly and honestly seek God. That example emerges primarily in your prayer life.

In your prayers, make sure you're looking for God's guidance. Look for God's activity in normal events. Pray specifically and look for God to answer in His own way. Write down your requests and go back to them a week or a month later to see how the answers have come.

Encourage your kids to pray on their own as well. Make sure they know that God is interested in whatever they're interested in. If they're dating, tell them to pray about that boy or girl and what kinds of goals they should have in that relationship.

You obviously can't force kids to pray, but you can structure the family so that everyone is alone and quiet at a certain time and expected to be reading the Bible. Perhaps you could make sure everyone's up by 6:30 A.M., and quiet time is from 7 to 7:15.

Our personal devotions weren't that formal, but our family devotions were very structured. Structure isn't bad. Teens need structure, direction, and authority. It can be a help to them if you create the place where something spiritually significant can happen.

Kids also need other Christian teens. Ask God for the blessing of a youth group or at least one strong Christian friend for each of your kids. At that age, if they're totally isolated, standing firm in their culture is tough. Even one friend can help them make it.

The central thread here is that God is a living God who is leading each of us to a particular place within His kingdom. Finding God's purpose for us takes some sweat.

Related Articles

RELAX AND LET GOD LEAD

Each of our grown children's theology has taken a slightly different bent from ours. That's because God has places for each of them to go where we cannot go. And He has things for them to do that are not for us.

We can trust His shaping. God won't just repeat to our children what He has said to us. They are not clones. So we can relax and let God lead them, and we can be willing to back them up.

The alternatives?

To keep them as little children. To overwhelm them. To make them unable to enter the adult world on their own.

Ray & Anne Ortlund

Out of the Church, into the World
Living the Christian Life Where It Counts

DAVID & KAREN MAINS

The Christian element of our society has become a self-contained unit to the degree that it has its own publishing houses, its own stars, its own personalities. When Christians become a part of the church scene, their whole world begins to revolve around it. And then they begin evaluating life on the basis of whether or not they are enjoying that subculture.

That's just the opposite of what God wants us to do. He wants Christians to be the salt in society. And though we will never change society, we can contribute to it, preserve it, and provide for it things that are pleasing to God.

One way we've helped keep our kids from developing a Christian subculture mentality is to refrain from talking about witnessing. They do share their faith, but that's because we say such things as, "How can we show love to that person? He's really hurting." Or, "Can you think of ways we can minister to them?"

This type of thinking showed when Melissa decided to go to a public high school her senior year instead of finishing at the Christian school she had been attending. It was a hard decision, and we weren't sure it was the right choice. But when she got to the public school, Melissa related beautifully.

She was a good listener and everyone started talking with her—girls who had had babies and then came back to school, girls who were then pregnant, the popular kids, kids with all the brains. Many of them commented on the fact that they'd never had a friend like Melissa.

Because that comment came up frequently, we sat down and talked about it. We discovered that Melissa demonstrated a care for different people, and one of the ways she showed it was to listen to what people had to say. Melissa didn't have to win the whole school to Christ. Her only goal was to show His love in whatever way she was able to do so.

Because we don't prod our kids to witness, the children relate beautifully in non-Christian environments. When Randall dates non-Christians, the conversations continually come around to Christian topics. Randy feels comfortable about his faith and has no trouble talking about it.

Their ease is quite different from what we experienced when we were growing up. At that time, people imposed on us how and in what ways we were to share our faith. This made talking about God very uncomfortable.

However, our kids are very comfortable with their faith. They know they are Christians. They know that to be a Christian isn't just something theological but that Christ lives in them and He teaches them how to love God and other

people. They are very good at loving other people. They can pick out lonely kids or ones whose feelings have been hurt. Then they reach out to those kids.

We've shown our kids that not all that is good or interesting is in the church. We point out fascinating books; we take them to Shakespearean plays. We've said that there are lots of things in the world around us that a Christian can learn from and legitimately enjoy.

We've also exposed them to the suffering world. When we were in the inner city, we didn't have very much money. But when there were opportunities for the children to travel to developing third-world nations, we'd scramble to get the money together so that, even as young as junior high age, they could go. That helped them see that most of the world does not live in a middle-class environment.

If parents want to begin to wean their teens from the Christian subculture mentality, parents have to be willing to explore. They have to reach out to people who aren't like them. They might invite a family of a different race over for dinner or spend Thanksgiving at the Salvation Army or a mission. Or, they may want to talk as a family about some of the people around them—people who are going through divorces or who have had crummy childhoods—and discover how they can understand and help these people.

You also need to talk about people as people, not just as Christians or non-Christians. For instance, a teacher can be a good or bad teacher whether he is a Christian or not.

We've also tried to maintain a relationship with the church that did not demand all of our kids' energy. That was one of the basic things David attempted when he started Circle Church. We tried to show that the church should equip you to be in the world and not consume all of your time. Thus, we only had Sunday morning services. Sunday evenings were for small neighborhood groups or for special projects. The whole thrust was to free the Christian family or the Christian single who was attending the church to have an outreach.

We've had a lot of different people in our home and have allowed each member of our family to ask those people questions. Not questions like, "What's your favorite color?" but ones like, "If you could be anybody else in the whole world besides yourself, who would you be?" or, "What are you learning spiritually?" They tend to ask questions that unlock the people. And these have been integration times, times when people of different ages and backgrounds can find out what each other is like.

We've worked at letting our kids fit into the church where they feel comfortable. Most churches divide people by age-groups, but that doesn't always meet people's needs. When Joel entered high school, he decided that he didn't want to be part of the small church youth group, but would rather sit in on the adult discussion groups. That was fine with us.

The kids' choices extend to the kinds of schools they attend. When we moved to Wheaton, we put our children in Christian schools. But after a few years, they were crawling the walls. (There's nothing wrong with the Christian schools; they were just too confining for our children.) The kids wanted to be out where they could test their faith, be challenged, and where they could see evidence of the blood of Christ at work in them.

Because the older kids both had good experiences, we put Joel into public school when he started high school. It's incredible to see the way he integrates his faith.

One way he does it is with contemporary music. He uses it as a fantastic entry point for spiritual discussions. Once he tried to do this by working on the dance committee. His goal was to be able to use some contemporary Christian music at the dance.

It didn't work. But a funny thing happened. One day our pastor asked for prayer requests, so Joel asked him to pray that they could have contemporary Christian music at the school dance. We were "dying," but it didn't phase Joel because that's how he was integrating his faith.

We try to let our kids make their own decisions as to how they move in and out of the Christian subculture. Of course, if we see areas that are potentially dangerous, we point them out. But if the children feel they want to go ahead, we usually allow them to do so. But we pray for them, discuss and talk about what's going on, and try to learn from things that don't work out the way the kids thought they would.

That takes us back to Joel and the dance committee. We had tremendous reservations about his plan because we thought that using Christian music at a dance was a clash of cultures, not an integration of cultures. Anyhow, it didn't work out because the school decided to hire a live band to perform at the dance.

But the Lord honored Joel's desire just the same. One of his teachers asked Joel to do his juggling routine in his class on the last day of school. Since Joel had put a track of Christian records together for the dance, he was able to use that music as the background for his juggling routine. And teachers from other classes who came and watched invited Joel to do his routine in their classes as well.

The intent of Joel's heart was to share something that meant a great deal to him, to communicate his faith in Christ. The Lord knew that and gave him an opportunity to do it.

Christian Friends Make the Difference

DAVID VEERMAN

Peers play a critical role in the lives of teens. This is often threatening for parents who see their influence diminishing with the years. Actually, they shouldn't be so surprised. With the first days of school, children spend increasing amounts of time with their friends and classmates. After they learn to drive, the hours away from home escalate dramatically. In addition, adolescence is the time of identity development. With fragile egos, our young people seek affirmation and a place to belong.

Aware of this influence, moms and dads are concerned about the quality of their children's friends, as well they should be. There's no question that peers can affect behavior. But usually our young people will choose friends who have needs *similar* to theirs. By associating with them, their values are reinforced, and they achieve a sense of security. The peer group, then, can provide a clue to their needs and desires.

Since peers exert so much influence, a group of "good kids" could push our teens in the right direction. This is where the church youth group and other Christian youth organizations come into the picture. They can provide Christian friends, a wholesome atmosphere, and solid content. But the fact that these groups are Christian is no guarantee that all of the members will be a good influence. (Stories abound of "good Christian kids" getting in trouble.) But certainly the chances are greater for *positive* relationships.

Another problem faced by teenagers is the pressure to conform. Often, in an effort to help Christian young people *resist* peer pressure, we put them under our own pressure to conform to *our* behavior standards. Though we will probably get the desired actions, we will have perpetuated the problem and not helped them learn how to resist.

Toward a solution, there are three key concepts to consider:

1. *Relationship.* Become a "peer" in your young persons' lives. I'm not suggesting you act like a teenager and try to fit into the adolescent world—that would be foolish. But it is possible to build an open, "influential" relationship by doing things together, talking and listening, and accepting them as emerging adults.

In addition, encourage their youth leaders to get to know them on a personal level. Hopefully, they will open up to these leaders, who often can get closer than parents.

2. *Dialogue.* If you want to steer your kids toward the right kind of friends, you must open channels of communication. Be sure not to throw out the typical phrases like, "Why don't you go to the youth group?—they're such nice children." Or, "I don't see what you see in those friends; they're so weird." Instead, show genuine interest in them and their activities, and spend time just talking things over.

3. *Open home.* Let your kids know that your home is open for their friends. Instead of condemning their peers and pointing out their faults, invite them to dinner or some other social opportunity.

Since peers play such an important role in our young people's lives, let us prayerfully and carefully lead them and help them learn from the experience.

Related Articles
Chapter 15: Resources That Help Teenagers Grow Spiritually
Chapter 16: What Can the Church Do?

ENCOURAGING CHRISTIAN FELLOWSHIP

How can you help your teens' spiritual development and get them involved with other Christian teens?

1. Start going to church with your family when your children are very young. Go to Sunday School and have your children attend a class too. Get into the habit of family worship right from the start (or right now, if you haven't already!). Then speak well of your church and its activities; don't criticize the church all week, then expect your kids to want to be there every Sunday or wonder why they don't like the youth leader.

2. Find out what your church youth group does—don't assume it's effective (especially if your kids have gone and not liked it). Find out what's happening. And don't let yourself think that your parental role is threatened by youth leaders—they can help; they're not competing with you. Support them. If your teen would rather talk to them than you and *does,* accept that at this point in your child's life and make efforts to improve listening and communication at home.

3. Be willing to take your kids (and their friends at times too) to the church-sponsored activities.

4. Look into options for your teens (other churches, for example).

5. If nothing is available, take the initiative to get something going. Seek out resources. Be willing to help. Get other teens' parents interested and involved.

6. Give your kids a choice—don't cram certain friends or even Christian fellowship down their throats. Respect their choice of friends while encouraging Christian contacts.

YFC Editors

Resources That Help Teenagers Grow Spiritually

JAMES C. GALVIN

Church libraries, public libraries, and Christian bookstores contain many resources to help teenagers grow spiritually. Often these resources are overlooked by parents or set aside because they don't know how to plug their teenagers into them. Some teenagers appear disinterested in reading books that would help their spiritual growth and others seem to be disinterested in reading altogether. Parents who have tried to get their teenagers to read often feel that you can lead teenagers to the library, but you cannot make them read. So how can these resources best be used? How can parents interest teenagers in reading to help them grow spiritually?

One approach is to take a monthly trip to the church library or public library to explore the selection of books which may be of interest to the teenager. Church libraries often make the newest and most interesting books for young people a top priority. Though this is the least expensive approach, some teenagers are just bored by libraries. A second approach is to purchase a book for a teenager and wrap it up as a gift. Rather than waiting for a birthday, giving this type of gift, for no other reason except love and the desire to see him grow spiritually, will be a surprise and may help him read that particular book. Of course, some teenagers may start to read the book and never finish. Given this situation, a third approach might be to set up a reading program where parents can take their teenager to a Christian bookstore to purchase any book of his choice. The only ground rules are the teenager must read the entire book that he selects and he may not select another book until the first book is completed. This approach will ensure the teenager is interested in the book, but he might not choose a book that the parents consider valuable for helping him grow spiritually.

Resources for spiritual growth, normally found in a Christian bookstore, would tend to fall into nine categories. The chart on the following page describes each and explains how it may be useful for helping teenagers grow spiritually.

For teenagers who like to read or are at least willing to do the hard work of reading to dig out some valued information, a book can be a very helpful resource. Many books are available that are written specifically for teenagers. Best-selling books, however, should not be overlooked. These are often self-help books with practical advice for a problem a teenager may be facing. Bible study books that are more detailed and academic in nature should also be considered for those who are bored by Sunday School classes or typical devotional materials. A more in-depth and adult approach may be exactly what they need to help them grow spiritually.

For teenagers who dislike reading, other resources such as magazines, music, and cassette tapes can facilitate spiritual growth. The text in these materials is often broken into short paragraphs with plenty of pictures, illustrations, and titles. Teenagers who might not ordinarily sit down to read a book would find it easier to use these resources. Even those who are poor readers can still grow spiritually through cassette tapes and Christian music.

In order to multiply the effectiveness of these resources, have teenagers study a book or listen to a tape together with a group of friends. This can be accomplished as a project in the youth group, or an assignment for a Sunday School class, or a special small group with an adult leader. Because of the influence of peers at this age, a group of teens reading through a biography, working through a discipleship manual, or reading through a best-selling book will do even more for helping teens grow spiritually.

Related Articles
Chapter 15: Helping Teens Live Their Faith
Chapter 15: What Teens Should Know about the Bible

TYPES OF RESOURCES	HELPS TEENAGERS GROW SPIRITUALLY THROUGH:
1. *Bible study.* Books about a particular section of the Bible or reference works, such as commentaries or Bible dictionaries. These examine the Scriptures in detail and also discuss the original language, history, culture, and archaeology.	Answering more in-depth, advanced questions about the Bible and theology; providing richer insights for living out their faith.
2. *Self-help.* Books dealing with a particular topic such as dating, loneliness, etc. or those by famous authors which are more general in nature.	Offering practical help with a problem area in life or additional information in an area of interest.
3. *Biographies.* Life stories of Christians who have faced particular struggles in life.	Inspiring them to follow the examples of other Christians; providing outstanding role models to pattern their lives after.
4. *Fiction.* Creative writing which takes the form of mysteries, poems, short stories, or novels.	Viewing human struggles and spiritual struggles in life from a fresh perspective.
5. *Devotional aids.* Supplemental material for daily personal devotions.	Challenging them to apply Christian principles to everyday situations.
6. *Discipleship manuals.* Workbooks for spiritual growth specifically geared for teenagers to study in small groups.	Establishing basic disciplines of prayer, Bible study, and church involvement, and examining their actions from a biblical perspective.
7. *Magazines.* General Christian magazines or those targeted specifically for teenagers such as *Campus Life.*	Presenting Christian truth through attention-grabbing, easy-to-read magazine format.
8. *Audio cassettes.* Tapes on a particular topic or from a speaker of interest to teenagers.	Listening to a dynamic communicator when convenient.
9. *Christian music.* Music with lyrics relating to spiritual growth or Christian living.	Expressing feelings and solidifying convictions about their commitment to Jesus Christ.

You're a New Christian Family: What Do You Do Now?

KENNETH O. GANGEL

Setting up a Christ-centered home doesn't have to be a traumatic experience for new believers. You begin by trusting God, asking Him to make up for all the lost years of communication and friendship your family could have had. Then commit your home to the Lord with an attitude of expectancy: "Lord, we're starting from scratch and need to learn how to put You first."

The home then becomes a little school where everybody is growing and sharing with each other. As family members learn new things from God, they reinforce value choices and priorities. Parents should communicate openly with their children and not be afraid to admit when they fail.

It's important to immediately establish family devotions or worship time. Even new believers with limited Bible knowledge should start by opening up to a passage and asking each other, "What does this mean?" "What should we be doing about it as a family?" The Holy Spirit will help teach the family as they explore God's Word together.

Children may be surprised to see authoritarian parents humbling themselves and making themselves vulnerable. At first, there may be a credibility gap—kids will stand back and say, "Prove your faith and leadership: show me you can pull it off."

Instead of getting defensive, parents should admit that they are depending on Christ to help them with their weaknesses. There's nothing wrong with admitting to your children that you need help being a godly father. Scripture teaches us to be vulnerable: "Not that we are competent to claim anything for ourselves, but our competence comes from God" (2 Cor. 3:5, NIV).

When children see this kind of honesty, they're not likely to spit on it and say, "Do your own thing and I'll do mine." Kids are ultimately more hostile to the authoritarian parent than the vulnerable parent. There are no formulas guaranteed to swing children around to the parents' side, but openness and communication often work wonders.

A new Christian family should also strive to include children in decision-making. Instead of saying, "We're going to the lake this weekend" and giving kids no choice, parents should let children have a voice and ask them what they want to do: "Would you like to go to the lake this weekend, or would you rather do something else?" Parents, of course, have the ultimate responsibility under God to make the final decision, but children should have a voice in the process.

One of the things our family did was to plan family vacations together. We plotted out map routes and scouted out parks to visit. A parental duty—vacation planning—turned out to be family fun.

We also had a family council, a time when family members could discuss whatever they wanted. Sometimes the kids would say, "We'd like to call a family council because we feel we're being asked to go to bed too early." Then we would get together and negotiate the issue.

One issue that families should discuss is what church they would like to attend. After visiting several churches, they can talk about what they're looking for in a church and where they think God wants them. Parents and children may need to weigh the importance of their needs— they may end up choosing XYZ church because of its growing youth program, even though it has mediocre preaching.

But even though a church may not be perfectly suited to all your family's needs, family unity in worship is important. My daughter attends a college far away from the church I pastor, but we're working hard to make sure we're still all together on Sunday morning.

Ultimately, after family worship, devotions, and decision-making have been discussed, the family of new believers can have an easier time adjusting than parents who have been believers all along but have not applied their faith at home. Instead of living down sixteen years of hypocrisy, you're starting anew. And that's an exciting, not scary, experience.

The Powerful Effect of a Parent's Prayer Life

EVELYN CHRISTENSON

In 1968, I was involved with a project organizing a telephone prayer chain. As the telephone would ring, my children watched me write down the request at the blackboard, hang up, and call the next person to start the chain. Then, I would go to prayer immediately. Thus, they were able to see the priority of prayer in my life and the discipline of stopping to pray no matter what was going on.

They also heard the phone ring and listened as the answers came in. This was a subtle example, and I didn't realize that they were paying much attention until they were older. But I knew what a tremendous impact this made on their lives when they began to ask for prayer if something was happening in their lives or in the life of a friend. They had watched the power of prayer in my ministry and my personal life, and it became a way of life for them.

Another part of my prayer life that affects my children is my intercession for them. I consider praying for my children to be the most significant thing I do for them. I spend, as a rule of thumb, two hours a day in prayer and they are at the top of my list. My motivation is that I believe God answers prayer. If I didn't, I wouldn't spend all that time praying.

When my daughter, Jan, took her internal medicine board tests, which involved eight hours of writing, two days in a row, I spent every hour in prayer for her. Only God knows what my life of intercession has done for my children, but prayer is a tremendous way we can help our teens, whether our teens are aware of it or not.

I reversed this process too, asking my children to pray for me. I admitted my needs to my children, even when they were young. I let them know that I didn't have it all together. I would tell them, "I'm scared; I have to do a program on TV and I don't know how to do it. Would you pray for me?"

As we admit our needs to our children, it becomes much easier for them to admit their needs to us. In doing so, we're not queens or kings sitting high on a throne, but people who need to change and who need other people to pray for us.

Praying *with* our children is also extremely important. When they are small, praying together is easily structured—at mealtimes, at bedtime. Our family had the practice of praying with the kids just before they walked out the door to school, even if we only had time for one sentence. That prayer not only helped them, it set my mind at rest, knowing that I had handed over my children to God for the day.

As children become teens, they can shy away from prayer, thinking it's kid stuff. The secret is to pray little short sentence prayers, with the parents not praying any more than the teen. Then, the teen is made to feel that his prayers are just as important as his parents'. The teen has equal time and equal worth in prayer; this is helpful, though sometimes hard for parents to remember.

Parents could spend the rest of their lives reading good books on prayer. But the important thing is to pray, rather than learn more about prayer. God answers prayer, not the study of prayer.

Prayer takes discipline too. Sometimes it means giving up a TV program or some other leisure activity that is not bad in itself, but is not a top priority. We need to

HOW TO PRAY FOR YOUR CHILDREN

What should parents pray for their teens? Most importantly, that God's will be done. This means that He will have His perfect will in them all day long, that He will be training them, making them holy, as He desires.

Sometimes this means praying for something hard to help a teen see his error, like "Lord, do whatever you need to do to turn that teen around." I've prayed that many times, but it is a difficult prayer because I know God might answer it by a hard experience.

My own mother prayed for my brother for twenty-seven years and she finally said, "God, do anything you need to bring my boy back to You." A little while later, my brother was in a serious car accident. He survived it and through it came back to God, but that is still a scary prayer to pray.

Then, there are specific things parents can pray for. Perhaps the teen has a test that day in school. I don't pray for all A's, but "God, you know if this child's self-image is not what it should be and if he needs some encouragement. So give him the test results he needs." Or I prayed, that if it was His will, that God would give my teen enough success to give him courage to enter into a certain field of study.

I also ask God to deliver my children from the evil one. I claim the blood of Jesus over them and tell Satan he doesn't have a right in my children's lives. If they are sinning, I ask God to rebuke them and pour coals of fire on their heads until they can't stand what they are doing. I probably pray some pretty peculiar prayers as a parent.

Evelyn Christenson

be willing to give up some of the little things we like, to spend more time in prayer. I've had to make sacrifices in order to pray but it has been worth it.

A prayer partner can also help. If both parents are Christians, then this is a natural. If not, a parent can pray and ask God to show him someone with whom he can pray on a regular basis.

Related Articles
Chapter 1: What Can You Do for Your Children?
Chapter 2: Parents Need to Change Too!
Chapter 15: Parents Set the Spiritual Pace

THE RICHEST POOR LADY IN TOWN

Grandma Rudy was expecting her fourth child when her husband died. He was a pastor of a small Iowa church, and in those days pastors of small Iowa churches had only enough money to keep food on the table. Savings were for others.

With three small children and another on the way, Grandma Rudy sought refuge in her brother's home, where she raised her family. There she remained for years, with no money, no way to earn money, and certainly no status or power. In all kindness, my wife Arlie's grandmother was a nobody with nothing.

But in her nothingness, Grandma Rudy began a crusade—praying for the salvation and Christian nurture of her children and her unborn grandchildren. This crusade kept going for years.

I knew all four children in their older years, one of them my saintly mother-in-law. Each bore a presence that clearly showed he or she had walked with Jesus. The seventeen grandchildren also put Christ first in their lives, and those who married chose Christian mates and affirmed that their homes were Christian homes. Six chose missions or ministry as a full-time career. More than fifty great-grandchildren, as far as we know, became Christians and several of them have chosen some form of ministry or missionary work as a full-time career.

Though she did not know at the time, Grandma Rudy was leaving a family heritage greater than all the wealth she could have passed on. She was indeed the richest poor lady in town. And we who remember her ministry of prayer recognize that she has bathed four generations, with a fifth coming on, in the practice of the presence of our Lord.

Gil Beers

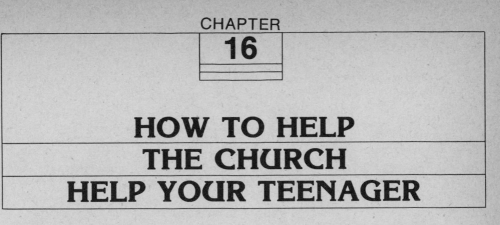

HOW TO HELP
THE CHURCH
HELP YOUR TEENAGER

- Why don't my kids like church?
- Can the church really influence teens' spiritual development?
- How to get the church involved with its youth

- Must your teens attend church?
- What can parents offer the church?
- The church exists for the family, not the family for the church

An enterprising, middle-aged businessman has moved twenty-three times in his thirty-five years of marriage and yet has one of the most successful families going. When asked how he managed this, he responded with a real pearl of wisdom. "Every time we moved to a new town," he said, "the first thing we did was look for a church with a program for kids the ages of ours. Then we found a house near it. We've been Methodists, Presbyterians, Episcopalians, Baptists, Assembly of God, and Free Churchmen. We've always felt that the key to helping our mobile family was to choose the church first, then the house."

It's important for parents to support all three of the great forces in young people's lives: the home, the school, and the church. All three are necessary to proper growth and maturity.

Why Don't My Kids Like Church?

RONALD P. HUTCHCRAFT

Society has changed. Only a few years ago you were the odd one if your car didn't leave the driveway on Sunday morning to go to church. Now you're the odd one if it does. The family is weaker; the neighbors don't go, and probably church is the ultimate example of that old saying, "You can lead a horse to water, but you can't make him drink." You can get your kid to church, but that doesn't mean he's going to get anything out of it.

You can do everything possible to navigate your teen's body through the church doors, and his mind can still stay home. Just getting his body to occupy a pew is not the point—occupying his heart with the Christian message and Christian fellowship is.

Why Kids Turn Off

Let's talk about some of the reasons why kids turn off *at* church—or *to* the church. One reason is *inconsistency*. They are quick to see the gap between what a leader is *teaching,* and how he is *living.* They may even see the inconsistency between what that leader is teaching and how his own children, who might be their friends, are acting.

Another reason is *irrelevance.* Teens feel, perhaps, that there is no connection between what's going to happen to them on Monday morning and what is being taught on Sunday morning. And when they don't see a connection, they say, "What's the use of being here?"

A third reason is *independence.* They seem to say, "Any time you want to make me do something, I want to show that I don't have to do it." And the more we try to force kids to go to church, the more their adolescent, independent feelings rebel against that. They have something to prove now; something to win. It's a power struggle.

A fourth reason some teens turn off *at* or *to* church is that there may be *a lack of others their age.* The most important factors to any teenager about any event are, "How many kids will be there?" and "Which kids?" And if he sees only a few kids his own age, that may just confirm his feelings that what's going on there is irrelevant.

A final reason is *school pressure.* Quite frankly, kids are in an academic and social pressure cooker at school. And if they're trying to make it in these areas, they may say that they don't have much time to spend at church. They have a time-management problem. They may really want to go to church but don't think they have time.

Freedom within Boundaries
Probably the best way to create a more positive attitude is to give teens latitude within limits; to give them freedom within boundaries. In other words, there are some things about their church relationship that *you* will decide. They won't get a choice. But *within* that structure they will have choices. For example, they will be allowed to choose with whom they will

sit. Within the boundary that they must go to church, give them some freedom to choose which services they want to attend. Perhaps the policy decision will be two services a week. If that is the decision, you may allow them to decide *which* two services. You may even decide to allow them the freedom to choose *which* church to attend. Sometimes parental ego comes into play here because we want our kids to go to *our* church and be seen by *our* friends. But if they find a church that better ministers to their needs, there are cases where we ought to allow them to choose another church fellowship. The point is to give your kids freedom to choose within your broader guidelines.

Now, what can parents tell kids to help them appreciate church and get more out of it?

Help Kids Appreciate Church
Help them realize that everyone at church is a becomer, including them. Nobody has "arrived"; everyone is "under construction," spiritually. No church is perfect. Fortunately, it's a place for imperfect people, or else you and I wouldn't be admitted. Yes, churches are made up of imperfect people, but people who are basically trying to grow up spiritually.

Encourage your kids to go to church to hear from God, not from people. Tell them, "You never know what you'll hear from Him. It isn't just the sermon; maybe it will be in a hymn, maybe in what the choir sings, maybe in the pastoral prayer, maybe in something that someone says before or after the service. But the point is: Go into the service saying, 'God, I'm here to hear from You. I don't know which person you're going to send it through.' That means you've got to be looking everywhere, because you never know where God will make that personal encounter with you."

Put yourself into it, and you'll get more out of it. If you're not getting anything out of it, you may not be putting anything

SURVIVING SUNDAY SKIRMISHES

"As long as you're living under this roof, you will go to our church!"

"What do you mean you don't feel like going? What kind of Christian are you anyway?"

"I don't care where your friend goes to church; you're coming with us!"

Sound familiar? In many Christian homes, teenagers resist going to their parents' church. Only after verbal warfare or outright coercion do they shuffle out and go along for the ride. Feelings range from silent apathy to open rebellion. Some parents simply give up and allow their children to attend another church or sleep in.

This can be painful for parents, especially when they are long-time church members. Church involvement represents years of commitment—tithing, teaching Sunday School, serving on boards and committees. They may have helped build the church and still have the zeal and vision that gave birth to their local assembly.

Other parents simply want to do what's right. They know a solid foundation in the Bible and church involvement is important in a young life.

Your teenagers are emerging adults and question every part of society, including its morals. They desire independence and the opportunity to make their own decisions. This is healthy, though it can be threatening to the older generation. Your child's Christianity needs to be deeper than a parroting of your views.

Be open to your teen's questions and criticisms, and learn from them. Encourage him to probe his faith at a deeper level and search Scripture for direction in church attendance. This present conflict can be an opportunity to discuss spiritual truths.

Take an honest look at your own church attendance. Why do you go to church? Do you attend church for social reasons or just out of habit? Admit when you're wrong and pray for a fresh touch of God's Spirit.

What kind of model are you? Is "roast minister" regular fare for Sunday dinner? Don't be surprised if your children pick up your critical attitudes. Though you can't undo years of teaching in a week or two, it's not too late to change. Speak in love and affirm the pastor, services, and programs.

What are your priorities? Is church really important to you? Does it make any difference in your life? Actions can be deafening. Some parents forbid their children to attend another church, but later allow them to miss their own church if they have to work on Sunday. Sometimes, the real reason parents require their teen to join them in church on Sunday is to save face. Are you embarrassed to explain your son's or daughter's absence? Your young people will see right through you.

Listen to your teen with sensitivity. His complaints may be symptoms of adolescence or echoes of your complaints from months ago. Then respond with loving acceptance and instruction.

"Provoke not your children to wrath: but bring them up in the nurture and admonition of the Lord" (Eph. 6:4, KJV).

David Veerman

into it. Start to take some notes; really listen; make an effort to make an application. Kids are used to spoon-feeding these days. They're used to TV and other media just handing it to them, and it takes a little work and extra energy to get something out of church.

Sit in an active rather than a passive spot. The church is one of the only places I know where people get there early to get a back seat; everywhere else you go, you get there early to get a front seat. You're saying by the position of your body, "I want to be out of here." I challenge kids for just one month to try sitting on the first three rows, taking notes, and really being active, front-end sinners. The closer you sit, the better it is. Don't sit in an active spot and be passively out of it.

Go to church determined to get a personal word from the Lord. Say, "God, I'm not leaving here without more of You. Somewhere here today I'm going to get more of You."

Go to church to *give* something, not just to get something. We tend to see the pastor and the choir as the performers, and we in the congregation as the audience, when in fact, the biblical concept of worship is that the pastor, the musicians, and the congregation are all the performers, and God is the audience. What we're doing in church is for Him. So the question might be, "Did God get anything out of this service from me?"

Look for a place to serve. Fans at football games spend a lot of their time criticizing what the players are doing. The players spend *their* time playing the game. If kids come to church with a fan mentality, they're going to sit and think about all the ways things could be done differently. My challenge is: Get in the game. Find a place to serve. Don't sit on the sidelines and criticize.

If you go to church determined that someone is there who needs a smile, a touch, a listening ear, an encouraging word from you, you'll be a blessing and a true servant of Christ. This way church can never be a failure for you.

Finally, prepare for worship before you go, whether that means reviewing memory verses on Saturday night for Sunday School, reading a passage you know the pastor will be tackling the next morning, or singing together or praying on the way to church. Create that air of expectation before you get there.

How Families Can Help

Here are some practical things families can do to help enrich the church experience for kids:

First, discuss applications. For instance, "Let's each of us talk about what we got from the Lord this morning and what we are going to do this week because of something we heard in church today." If that becomes a regular fixture in the family agenda, you'll all tend to be looking for something to talk about. *Tie the lessons of Sunday into your daily family devotions during the week.*

Second, minimize the Sunday morning hassle. We've all been guilty of bickering all morning long, then suddenly putting on a smile as we walk through the church doors. But, of course, that behavior doesn't exactly create a climate in which the Lord can speak to us. Why not plan ahead? Get the clothes ready Saturday night. Set the alarm a little earlier. Eliminate the things that tend to make Sunday morning a negative time; try to make it peaceful and positive so that the family goes to the house of the Lord with that attitude.

Third, invite church families to your home who match your family. This will help create a sense of social-ness as well as spiritual-ness about what goes on at church.

Fourth, do all you can to encourage your kids with church friendships. Invite those kids over; have parties at your house for them.

By doing the things I've mentioned, you're saying to your kids, "Listen, for the next three months, six months, or whatever, I want to see you give our church your best shot. After that, if you've really given it your best shot, and your spiritual needs are still unmet, we are willing to let you start to search for another church." That's the way kids should earn the right to make their own choices about church.

Teenagers and Church: Why the Two May Not Mix

HOWARD G. HENDRICKS

One reason teens and church may not mix is because teens go unprepared. Most people have never been taught how to get something out of church. They walk through the church doors and expect something magical to happen to them. Of course, too much "get" and too little "give" isn't right either. We need to honestly ask if we go to church to delight God's heart, or just to get our spiritual "goodies."

Another reason our teens may resist church is because we don't debrief them afterward. In other words, do we discuss at the table what went on at church? Do we ever ask, "What did you think of the sermon?" "What are your questions?"

As parents we also have to ask ourselves if we build bridges with the pastoral staff. Do we have them over to the house? Do we support the church or do we criticize it?

Parents often criticize the youth leader and then wonder why their teen doesn't want to be involved. Once there were two couples slicing the throat of our youth director. Their kids were giving us more grief than anyone else in the group because the parents were undermining the director's position.

We finally called them before the board and asked them to tell us all of their criticisms. We told them we would work with the youth director on the problems, but that we didn't want them criticizing the youth director in front of anyone. When the parents stopped criticizing the youth director, the teens became more involved.

Should Parents Make Teens Go to Church?

Developing a positive attitude for going to church starts when the children are small. If the parents go to church with a sense of enthusiasm, the children will pick this up and model the positive attitude.

But if a teen doesn't want to go to church, I would treat the situation with a precision touch. I wouldn't *make* him go to church but, on the other hand, I wouldn't *ignore* the problem. I would explore it at a deeper level.

Not wanting to go to church is often a sign of independence. Somewhere along the line, the teen has to tell you no just to "try it on for size," to find out if he really is independent. If the parents have a good sense of humor and don't make a big issue out of it, they might nip this behavior in the bud. They might respond with something like, "Oh, come on,

371

you're going along. We're all going as a family. You can't let us down." They sweep him up, and they have a lot of fun, and go out to eat afterward. By the next Sunday, he's probably forgotten about it.

If the teen has a serious gripe about going to church, parents could replace church attendance with another assignment. Options the teen could be given might include personal Bible study or getting involved with other people in ministry. By doing this, you get away from outward conformity and concentrate on inward conviction. Maybe the family needs to find a new church. Of course, in some communities there are no other churches, and the parents have to face that realistically.

The key is to keep the relationship open between you and the teen. If you have a knock-down, drag-out fight and you lose the relationship, then whether the teen goes to church or not is really quite immaterial.

It's like the parents whose daughter comes home announcing she is going to marry a certain man, and the parents reply, "If you marry him, you'll never step in this house again." I've known young women who go out and marry the man, and when I ask them why, they say, "I hated the man, but my father said if I did it, I'd never come home again. I thought, *Well, I'll show him.*"

We need to guard against church attendance becoming a battle like that— where teens feel they must show us we don't have power over them.

DOES YOUR TEEN HAVE TO ATTEND YOUR CHURCH?

Two of the goals that Christian parents are trying to achieve with their children are family togetherness and individual spiritual development.

If a teenager doesn't want to attend your church, it can be for a variety of reasons. He's either trying to get away from you or he finds something attractive in another church. Maybe he's avoiding some difficulty at your church.

It's important that you attempt to find the real reason. If he's trying to get away from you, then the issue is one of conflict resolution between you and the teenager. If he finds spiritual fulfillment or excitement at another church, then you must evaluate its spiritual health (doctrine, leadership, approach to issues, etc.), your reasons for staying where you are, and the time when the family can be together.

If there is a difficulty or problem that he is trying to avoid at your church, then you need to evaluate whether it is worth trying to solve. In this situation you can either try to change a legitimately negative situation, or you can teach your teenager what it means for him to provide positive leadership and not to run in the face of difficulties. Since there are different answers for different problems, we must follow the advice of Solomon and seek wisdom from a multitude of counselors (Prov. 11:14).

Larry Kreider

What Teens Should Learn at Church

WARREN W. WIERSBE

Creating the right church environment is a very delicate thing. Many churches fail because they use the Bible as a weapon to fight with instead of a tool to build with. The atmosphere becomes vindictive rather than eager and creative. When kids are beat over the head about their music or clothing styles, it's no wonder they don't want the Bible.

The right atmosphere is one where the Word of God applies to everyone: adults, teens, younger children. Everyone, even the preacher, must be under the authority of the Word of God.

Yet each church also needs to have distinct aims for its youth ministry. Five basic aims I see as important are to help every teenager develop:

1. A working knowledge of the Bible.
2. A set of standards (not rules) based on biblical convictions.
3. An appreciation for his heritage—family, country, and church.
4. A real concern for his own generation.
5. A growing awareness of his own gifts and abilities.

After reading these aims, the natural question arises: What if my church isn't emphasizing these things? First, recognize that these things are as much the responsibility of the home as of the church. My wife and I never expected the church to do it all. All of these things

SEX EDUCATION IN THE CHURCH?

I believe that the home and the church are the two best places to educate young people about sex. Unfortunately, it's too often ignored in both places. I've spent my lifetime dealing with teens, and I guarantee you that few got their sex education from their parents. It's just too threatening to parents.

Now, the church is ideal because it provides a context in which the spiritual, emotional, *and* physical aspects can be brought together. *Keep in mind that sex was God's idea.* The most beautiful relationship two people can have is the intimate relationship that is tied together through their sexuality. It's a matter of humanity, fidelity, trust, love, caring, sharing, giving, and forgetting about yourself.

When sex education is done tastefully and reverently, respecting the sanctity of this as part of God's Creation, I think it can be a beautiful thing. Children don't have to sneak around and act as if sex is something bad, but can grow up with a healthy understanding of sex and have it in context to the glory of God.

Jay Kesler

we tried to do, to some degree, in our home.

On the other hand, you need to help the church do what it can. At one point, we had four teenagers in our family. I sat down with the person in charge of youth ministry and asked (nicely, of course) about his aims—"You've got these kids. What are you doing with them?"

The preceding list isn't the only way a church may articulate its aims. The basic purpose, however, should center on maturity. What you don't want to hear is that kids are basically being entertained. Teens want enrichment, not entertainment. Christian teens, especially, want to get at church what they can't get other places. They don't want to watch TV at church; they want to learn how to live as Christians—in a relevant way, of course.

The greatest compliment to my preaching I ever received came from a ten-year-old boy who said, "I listened to every word, and I understood it, and it did me good." I felt like crying.

Related Articles
Chapter 16: Why Don't My Kids Like Church?
Chapter 16: What's Behind Your Teen's Sunday School Lesson?

What the Church Can Do
Getting Teens Involved in the Body

B. CLAYTON BELL

A church has to be careful not to equate its activities with living the Christian life. The church's program should be a supplement and an encouragement to a person's relationship with the Lord. It should not be *equated* with one's relationship to God. Even a church's teaching ministry should be a supplement to Christian teaching in the home. Unfortunately, a lot of families don't realize this and rely entirely on the church for Christian training.

A church should provide wholesome activities for its youth, but these should simply supplement, not compete with, what the family does. The youth activities provided depend on the size and resources of the individual church. We have tried various things in the different sized churches my wife and I have served. These churches have run the gamut from 110 members where there was no other staff, not even a secretary, to the very large congregation we're in now.

In the smaller church, we had an open house for the young people where we sat down with them and discussed their needs. Occasionally, we took them places and once a year we went to a conference together. We didn't have any bang-up program going, but the kids knew that we were interested and concerned, so they responded. They felt like I was not just the adults' pastor but their pastor too, and that made a difference. We also planned cooperative youth programs with other churches in the community for cookouts, discussions, and other events.

In the very large church I pastor now, we have six people working just with young people, so we are able to provide a wide variety of activities. We have a gymnasium, take more than 100 kids each year to out-of-state conferences, have parties in homes, and schedule many events. We plan some of our youth activities just for sheer fun. Kids like to get together, so we often get two bus-loads of kids and take them to an out-of-town football game and stop for pizza on the way back. That way the kids get together; they are able to do something wholesome; there are just enough parents involved to make sure everything is on the up-and-up; and yet it's a large enough group to make the kids feel they are on their own.

A church should plan its youth programs and activities in conjunction with the parents. We've encouraged each of our youth ministers to counsel with parents and some of the young people on a regular basis, so that they can get periodic feedback from both groups on how the programs are going and what the needs and opportunities are.

It's a debatable point, however, as to how much responsibility teens should be given in the life of the church. Some people believe that church government needs to be shared by the youth. They strongly emphasize the importance of having young people serve on official boards. Other people believe that the official government of the church must be in the hands of the spiritually mature, though these leaders need to have their ears open to what the young people are saying.

I think that young people should be supplied opportunities to give their input into what's going on in the church. As far as getting them to help serve, however, their attention spans are often too short to sit through long committee meetings. And you can't expect a young person to be as seriously interested in everything that goes on in the church as an adult is. To expect that is to frustrate him and disappoint the church.

A different type of problem occurs when a church leader's teenager doesn't want to attend the youth programs, which can be pretty embarrassing to the parent. You're asking for rebellion, however, if you tell teenagers they have to attend because of the leadership role you play in the church. And your embarrassment if they don't go is no strong motivation for them to respond in a different

way. Besides, their responsibility is to the Lord. In such situations, I talked to my

HOW PARENTS CAN HELP THE CHURCH

The best thing parents can do to help the church do its job better is to raise a good kid. Then that kid will help other kids.

In every church, certain teens are the transformers, the Daniels and Josephs. They can have more spiritual influence than a legion of adults. So as a parent, my first responsibility is at home.

If, however, I find my teen being harmed by what happens at church, I must do something. Of course, I'll be careful not to make hasty accusations because maybe, just maybe, it isn't the church's fault but mine—or my kid's.

But if the problem genuinely seems to lie with the church, I'd go to the youth leader—not the pastor. I'd say something like, "I've noticed our kids aren't spending much time with their Bibles," or "I've been quizzing my son and he isn't remembering anything from Sunday School. What can we do to help?" By offering your concern and assistance, you're much more likely to find the youth leader willing to make changes.

One other specific suggestion: get parents and youth workers together every couple of months for a "Christian PTA" meeting. We did that, and though it wasn't highly organized, it greatly aided parents in knowing what their teens were doing and how they could reinforce the lessons at home.

Warren W. Wiersbe

teenagers about being salt and light in a group and suggested that they go and try to make it a better group. Sometimes I pushed our kids a little to be involved but, every now and then, I also let them get out of participating.

This is where parents need to set the example for their children. If parents continually complain about the church, the minister, the music, etc., and go only sporadically themselves, the kids will quickly get the message that they don't have to go and that church is not important. No matter how poor the preacher is, I have found I can always worship the Lord in church. But if the church is so bad that you can't do even that, then you should look for another church.

If you as parents don't like what is happening in the youth program, then talk with the youth director and explain

RETREAT!

"Retreat" is a curious name for a weekend experience designed for spiritual and physical renewal and for personal challenge. In reaction, some have renamed these experiences "advances." Whatever the name, retreats, camps, and conferences provide excellent opportunities for reflection, fellowship, and renewed commitment.

If the budget and schedule permit, teenagers should be encouraged to get away and spend time "retreating" occasionally. (Of course, the trips should have reputable and responsible organizers and sponsors.) Often, however, our kids don't want to go or react with benign disinterest. This is especially true for younger teens (their first retreat). In these situations, it would be counterproductive to force them to go. Instead, we should find out why they are uninterested. Perhaps they are afraid to leave home; they don't think *they* can afford it; or they haven't been "sold" on the trip. Usually, however, the block involves their friends. It's threatening to go *alone* (adults have the same feelings).

Most of these obstacles can be overcome by careful and loving help. If money is the problem (and we really want them to go), we can offer to pay for part or *all* of it. If they just aren't convinced of its value or that they will have a good time, we can enlist the help of the youth leaders. They will be happy to encourage our son or daughter and to reassure him or her of their presence and friendship.

Working with other parents will help encourage *groups of friends* to make the trip. These parents may also want to chip in for a "scholarship fund" to help those who really can't afford the cost.

If there isn't a specific camp or retreat on the horizon, we can research camps together and find one that meets their needs (a "sports" camp would be inappropriate if they aren't athletic). To help them make the decision, we can offer incentives.

Before and after camp, we must respect their feelings, allowing them to honestly evaluate the experience. (If they didn't like it, we should drop it.)

Hopefully, they will have had a wonderful time retreating from the daily schedule, meeting new friends, having fun, and deepening their understanding of themselves, others, and God.

YFC Editors

the problem that's bothering you. If necessary, sit down with the minister or with the church board and explain how you think things should be changed.

The greatest thing that parents can offer the church is to realize that the church is not an end in itself; it is a means to an end. The church is to help us grow in a relationship with the living Christ, to assist our learning about and worshiping Him, and to provide us this channel through which we can express our loyalty and worship. Parents need to communicate to teenagers that their loyalty should be to the Lord, and the church is just the channel through which they serve Him.

—————

Related Articles

Can the Church Solve My Teen's Problems?

JOHN PERKINS

Theologically, we have to believe that the church is able to save what society has allowed to deteriorate. If the church is going to be the salt of the earth, then we have to believe that the church always has the possibility of recreating society's failures.

The church ought to be making strong families. When weak families come to the church, they should find a family within the church, the family of God. The weak family then has an opportunity to be recreated through the church family's help and example.

When there are families in the church who have the virtues of love and compassion and the desire to share them, the church can provide that sense of family. The leadership of the church and the elders can find ways for these families to provide an outreach within the body of Christ.

The church can be an extended household. I was once in Portland, Oregon and met a wealthy woman who had raised her family in a beautiful thirteen-room house. She was only using a small part of it, and she asked me how she could use that house so it could continue to minister to other families, like it had ministered to hers. The home was near a medical school and I encouraged her to open her home to provide an extended family to several interested med students.

God creates man in an environment. We have to make certain our faith is affecting the environment in which we live—our neighborhood. The weakness of the church is that we have lost the sense of parish, the sense of neighborhood. We are concerned about church growth, not about community effectiveness.

Middle-class Christians are not using their gifts and their homes. They are trying to help the community through time they give to the Boys' Club or Boy Scouts. While those programs are worthy ones, we also need to open our homes so that these young folk can experience a healthy home environment. They need to see morality and righteousness and love firsthand instead of expecting all the love to come from institutions.

It is what we do outside the church building that counts. There *does* need to be an incentive to worship and there *does* need to be sound biblical teaching, but what we actually do in the community is

377

the final judgment on the effectiveness of the church.

Churches are really doing their jobs when their people have turned their homes into extensions of their churches. I am seeing it all around: families who make their swimming pools available to young people, families who have Bible studies in their homes, or who have home fellowship groups.

Teens sometimes feel that the church doesn't care about them because the church is concentrating on itself rather than being out in the community. But when a church adopts a high school or helps some troubled teens, it is showing people it cares about what happens outside its walls, its circle.

In Fresno, California Youth for Christ has set up a "Grandmother adoption program." A grandmother goes to the juvenile center and adopts one or two of the teens, visits them regularly, and provides much needed love and affection. I want those grandmothers to see that outreach as a direct ministry of their church. Churches need to look for those kinds of avenues and get people to do those kinds of things. It's a sign of healthy bodies.

Related Articles

Chapter 16: What Can the Church Do?
Chapter 24: Can the Church Help the Troubled Teen?

What's Behind Your Teen's Sunday School Lesson?

WARREN W. WIERSBE

The curriculum a church uses can have an important influence on teenagers. It determines the Bible content they'll study. It provides the direction of the lesson and many of the applications. And to varying degrees, it will help inspire the teacher with ideas and methods.

But curriculum is a limited tool. It's only as effective as the teachers. Good curriculum can't make up for poor teachers. The church's biggest job is to get teachers who can handle teenagers.

How do you do that? Naturally, as a pastor, I think it begins in the pulpit. We reproduce after our kind. If the pastor is excited about the Word and makes it meaningful, he will grow people like that. If you don't have a pastor like that, you have to look doubly hard for teachers who are already excited about the Word.

The most important characteristic for teachers of teens is to be people who practice the Word. A man may have a sixth-grade education, but if he's excited about Scripture and practices it, he'll teach better than a person who has a university degree but little zeal for the Word.

Our kids were fortunate to have excellent Sunday School teachers. Even today, they still talk about one or another of their teachers who excited them with learning. The Word must always be made flesh. John 1:14 isn't just a Christmas event; it's a continuing ministry. Unless the Word is "made flesh" so my daughter can see someone come through sorrow and sickness with triumph, all the teaching in the world doesn't do any good.

Once spiritually minded teachers are secured, then attention can be turned to how the curriculum is used.

The church and home ought to coordinate their efforts. Let parents know what

378

their kids will be studying for the next three months. Suggest that they have both private and family devotions in the same Bible portions. Scripture has the most impact when it is met under a variety of learning conditions. Repetition won't be dull. It will make the passage glow with ever brighter light.

The pastor can also reinforce the lessons. Occasionally, I used to say from the pulpit, "Now this past month our teens have been studying the life of David, and we see the same lesson here. . . ."

The teens think, *Wow, he knows.* It affirms the importance of their class, and it confirms the point they were studying.

Finally, good curriculum always translates the Bible into life situations. I often used to ask our children after Sunday School, "What did the Bible lesson mean to you? How's it going to work at school or at football practice?"

The important thing is not accumulating content but deciding intent. The purpose of a sermon or a lesson is not to explain a subject but to achieve an object. Not many people care what happened to the Jebusites, but they desperately need to know how they can keep their homes intact.

The Bible, when properly taught, can help keep homes intact and lives growing into maturity.

Related Articles

You *Can* Become an Effective Youth Volunteer

JAMES C. GALVIN

Perhaps you have been asked to become a volunteer working with the teenagers in your church's youth group. Other adults have not lasted very long as volunteers. Those who have been around for a while don't seem to help kids very much. Becoming a volunteer in a youth group is a difficult task because of the range of talents and abilities needed to be successful. However, you can become an effective volunteer through (1) being a good example, and (2) sticking to the type of ministry which you do best.

Being a good youth worker really has more to do with who you are than what you do. Whether you lead the meeting or merely stand on the sidelines, you are a role model for teenagers. You are acting and living as an adult and teenagers are watching for clues as to how they will have to act and live when they become adults. Teenagers are searching for an answer to the question, "Who am I?" They often try on the identities of other people in search of their own identity. They look to you as an example. So who you are speaks more loudly than what you do. Those who are good examples are not the ones who seemingly live well-disciplined and perfect Christian lives, but those who allow teenagers to look in to see what they are really like. So to be a good example, be genuine and open to teenagers. Be willing to share struggles that you face and feelings you encounter. Let them see you in many different life situations, not only in the youth group meeting room or church sanctuary.

Youth ministry occurs in three different settings: large groups, small groups, and one-on-one. Volunteers are not normally gifted or talented in all three areas. As a result, you need to select and stick with the area in which you do best. This acknowledges an understanding that people fulfill different functions within the body of Christ and are gifted in different ways. Those who desire to work with kids in an individual setting need to be good at listening, counseling, and leading kids to Christ. Those who want to work with kids in a small-group setting should be good at leading discussions, teaching the Bible, and building relationships in a small group. Those who want to work with kids in a large-group setting should be good at planning or running meetings. This could range from speaking, to leading games, to providing music or media, or meeting new people.

If you make sure you are being a good example of the Christian life and focus on one setting for ministry at which you are best, the chances are better that you will be an effective volunteer. However, the situation of the youth group also impacts your effectiveness. Is there a full-time youth director? Does the youth director know what he is doing? Are there any other volunteers and what are they like?

If you have a full-time youth director who is in control of the program and uses volunteers appropriately, becoming effective will be fairly easy. In this situation, just move in and work out expectations with the leader; follow through on all your assignments; determine whether you work better with individuals, in small groups; or in large groups; and strive to be a part of the team.

If you have a weak or incompetent youth director, being an effective volunteer becomes a little more complex. The youth director could be either full-time or a volunteer, but he just doesn't seem able to accomplish the job or help the volunteers to do their work. As a volunteer in this situation, you may be asked to do too much in areas where you are weak. If this happens, clarify the number of hours which you can contribute each week and focus on that aspect of youth ministry which you do best. Learn to say no to other responsibilities which may not be among your strengths or interests.

On the other hand, you may have a youth director who doesn't ask you to do anything. Sometimes, youth directors are "do-it-yourself" types of people who find it very difficult to assign tasks to others, even volunteers who want to help. In this situation, stand close by and look for ways in which you can help out. Look for assignments that are within your areas of strength. Sometimes any outside ministry you perform with kids on an individual or a small-group basis may be viewed as a threat by the youth director. If so, you need to consistently reassure and show your support for his leadership.

You may be asked to volunteer in a youth group where there is no youth group leader. You will have to take over and fill in until another leader is found. In this situation, do your best, knowing that the results may not be ideal. Find others to get involved with you, either other adult volunteers in the church or students who can help lead. If needed, seek advice from other youth group leaders in other churches. Don't try to do all the youth ministry yourself. As a leader, your main duty is to make sure each person is doing his part. You may find that all of your time is taken up by running a large group and you have very little time left over for working with teenagers in a small-group or individual setting. But don't be discouraged. The Lord knows when you've done your best, no matter how trying the circumstances. And He will produce fruit as you faithfully minister.

Related Articles

The Church Exists for the Family, Not the Family for the Church

J. SCOTT SUSONG

I first heard this story from Dr. Howard Hendricks. It goes something like this: A young, enthusiastic pastor held up the church bulletin and proudly said to his wife: "Look at that, Honey, an activity on every night of the week!" His wife, not nearly so enthusiastic, said, "That's nice, Dear. Tell me, are you interested in seeing families grow together and develop in the Lord?" The pastor, a little perturbed that his wife would ask him a question with such an obvious answer replied, "Why, of course I am! After all, that's biblical." This very wise wife then said, "I see. I was just wondering, on what night of the week do you suggest they do that?"

The point was made loud and clear. This pastor, in his desire to build the church, was wiping out the family times of his members. He failed to see both dimensions of his ministry—that the church exists to serve families as well as families existing to serve the church. Actually, it's not a question of either/or; it's a question of both/and. That is, the church must serve families by preaching and teaching the Word, through pastoral care, youth groups, etc. All of these things should point in one direction: helping youth and adults come to know Christ as Saviour and to grow in that relationship. This produces men who take leadership in their homes, women who are godly examples, and young people who obey and respect their parents. In turn, strong families become the heart and soul of an effective church ministry. Churches must give direction, teaching, and encouragement, but then allow families to be together and practice what

they are learning. Obviously, a family cannot grow in the Lord if they are always at the church, building the kingdom of some misguided pastor!

How can the church best serve the family? I want to suggest several ways:

1. *The pastor must be a good family man.* Quite frankly, this one point can cover a multitude of other sins. People who study such things will tell you that after two or three years, the congregation will take on the personality and priorities of the pastor. If the pastor is a good family man, chances are it will filter down and strengthen the families in his church. Notice, I am not talking about teaching or preaching about the family, I'm talking about the pastor *modeling* biblical principles in his life. Now, modeling in what areas? I feel these areas are most important (pastors, pulpit committees, take heed!):

• *Loving his wife.* Many pastors can expound volumes on Ephesians 5:25-33, but do they demonstrate it? Teenagers today are in desperate need of good models to follow. Many young people know what the Bible says about a godly husband and father, but they've never *seen* one! Pastors, who live in a "fishbowl" anyway, can do a world of good for teens if they will simply love their wives. By loving their wives, I don't just mean opening the car door for her or letting her go ahead in the fellowship dinner line. The love that Paul speaks of in Ephesians 5 is the same love that God displayed when He gave His only Son to die for us (John 3:16). It is a sacrificial love that says, "I want to do all I can to help you be all you can be in the Lord." It is a love that is expressed in forms such as: listening with the inner ear, respecting her opinions and ideas, *asking* her opinion, praying with her, protecting her emotionally from the kids, building her up, etc. I'm not perfect, I've got my weaknesses, but I feel one of the strongest areas of my ministry is the relationship I have with my wife. This dawned on me one day when a woman in our church approached my wife and said, "When I saw the relationship that you and Scott have, I knew that I didn't have to settle for mediocrity in my marriage." She didn't come because of some grand sermon I preached but simply because my wife and I love each other. I'm the pastor, but she's the "pastoress."

• *Loving his kids.* We try to make it a practice in our family not to involve the children in the church any more than any other children normally would be. The church activity calendar is secondary to my children's needs. I want them to be good examples as Christians because that's what God's Word says, *not* because I'm the pastor. This carries over into their school activities as well. What they can and cannot do at school is governed by the fact that their mother and I are Christians trying our best to rear them according to God's Word. The fact that I happen to be the pastor of a church has no more to do with my parenting style than if I were a doctor, lawyer, or plumber. In a nutshell, rearing our children in the Lord means not neglecting them. When I'm with my kids I'm *all there:* wrestling, reading, building a fire, sleeping in the tent, talking, trading jokes, praying. It requires both quality and quantity time. Teenagers today not only need to see a pastor who loves his wife, but who loves his children as well.

2. *Church leaders need to be good family men and women.* Everything mentioned about the pastor holds true for the leaders of the church. Elders, deacons, committeemen and women, teachers, staff personnel, and youth leaders all should be good examples at home. Now, I'm not saying that these people cannot be leaders unless they are married. However, it is not within the scope of this article to discuss the single-married issue. One of the most important qualifications of an elder is that he "manage his own household well" (1 Tim. 3:4). The idea is that if he can't cut it at home, don't enlarge his sphere of responsibility! I'm not saying that a man or woman must be perfect before he or she can take a position of leadership. The church is made up of sinners saved by grace, but sinners just the same. The church leader doesn't have to be perfect, but is he progressing? Does he take his biblical responsibilities in the home seriously? His effectiveness at home is the proving ground for his effectiveness in church leadership.

The youth of today need to see pastors and church leaders whose walk matches their talk, and the Christian walk begins at home.

What else can churches do to best serve families?

3. *Preaching and teaching biblical principles of family living.* Let's face it, God created the family and He knows how to make it work! I would suggest in sermons and Sunday School classes that these passages be covered: Ephesians 5:22-33; Ephesians 6:1-4; Colossians 3:18-21; 1 Peter 3:1-7; Deuteronomy 6:4-9; and many more. As with any teaching, practical suggestions and applications should be made. These applications are most effective when they come directly from the experience of the teacher or preacher.

4. *Counseling.* This doesn't always have to be done by the "professional." The listening ear of an elder or a Sunday School teacher can do a world of good. The pastor should make himself readily available for counseling and have a good Christian "professional" to whom he could refer people.

5. *Youth ministries.* If there is any way

that pastors and churches can cooperate with these fine organizations, they should do so. I can personally recommend Youth for Christ (Campus Life), Campus Crusade for Christ (High School Division), and Young Life. These people know how to work with youth and parents, and would be a valuable resource to any church ministry in serving its families.

6. *Literature.* Our church has a book rack containing a generous supply of material on the family. Unfortunately, the market is flooded with material on the family and people become confused as to what they should buy. I would personally recommend these authors: James Dobson, Norman Wright, Charles Swindoll, John MacArthur, H. Page Williams, Tim LaHaye, Joyce Landorf, and Howard Hendricks. No doubt I have neglected to mention someone's personal favorite, but this is only a partial list.

7. *Seminars and films.* Our church makes these available to our people from time to time. There are too many film series or seminars to mention, but I would personally recommend any film series by James Dobson, Charles Swindoll, or John MacArthur. I would also recommend the weekend seminar on the family offered by Campus Crusade for Christ.

Only the surface has been scratched in this article as to what churches can do to serve families. Volumes could be written on this subject. Churches must *serve* families, not *use* them. Pastors and church leaders can't do everything, but they *can* do something. The job is to serve; the time to start is now.

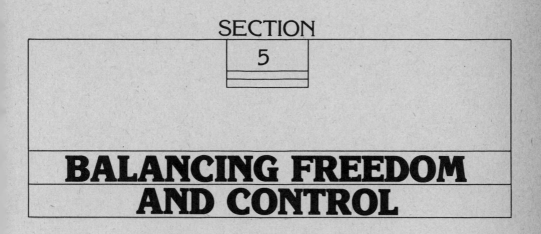

SECTION

5

BALANCING FREEDOM AND CONTROL

17

MANAGING THE HOME
WITH LOVE AND AUTHORITY

- When does your teen's business become your business?
- The importance of rules in the home: Learning to be flexible without sacrificing principles

- How do you get teenagers to obey?
- Should parents always get their way?
- How to avoid power struggles
- Are you spoiling your teenager?

Young people do not resist having a fair and compassionate authority over them. In fact, without walls and edges in their lives, they flounder and cannot feel secure. But authority is not something we parents can demand. It is something we command.

We begin to command authority when we pick up and hold and love our infant children. As they grow in understanding, we establish guidelines and boundaries for them. They respect our authority to do this because we are willing to explain the logic behind our requirements, to discuss our concerns, to confess our fears for our children's well-being if they violate them. As we do this, we establish not only our own authority but God's also. Our children will come to see that God loves us, that He hates sin because He doesn't want us to be hurt. They will not find it difficult to love and follow a God whose loving authority they first saw in their parents' actions.

When Should You Mind Your Teen's Business?

JAY KESLER

Some young people and their parents have excellent communication with each other. The parents are genuinely interested in their children's activities. They are willing to listen and share, but they do not attach value judgments to everything their children say. They are able to make observations that do not make the children feel pressured to change.

"That's interesting," they may say. "I've had the same kinds of questions myself, and I've approached them this way." Or, "I remember I used to struggle with that too, and I failed almost all the time with that particular thing."

Such an atmosphere of openness and vulnerability makes two-way communication possible, because the young people do not feel threatened. When something goes wrong, the teenagers are unafraid to share. When the parents are fearful, they can ask questions without making their children feel like the jig is up and everything is going to come unraveled. The young people already know how their parents deal with difficulty and defeat and

387

failure. They are willing to believe they can risk discussing this sensitive topic with their parents as well.

One of the most heartwarming things I hear from parents is this: "If that's what my child said, then I know it's the truth." Though occasionally parents are fooled, I always like to think they know enough about the young person to know that he or she tells the truth even when it is not pleasant.

The same kind of trust is evident when a young person says, "Hey, we can tell my dad about it because I know he'll understand." I constantly try to tell young people that most parents are more understanding than teens think they will be, especially in the big issues. For instance, I have gone with young people to tell the parents that the daughter is pregnant. Now this is a very extreme and severe circumstance, yet every time I've done it, both the teenager and I have been amazed at how well the parents have handled it. Parents tend to muster more strength and maturity and tolerance with the big issues than they do with the small ones.

When we have established with our kids that we can handle these things without coming unglued and making a federal case out of everything, then we're able to pry. When we begin to see trouble signals in the kid's life—she's falling behind in her schoolwork, he has suddenly gotten lazy, we have found drug paraphernalia around the house or have noticed strange smells or conduct—it's time to say, "Is there anything we ought to talk about?" Or, "Tell me what's going on." Or, "Is there any way I can help you with this?" Or, "You need to reassure me—I think something's wrong, and I want to know."

I believe it's a parent's duty to ask some questions, even at the risk of making the young person feel temporarily distrusted. If the investigation shows that there is no real cause for concern, then it's time to say, "I'm very sorry if I seemed to distrust you, but I love you so very much that I didn't want you to be hurt. Sometimes we're into something over our heads and we need somebody's help, and I always want to be available to help you. That's why I was probing.

"HONEY, I LOVE YOU"

Some parents have been so busy with their work and church activities that they never have developed a relationship with their children. These parents can't afford to be hard-nosed with their children, because they don't have the relationship that would support tough demands.

Parents have to let their children make a few mistakes. They have to learn to listen without reprimanding and correcting. I'm convinced that in most situations, if the parents will just listen, many of the problems will be dealt with. Sometimes parents have to say, "Son, I don't agree with that, but if that is what you want to do, I'll support you in it." That's not the same as saying, "Go ahead and do it."

A real problem for many parents is their own reputations. I am very visible in evangelical Christianity. It's easy for me to reason, when I discipline my children, "If I don't do this, what will people think?" That is the wrong motivation for discipline. I have to face it—the time may come when my children will embarrass me. I've done books on sex, love, and dating—what if my daughter got pregnant? I trust God would give me the strength to turn my back on the people who criticize, put my arms around her, and say, "Honey, I love you."

Josh McDowell

388

Please forgive me for misjudging you. And let's keep talking, because any time something difficult comes up in your life or mine, we need to be available to help each other."

What do parents do if the investigation proves that the child *is* in trouble? Parents who have found a contraband item in their child's room might say something like this: "We want to apologize to you. We have been seeing some danger signals, and we became suspicious. We began to look through your personal things, and this is what we found. We're sorry you felt you had to keep this from us, but let's deal with the situation now."

I think young people ultimately expect this degree of interest in their well-being, and when they don't find it, they think less of us.

Related Articles
Chapter 17: Teenage Rights vs. Family Rights
Chapter 17: When Teens Test the Rules
Chapter 18: Discipline: A Family's Friend or Foe?
Chapter 19: When Your Teen Betrays Your Trust

Why Teens Reject Parental Authority

RONALD P. HUTCHCRAFT

The concept of parental authority has changed in our society. Many parents can remember when the end of any argument used to be, "Because I'm your father! (or mother)" Today that view of authority has changed. Our position as parents does not automatically invest us with authority, from the teen's point of view. Today authority has to be *earned,* not just demanded.

It's true that the Bible gives parents a special position of authority over their children. But whether or not parents enjoy that position in the eyes of their teens is another matter. You may be interested in several studies that have been done about the long-range effects on teens who have very authoritative parents. An authoritative parent is one who doesn't give much support to his children, but who exercises very rigid control over their behavior. The research says that the parent who demands obedience to his authority, and is big enough to get it, will get short-term compliance, but long-term rebellion. The authoritarian parent feels like his kids are "toeing the mark," but they're really just biding their time until they can do everything the parent detests. So, while it may look like the parent is succeeding, the true test of what's been done as a parent is what kind of men or women the teenagers become. Generally speaking, the studies indicate that rebels come from homes where there has been a very authoritarian climate.

Here are some of the reasons kids reject their parents' authority:

1. *"I don't feel respected."* If a young person doesn't think you take him seriously or that you don't respect him as a person, he probably won't respond with respect. Teens are best taught respect by being shown respect. So if you're not enjoying respect from your children, ask yourself: "Do I show them respect?"

• *Respect their friends.* Perhaps the most important choice in a teenager's life is his choice of friends. If you don't respect his choice of friends, even if you're not wild about them, you have basically said to your teen: "I don't respect your right to choose or your choices." You will have more clout in your teenager's life by making his friends feel special than by rejecting the friends you don't happen to like or appreciate.

• *Let them make decisions.* Give them time; give them space. Ask questions; give guidelines. But don't panic if they don't immediately see things your way. Give them room and the right to make some of their own decisions.

• *Respect their privacy.* One of Billy Graham's daughters said that one of the great memories she has of her dad is that he never entered her room without knocking. Say, by your actions, "I respect your privacy, your mail, your room, and your conversations."

2. *"They don't really hear me."* Kids reject parental authority because they don't feel their parents really hear what they're saying. The reason why many teens don't talk to their parents is not because they aren't looking for someone to talk to. They usually do their share of talking, but to one or more of their friends—which is a little like talking to somebody mired in quicksand about how to get out of it.

The reason teens prefer to discuss their problems with their friends is that they usually get better results (from their point of view) than they get when they talk to their parents. They feel that when they talk to their friends they've been *heard,* not *had.* If your teens don't talk to you it may be because they feel you don't really know where they're coming from, and therefore don't have the right to tell them how to run their lives.

How can you encourage them to talk? Ask for their advice. Let them know that you value their ideas and suggestions. Spend time with them. Go to their games and to other events that are important to them. Try to be with them in formal settings too, where you are forced to talk to one another. Ask a lot of questions before you respond to them or try to unload your point of view. There's a tendency for us as parents to fire off an immediate response to our kids' first sentence. Ask God to help you control yourself and to realize that unwise and hasty responses on your part may close the door to future input from them. Try rather to say: "Oh, I see. Now, how do you feel about that? Tell me some of your reasons." Or, "What do your friends think about that?" If you ask a lot of questions *before* you respond, you'll end up responding with greater authority in the eyes of your teens. Proverbs 18:13 has some good counsel for us parents at this point: "He that answers before listening— that is his folly and his shame" (NIV).

When you *do* listen to your teenagers, be sure that you're not preoccupied. If you aren't able to talk with them at the moment say: "Listen, this isn't a good time. But I really want to hear what you have to say, so give me a half hour, and then I'm all yours." And be sure that you

GOD, THE SOURCE

The Bible does not teach prohibition of sin simply because God is looking for something to prohibit, or even because God will be embarrassed by our sin. The Bible teaches prohibition of sin because the consequence of sin is death!

Therefore, we as parents ought not to be motivated by our need to establish our authority. Our motivation should be love for our own children. God is not an added problem in our relationships with our family. *He is our Source!*

Peter Sjoblom

give them those "all yours" times.

3. *"I think parents are inflexible."* Kids don't have much respect for parents who are "never wrong." And if you are never wrong, never apologize, or never seek forgiveness, you seem unapproachable to them. In their eyes, it's an impossible, no-win situation. You choke off dialogue and any kind of respect. While you may be able to force them to do what you want them to do, you really don't have positive authority in their lives. So don't expect them to do all of the changing. Since you *can* be and *will* be wrong now and then, simply admit it, rather than try to over-power them. Be approachable. Otherwise teens will just shrug their shoulders and say, "What's the use of trying to talk to them? I already know the outcome."

4. *"I don't feel trusted."* One of the most common complaints I hear from teens is that they don't feel that their parents trust them. When I talk to teenagers I stress the importance of being trustworthy. The parents' side of this is to look for ways to show trust in teens—let them handle some money; let them use the car under appropriate circumstances; give them some freedom, within limits, to manage their time; and allow them to have input into policies that affect them. Show them how they can get even more freedom from you. Say yes to them as often as you can. All of these things communicate a sense of trust to your teenagers.

One of the things that happens in the trust business is that we parents tend to react, not on the basis of what is happening, but on the basis of what *might* happen. We know what *can* happen so we react with fear and suspicion. We bombard our kids with questions. We accuse them of sins that they haven't committed. So they feel untrusted and pushed. Our panic has a way of convincing our teens that we don't trust them. A better approach is to ask some thought-provoking questions. Trust in the Lord to protect the teens you've prayed for all

their lives. Authority ought to be based on mutual trust between you and your children.

5. *"I don't know what the boundaries are."* Another reason why kids reject parents' authority is that parents sometimes aren't clear about establishing definite boundaries and penalties. Take football as an example: You know where the yard markers are and where out of bounds is. The players go into the game knowing clearly what the rules are and what the penalties are for breaking the rules. That's how it needs to be in a family. When the boundaries keep changing and the penalties aren't consistent, kids become confused. As much as possible, decide on the boundaries and penalties early in the game and enforce them fairly and consistently. When kids feel unsure about boundaries, they will test them constantly and will take advantage of any inconsistency or confusion. This ultimately breeds rebellion.

Something else that makes kids unsure of the boundaries is if Mom and Dad are divided on discipline. I believe it's better for parents to be united on a disciplinary decision than to be totally right about it. Greater damage is done by parental disagreement in front of teens than by letting the other parent follow through on discipline, even if it is flawed in some way. Parents should talk about the flaw later when the children aren't present. Kids are quick to exploit the "divide and conquer" opportunities that come their way. And divided authority makes them disrespect the authority of *both* parents.

6. *"My parents are poor examples."* Another reason why teens reject parental authority is that they don't think their parents set a good example for them. They feel that parents expect one thing of them, but do not practice what they preach. They want their parents to be good models for them—to show them by their own lives how they as children should live and respond to various situations.

Ask yourself: "Is my attitude, my example, such that I really want my kids to do what I do, to follow and obey me? Do I tell them to hang up their clothes, but not do it myself? Am I asking them to respect me, but show them little or no respect? Do I tell them it's important to have a strong relationship with the Lord and yet they never see me reading the Bible or showing interest in spiritual things?"

How Do I Get My Kids to Obey?

V. GILBERT BEERS

"**H**ow do I get my kids to obey?" That depends on your view of obedience. It may be possible to brainwash a child to do anything you say, whether it is good for him or not.

But what intelligent parents want complete and unquestioning obedience from a child? You may as well turn your child into a robot and set the controls to please you. That kind of thinking assumes that you are always right, that you know exactly what your child should have, and that you never want your child to grow up and make his own decisions.

I remember a man in his forties who hated his father because the father did all his thinking for him and never allowed him to grow up as a decision-making adult. Now the father is no longer able to make the decisions and the son has found it difficult to learn how.

Before you expect obedience, be sure you deserve obedience. Are you asking something, or demanding something, because you truly know it is best for your child? Or is it possible that your teen really does have a better idea?

It is assumed that parents know what is best for a very young child. But this may change somewhere along the way. As a teen grows and becomes mature, he needs to make certain decisions, even at the risk of failure or hurt.

So the first part of the obedience matter is to be sure you are right, and not to assume your child is always wrong. Even a small child isn't wrong all the time.

Having said that, let's assume that you, the parents, are right most of the time, especially for younger children and their needs. Why then are you not getting the obedience you think you should get?

Several reasons may emerge. One may be that your child does not respect parental authority. There is a time when a child should obey his parents because his parents are right. But there is another time when a child should obey his parents because it will please his mother or father.

Part of the process of parenting is to build in your child's mind the proper view of a parent. Parents are not unnecessary baggage to put up with until you can "get out of this house." Parents are ordained by God to care for the best interests and needs of children until those children have developed the maturity to take care of themselves.

Perhaps you should spend more time in the earlier years establishing the right parent-child respect and love (mutually), and less time worrying about blind obedience. Most obedience comes out of love and respect for the person we obey.

Should we "buy" obedience with gifts? Of course not. Gifts express love, but they do not buy love. If you or I love someone because that person gives us gifts, our motives are warped. We love the gifts more than the giver. But if we love gifts because of the giver, we have put the person ahead of the merchandise. You or I cannot bribe someone into loving us, and we also cannot bribe someone into cheerful, willing obedience.

If you must repeatedly "discipline" your child to command obedience, perhaps you should begin to ask about the love relationship between you and the child.

Of course, your child may love you very much and still not obey you because of competing loves and loyalties. Some teens foolishly assign more importance to peer pressure than to love of parents, perhaps without realizing it. If you believe your child loves you and does not obey you, it may be wise to gently probe to find competing pressures, loves, or loyalties. Be prepared to discover that your child may not be able to define these himself. And even if he can, he may not have the strength alone to pull himself away.

Love is still the greatest motive for obedience. We obey most whom we love most. And we love those who first love us. Perhaps that is the best way to win obedience. Love your child unconditionally. Love your child because you should love him and do love him and not because that's a way to get what you want. If your love is so compelling, it will strike fire and your child will love you back. And unless there are competitive forces pulling stronger than your love, he will obey, not because he must, but because he desires it.

TEMPTED TO DISOBEY

A boy was once tempted by his friends to pick some ripe cherries from a tree which his father had forbidden him to touch. "You need not be afraid," they said, "for if your father should find out that you had taken them, he is so kind that he would not hurt you." "For that reason," replied the boy, "I ought not to touch them; for though my father would not hurt me, my disobedience would hurt my father."

The Biblical Treasury

Related Articles

Teenage Rights vs. Family Rights

GARY R. COLLINS

I have a problem with the word "rights."

When we start talking about rights, we've already created a tense situation. There are women's rights, black rights, student rights, gay rights, union rights, etc. When we talk about teenage rights, I automatically think of a teenager I know who bought the radio for his family's car. Now he thinks it's his "right" to play "his" music regardless of who else is in the car. He forgets that the radio is in his parents' car.

I much prefer the word *respect*. As parents and teenagers, we need to respect each other.

In our family the radio came with the car. So, based on our respect for each other, we decided that the parents would choose the music on the way to a destination, and the teenagers would choose the music on the way back. If, in either case, the music got noticeably bad, we would respect each other enough to turn it off. Along the way, we've had to admit that we like some of each other's music, and good conversations have been the result.

Respect should go hand-in-hand with *understanding*. If I try hard to understand that my kids have a different perspective on music, for instance, then I can say, "Hey, let me tell you where I'm coming from." Kids are willing to listen to us if we're willing to listen to them.

At home, like in the car, we try to understand each other's taste in music, and we respect it. Instead of turning on the Chicago Symphony nice and loud, I try to keep it down. And the kids make the same effort with rock music. At dinnertime, we compromise and choose something that is in-between, such as a contemporary Christian album or tape. And we keep the volume at a reasonable level.

In counseling troubled teens, one of the complaints I have heard the most is, "My parents don't understand me." But if parents are willing to say, "All right, I don't understand—help me," then they have demonstrated that they are trying to understand their kids. The admission of desire is the first step to understanding.

But it is never easy. It requires effort. I do not understand why my fifteen-year-old daughter wants to put silver paint on her hair. I know that she wants to look "punk" but I do not understand it. I have less trouble with her clothes and can accept the fact that they are stylish right now. But I am trying to understand, and she can see the effort.

To understand each other as parents and teens, we must *communicate*. We must make time for mutual sharing. Family discussions are great, but let's be realistic: they're almost impossible to maintain on a regular basis. So I try as often as possible to take my kids out to lunch. Sometimes I take them both at the same time, but most of the time I take them separately. I'll ask them how their social life is going, how school is going, etc. The simple fact that I'm showing some interest makes them willing to talk.

And again, respect is the key. You can't always treat them as adults, but you *can* treat them with respect. And in respecting them, sometimes you have to be willing to let them learn by their mistakes.

One of our kids once developed a friendship with someone we felt would be a very bad influence. So my wife and I were faced with two options: (1) we could refuse to let our daughter see this friend; (2) we could express our disapproval, listing the reasons why, and then let her decide for herself what course of action to take.

The first option would do nothing but create a power struggle, and immediately there would be the potential for dishonesty as our daughter might try to see the

BE A SYMPATHETIC PARENT

In my church last year, I listened one Sunday to a group of teenage musicians whose music I did not appreciate. But my kids loved them.

Sitting in front of us was a music teacher I knew, so I leaned forward and said, "George, what do you think about this music? I'll bet you don't like it."

"No, I don't," he said. "But I think of it as folk music. Where there is Hispanic music, black music, Slavic music, there's also teenage music. So because I look at it as folk music, I try to appreciate it as such. And I have to recognize that my highbrow Beethoven is not the only kind of music in the world."

George's answer drove home an important point in developing a sympathetic attitude toward teen perspectives: Don't always assume that because you're parents, your way is right. Who's to say that church music by Bach is any better than church music by the rock group, Petra?

To a teenager, the Bach or Petra question is authentic. But so often we refuse to entertain such questions because we're convinced *we're* right. By our words and attitudes we say, "You are wrong. Don't ask any more questions."

Instead we need to say to ourselves, "Maybe they have a point." "Perhaps theirs is a valid perspective." And once we've made that initial step, we open a door for being truly sympathetic.

Sometimes all that's needed then is a pat on the back or a note of encouragement. Teens respond to active encouragement.

Recently, a teenage boy I know walked out of church. I saw him outside and said, "How's it going?"

"I'm mad," he said. "It's just not fair." He was angry at his father for some reason.

Not wanting to take sides, I said simply, "I can appreciate that. I get angry too sometimes."

I went home and wrote him a short note of encouragement because I knew his father wouldn't mind, and I dropped it in the mail. The next Sunday he said, "Thanks, I got your note; it was nice of you."

He didn't say another thing, but knowing my own teenagers, I suspected that his words fell short of what he was really feeling.

Gary R. Collins

person behind our backs. On the other hand, the second option left her with a choice to make based on what we, as parents, had shared with her. She will realize in time that we respected her enough to give her some freedom.

Over time, she began to see our position. She never actually came back and admitted that she was wrong and we were right, but one day she said, "Boy, that person really is not good for me."

If we had forced the power struggle, I think we all would have lost. Sometimes, of course, parents have to say no. But even then teens know if they are respected, and they know where parents stand. Often that is beneficial to all concerned.

───────

Related Articles

How to Avoid Power Struggles

DAVID L. McKENNA

To avoid power struggles between parents and teens, there must be mutual respect. And that relationship of respect is lived out day-to-day in three major principles: love, praise, and consistency.

Love must be lived as well as spoken. Homes of love have a certain spirit about them. Unlike the "Spock-marked" generation of the 1950s when Benjamin Spock opposed punishment, we know that if love is present and evident, you can punish a child and it will not be a negative experience. You have to be discreet and consistent in the punishment, but children who know that they are loved can accept it.

In the best-selling book, *The One-Minute Manager,* authors Kenneth Blanchard and Spencer Johnson suggest that an employer praise an employee for one minute and then reprimand him for one minute. The rule is, "Change the performance, but save the person." In the one-minute reprimand, the employee gets immediate feedback. If his words or actions have been misinterpreted, he can meet the problem at the issue.

In the home as well, you must first let the child know that he is valuable to you. Character flaws and performance failure are two different things. There must be a love base so the reprimand is not mistaken as a loss of love. Second, you must communicate that the performance is being reprimanded, not the character or the person. What a difference there is between saying, "You lied" and, "You are a liar."

There is not a more meaningful motivator than *praise.* When John Wooden, the former great basketball coach, was asked how he motivated his players, he said, "I try to catch them doing something right." I think we have so many frustrations and expectations with regard to our teenagers that we don't praise them when we catch them doing something right. If a praise foundation is established, a reward becomes a natural outgrowth, rather than a manipulative tool.

Finally, there is no substitute for *consistency* in the home. If teens can't see consistency, they become confused as to what is actually right.

When we have a foundation of love, praise, and consistency, there will be

KEEPING MOLEHILLS MOLEHILLS

There are four keys to preventing molehills from developing into mountains.

First, before parents take "official action," they need to count to ten. Better yet, a hundred and ten. They need to listen a lot, think a lot, and pray a lot.

Second, parents should be secure. If they aren't secure, then they should at least act like it. When parents are insecure, they often try to prove themselves. Afraid that their power is eroding, they're quick to make their teenagers knuckle under. Teens need parents who serve as leaders and counselors, not as overlords.

Third, before making any pronouncements, parents do well to say to any new idea, "Let me think about that a little bit."

Fourth, if you have a spouse, work through the decision together. Double-teaming is an effective strategy in basketball and in parenting.

Harold Myra

---

mutual respect. Where there is respect, there is no need for manipulation to gain power. Parents and teens *can* avoid power struggles.

Related Articles

Chapter 17: Why Teens Reject Parental Authority

Chapter 17: Who's Taking Advantage of Whom?

Chapter 22: Rebellion: Can It Be Prevented?

Rules or Rebellion?

It's Your Choice

NORMAN WRIGHT

Without rules, you have anarchy. With too many rules, you can deaden a teen's spirit or incite rebellion. Openness and preparation may be the keys to finding a balance between these extremes.

Before our daughter, Sheryl, was old enough to drive—two or three years before—we started discussing the subject of driving with her. When she turned fifteen and was able to get a learner's permit, it was time to set rules concerning use of the car.

We decided to come up with a driving covenant. I asked Sheryl to think of several guidelines; my wife and I did the same. Finally the three of us sat down at the "negotiating table" and worked out a contract. The agreement included rules governing how often our daughter could drive, how many people could be in the car, who would pay for insurance (and the deductible in case of an accident), and more.

It wasn't all democratic. There were a

couple of provisions that I didn't leave open to negotiation. But we gave and Sheryl gave, and when the covenant was complete we signed it. Those rules stayed in force till Sheryl was eighteen, and we had practically no problems with it. Once in a while the terms were adjusted as conditions changed—but when they were, we all talked about it. Nothing was done behind our daughter's back.

I think covenants apply to many areas, not just to driving. We did the same thing with a dating contract—number of dates allowed per week, curfew, and so forth. Whether the rules are written is less important than that they're specific, mutually agreed on, and tailored to the individual teen.

What about punishment? When we hammered out our covenants, we didn't set penalties for infractions. We preferred to give our daughter the benefit of

the doubt, to proceed on the assumption that she'd be able to obey. "If you love someone . . . you will always believe in him, always expect the best of him" (1 Cor. 13:7, TLB). On that basis, we gave her a chance.

When a rule is broken, of course, there should be a penalty. That's the time to sit down with your teen and say, "OK, this rule was broken. What do you think ought to happen because it was broken?" Once you've determined the "sentence," be sure to talk with your teen about how he or she will avoid breaking the rule in the future. Always look toward the future.

Balancing rules and freedom can be tricky. As parents we often want to clamp down because we're afraid we haven't done a good job so far. We want to make sure the child performs or the adolescent conforms. The problem with that approach is that the young person may

"I'M LISTENING"

When people ask me, "Do you think the reason why your teens were able to abide by your rules was because of the foundation that you had put down earlier?" I heartily agree. In the first ten years of their childhood, we worked hard to establish in our kids a total acceptance of one another—with open communication lines. So our kids entered the teen years knowing that there was nothing they couldn't talk to us about. From their earliest years, the kids always felt free to express their thoughts and feelings. If we disagreed with them, we told them why. We never punished them for raising an issue. We never made them feel small. I think when that kind of trust is built in the first ten to eleven years, then the kids go into the teen years feeling that they are thoroughly free to express their feelings.

I've also discovered that there is a great uniqueness to teens—what I call a cross-sexual relationship. My son finds it much easier to talk to my wife about some personal matters, while my daughter has always found it easier to talk to me. I think there is a certain element of mystery when you talk to a member of the opposite sex. It has been good for that kind of cross-sexual friendship to exist. The kids have pursued this and feel good about it. It might be because a daughter thinks her mother knows too much about women and the son thinks that his father knows too much about men. Perhaps they think they can guard their dignity a bit more easily if they talk to the other parent.

Gordon MacDonald

throw off the rules—and all the other standards you've tried to instill. On the other hand, a teen without rules will flounder.

To make sure you're striking a balance, keep the lines of communication with your teens open. They don't always have to agree with the rules; but if they're willing to go along with them without always agreeing, you're on the right track. Getting a clear reading on this is difficult, since adolescents switch from "pro" to "con" on short notice. Keeping your eyes and ears open and staying flexible will help.

Rules are to be obeyed. But the ultimate goal is to internalize those values behind the rules. You don't want only lip service. Talking with your child about value systems and the reasons behind them should begin when he or she is about eight or nine, and continue through adolescence.

When Teens Test the Rules

CHARLES R. SWINDOLL

"**C**orrect your son, and he will give you comfort; He will also delight your soul" (Prov. 29:17, NASB).

Fact of life: Teens will test the rules.

I don't know of a teenager today who doesn't really want to know where the boundaries are. There is a security in knowing the limits.

What teens *don't* want is to have the boundaries hammered on their bedroom door like Luther's ninety-five theses. They don't want to hear the rules recited every morning when they awaken. But teens *do* want to know the rules and have them enforced. And they'll test them to the ultimate!

For example, we had a rule that our children would not single date until they were sixteen. That rule was tried and tested and pulled and argued until they turned sixteen and got to single date.

Now there was a time or two when we had to make an exception. But those were *very* unusual situations. We weren't able to pull things off logistically, so a boy our daughter happened to be interested in had to bring her home. But it wasn't a date, as such. We enforced the rules, and it paid off.

The *way* you enforce rules is important to the effect they have on teens—and it has a lot to do with whether or not the rules will be obeyed.

Our kids had time limits like everyone else. But instead of arbitrarily insisting, "Be home at 9:30," for every event, we tried to think of what was reasonable for the situation. If an event wouldn't be over until 9:15 and it was an hour away, we would extend the normal 9:30 time to 10:30.

We also asked our kids to call us if they couldn't make the time limit. If it had to be a long-distance call, we told them they could call collect, but they were to get in touch with us. And I can't remember a time when our kids didn't call us if they were late and were able to get to a phone.

We let our children help set their own boundaries in other areas. It has been remarkable to see how the older children will reinforce some of the rules with the younger children because they saw the value in them. I've heard them tell the younger ones, "You don't think that's going to work, but when Mom and Dad did that for me. . . ." What's better than a testimony? Watch *how* you do what you do.

Hold your children in high esteem. Nobody likes to live with a Stalin or a Hitler. Nobody likes to take orders when they are embarrassed in public. When I use my children as an illustration for a message, I ask their permission first. If I've mentioned them in a book, I ask them to read over the material and give their consent.

The effects of enforcing the rules are that our kids have been our greatest fans. I've asked them if it bothers them when people come over to our table in a restaurant and start talking to me. They said it's a bit of a hassle, but that it's also a real privilege and that they're honored.

YOU CAN'T BREAK OUT
OF MY CIRCLE OF LOVE

My circle of love began with our first child, Kathy. Like all parents who are concerned for their children, Arlie and I entered into our first child's teen years with fear and trembling. We had heard all the depressing stories you have heard about teen problems. By the time your second, third, fourth, or fifth child comes along, you know what to believe and what not to believe about teens. But we are all terrified as our first child approaches the teen years.

You can't go with your teen everywhere (although you might want to!). You can't lock the door and throw away the key. And you can't set up a spy network to keep a teen out of whatever he should not get into.

So you, and we, worry. And we pray. Sometimes that's enough. Sometimes it isn't.

I learned much later, when children in their twenties get close to parents and tell them about their teen struggles, that something else had really worked.

"Do you remember your circle of love?" Kathy asked me one day. Of course I remembered it. I had drawn that circle around her a number of times. I had told her in her teen years, "I have drawn a circle of love around you. I can't be there to keep you from doing what would hurt your mother and me. But my love is always there, in a circle around you. Within that circle you have freedom to move and grow and do your thing. But when you are tempted to do wrong, you will bump up against that circle of love and it will restrain you."

"It really worked," Kathy told me. "Several times I ran headlong into that circle, and I knew my father's love was there to keep me from going too far."

Our Lord has drawn a circle of love around each of us. Within that circle we move about in a spirit of freedom and growth. But His loving arms are there to restrain us when we are tempted to go too far.

Gil Beers

I think that's terrific!

Teens want to know the limits. They want to see the rules enforced. And in the long run, it will have positive effects— your soul will delight!

Teens Are People Too

Do You Treat Them That Way?

RAY & ANNE ORTLUND

Just before our first child was born, Anne's dad gave us some advice on how to be good parents. "Treat your children like real people," he said.

Sometimes we forget. Once at a restaurant we were ordering food and Nels told the waitress he wanted a hot dog. We said, "Nels, we think you ought to have something more substantial." But the waitress wrote down "hot dog" and walked away. Nels looked after her with awe and delight, and said, "Hey, she thinks I'm real!"

If we can learn to treat our children as we treat the people we work with, like adults, as often as possible, they will begin to see themselves as responsible and mature. They probably won't even die from too many hot dogs!

It's important to openly, deliberately trust our children in all the areas in which they can be trusted. Over the years, the two of us have sought to do this with our four. We frequently asked their advice or help with things we could probably have figured out ourselves. We deliberately leaned on them sometimes, admired them when they did well, confided some of our own insecurities to them, and asked them to pray for us. We tried to relate to them the way we relate to adult friends that we know and love and trust.

Sometimes teenagers' ideas of what it means to be trusted may differ from their parents' ideas. Ours have from time to time! Some seem to think that to be trusted means to be permitted to go anywhere and do anything they want to do, until all hours of the night if they choose. That's not really trusting; that's being careless. Teens need to learn to trust us and our guidelines for them, just as we need to learn to trust them.

Our son, Nels, came in late the other night, and Ray was up to meet him when he came in. He told Ray he'd had a big disappointment that day, so he went down to the beach just to look up at the sky and think.

"When you were out there alone," Ray asked, "did you think we would be concerned?"

"Yes," he answered. "I tried to phone once but the pay phone was broken. So I didn't do anything else about it."

Ray told him it was fine for him to be alone and to work through his problems, but not till late at night when we didn't know where he was. His attitude was, "Dad, you don't trust me."

Ray said, "Look, when you're out that late and nobody knows where you are, we think of all the dreadful possibilities. We see you splattered on the freeway, hurt, unable to get help. We trusted that you were not out carousing, but you were not trusting us with information we needed to be relaxed about you." Nels had to learn that trust must work both ways. He got the message.

One way to help teenagers feel that you respect them, that you are treating them like adults, is simply to introduce them to others in a way that shows your respect. It's wonderful when parents obviously love to show off their kids and show their delight in them.

Sherry, our oldest, is now thirty-six, in ministry with her husband, and a vibrant yet thoughtful Bible conference speaker.

TRUST AND OBEY

In raising children, there is a time to trust and a time to obey. Both of these approaches need a longer time for application than most of us are willing to spend. The results may be a long time in coming, but as we wait, there may be some things to keep in mind.

If we are trusting our teenagers, and still seeing no results, maybe we should ask ourselves the question, "Is there some area of obedience in which I need to follow Christ more closely?"

On the other hand, if we are obeying God and still seeing no results, we may need to rest in trusting Christ until more light is available.

Let God do His job description in the cosmic economy; and make sure you don't abandon yours. Never ask God to do the things you should do for yourself. And never do yourself the things only God can do.

YFC Editors

Sherry still talks about the year she graduated from high school and visited her grandparents on the East Coast. Her grandmother took her to meet every one of her friends. She went from house to house—obviously showing her off. Sherry has never forgotten the thrill of knowing that her grandmother was that proud of her.

That's an important role for parents to play too. When we're with our adult friends, let's not leave the kids off in a corner. Invite them away from their reading or television long enough to say, "I want you to meet my son or daughter." This means a lot to kids.

Another thing we believe helped our children know our confidence in them was to let each of them take a trip alone right after high school. Sherry earned enough money to join a tour of school teachers going to Europe. Nels went to South America to work with missionaries. Margie went to the East Coast, and because pilots were on strike, she had to make her own way, twenty-four hours a day, by train and bus. We felt the kids were grown up enough to do this.

Driving is one area in which we tried to show our trust in our children. Once they got their licenses, we felt we ought to let them share the car with us. Of course we set up guidelines and we prayed like mad! But if they obeyed the guidelines, we let them take the car more often.

The guidelines involved more than just handling the car. If our sons were dating, they had to keep their promise to the girl's parents to have her home on time. They had to go where they said they were going, and they had to practice a reasonable amount of etiquette. We trusted them to do these things.

The summer Bud finished high school, he had to decide whether to attend the local community college or go away to Wheaton. He had not yet made up his mind by August when we had to leave to speak at a Bible conference. If he was going to go to Wheaton, he would have to make the decision, pack, and leave home before we returned, in order to get there in time for the football season.

"Bud," we said, "we trust you to make that decision. We're praying that whatever you decide will be God's will for you." We hugged him and left, and sure enough, when we got back he had left for Wheaton. The important thing is that we trusted him with a major decision affecting his own life. It wasn't easy, but what else can you do? You have to let go of those reins sometime. It was good for him and for us.

But here's an important point. We have to be able to draw the line between where kids can be completely trusted and where they should not be. For instance, our daughter, Margie, was out on a date, and afterward she and her boyfriend sat out in the car in our driveway for about an hour. When she came in, Ray said to her, "Don't you ever do that again. If you want to talk, come into the living room, but don't sit out in the car."

Margie said, "Dad, don't you trust me?"

Ray replied, "If I were your age, I wouldn't trust myself that long in a car with an attractive date! Why should I trust you? We're all just human beings with good red blood, and there's no sense in asking for trouble."

Ray didn't imply that she was less trustworthy than himself. When he put himself down on her level, she could take his rebuke and keep her dignity.

So one challenge of parenting teenagers is to know the areas where they can be trusted and the areas where indeed they should not be. These areas will differ from child to child, even if they are brothers and sisters in the same home. But how important it is to try to keep the areas where they can't be trusted to a bare minimum and not talk about those any more than we have to. And to talk openly about those areas where they can be trusted. The idea is to let them feel our confidence in them—in all the numerous and important areas where they are totally trustworthy—and then not to forget the quiet but crucial warnings where they are necessary.

You, as parents, are the world's greatest authorities on your own teenagers. Nobody else knows as much about them as you do. You've watched them grow from babyhood up. You know their weaknesses and strengths. You know what temptation might make them succumb, even if it would not affect another. You know your children well, and your experience should inform you correctly of confidence areas and danger zones.

Cover it all in constant prayer.

Emphasize as much as possible the areas where you know they can be trusted.

Then, God helping you and them, every year they will grow to be more and more worthy of your trust.

Related Articles

Being Flexible without Sacrificing Principles

MARSHALL SHELLEY

Sometimes parents are put in ticklish situations. Perhaps your daughter wants to go out with a guy who's a known drug user. How do you maintain both your relationship with your daughter and your principles?

First, and undoubtedly toughest, you have to decide what your absolutes are and what you're willing to negotiate.

There may be certain things you will absolutely forbid, even at the cost of losing your son or daughter—things to which you will reply, "No way. Not under my roof. If you insist on doing this, you're on your own." The trouble with that approach is that it's a verbal nuke—such a powerful weapon, you dare use it only once. If you threaten it repeatedly, your relationship disintegrates.

Other times you'll have to say, "I don't like what you're doing, and you know why, but I respect your personhood. I'll continue to love you, but this makes me unhappy."

In between, there are countless situations where you're forced to negotiate. "If you do this again, you won't use the car for two weeks." Or, "Until the grades come up to a C average, the TV stays off."

How do you decide which behavior warrants which response? I wish there were an easy answer, but there isn't. Every set of parents must draw their own limits. Different parents will draw the lines differently. The crucial thing is for husband and wife to present a unified policy to the children. Making a bad decision together is better than telling kids two different things.

Personally, in the gray areas, I would rather err on the side of leniency than risk destroying the relationship with the teen. God has ways of drawing stray sheep back to Himself. Our job as parents is to let children know what we expect, enable

---

BE A PARENT AND A FRIEND

There is a fine balance between being a friend to your teen and maintaining proper authority and control. Teens want to be independent and yet they still need controls in their lives.

When the two seem mutually exclusive, the parents must demonstrate the ability to defuse issues. To defuse issues, keep talking when you can, and keep silent when obviously false claims are being made. Often parents personalize issues that didn't start out to be personal at all. Try to get to the *real* issue at hand.

Be interested in your teen and let him know that you are available for him. But parents do have authority over the teen and the teen should respect that.

David L. McKenna

them, encourage them, and show them our trust. That spirit, that atmosphere of respecting the intelligence of our children should be developed throughout the childhood years. Hopefully it will continue to pervade the relationship through adolescence.

Two of the things parents must learn are listening and avoiding snap judgments. When your teen takes you by surprise with a request that makes you uncomfortable, the greatest temptation is to render an immediate verdict. Sometimes the wisest decision is not to make a decision—at least for the moment. Buy time. Ask your teen to help you think through the pluses and minuses. Rarely will this hurt your decision-making ability; almost always it will help.

Parents needn't forfeit their leadership. Teens still need parents to direct them, but that leadership is based on understanding and humility.

Related Articles

How Teens Use Guilt to Their Advantage

DAVID L. McKENNA

Teens use parents' guilt to their advantage by playing on the parents' sympathy, making them feel as if an injustice has taken place. To make right the perceived injustice, the parents usually submit to the teens' wishes, thereby attempting to absolve their guilt.

For instance, my son, Rob, wanted to go to a rock concert. As we talked about it, he became defensive. He began arguing that if we hadn't moved from Seattle to Kentucky, I would have let him go. His reasoning was that in the city of Seattle he had more freedom. In our little rural town of Wilmore it became inconvenient to travel to events; therefore, he was getting the shaft.

Rob had been taken from his friends and his Christian high school to a new community and a public school. He wanted to "punish" me by calling my memory back to the area where he knew I hurt the most. He had saved that bit of garbage for an appropriate moment, to play on my sympathies.

You see, Rob knew I felt guilty about how the family's move had affected his life. He soon learned that he could get anything he wanted because Dad felt guilty about it. Fortunately, I eventually realized that I was using a reward system to manipulate my son to accept our move, and that he had been capitalizing on my distress.

Because I recognized Rob's behavior about the rock concert was another of *his* manipulative techniques, I had to say, "Rob, this is totally independent from Kentucky. We'd be asking the same questions in Seattle." I confronted him.

Now my son's friend had asked his parents to attend the same rock concert. Only he used a slightly different technique. He told his parents if they didn't let him go, it meant they didn't love him. That is another spot that really hurts,

405

and another way to punish unyielding parents.

Teens can capitalize on parents' guilt by using it as a manipulative device to work for their own advantage—whether it's to do certain things, or to get material goods. Parents must first recognize what is happening, and then confront the issue head-on.

Are You Spoiling Your Teenager?

DAVID VEERMAN

The classic "spoiled-child syndrome" is a seven-year-old girl throwing a tantrum in a toy store or a boy questioning the value of the gifts at his tenth-birthday party. But is "being spoiled" limited to the very young? According to the dictionary, *spoiled* means "demanding or expecting too much because of overindulgence." Obviously, spoiling can cross all generational lines.

High schoolers can be the epitome of "spoiled-ness." Personal demands and reckless use of money characterize their lives. During the '70s we experienced the "me generation," and we seemed to be innundated with self-indulgent young adults who had been reared in an atmosphere of me-first materialism.

Instead of decrying the past (the spoiling process) and bemoaning the present, what can parents *do* to avoid spoiling their teens (or to effect a "mid-course correction")? This is an important question since our high schoolers will soon be out of our homes, turned loose on the world. We certainly do *not* need more ego-oriented adults. The first step is to discover the potential (or actual) cause of the problem. Then we can take the appropriate counteraction.

One of the main causes of spoiled kids is spoiled parents. In other words, we may set an example of self-indulgence, spend-ing mounds of money on comfort, surrounding ourselves with adult toys, and pampering our bodies with "good" food and clothes. Our children follow those footsteps. To counter this cause, we must begin by "unspoiling" ourselves. A healthy dose of self-sacrifice will do wonders.

A very natural part of the spoiling process for children is a misconception they have about life . . . that pain is the exception and must be avoided at all costs. Most young people have this jaundiced view. After all, from birth through college, all of life's necessities are provided, and youthful vigor has sheltered them from physical deterioration. It's not surprising that they expect pleasure and a personal comfort zone. The only complete cure is age (and thus, experience); however, we can provide helpful medicine. By opening our "life files" to their inspection, teenagers will see the other side and gain a broader perspective. This means sharing some of our very real struggles with our children. Often we hide our problems, not wishing to burden the kids. Certainly I am not suggesting that we unload everything— that could be devastating—but we can open the door a crack to let them see. Praying together can also alert them to reality.

Another spoilage factor is money. Many teenagers are pushed (by their needs and the parents' feelings) to part-time employment. These jobs are justified on the basis that they teach how to handle money, but often the opposite occurs. The paycheck is seen as "my" money, and it is spent like water. And usually a car is involved. That is, they buy a car for "the job" and then work to keep up the car. A more constructive plan would be to work on "work" together. Allow them to be gainfully employed and design a budget for the income including saving toward a goal. Instead of investing in a vehicle, cooperate for their use of the family car.

By identifying contributing factors for spoiling our teenagers, we can act to avoid them and to "unspoil." In addition, here are other suggestions:

- We must continue to discipline them when necessary—the discipline should be different than for young siblings.
- We can encourage them to give creatively to family and friends—designing homemade cards and offering "moneyless" gifts.
- We can take the family to a nursing home for caroling and to spend time talking to various residents, asking them about life. Later we can discuss the experience at home.
- We can plan a family service project in the neighborhood or out of town during vacation (paint a church, weatherize homes of the elderly, deliver food, etc.).
- We can open our homes to visiting missionaries, foreign students, and others who will share a broader world view and model a sacrificial lifestyle.
- We must teach tithing.

Who's Taking Advantage of Whom?

Techniques of Parent-Teen Manipulation

DAVID L. McKENNA

I think we're all manipulators, parents and teens included. Both attempt to manipulate each other to get their way, sometimes unconsciously. But when it's conscious manipulation, we need to recognize it and confront it.

Methods of manipulation popular among parents and teens include the "garbage can" technique, the threat to withhold privileges, and the reward system.

To make the "garbage can" technique work to perfection, an individual stores a lot of junk in the garbage can for future use. Then when something comes up that appears to be a very minor issue, he takes the lid off the garbage can and rummages through it to come up with something smelly to wave in the face of the other person. Usually he calls to mind the area where the other person will hurt the most. This old junk smells so bad that the victim will often retreat and let the garbage thrower have his way.

Parents usually have the leverage to execute the withholding-of-privileges technique and the reward system. These old standbys capitalize on the power issue. Teens can also use the former, to a limited extent, for example, threatening to withhold love from their parents.

The reward technique, though, is

probably best used by parents. Like dangling an apple in front of a horse to keep him plowing, parents can promise a great reward to get a teen to do something. At times this can foster healthy encouragement. But often it is manipulation.

Manipulation is a form of persecution where the free will of the person is "taken away," or diminished. *Webster's Dictionary* defines it as controlling or playing on by artful or unfair means to one's own advantage.

You know you are being manipulated when you recognize one of the preceding techniques. If a family member begins bringing up things from the past (out of the garbage can), seemingly unrelated to the issue at hand, in an attempt to make you sympathetic to his or her argument or cause, you are being manipulated. Or when a privilege is being threatened or a reward suddenly enters the picture to sway your stand, stop and consider if manipulation is at work.

Related Articles

ARE YOU BEING MANIPULATED?

The teen years offer opportunities to expand and grow as individuals and to become independent. Yet the safety and security of childhood still loom important and desirable. This "push-and-pull" is ever present in a teen's life.

Much of the underlying feeling of security comes when clear limits are communicated to the teen. Yet, knowing the limits and obeying them may be two different things. Of course, the limits are not always tested overtly by what we usually perceive as "rebellion." A subtle rebellion may take the form of manipulation—pushing the limits covertly.

Manipulation sounds so "crafty," but usually it is not. Asking continually for small favors might be a way to "win your favor." Saying, "I'm sorry—I didn't mean it," may be the way to get you to soften up. Telling a story about the day's events with intensity (e.g., "Everything was *so great*—I want to go back again!") could be a way to play up an idea so that it won't be shot down.

Here are some guidelines to know if you're being manipulated:

1. If you find you are becoming tired of a certain "topic" which seems to be discussed over and over, watch out.

2. If you find yourself constantly negotiating and compromising and feeling edgy, you are being tested.

3. If you see Mom played against Dad, and big brother against little brother, etc., limits are being pushed.

4. If Mom is doing all the disciplining, you're being tested.

Remember, the only positive solution is to be *clear* and *consistent* in your expectations, rules, and discipline.

Tom Perski

MANAGING THE HOME
WITH DISCIPLINE

- How to discipline your children without alienating them
- What are the different ways of disciplining teens?
- What can parents learn from God's model of discipline?

- Grounding your teenagers—is it effective?
- What is the difference between discipline and punishment?
- How to discipline with consistency
- Is there a difference in disciplining younger and older teens?

Ultimately, discipline is the friend of freedom. A person who knows no discipline has no freedom. Discipline enables us to live life to its fullest. As we communicate this to our families, discipline ceases to be a terrible burden.

Whether we are talking about the discipline of getting to bed on time so we can wake up and function the next day, or the discipline of getting our household tasks out of the way so we can go water skiing, we must teach our children that the whole process of discipline exists for their benefit and ours.

Sometimes, of course, discipline is painful. Children find it hard to believe that "this hurts me more than it hurts you," but they will understand this when they have sons and daughters of their own.

Be Disciplined

WARREN W. WIERSBE

Discipline often gets bad press. People think of discipline as punishment, and at least in the Bible, that's not the intended meaning at all. Both in Hebrew and Greek, the words we translate "discipline" actually mean training or education. Discipline may come through words, deeds, or circumstances, but the purpose is always to develop maturity.

Hebrews 12 is the key passage in the New Testament on discipline. Even here, where the writer talks about hardship as discipline, the purpose is not punishment or upholding justice or maintaining authority. God's purpose is the maturity of the child. That should be our goal in administering discipline too.

Maturity is when the child knows himself, accepts himself, controls himself, and is able to use what he is and has creatively and constructively.

The philosophy in our home began with the conviction that discipline was more an attitude and atmosphere than an action. The reason many parents cannot discipline children is that they cannot discipline themselves. I've seen some parents who won't clean up the table, won't groom themselves, who are just sloppy people. They bawl out their kids, but it does no good. As Dr. James Dobson has pointed out, if a child finds an undisciplined area in a parent's life, he'll use it as a point of control. If the attitude and atmosphere are absent, the action does no good.

A second aspect of our philosophy: discipline means we are under authority; we don't just exercise authority. You can't demand respect; you command it. That, of course, means character and example.

Third, discipline is a tool, not a weapon. Too often, if you've raised kids, you find yourself on the offensive, acting out of spite or irritation. Discipline must be an expression of love, not anger. This is true of God—whom He loves, He chastens. If our children feel they must earn our love, we're in trouble. No, they must see discipline as an evidence of our love, a tool to help them grow.

Fourth, discipline is a process, not a crisis. We didn't always succeed, but we tried never to discipline in the heat of the moment. Crisis discipline is inconsistent and confusing. What's needed is that constant process of working in love, speaking the truth in love.

These were the principles we tried to use with our children, and they seem to have worked, though we certainly failed on occasion. Each child is different. For example, we could just look at one of the children and she'd cry. But we could beat another one with a girder and he wouldn't budge! You have to find each kid's hot button. There are plenty of tools: words, appreciation, rewards. And don't underestimate the spiritual tools: the Word of God and prayer.

As kids grow, naturally methods of discipline must change. At fifteen or sixteen, my boys were bigger than I was. Spanking wouldn't work. So we prayed they would get to the point where they obeyed not because they didn't want Dad to hurt them, but because they didn't want to hurt Dad. And that's a big difference.

Of course, we still needed some form of correction. We found that depriving them of something they enjoyed was most effective. The important thing is that we never surprised them. We tried to make

BUILDING A FIRM FOUNDATION

If a firm foundation in discipline has not been laid, one struggle parents can expect is in the area of faith. Children who have not been disciplined are not going to believe their parents. Discipline creates trust and respect. Without discipline there is no basis for trusting the parents' values or faith, and no respect for their viewpoints.

Discipline is important in helping our teens feel loved. In fact, discipline is a fruit of love. In some cases, parents are never able to show outward affection or verbal affirmation, but the kids discover love in their discipline. I am not talking about rules here, but the kind of strictness that produces respect. I have heard many young men say that their fathers never took them any place, but they cared for their fathers because they were strict and the sons knew the strictness came out of love. Discipline without love is not going to be effective. The love might be buried underneath, but it has to be there.

The person who helped me the most with this aspect of life was a step uncle. I was afraid of him. I don't recall that he ever "whopped" me, but I never wanted him to. He didn't express much outward love, but he created an environment where I had to respect him.

John Perkins

the conditions clear—"If you do this, then this will happen." And we tried never to break those promises.

Parents do need to be flexible, however. I think God is a flexible disciplinarian. He knows how much we need. He knows our motives, our struggles, our weaknesses. As a parent, I don't always have that knowledge, so I shouldn't pretend to play God. A.W. Tozer once said, "God is not hard to live with." That helped me tremendously. God's standards and demands are high, but His resources are great. I want to be like that as a father.

We didn't have many rules—only when the kids were little: don't go near the highway; don't leave the back door open for the baby to fall down the stairs. As they got older, we tried to raise them by mercy and grace, love and truth—the way God raises His children.

If I err, I want to err on the side of forgiveness. There were probably times when I should have walloped the kids. Only now am I finding out things they did I never knew before—by listening to my son preach! He'll tell a story from his teens, and I'll say, "I didn't know about that." But they seem to have come through.

On the other hand, there were times when we disciplined the kids for things they didn't do. I discovered the truth later. Fortunately, where there's love, openness, honesty, and fun, kids somehow survive those injustices.

Oh—a sense of humor really helps!

Related Articles

The Difference between Discipline and Punishment

GORDON MacDONALD

When I wrote *The Effective Father,* I included a chapter on discipline and punishment and assigned my own practical definition to those words. To me, discipline is the deliberate creation of stress in a relationship with your children in order to help them grow and learn. Discipline is setting them to a task to exercise, strengthen, and help them mature. Discipline is forcing them to face painful questions that need to be wrestled with. What a coach takes a team through *before* a contest is discipline.

A Matter of Justice

Punishment is a matter of justice—something that happens when an action violates the covenant of family life or the family laws. At first, punishment tends to be artificial, like a spanking. You create pain, hoping it will be equated with the seriousness of the act and associated with wrongdoing. Later on, when the child is older, punishments change from artificial pain to ones with specific, measurable consequences.

For teenagers, a typical punishment is grounding, a fairly significant consequence. Obviously, grounding a three-year-old wouldn't be very effective! It's important to pick a punishment that approximates the significance of the infraction. Then children will be impressed by the seriousness of the act they

411

committed. Most parents tend to either make the punishment greater than the seriousness of the act, or to make it less serious than the act. So the child ends up thinking the punishment was too great for the act or that it really wasn't too high a price for what he did.

One of the worst things is when parents are inconsiderate about their punishment. Parents may tell a teenager, "Be home by 11 P.M. or else." The first problem is not defining "or else." The second problem is that parents should never have to say "or else." If the discipline and punishment were handled properly in the early years, it is much less likely that a teenager is going to violate a curfew.

The Problem of Interpretation
When kids get home, they may ask, "Did you mean 11 o'clock or did you mean plus or minus twenty minutes?" Teenagers will press parents all the way. They may say, "Well, you said 11. It's 11:09, but we left the restaurant at 11." Or, "We were on our way home and got caught in traffic." Then parents get into the problem of interpretation. The wisest thing parents can do is this: Long *before* those situations develop, lay down definable, livable rules so that no one is in doubt as to exactly what the rules are.

Instead of telling my children, "Be home at 11; there's nothing negotiable," I said, "I want a phone call at 11 if you'll be late." That's not unreasonable because there are phones all over. If a problem develops, I can sit down with my daughter and say, "Honey, I notice that three times in a row you've called telling me you're coming home late. That doesn't sound like you're planning well. I don't mind a midnight once in a while when your reasons are good, but three in a row is not acceptable. Let's get the act together."

Look Downstream
Parents always need to be looking downstream, trying to pick up signals and patterns of where things might be headed. This may sound like bragging, but I can't remember the last time I punished my children. We established a rapport with both of our kids by the time they were about nine, and our kids never disobeyed us in the teen years.

A few times my children failed to do what I asked, but inevitably there was a misunderstanding that was often my fault. Of course, there were the minor incidents that every family has. My wife might say, "Kristi, would you clear the table?" She would say, "Yeah, I'll do it in a few minutes," and then go downstairs, forget, and three hours later the table's still uncleared. But we haven't had flagrant violations of our rules. In the first ten years, our kids learned that we meant what we said.

Discipline: Stretch and Build
The role of discipline is to create situations that slowly stretch and build your kids so they can handle difficult situations. Let me give you an example: A week after our son got his driver's license, he wanted to use our pickup truck to take his date to the middle of Boston on a Friday night. Boston isn't a good place for driving your lovely red pickup truck in Friday night rush-hour traffic.

My first instinct was to say, "No way am I going to permit this!" But I decided I wouldn't immediately react with an answer. I said, "I'll tell you what. I need about three hours to think about that." It was important to say how much time I needed instead of saying I'd let him know "in a little while." An indefinite time period creates unnecessary anxiety for a young person. But if you say you'll have an answer in three hours, that usually puts everyone at ease.

When the three hours were up, I said, "Son, I'll tell you what. The truck is yours on Friday night with one condition. Thursday night you and I will drive the full length of the route of the date as if I were the girl. I'll be free to simulate conditions you may encounter on your date. Good enough?'' He agreed.

On Thursday night at the same hour as his Friday night date, we started driving up the freeway toward Boston. Suddenly I said to him, ''Son, your right front tire just went flat.''

He said, ''No, it didn't.''

''Yes, it did. You remember I said I could create any conditions.''

''Well, what do you want me to do?''

''When a tire is flat, you pull over and change it. Do it.'' So he pulled out of traffic to the side and got out. He couldn't believe I was going to make him do this. Again I said, ''Change it.'' I sat on the guardrail while he got under the truck to find the jack and the tire.

He couldn't find the jack and after several minutes of clowning around, he said, ''Where's the jack?''

''Son, I'm not here. I'm the girl, remember?'' So he went back and, for fifteen minutes, looked for the jack. Finally he found where a jack is stored on a pickup truck—under the hood. When he got the truck jacked up, I let him put it back down without changing the tire. But now he knew what to do.

Then we drove to the ramp where he was supposed to exit. I said, ''Sorry, the ramp is closed due to construction.'' So he had to find a new way to get to his destination. On the way back I simulated an engine breakdown. Then the questions were, ''Do you leave the girl in the truck and go for help, or do you wait for the police?''

I disciplined my son by helping him learn how to cope with a series of stress situations. The next evening he had minimum nervousness because he knew how he would perform under difficult situations. That's what I mean by discipline.

Barriers to Discipline
Many parents clutter their lives with so many things that all they can do is react to their children. Most parents try to

crowd too much into their lives: trying to establish careers; working too much during the most formative period of their children's lives. Some fathers have two jobs, and the mother may be pursuing a career as well.

Parents may also get preoccupied with all sorts of recreational pursuits and hobbies that become all-encompassing. Then, in spare moments, between all the busyness, parents try to give attention to whatever is ailing the kids. You just can't promote a healthy lifestyle that way.

When our children were infants, my wife and I decided that raising our children was our number one priority. There was going to be a parent on site at home as long as our kids were young. Now that our children are older, my wife is enjoying a new phase of life—traveling, speaking, and writing. People look at her and envy many of the things she is into. But ten years ago, she gave ninety percent of her time to the children. She was always there when the kids were home.

Only after the kids entered high school, started driving, and began to spend more time in their own activities did she become increasingly involved outside the family. When the kids left the nest, she found more than enough things to do from another perspective. But while the kids needed a parent around, she never compromised her availability to them. That's where I think most modern parents are jeopardizing their relationships with their kids, making them only one of a number of priorities. You just can't do that.

Another barrier that can prevent parents from taking time to discipline children adequately is the church. Many churches consume almost all of the free hours of well-meaning young Christians. Many people are at the church every time the doors open; there's a program every night of the week. A willing Christian man is going to be asked to do everything the church needs. A lot of Christians are driven by guilt and simply don't know how to say no, even to the church. But there *is* a time to say no to the church—when it's improperly infringing on your family time.

Learn to say no to *anything*—careers, recreation, hobbies, or even the church—

that continually comes between you and your children's needs.

Related Articles

   Chapter 18: Discipline: A Family's Friend or Foe?

   Chapter 18: When Should You Ground Your Teenager?

How to Discipline Kids without Alienating Them

KENNETH O. GANGEL

Picture this: A teenage boy has just finished two weeks of being grounded, during which he missed seeing his high school basketball team win the league championship—in double overtime. In a spirited conversation with his parents he tells them, "That was a terrific grounding! I had a lot of time to think about my role in our family. It was a wonderful experience. Thanks a lot!"

I doubt if you would ever hear such a comment from a teenager. More likely, he would hold a considerable amount of resentment. It is not always possible to punish without creating some alienation, at least for a time. This fact scares some parents. Through the years that I've spent as an adult Christian leader, again and again I have witnessed the parent cop-out syndrome. Parents throw up their hands and say, "It's just not worth it; let the kid do what he wants! We hope he'll turn out all right."

Despite the bitterness and alienation that may result from meting out punishment, however, wise parents realize they are operating on a solid biblical principle. They know that in the long run—if the punishment is properly carried out in love —God is going to work everything out for good. God sets the example in His own

dealing with mature Christians:

"We have had fathers of our flesh which corrected us, and we give them reverence: shall we not much rather be in subjection unto the Father of spirits, and live? For they verily for a few days chastened us after their own pleasure; but He for our profit, that we might be partakers of His holiness. Now no chastening for the present seems to be joyous, but grievous: nevertheless afterward it yields the peaceable fruit of righteousness unto them which are exercised thereby" (Heb. 12:9-11, KJV).

There is a dynamic parallel between the spiritual realm and the physical realm of the family. At the end of that disciplinary section in Hebrews 12, the author states: "Wherefore lift up the hands which hang down, and the feeble knees; and make straight paths for your feet, lest that which is lame be turned out of the way; but let it rather be healed" (12:12-13).

Essentially, I believe the writer is saying: "Those of you who have the responsibility for discipline and punishment are going to be constantly tempted to back off and not do it. But strengthen your feeble arms, strengthen your weak knees. This molding of mature persons is going to take work and you'd better be prepared for it."

Realizing that they probably can't punish their child without creating some resentment, wise parents look at the child's future rather than the present state of discontent. If punishment is in order, it is delivered—but not without full consideration given to the offense and the proper response.

Insofar as possible, punishment ought to be based on correcting inappropriate action. "Let the punishment fit the crime." Corporal punishment—either light or heavy—would probably not be effective correction for a teenager who consistently neglects his schoolwork. The teen has a time-investment problem, and correction should be geared to the way he uses his time. Revocation of TV rights or of going out to play basketball with the neighborhood kids for an hour after dinner would be a direct confrontation of the specific problem.

When revocation of rights is instituted, it is important to attack the problem— and not the child. He should be assured that the parents' love remains constant, though his actions may require correction. A time should be set for future review of the situation. A definite date should be established—not a vague "when your work improves." On the given date, an evaluation of the situation must focus on measurable results: homework completed on schedule, for example. Future action will be determined by progress made—resumption of privileges or continued revocation of rights, again for a specific time period.

In the case of disobedience, not only should the punishment fit the crime, but the punishment ought to be administered by the parent who was wronged. If one of the children was disobedient to Mother during the day, punishment should not be saved for Dad to administer, even though Dad may be a stronger disciplinarian. Such action tends to convey the concept that Dad has more authority than Mom. If

TIME AND TIME AGAIN

"I asked you to clean up that stuff, and it's still there! What's the matter with you?" Sound familiar? The scenario is simply this: You've asked your teen to do something, and it has not been done. Now it's a big issue. Often the real question is timing. That is, is it fair to demand an immediate response every time?

Unfortunately, we parents usually confront our kids *after* we have reached the boiling point. We don't like to be interrupted in the middle of another task (but neither do they).

Often we ask for something to be done, like "Take out the trash," but we don't say when. It would be much better to say, "After dinner, I'd like you to take out the trash" or "*When* are you going to. . . ?"

We should set specific guidelines with our kids, agreeing on the job which is to be done, how, and when, and the reward for doing it without being nagged.

Also, it is important not to treat each child the same. There are many differences to be considered. With some chores, specific strengths and abilities will be needed to get the job done (age, size, strength, sex, etc. will be factors). On routine tasks, however, the kids can take turns (guys can do the dishes too).

Finally, we should let them know what we expect of them as contributing members of the family, and we should encourage their suggestions and their initiative to do things before we ask.

YFC Editors

Mother is wronged, Mother must carry out the discipline.

The important thing for parents to keep in mind is that they are molders of lives entrusted to them by God; they are not participants in a popularity contest. If established family guidelines are violated, the action should be dealt with as quickly as possible. The discipline should focus on the offense and not the offender. If the correction results in alienation, the resentment will pass in time.

However, if every family member understands clearly what the guidelines are, why they have been established, and that they must be adhered to—the atmosphere has been set for compliance. Correction of individuals veering from the established course will be viewed as an important part of maintaining an orderly family.

Do You Discipline with Consistency?

J. ALLAN PETERSEN

Parents need a planned approach toward discipline. And the first step, even before deciding what style you're going to use—authoritarian, permissive, or something in between—is to agree on your objective for your child. What are you training your child for?

In our situation, we tried to see God as a model parent and determine His objectives for our children—being responsible, mature, Christlike, and so on. An important aspect is realizing that "a man shall leave his father and mother." We don't prepare our children to stay; we prepare them to leave us. This means, then, that we've got to give them the worth and confidence they need to live on their own and replicate what we've shown them.

To do that, however, both parents need to agree on forms of discipline. They must see that discipline is broader than punishment; it's training, discipling, growth.

In addition, they must agree to support one another in front of the children. When differences crop up regarding discipline, parents must agree to disagree only in private so a child can't work one parent against the other.

A united, consistent approach with children, even if you make occasional mistakes, is far better than trying to second-guess your mate in front of them. Not only does it damage the marriage relationship, it confuses the children.

One of the keys to effective discipline is learning to react to bad behavior, not just because the kids are getting on your nerves. How? Try never to discipline when you're angry. And when you do, admit it later—apologize for your attitude: "I was wrong. What we were talking about is right, and something had to be done, but my attitude was wrong. I lost my cool. I'm sorry." This is where parents need each other—if I'm angry, it's better

416

to let my spouse handle this situation.

Psychologist Bruce Narramore pointed out some helpful things about God as the model parent and how He disciplined His first children, Adam and Eve. Notice the order of God's actions: First He provided for their needs; then He instructed them; then He corrected them. So often I do just the opposite: correcting my kids before ever thinking about their needs.

God provided Adam's and Eve's physical needs in the garden, their social needs in each other, their need for responsibility in tending the animals, and their spiritual needs in His daily presence with them. Before He did anything else, He provided their needs.

Before we correct our children, we too must ask, "Am I providing their needs for love—belonging, confidence—competence, worth—value? Are they doing these bizarre things because some basic emotional needs aren't being met?"

Second, God gave clear instructions: Don't eat from the one tree. Do I give clear instructions? Do my children really know what's expected? Many of us are guilty of disciplining a child without him knowing what we expected.

A final note about the Adam-and-Eve account so Christian parents don't take all the responsibility and think "Everything's my fault" if things don't turn out well: God, the model parent, did everything right . . . and His first children disobeyed. Children share the responsibility for their actions.

Some people wonder, *Can parents overcorrect, overdiscipline?* Very much so. Often parents' biggest mistake is fighting the wrong war. They don't distinguish between rules and principles.

We need to teach children principles to live by rather than just rules to obey.

Way back when, we were always taught "Don't go to dances." Why? "You just don't do it." But no one said anything about driving a date home along a lonely road. Nobody gave us principles.

We've tried to teach our kids princi-
ples. We never, for instance, told our sons not to smoke, but we stressed over and over the importance of our bodies, that we're valuable, that God has given us bodies and minds that are too important to ruin.

By stressing principles rather than rules, parents can make their discipline more consistent and more effective.

Related Articles

WHEN PARENTS DISAGREE

If parents disagree about discipline in a particular situation, they need to get behind closed doors and say, "If we can't agree on discipline, let's at least agree that it's more important for the kids' welfare that we be united than it is for either of our opinions to prevail."

Children need to see unity between their parents, and it's the parents' responsibility to be united even if it means fasting and praying until you starve. At times, you may have to do something you don't feel quite right about. Again, your opinions aren't as important as the children's welfare.

To do something in a united way is better for the children than for the better idea to prevail with one parent openly dissenting. It's like a football game: It's better for everyone to execute the play the quarterback calls than for half the team to do one thing and half to do another.

Larry Christenson

417

CONSISTENTLY INCONSISTENT

Many parents are consistently inconsistent in the way they discipline their children. They let their daughter tie up the telephone for two hours one night because "we're too tired to argue," but the next day, they scream and yell when she talks for ten minutes. It's enough to mess up the psyche of the most balanced adolescent.

Consistency in discipline is necessary if children are to learn what is expected from them. Kids often complain, "I didn't know you wanted me to do that," and though you may think you've told them to do it over and over, did you tell them *consistently?*

Inconsistency in discipline may occur when parents aren't sure how to handle family training and discipline. They may not realize how important it is to set up unchanging guidelines for their children's behavior. Even when they do attempt to set up rules, they may be too lazy to enforce them all the time. It is difficult to discipline someone when your own life is un-disciplined.

But parents who examine their behavior and see inconsistencies in their disciplining shouldn't give up hope. God can change an inconsistent person into a consistent one, just as He can cure the alcoholic from his habitual drinking problem. We "are being transformed into His likeness" (2 Cor. 3:18), and this transformation includes the freedom from negative patterns such as inconsistency.

The inconsistent parent should make himself vulnerable to God and communicate with his family. He shouldn't be afraid to pray for his children and their disciplining while they're present. I love to go to a home and hear a father pray with his family, confessing his shortcomings. When a family expects the miracle of consistent disciplining to take the place of chaos, their ready hearts pave the way to answered prayer.

Kenneth O. Gangel

Discipline Requires Communication

LARRY RICHARDS

When my son was in the third grade, we went shopping for clothes. He wanted to buy a particular shirt—a shiny green thing that was seedy looking, poorly made, and overpriced. We tried to talk him out of it, but he was set on it. Since we felt he was old enough to manage his clothes, we let him get it.

But the first time the shirt was washed, it bunched up and started to fall apart. Needless to say, my son was heartbroken. However, this became an opportunity to teach him about buying clothes. We sat down together and talked about how to pick out a shirt in terms of price and quality.

This story illustrates one reason why communication is crucial to discipline. The role of discipline is not to impose our wills on our children but to help them develop the ability to make right choices as well as the desire to make them.

Short-term discipline which says, "Sit down and do this right now" is detrimental to this goal. Too often it becomes a clash of wills, with the parents trying to force their prejudices and opinions on the children. We could have just told Paul that we absolutely would not get him the shirt. But the purpose of discipline is not to impose our clothing tastes on our children but to help them develop the ability to desire right decisions. That's something that can't be done without communication.

When children reach adolescence, communication becomes even more important because there are many things in the adolescent culture which parents simply do not understand—issues and decisions facing a young person which parents don't realize. So if parents are going to help their teen make right decisions, they have to provide a context in which the son or daughter is free to communicate and explore tough questions with them.

To keep the lines open for communication, parents need to be careful not to jump to conclusions. Often young people will not present what they really believe because they're not sure what they believe. So they'll say things in a discussion that they might not believe, just to see how their parents react. That's when parents need to keep especially calm and cool.

Two Communication Helps

Any parent knows that communication isn't always easy, but two pieces of advice will help. One is for parents not to try to help the teen avoid all the mistakes he's going to make. For instance, if parents know their young person is procrastinating on a very big assignment at school, they shouldn't keep nagging about it. The teen may get an F, but it won't kill him. In fact, it just might teach him to learn better work habits.

The other thing parents can do is to develop a pattern of natural consequences. If the teen has become habitually late for dinner, parents can remind him of the times when meals are scheduled and point out that it's not fair for everybody else to wait. The teen learns that if he's on time he gets to eat and if he's not, he gets leftovers.

There is no battle then. Eating dinner doesn't become a conflict of wills. The parents have simply established a pattern of natural consequences by communicating what the teenager can expect to happen.

If parents have helped their teen from a

GET THE FACTS

Parents of teens have to learn not to get uptight too fast. It's easy to react without knowing the facts. For instance, one day Ray came home and found a brown bag full of beer cans in the kitchen, and his mind began to dance with fantasies and fears. When our son came home, Ray said to him, "Hey, what are those beer cans doing in the kitchen?"

Nels said casually—and immediately Ray knew it was true—"Oh, I found them out in the yard and I hauled them in to put in the trash compactor. Sorry I left them out—I'll go take care of it."

Ray thought to himself, "Whew! I'm so glad I didn't make a fuss first, before I got the story."

How important it is not to jump to conclusions! Teenagers and parents of teenagers need to react first by giving each other the benefit of the doubt. *Ray & Anne Ortlund* young age to make choices, and have allowed him to experience the natural consequences of those choices, then by adolescence, there won't be many problems. If parents haven't done this and decide to change from short-term to long-term discipline, they need to communicate the ground rules clearly. It will help if parents focus on one or two key issues instead of making an issue out of everything.

Related Articles

Teaching Teens Responsibility for Their Actions

D. BRUCE LOCKERBIE

When my son, Kevin, was six, he and a playmate were playing in our yard. I was on the porch typing, so I could hear what they were saying. Kevin had taken his friend to a particular part of the yard where he knew there was a hornet's nest, and was repeating, "Come on, bees, sting Mark. Come on, bees, sting Mark." Lo and behold, a couple of those hornets actually did fly out and sting Mark. Kevin, who was expecting them, was smart enough to take off before they could do him any harm.

I'm not too sure I'm proud of what I did, but I went out and said, "Kevin, you stand there, shake the shrubbery, and say those same things." He did, and he got stung too. If he hadn't gone through that experience, I'm not sure he would ever have fully understood the pain he had inflicted on his friend.

As soon as a child begins to reason for himself—perhaps as early as age two—he needs to be instructed lovingly and step by step that water drowns and fire burns. Then if he sticks his hand in a flame, he begins to see that it is his responsibility not to do it again. If a child standing one and a half feet tall reaches up and pulls the tablecloth (and everything on it) off the table, he must be told

that his action was not amusing. The parents should explain how hard the people worked to prepare the meal and to buy the dishes, crystal, and so forth. It is not right to pass off the action with an attitude of, "Oh well, he's too young to know any better."

A child needs to see the results of the havoc he has caused and be frightened of the consequences if he does it again. By "frightened," I mean to have a righteous fear. It's not very popular these days to talk about righteous fear. We hear a lot more about, "Smile, God loves you." You don't see too many bumper stickers that say, "The fear of the Lord is the beginning of wisdom." But we need to teach a child righteous fear for his own good. He can be taught the consequences of his actions progressively, without brutality or abuse. It begins when the child is chasing a friend around the playground with a sharp stick, and continues throughout his teenage years, when the younger driver takes over the family car.

In the Parable of the Prodigal Son (Luke 15), I'm quite sure the father tried to reason with his son before the son took off with his share of the estate. But once he left, the father let him be responsible for his own welfare, even when things didn't turn out too well. The father didn't send any people to bring him back, any money, or any help of any kind. He simply let the son experience the pigpen, and eventually he came home.

The Word of the Lord to Ezekiel is even more powerful: "The soul who sins is the one who will die. The son will not share the guilt of the father, nor will the father share the guilt of the son. The righteousness of the righteous man will be credited to him, and the wickedness of the wicked will be charged against him" (Ezek. 18:20, NIV). Everybody experiences pain and suffering, and Scripture teaches moral accountability as individuals. So parents must begin working with their children while they are still young to develop this moral accountability and continue the training as they grow older.

No pleasure comes without responsibility. I tried to impress this truth on my children during their dating years. I made it very plain that in this family there would be no abortions nor financial support for any other alternative in the event of pregnancy. I told them that sexual relations meant marriage, and that they had better be prepared to face the full responsibilities for any actions they took. They knew that if they became sexually involved, they were likely to become members of their own households earlier than they had anticipated.

OVERRULING YOUR TEEN

It's tough when you tell a teen certain behavior is unacceptable, and he or she stomps off and slams the door.

But if you've discussed the issue and made a decision, you can't abandon it because the kid takes exception and starts acting in disrespectful ways. Slamming the door, for instance, is another way of saying, "Drop dead."

I remember dealing with some teenage girls a few years ago in our school. We had some strict rules, and one of them was that any impudence or backtalk would be punished. I called the problem girls in one day and said, "How many of you know you can tell someone to drop dead without opening your mouths—just in the way you toss your head and the way you look?" I saw that knowing look come into their eyes.

"From now on," I said, "your body language will be judged by the same standard as verbal language." They understood what I meant. When they had disagreements with a teacher, they could present their cases respectfully, but any disrespect was unacceptable.

Of course, there are times when a teen will brood for days. That's when you must remember you aren't trying to win a popularity contest with your kids—unless you're going for the one twenty years from now. Then the kids will be able to see these situations from a little better perspective.

You have to be willing to be unpopular at home—just as you tell your kids they may have to take an unpopular stand at school. Recognize that sometimes you'll make mistakes, and yet you'll be doing it with the best light you have.

When you see that you were wrong, admit it and ask forgiveness. But don't let the possibility of making mistakes prevent you from exerting your leadership.

Larry Christenson

Of course, the other side of the story is that there *are* a lot of young people in the world trying to head a family who are barely able to run their own lives. But you can't teach responsibility by ignoring the potential negative results of a child's action. I'm not a fan of Jesse Jackson's politics, but I like what he tells high school students: "You're not a man because you can make a baby. You're a man because you can care for a baby." I think sex is one of the areas where parents are a whole lot less willing than they should be to enforce the consequences of a child's misuse of responsibility.

Another thing I told our children was that we expected them to behave properly in school—that if they did anything to bring shame on themselves, it would also bring shame to us as a family. I made it very plain that my expectations for them exceeded whatever might be normal teenage behavior. I expected their loyalty to what our home represented and gave them a very clear understanding of what lay in store if they decided to rebel.

Someone might accuse me of being pessimistic and not trusting my children, but it isn't a matter of trust. First you lay out parameters for them, and *then* you trust them. My earliest childhood recollection is living in the parsonage across the street from my father's church. Our house was on one of the main industrial corners of the city. I wasn't even three at the time, and I had a little kiddie car. I can remember very well my mother drawing lines at the end of our gravel driveway and telling me not to cross that line or I would be closer to the street than she wanted me to be. I also remember going into the house and telling her that the lines had disappeared (into the gravel) and

MAKING DISCIPLINE WORK

When teenagers need discipline, parents sometimes find themselves not knowing what to do. Spanking becomes ineffective because it only tends to intensify any feelings of rebellion a child may have. I believe teens generally respond best to privilege deprivation.

I also think discipline works most effectively if the consequence fits the problem. If teens are late to a certain number of meals, have them go without dessert for a period of time. If they misuse their driving privileges, restrict their use of the car for a while. Grounding is usually a suitable punishment for more serious offenses.

Once the punishment has been decided on, set a definite, limited time and follow through with it. Too many times parents threaten some type of punishment, but then fail to follow through because it's too inconvenient for them. Teenagers respect parents who carry out the punishments they set, and the teens expect to be grounded when they do something wrong.

In fact, teens will often set a harsher discipline for themselves if given the chance. The next time you need to establish a punishment for your child, ask him, "What do you think will help you learn your lesson so you won't do this again?" Your teenager doesn't want to be a bad person with undesirable qualities. If you have a reasonably good relationship with him, it is uncanny how he will come up with something stricter than what you had in mind. And he will probably learn more from his self-imposed discipline too.

Grace Ketterman

would she please come back out and draw them again. I'm sure that kids are a lot more comfortable knowing where the lines are.

Parents can draw those lines without alienating their children. They must accept that responsibility, because that's why we are parents and they are children. The whole "palsy-walsy" notion that "My son is my best friend" is wrong. I am very happy to have two friends who happen to be my adult sons and a third who is my adult daughter. But those relationships have formed because first I was their father and they were my children. It was up to me to draw the lines with a certain measure of wisdom and compassion.

I also had to recognize that a thirteen-year-old should have more privileges than an eleven-year-old, and it was my task to enforce the distinction for the younger child. In my book, *Fatherlove,* I tell the story of the first time we let our older son go to New York on the train with his best friend. While those two went off like a couple of heroes, their younger brothers both had their noses seriously out of joint. The other father and I got together, measured their maturity, and came up with something else for them to do, but there was no way we were going to give them the same privileges as their older brothers just because they complained.

Parents with teenagers would do well to model the system used by the government in issuing driver's licenses. The state expects to see some maturity and responsibility before they hand out the right to drive an automobile. Teenagers don't get a driver's license just because they want one or because they are old enough to receive one. They must earn one by demonstrating competence and a certain measure of common sense. If parents begin to hold back on privileges until their teens can prove that they are ready to handle them, they should see their children mature quickly into responsible adults.

Related Articles
Chapter 18: Discipline: A Family's Friend or Foe?
Chapter 18: When Should You Ground Your Teenager?

WHO DECIDES THE PUNISHMENT?

The next time your teenager does something he knows he shouldn't have done, ask him to suggest his own form of discipline. I think it makes good sense for parents to say, "What do you think will help you remember never to do this again?"

I remember an instance when my two sons rode and damaged the bicycle of their little sister's friend. I didn't need to tell them what the penalty would be. I said, "What is the right thing to do in this case?" and they answered, "We've got to pay for repairing the bicycle."

It was an unintentional offense which didn't deserve physical punishment. But in this case it meant opening piggy banks and cleaning out savings accounts to make things right. If I had laid down the law, my sons might not have been so willing to settle the matter. But since I let them pass judgment on themselves, they couldn't argue with the verdict.

D. Bruce Lockerbie

Discipline: A Family's Friend or Foe?

KENNETH O. GANGEL

When a father says, "I had to discipline my kid last night with an old-fashioned thrashing," it is apparent that he does not know the meaning of the term *discipline*. What this father applied is *punishment*—not discipline. To develop an effective system of family management, it is imperative that parents understand the difference between discipline and punishment.

Let me point out at the start that I am not making a case against corporal punishment. I believe it is a basic responsibility of parents. However, it is not an appropriate method of dealing with teenagers. Nor is it effective. Parents who find themselves frequently resorting to punishment need to check out their discipline structure.

So just what is *discipline?* It is the orderly working of the family. It includes rules and guidelines—a mutual understanding of what has to be done, when it has to be done, and how it has to be done. *Punishment* is what is applied when discipline breaks down.

I like to compare the effective parent to a good fence-builder. The farmer who puts up a fence to contain his livestock does so for the welfare of his animals. Their grazing land is defined by the fence boundaries. As long as they are content to stay within the boundaries, they are well cared for.

Discipline in the family is keeping such an orderly maintenance of "fences" that family members know exactly where the boundaries are. As long as they stay within the defined boundaries, punishment is not necessary. In establishing boundaries, it is important that both parents agree. Two extremes must be avoided:

One is to erect the fence so far away from the house that the children can virtually do anything they want and still be within boundaries. This kind of fence-building provides a nice cop-out for parents. They can say, "Oh, our child never disobeys." As long as there are no rules, there is no disobedience. But this merely decriminalizes disobedience. It would be as if there were no traffic guidelines. A person could drive 100 mph—but who cares? He's not breaking any law, as long as there is no law to break.

The other extreme is to build the fence so close to the house that there is no room for the family to breathe. Trying to maintain that kind of fence requires almost constant vigilance and often leads to constant punishment. The frustration and frequent abrasion that come between parents and children who are too confined fosters disobedience.

Fence boundaries should be appropriate for the age and temperament of the child, and the boundaries must be redefined as the child matures. Different fences should be established for different children in the family. Fence boundaries may be changed by virtue of age, increasing responsibility, proven capability to handle wider fences, and other considerations. One of the major parental responsibilities in a multi-child family is explaining to the younger ones why the older ones get to do things they can't. But any thinking parent understands that there are things a fifteen-year-old may do that a ten-year-old may not.

The first step in building family fences is to establish the boundaries. The second is to explain the boundaries. This is where the family council can come into play. It is important that children understand why the boundaries are where they are. It is *not* necessary that the children agree with the placement of the boundaries.

Parents should ask adolescents, "Do you understand me?" rather than, "Do you agree with me?" A fifteen-year-old might not be enthusiastic about where the fence boundaries have been placed. He should understand, however, *where* the boundaries are and *why*—even if he doesn't appreciate the boundary lines.

Parents who wish to establish discipline in their home correctly and properly will be ardent and regular students of Hebrews 12. This passage explains how God the Father exercises discipline with His spiritual children. It points out that the motivation for discipline is love. The constant implication throughout the passage is that God's dealing with His children represents a model of discipline for the Christian parent:

"My son, do not make light of the Lord's discipline, and do not lose heart when He rebukes you, because the Lord disciplines those He loves . . . Endure hardship as discipline; God is treating you as sons. For what son is not disciplined by his father?" (Heb. 12:5-7, NIV)

A family needs to operate within clear-cut boundaries, with a disciplinary system that is understood by all. Some families even have guidelines written down. Occasionally, however, parents are confronted with a situation for which there are no established guidelines. Then, in love, they have to say, "Wait a minute! We don't have a rule for this. You'll have to trust our judgment."

The child who has been given good reasons for boundaries ninety percent of the time will be willing to trust the parents for the other ten percent.

DISCIPLINE PREVENTS PUNISHMENT

Discipline is the act of stretching the mind and body of a person so that when the performance comes, it can be a pleasure because of the pain a person faced in the practice.

As I define it, discipline comes *before* the act, and punishment comes *after* the act, if the act isn't done well. If you consistently discipline well enough and thoroughly enough, there isn't any need for punishment because children have learned how to act.

Most parents live on the basis of reaction and response rather than initiation. That's the whole name of the ball game.

In *The Effective Father*, I have a chapter about a canoe trip through white water. There are two ways to paddle a canoe through white water. You can wait until you get into the rapids and then decide what you're going to do. But you'll probably end up falling into the water. Or, you can keep your eyes fifty yards downstream, picking out your route so you know exactly how you're going to act before you get there. Many parents make their errors by failing to plan ahead.

Gordon MacDonald

Related Articles
Chapter 17: How Do I Get My Kids to Obey?
Chapter 17: Why Teens Reject Parental Authority
Chapter 18: Be Disciplined

Dealing with the Disobedient Child

What Works and What Doesn't

LARRY CHRISTENSON

There's a difference between discipline and teaching kids a lesson.

At times you have to use something unpleasant to reinforce a lesson they need to learn, but that's not discipline. For instance, one mother caught her young son fighting with a playmate. She sent him to his room and said, "Now you think about the kind of neighborhood this would be if everyone were always fighting the way you and Johnny were." That's not discipline; that's reinforcing a concept.

That kind of education is necessary to teach a child what he does not know or what he hasn't internalized. When the child fully knows what's expected, however, and willfully disobeys, then discipline is necessary. By discipline, at least in this article, I mean correcting willful disobedience.

Basically, there are two forms of discipline: spanking and consequential discipline.

When children rebel against their parents, whether verbally or by body language, a spanking is called for. Scripture indicates those who spare the rod hate their children, but those who love them are diligent in their discipline (Prov. 13:24). It's especially important in the preteen years to lay the groundwork of

---

WHAT IS CHILD ABUSE?

Child abuse and neglect are serious social problems in the United States. The *nonaccidental* emotional or physical injury to an individual under eighteen by a parent or guardian generally constitutes the act of abuse, while the deliberate failure to meet the physical and psychological needs of the child is generally regarded as neglect (though the degree of failure and deliberateness to meet the child's needs is generally imprecisely defined). Controversies over the appropriate definitions of abuse and neglect influence all efforts to deal with the problem, including deciding how often it happens and when a parent is in the wrong.

Individual states vary with their definitions of child abuse and neglect, and often their statutes are difficult to interpret and apply. Gradually, researchers are becoming aware that no simple element can provide a sufficient explanation, and they are being trained to consider that the child + parent + situation = abuse. Consequently, in most cases, legal definitions offer marginal safeguards for the child without interfering with a parent's reasonable discipline.

For specific definitions and what they mean to you as a parent, contact your county juvenile court.

Dwight Spotts

disciplining in love.

There's only one place for a spanking— on the back end. You should never cuff, hit, or abuse a child. Biblical discipline is the antithesis of child abuse. Child abuse comes from undisciplined parents who spill their uncontrolled emotions onto the kid.

I saw a neighbor cuff his son around the ears, and I took him aside and said, "Never hit a child like that. You'll become combatants rather than a father and son."

God created the rear end with lots of padding and lots of nerve endings—a perfect combination for discipline.

Spanking, however, generally tails off around age twelve or thirteen. Hopefully by that time, the parents' authority is established. You and the kids may have differences of opinion but usually not out-and-out rebellion. You should be able to reason things out.

If reason doesn't work, consequential discipline is required. You establish the conditions and results. For instance, if you've told your daughter she can have the family car but must be home by 11 o'clock, and she pulls in at midnight, then the consequence is the next time she asks, you say no. It's punishment appropriate to the offense.

Some forms of discipline are *not* effective—nagging, sarcasm, verbal put-downs. That sacrifices your authority; it's just will against will, and you're not exerting any real leadership.

Sending kids to their rooms is another loser. It's counterproductive! They go with emotions churning, and alone in their room that hate and resentment just smolder. Spanking or some other punishment deals with the issue decisively. It's over—and you never let the child out of the embrace of the family.

Personally, I feel fathers should do the disciplining except in situations when they're gone, and then the mother should do it without delay. An exception might be when children get a little older and are big enough to fight back. When that happened in our house, my wife said, "Now you either lie down on the bed and let me spank you or else Dad will do it when he gets home." Most times they chose Mom's spanking because it wasn't as hard. The important thing was they realized Mom and Dad stood together in the discipline.

Related Articles

When Should You Ground Your Teenager?

D. BRUCE LOCKERBIE

When a teenager commits an offense for which he needs discipline, the parents should try their best to make the punishment fit the crime. A massive punishment for a small offense is likely to prevent the teen from seeing the correlation between the two. And more often than not the result is resentment.

In my book, *Fatherlove,* I humorously said that every family has its own set of do's and don'ts, and I listed four of Lockerbie's Laws:

1. If it is right, enjoy it.
2. If it is wrong, you know what to do.
3. If you aren't sure whether it is right or wrong, it is probably wrong.
4. Under any circumstances, no matter what the hour, find a phone and call home if you're going to be later than you told us.

(This Law ends a lot of anxiety on the part of those who are waiting for the car to drive up and wondering why it hasn't yet arrived.)

When my sons were in junior high school, their school had only recently acquired coeds. We were at a football game one Saturday when it started to rain. When I looked for my sons, I couldn't find them. I followed the crowd that was leaving to one of the dorms. I found Donald and Kevin in the lounge of the girl's dorm watching the football game on TV. Since they seemed to think that they were such hotshots that they could entertain and be entertained by the ladies while their schoolmates were playing in the rain, I thought a couple of days of hard work would be a good antidote for the soft life.

First we watched the rest of the game (in the rain, not on television). Then that afternoon and the next I introduced them to a pick and shovel and let them help me do some yard work that I had been planning to hire some stronger boys to do.

I'm not saying that all punishment ought to be household chores or that kind of thing. But I think it is pretty important that we share the experience with our children whenever possible. Parents shouldn't just say, "You go do so and so." Instead they should say, "Your behavior has caused me a lot of anguish, and I think we need to work something out."

I also don't think it's a good idea to use what could be a positive experience as a form of punishment. For example, it's a most disagreeable thing for a schoolteacher to punish a student by having him write a composition. Having been an English teacher, I don't like to see the act of writing used in such a negative context. The privilege and ability of writing are gifts from God, and I would prefer that

SCOLDING WITH EFFECT

Scolding has bad connotations. It usually degenerates into nagging, which is not only ineffective but downright destructive in a relationship. But if done on the right occasion and if the Spirit releases you to do it, scolding can have good effect.

The key is making sure the scolding is rare. The shock value is lost if you scold more than once a month. In fact, for younger kids I think spanking should be the first resort and a good scolding the last resort. If you scold too often, they know right away it doesn't mean anything, and they'll push you to just short of the spanking point. They manipulate you, rather than you controlling them.

The biggest mistake parents make in this area is punishing with the voice rather than taking definite action.

But on rare occasions, when the situation calls for it, make use of the genuine emotion you feel, and read the riot act. But make sure the issue is truly significant, not just something that irritates you.

Larry Christenson

the teacher find a more suitable form of punishment.

Christian parents are similarly guilty of assigning wrong forms of discipline. We should never use spiritual matters to punish offenses. Yet we say, "Just for that, you have to go to Wednesday night prayer meeting," or we force younger children to memorize Scripture. Consequently, they see these church activities as distasteful. We need to be aware of the hidden results of many of the punishments we assign.

In fitting the type of discipline to the offense, I reserved grounding for extreme cases. Every once in a while one of my children did something where I was sufficiently outraged to say, "OK, for that action you cannot have the use of the family car."

With a little thought, parents can make discipline a positive experience for their teenager. By selecting a fair punishment and not overreacting, each period of chastisement can be a growth experience for the child and an opportunity for the parents to grow closer to their son or daughter.

Does Discipline Change as Teens Mature?

DAVID VEERMAN

"**S**pare the rod and spoil the child" is a Bible verse familiar to most Christian parents. They believe it too, but its application is where things get sticky. Each child is different—spanking is effective with one but seems to break the spirit of another. Then there's the second-guessing, always questioning the appropriateness of the response. So we make scores of threats and seldom follow through.

Discipline is difficult at any age, but the problems seem to be magnified as our children move into adolescence. What discipline is most effective with teenagers? Should our methods change as our children mature?

First, it is important to realize that our older children still need discipline. In the throes of identity crisis and peer pressure, teens desperately need security. Firm and reasonable discipline is like a wall providing protection, defining limits, and demonstrating care and concern. This wall is necesary—not for shelter—but for teenagers' growth and readiness for life on the outside where they will need self-discipline. The goal of discipline, then, is to help prepare our young people for life without us.

As our kids mature, it becomes obvious that physical punishment is increasingly difficult to administer. (How does a five-foot-five mom spank a six-foot-two son?) Unfortunately, most parents resort to yelling, and soon the discussion escalates into a full-scale blowup. Instead, there must be concern, commitment, and creativity.

If we truly want our children to be ready to leave our care, we must give them increasing amounts of freedom, privilege, and responsibility. This involves time (curfew), money, use of the car, dating, and other "adult" areas. Teens want to be trusted as they push for independence, and we should prod them toward trustworthiness.

Our methods of discipline should parallel this process. As our children enter junior high school, we can take them aside individually and explain the ground rules—that our goal is to help make them move toward independence, that there will be no more spanking or threats, that discipline will involve their freedom and privileges, and that we will be firm, fair, and consistent.

At first, the affected areas will include the upkeep of their room and belongings, obeying the "house rules," their treatment of their brothers and sisters, and their study habits. Later (especially with the advent of the driver's license) the list will expand to include curfew, use of the family car, choice of activities, dating, and money. Each reward and punishment must be thought through *before* the problem arises—this will ensure fairness and learning.

Here are some possible situations:

- If grades are maintained at the desired level, he or she may become involved in special extracurricular activities. If the grades fall, however, the activities will be curtailed.
- If there are problems at school or other flagrant disobedience (drinking, etc.), privileges will be curtailed through grounding, loss of TV watching time, etc.
- If curfew limits are honored, they will be expanded; if not, they will be cut back.

It is imperative that:

- Reward and punishment are a part of every rule.
- Communication lines remain open. We can treat the rules like a contract, perhaps even putting the guidelines into writing.
- Responsible independence is seen as our ultimate goal.
- A person is assumed to be trustworthy until proven otherwise.

Watch out—don't discipline with helpful (life-changing) activities (e.g., withholding attendance at church youth group socials) and don't use the Bible as a weapon (requiring Scripture memorization as a punishment).

Related Article
Chapter 6: Changing Roles

Give Your Teen a Wall and a Towel
DAVID VEERMAN

"**T**hat kid is driving us berserk!" Though her voice bristled with anger, I sensed deeper feelings of hurt and discouragement.

"He fights us at every turn. It's not just the arguments, but his whole attitude. We don't know what to do."

"That kid" is a disobedient teen—and too big to spank. So how can parents discipline? We have heard a wide range of contemporary answers from "grounding" to threats of "kicking them out of the house." We love our children and desire the best for their lives. But how do we influence them to choose the best way for their lives?

If only a simple formula for adolescent discipline were discovered which, when applied . . . *poof*, a mature man or woman appears. But unfortunately, there is none.

Life is too complex, and each person is a unique creation of God. To approach our sons and daughters with "three easy steps" violates their individuality.

But before we raise our hands in despair, let's grab some hope. Scripture abounds with God's promise that people, their directions in life, and even their personalities can change (Luke 19:1-10). Look at the apostles, Mary Magdalene, and Zaccheus. With God, nothing is impossible (Luke 18:27).

At the same time, it helps to know that most of the things our teenagers do are quite normal. Our kids are caught in the difficult transition from childhood to adulthood. They are experimenting with independence and identity while maturing emotionally. The process is as exhausting and confusing to them as it is to us.

Biblical principles can guide us through these normally difficult teenage years. First, we should immerse ourselves and our children in prayer (Matt. 21:22). This means much more than simply asking for God's blessing and protection. We need to lay out openly before Him all of our deep feelings and fears. We should expect a struggle as we try to release ownership and expectations to Him.

Prayer is basic and foundational. But it is only the first step.

We must act with both love and discipline. The Bible holds these in tension. As parents, we are instructed not to "spare the rod" (Prov. 13:24). As Christians, we are to live in love (John 13:35). The application of this tension is

A QUESTION OF DISCIPLINE—WHEN AND HOW OFTEN?

One of the toughest problems for parents of teenagers is the question of discipline. We know they still need it, but they're too big to spank. Obviously there are no easy answers, but here are some guidelines.

1. There is a difference between punishment and discipline, though they are tied together. "Discipline" is the means of moving someone toward *positive* goals.

2. It is important to continue the system of punishment and discipline which was consistently carried out from an early age. In other words, don't change the rules or the broad guidelines, just the specific disciplinary actions.

3. Learn to know when "enough is enough," and look for the deeper reasons for bad behavior. Punishment becomes useless if you are constantly punishing repeated problems. The teen's action is a symptom of a deeper problem which needs attention.

4. Punishment should not be an exercise in anger or an expression of frustration. Try to calm down before meting it out.

5. Give two sets of consequences and a positive alternative. For example, if you banish him to his room for swearing at his mother, lay the responsibility on him: "If you go a week without swearing at your mother without being reminded, then we will do this; if not, then this will happen." This is preferable to saying, "Never do that again." (A week is easier than never.)

6. Enlist the teen's help in designing discipline. Ask him what would be a fair and motivating punishment (and reward) in specific situations.

YFC Editors

so important that we dare not miss it.

On the one hand, we are to surround our children with a *wall* of discipline. Rules, limits, firmness, specific penalties (or enforcement principles), and punishment are involved. This wall provides security.

Especially with high schoolers, communication is vital. We must talk out the family's rules and guidelines, and perhaps even put them in writing to avoid confusion. Both positive and negative elements (rewards and punishments) may be included. At the appropriate time we give swift, firm, and fair enforcement. Imagination is the key. We and our kids *together* can think of new disciplinary actions. And if we agree on the ones suggested, so much the better.

Within the wall of discipline we must look for creative ways to "wash feet" (John 13:14-16). Love begins at home. The love Jesus demonstrated involved the humility of a towel. Usually, we will respond to our children when a problem arises. But if they seem happy and quiet (especially quiet), we leave them alone.

I am suggesting that we discover their needs and serve. Investigation will help. What do they desire? Let's ask, then take the initiative—providing concert tickets, preparing favorite foods, repairing broken sports equipment, planning enjoyable activities together, offering the use of the car, and other surprises. We do this because it is *His* way of loving. As we wash the feet of our children (especially teenagers), we model Christlike love; we build meaningful relationships and win the right to be heard.

Finally, our biblical response should include patience and faith. God expects us to be faithful stewards. The results are up to Him. In faith, let's build our walls and wield our towels. Then relax—He will be at work.

Adapted from an article in *Moody Monthly* magazine. Used by permission.

Related Articles

MANAGING THE HOME
WITH TRUST

- When can you trust your kids?
- What should you do when teens violate your trust?
- Don't project your failures onto your teens
- When should teens be left home alone for a night or weekend?
- What are the biblical elements of trust?

At the top of every list of pet peeves ever received from teenagers is this: "My parents don't trust me." Along with love, trust is one of the most powerful tools we have in helping young people develop toward maturity. Of course, it has its inherent dangers. Can there be good without bad, light without darkness, top without bottom, full without empty? Probably not, and neither can there be trust without failure and disappointment. But when trust shines brightly and the young person comes through, both parents and teen reap the rewards.

When Can We Trust Our Teenagers?

JAY KESLER

Your teenage daughter breezes into the living room and plants a loving kiss on your cheek. Casually she mentions that her room is spotless, homework done, the dishes have been cleaned up, and tomorrow there are no exams at school.

You glance quickly at your spouse, and without a word you ask each other, "What does she want?"

You don't have to wait long for an answer. "Mom and Dad, is it OK if Jim picks me up at 7:00? [It's 6:55.] A bunch of us are getting together tonight. I promise I'll be home by 10:00."

Staring at the bedroom ceiling, you lie awake waiting for your daughter's return. At 11:07, she tries to sneak through the back door, but of course you hear her. The worry is over, but with a sigh you wonder aloud, "When can we trust our kids?"

Do you know what trust involves? Do you know how to develop trust within yourself and within your children? These are difficult questions for all of us, and no one has all the answers. There are certain biblical guidelines, however, that relate to trust and that can help parents make good decisions.

1. *Get to know your children.* You do not trust someone you do not know. We must reach kids where they are, not where we wish they were. Earl Wilson, in his book, *You Try Being a Teenager,* explains it this way: "Without respect, there cannot be love, and without love, there cannot be friendship (or trust). This friendship is much more than being chums with your son or daughter—it is

in-depth knowing, caring, respecting. Be available to your kids. True friends play together, work, think and feel together, solve problems together, share dreams together, and interact with God together."

Some parents worry, "If we get too close to our kids, they'll walk right over us." In fact, the opposite is usually true. Parents maintain greater respect and authority in close, healthy relationships.

2. *Be an example.* Parents who are forced to say, "Don't do as I do; do as I say," lose the strong influence of a good example.

3. *Build their self-esteem.* It is a good idea to affirm in public and discipline in private. My collie will get up and walk the length of the yard for a pat on the head, and so will most of us. Kids are no exception. Be generous with your praise.

4. *Communicate with your kids.*

"WHY DON'T THE KIDS TRUST US?"

Trust is a valuable gift, and losing it is tragic. Unfortunately, however, the "trust-thread" is easily snapped. A broken confidence or a promise forgotten may destroy a friendship that took years to build.

Trust is a word often used in parent-teen relationships. The high schooler confronts with, "What's the matter; don't you trust me?" and Mom and Dad wonder why the kids don't confide in them like they did when they were younger.

This is a difficult area for parents to handle emotionally. They know the kids aren't taking their advice, and they feel threatened by their listening to and confiding in others.

This happens mainly because teenagers are trying to grow up and be "on their own," and this involves "apron-string-cutting." It may also be that they are afraid of disappointing or hurting Mom and Dad, so they don't tell them *everything.*

Often, however, parents exacerbate the problem through their actions. We may say one thing and then do another—inconsistency breeds mistrust. Or we overstate the case (e.g., an overprotective mom says, "If you kiss a boy, you'll get pregnant")—when the kids learn the facts, they also learn not to believe everything we say.

There are no easy answers to the trust question, but here are some suggestions:

1. We shouldn't confuse their desire for independence with a lack of trust in us.

2. We shouldn't try to be infallible. Instead, we can give our kids two *good* choices and let them choose.

3. We should be willing to tolerate conduct which differs from our own opinions (we expect *them* to do this) and not hold it against them.

4. We should communicate honestly and on a *feeling* level (e.g., "You can do this, but I'm not for it"), again letting them know it won't be held against them.

5. We should hold confidences and *never* share their secrets with others.

YFC Editors

Remember that communication is a two-way street. Teens won't share their inner feelings if they sense that their answers will be graded like an exam or ignored because the expected response wasn't given. By demonstrating a sincere interest in what your children say, you will begin to develop strong, lifelong relationships with them.

5. *Develop values in your children.* "Values and morals cannot be taught without consistent discipline," says Wilson. "By the time your children become teenagers you can no longer impose your values on them. The only alternative is to try to build a relationship with your teenagers in such a way that they see you as someone who is helpful to consult in developing values." Help your teens use their values when making decisions.

6. *Develop responsibility in your children.* Let your teenagers know that you want to give them more freedom and independence, but that in the process they must learn to take on more responsibility. For example, if your son has difficulty getting home on time, then he is not ready to take out someone else's daughter.

As your teenagers begin taking on more responsibility, make trust an automatic part of the process. Tell your teenagers that you trust them to take care of the car when they use it, or that you trust them to take care of the house when you are away for the weekend. You can't give your teens responsibility without using trust.

When teenagers leave home, the choices they make will be their own. Hopefully your trust will have developed within them the character and independence they need in order to stand against things which don't agree with their values.

7. *Understand what it means to be a teenager.* Realize that to be young is to be different. To be young is to be in rebellion. To be young is to question and to test. It doesn't mean that your kids are hostile, or

that they will leave the time-tested things permanently. It just means that they are trying to find their own set of values.

8. *Recognize the emotional turmoil caused by a changing body.* Complexion problems, small stature, protruding ears, dental flaws, and glasses are all factors that can affect young people. Most of us can look back at those struggles and laugh. But while we were going through them, there was no humor in the situation at all.

These tremendous physical changes put great emotional strain on your teens. They will be attracted to someone who is sympathetic. If you aren't, someone else will be.

9. *Understand and empathize with your children's social lives.* The social area is the most threatening and fear-filled of all for many young people. Teenage society can be quite cruel. Often parents can't figure out why their kids are in one group when another looks so much more constructive. The truth may be that your children prefer the other group but have been rejected by it on an arbitrary basis such as looks.

10. *Discover your children's strong points.* Focus attention on those strengths. It is very difficult for trust to thrive in a negative atmosphere. This is not to say that we can never correct our kids. Pointing out failure is only effective, however, when kids are secure in our love and esteem.

These ten guidelines help us discover how to develop trust within a family atmosphere. If we put these guidelines to work, can trust become a regular part of our lives? Let's look at some specific examples.

Rather than doling out money to kids, give them an allowance and trust them to have the ability to budget it according to their needs. It is important not to bail out your teens if they run short of cash. Let them go without until the following week when they again receive their allowance. Hopefully they will learn how to do a better job of budgeting.

Help your teens to understand that they give account of their time as a matter of respect for others (so that no one will worry about them), rather than as a means for you to check up on them. Ask your teens, "How much time do you think you need after this school activity? What time do you think you should be in?" Demonstrate your faith in their ability to set some of their own time standards, but at the same time, make them stick to their commitments.

It is good for children to see the connection between responsible behavior and privilege. As they learn to be responsible in their actions, they should be given more privileges. This type of trust builds maturity.

Trust must be encouraged and reinforced, but keep in mind that your kids are not perfect. When kids fail, however, many parents make the mistake of removing all trust. They say, "We can't trust you again until you prove that you can be trusted." But if the children are not given trust, how can they prove that they are worthy of it? When parents say, "Earn

CAN PARENTS CONTROL THEIR TEENS' ENVIRONMENT?

GIGO (*G*arbage *I*n, *G*arbage *O*ut)—this computer cliché is a good description of what happens with us. A continuous diet of "garbage" produces all sorts of problems in our lives (from the thought life to lifestyle). Unfortunately we are surrounded by the stuff. Politicians, neighbors, movies, TV, and magazines all produce a "polluted" environment. It's hard not to be overly dramatic, but let's face it, the values of our society are patently non-Christian.

As our children are growing, we can't help but be concerned about what they are being fed. And, in addition to the "me first" and "sex saturated" values, they find it easy to take shortcuts intellectually, socially, and spiritually.

Obviously, we cannot "force feed" our kids (especially teenagers), but we can help them develop "taste." This needs to be started early in their lives. But instead of trying to control their environment (or shelter them), we should provide positive alternatives.

Here is where our homes are so important. We should ask ourselves, "What values and priorities are being taught in our family?" To provide a positive and wholesome environment means a responsible use of the television, a priority of church and family devotions, reading books of high quality, and choosing good entertainment. It also means exposing our children to the fine arts, good music, and great literature. They can't be forced to like these things, but at least they will know they exist. (They will *never* appreciate them if they're never exposed to them.) No, we can't control their total environment, but we *can* provide options.

It is also important to help our teens learn how to read their environment—seeing through the surface to the actual values espoused—and to help *them* make mature choices. We must remember that soon they will be on their own and totally responsible for "feeding themselves."

YFC Editors

my trust," they are actually demonstrating an attitude of distrust.

This attitude is unrealistic and unfair because your children may be very responsible in other areas of their lives. You may have to take away certain privileges for a time, but keep communication going. Tell your kids why these consequences are necessary. And as soon as possible, give them another opportunity to be responsible.

We must also be careful not to project our own bad performance onto our kids. For instance, fathers often feel that when their daughter goes on a date, they know just what the boy has on his mind. Now the truth is that they don't know at all what that boy has on his mind. All they know is what they had on their minds when they were seventeen. Many Christian kids wouldn't think of doing some of the things their parents did before they were saved. Everyone ought to get a chance to prove they are trustworthy.

Though we take the risk of being deceived, it is still more powerful to trust our children than to protect ourselves from being fooled. It is important for your children to know that your love for them is unconditional and unshakable even in the face of disappointment and fear.

Can you be certain everything will work out right? No, you can't. But remember that developing trust is like a baby learning how to walk. You must take the first difficult step toward a lasting relationship. There is risk of humiliation, failure, and rejection. As you demonstrate faith in your kids' abilities to act responsibly, as you step out to give them another chance, the effects of your trust begin to work. The results are slow and unsteady at first, but over time your family should reap the rewards.

From an article first published in *Christian Herald* magazine and adapted from *Too Big to Spank* by Jay Kesler, © 1978, Regal Books. Used by permission.

Related Articles
Chapter 14: Giving Teens Room to Grow
Chapter 17: Teenage Rights vs. Family Rights
Chapter 17: Teens Are People Too—Do You Treat Them That Way?

The Ingredients of Trust

ADRIAN ROGERS

I have told our children through the years that we will always trust them, but that we'll not always trust their judgment. I think this distinction between trusting them and trusting their judgment is important. I may trust my son, but that doesn't mean I'm going to let him do brain surgery on me if he's not qualified. Trusting him as a person has nothing to do with it; it's his judgment, his experience, that I don't trust.

I explain to my children that though they already have my trust in their character, they have to earn my trust in their judgment. "As you display better and better judgment," I tell them, "you will have more and more freedom and responsibility. Freedom and responsibility are mutually corresponding. The greater responsibility you assume, the greater freedom you can have."

Teenagers, young people in the process of becoming adults, need to assert their independence. They need to be trusted to do things for themselves. They are getting ready to break away from their parents, and this is right. A father and mother are successful when their children no longer need them.

Many times, however, when the teenager no longer needs his parents, or at least does not need them as much as he once did, the parents still need to be needed. So they try to create artificial needs in the teenager. But the child rebels against those artificial needs and says, "I want to be trusted. I don't want to be tied to your apron strings. I don't want these restrictions placed on me."

This is a natural response on the part of the teenager. It's part of growing up. But some parents react by accusing the child of rebellion. At that point, the teenager actually does rebel. He thinks his parents don't trust him. And indeed there is a lack of trust, but it's not the teenager the parents aren't trusting. It's themselves. They do not trust themselves to be able to continue without being needed by their child. And by needing to be needed, they actually cause a split.

Of course, there are teens who shouldn't be trusted. The Bible says that "foolishness is bound in the heart of a child" (Prov. 22:15, KJV), and certainly children need discipline. But if parents are having difficulty showing trust when trust is called for, they may need to talk with someone who will help them realize that it is themselves and the Lord they are not trusting, as well as the teenager.

It is important to give our teenagers more and more trust, more and more responsibility, until they can function without us. We will work ourselves out of a job that way, but not out of a relationship. As a matter of fact, the relationship becomes more beautiful and meaningful. I am enjoying my children more than ever before because I don't have to ride herd on them. I'm not superintending everything they do. We don't have to discuss trust anymore. I now have four wonderful friends with whom I enjoy fun and fellowship and friendship.

CAN PARENTS BE TOO TRUSTING?

As parents, you cannot be too trusting—in fact, you have everything to gain as you trust your teen's integrity. Mutual trust is one of the blessings of parenthood; if you feel that your teen trusts you, you really value that, and vice versa. Trust breeds responsibility. Give your teens the opportunity for independence, and communicate your trust to them by saying yes as often as you can.

Trust that is earned by good judgment increases as children learn to make decisions. Don't trust your teens too soon in areas where they are likely to fail; don't give trust where direction or more maturity is needed; don't trust when there is not enough knowledge or experience or confidence to make a good decision. A teen's repetitive bad choices are sending a message that your help is needed in learning to make positive and constructive decisions.

Teach your children how to make wise choices; then as they become teenagers, allow them frequent chances to make their own decisions. As you encourage their independence, give yourself and your children to the Lord. Can you trust God too much?

YFC Editors

When Your Teen Betrays Your Trust

NORMAN WRIGHT

Your son or daughter has let you down, violated a trust. You trusted him or her to take good care of the car, get home by a certain hour, adhere to certain standards of sexual purity. But your belief in your teen has been betrayed—and it hurts.

Now's the time to ask why you're hurting, so that you can deal with the pain. Ask yourself: "Am I hurt mainly because I've been let down, lied to? Is it because I fear what other people may think? Or am I genuinely hurt because a good rule has been broken and I'm concerned about the consequences for my teenager?"

You have a choice of two ways to deal with your hurt, your disappointment. You can (1) rail against your teen, try to put him in a box and control him; or (2) use the broken trust as an opportunity to help keep it from happening again. This doesn't mean you have to submerge your hurt; you need to discuss it in a way that keeps the future in mind.

Sit down with your teen and discuss what has happened. Ask, "Why do you think this occurred? What do you think we should do now?" Once you've set the penalty, work toward rebuilding trust.

If the violation has been major, you'll probably want to reestablish trust in small steps. Give the teen more freedom as he or she regains dependability.

Repeated violations of a rule, however, show that the young person isn't learning from experience. Let's say your son goes out and gets five traffic tickets, has four minor accidents, and then says, "Hey, let me use the car."

"No," you say.

"You don't trust me," he says.

You could say, "You know, you're right. In this area, we don't trust you. We trust you in other ways, but in this one it's hard. You've had several chances." Now that you've identified the problem, you can propose the solution: "So that we can trust you in this area, here's what we would like you to do. We're going to send you to a driving school for a while, or a class the police department holds for traffic offenders.

"Then we want you to drive with us for a month. After that, we'll gradually give you more freedom in this area. But for now we can't afford to, because there's an insurance problem—and you could kill somebody with a car that's out of control."

Sometimes a pattern of offenses develops, and the teen doesn't respond to your increased trust. He may use drugs or alcohol, for example, and when he drives he poses a clear danger to others. If he persists, you give him a choice: "As long as that happens, we cannot allow you to use our car. If we can be assured that you're not going to use drugs or drink, fine. It's your choice." Teens need to learn that life is full of choices—and consequences.

Trusting your teen means running the risk of having that trust broken. It might be nice if you could get your adolescent to promise in writing not to betray your trust; you could even get it notarized. But it would only be a piece of paper. As in any love relationship, you have to risk being hurt. You'll be disappointed, just as I've been at times. That's the price of saying, "I still love you."

THE TEST OF UNCONDITIONAL LOVE

All our children rebel in some form or another, whether quietly or noisily. Part of growing up is to test the waters and the boundaries. The question is, "When our children do things that are difficult for us to accept, can we still love them?"

Probably the single most important factor why children reject parental authority is that the kids don't feel loved unconditionally. Unconditional love is the most powerful change agent on earth. There is a point where you can no longer overpower your child. He has too much freedom, too much time away from you, and he's just as big as you are. Then the most powerful control you have on him is your unconditional love. That kind of love gives a child the feeling he's loved as much when he gets F's in life as when he gets A's. While unconditional love cannot guarantee all happy chapters in the book, it may guarantee a happy ending.

Of course, the test of unconditional love comes in times of failure. That's how we test God's love. While we were yet sinners, God demonstrated His love for us (see Rom. 5:8). That is the model of the ultimate Parent. He made the supreme sacrifice for us when we were in total defiance against Him. That is the precedent for how we should love our children and a demonstration of the power of this love to deliver.

It is not humanly possible to consistently love our children. That's why we need the resources of Christ to love a child in the moments when he's unlovable. Those are the moments when he needs our love the most.

You can make many mistakes, but somehow love does cover a multitude of sins and a multitude of parental errors. Unconditional love will eventually win, I believe. It won us to God, and it continues to win.

Many children have to drive to the end of a dead-end street before they'll accept help and change. And when they get to that end, they'll turn to the person who loved them the whole time they were on that street. The prodigal son is a classic example. The son knew there was only one person to whom he could go—to his father, the one who had demonstrated unconditional love to him throughout his life.

Ronald P. Hutchcraft

Separating Your Teen Years from Your Teen's Years

GLANDION CARNEY

Parents must not project their own failures or successes onto their teenagers. Just because a parent did something wrong as a teenager does not mean that his teen is doing it or even thinking it! Parents can learn to trust their teens not to do the same things they did as teens.

Realize that we live in a different world at a different time. The things I did as a teen are entirely different from the things my teens will do. Value systems and the whole way of life are different today than yesterday. It's not fair to say to a teenager, "When I was a kid, we did things like this."

When I was a kid, we lived in a society where cruising in the car was a big thing. We were embarrassed to walk into a drugstore and buy a prophylactic, and kissing on the first date was barely acceptable.

Nowadays, kids don't give a second thought to buying birth control paraphernalia. Our promiscuous society preaches that if you don't have sexual relations with your girlfriend or boyfriend, something must be wrong with you.

If you can understand the environment in which your child is growing up, and realize the complexity of it, I think you can begin to deal with your child in an honest, open way, by talking about what's out there. It's honest to say, "You know, I just feel that you need to be aware that I know what's out there. I think you need to know that you can always come and talk to me when you feel the pressures of the world pressing in on you."

Projecting your failures on a teenager and talking about failure are two different things. You can talk about a failure and say what you learned from it. Or you can dwell on your failures, acting overly fearful and believing that your teen will fail in that area also.

The flip side of projecting failure on your teen is projecting your success on your teen. Though you may not see the success of your job or status, children are quick to recognize when Dad or Mom is considered successful. They often live under the pressure of your ideas of success. They feel as if they have to be just as successful or even more so.

Learn to trust your teen implicitly. It is wrong to impose your insecurities on your teenager, to assume that he has the same weakness that you do. Trust your teen to make the right decision, until he proves irresponsible. Develop an atmosphere of trust in your home.

Some families are living under the auspices of suspicion. The consequences are parallel to what we see in a dictatorial environment or in an Iron Curtain country. With no trust, you have to create a police system, complete with interrogation. Your relationship becomes so strained that you end up at odds, with a vast distance between you.

Keep in mind that sometimes teenagers give their parents reasons *not* to trust them. I've seen a lot of parents who begin very innocently to create an idealistic trust factor, and operate in an open atmosphere with their children. Then one of the children takes advantage of that trust, using it to his own advantage. And when trust is gone, it is *very* hard to win back.

When a teen fails, or breaks a trust, parents need to respond in an appropriate manner. In other words, is the failure major or minor?

If, for example, your child were to steal something from church, it would be hard to understand the reasons behind that action. Chances are, you would feel hurt and frustrated. Because stealing violates a high family value, it may be difficult to come to the point of forgiving him. It would be tempting to bring his failure up again in an argument. But that's not true forgiveness.

It's hard to give a teen a clean slate after he's broken a trust. I think it's more of a burden for the parents to wrestle with than for the teen. The teen commits a wrong, forgets about it, and his life mends easily. But the parents often continue to struggle with that broken trust.

For example, if Christian parents trust their child, and the child goes out and has a sexual relationship, that action would violate a standard that the parents feel is very sacred in the area of marriage and family. If the child becomes pregnant, the parents have even a harder time. Long after the teen deals with the sin and her life is mended, it still eats away at the parents. They feel as if they have failed their child, and often the incident remains a lifetime scar.

Projection can be positive for your teen if it's in the form of hopes and desires for his future. Project success and achievement in the form of encouragement that says, "I believe in you."

Especially in a poor or minority environment, you need to project some form of success in the child so that he has a dream to strive for.

In a middle-class environment where there is probably an overabundance of success, I think parents have to watch what they say and do, and temper any form of projection. Raising a child in white suburbia is radically different from raising a child in a poor or minority neighborhood.

Projection in the sense of encouragement may stimulate the teen to personal success and satisfaction. But becoming too pushy in projecting your own failures or successes onto a teenager will only bring grief.

When raising teenagers, parents can learn a lesson from a prizefighter. They have to know when to take the bad, when to get in the best shot, and when to back off.

Related Articles

When Should Teens Be Left Home Alone?

For How Long?

DAVID RAHN

No formula exists that yields the answers to these questions. Trust is a function of a healthy relationship. When two persons get to know one another, clearly understand their expectations, are aware of their strengths and weaknesses, and have a sense of the pressures to be faced, mutual trust seems to emerge naturally.

Kids are desperate for their homes to be safe places, places where they can share their fears, struggles, and dreams in the certainty that they will be answered with love, confidence, and direction. Where such a climate exists, parents ought to be able to reduce the risk involved in trusting a child by eliminating many of the critical unknowns. Parents might find the following questions helpful as a self analysis:

• How well do you know your teen? Are you current? Pressures on teenagers can create a volatile atmosphere and last month's son or daughter may not be the same this month.

• How well do you know the world of your teen? his friends? the current temptations and battles? Good kids can be subject to lots of pressure when party-seekers discover that they're home alone.

• Does your teen clearly understand your expectations? Are they agreed on by all concerned, or simply handed down from a parental Mount Sinai?

• Has your child demonstrated a fundamental trustworthiness in the past? This is not to imply perfection, but rather a genuine pursuit of the expectations you've agreed on, and an ability to meet them.

Where the preceding questions can be answered satisfactorily, trusting a teen home alone is not only a good risk, but may be a rewarding experience in a relationship. Remember that children learn to be trustworthy by being trusted. The parents who expect the best of their kids and the parents who expect the worst of their kids often watch their expectations become self-fulfilling prophecies.

20

PREPARING YOUR CHILDREN TO MANAGE THEMSELVES

How to Help Your Teens Become Independent

- Preparing to let your teens go
- What is the parents' ultimate goal for their children?
- What do you let go of first, and when?
- How to prepare your teens for the "real world"
- The secret of keeping an open home

- What's right for you may not be right for your kids
- The empty nest: What should parents do now?
- How to make the transition from adult-child relationships to adult-adult relationships

The empty nest is a frightening prospect, especially when you have built your entire life around children and family life. Yet our children's independence is the ultimate goal of parenting. Their ability to function on their own outside the home is parenthood's final exam.

Our own attitudes as well as their behavior are on trial. Has our husband-wife relationship been simply a child-raising partnership, or have we truly grown to love and care for one another? Do we derive our meaning in life from the ego boost of having children depend on us, or do we receive joy and happiness from seeing them succeed on their own?

In this empty-nest stage, some of our deepest feelings are revealed. David prayed, "Search me, O God, and know my heart: try me, and know my thoughts: and see if there be any wicked way in me, and lead me in the way everlasting" (Ps. 139:23-24, KJV). These experiences truly search our hearts, and through them we are refined as we move toward lasting goals.

Preparing to Let Them Go

RAY & ANNE ORTLUND

When Jesus was twelve years old, He backed off a bit from His earthly father for the first time. The story is found in Luke 2. Jesus remains behind at the temple to talk with the rabbis while His parents, thinking He is in their traveling group, leave without Him. When they return and find Him, His mother chides: "Your father and I have been anxiously searching for you" (v. 48, NIV).

Jesus replies, "Didn't you know that I had to be in My Father's house?" (v. 49, NIV) He wasn't talking about Joseph, even though Joseph was legally His human father. He was talking about God—and thus gently putting a little distance between His human parents and His heavenly One.

From about age twelve on, our children may begin to feel readiness to start getting a few directions not just from us but from their heavenly Father. We need to speak to the children about this. Assuming that they have already had the new birth experience—"Listen," we might say, "we know that from now on, the Lord will be coming more and more into your life, and the more we see you getting your orders from Him, the more we can back off. Probably by the time you're twenty or twenty-two we won't have to tell you what to do at all. You'll be getting your orders from God, and we'll just be your good friends!"

If we say this to them from time to time, gradually they'll get the picture, and they won't have to wonder how long we're going to stay on their case. They'll know they won't have to rebel to get their way. They'll know that we fully intend to gradually withdraw our authority over them as we see God taking over.

We met a mother at one of our meetings several years ago who seemed almost like Susannah Wesley herself. Her five kids looked great as they sat like little stairsteps beside their mother in the pew. She described to us her amazing program of mothering. She had a goal for each child each year, and she scheduled their Bible study and prayer times, their music lessons, ball games, family devotions, family social times, family educational trips—we felt worn out just listening to this 100 percent mother.

Finally Anne asked her, "How do you plan to release them as they grow up?"

The mother looked a little startled. Anne went on, "I mean, when they get older will you still have them follow the same regimen?"

"Of course not," the mother answered. "They'll be married and have their own kids."

"Well," Anne said, "what about the transition time? One of them is going to

be a teenager in a couple of years. How do you plan to loosen up so that that child will not rebel?"

"I really hadn't thought of that," the mother said.

It's important that we plan for the time when we'll begin to let go of our children. We need to tell them, "The day is coming when you're going to leave the house and go off to college, and home may never really be the same to you again. You'll be becoming your own person. You'll come home again, but it will probably be different."

It happened with us, and it happened with our children. They went away and got new ideas and discovered, for example, things to criticize in their home church. As they continued to go away and return home, their criticisms changed—they became more accepting of the church and less of some other things—but each time they returned, they had new observations about the home and community that used to be their whole world. This is a normal and desirable part of growing up.

As kids grow older, parents need to push them out more and more. We saw a cartoon one time of a mama dog standing in front of her puppies, and she seems to have both a tear in her eye and a grin on her face. "The time has come," she was saying to her pups, "for each of you to find a little boy to follow home." That's in a sense what parents eventually need to say to their children.

Preparing children to leave the nest is a gradual process that happens all through childhood and adolescence. If Jesus is our clue, the distancing may begin around age twelve. Sometimes you have to let go more, and sometimes you have to retighten your grip. Some kids, given freedom, become more and more independent, while others need a little more supervision.

When teenagers revert to childishness along the way, the parents have to revert to more controls. When they have a spurt of maturity, the parents need to affirm them and back off. You have their eventual independence in mind. Sometimes you need to say, "When you're controlled by the Lord, you're moving in the direction of total release from our guidance, but if you get in trouble, we'll be there to take more control again." They need to know you understand where they're going and that you will recognize their increasing maturity. They need to understand the process you have in mind.

One of our two sons is Nels, born fifteen years after the other three, and adopted at birth into our family. Several years ago he made his own decision to go 3,000 miles away to a private Christian high school—a very wonderful one. But by Christmas vacation he'd decided that he wanted to return home to stay. He was frightened by the heavy scholastic demands and just plain homesick.

We waited until a few days after Christmas, and then we spent a day together out in the desert to discuss the decision. We had fun, but we also talked tough with him. "You really are going back," we said. "We're not changing our minds. We don't want you to remember this as the year when you were a quitter. Next fall you can finish high school here at home again."

He was only fifteen but he was already over six feet tall, and it was hard to see this great big boy crying.

"You can't really mean it," he said, and we said, "Yes, we really do."

By the end of the afternoon he said, "All right, I'm going. I don't want to, but you guys are making me, so I'll go. But I want you to know one thing. Even though you're forcing me to go, we still love each other and we're still on the same old terms." It absolutely melted us!

But when Nels showed that he didn't yet have the stability to hang in there without our demanding it, we had to step in and provide the demand. We insisted that he complete the year he had started. By spring he had adjusted and he loved the school. Now he thanks us for making him stay.

Sometimes teens want more independence than their parents think they can handle. The parents are still responsible for their children's decisions, and this can create tension. For instance, if a son pays for his own car but Dad signs for it, who makes the decision if the son wants to trade it in or rebuild it? The decision affects both of them, so it has to be mutual.

Or perhaps a daughter wants to get married before her parents think she's

---

LETTING YOUR TEEN GO

We raised our children with the attitude that when they turned twenty, we'd help them pack and shove them out because Dick and I wanted to be alone. Though we always kidded them about it, they knew we weren't joking. They also knew our desires were prompted by love, not selfishness. We told them over and over again, all the time they were growing up, that they were going to make wonderful adults, and when they were adults, they weren't going to live with us. They knew they were going to have to make their own home. We started preparing them for that when they were very young.

It's not nice to pull that line on your child at sixteen. As soon as a teen turns sixteen, some parents give him his free will, loosen the reins, and all of a sudden become permissive parents. That isn't fair. We need to make letting go a gradual process that begins when the child is young.

Joyce Landorf

ready. It's perfectly fair for the parents to say no! Tensions may be there in abundance, but parental control is necessary when children are not yet ready for full responsibility. Tact, prayer, and mutual love will probably iron it all out.

Last year when Nels turned eighteen, we got a new line: "If I'm old enough to be drafted and killed in a war, then I'm old enough to do so and so." He thought that should work on any issue. We had to say, "It's true that you're old enough for this, but you're not old enough for that, and that's how it is." We also said sometimes, as we've said to each of our four, "You're an Ortlund. Maybe other kids can do so and so, but you can't. We're not responsible for how the other kids turn out, but we're responsible for you and we love you too much to let you do it." Nels has responded to that beautifully.

We gradually turn our children over to the Lord's total direction. We gradually prepare them for adult life. And gradually we also allow them to discover that failing is not the end of the world. They can pick themselves up and get going again. At points of failure we need quickly to identify with our children and recount some of our own failures. We can be so threatening to them if we appear to be only supersuccesses. In us they ought to be able to see that failure is not the end, and that life isn't really as risky as it looks, because our loving God is in control of both our failures and successes.

The ultimate goal is that our children become godly adults. They can't ever learn this unless they practice it. It's like learning to swim: you have to get in the water. And even though they're inexperienced, we have to let them practice being adults. Like the swimming instructor, we can stand by to help, but we can't do the swimming for them.

During your children's teen years, expect tensions, and don't feel guilty when they come. Tensions are the only way kids will ever get out of the nest and get on their own. There's no way to escape the push-pull of control and release, and the heat and friction caused by the process. There will be differences of opinion. The children will feel more mature than their parents think they are. All this will be at once both painful and normal—even healthy, because it eventually gets the children out on their own.

So there you have it: communicate well in advance that separation is coming. Communicate along the way that tensions happen to everybody. And communicate over and over that you still think your children are coming along fine and are going to turn out great.

Related Articles

Keep an Open Home!

V. GILBERT BEERS

Being a parent is a strange business. Our most important job is to work as hard as we can to work ourselves out of a job. I can't think of any other business quite like it. Can you?

We parents are, or should be, wholly committed to the job of gradually making our children independent, less and less dependent on us.

This whole process plays tricks on our thinking. We become increasingly involved in the lives of our teens to do our best job as parents. But as we become increasingly involved, we simultaneously become increasingly disengaged. The better we do, the less we are needed.

Let's put it this way. Ultimately a measure of your parental success will be how well you have given your son or daughter independence, and equipped that young person to live and lead life as an independent young adult. But to do this task to the best of your ability, you must spend much time, invest many prayers and much interest, and become deeply involved in that young person's life.

At first, it seems that these two run across each other's grain. But they don't. Increased involvement means turning up the love and sacrificial giving while you gradually loosen the strings that bind your teen to you. Loosening those strings is really not giving up your teen as much as it is building Christian maturity in that teen and refocusing his purposes and energies on living the Christian life as a mature adult.

Involving yourself in your teen's life is a building process, being a role model, a guide, and a counselor in his growth into Christian maturity. You also grow simultaneously, maturing in your view of a parent's ultimate role. As your young person matures into Christian adulthood, you become increasingly delighted as you become decreasingly responsible for that maturity.

What is more exciting and more fulfilling than to see your child become a responsible Christian teen, and then a mature Christian adult? What is more rewarding than knowing you have had an important part in this process? What is more wonderful than to see your teen, or older, become all you want him to be?

Parents who keep on thinking of their children as *dependent children* face an agonizing dilemma as their children head toward independence. Our job is to work as hard as we can to change our thinking and his—ours toward less dependence, his toward more independence.

Independence does not mean your child will love you less, or think less of you as a parent, or be less grateful for your parenting. It simply means an emerging view that your job is moving toward completion and his job is moving toward increased responsibility.

Parental attitudes during this process come to focus on the home, and the way you teach your teen to think of his home. Moving out of a home that has been a prison is easy. A young person wants to leave, not because he has matured and is ready to leave, but because he wants to get away from an undesirable atmosphere. That's the wrong way to send your young person into adult life.

Or if your older child is anxious to leave home because it is a place of tension, he will not likely move into a mature Christian life away from home. A home atmosphere saturated with love and affirmation—between mates, and between parents and children—will graduate young people excited about the idea of starting their own Christian home and family.

The Christian home should be a place where teens learn respect among family members, and thus love for one another. It is a place where Christ is an active member of the family, and will continue to be in their new home setting.

The Christian home is an open home, a home without prison walls that restrain the teen and thus create the illusion that he is locked in. An open home is a home with such love, warmth, acceptance, and affirmation that the teen will gravitate toward its magnetic center and seek to duplicate it later in his own home. It always remains a haven in life's storms.

The open Christian home is one where the teen can proudly bring his friends, and later his family. The subtle suggestion is, "I'm secure to move out beyond my home when I should, but I'm pleased to return to its magnetic Christian warmth at any time. And I know I will be welcomed with open arms."

Open home. Open arms. Children who

LIFT THEM UP

A while back we learned three techniques for effecting changed behavior in others from Sally Folger Dye, a missionary who shared her master's thesis with us. She called them "shape up," "pull up," and "lift up." She actually had in mind counseling techniques—but we immediately thought of child-raising.

The "shape up" technique is great for two-year-olds: "Shape up and obey me, or I will punish you." Simple, direct, effective for preschoolers.

The "pull up" technique works for the elementary school age child: "I will create goals for you, and I will pull you up toward them and help you achieve them. When you do, I will reward you." In other words, "Make your bed every day and we'll put stickers on the refrigerator, or do the following six things and earn a Scout merit badge."

Now the "lift up" technique requires an older age. It is much deeper, much more difficult, and much more wonderful when it is achieved. It says, "I will humble myself, and get under you, and lift you to act as you should." Using this technique is very risky. We lose our authority. We treat our children not even as equals but as superiors, and they may take advantage of us when they see they have the upper hand. We say to them, "Look, I know about your weaknesses because I have them too. If you pray for me, I'll pray for you, and let's help each other grow in Christ."

The "lift up" technique is the way Jesus chose to relate to us. He lowered Himself—this is what Philippians 2 is all about—in fact, He took a lower position than any of us has ever taken. He did it in full knowledge of the risk of being misunderstood or taken advantage of—but He did it knowing its power to "tenderize" us and humble us and make us repentant and desirous of change. It can have the same effect on our kids. Take off your mask.

Ray & Anne Ortlund

grow up in that atmosphere will surely want to duplicate it when the time is right.

The Battle for Independence

JIM & SALLY CONWAY

If, as parents, your target is to help your children mature, then while they are growing up, you will try to teach them every skill needed as adults. If you have done that, independence will not be a big hassle as the children enter the teen years. In many ways they will already be independent.

It's not a matter of saying, "OK, now you're sixteen. I'm going to teach you to be independent." If you have taught your child to handle finances, to purchase and care for his own clothes, to shop for groceries, to care for his room, to relate to people, to walk spiritually, to balance work and leisure, and have given him adventure along the way, then you have helped your child to become independent.

Our goal was to gradually give our daughters their independence as they were mature enough to take the responsibility and freedom that go with it. One way we did this was to teach them about finances—how to save money and how to spend it. It began with separate little jars in their dresser drawers. One jar was for money they would give at Sunday School, another for Pioneer Girls, and other jars were for other funds. One jar was for their own spending money.

To encourage saving, we always matched what they saved. If they had five

dollars, we gave another five. They also had a gift fund so that they would have money to spend when it was time to buy a birthday present. By letting them make their own saving and spending choices, we taught them independence.

When they got their driver's licenses, we let them take the car by themselves and practice around town. We had an agreement that they could not drive with anyone else in the car until they had a certain number of hours of experience. We didn't want them to be responsible for having other kids in the car until they had enough driving experience to handle it. They learned that along with the freedom of being able to drive came the responsibility to be safe drivers.

We also gave them errands to run for us. That way they got to use the car a lot and this also met their need for adventure. One daughter was allowed to take the car several times to visit her sisters in college three hours away.

Another way to encourage independence is to send your teens to the grocery store with a shopping list of certain items. If some of the items aren't available, they learn to make suitable substitutes, and then you can affirm their good choices. Or they can have responsibility for the upkeep of the car. Make these activities privileges, not assignments they have to do.

Jim showed our daughters how to put up dry wall when we were adding an addition to our house. Later they helped him build a fireplace. They know how to take care of the car, mow the lawn, trim the bushes, and work with plants and animals. They also learned how to cook and clean the house. Such abilities stimulate confidence. If teens feel you are pushing independence and encouraging it, they won't have to challenge you to get it.

But along with helping them gain independence, you can't forget that they still need some limits. There are times when you need to forbid them, flat out, to do something. We said to the girls from the beginning that we didn't want them involved in drugs. Driving fast in an automobile is something else we said no to.

We told them where the fences were. In between they could roam and do whatever they wanted, but they couldn't go outside those fences. That wasn't just because we said so, but because going outside the fences would cut off their future potential or damage them.

Perhaps we really need to teach children *inter*dependence. It would be a better focus for the teen years to reinforce that we need each other and we care for each other. Independence, after all, can be an escape. After you learn to stand on your own and know who you are, you need to

EMERGING FROM THE COCOON

Caterpillars spin and moths emerge and fly off on beautiful wings. It's a natural process that only takes time and the right environment. Our teens are trying to emerge as adults and fly on their own, but children are not insects, and parents are involved.

As loving parents, we realize (mentally) that one day our sons and daughters must leave home and live as adults. After all, that's what all our discipline and nurture have been about. But *emotionally* it is so tough to let go. The apron strings give us a sense of worth and a reason to live.

Also we are afraid that they may fail, be hurt, or repeat our mistakes. These are legitimate fears, but still we must let go.

The two key words in this process of "breaking away" are *relationship* and *trust*. *Relationship* means really knowing our kids, their strengths, weaknesses, dreams, fears, desires, and feelings about us. If the relationship is strong, we will be able to express honestly *our* fears for them, and we will be ready for their move. Distance and age cannot break the bond of love, and we can be secure in knowing this.

Trust means giving them responsibilities without checking up on their slightest move. It means avoiding those condescending remarks, and giving them opportunities to be "adult." This is not a "carte blanche" invitation to do anything they want, but it does mean giving them guidelines with the understanding that they can gain freedom by playing by the rules (for example, encouraging them to call if they know they are going to be late). When you give them an assignment, decide on a checkup time so your teens are expecting it and won't feel like they are being nagged. Trust is built piece by piece but may be destroyed in a moment. Build it together.

YFC Editors

learn how you can use your knowledge and skills to help other people.

The teen years were really fun years for us. Our daughters could think about ideas with us and we could talk on an adult level with them. They were very involved in caring for others and were friendly with a broad spectrum of people.

Sometimes our first reaction was, "Don't have anything to do with these kids because they will lead you astray." But our girls appreciated them as people, focused on their good qualities, and then reached out to help them. We would overhear phone conversations where they would guide friends in reading the Bible and thinking through issues of life.

This also drew us into a peer relationship with our teens. They would share a discussion they were having and ask what we thought.

Some parents have an internal resistance when their kids start to become *inter*dependent, because they haven't worked it through themselves. Parents who are secure in themselves can take an objective look at their relationship with their children and allow them the freedom to grow up.

As Christian parents, we have a strong desire to have our kids turn out right. Some parents get very rigid with their teens, hoping a tight structure will ensure success. But pat rules and a strict framework is not the answer. Rigidity is not the way to bring about maturity. In our family we found that flexibility and openness were much more helpful.

Related Articles

What's Right for You May Not Be Right for Your Teen

EVELYN CHRISTENSON

I remember Nancy saying to me one day, "Mother, is it still sin to do what was sin when you were a girl?" I said, "Well, Nancy, what does God's Word say about that? Let's go to where you are reading devotionally."

She happened to be in Ephesians 1, so we sat down and read it silently together until God stopped Nancy at verse 8, which talks about God's wisdom. She looked up and said to me, "God's saying to me that I will be judged not by what I think or what you think but by what He thinks."

Nancy was right. When a teen has a different viewpoint than the parent, the parent must realize that if the teen is a Christian and God is working in that child's life, then God is number one. Just because a parent thinks the teen is wrong doesn't necessarily mean that the teen is wrong. It does mean, however, that we had better find out what is right; and to discover that, we have to go to the Bible. It doesn't matter what either of us thinks. We both may be right or we both may be wrong.

By going to the Bible, parents teach their teenagers that God's Word is where to find answers. It's not easy to say, "Just because I think it, doesn't mean my opinion is right. Let's go to the Word and find out what God says." But the fact remains that God's Word, not the parents', is the final authority.

All parents look back and see things they wish they had done differently, things they wish they had not said, or decisions they had not made. Because parents can be wrong, they need to rely on God's Word instead of trusting their frail, imperfect human understanding.

Of course, there are gray areas, where God's answer is neither black nor white. In those cases, parents have a responsibility to talk with their teens, and pray *with* them and *for* them. This happened many times with my teens and my prayer was, "God, You deal with that teen the way You want to. If what that teen is doing is not right in Your eyes, then rebuke him, send reproof into his life, make him so miserable he can't stand it. But if this is the way you want him to go, then Lord, send peace and assurance into his life and undergird him in it."

There were times when I simply had to say, "That's my teen's business, not mine." Parents have to realize that their teens are responsible to God. This doesn't mean we don't talk with them, that we don't multiply our prayers for them. We let them know we still love them, but we also let them know exactly where we stand and that we don't approve of what they are doing.

When Bad Is Bad

There are times when a teen and his parents go to God's Word and it's clear the parents are right. In dealing with this situation, it helps if we have already built a foundation of the importance of obeying God. We then can point out that the teen is a child of God, and has been brought up to obey Him. We can remind the teen that obeying God makes things turn out for his good. Then, all we can do is pray about it and trust God.

The teen might repent and obey, but there's no guarantee. After all, we don't always obey everything God tells us, either. We still rebel and go our own stubborn way and do things that are the opposite of God's will.

So we need to remember that, like ourselves, our teens have a free will and they can rebel against God. They can rebel against God even if they know what His Word says. Or they might try to twist His Word and look at it from a worldly point of view, saying, "*This* is what feels good to me and I can't believe that the God of love would expect *that* of me."

I've had parents ask me what to do if their grown son or daughter is living with someone and the two of them come home for a visit. If I were in that situation, I would explain that we have rules in our house, God's rules, and if they want to live in absolute rebellion outside of God's will (which cohabitation obviously is) there is nothing I, as a parent, can do about it outside of my house. But in my house they won't live like that. The parents can pray for them, counsel them, and love them, but they don't have to accept that kind of behavior in their house.

It's important to remember that the teen, not the parents, is ultimately accountable to God for his actions. Many times, as parents, we like to play God and give the impression that we are ultimately responsible. But as much as we might want to be, we're not. Starting at about ten years of age, we made it clear to our children that we had taught them what was right, and they knew what was right. If they still did what was wrong that was their business, but God was not going to hold us as parents responsible.

Raising Teens to Make Right Choices

GORDON MacDONALD

I'm responsible for one thing—to create an environment in which my children can grow to a point of maturity where they can make good choices. I am not responsible for the choices they make. I'm responsible only to the extent that I've made them free to make good choices.

All of us have seen homes where, though the parents have done a bang-up job, the kids turn out to be monsters. We've also seen terrible homes where the kids turn out to be saints. To blame parents for the way their kids turn out would be like blaming God because every human being hasn't turned out to be a beautiful person.

When God created us He gave us His image and certain capacities and gifts. Ultimately, He gave us the choice-making responsibility. I think that's what a parent does. He raises his children to make good choices. And that process takes twenty years. We have a little saying at our house. It started when Kristi was in seventh grade. She was trying to decide whether or not to stay in the public school or go to the local Christian school. She was under strong peer pressure to go to one place or the other. It was really hard for her to decide. She realized that if she went to one school some friends would turn against her and if she went to the other school, she would lose other friends.

Tulip or Oak?

One Sunday evening I took her into the living room and said, "Honey, let me put your problem this way: Girls and boys are sometimes like tulips, and sometimes like oak trees. When an oak tree is in your path you walk around it because it is very strong and it can stand by itself. But when there is a tulip in the path you sometimes build a fence around it because someone might step on it. We need to know on any given day whether we feel like an oak tree or a tulip. I want to know on the basis of where you are right now, are you a tulip or an oak tree?"

She said, "Daddy, I'm a tulip."

So I said, "OK, then God provided your mother and father as a fence. And what I am saying is, if you are a tulip, then we're prepared to help you make this decision to protect you. We may be able to see a larger part of the decision that you can't right now. Let's make it together instead of you making it alone." That made a lot of sense to her.

Since then, as the years have gone by, we've used that code phrase on many occasions when she was wrestling with a decision. I would ask her again if she was a tulip or an oak tree. More and more frequently she has come to the point where she is an oak tree. That's just fine. If she has come to me and said, "Dad, today I feel like a tulip," I say, "OK, let's put up the fence."

I think teenagers need that kind of relationship with their parents. A daughter has to know that at any moment she can revert to girlhood or spring up to womanhood and that her father will play the game either way. I guess that is what we learned over the years in our home. Within reason we allowed our kids to be either children or adults. We would relate to them on whatever basis seemed best.

Selective Release

I think it's important for parents to pursue what I call *the process of selective release.* You learn to recognize when your children move from tulips to oak trees. They are going to do it unevenly and in specific areas of their lives. Some will do it in their fourteenth year and others in their seventeenth year. It will vary from child to child and from family to family. That means several things.

First, parents should never be intimidated by what another family is doing or not doing. Back in the tenth, eleventh, and twelfth years of our children's lives, we said, "Now don't ever assume that we're going to bend our wills because you have a friend whose parents are doing such and so. We are going to run our family the way that is best for us. No other family is going to dictate our decision-making."

Second, even the kids in the family must not become the basis for how parents relate to another person in the family. Because I allowed Kristi to do certain things did not mean that I was going to allow Mark to do the same. I wanted to practice this principle of selective release. As a child showed maturity he would earn the right to a greater amount of release. I'll give you an example that goes back many years. When Mark was eight or nine, I noticed

that I never had to tell him to go to bed. He always went to bed at the same time whether or not anyone mentioned it. We never had a specific "bedtime" for Mark for about six or seven years because he showed very early the ability to choose his own bedtime responsibly. On certain occasions when he chose to stay up twenty or thirty minutes later I wouldn't say a word because I knew it was just a break in his normal pattern. Kids who stayed overnight would go home and tell their parents that we didn't have any bedtime for our children. The parents would come to us and ask if our kids had to go to bed at a certain time. We just replied that we never had to set a bedtime; that our kids just did it on their own.

I think as kids prove themselves in various categories of character and development, parents should be quick to release them. Maybe even five to ten percent ahead of the exact moment when they deserve the release. We have tried to practice that with both of our kids. We allowed them to earn rights and privileges. The minute that they got very close to a mark, we granted the earned privilege.

Related Articles

How to Help Your Teenager Become Independent

DAN SARTIN

During the seventeenth century, an isolated British island known as St. Kilda, 110 miles off the coast of Scotland, was a thriving community. Its lifestyle was dictated by the geography of the land—a plateau surrounded by sheer rock cliffs plunging 200 feet to the ocean below.

For some reason, the cliffs attracted thousands of birds which nested at the base of the rock walls, so naturally the tiny island focused its economy on catching those birds for food and commerce. The feathers brought good prices from an occasional ship passing by on its way to England or other distant places.

The island people were known as cragsmen and became very efficient at catching these birds. They did it by securing a rope over the cliff and swinging down to snatch a bird.

By age sixteen, boys were full-fledged cragsmen, displaying great courage and skill. They were considered mature and ready for marriage when they completed what was called the "Ritual of the Mistress Stone." The young boys were required to balance on one foot at the very edge of a sheer precipice that fell 200 feet to the ocean waves pounding on jagged rocks. It was necessary for them to hold this position until all their friends were satisfied. Needless to say, some did not make it.

The story of the cragsmen gives us a vivid example of how *not* to give responsibility to our children. It illustrates one of the main reasons why we as parents should be in control of the release of our children. If we do not encourage their quest for independence, others will take our place and assume that position. If your children are not able to gain your approval of their adulthood, then they will resort to proving it in front of others and it could be dangerous to psychologically place your child on that same type of cliff.

Where, then, can we find a good method or program for helping our children become independent adults? I feel that the following steps would be wise and advisable for you to consider.

First, you must seek to understand yourself and present to your children the most mature adult model you possibly can. You can continue to positively influence your children for many years if your life presents a desirable model for them to follow.

Second, you must be willing to help them recognize the responsibilities of adulthood. Begin to identify the responsibilities you have been required to carry since you became an adult. I'm sure you will include such items as: handling a budget, personal grooming, work responsibilities, health and exercise, spiritual growth, social graces and handling people, recognizing weaknesses and correcting them, making decisions, handling a sex life, and coping with stress in our fast-paced society.

Once you have carefully decided the areas you feel are important for your children to understand, it is time to begin showing these areas to them one at a time. As each child becomes older, the need for structure and control diminishes. So, you should begin to give responsibility to your child and help him or her carry the areas that are difficult.

The key to helping your child carry responsibility is first to allow him to discuss it with you, and if at all possible to see *you* handle it. This should involve creative learning experiences where the two of you do something together in hopes that your child might learn from it.

The traditional Passover supper is one example of this principle being used to help children remember the Exodus from Egypt. The children were deeply involved in the whole experience, from searching for the unleavened bread to the traditional questions asked by the youngest child about the entire proceeding. After such an experience, few children could forget how it was performed.

Ken Poure, in his book, *Parents, Give Your Kid a Chance,* uses a birthday box each year to give certain areas of responsibility to his children. The idea is that total responsibility is given in progressively larger areas of life. Each birthday brings a new box, and whatever goes into the fourteen-year-old box is completely dependent on how well the child took care of his thirteen-year-old responsibilities. The contents of each box are decided by the parents and the child.

These *total responsibilities* you give to your child (the areas in which he or she is completely responsible) should be combined with *shared responsibilities* (those areas in which you still help your child). After a specific amount of time, each shared responsibility is placed in the total responsibility box. From that point forward, that responsibility rests totally on the child and it then becomes the parents' unique role to give assistance when the child falls.

On pages 458-460 you will find a suggested program for helping your children grow into independent and mature adults. It covers the junior high (ages 13-15) and high school (ages 16-18) years, and outlines specific ways to begin the process of releasing your children from your authority.

Starting with a child's thirteenth birthday, there are three key things you should do during each year of his or her adolescence. First, determine to have discussion sessions with him to study and learn things that may be unclear to him (called the "Rap Session"). Second, determine the responsibilities that you should share with your child over the next year (called the "Yoke Box"). Third, determine the responsibilities that should be totally on the shoulders of your child (called the "Birthday Box"). It should be noted that the examples of the various responsibilities listed under each age-group are only suggestions. Remember that each family and each individual child are different and unique, and children will therefore progress at varying paces.

Related Articles

SUGGESTED PROGRAM FOR PREPARING TEENAGERS FOR INDEPENDENCE

Junior High School (ages 13-15)
Age 13

This Birthday Box is very special because it is the first one. It should be introduced in a special way with a party or an evening date. Together the parents and child should decide what ingredients should be contained in the boxes.

The Rap Session
(family discussion time)
Parents should recognize the physical and sexual changes occuring in their child at this time and be prepared to discuss sex with him. Studying a book together, such as *The Stork Is Dead,* by Charlie Shedd, or *Preparing for Adolescence,* by James Dobson, could give good structure for discussions. The important thing is to help the child feel free to seek advice and help from you. Give him enough information to make wise decisions concerning sex.

The Yoke Box
(shared responsibilities between parent and child)
  • Maintenance of the lawn equipment
  • Personal grooming and dress
  • Handling money and a personal budget
  • Family Bible study

The Birthday Box
(child's exclusive responsibilities)
  • Design and organization of room
  • Maintenance of the yard
  • An allowance mutually agreed on

Age 14

If the child fulfilled the responsibilities of the Birthday Box for last year, then the box is expanded to include new areas. If the responsibilities were not fulfilled, then privileges and freedoms are removed. Parents should not always bail out the child who has wasted his freedoms and not fulfilled his responsibilities. A child must recognize that there are consequences to mistakes. This is an important factor in learning responsibility.

The Rap Session
The social struggles children suffer at this age make this a good time to work through books on social graces and presentation. *Man in Demand* (for boys) and the *Christian Charm Course* (for girls) are excellent for this purpose.

The Yoke Box
  • Decisions concerning group social events
  • Maintenance and repair of the family car
  • Setting a family budget
  • Planning a family supper

The Birthday Box
  • Maintenance of lawn equipment and yard
  • Choice of clothes
  • Handling a personal weekly budget
  • Curfew of 9 P.M. during the week, 10 P.M. on weekends

Age 15

This is the year that many states allow teenagers to acquire a learner's permit for driving. So parents need to become actively involved in helping their young person learn about automobile safety and responsibility.

The Rap Session
Many young people drop out of church at this age because they lose interest in something that is not personal. Now is an excellent time to discuss with them the facts of faith and the reasons behind it. *Know What You Believe* and *Know Why You Believe,* by Paul E. Little, are more than adequate for these discussions.

The Yoke Box
  • Driving the car with parents present
  • Balancing the family checkbook
  • Group dating
  • Planning a family vacation
  • Part-time jobs

The Birthday Box
  • Passing driving test for license
  • Choice of friends
  • Balancing a monthly budget
  • Leading family devotions for two months
  • Telephone time limit
  • Maintenance of family automobile fluid levels, rotate tires (with supervision), and change oil once during the year

High School (ages 16-18)
Age 16

The beginning of high school is very exciting for young people, and also very fearful. Parents must try to be sensitive to the feelings of their sixteen-year-olds. It is important to recognize the pressures teens face from their peers, and the great desire all young people have to feel accepted. In the midst of these troubles, children need your support, not your condemnation.

The Rap Session
(family discussion time)

Learning how to get along with other people is very important during this time. Family discussions on friendships and how to treat others would be of value. *Building Up One Another,* by Gene Getz, would be a helpful resource for these discussions.

The Yoke Box
(shared responsibilities between
parent and child)

- Let your teen observe how you acquire tags, inspections, and insurance for your auto
- Help your teen select a physical stress camp to help him establish personal confidence (examples: American Wilderness Institute, Outward Bound, snow skiing, etc.)
- Let your teen observe you or your spouse at work several days during the year
- Let your teen select and implement a family ministry project at a special time of the year

The Birthday Box
(child's exclusive responsibilities)

- Balancing the family checkbook for three months
- Choosing one spiritual conference to attend during the year
- Driving the car alone
- Double dating
- Having a personal activity with each family member sometime during the year
- Require forty hours of volunteer work at any church or civic organization
- Curfew of 10 P.M. during the week, 11 P.M. on weekends

Age 17

The parents' job of developing maturity and independence in their child is almost complete by this age, and a young person is usually looking for direction concerning the future. Patience is of great value during this time of confusion, but parents can help their child consider options concerning those tough decisions.

The Rap Session

This is an excellent time to discuss areas such as finding God's will, making good decisions, and setting priorities in life. You will find a multitude of good books focusing on these areas.

The Yoke Box

- Assisting in the maintenance of the home
- Touring colleges for consideration
- Opening a personal checking and savings account
- Selecting part-time jobs

The Birthday Box

- Paying at least one-half the cost of all social events
- Assisting in family driving needs
- Balancing his own bank account
- Selecting a personal ministry project
- Single dating
- Curfew of 10:30 P.M. during the week, 12 A.M. on weekends

Age 18

For many young people, this is their last year at home. College, marriage, and work soon sweep them into their own independent lives. Treasure these precious moments.

The Rap Session

Graduation from high school is the consuming thought of the year. This is a good time to discuss marriage, loneliness, and how to interview for a job. *After Graduation,* by Tim Stafford, is a good book covering the many concerns of this age-group. It should stimulate a good family discussion.

The Yoke Box

- Assisting in income tax preparation
- Assisting in buying a car (50/50?)
- Learning how to wash clothes, iron, etc.
- Learning how to cook
- Assisting in college financing

The Birthday Box
- Maintaining the house
- Responsibility for his car's gas, tag, insurance, and upkeep
- Selecting and keeping a job
- Selecting a college or trade
- Curfew of 11 P.M. during the week and 1 A.M. on weekends
- Attending church

Age 19 Until Separation

This age-group is considered mature in our country by most legal standards. Young people this age are characterized by a great fear of failure coupled with a great excitement about the new freedom they possess. This is one of the most crucial times of their lives because for the first time they become almost totally vulnerable to negative influences. As new adults, they must stand on their own two feet.

It is true that as adolescents mature, their affection for friends increases. However, there is no evidence that this results from a diminished affection for parents. Thus, for older adolescents to care for friends more does not mean they care for their parents any less.

Once children leave home to attend school or get married, parents should help them in every manner possible to set up house. Encourage them in their faith and give them lots of positive feedback about the life they have chosen. If mistakes are evident, then certainly give guidance, for it will usually be welcome if you have prepared your children for independence in an open and flexible manner.

Your child's development in most areas of independence is near completion. Parents now have another adult under their roof. At this point many parents ask their teenagers for a cut-off date, a certain period of time or a certain age when they plan to move out of the house for good. This gives a teenager latitude to consider the direction of his or her life. If parents have communicated love through the whole growing-up experience, then the child will respond in genuine love as well. Now all you have to do as parents is sit back and watch the results!

In summary, this suggested program for helping your children grow into independent adults is not meant to be a complete guide or program. It is really meant to be a tool that can and should be adjusted to fit any particular young person. The boxes of responsibility can be filled with any activity or job, at the discretion of parents and youth. But as mentioned earlier, keep in mind that all children are different. The boxes suggested may need different time frames depending on the circumstances and the child. A young person may need more than one year of assistance in carrying a certain responsibility, but for others it may take only a few months.

James Dobson has said in his book, *Dare to Discipline*, that parents must gain their freedom from the child, so that the child can gain his freedom from the parents. This method of combining shared responsibilities with total responsibilities should provide the motivation for your child to be a self-starter.

The end product should consist of a young adult who can handle the responsibilities of life. And for you as parents it will provide an ongoing relationship with each of your children in the years to come.

You should seek, as parents, to be authentic and honest in your evaluation of yourselves. You should seek to become proper adult role models for your children. But most importantly, you are to help your children recognize the responsibility they must carry when they are on their own. Hopefully you can accomplish this by helping your children carry the yoke of responsibility just long enough for them to become accustomed to it.

When to Start Letting Go

DAN SARTIN

Sooner or later there must come a time of decision when you say to each of your children, "Now you will begin to carry responsibility for yourself, because you are no longer a child."

In Bible times, children were usually weaned at between two and a half and three years of age, and became responsible adults at thirteen. As a result, both boys and girls often married when they were very young. Later, the rabbis fixed the minimum age for marriage at twelve for girls and thirteen for boys.

Adolescence appears to be a phenomenon of the past century, since the Industrial Revolution. Since that time the legal age of marriage has risen from thirteen and fourteen for girls and boys respectively, to eighteen and twenty-one. At the same time, the age of puberty has fallen from eighteen to thirteen. Today teens are becoming sexually mature five to seven years before they are free to marry or be accepted as adults.

There is no specific Greek or Hebrew word to characterize adolescence in the Bible. The common word for *youth* is translated "boy," "lad," or "youth," and can be speaking of a lad just weaned (1 Sam. 1:24), or of someone of marriageable age (Gen. 34:19).

In an article aptly titled "Growing Up Too Late, Too Soon," Ronald Koteskey writes, "Until recently the age for responsibility has been twelve or thirteen. Hebrew boys go through bar mitzvah at age thirteen and read a part of the Torah in the synagogue as their first religious acts as adults. From about age six or seven, Roman boys were the constant companions of their fathers on the farm, military field, or in the forum. They learned in the school of life. During the Middle Ages, German youths were freed from their fathers' authority when they were able to bear arms, about twelve to fifteen years of age. Among Anglo-Saxons, boys were made freemen, responsible for their own behavior, at the completion of their twelfth year" (*Christianity Today,* March 13, 1981, p 24).

As you can see, it is certainly possible that adolescence could be unique to this century, and therefore causes greater anxiety for parents in handling the process of "letting their teens go" to become adults.

In helping your teenagers move toward independence, one of the most helpful things is to set an age at which you will begin to release your children from your authority. But while this is helpful, it is one of the most difficult things for parents to do. Why? Because sometimes you might receive a sense of meaning and even power from being in charge, or in control of your household (Jay Kesler, *Too Big to Spank,* p. 37). Or, it could be that you do not want to face the fact that your children are growing up. Still another reason is that some parents have an emotional dependence on their children. In essence, the husband and wife are emotionally separated and it is the children who are keeping them together. Finally, there may be a fear that you have not done a good job as parents, and that your children will fail when they strike out on their own (Charles R. Swindoll, *You* and Your Child, pp. 145-148).

But, there does come a point when you are accountable, though not responsible, for the actions of your children. You must loosen the reins to allow them to make decisions on their own.

It appears to me that age thirteen is a good time to start, because at this time your child has entered the "blooming body" growth spurt. In addition, the sexual onset of puberty is beginning around this age. It is a good point in life for you to start making changes with your child. Ken Poure and his family have done just that: "We started our program when our kids first became teenagers. All kids look forward to that day, so we made it special. We had what we called a 'growing up' party, or a spiritual 'bar mitzvah.' From that point on we recognized our children as young men or young women"

(Parents, Give Your Kid a Chance, pp. 83-84).

If your child has passed his thirteenth birthday, then release should begin as soon as possible. This could also be an excellent opportunity to establish good communication with your child who may want little to do with the family at this point in life.

If you fail to set an age of release, and don't faithfully work toward it, your child's adolescence could be prolonged to age twenty-two, twenty-three, or twenty-four. Help your child to begin early, so that by age eighteen or nineteen he can make wise and intelligent decisions concerning his own life.

Related Article
Chapter 20: How to Help Your Teenagers Become Independent

The Empty Nest

EVELYN CHRISTENSON

One secret of adjusting to an empty nest is for both parents to find places where others need them before the nest empties. This eased my transition to an empty nest. As the children were growing up but still at home, I taught several studies on prayer, but I was only gone for an evening or two a week, and rarely more than two weekends a year.

When the children finally were independent and no longer living at home, my ministry just exploded. I believe this was because I had been faithful in raising my children and God knew I could be faithful in even bigger things.

If parents are doing something part-time prior to the children's departure, all they need to do is to expand their ministry and go full-time when the children leave.

Though it will still be hard to see the children go, the parents can be thankful that God has called them to a different ministry, whatever it may be.

So, while we're raising our children, we shouldn't ignore God's call to other areas. We can develop obedience to God's call while the children are still at home, and then as they leave, we can thank God that we will have more time to do the job to which He has called us.

Redefining Your Role As a Grandparent
One way I've redefined my role with my daughters now that they are married is that I don't call their husbands sons-in-law, but sons-in-love. I didn't realize before my daughters were married that I

462

could love my sons-in-law as much as my own children, but I do. In all my dealings with them, I try to love them selflessly. I don't attempt to control them though. They control their own homes, children, and lives.

As my daughters have had children, I've become even closer to them, as they understand more of what I went through as a parent. Being a grandparent is the greatest thing that's ever happened to anybody. My daughters tease me and tell me that I'm absolutely bananas over those children, and I am.

I've found that praying for my grandchildren is so important. The minute I

GETTING TEENS TO LEAVE THE NEST

I've seen a number of parents who have been too giving when their teens need a firmer hand. By going along with their adolescents' refusal to take on responsibility, these parents have contributed to their kids' eventual downfall.

Take the example of the adolescent who doesn't want to leave the nest. He's eighteen, but he doesn't want to go to school or get a full-time job. So he gets a part-time job and spends the rest of his time drinking and running around with friends.

"Look," his parents say, "you're going to have to get a full-time job and move out on your own. You're eighteen and you're not going to school."

"I can't move out unless I have a full-time job," he says.

"Well, go get one," the parents reply. But when it comes to really looking for a job, the kid won't do it—he doesn't want to leave home. So the parents let him stay.

The parents may think they're rescuing the child by letting him stay, but there comes a time when too much rescuing simply contributes to the young person's irresponsibility. The teen learns to think, "Hey, why bother to go out and earn a living? I've got free room and board here, as long as I can con my parents."

We have to be like eagles then, pushing our kids out of the nest—even though it can cause us agony. In one case, the parents had to take all the teenager's belongings and pack them in his car. "You're on your own," they told him. "We gave you two months to look for a place; you didn't look. We told you that on this date we would move you out, and here it is."

The shock got that teen moving. Perhaps in another case the adolescent would have responded by living in his car and continuing to bum around with his friends. But that would have been *his* choice.

This is especially important when other family members are adversely affected by the teen's presence. Let's say there are four children in the family, and the oldest at seventeen is using drugs. The other three kids are young and impressionable. If that seventeen-year-old is incorrigible, the parents might have to decide to move him elsewhere for the sake of the other three.

That's one of the hardest decisions you can make. But it's better to have a chance with the other three than to waste all your effort in a futile attempt to help the one who refuses to be helped.

Norman Wright

learned they had been conceived, I started praying every day that God would fill them with Himself, even while they were being formed in the womb. I prayed for whatever was being formed that day—a little finger, or an attitude—that God would touch them with His Spirit.

The Gospels talk about how people brought their babies to Jesus and how He held them and touched them and prayed for them. I've asked God, since Jesus isn't here to do those things bodily for my grandbabies, that through me my grandchildren will feel Jesus' touch; that my touch will be Jesus' touch, my words Jesus' words, my prayers Jesus' prayers. I want them to experience Jesus through me.

Related Article

Chapter 20: Keep an Open Home!

WHEN A CHILD DOESN'T WANT TO LEAVE

I've met many parents whose children don't want to leave home. Yet there comes a time when parents must encourage their child to leave. Why? For one reason, it's not fair to the child because he's not able to develop as he should if he remains at home. He's not learning to become an independent and responsible person. His parents are allowing him to lean on someone else.

It's also not fair to the parents to have to keep doing the laundry, grocery shopping, and cooking for an adult child. There comes a time to tell, or gently show, the child that he needs to be independent of his parents.

Evelyn Christenson

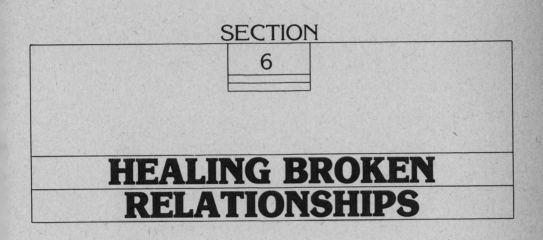

SECTION

6

HEALING BROKEN RELATIONSHIPS

WHEN THE FAMILY SPLITS UP

- Divorce and separation—how is the teenager affected?
- Raising teenagers as a single parent
- The challenges of stepparenting
- The absent parent—"I live with my
- kids but don't really get to see them much"
- What to do when family members (including children) are too busy to interact with each other

Few words are as filled with pathos as the word *separated.* When separation results from death, children face one kind of pain. In our culture, however, most separations result from incompatibility between husband and wife, a breakdown of commitment, estrangement, and finally divorce. Many of us who work with young people believe there is no disjuncture as serious as that caused by divorce.

Teenagers hurt by divorce may blame themselves or society, or they may be unable to blame anyone. They may simply lash out and destroy themselves or those around them. In a common laboratory experiment, mice are put on an electrified cage floor. As electricity is run through the wire mesh, the mice, unable to locate the source of their pain, begin to attack each other or to mutilate themselves. This is a picture of many young people who are forced, through no choice of their own, to live with only fragments of their original families.

Divorce and Separation

How Your Teenager Is Affected

JAY KESLER

It is not the purpose of this article to deal with the pros and cons of divorce or even the biblical arguments for or against divorce and remarriage. To spend a lot of energy on "We ought to," "We should have," "Why didn't we?" "How did it all happen?" is often unproductive. The simple facts are many people have divorced and society has given tacit approval to divorce as a solution to marital conflict. Now what?

Divorce, like all other sins, is not condoned by God. In fact, in Matthew 19:3-9, Jesus had a lengthy discussion with the Pharisees about the issue and indicated that divorce was a part of that culture not because God desired it; but because of the hardness of the people's hearts, He permitted it. Divorce is, in some senses, by its very nature an object lesson of the nature of sin. Sin is disjuncture. Sin is alienation. Sin is fragmentation of relationship. Sin is division. All of these things can be said of divorce. And so one can expect that the results of divorce will be very severe for all concerned.

I have spent a great deal of time with divorced people, talking with them about their lives and relationships. Seldom, if ever, have I met people who would honestly say that divorce was, for them, a good experience. It is often the least objectionable of their alternatives and has led them from deep pain to a new start in life, but all say that the experience itself leaves permanent scars that time, indeed, does not heal.

God, of course, is able to forgive all of our sins through Jesus Christ—that's one of the miracles of the new birth. God does not put divorce outside of His promises. People can be forgiven for having divorced and can be healed of the scars of their divorces in the same way that they can be healed of other scars. There is, however, scar tissue that remains in the lives of all those involved. Children who are victims of divorce carry permanent, lasting marks on their persons and characters. This is not to say that they cannot understand these, cannot work through them, cannot overcome them, and even be better persons for having struggled. But they are facts of the relationship just the same and will always continue to affect the family.

In order for the miracle of forgiveness and reconciliation to take place in a family fragmented by divorce, I believe responsible parents need to do several things. First, each person must acknowledge before God his or her own contribution to the situation and acknowledge it forthrightly as sin—sins either of omission (indifference, insensitivity, carelessness, etc.) or commission (unfaithfulness, abuse, etc.). Until divorced persons bring to God the sin of divorce and the thousand other sins committed in the process and seek His forgiveness, they'll never truly get beyond it.

Having confessed the sin to God and having allowed Christ's forgiveness to cover it and put it in the past, the parties need to go to one another and acknowledge that they realize there are two sides to every issue. (You can't slice bread so thin that there aren't two sides.) Unless they are willing to acknowledge their contribution to the breakup, and ask forgiveness of their ex-mate, they will never really have peace of mind.

Third, the husband and wife involved in divorce have to conscientiously and before God look at their responsibility toward children and others—family members and friends—who surrounded them and were part of their lives while they were married. This is obviously easier to do when both members of the marriage feel some responsibility toward

WHO GETS THE KIDS?

Who gets the kids is an issue which, on the surface, seems relatively easy to resolve, especially for the adults involved in a divorce. Too many times this issue is settled based on what is best for the parents rather than what is best for the children. The children become like pawns in a chess game—moved wherever and whenever it is convenient.

This is very true in the area of visitation rights. The question is not, "What do the children want or desire or need?" but "What is best for Mom or Dad?" The same holds true when splitting the children up for the summer if there is more than one child. Once again, are the children's feelings and desires considered or is it simply a matter of what is the most convenient for the parents?

Custody and visitation rights may be mere legal red tape to many divorcing parents, but to kids caught in the middle, it can do irreparable emotional harm.

Al Cocannouer

God and some desire to rectify things in His eyes. If they don't agree on this issue, then surely the believing spouse must do all he or she can do to bring about as positive a situation as possible. This involves sitting down with the children and explaining to them that often adults get involved in situations that they don't truly understand and act sinfully and unworthily.

I think each parent owes the other one the courtesy and dignity of telling the children that they dare not go through life feeling that one party was totally guilty. The parents must accept mutual responsibility for the breakup and allow the children to understand that here are two adults unable to solve their problems and honor their commitment. It is also important to expose the children to the pain, personal hurt, and frustration that exist because the parents have chosen this "out." Kids need to hear their parents say how painful divorce really is and how lacking it is as a solution. It would have been better if things could have been worked out.

Parents owe it to children to tell them that they (the children) were not responsible for the divorce. Many children, deep inside, feel that they caused the divorce because while Mom and Dad were having their marital battle, the kids were having their own problems with behavior and obedience. Thus these children feel that divorce is God's way of punishing them for their misdeeds. Responsible parents must sit down with children, especially younger kids, and help them understand that these things are totally unrelated. Of course, older children are generally more aware of the family situation and what led to the breakup. Still, parents should not assume too much.

Both of the divorced parents need to continually reassure the children that they love them. They should also commit themselves to fairness in their relationships with the children and determine not to cut down each other or drive a wedge between family members. In short, they should commit themselves to make the best out of a very bad and difficult situation. I believe people involved in divorce and separation need to do the same kind of thing with their friends, rather than seeking allies or further sandbagging themselves against their former spouse.

The New Testament admonition that "love covers a multitude of sins" (1 Peter 4:8) is speaking of the application of loving principles to very difficult and sinful areas such as divorce. Responsible people who have divorced should attempt to apply love (i.e., responsible behavior) by lessening divorce's effect on innocent parties. Though they *can't* undo the wrong that's been done, they *can* try to ease the pain. To start off on a new foot without giving care to the rebuilding of these broken and bruised relationships is to build one's future on a foundation that is crumbling.

What about remarriage? There is a rather old pop tune that extols how much better things are the "second time around." It is possible; they can be. But one dare not start the second time around and repeat the same old mistakes or he is guilty of the grossest of all insensitivities. This is perhaps the reason why, as you read the New Testament, you sense the severe nature of the prohibitions against the breaking up of the family. It is in the family that we can enjoy the deepest relationships with God, but it is also in the family that we can hurt one another the most.

Divorced persons need to team with other divorced persons in the church or other Christian context. They need to learn from one another, support one another, and help one another in the rebuilding process. It's not so much a matter of doing it once, that is, sitting down with the children or sitting down with one's former spouse or explaining things to friends and neighbors; it's a matter of entering into a quality of life that is redemptive in its very nature and demeanor. I suppose there's a sense in which a formerly married person is always a formerly married person; therefore there's a certain sobriety and seriousness about the way he or she approaches relationships now that is uncharacteristic of people who have never experienced the hurt. It is this contriteness and humility of heart, this willingness to seek forgiveness and increased concern to bring about understanding relationships that cause God to smile and say even to a person who has gone through this most serious of human experiences, "Well done, good and faithful servant."

Life As a Single Parent

RONALD P. HUTCHCRAFT

The single parent is a new and growing challenge for the church. Twelve million children under the age of eighteen now live with a divorced parent. And that number is growing by one million each year.

Studies indicate that divorce has mixed effects on children. One five-year study revealed that one-third of the children of divorce came out resilient through the experience. Another third could be described as only muddling and coping. The third group would have to be described as very bruised. You ask, "What makes the difference?"

In a single-parent situation, particularly where a divorce is involved, there are three steps you can follow to make sure your child ends up on the positive side of those statistics.

Clean Up the Wreckage

The first step is to clean up the wreckage. Again, this relates particularly to a broken home. As a single, divorced parent you have two choices. You can nurse your own wounds, or you can help heal your children's. Rather than focusing on your own feelings, the greatest therapy for you will be to give your life away to them. And in the process you will find your own. In trying to heal them, you'll heal yourself.

Because of the survival mentality after a divorce, there is a tendency toward selfishness, toward self-protection, toward thinking, *How am I going to take care of myself? How am I going to meet my needs? How am I going to put my future together?* During that process, you further isolate a child who is already devastated by the loss of his relationship with his dad or mom.

Wreckage after divorce takes three forms. First, there's *bitterness*. In Ephesians 4:26-27, the Apostle Paul talks about not letting the sun go down on your anger, and then says not to give place to the devil. We often miss the point that you give place to the devil by letting the sun go down on your anger.

Hebrews 12:15 says, "See to it that . . . no bitter root grows up to cause trouble and defile many" (NIV). If by bitterness we blight or blot out one half of a child's emotional identity, we have crippled him for life. A child needs to have *both* a mother and father that he can relate to emotionally.

As a single parent, you can help a child understand the weaknesses of the departed spouse—perhaps that parent's background and some of the reasons he (or she) acted as he did. Learn to pray together for the departed parent. Don't force your child to divorce one of his parents. The fact that Mom and Dad have divorced each other ought to be enough pain for a child to handle.

The second piece of wreckage is *guilt.* Research shows that children of divorce tend to assume blame, or at least part of the blame, for the failure of that relationship. They say, "Well, maybe I made too many demands; maybe they spent too much money on me. They argued about me a lot of times."

Help the children understand that they are not to blame, that the decision to get a divorce was Mom's and Dad's responsibility. And certainly, don't lay any more guilt on your children to get your way with them, like: "You're *all* I've got. *Please* don't let me down. How can you *do* this to me?"

The third piece of wreckage is *the tendency to withdraw.* When relationships have hurt us, we tend to pull in, withdraw, and not talk, love, or care. So it's more important than ever that the single parent do special things with the children to help pull them out of those feelings.

Plan fun times and special occasions to be *together.* This creates a climate for communication. It's important too for the single parent to share *some* of his or her own struggles and feelings. This will help *the parent* to not withdraw and will provide the children with a model of "reaching out" rather than "pulling in." And when you can't talk to each other, write notes. Fight withdrawal at all costs. Clean up the wreckage.

Create a Stable Home Life
Concentrate on *stability.* Now perhaps more than at any other time, everything is up for grabs. The single parent needs to devote himself or herself to creating as stable an atmosphere as possible. Here are some steps:

1. *Try to maintain the daily routine.* Make life as predictable as possible—getting-up times, going-to-bed times, mealtimes, special traditions in the family, celebrations. Provide as much structure as you can.

2. *Make a fuss over the special days in their lives.* See that there is a festiveness and a spirit of celebration for birthdays and holidays—even the birthdays of other family members and friends. Make special days *special.*

3. *Include the children as partners in the decision-making process.* Don't expect them to become a substitute for your marriage partner but give them a more-than-average say. Let them serve as your prime advisers and chief consultants on decisions you need to make. They need to feel that they are part of the destiny of the reconfigured family unit.

4. *Affirm their worth regularly.* Their self-esteem may have taken a beating. Studies show that many young people from divorced families feel that they're worthless. Let them know often that nothing that *can* or *has* happened will change their great worth to you.

5. *Encourage parent substitutes in their lives.* Use hospitality in your home as a way to build an "uncle-ness" and "aunt-ness" and "cousin-ness" with other people. Encourage a grandpa or a dad in the church to adopt your son for the next father-son banquet. Invite families over who are good role models.

6. *Don't marry your children.* Don't become so emotionally dependent on, or protective of, your children that you force them to try to take the place of your absent spouse. They can never do that. And don't rob them of their own childhood. It's important that they have their own adolescence.

7. *Keep consistent boundaries.* Sometimes there's a tendency to compromise firmness because you fear risking the rejection of those who remain in your family. But don't let tough love become soft or you will lose both the respect *and* the love of your children. And maybe,

because of that, you might even lose them spiritually. Keep the boundaries intact, where they were before the family split up, unless you can better define them.

Convert Minuses into Pluses

Certainly a broken home or a broken marriage is one of the biggest minuses in life. But there are *some* pluses that can be derived from that tragedy.

A story is told of twin boys who grew up with an alcoholic father. He was absent most of the time, didn't work much to support the family, and was unfaithful to their mother.

One of the twins married early, didn't go to college, didn't hold down a job, was abusive to his wife, and ended up divorcing her.

The other boy went to college, took his time getting married, had a great marriage, a very successful career, and beautiful children. Later in life, both of them were asked why they became what they were. Strangely enough, both gave the same answer: "Because of my father."

What had happened? Out of the one son's negative experience came depression; out of the other son's came determination. Really, the situation can go either way. A negative can either create another negative or it can create some positives. Those positives might include:

1. *Strong bonds.* In spite of the pressure and the survival needs you and your children have, the possibility exists for you to become bonded to each other in a close relationship you might otherwise have never experienced. (And perhaps closer than many children experience in two-parent families.)

Remember that diamonds are formed under great pressure, and that many children have emerged from broken families as diamonds because the pressure formed very strong bonds.

2. *Strong children.* Another plus can be strong children—children who have to step up to greater maturity, greater responsibility sooner than other children do.

James 1:2-4 tells how trials develop a stronger, more persevering and enduring character. If we approach single parenting in this way, we can help our children see the situation as an opportunity for personal spiritual growth. We can show them how they can be far ahead of their peers in understanding, cooperation, accountability, responsibility, hard work, decision-making, and character and that this will help make them better persons for the rest of their lives.

3. *Strong lessons.* Strong lessons can be learned from negative experiences, if the single parent approaches the situation saying, "I want you children to learn from this mistake, these problems, this failure, in order to provide a solid foundation for your lives."

The parent can even point out personal mistakes he or she made to teach lessons to the children. "Wouldn't it have been good if I had waited a little longer before I had decided to get married?" "I wish I had been older." "I wish I had kept sex in its right place." "I wish I had married a spiritual leader; I didn't realize how important that was." "Here's how our communication broke down...."

If those lessons become part of the character of your children, they may very well become equipped to build rich family lives of their own.

4. *Strong faith.* There's something about desperation that builds a new reliance on the supernatural. If you're desperate, you don't just pray, you *cry out* to the Lord. And if you and your child, or children, together say, "Lord, we just can't make it; we're desperate," the possibility of a strong faith, of seeing God become a father or mother to your family, becomes part of the solution of the substitute parent situation.

God provides where you can't. He can give love and support where you cannot.

He gives you and yours the strength you need to face life. You may come to experience God's love and power in ways people who have the security of a whole family have never experienced.

The Challenges of Being a Stepparent

GARY D. BENNETT

Most families want their children to enjoy life and be happy, healthy, well-adjusted family members. Few parents actually choose to be grouchy or grumpy caretakers of their children. Nevertheless, raising children is one of the most demanding and responsible jobs that any adult ever assumes. And the job of being a stepparent makes the responsibility even more difficult and frustrating.

Though there are no absolute standards for being a "good parent," there are some basic practical principles which, when applied, can make the task of helping to raise someone else's child a more fulfilling experience.

Separation and Loss

One of the best ways to help a teen accept your remarriage is to understand what he may be feeling. Splitting children between their parents is always traumatic. In most instances, a child views his parents as important love objects. It's important to remember that separation represents a significant loss, even to the adolescent. In fact, many of his feelings are similar to those everyone goes through when faced with the death of a loved one. The adolescent may deny or repress the importance of the person or place he has left. Sadness, anger, guilt, and ambivalence are always present to some degree. When the stepparent and biological parent help the child to acknowledge and identify these various feelings, then the teenager's acceptance of the remarriage is enhanced and the developing new family becomes strengthened.

Supporting the Old, Developing the New

Most families provide growing teenagers with memories of their past and help them keep memories alive. This helps maturing children to develop a sense of self. But it's something usually lost in cases of divorce and remarriage. In these situations, a child's past is often minimized by criticizing the "other" biological parent or by encouraging the youngster not to talk about earlier childhood experiences. Often the adolescent's future is minimized because no one is sure what will happen in the future. Perhaps no one can even tell the teen who will be taking care of him next year. By focusing only on the here and now, the adolescent's sense of self becomes distorted.

It will always be necessary for the stepparent and spouse to support the "old" family members. Doing so will

473

enable the teen to develop a wholesome sense of self in the least traumatic way possible. Keeping pictures of "old" family events and speaking respectfully of the "other" biological parent are two of the best ways to ensure the teen's acceptance and adjustment to your remarriage and new family.

Though reactions of relatives to your remarriage will vary (sadness, blame, embarrassment, shame, avoidance, helpfulness, etc.), don't overlook the importance of including them in the teenager's life. Whether it be grandparents, a favorite uncle, a special cousin, everyone will add something worthwhile to your adolescent's emerging sense of self and identity. Since significant relationships usually override legal status anyway, refusal to allow contact with former relatives may backfire and cause more frustration than is necessary.

On Entering Your Family

The problem always comes up of what the child should call his stepparent. The very young child is almost always going to parrot whatever everyone else calls you (i.e., Mommy or Daddy). But the teenager often feels caught. On the one hand, he doesn't want to call you the same name he calls his real parent, yet he may be the only one in the family not calling you Mom or Dad. Adolescents may feel OK using first names if the stepparent is comfortable with this. Some teenagers have solved this dilemma by referring to their stepparent as Mother or Father, and then referring to their real parents with the customary Mom or Dad. Other teens have used a combination of the title and the stepparent's first name, such as Mom Susan or Dad Tom. This is a good thing to talk about, so that you agree on something that is both easy and comfortable for everyone involved.

Don't be surprised if, after entering your family, your stepchild drags out all his worst behavior and perhaps some surprising new behavior to see how much

he can get away with. He may test the limits to see what the rules really are in this new family. Remember, this is normal and the natural way all children learn; so don't panic and feel that "he's worse than he was before." And if your stepchild doesn't misbehave, expect your own children to. Simply set realistic limits, state your rules, and follow through with the consequences. With no consistent boundaries, they will keep on testing everything until each knows what his new role is and what is expected of him in the new family. All of this will settle down eventually.

Building and Promoting Healthy Relationships

Social interaction, not routine care, is the most important part of stepparenting. The more social interaction an adolescent has with you, the more strongly attached he becomes to you. It is easiest for stepparents to begin initiating positive interaction with a teenager as the family begins its new life together. If you happen to get off on the wrong foot in your relationship, don't give up. The following suggestions are good ways to build and promote a healthy relationship between stepparent and child:

1. Show affection: hugs, kisses, physical closeness.

2. Help your stepchild to meet expectations of the other parent (your spouse).

3. Show genuine interest in his activities.

4. Support the adolescent's outside activities by providing transportation or being an adult sponsor for one of his activities.

5. Display interest in your stepchild's school performance. Help him with homework when he needs it, but don't expect him to ask for help. Be careful not to nag.

6. Help your stepchild to understand your family "jokes" or sayings.

7. Read together, or play games

together. Being together and doing things of common interest is a tremendous aid in building relationships.

8. Go shopping together and on special outings. If your remarriage involves mixing sets of kids, try to take them out together sometimes and separately sometimes. Taking turns can be very fun. You won't be so tired and each child can have a little special time alone with you.

9. Teach your stepchild a new living skill: cooking, baking, changing spark plugs, repairing a door. Involve him with you as you carry on the normal tasks of maintaining a home.

10. Trust your stepchild.

11. Show interest in and acceptance of his friends.

12. Stand by your stepchild if he gets in trouble.

13. Be affectionately firm and consistent in discipline. It is extremely important that both parents agree on the standards and discipline. And be fair and loving as you administer the discipline. Your stepchild will respond if he has understandable reasons for his expected behavior.

14. Accept your stepchild as he is. God made each of us with little differences which make us interesting. Appreciate your stepchild for the person he is without forcing him into your mold.

15. Cultivate a love for him and make it known. Tell your stepchild you love him and show it. Most teenagers need to see love in action as much as they need to hear it.

16. Give your stepchild a place of importance in your home. Make him an integral part of the family unit by giving him a voice in family decisions and responsibilities in the home.

17. Remember, shared laughter and shared tears are powerful bonding tools. Allowing yourself to be vulnerable will strengthen your relationship.

As previously mentioned, the responsibility of stepparenting is a demanding and difficult task, but it's also one which can be extremely rewarding and fulfilling. As a stepparent, it will be of vital importance to always be honest with yourself and the youngster, to be realistic, to be positive, and to be prepared to have your feelings hurt along the way. At times it may feel like it's a thankless job, but keep in mind that you are helping to raise the future parent of your "grandchildren." Doing your best today will pay off in greater dividends later.

Absentee Parents

Does It Pay to Be Away?

JAY KESLER

The demands of our culture have created a situation in which more and more young people are being raised by absent parents. In fact, in any group of ten teenagers, you'll find that six or seven of them live in a home where there is some disjuncture. In its most serious form it involves divorce or the death of one or both parents. In other situations it involves alcoholism, emotional illness, or time abuse.

The term *workaholism* has been coined to describe one form of time abuse. The well-known football commentator John

Madden said on national television that he left coaching because one day his wife said she was taking their son to get his driver's license, and he thought the boy was still twelve years old. He had been so caught up in his work that he had missed four years of his son's life. This happens with a lot of parents, and I give Madden a great deal of credit for leaving a prominent career to devote more time to the more important concerns of his family.

Today about half of the mothers in America are working, and many of the fathers are traveling. Inevitably, a large number of children are being raised by absent parents. I believe it is possible to raise a family successfully in this atmosphere. People can overcome the difficulties caused by both parents' working. But they must be seen as difficulties, factors that must be dealt with.

It is like having a son or daughter with a physical handicap. We do not help the child by ignoring the problem; it is there, and it must be taken into account. Special effort must be made to overcome it. A child can cope with one arm, but it isn't easy. It takes extra effort. A child can cope with one parent, or with two parents that are too busy to give him much time, but it isn't easy. It takes extra effort.

When parents are absent, other responsible people must be left in charge. There have to be very specific understandings about where people are going to be and what they are going to do. Involvement in a church community can help plug the gaps. One of the most wonderful things about the body of Christ is that it provides an extended family for us while we are struggling in this "wicked and perverse generation." We can have surrogate aunts and uncles, grandparents and grandchildren, brothers and sisters, who can help make up the differences.

To raise children successfully in an imperfect situation, we must make every minute count. We'll have to cut out activities that other people may enjoy. Other men may have time to play golf, but a man who's often on the road needs to devote Saturdays to his children. Other women may have time for club work or community activities; a working mother probably does not. Both parents in two-career families, as well as all single parents, rarely have time for anything beyond family and work. And everything has to suffer to some degree.

Churches are wrong when they provide endless activities for busy people, time-consuming programs going from morning to night, day in and day out, from cradle to grave. Families with absent members or with heavy work responsibilities must intentionally guard against overcommitment, even to church. Too many outside concerns can destroy the family.

I have met hundreds of young people who have been raised by one parent or by working parents and who have done very well. But it didn't just happen. It came about because someone cared a great deal and put forth a great deal of extra effort.

Related Articles

The Family That Is Too Busy for the Family

GARY R. COLLINS

It's an old false remedy to fight stress with busyness. I'll give you an example.

I know of a successful professional man who began having trouble with his children. So he took on more responsibilities with his business, and he let his wife handle the kids. The busier he got, the farther apart he and his wife drifted. Eventually the kids grew angry and resentful at his self-imposed alienation. The family finally broke up.

Sometimes stress will allow negative attitudes to enter our lives. It's easy to think, for instance, that we haven't got time just this moment for our family, but we'll have it soon. This attitude carried from day to day usually means that we're never going to have the time.

We have to say, "I'm going to make the time. Period."

One way to take that step is to grapple with the fact that our kids are not going to be with us forever. When the time comes for them to leave home, what kind of shape will our relationship with them be in? Will it be warm and communicative or cold and dusty from lack of use?

Do we create space for our kids?

Some time ago, my wife and I made it a priority to fix up the basement as a place where our kids could bring their friends. It's also a place where we can be together as a family. We're a little low on furniture in the living room, but we decided that the communication the basement would facilitate would be a lot more important than new lamps.

You have to have priorities, even if they're as seemingly insignificant as making it a point to go places in the family car together. We do that. If the drive lasts long enough, it's a good opportunity for conversation.

Lack of communication causes us to lose sight of each other. And as individuals, we grow differently and cannot predict each other's growth patterns. Families evolve and mature just like individuals. Five years from now, for instance, I might have a son-in-law. I might be a grandfather. My parents might not be living. Time changes things, and I want to keep abreast of those changes through daily communication.

One of the worst dilemmas the "too-busy family" will face is the natural parent-child modeling that becomes replaced by busyness. Modeling is so important for teenagers. Day to day, they need to observe a healthy marriage. My kids need to see that it's OK to goof off once in a while; that it's OK to laugh, cry, and console.

They may not want to sit with you in church all the time, but they'll be watching you if you're not too busy to be a good model for them.

Related Articles

WHEN THE KIDS COME HOME

The scenario: The kids have been at college for a year, and now they're coming home.

The situation: During any long separation, whether it's summer camp, college, or something in between, young people will grow and change (and so will you!). How can we begin to rebuild the relationships at their return?

The solution: First, we must work back into their lives slowly, giving them time to work into ours. (Note: After an *extended* separation, we should understand that we are building something new and not rebuilding the past.)

Next, we should take time to hear the details of their experiences while away, exploring the facts and listening for their feelings.

Finally, we should plan "traditional" activities, those family rituals and special events which will provoke pleasant memories and feelings of togetherness.

The snag: What about sending kids away *against their will* (i.e., to camp, boarding school, etc.)? Here it is imperative to examine our motives. Are we getting them "out of our hair", and avoiding our responsibilities or are we doing it because it's socially "the thing to do"? (There are parents who have no choice because of geography or employment.) In any case, we should engage in honest introspection.

The deeper question to ask is, "Is this separation truly beneficial?" If our honest answer is no, then we shouldn't force the issue. The negative repercussions, including communication breakdown, the search for new parental models, resentment, and emotional confusion can be devastating for the children and the family.

If, however, the separation is in the family's best interests, it is important to communicate the facts and our feelings. This should be done quietly, firmly, and lovingly. Our kids need to understand that *they* are not being rejected or avoided, and that we will welcome their return.

YFC Editors

WHEN THE FAMILY FALLS APART

- Rebellion—why it could happen to your teenager
- Dealing with the pain over wayward children
- How should parents handle teen rebellion?
- Is rebellion ever good?
- Why do kids from good homes go bad?
- What to do if your teenager runs away
- How to pick up the pieces and start over
- Will things ever be the same?

The Parable of the Prodigal Son transcends language and culture. Anyone, no matter what his background, can relate to the story of a boy who repudiates his father's lifestyle, runs away to a far country, and eventually sinks into misery and despair.

Not all prodigal sons come to themselves and decide to return; not all rejected fathers put aside their pride and hold out welcoming arms. But Jesus' story in Luke 15:11-32 ends very well because father and son are eager to be reconciled.

When a child rebels, nothing need be permanently lost. Reconstruction and redemption can follow rebellion. Success comes not simply from winning the race, but from getting up whenever we fall. If our children fall, or if we are knocked flat by their behavior, we need not sink into permanent despair. God's entire redemptive effort is aimed toward picking us up and setting us on our feet again.

Dealing with the Pain over Wayward Children

JOYCE LANDORF

Hundreds and hundreds of people have talked to me about the pain they have experienced over children who have chosen a harmful lifestyle or gone totally off the deep end. I know what this is like because my daughter, Laurie, left home when she was eighteen and didn't come back until she was twenty-two.

Parents suffer from a lot of unnecessary guilt when children go astray. In Proverbs 22:6 we read, "Train up a child in the way he should go: and when he is old, he will not depart from it" (KJV). We take this as a promise and then feel guilty and wonder what we did wrong when our child doesn't turn out right.

This verse is not a promise, but a proverb, a wise saying. Though its principle is sound, it can't be a promise because God never violates our free will, nor our child's free will. If our child wants to go off the deep end, he has a right to do so because he has a free will. We can't force our children not to depart from the path we showed them.

The first parent who ever felt guilt was Eve. Eve could not believe that her older son, Cain, murdered her younger son, Abel. I know for a fact, even though the Scriptures don't explicitly say, that she went screaming to Adam and said, "What have we done? We've fed them the same porridge; they slept in the same tents; they did everything the same except one was in the fields and one was hunting. We did everything for them; we trained them; we told them the story of the Garden of Eden; we told them about God; and look what one has done to the other."

It was hard for me to accept my daughter's free choice when she left. But *she* chose it and I did not pull her back home. I still had the right to say to her, "I think your choice is lousy." When I found out she was living with a guy, I did not tell her she couldn't do that anymore. I told her I disagreed violently with her choice, and I thought it was wrong. But I still loved her.

I could not approve of her lifestyle, which was contrary to Scripture, but neither could I prevent her from exercising her free choice. Later she said the thing that sustained her, after the man set three wedding dates and canceled all three times, was that she knew we loved her. She didn't want to force him into marrying her because she knew she would not get our blessing.

When a child is sixteen, seventeen, or eighteen years old and chooses habits or a lifestyle against Scripture, we can't prevent the choice. Neither do we have to sit back and be silent. We can tell our teen that it is wrong, that we are not going to support him, that we can't give our blessing. But at the same time, we need to reinforce the fact that we love him.

This happens all the time. Children are raised in Christian homes and leave, either emotionally or physically, to test the principles they saw lived there. They eventually come back about age twenty-five or thirty, especially if the parents were Christians before the child was seven. The Roman Catholic Church used to say, "Give me a child until he is seven, and I'll have him for the rest of his life." Even if there is only one godly parent, they will usually come back.

But if Christianity has not been lived in the home, the ending is generally not a happy one. Children see what parents are, not what they say. If the parents, even one of them, has really lived the faith, the

WHY A TRAGEDY OCCURS DESPITE OUR PRAYERS

A dedicated prayer life is not protection against tragedy. Sometimes after a person has done the most praying, the biggest tragedies occur because God's ways and answers are not human ways and answers. If we pray faithfully and a tragedy happens, we think God didn't answer our prayer. But that's faulty thinking because God doesn't make mistakes. It's just that He sometimes answers prayer in ways we would never do.

As a parent, I would never desire a tragedy happen to my child in order for my child to become, for example, more patient. But patience doesn't come by sugar coating. In fact, none of the good personality traits come easily. We would dump a carload of sugar on our teens, but God has a different economy. He changes people from the inside out. Sometimes He does that by encouraging them; other times He does that with hard times. But that's His choice, not ours.

Evelyn Christenson

480

kids will come back to it because it is so powerful. This is the reality that validates the principle of Proverbs 22:6.

It's also important to understand that God may have had you make mistakes for the child's development. Laurie learned more in the four years she was away from us than at any other time of her life. It was painful for her, but she is the mother and wife she is today because she knows how rotten life can be. God doesn't waste mistakes.

How to Affirm a Wandering Child

DAVID HOWARD

Our son began to stray from the Lord when he was in junior high. As he entered high school, the separation between us was growing wider and wider. It became more and more difficult to relate to him as he went through a typical adolescent stage. But through all of his wandering, we tried to keep open communication with him.

One way I did this was by making a point always to be at his high school wrestling matches. In fact, I had a basic rule that I would never accept speaking engagements on weekends from November through February because that was wrestling season.

I didn't make a big point in telling our son about this, but he knew that it was my rule and I was going to be there every Friday night and Saturday afternoon. I know he appreciated my being there and it gave us something to talk about. Having been a wrestler myself, I understood the sport and could talk to him intelligently about it. It was one area where we could maintain good communication.

Doing things together is another way parents can keep reaching out to their wandering child. There were occasions when I could take our son on a trip. While he was in high school, I was working with the Lausanne Committee for World Evangelism. When I had to go to Asia to prepare a conference, I decided to take him with me.

The school principal agreed that three weeks in Asia would be a better education for him than sitting in a classroom, and he gave me permission to take my son out of school. Even though it was expensive to take him along, I decided it would be a good investment of money.

I felt that having him with me for three weeks, day and night, would be good; and it was. The trip gave us a lot of things to talk about. I don't know what immediate or long range effect it had on him, but it was important for me to do it.

While he wandered I felt that no matter how hard it was, maintaining some sort of communication was crucial. If communication had broken down between us, I don't know how I could have handled it.

Parents can continue to affirm their child no matter what happens. Many times I told our son that I loved him and appreciated him. Sometimes I did this with notes, which seemed to be easier for me to handle.

WHO'S TO BLAME FOR A BROKEN RELATIONSHIP?

When a teenager rebels against his parents and the family relationship is shattered into a thousand pieces, who is to blame? Certainly it is someone's fault, isn't it? Who started it?

But is that the real question? Does it really matter who's responsible? Our advice would be to pin the blame on no one. What you really need to be concerned about is healing the wounds between yourselves and your child.

Between any two people you have *relationship-builders* and *relationship-breakers.* Relationship-builders include love, trust, credibility, genuineness, faithfulness, hope, and the other fruits of the Spirit.

Relationship-breakers include guilt, hostility, fear, and anger. When you apply these traits to an already broken relationship, you will only drive the wedge deeper between you and your child.

Too quickly we judge ourselves to have reached the point of irreversible behavior. "They'll never change," we say. Or maybe we think, "I just can't forgive them for what they've done." But if God truly lives in our hearts, nothing can ever get that bad.

Are you having trouble building or rebuilding a relationship with your teenager? Start over again with the relationship-builders. Apply these as salve to the open wounds, and watch how those ugly sores heal!

YFC Editors

During his senior year of high school, he dislocated a finger in the middle of wrestling season which hindered his performance. I wrote him a long note just before the tournament that would determine whether or not he went to the state championships. I told him that I admired the way he had taken the injury and his dedication to be willing to go out and perhaps make a fool of himself.

He never said anything about the note, so I don't know what effect it had on him, but it was helpful for me. I needed to know I was doing as much as I could to love him and affirm him.

Related Articles

Rebellion: Can It Be Prevented?

GRACE KETTERMAN, M.D.

I love the symbolism of the Jewish bar mitzvah ceremony, which celebrates a boy's transition from childhood into adulthood. There is nothing comparable in our society or in the Christian religion, but we need an equivalent procedure to welcome our children into the adult world. I suppose a girl's menarche or a boy's first wet dream makes us aware that our children are growing up, but the recognition is in the mind of the parents and not the children themselves.

When parents fail to allow their teenage children the freedom to begin to make certain decisions on their own and to voice their opinions on matters that concern them, the usual result is rebellion. And I think the parents need to see their responsibility for the rebellious attitude of the teenager. I've worked with a lot of troubled kids, and without exception they rebel because their parents' demands are too frequent and too rigid. Both quantitatively and qualitatively the parents are unbending, do not allow for the growth and change the young person is going through, and expect the same kind of instant obedience from their fourteen-year-old that they expected when the child was two or three.

If parents refuse to allow their children to grow, a vicious cycle can develop. As parents become more unyielding, the child becomes more guilt-ridden. The more hopeless the child feels, the worse he acts, because he doesn't know how else to express the way he feels inside. And the worse the child acts, the more determined the parents become to make him behave.

When the parents can admit that they may have made mistakes, the negative cycle can be broken. Usually, the child is so amazed that he is not the only culprit, that he is more than willing to begin to talk and to make some positive changes in his behavior.

A good first step for parents is to begin focusing on their child's strengths and not just his rebellious attitudes. Every time parents need to say, "Look, this is a bad thing you are doing," they also ought to say, "but here is something you are doing well." Balancing weaknesses with strengths can give the child some kind of hope. I've talked to kids whose parents had put them down so badly that they didn't even think God could forgive them, much less their parents. No situation should become that hopeless.

Counseling can often help parents who find it hard to give their children the freedom they need. But often the adults who are most strong-willed are the ones who won't admit they need help. I know that some of those parents aren't going to be able to hold on to their kids for long.

When parents come to me for counseling, I do with them what I tell them to do with their children. I point out the things I see they are doing that show they are concerned about their teens, and I tell them what they are doing right. By giving them some ground to stand on, I can then begin to think logically about what their major problems are, why they exist, and what the parents can do to solve them. You can't win them all, but that method has won a great many teens back to their parents.

Teens often misbehave for one of three reasons. *Rebellion* is only one of the reasons. When parents are obviously too strict, children rebel to draw attention to the fact that they are growing up. But the same misbehavior is much more com-mon among children whose parents are terribly inconsistent. I label the actions of these teens *testing-out behavior,* because they aren't actually rebelling. They are

GETTING THROUGH TO MY TEENAGE "REBEL"

My youngest daughter wasn't asked out much when she was a young teen. She became convinced she would never have a boyfriend or get married, and she was really grieving about it. I can't describe what a wonderful, loving, cooperative person she was, but her lack of being asked out was getting her down.

Then a guy in school asked her out several times in a row. We liked the boy and were excited about our daughter beginning to date. But the first night she went out she got in almost forty-five minutes later than I expected.

We had a chat that night, and I told her I was disappointed that she was late. I explained that I was worried that she was going to rebel like the troubled kids I worked with. Of course I trusted her, but it seemed that she was just waiting for her chance to see what I would do.

She reminded me that I had not set a specific time for her to be in, and I admitted she was right. In the excitement of the evening I had forgotten to tell her what I expected. She had another date a night or so later, and believe me, I made sure she knew exactly what time she should be in. But when that time came, she still wasn't home.

My worst fears seemed to be verified—my teenage daughter was going to be a rebel. You can't imagine how upset and angry I was as I sat there and tried to decide how I would discipline her. But fortunately the Lord let her stay out long enough for me to get worried enough to turn everything over to Him. I prayed, "Lord, if You were her father, what would You do when she finally gets in—*if* she ever does?"

In answer, the most wonderful remembrance came to my mind. I recalled my daughter's third Christmas, when she was so excited over so many special toys all at once. It was an unusual time. She couldn't really enjoy herself because there was just too much to absorb.

I suddenly understood what she was going through with all her dates. She had the same frantic, out-of-control enthusiasm she had felt during that Christmas when she was three. At the moment I remembered all of this, she came in. All I did was pull her down on my lap in one of our big old chairs and I told her that story. I didn't even interpret it. I just told her what I remembered.

The next day I heard her on the phone as she said, "Well, Steve, I can go with you, but I have to be home by 10." There was a pause, and I knew what he must be saying. But she replied, "No, I have to be in the house by 10."

You see, I could have sent her into rebellion if I had overreacted or acted in my own strength. But by listening, praying, and seeking God's guidance, I grew closer to my teenage "rebel."

Grace Ketterman

only trying to find out if the parents care enough (and are powerful enough) to stop them. The bad behavior is very similar, but the reason is just the opposite. Rigid parents need to let up a little and be flexible. Inconsistent parents must tighten up and set some standards. The third condition I call *wild behavior,* which is exhibited by some children as an attempt to get away from their emotional pain. Many kids have their own variety of pain—broken homes, loss of a parent, etc. So they act out their feelings, and their actions are interpreted as rebellion. When a child misbehaves, the parents need to analyze the situation to see which condition the teenager may be reacting to.

My oldest daughter began to rebel at fourteen, and I think it was only divine guidance that got us through it smoothly. I began to treat her more like an adult friend, telling her about my job and how my day went. That small change on my part cut short her rebellion. I still had to be her mom sometimes and set limits, but she accepted them better when she felt I respected her.

At the same time I began to work with our son, who was four years younger. By the time he was thirteen, we had a pretty smooth relationship. I've sensed no rebellion at all from our youngest daughter. I guess if she is ever going to rebel, it will have to be against her husband, but I don't think it will ever come to that.

Even young children are more willing to obey if parents explain *why* they make the demands they do. And as they grow, you can reason with them as to what kind of freedom they expect. If they want to stay up later at night, you can remind them of their responsibility to make it to school on time the next morning. If you balance new privileges with new responsibilities, you may be able to prevent teenage rebellion and develop well-adjusted young adults in the process.

Related Articles

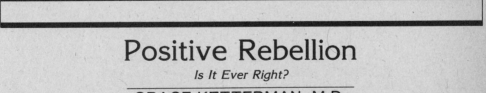

Positive Rebellion
Is It Ever Right?

GRACE KETTERMAN, M.D.

Is rebellion ever good, or necessary? I think it is in those cases where the parents are so restrictive that the young person cannot be himself. I knew a twenty-two-year-old man who was out of college, employed, and about to become engaged to the girl he was dating, but his parents still made him get in by 10:30 every night. Now that man needed to rebel in order to establish his identity and to prepare for the responsibility of his own home.

I would never recommend that rebellion be expressed in a wild or angry way, but I advised that young man to sit down with his parents and explain that they had waited much too long to give him his freedom. If handled with calmness and cooperation, rebellion can be a positive experience.

The biggest challenge a teenager has is to develop his own personal identity and establish his independence. If not given a chance to break free from the dominance of his parents, at least to a degree, he is likely to face problems as he becomes interdependent with others during dating, marriage, and parenting. Unless teenagers are given a chance to explore and establish their own beliefs, values, and behaviors while they still have parents to guide them, they tend to turn to their peers for that guidance. I would rather see teens rebel a little against their parents than become overly subservient to the wrong kind of peers.

I learned this lesson from my oldest daughter. Since she was four, she had always made her bed and kept her room neat and organized. Suddenly at fourteen her room began to look like a disaster area—absolute bedlam. I scolded her over a period of time, and one day she said, "Mom, everybody has to rebel. You should just be glad I'm not rebelling in worse ways."

I decided she was right, and told her it was OK to leave her room a mess. After I did, it wasn't long before she started cleaning it up again. A girl's room is a small thing, but it was a big enough issue to let her know that I respected her right to have an area of her life that she could govern as she chose.

Some parents think it will be hard to "let go" of their child as he goes through this stage of rebellion. But as soon as I understood *why* my daughter was rebelling, I felt all right. I took it harder when I thought she was developing bad habits and being just awful for no good reason.

If it seems that your child is rebelling for the sake of rebelling, try to discover *why*. Have you been holding on too tightly? Have you been too strict? If so, work with your child to reach a compromise. Negotiate an arrangement you can both live with, that will protect your feelings and also meet the needs of your teenager.

My son was staying out later than I thought he should, even though it was with a really neat Christian group. I knew he was OK, but I still worried about him while he was out. We negotiated the situation and agreed that he could stay out, but if it looked like he would be out longer than he originally thought, he should call to let me know. We also agreed that when I got over being worried

WHEN TEENS WANT TO MOVE OUT

When teenage rebellion is not dealt with properly, it usually tends to intensify. When that happens, the question often arises of whether or not the teen should move out of the house. I generally would not advise that a child younger than eighteen be allowed to do so. If one of my children wanted to move out because of a problem I couldn't resolve, I would probably head for counseling so quickly that all you could see would be my dust.

If necessary, I would put a younger teen in an institution to keep him from moving out on his own, because the other option has too many grave dangers. I've seen too many kids leave home before they have the maturity or responsibility necessary to lead their own lives. Pregnancy and other sexual involvement, stealing, drugs, and crime are terrible temptations for young people out on their own.

Now with older kids—those out of adolescence and of legal age— the reverse is sometimes true. Sometimes you need to let them go (or *make* them go). But with younger teens it is always preferable to work out the problem instead of forcing the issue until leaving home is the only answer that seems to be left.

Grace Ketterman

about his being out late, I'd tell him so he could quit calling. The arrangement worked out beautifully.

Sometimes rebellion can draw families closer to each other and to God, but the consequences of rebellion must be lived with. I worked with unwed mothers for several years—many thousands of them. Many times their pregnancies were the result of nothing more than a rebellious act. But in almost every case, I saw that apparently bad situation work for good to bring the family back together in dependence on the Lord.

Rebellion *can* be positive. Sometimes it can teach teenagers lessons they won't learn any other way. Occasionally they have to learn something the hard way, but when they do, it is a lesson that really sticks.

Related Articles

Runaways
*Why Your Teenager Might Leave Home
and What to Do about It*

GARY D. BENNETT

As many as one million young people between the ages of ten and seventeen run away from home each year, according to recent estimates. At least half of all youth who run away from home stay within the town or vicinity in which they live, many going to a friend's or relative's house. Most runaway episodes seem to be poorly planned, reflecting impulsive behavior, and most runaways return within a week. Generally, the length of time gone from home increases with age (Debra Klein Walker, *Runaway Youth: An Annotated Bibliography and Literature Review,* Department of Health, Education, and Welfare, May 1975).

Reasons why a teenager may run from home include:
- To avoid feeling a lack of love
- To escape a "situation"
- To avoid punishment
- To respond to friends
- To seek attention
- To ease emotional problems

- To act out feelings the teenager has about parents, siblings, or other "important" people in his life
- To find a meaningful family relationship (often a teenager may be detached or rootless)
- To avoid disappointing parents when the teenager feels something he has done will not please them
- To attempt to control; i.e., he exploits the threat of running away in order to manipulate the parent
- To test independence and prove he can make it on his own without parental supervision.

Though the preceding list is not all-inclusive, teenagers generally are either running *from* something or running *to* something. Understanding this distinction should prove helpful in determining clearly what motivated the flight.

What can parents do when a teenager runs away? First of all, whenever a minor runs away, it must be reported to the police immediately. The police will place the basic information regarding the child into L.E.I.N. (Law Enforcement Information Network), a nationwide computer system. This must be done for the safety and ultimate return of the child. Next, if the child is gone more than a week, the National Runaway Switchboard should be contacted. This is a neutral channel of communication between runaway young people and their parents.

National Runaway Switchboard
Toll-free phone: 1-800-621-4000
In Illinois, phone: 1-800-972-6004

Switchboard staff can take a message from a runaway youth to be delivered via phone to his parents. They will also relay messages back from parents to youths. With the ability to make a telephone "patch" through Switchboard, a youth and his parents can talk to each other directly. In addition, Switchboard can use its resource file to refer a runaway youth to a local shelter facility or a needed service (such as health care); and will explain to a young person who is thinking of running away what can be expected when one is "on the run" (*Youth Reporter,* Department of Health, Education, and Welfare, November 1974).

After the teen has been safely returned home (or returns on his own), it is important to deal with the situation in light of the circumstances which led up to the departure. The teenager will need help in dealing with his underlying feelings or problems and in dealing with the consequences of running.

Leaving home is the least of the runaway's problems. Survival becomes a critical dilemma since most runaway episodes are poorly planned. Food is obtained by panhandling or shoplifting. If shelter isn't available with friends, then a runaway must resort to living and sleep-ing in cars, laundromats, storm drains, garages, etc. When money runs out, work is usually impossible to find because the runaway is underage and doesn't have the skills, maturity, or legal acceptability to be hired.

Problems with the law are inevitable because running away and the necessities of survival create circumstances which lead to illegal behavior. A runaway may be charged with such offenses as disorderly conduct, hitchhiking, possession and use of alcohol and other drugs, being declared "wayward" or "uncontrollable," and shoplifting.

Other problems include susceptibility to sexual abuse, rape, and prostitution; drug addiction; malnutrition and poor health; and susceptibility to physical assault.

Should parents let their son or daughter come back home? Generally, the answer is yes! It is important to try to understand why the youngster ran and to express concern about his well-being. At whatever stage one becomes involved in the teenager's return, reassurance and protection should be the message the child receives —certainly not fear of discipline. Though the youngster should, in some cases, be restricted by curtailment of some sort of freedom, parents should be sympathetic, understanding, loving and, of course, willing to seek outside professional help. He is still their child, and they are still his parents (Walker, *Runaway Youth*).

Related Articles

Why Kids from Good Homes Sometimes Go Bad

GRACE KETTERMAN, M.D.

When our son was in the eighth grade, he developed a desire to hang around with the tough kids. I didn't know exactly why he wanted to leave the friends that his father and I approved of, but I suspected that a big part of the real problem was his small size. I finally got him to talk to me, and he said that all the kids called him "Shrimpy." He felt weak and inadequate and wanted to start hanging around with the tough guys so they would protect him and give him a little status.

When I began to talk over his problem with him, I discovered that he was hiding more pain than he wanted to show. As I tried to help him understand that he might always be a little smaller than average, we went through a period where he got mad and yelled and cried. I cried with him too, because I was beginning to discover that I had been nagging him too much. My regular criticisms and reminders were only adding to his feelings of inadequacy.

I believe there are reasons for every hurt. In order to eliminate the hurt, we must discover the reasons for it. We found out part of our son's problem was physical in nature, and the doctors helped him in that area. We also started sending him to a different school. Sometimes the answers to teen problems are varied, but they are there if we look for them.

Kids from good homes sometimes seem to go bad, and it can be for one of several reasons. Often parents in "good" homes are a little too rigid, and try to hold too tightly to their child for too long. Sometimes a child who is a slow learner feels left out, inadequate, and not as good as the other children in the family. Or a child may compare himself to teens in other families and come out on the bottom in his own mind. Sometimes there are special circumstances, such as a child who is ill a lot of the time. If he receives a good deal of physical and medical attention as a little kid, he might unintentionally become spoiled. Then as his body grows stronger he loses the special attention he had, and he begins to "go bad" to get it back. In still other good families I find that parents might have had a lot of problems when one child was small. If they focused their attention and energy on their problems, the child might begin to misbehave as he grows up in an attempt to make his parents notice him.

I often take for granted that parents know about and try to avoid sibling rivalry, but I know that is not true. A lot of parents unconsciously single out one of their children as the one who best fits their concept of a model child. If that child happens to do well in everything that is important to his parents, he will get a lot of praise. The other children may do just as well in other areas, but the parents aren't usually as vocal about those accomplishments.

A teenager who feels he is loved less than his brothers and sisters will be hurt, and often becomes angry to cover his pain. His hidden hurt is seen as rebellion by his parents. Even parents in good homes are likely to face this kind of problem. If they wish to keep their children from going bad, they need to

CAN YOU DISCIPLINE REBELLION?

Trying to discipline a rebellious teenager is like asking a baby to ride a bucking bronco in the rodeo. It just won't work. Punishment won't solve the problem. Why? Because you are dealing with a symptom and not the real cause of the rebellion.

The first, and most helpful, step is to determine exactly *what* your teenager is rebelling against. Almost without exception, teens are not rebelling against their parents, but against some value or rule the parents stand for. More important, many kids are confused because quite often parents keep changing the ground rules, and kids don't know if they should follow the old system or the new.

When communication breaks down, don't withdraw from the negotiations. Instead, invite dialogue. Isolating the teenager only encourages rebellion.

Don't dominate or try to use power to get your way. When kids rebel they are trying to equal the balance of power. If you continually crush their attempts to communicate to you as an equal, you are setting yourself up for a great power struggle.

Realize also that you may need to find a trusted third party to run the negotiations smoothly. A counselor is an expert at leading a smooth conversation that sticks to the important issues.

Your teenager's rebellion may or may not be his own fault. But he probably won't take the first step to change things. The fact that parents are willing to change communicates more to kids than anything else.

YFC Editors

understand the hurt the kids might be feeling. Hurts can't all be prevented, but with the patient help of the parents, they *can* all be healed.

Related Articles

How Do You Pick Up the Pieces and Start Over?

JOYCE LANDORF

When a wayward child decides to come back home, parents need to start rebuilding the relationship very slowly. You are on tenuous ground, so you shouldn't push your child. Let him come back on his own terms. Sometimes the young person starts to come back with a phone call. That's all. Then weeks go by and there is another phone call, but this time he asks if he can meet you at McDonald's. Then, gradually, the distance between you and the teen disappears.

Other teenagers come back without notice and are totally transformed overnight. But with most it takes a long time, so it is important for parents not to become overanxious to push them back into the home routine. Let them come back at their own speed and in their own time.

Parents should resist the temptation to drag a runaway child back before he is ready because it may have been this overeagerness that caused the child to leave home in the first place.

The prodigal's father threw a party for him (Luke 15:11-32), but he didn't kill the fatted calf until he saw his son coming down the road. And the son was coming back on his own terms. The father was not pulling him home by the coat collar. This brings us back to the matter of free choice. The runaway child still has a choice, and he must be the one to decide when and how he wants to return.

When parents get anxious and tense as their teen seems to once more be reaching out to them, they are not trusting that the Lord is in control. Unfortunately, Christians have misused and overworked the phrase, "Trust in the Lord," so that it is no longer meaningful. Someone says, "I'm hurting because of what my teen is doing," and we reply, "Trust in the Lord. It will be all right." That makes hurting parents want to punch our lights out.

The time to say it is when it looks like the child may actually be coming home. If it looks like the child might return that weekend, then we can point out that the Lord has been working all this time, and we can trust Him to bring His work to completion.

The prodigal son's father must have had tremendous faith in God. He knew his child was in God's hands, and he trusted that his runaway son would one day walk through the gate.

And why did the son return? It wasn't the three-bedroom house or the swimming pool. The son came back because of the life the father led. The father must have been a just employer, because the son knew the servants were better off than he was in the pigpen. The values his father had taught him brought him back.

Our Prodigal's Return

Our daughter, Laurie, came back rather quickly, thanks to the man who is now her husband. She met Terry at the same time she met the man she had lived with, and Terry had fallen head over heels in love with her. But she would not give Terry the time of day. He would ask her for a date and she would refuse.

After four years, when Laurie was in the worst state physically we had ever seen her, Terry decided to phone her one last time. She still said no, but invited him over for dinner to meet a girlfriend of hers. He came, and at the dinner table he bowed his head to say grace.

Laurie remembers sitting at that table and taking a second look at Terry because he said he was a Christian. The guy she was living with claimed to be a Christian too, but he didn't act anything like Terry.

Terry looked at Laurie and said, "Since I've become a Christian I've only had one prayer, that the Lord would let me marry you." He asked her to dinner for the next evening and to her surprise she said yes.

Two weeks later she called me and told me she was in "like." This was our little thing, because I never asked her if she was in love, I asked her if she was in "like." I figured you shouldn't marry someone you don't like.

She asked if she could talk to me. I told her I was on my way to a speaking engagement, but that she could go along. Up to this point, during the entire four years, she wouldn't go anywhere with me. But she said, "Oh, I'd love to." On that trip, she began to talk to me for the first time. I just listened. I didn't give any lectures; I didn't make any comments.

After a week she called and asked if she could come over to talk with us. We were on our way shopping so we picked her up

"WILL YOU FORGIVE ME?"

Forgiveness means "to-give-for." Sometimes we need "to-give-for" our teens, sometimes for ourselves; and sometimes we need to ask our teens "to-give-for" us.

If you need to forgive your teen, first make sure you are acting on reason, not just reacting to a personal irritation. When you find out *why* the behavior occurred, there may be no need for an apology; there should only be an apology if a wrong has been committed. Think it through. Then focus on the behavior, not the person, just as God accepts the sinner but not the sin.

In forgiving yourselves, realize that you can make a lot of mistakes, and your kids will still turn out OK; but *not* forgiving yourselves or them *is* a mistake. Be specific about what actions you need to self-forgive, then take those to God and ask Him for His forgiveness and for the ability to forgive yourselves. Once forgiven, forget it; focus on the future and on appropriate changes and actions you can take.

Let your teens know you are not perfect by asking their forgiveness when you need it. In the long run they will respect your authority and control more readily because they know they can relate with you. Identify what you did wrong and specifically ask them for forgiveness. At first this may not be easy, but with practice you will become more comfortable as you realize the personal and family bonds that are created. You will also take a lot of parental pressure off yourselves and have more fun with your teens in a relaxed atmosphere.

In any "giving-for" situation, once the gift has been accepted, don't bring it up again. If any retribution or punishment is necessary, follow through, but don't dwell on the now-forgiven behavior. Blot out the iniquity, and restore the joy (Ps. 51).

YFC Editors

and parked in the store parking lot. We never got out of the car. We had a long talk and she asked our forgiveness. Then within five days she went to all her friends and her brother and asked their forgiveness too. Nine months later she walked down the aisle to marry Terry with our full blessing. Today she is a godly mother and wife.

P.S. Can Things Ever Be the Same?
Things are so much better after the child returns. I practically worship the ground Laurie walks on because she has become so special to us. It's not that she wasn't always special, but when you've lost someone, and then find out the gory details, you are so thankful that person is back home.

I'm sure that the prodigal son's father felt the same way. When he found out that his son had been in a pigpen caring for the pigs, I think he must have just put his arms around him, cried with him, and said, "I'm so glad you're home!"

When we were looking for a wedding gown for Laurie, we found a gown that was perfect, but very expensive. We looked and looked and found others that would have been all right, but I kept coming back to that one. I went home and told Dick about the gown. He said not to worry about the money because we were so pleased about Laurie marrying Terry.

I didn't want to spare any expense because she had come back. We were so thrilled. I've never regretted buying her the dress; I don't miss the money. When kids come home, the joy overshadows the pain. It's like being in labor for twenty hours and then giving birth. You are so excited about the baby that you forget the pain.

Related Articles

Too Late for Reconciliation?

GRACE KETTERMAN, M.D.

I like the Parable of the Prodigal Son, because the father never gave up on the son who had left home. With few exceptions, I don't think it is ever too late for parents and children to reconcile their differences. It may seem like there is no hope when a child has left home or gotten into drugs, but I've seen so many "hopeless" kids return. At the psychiatric hospital where I work, we have close to an eighty percent success rate in reuniting parents and children—even children who are drug addicts and have been away from home for several years.

Of course, there is the tragedy of teenage suicide. That is one of the exceptions I mentioned. And sometimes accidents or overdosing that lead to permanent brain damage will prevent reconciliation. Otherwise, most conflicts can be resolved if both parents and children finally agree to work together and receive some objective outside counseling.

But until the children are ready to work things out, parents must learn to forgive themselves and their mistakes. Parents who blame themselves for their child's rebellion struggle the most with all kinds of guilt. They feel like the separation was all their fault.

I don't know any parents who don't do the best they know how. Sure, everybody could look back and recall some things they would do differently if they had another chance. But it is also important to recognize the good efforts and positive things they have done. Then they must receive God's forgiveness for the mistakes they made, apologize and try to make it right with the child, eventually forgive themselves, and finally quit giving in to their remorse.

Parents grieve the loss of a child through rebellion much as they do the death of one. But I think their grief for a living child may even be worse, because it is ongoing. Sometimes they see their teenager go through his rebellious, problem behavior for years, possibly ending up in prison. Healthy grieving, however, is a process that will eventually end. If parents don't get caught in the detours of self-condemnation and permanent remorse, they can turn the matter over to the Lord and make the most of the rest of their lives. After all, God loves their rebellious child even more than they do, so they should get ready for Him to work in their lives by preparing to receive their teenager back in forgiveness.

My husband had a female patient who was heavily into drugs. She reached the point where she had to turn to prostitution and theft to support her habit, and finally overdosed. As she lay semiconscious in the hospital for several days, she had a vision of the presence of Christ beside her bed. It reminded her of her mother's prayers. When she got better she called her mother, went back home, and really committed her life to the Lord.

It takes a strong person to say, "I'm sorry. I was wrong." Sometimes the child comes to that recognition. But if the parents take the first step, it can really shock the child back into the realization that he has gone wrong. Then the child can start to look at his rebellion objectively and want to change.

If parents have been too lenient and permissive with their child, they need to take that first step and say, "I was wrong. I was so busy working that I didn't spend any time with you. I'm sorry. I was really working for you, but I see now that it isn't what you wanted from me." It is usually good for the child to know why the parents acted as they did.

Reconciliation may take a long time, but it is never too late. It demands consistency and sticking with it, which is where many parents falter. They think, "It's no use. I've tried for six months, and he's just not going to change. I quit." How can you quit when you know you're doing the right thing? Just stick with it, and one day your determination will be rewarded.

Related Articles

WHEN THE FAMILY
FACES CRISIS

- Why do all these problems happen to my teenager?
- How to respond postively when your child faces a crisis
- What should you do if your daughter gets pregnant?
- What if you find your teen using drugs?
- Preparing teens for the alcohol epidemic
- Helping your daughter cope with rape
- Why do teens smoke?
- Battling anorexia nervosa
- When to seek outside help, and where

No son or daughter is raised in a sterile laboratory environment under a bell jar. We live in a world full of the germs of a fallen and broken culture. Many of today's evils did not exist when the Bible was written, and many others were far less prevalent. Surely those connected with the media, with subliminal messages, and with extreme substance abuse are unique to our day. And yet Scripture contains principles that are helpful to our lives. A loving family that is grounded in scriptural principles can be a strong antidote to today's societal aberrations.

"Why My Teenager?"
DAVID HOWARD

When our youngest son strayed from the Lord, it was the most devastating thing that had ever happened to me. It was so easy to ask, "Why should this happen to my teen?"—partly because I had never expected it would happen. It never entered my mind that I would have to face this situation.

During this time, the most helpful book in the Bible was Job. Job and his friends asked questions all the way through the book, yet Job didn't get any answers. Even when God started to speak in chapters 38—41, He didn't answer a single question. All He did was ask more questions.

Reading Job, I learned that there are times when God doesn't answer our questions. There were times when I couldn't get answers to my questions about my son from God. Maybe it was none of my business. Maybe it was part of God's plan.

With Job, God *knew* what He was doing, but He didn't *tell* Job. Job had to be faithful even when he didn't understand what God was doing. There were many times when I simply had to accept that this was God's way of dealing with our family. My part, like Job's, was to be faithful and hold on to the Lord no matter what.

Still, parents can do several things to move on from questioning "Why me?" or "Why my teen?" First, believe in the sovereignty of God. God is God. God is sovereign. He is under no obligation to give us explanations. God may or may not choose to answer our questions. If He does not choose to answer, we still must hold on to Him.

Second, even if we don't know what is going on, God does. He knows exactly where we are. This was one of Job's great character traits. A lot of what Job said was negative, but one of his positive outbursts came when he cried, "Oh, that I knew where I might find Him [God]. . . . I go forward but He is not there, and backward, but I cannot perceive Him; when He acts on the left, I cannot behold Him; He turns on the right, I cannot see Him" (Job 23:3, 8-9, NASB).

But then Job said, "But he knows the way that I take; when He has tried me, I shall come forth as gold" (Job 23:10, NASB). As I read that, it encouraged me. I may not know where God is in all that happens, and I may not know what He is doing. But, He knows where I am. He knows the way that I take.

Incorporating this knowledge into my life was difficult, but I went back again and again to the Scriptures and held on to what I knew intellectually to be true. Accepting it on the emotional level was the hardest part, but that came gradually with continual reminders to myself that God did know what He was doing.

A continued acceptance of the child himself is another key. This doesn't mean an acceptance of what the child is doing, but accepting the child as my son (or daughter) and *letting him know I accept him.* I have to accept God for who He is and what He is. I also have to accept my child as one whom God has given me to love.

Even if there is nothing else parents can do for their child, they can love him and accept him. I used to say to our children, whether they wanted to hear it or not, "We want you to know this is always your home. We're your parents no matter what you will ever do in life, good or bad. You will always be accepted here."

Related Articles

How to Respond to Family Crises

GLANDION CARNEY

Dealing with crisis calls for being calm, level-headed, and for trying to gather as much direction as possible to make the right decision. A crisis causes tension and polarization. Sometimes it brings people together. On occasion, it pulls people apart.

How should parents respond, ideally, to crises? How can parents help teens respond? And how can a family bring itself through these situations with positive results?

First, I think parents should respond in a way that helps them to feel that the crisis is not overwhelming. God is bigger than any crisis and He will help them through it. What parents say to their teen, the community, or others is the witness of God's control. The sovereignty of God is at work. Parents have to believe that and respond properly to what the Bible says about the nature of God.

It's almost like when the President of our country says on a telecast that we're facing a national crisis, but we have the "means" to deal with it. As Christians, we have the means to deal with crises, and God is that means. We have to rely on God, and trust His sovereign authority in our lives. Though that doesn't lessen the crisis, affirming God's control should relieve some of the tension or at least give you a solid basis to deal with the tension.

Parents can help their teens respond to an adolescent crisis—be it drugs, alcohol, or a pregnancy—by getting counseling themselves. Especially in a serious crisis, parents tend to look at the situation emotionally, as though it's a personal

IS YOUR TEEN A BAD APPLE?

The newspapers scream their reports of teenage drug abuse, premarital sex, drinking, suicide, and other assorted modern plagues; and the natural response of concerned parents is worry and fear. Questions like, "I wonder if Michelle is involved?" or "How can I send Bill to that high school where so many terrible things happen?" fill their minds.

Of course, some of these anxieties are well-founded—pressures, problems, and temptations are prevalent. Most "good" kids, however, are not nearly affected to the degree of our imaginations.

"But just suppose my teenager *is* involved in a terrible habit—how would I know?"

This question is relevant, but the answer is not easy or simple. Here are a few guidelines:

1. *Know your kids.* This involves spending time together and building strong relationships.

2. *Be a model.* There should be no double standard in the home. You can hardly expect the kids not to drink if they observe Mom and Dad turning to the bottle for fun, to relieve stress, to escape problems, etc.

3. *Use loving firmness.* As the children move into adolescence, set aside a few hours together for a good, solid talk about what they can expect and about your values, guidelines, and rules. Make sure they understand the constancy of your love, but also the inevitability of your discipline when the need arises.

4. *Encourage open communication.* Honestly share your own daily struggles. When they open up and share a problem or a sin, treat this act as a gift and protect their vulnerability. (Don't use the information later in an argument or allow it to erode your trust.)

5. *Build on trust.* This means that the kids are assumed innocent until proven guilty. Don't assume guilt because of rumor or hearsay, and then accuse.

6. *Research.* Read pertinent literature, attend seminars, become active in "preventive groups" and PTA, and talk to other parents.

7. *Use community resources.* Teachers, "hot lines," crisis centers, counseling services, alcohol treatment facilities, and others offer solid counsel and information. No parent can know all the symptoms for every possible problem, but these specialists will help.

YFC Editors

failure in their own lives. I think it helps to talk to someone—a pastor, a close friend, or a Christian psychologist. Be open and honest and try to listen to the counsel of God through others. Of course, be willing to wait on God for direction.

Eventually, the parents will have to approach their teen. Most important is the *way* you approach the teenager, and the *timing.* Perhaps you will need to wait a week or two. Consider sending the teen to visit Grandmother or an aunt and uncle for a while. Give yourself some distance and time to get your head together. If you deal with the crisis immediately, I think it's going to hurt you and perhaps hurt your teen, by saying and doing things that you might later regret.

When your time of contemplation is over, be man or woman enough to sit down and deal with the crisis. Don't be afraid to share your disappointment or your hurt and the fact that it's going to take time for you to get over it. But make it clear that you hope to come up with some answers in the struggle.

Positive things can come out of crisis situations. The teenager might learn from the crisis experience itself, or from your example of coping. Throughout the years, it might continue to influence him for the good.

What Creates Crisis?

I think crisis is created by not having the alternatives at your disposal to deal with life's trials. For example, if your child does something that puts your family in a crisis situation, you probably don't have a plan to handle it. You haven't thought ahead. Of course, some families live in crisis all the time—something is always wrong with someone. But that's the exception.

When you are raising children, you almost have to be prepared for a crisis. I'm not suggesting that you should walk around paranoid, saying, "Crisis, crisis!" but you do need to develop a mindset that reasons, "If a crisis comes, I'm going to

try to be relaxed about it—with God's help I'm going to try to handle it."

It's almost like the cruise-control button in your car. When you reach a certain speed, you press that button and it lessens your gas usage as well as the wear and tear on your engine. Similarly, you must say to yourself, "In this world, we all have tribulations and trials. I'm going to have them from time to time, so how will I deal with them?" Such an attitude will lessen the wear and tear on you emotionally, mentally, and physically.

For example, when I was a pastor, a mother once called me because she found a prophylactic in her son's room. It was a crisis to her. We talked about it, and I told her to try and understand the environment her son was growing up in—his home life, his academic experience, peer influence, etc. I then said to this parent, "Lay down what you feel are your Christian moral responsibilities in raising him. Think of what you expect of him. You have to let him know that you weren't prying. You weren't looking for what you found, certainly. It just happened that you found it.

"If he continues to violate your principles, I think to a degree you almost have to abandon your child. Teenagers are going to do what they will. That sounds cold and cruel, but they too have been given a free will to exercise."

I can't think of one family that has never experienced at least one crisis. Crisis is a fact of life in our fallen world. But God can bring good—especially spiritual maturity and family unity—out of even the worst circumstances.

Talk with the youth pastor at your church and develop a rapport so that you can confidently go to him with intimate family problems when they arise. Start a coffee group among parents who have gone through crises and ask to be a part of the process of sharing their hurts and frustrations. Be open with one another, read books, and try to have a contingency plan for the future.

Preparing Your Child for a Drinking Society

DAVID VEERMAN

Chris is from a strict Baptist family where alcohol is banned. In high school, though, his continued success on the football field provides a reason for post-game celebrations with his teammates. A drinking habit is the result.

"I feel so rotten," he confides, "I don't want to drink. My parents would kill me if they ever found out."

According to a recent survey, twenty-four million high school students drink, seventy-five percent of them regularly, and one out of every five seniors admit being drunk at least once a week. Alcohol leads marijuana as the most abused drug on campus.

The results are devastating. *Better Homes and Gardens* magazine reports that more than 4,000 teenagers will be killed this year and more than 40,000 will be injured because they mix driving with drinking.

Teenage drinking affects most American homes, including many Christian ones.

Children learn that drinking is an accepted American social institution by observing either their parents or people on television. Situation comedies laugh at drinking, advertisements plug it, dramas make it a mysterious god, talk-show hosts laugh with guests about their drinking bouts. Even the strictest, nonalcoholic family cannot shield its children from this reality. A child's curiosity is built by the mystery and excitement of "grown-up" beverages.

What can Christian parents do? Our actions fall into two areas: prevention and response.

To prepare your child for a drinking society, first ask yourself, "What does my life preach?" Regardless of what you say, your example will teach most.

The older I become, the more I realize how much I am like my dad. When I discipline my children, familiar phrases roll off my tongue, words I heard many times but never thought I would repeat. My father modeled life for me and was the only father I witnessed in action. Now the cycle continues, and I know my children will mirror me. This is a tremendous responsibility.

If you drink to relax or to make life more bearable, don't be surprised if your child turns to alcohol too. We are hypocritical if we expect our sons and daughters to be straighter or more spiritual than we are.

Marty's mother and brothers watched helplessly as his alcoholic father withdrew from them, stole from the family business, and destroyed himself, bottle by bottle. After a Campus Life meeting one evening, Marty poured out his frustrations and bitterness. Marty's turning point came when he realized he was becoming like his father by drinking to escape problems and stress. Marty gave his life

499

to Christ, and God's life-changing process began.

Second, communicate with your child. The media presents alcohol as fun. Your task as parents is to balance the picture. Explain at a level he can understand what alcohol does and what motivates drinking. Answer questions honestly, even the embarrassing ones about Uncle Bob or Daddy's business friends.

Search the Bible together to see what God's Word teaches about alcohol. Teenagers especially need to know how the Bible says we should treat our bodies (1 Cor. 6:19-20), who should control our lives (Eph. 5:18-20), the example we should be for others (1 Cor. 10:23—11:1), and our responsibility to be good stewards of God's gifts (Matt. 25:14-30).

Third, take the time to develop a close relationship with your child from an early age. As he matures, he will be open to your counsel and more likely to come to you when he faces problems and temptations.

Prevention is great, you may say, but what do we do when the problem hits home? How should we respond when we find that our child has a drinking problem?

Even when confronted with the evidence, many parents deny that their teen could be involved with alcohol or drugs. And one form of denial is blaming others, often the son's or daughter's friends. "It isn't Scott's fault," they tell each other. While a teen's peers may reinforce bad behavior, they really reflect his or her problems; they don't cause them. And if parents continue to be blind to their son's or daughter's drinking problem, this hinders help.

At the other extreme, parents may blow up when faced with the evidence. This only serves to alienate and polarize. It may be a natural response, but it aggravates the situation.

Balance is the answer. Without falsely accusing, face the facts. Don't close your eyes to the problem. Don't come on too strong.

If this is your teen's first offense, talk it over with him and try to discuss *why*. Describe your feelings without attacking. Even if it is a repeat occurrence, be "slow to speak and slow to anger" (James 1:19) and quick to forgive (Eph. 4:32). This does not mean that firm discipline is out, but your goal should be to keep communication channels open and find answers together.

Be honest with yourself too. Are you genuinely concerned for your teen or are you more worried about what your own peers will think and say? Or perhaps you feel guilty, believing you've failed as parents. Your teen has to believe you accept him and want the best for him, regardless of the cost to you, before he will be open to your counsel and guidance.

Drinking is not the real problem. Usually it is a symptom of poor self-esteem or a need for peer acceptance. Use this crisis as a chance to reaffirm your acceptance. Embrace him and let him know his worth and your love. This can be a dramatic life-changing turn toward deeper communication.

John was caught by school officials drinking in the parking lot with friends at a football game. He was terrified. What would his parents do?

They didn't hide their hurt or anger But they also showed their love and concern. Hours of talking, confessing, weeping, and praying deepened their relationship. John still faced discipline, but he learned a valuable lesson—his parents really cared and wanted to understand.

It's common for parents to want to bear this burden privately, for fear of what others may think. The Bible says to "bear one another's burdens" (Gal. 6:2). Selectively share your needs with your pastor and with Christian friends. They will offer prayer, counsel, and information. It is likely they have experienced similar situations, and certainly your pastor has counseled other parents. The church is strongest when it loves (John 13:35). Give it a chance.

Why Do Teenagers Smoke?

TIMOTHY SKRIVAN

Over the past four or five decades new issues have faced parents, including drugs, the availability of birth control, and rock and roll music. One issue hasn't changed. That is concern about young people smoking cigarettes.

Information on the harmful effects of smoking has been accumulating over the years. Even with the conclusive evidence that smoking is a serious danger to health, one-fifth of all high school graduates are addicted to cigarettes, specifically to nicotine. (All statistics are courtesy of the American Cancer Society.)

Similar to the clothes one wears or the hairstyle one chooses, smoking is a statement of *who I am*. Let's take a look at what a teen is trying to communicate through the use of tobacco:

• *I belong.* Almost universally, the first time a young person smokes is in a group situation. Nicotine is a poison and usually causes nausea the first few times of smoking. It takes encouragement from friends and some perseverance to get to the point of enjoying or craving cigarettes.

• *I am grown up.* There are very few adults who would judge a young person's maturity by the amount of tobacco consumed because adults see maturity in relationship to responsibilities. Children, on the other hand, view maturity in terms of privileges. We communicate that smoking is an adult privilege.

• *I am tough.* No one wants to feel that people are taking advantage of him. One of the ways a person protects himself is by letting others know he is tough. Smoking communicates toughness to other people; even the brands of cigarettes communicate various degrees of toughness.

• *I am angry.* Many young people are growing up angry. The reasons are many, and the focus of the anger may be toward authority, parents, or themselves. When a teen is angry, smoking may be used to hurt someone.

The final reason young people smoke is that it is truly an *addiction*. Once smoking has left the experimental stage and has become a habit, there is a very definite addiction to nicotine. Heart rate, digestion, blood pressure, sleep, and temperature are all affected by smoking. The body becomes "used" to functioning with the drug and does not want to revert to functioning without it.

Eighty-five percent of all smokers wish they could quit. The evidence that smoking is harmful is overwhelming. It is reinforced when a teen's lifestyle is affected by bouts of coughing and short-windedness at an age when he should be at the peak of health.

The solution at face value is simple: the risks of smoking need to outweigh the benefits. However, the desire to quit smoking has two enemies—the addiction and the statement that is being made.

501

Addiction may be easier to solve than "the statement." Ninety-five percent of people who quit smoking do it "cold turkey." They do not need the aid of pills, shocks, or counseling. They are willing to make the statement of who they are in less destructive ways and combat their addiction to nicotine.

As adults and parents, we do not want to see our children grow up "chained" to a destructive habit. In combating this difficult problem, our goal should be to teach our teens the ability to enjoy and express their uniqueness constructively.

Playing with Drugs Is No Game

GREGORY MONACO

Over seven million people in this country have tried PCP, an animal tranquilizer that disorients, causes hallucinations, and sometimes kills. PCP is the third most widely abused drug, behind alcohol and marijuana.

A recent New York study of two million students revealed that 276,000 of them had tried PCP and 12,000 were using it ten or more times a month. Today alcohol seems to be replacing pot as the choice of drug users, but by no means have drugs disappeared. With a rising tide of evidence relating to heart, lung, brain, and reproductive system damage, drugs are still an overwhelming force to be reckoned with. In a recent national survey, one out of every ten high school seniors said he was using marijuana about once a day.

And if that isn't evidence enough, the "head shop" business—the sale of drug related paraphernalia—has annual sales of almost 1.5 billion dollars. Add to this the multi-billion dollar alcohol industry and you can see what our young people are up against.

So what does all this mean to you as parents? Let's look back at some statistics. One out of every ten high school seniors uses pot on a daily basis; three out of every four junior and senior high students are drinkers, one out of every five a problem drinker; one out of every

eight students in New York has tried PCP.

The odds are good then that your son or daughter will at least try drugs or be in close contact with someone who does. A student in one city said dealing drugs was so easy it was funny. He sold all over school—in the bathroom, the hall, even through a window of a class in progress.

Here in my quiet suburb of Chicago, a respectable place, two drug busts took place this winter. One involved two million dollars worth of cocaine. The other involved a "mom and pop" business selling bags of marijuana out of their townhouse. The bags were marked with Donald Duck and Mickey Mouse stickers which were being sold to elementary school students! The worn-out excuse that "everyone does it" is becoming dangerously close to reality.

As parents, what can you do if you suspect your teenager is using drugs? Here are some suggestions:

1. First, don't deny your suspicions. Addiction to any drug takes time, but the younger abuser has a faster rate of addiction than the adult. What may take years for an adult can take only months for a teen. Therefore, if you suspect your teen is using drugs, act on your suspicions. Don't hope it will go away, and don't deny the obvious. You are only

giving up precious time.

2. Learn to recognize danger signals— the symptoms of drug abuse (see next page). At the end of this article you will also find a list of places to write which can supply helpful literature and other advice concerning these signals. Your local hospital, youth agency, or a high school counselor can also supply you with this information.

3. Deception and secrecy are two of your major foes. Remove the cloak of secrecy from your child's actions by talking with his friends' parents, his teachers, and even your neighbors. This assumes, of course, that you are willing to put his welfare above your personal embarrassment. Remember, you didn't cause the problem, but you can prevent the cure out of pride.

4. Be consistent. Develop clear rules in the areas of curfew, accountability for allowance, and where your teen spends his time. Then stick with them. Sometime it's best to do this with the help of your pastor, some friends, or another suppor-

tive third party. This keeps you from overreacting and allows you to lend support when it comes time to follow through.

5. Become involved in community efforts to combat drug abuse. Contact your school or your city or county government to find out if your community has a task force on drug abuse. If it does, join it. If it doesn't, get one started.

6. Most importantly, keep lines of communication open with your child. Know what you are talking about. Discuss your plan with other helpers to ensure your objectivity before you talk to your child.

7. Finally, be ready for a tough time, and don't get discouraged or quit if you don't seem to be making headway at first. Your unconditional love is a force even more powerful than drugs.

RESOURCES

In your phone book:
  Tough Love and *Families Anonymous*

THE FACTS ABOUT MARIJUANA

Dr. Harold Voth, M.D., has served as senior psychiatrist and psychoanalyst for the Menninger Foundation in Topeka, Kansas and is also associate chief of psychiatry for education at the Topeka Veterans Administration Medical Center. These are his words:

My own family has provided a major stimulus for me to become involved in the problem of drug abuse. Seeing our three sons grow into wholesome manhood provides such a vivid contrast to those youngsters I have observed over the years whose lives have been damaged or destroyed by marijuana.

Witnessing a young person harm himself is a tragic sight; it is heartbreaking. I think of what might have been for all of them, of their parents' broken dreams, and of the sadness that has beclouded the lives of their families.

Therefore, to prevent others from walking down the path of deception offered the potential drug user, I refer you to the following facts.

• All parties agree, even those dedicated to the legalization and open distribution of marijuana, that children, teenagers, and young adults whose minds and bodies have not yet matured, as well as pregnant women, should never smoke marijuana.

• Ninety percent of those using hard drugs, such as heroin, started with marijuana.

- Five marijuana cigarettes have the same cancer causing capacity as 112 conventional cigarettes.
- Marijuana stays in the body, lodged in the fat cells, for three to five weeks. Mental and physical performance is negatively affected during this entire period of time.
- A person smoking marijuana on a regular basis suffers from a cumulative buildup and storage of THC, a toxic chemical, in the fat cells of the body, particularly in the brain. It takes three to five months to effectively detoxify a regular user.
- The part of the brain that allows a person to focus, concentrate, create, learn, and conceptualize at an advanced level is still growing during the teenage years. Continuous use of marijuana over a period of time will retard the normal growth of these brain cells.
- A study at Columbia University revealed that female marijuana smokers suffer a sharp increase in cells with damaged DNA (the chemical that carries the genetic code). It was also found that the female reproductive eggs are especially vulnerable to damage by marijuana.
- A second Columbia University study found that a control group smoking a single marijuana cigarette every other day for a year had a white blood cell count that was thirty-nine percent lower than normal, thus damaging the immune system and making the user far more susceptible to infection and sickness.
- One marijuana cigarette causes a forty-one percent decrease in driving skills. Two cigarettes cause a sixty-three percent decrease.

Symptoms
According to Drug Abuse Central in San Antonio, Texas, the symptoms of marijuana use are as follows:

1. Diminished drive, reduced ambition
2. Significant drop in the quality of schoolwork
3. Reduced attention span
4. Impaired communication skills
5. Distinct lessening in social warmth; less care for the feelings of others
6. Pale face, imprecise eye movements, red eyes
7. Neglect of personal appearance
8. Inappropriate overreaction to mild criticism
9. A change from active, competitive interests to a more passive, withdrawn personality
10. Association with friends who refuse to identify themselves or simply hang up if parents answer the phone
11. An increased secretiveness about money or the disappearance of money or valuables from the home

James Dobson

From *Dr. Dobson Answers Your Questions*, by James Dobson, Tyndale House Publishers, Inc., © 1982. Used by permission.

(help for parents)
City, township, and county governments (anti-drug groups)
Your local hospital or substance abuse treatment center
Your local school
Your health insurance company (for information on Alcoholics or Narcotics Anonymous)

Other resources:
The National Institute on Drug Abuse
P.O. Box 2305
Rockville, Maryland 20852

Phoenix House
164 W. 74th Street
New York, New York 10023

Drug Enforcement Administration
U.S. Dept. of Justice
1405 I Street, N.W.
Washington, D.C. 20537

Youth for Christ/Youth Guidance
P.O. Box 419
Wheaton, Illinois 60189

Pregnant and Unmarried

JOHN W. WHITEHEAD

Compassion is a quality that is all too rare in our day. Of course, it has always been rare. In John 8 we read the story of how the Pharisees caught a woman in the act of adultery and brought her to Jesus, seeking to stone her. Jesus didn't condone her sin, but He didn't condemn her either. He showed compassion, quieted the hostile Pharisees with calm reasoning, and sent the woman on her way with the instructions to go and sin no more.

We admire Christ's quiet wisdom in handling such a sensitive problem, but when parents face the same problem in their own family, it is hard to imitate the calmness that Jesus displayed. Yet if a teenage daughter comes home and tells her parents she is pregnant, I think it is important for the parents to remain as calm as possible and keep the lines of communication open. It is not a time for sledgehammers.

If the teen is remorseful for her actions (or *his* actions in a case where a boy has gotten a girl pregnant), I think it is more important to decide where to go from there than to dwell on what has already

been done. The teen faces several possible alternatives, and it is important that the parents provide guidance to help their child select the best one.

The first step is to sit down together and discuss what the Bible says about the sanctity of human life. The Ten Commandments (Ex. 20) and the Sermon on the Mount (Matt. 5—7) both emphasize the value God places on human life. Teens may think that abortion is the easiest way out of their situation, but they need to see it is not the way at all.

The next step parents should take is to acquire literature that will educate the teen as to exactly what is growing in the womb. Several excellent books by secular publishers show photos inside the womb at all stages of fetal development. The pictures are very important because they impress on the teen that God cares about the life that the teen is now responsible for. Pro-life groups, such as Birthright, can also provide materials which go into detail on the process that is taking place within the girl's body. Parents should first do some research and become versed on the issue, and then pass the information on to their daughter.

Once the teenager reaches the point where she says, "I thought about abortion, but now I realize that it would be the wrong thing to do," there are still a number of alternatives. Parents should be supportive and compassionate of her desire to have the child. Then they should help her decide what her next step should be.

I think if I had a daughter who became pregnant, my wife and I would offer to take care of everything. We would pay for the baby to be born and make sure it was taken care of. If my daughter didn't want to keep the child, I would even offer to adopt it. Compassion would say, "Why don't you let us keep the child for you until you're ready for that responsibility?"

In my legal work, I've seen a lot of mothers give up their babies and then want them back ten years later. Parting with a child is a very spiritual thing. If the parents are willing to care for the child at first, the teenager is likely to take over with time.

But sometimes conditions exist where there is little if any chance that the teen will ever want the baby. One extreme instance is rape. If the teenage girl is totally abhorrent to the idea of keeping a child, especially if rape was the cause of pregnancy, even more compassion than usual is needed. But you still need to explain that abortion is not the right answer to the problem. You are dealing with an absolute issue. A human being has been created in the womb. It makes no difference whether it was formed by

---

HELPFUL RESOURCES FOR PARENTS OF PREGNANT TEENS

Whenever a teenager comes home and announces her pregnancy or his involvement in a pregnancy, it is important for the parents to remain calm and compassionate. But it is also important that they educate themselves concerning this important issue so they can in turn educate their child. I recommend the following resources:

Books: *A Child Is Born, by* Lennart Nilsson. This book has drawn acclaim from everyone. Nilsson is a photographer who took pictures, using a special camera, of unborn children inside the womb. The pictures are just fantastic, and are most effective for getting teens to realize that the child they have conceived should be given a chance to live.

Whatever Happened to the Human Race? by Francis Schaeffer and C. Everett Koop. Schaeffer is a deep-thinking theologian who is not afraid to deal with complex moral issues, and Koop is the U.S. Surgeon General. I have seen a lot of young girls change their minds about abortion after being presented with the facts in this book.

Film series: *Whatever Happened to the Human Race?* by Franky Schaeffer. This series of five films is based on the material presented in the book. Every pastor and parent of teenagers should see this series.

Pro-life groups: *Birthright* and *Christian Action Council*

These groups and others can provide excellent materials for you and your teenager.

John W. Whitehead

rape or by moral indiscretion—it is not right to kill a person. We don't have a right to play God or choose the circumstances.

The best answer in these situations is usually putting the baby up for adoption as soon as it is born. Many people who want to adopt children today have to wait two years. The abortion rate is so high that adoption agencies can't supply all the requests.

Some churches are opening or helping finance adoption agencies to place unwanted children in Christian homes. I urge more to begin similar programs. Other churches are setting up pregnancy crisis hot lines or pregnancy crisis centers. Church counseling is helping fight the emphasis on abortion that is so prevalent today.

A pregnancy crisis hot line doesn't cost a lot to operate. It can be set up in the church, a home, or an office. Ads can be placed in the phone book and local newspapers, so people who have questions about abortion or pregnancy can call a number and receive good advice. A crisis center is one step up, where people with problems or questions can actually come to the church and talk to a paid counselor. Churches are opening up to these kinds of programs, which I think is a very good sign. They take seriously the biblical admonition: "Faith by itself, if it is not accompanied by action, is dead" (James 2:17, NIV).

The role of the church is very important in helping teenagers who are facing the result of their sexual sin. The pastor needs to be right there with the family as they work things out. He should be prepared ahead of time to face such situations. Above all, he should avoid condemnation. If pastors or church members give teenagers a hard time because they are Christians or have been reared in a Christian home, the teens are much less likely to listen to the Gospel and what the Bible has to say about the situation.

Parents, especially, might have a hard time getting over the hurt and forgiving their child for his actions. The only way they can accept what has happened is to

THE FACTS ABOUT TEENAGE SEX

- Eighty percent of all teenage boys and seventy percent of all teenage girls will have sexual intercourse before they graduate from high school.
- 1,100,000 teenage girls will become pregnant this year.
- 30,000 girls who become pregnant each year are under fourteen years of age.
- 400,000 teenage girls will abort their babies.
- 600,000 teenage girls will give birth out of wedlock; ninety-six percent of these girls will keep their babies.
- Eighty percent of the pregnant teens will drop out of school.
- Seventy percent of the unwed teenage mothers will go on welfare.
- Sixty percent of the teens who marry because of a pregnancy will be divorced in five years.
- Sixty percent of these girls will be pregnant again within two years.
- The typical high school student today encounters more sexual temptation on his way to and from school than his grandfather ever found when he went out as a young man on a Saturday night looking for it.

let the Holy Spirit act in their lives. It all comes back to compassion. I would say that Christ is the perfect example of compassion for those who have gone astray. He is the Good Shepherd, and a good shepherd does not beat or belittle his sheep. He counsels and takes care of them.

By the way, pregnancy should be no less a problem for the boy who is involved than it is for the girl. The honorable thing used to be for the boy to offer to marry the girl. He should at least offer to take care of the child. I would go so far as to say that the parents of the boy should raise the money for the girl to have the baby if she is willing to do so.

Some churches are beginning "human life funds" for similar circumstances. Sometime the day comes when they can actually use that money to make it possible for a baby to be born—to save that life. I have been an advocate of such programs for quite a while.

The importance of compassion cannot be overestimated—compassion for the teenage couple and compassion for the child inside the womb. We should exhibit the same strong love for small children that Jesus demonstrated. When we display that degree of love and compassion, God can work miracles. He can take these bad situations and use them for good. Many times a teenager will come to Christ because of this kind of experience, and all sorts of wonderful things can happen. The key is to allow the sovereignty of God to work, and not try to play God ourselves.

Related Articles

God's Answer for Teenage Sex
YFC EDITORS

"**I** recently had an abortion. I didn't think it was wrong. The counselors at the clinic told me the positive points of abortion, but they never told me the negative, emotional side effects. I'm a new Christian, but now I feel God doesn't want me back."

This girl, a senior in high school, isn't alone. One out of every ten teenage girls in America becomes pregnant every year—30,000 under the age of fourteen!

Why Teens Get Pregnant
For many girls, pregnancy seems to be a cure for loneliness. "I'll have someone to love who will love me back." Unfortunately, they never see beyond the happy, clean, dry baby pictured in a magazine. Then, reality hits.

Others believe pregnancy results in maturity and independence. You can quit school (eight out of ten do), get out on your own, and have a regular source of income (welfare). Having a baby means you can be your own boss.

False expectations lead many girls into sexual intercourse. "I thought he'd hate me if I didn't. "But you can't get pregnant the first time." "I thought being pregnant would make him marry me."

In spite of society's efforts, teenagers are often ignorant about sex. *Many teens never connect "sexual experimentation" with having babies.*

For those and other reasons, over a million teenage girls will get pregnant this year. Urban, rural, poor, or wealthy—the problem isn't limited to any class, race, or community.

How to Help

First of all, accept and love the pregnant teen. She doesn't need isolation from church, friends, or family. Rejection is not a solution. It doesn't help to try to establish guilt. We musn't make the teen feel unacceptable to God. *Remember, the pregnant teenager is not the only one who has ever sinned.*

Second, you can logically help the teen explore her options: adoption, single parenting, or marriage (abortion is not an option because of God's teaching in Scripture). Find out what services are available in the community. Are there clinics, hospitals, or counselors especially trained to help the pregnant teen? What are the alternatives and consequences of each decision?

Be willing to talk about sexuality and

THE VALUE OF LIFE

Have you ever noticed how much harder it is to demonstrate respect or love to someone who isn't present?

The person we're with gets encouragement, appreciation, human warmth, and the show of respect. But if we're honest, we'll admit the one not present is more likely to get blame or criticism and is harder to love.

It's human nature.

In many ways, human life at its beginning seems to be someone not yet present, even to the mother, let alone to anyone else. That's one reason why pregnant teens and adults have made decisions that fail to show love or even basic respect for God's creation of human life.

But God has made it clear that a human life is important, even in the womb.

Our authority, as children of God, is Scripture. But since Scripture does not explicitly prohibit or permit abortion, we must carefully search the Bible for God's teaching about the value of human life.

1. Life begins in the womb (not at birth).
   - John the Baptist leaped in his mother's womb (Luke 1:41).
   - David claimed God was his God from his mother's womb (Ps. 22:9-10).
   - Jacob and Esau battled in the womb (Gen. 25:21-24).
   - Jeremiah's destiny was determined while in the womb (Jer. 1:4-5).
2. God is actively involved before birth.
   - We are formed from the womb (Isa. 44:2).
   - The unborn child is protected (Ex. 21:22-25).
   - God ordained the unborn child's future (Ps. 139:13-16).
3. We are commanded not to kill.
   - All humans are made in the image of God (Gen. 1:26).
   - All life is valid because it was made by God (Ps. 119:73).
   - Children are a gift and a reward (Ps. 127:3).

YFC Editors

pregnancy. She is often confused about contraception, birth, and child-raising. Be honest. Talk about the good and the bad. Ignoring the pregnancy, even though the girl has chosen adoption, isn't a solution. She needs to feel your support and your interest. Don't leave her emotionally abandoned.

Recognize the final decision must be made by her. She must live with the consequences of her choice. *No one can force a decision and expect the teen to accept it.*

Finally, remember that love is action. It means caring for the pregnant teen, and helping her assess the situation and her options. It means work and honest compassion. And it means confronting her with God's truth and His view of love.

Related Articles

Helping Your Daughter Cope with Rape

JANICE SHORT

Rape can happen to anyone—including your daughter. It is one of the most misunderstood crimes in America. There is no such thing as a woman who is "asking for it" nor is rape a reflection of her moral character. It is a crime not of sex, but of violence, committed against an unwilling or defenseless victim. It happens to young and old alike, to the attractive and unattractive, and in lower-, middle-, and upper-class neighborhoods. It is very likely that someone you already know has been a victim.

When rape occurs, it is not just an individual affair. In many ways, the whole family is violated by this trauma. As parents, you feel responsible for your daughter's physical and emotional well-being. Many parents, particularly fathers, feel shattered by their own helplessness to prevent the rape and its consequences. Powerful emotions of rage, fear, and guilt are experienced by both the parents and their child.

How the family holds together and responds to the rape victim becomes important to her recovery. What can you, as parents, do? Following are some practical guidelines for responding to the shock of your daughter's rape:

1. *Believe her story.* Parents and family members are the most difficult people to tell about a rape. Few girls are comfortable discussing sex with their parents, let alone the private reality of a rape. It is a compliment when your daughter shares this information with you. Believe her. If you have any doubts at all, share them with a trusted friend, counselor, or worker from your local rape crisis or women's center.

2. *React to the news of her rape with a nonjudgmental, supportive attitude.* All rape victims experience feelings of guilt in varying intensities. Thoughts like, "If only I hadn't accepted that ride!" or "I should have tried harder to get away" are common. Because they don't understand why, they feel partly responsible. None of these things make any difference. A

foolish mistake is no reason to be raped! Remember, rape is not a crime of sex or a matter of choice. Your daughter is the victim, not the perpetrator.

3. *Don't treat your daughter like she is damaged property.* If your daughter was a virgin before the rape, she is still a virgin afterward. Being or not being a virgin is determined by a woman's choice. Since there is no choice in rape, and its purpose is not sex but violence, your daughter still retains her virginity. She is *not* damaged property.

4. *Talk openly about the rape.* As in any major crisis, she needs to accept and work through her feelings. Talking can help to ventilate her emotions and speed up the recovery process. Trying to distract her from the rape with other activities is *not* helpful. It won't go away. To deny open discussion about the rape communicates that it is a terrible secret, confirming her worst fears. Let her know it is OK to share her feelings. At the same time, don't push her to talk. All rape victims go through a period of denial. Let her work through the rape on her own time, not yours.

5. *Avoid being overprotective or patronizing.* Despite the rape, life goes on. Your daughter needs to return to a normal routine. To limit her activities makes her feel punished, as if she had done something wrong. It will not protect her or lessen her fear. During the rape she lost control over her own life. She needs to believe she can regain it. Therefore, involve your daughter in any decisions that concern her. Let her make her own choices as soon as possible.

6. *Accept her emotions, even if you don't understand them.* Working through the trauma of a rape takes years. Be sensitive to her needs. Watching a rape scene on TV can trigger an emotional flashback even a year after the event. Or two years later a date's innocent kiss may cause her to panic. These feelings are not stupid or unusual. What she needs from you is reassurance.

7. *Seek counseling for yourself.* You will have to cope with your own hurt and anger. The rape crisis center or a counseling center in your area can help you understand the physical, legal, and emotional consequences of rape. These agencies can be a sounding board for your feelings and help you know how to respond to your daughter.

Related Article
Chapter 23: Pregnant and Unmarried

Venereal Disease: A Well-kept Secret

THOMAS MORRIS

In the midst of the "sexual revolution" of the 1960s, venereal disease (VD) was seen as no real problem due to protection and antibiotics. Today the tables have turned. VD is a "plague" to be feared and has truly reached epidemic proportions. Not only are young people visiting their personal physicians and public health clinics, but are frequenting the couches of counselors due to VD.

Until a few years ago, the feared venereal diseases were syphilis and gonorrhea. Now herpes is without a cure and new strains of syphilis and gonorrhea are defying modern antibiotics.

Venereal disease causes a reaction in modern-day parents and young people much as leprosy would have in the past—fear, desire for separation or isolation, and more fear. Even in our educated age, many adults and young people still don't know the facts about VD. Here are some of them:

• How people contract VD. Contrary to rumor, the vast majority of venereal diseases cannot be transmitted through dirty towels or toilet seats. Neither is VD transmitted in the air, through insects, by food, water, or unsanitary objects. It is transmitted through close physical contact.

The words "close physical contact" were carefully chosen because, due to the proliferation of oral sex, VD of the mouth can be transmitted through deep kissing.

• How many kinds of VD are there? Many. The most common are gonorrhea, syphilis, AIDS, and herpes. There are at least ten other varieties that are not as prevalent.

• Gonorrhea. Commonly known as clap, morning drip, or gleet, this infectious strain of VD is caused by gonococcus bacteria and involves the moist mucous membranes. It can affect the genital organs, the joints, skin, mouth, and anus. It has haunted mankind since the late Middle Ages. Until 1792, it was confused with syphilis. Gonococcus are fragile and do not survive outside the human body.

Symptoms don't show until one to seven days after contact. In men, there is pain in urinating and a discharge of pus from which stem the common names. In women, there is usually no external symptom at all.

• Syphilis. Also called Old Joe, siff, or the pox, syphilis is caused by treponema pallidum, a corkscrew-shaped organism. As with the gonocuccus in gonorrhea, the treponema die in seconds away from a body. Syphilis is by far the most deadly strain of VD.

Symptoms typically start out as a rash or open sores in the infected area, which will disappear and recur. Syphilis, untreated, can eventually lead to heart problems and brain damage. For most cases, antibiotics will kill off the treponema, but some strains are proving resistant.

• AIDS (Acquired Immune Deficiency Syndrome). This is a disease experienced mainly by male homosexuals, Haitians, and hemophiliacs. As the name implies, it is a loss of the body's natural ability to prevent disease and is suspected to be caused by a virus that is transmitted through the blood or semen. In 1983, 6,000 cases were reported with 1,000 deaths.

Symptoms are similar to those of the flu—chronic cough, weight loss, diarrhea, and fatigue. Though this strain of VD is not easy to catch, seventy-one percent of the victims clearly contracted AIDS through sexual contact with homosexual males.

The U.S. Public Health Service can give more specific information by calling 1-800-342-AIDS.

• Herpes. Herpes symplex A and B are viruses. Today both strains of herpes— even the type which is behind the common cold sore—can cause VD. Herpes has the most traumatic effect on its victims, for there is no cure. The virus resides in the skin and can be triggered into multiplying rapidly into a reaction. Some of the triggering factors are known; others are not. Some of the "known" triggers are fever, constitutional disease, the physical skin trauma of intercourse, premenstrual (period) tension, and emotional tension.

Herpes occurs much like cold sores on any part of the body. The sores can be both internal and external. Reactions can either be small or large, and are unpredictable in size as well as in timing. Worry about an attack can prompt new attacks.

After the Fact

More than likely, as parents, you have counseled your teen not to become involved in premarital sex and, at the very least, you have given him or her the message, "Be careful." So when your son (or daughter) tells you he thinks he has VD, or when you get that information from a third party, the news can be devastating. Not only do you sense the "failure" in your child but, also, it emotionally boomerangs back to you. When people feel a sense of failure, it can make them frustrated or even angry. As parents, you need to understand your own emotions, and not let them hinder you in being supportive in a time of crisis.

First, let's understand that the young person made a mistake—a serious one, but at this juncture what is needed for your son or daughter is not a reminder or a lesson on "How you blew it." What is needed is not acknowledgment of the error, but understanding and empathy. He or she needs a friend.

Approximately sixty percent of the young people sixteen to nineteen years of age who contract a venereal disease do not discuss it with their parents. Most go to public health clinics for help. They fear being merely judged when they are scared and afraid and certainly don't need added guilt or pressure, for they feel that in themselves.

The heartbreak of VD can be an opportunity to get close to your child. Probably in the months or years prior to his or her bout with VD, there has been an ever-growing barrier to your communication. This opportunity to empathize and to reestablish rapport should not be short-circuited by your hurt or anger. It is also an opportunity to minister to your child about Christ's forgiveness and his or her need for repentance. VD is also a clear illustration of the consequences of sin.

Jesus' example in John 8 concerning the woman caught in adultery is appropriate as a model for parents' actions and attitudes.

A Pound of Cure

Parents, the best prevention tactic is to speak with your children early about sex and the possibility of disease from other people. Tell them how VD is acquired. Tell them about sex—its value and beauty—and that it is not to be misused. It could save you and your children from the heartbreak of VD.

If your teen is defiant about Christian sexual ethics, I would recommend informing him or her about cleanliness and the use of condoms. Remember too, your teen's acceptance of Christian sexual ethics is dependent on your own example and your family relationship.

Related Articles

Battling Anorexia

O'ANN STEERE

Anorexia nervosa. One of these days it might be called "Karen Carpenter's Disease" or maybe, in evangelical circles, "Cherry Boone's Disease." Whatever you call it, this once-rare illness affects up to a half million people between the ages of twelve and twenty-five every year.

What is it? What causes it? What are the warning signals? How can it be treated?

Anorexia nervosa is an eating disorder. It is self-imposed starvation. Sufferers rigidly restrict their food intake as their bodies are gradually destroyed.

Anorexia can be fatal. Fifty years ago it often was. Even with advances in identification and treatment, estimates run between a one and ten percent fatality rate today. Death usually results from heart failure, caused by the buildup of electrolytes or lack of serum potassium.

Victims are ninety-five percent female. They are usually from middle- or upper-class white families that are characterized as warm and close. These young women are bright and often achievement-oriented. They are described by peers as having "everything to live for."

What causes these "good girls" to stop eating? Why do they starve amid plenty?

There is no single cause. Societal pressure appears to play an important role. Anorexia is unheard of in Third World countries. But in a culture where advertising tells us that thin is beautiful and where strong emphasis is placed on physical appearance, these young women overreact. Ballet dancers, gymnasts, and models who must stay at low weights for professional appearance are particularly vulnerable. A high proportion have mothers who are very weight conscious. (Over ten percent of mothers or sisters of anorexia victims also have eating disorders.) Remarks such as, "If only you would lose a few pounds you would be more . . . attractive, outgoing, saleable, etc." can be very damaging.

Some victims see food as one area of their lives that they are able to control. Coming from what outsiders describe as "ideal" families, these women fight to achieve an individual identity or live up to family standards.

For some, anorexia is a rejection of sexual identity and adult responsibilities. The anorexic invariably diets away her secondary sexual characteristics. Her breasts shrink and her periods cease. One victim pointed out a woman who looked exactly like she would like to. Her ideal? A ten-year-old girl.

Some experience a loss of body identity similar to the experience of being pregnant and asking your husband, "Am I as big as X or bigger than Y or Z?" A twenty-one-year-old being placed in a hospital protested that she was energetic and feeling fine. Yet she had been dieting for eleven years and weighed only forty-five pounds.

Anorexia is an excellent tool for manipulating others. The dieter gets attention from family and friends. They may beg, threaten, or plead but remain powerless to make her eat. One seventeen-year-old, having heard her mother's plea to "Eat things like diet peaches and cottage cheese for lunch rather than starving yourself" reacted by eating nothing but those peaches and cottage cheese for a full year, thereby gaining a measure of control over her guilt-stricken

514

mother.

Some initial research indicates that there may be a hormonal cause for anorexia. It is still uncertain whether the chemical characteristics are cause or effect, but it is an area offering some hope.

Treatment is distinctly more effective if begun early. A victim must be helped to regain a certain level of health before further treatment can begin. Some therapists seek to find psychological causes for the behavior change. Others concentrate on changing the behavior. Most use a combination of these two approaches.

It is a slow process of discovering what benefits the woman derives from denying herself food and teaching her to adjust her attitudes toward eating. She must be convinced both that there is enough challenge in life to make it worth living fully and that there is enough value in herself to make her worthy of doing so. Johns Hopkins statistics show that twenty-five percent of severe anorexics are not helped by treatment, twenty-five percent seem to recover completely, and the rest improve but remain vulnerable.

Treatment success is not without its pitfalls. Prolonged starving can shrink the brain and change the size of the heart. Going several years without menstruation can damage reproductive organs permanently. An emotional crisis later in life can often trigger the disorder in a woman whose anorexia had been under control. Research in Sweden suggests that long-term victims have a mortality rate twenty percent above the overall population. They are more vulnerable to other illnesses and suicide.

The sooner anorexia is detected, the easier it can be treated. What signals should you be alert to in your own youngsters?

1. *Dieting that seems to be getting out of hand.* A classic definition of anorexia is the loss of twenty-five percent of normal body weight. Use your own power of observation. Is the target weight getting lower and lower? Is someone already thin trying to get thinner and thinner?

2. *An excessive interest in food (as opposed to eating).* Anorexics talk about calories and recipes, but not tasting. A fifteen-year-old was admitted to a hospital for treatment on the condition that she could bring along her file box. It contained hundreds of recipes, including fourteen different ones for pecan pie.

3. *Rituals of eating.* Be wary of the need to organize the food on the plate in a specific way so that nothing touches each other. Some anorexics decide that every bit of food must be cut into tiny symmetrical pieces or chewed a specified number of times.

4. *Consumption of diet sodas in great quantity or the excessive use of laxatives.*

5. *Going to unusual lengths in exercise, such as refusing to eat until five miles have been run or 200 sit-ups are done.*

6. *The cessation of menstruation.*

7. *Major social changes, such as isolation from friends.*

Obviously, one of these symptoms alone or for a short period of time does not mean that your daughter has anorexia nervosa. But, when they appear, investigate. One of the difficulties in screening for anorexia is that the victim has become acutely sensitive to food and areas surrounding it. She will likely be unable able to identify the problem herself and may be proficient at hiding her eating irregularities. If the problem persists for any prolonged period of time, get the help of a professional.

Anorexia Nervosa and Associated
   Disorders (ANAD)
P.O. Box 271
Highland Park, Illinois 60035
312-831-3438

Is Your Teen a Homosexual?

CHRISTIE STONECIPHER

Vividly, I recall the night Sandy and Kelly told me they were gay. To their surprise, I responded to their revelation with a quiet, simple reply, "I know." Though it had taken the girls several months to make such bold self-disclosure to an adult, the signs had been there all along. The hand-holding under the table; the girls constantly making body contact with each other at inappropriate times; their mutual lack of intimate male friends; their denial that they were too close or saw too much of each other; the need to always be together; the fabrication of stories to their parents as to where they were and who they were with; Kelly playing out a more dominant masculine role, and Sandy demonstrating a nurturing, passive female when the two were together; Sandy soon becoming more defiant and unreliable at home, and Kelly becoming more manipulative and secretive with adults in general. Each in her own way had, consciously or unconsciously, tried through her actions to tell those closest to her that she was changing. Unfortunately, the changes were not healthy ones.

Who were Sandy and Kelly? Sandy was the eldest of eight children. She came from a successful, normal, and caring family. Even though Sandy had a strong relationship with her parents and they had always demonstrated support and love, she had never experienced the freedom to be her own person. Sandy's identity had been molded by her parents' expectations as well as her younger brothers' and sisters' demands for a strong, capable older sister. Her grades were superb, her friends impeccable. Teachers saw her as a model student; all those around held her in high regard. Everyone that is, but Sandy herself.

Kelly was in many respects the opposite of Sandy. Kelly had been raised in a home which fostered bitter anger and hostility. Scenes of fighting, parental drug abuse, and experiences of sexual harassment by her brothers never departed from Kelly's mind. By the time Kelly was sixteen, she had participated in a number of gay relationships. Such affiliations were not primarily because Kelly wanted to be gay, but because she desired someone to hold her and love her, to tell her that she was OK. Boyfriends? No, Kelly's fear was too ingrown—they would hurt her like her brothers had. Sandy, on the other hand, never felt pretty enough; she avoided such intimacy.

Needs that have been denied is a constant theme for young people, particularly homosexual youth, desperately trying to cope with their pain. Sandy and Kelly, by announcing that they were gay, were not necessarily demonstrating blatant defiance to their parents and to God. Rather, they were hammering a stake in the ground to define: this is where they stood, this is who they were, this is what they felt could meet their needs— Sandy's need for identity and Kelly's need for love.

To stand and condemn these young girls would only force them to hammer their stake deeper into the ground. Their want now was for someone to listen, to touch their pain, to acknowledge their cry, and to grant them integrity. In order for parents to respond appropriately to such a young person, they need first to be clear with their own thinking and feelings regarding homosexuality. Homosexuality is not the "unpardonable sin." Though the Scriptures are clear in teaching homosexuality as sin (Rom. 1:24-27; 1 Cor. 6:9-10; 1 Tim. 1:8-10) and therefore an unacceptable lifestyle, they also teach that God's love can forgive such sin. His grace will also bring healing to the pain that abides in young people such as Sandy and Kelly.

Second, parents need to understand the dynamics in their teen's life which have led up to such a decision. What or whom has been influencing him? Who has hurt him? What does he want that he is not receiving? What does he desire to communicate by making such a stance?

Third, the homosexual youth needs the support of Christian adults and peers who will directly involve themselves in his life, not push him aside.

Fourth, a loving but firm stance regarding the unacceptability of homosexual relationships needs to be clearly explained.

And last, the homosexual teen and his parents should be encouraged to involve themselves in competent, godly counsel.

As seen in the lives of Sandy and Kelly, their reasons for choosing a gay relationship were different. Thus, they would each require different kinds of therapeutic counsel. Nevertheless, direct parental/adult intervention and involvement can most often be the primary vehicle to bring homosexual youth back into normal and healthy relationships.

Dealing with Death

GARY D. BENNETT

At some time in their young lives, children will be faced with the death of someone close to them: a parent, sibling, grandparent, other relative, or a school friend. When this happens, the impact on each child varies according to age, as well as the relationship to and the age of the deceased. Of course, the death of a parent will usually have the greatest impact.

Any death produces strong feelings of sadness, bewilderment, anger, and guilt; and the grieving person passes through specific stages. For parents to be helpful, they should remember that the young person should experience and work through each of them. Simply stated, the five stages of grief are:

1. *Shock*—seems stunned.
2. *Denial*—feels it couldn't have happened; it's a mistake.
3. *Anger*—blames other people, fights, screams; may suppress rage but internal-

ly is angry.
4. *Depression*—becomes withdrawn, blames self, experiences guilt, sadness, etc.
5. *Acceptance*—begins to pick up the pieces; makes a healthy adjustment to the loss.

It's important to realize that there is no timetable for working through the stages of grief. Some people complete them within a couple of hours; some remain for some time at one or more stages and don't come to acceptance for years. Sometimes the stages happen simultaneously, and at times, there is regression to earlier stages.

When notification of a death is received, several decisions must be made. These include the choice of the appropriate time and place to talk and the person who will tell the child. The youngster does not have to be told immediately; there may be a better time. For example, if the call comes during the night and the child is sleeping, the news could wait until morning. Since the tragedy and the child's reaction to it are very personal, a quiet place away from everything and everyone is preferable (especially if the child is at school). The news should be shared calmly and sympathetically, with the knowledge that there really is no "right" way of breaking it. Appropriate questions about the deceased are in order; these will help the child begin to experience the reality of his loss.

The grief process will begin with the child's expression of feelings. Parents should encourage crying as a legitimate way to show these feelings, not as a sign of weakness. Statements such as "Hold your chin up" or "Be brave" should be avoided. It's better to remain quiet and supportive than to say anything that will interfere with the grief process. Under no condition should statements be made that depreciate or deny the awful reality of loss. These denials betray one's own refusal to share the youngster's grief.

Occasionally, it may seem that the child's expression of grief is over-exaggerated in light of his relationship to the deceased. It is important to remember, however, that previous losses may be connected and mourned with this one. Participating in the funeral would also be helpful in the grief process. Whenever possible, the child should attend the funeral with the family and participate with them in their grief.

Time and the Lord's grace will ease the pain, so it is important not to push immediately for the child to get on with the business of living. He will probably do this eventually. The child must work through his grief and make a "healthy" adjustment to the loss. Supportive love and emotional nurture will never be needed more.

_____

Related Article
Chapter 23: Suicide

Suicide
TIMOTHY LOEWEN

The word elicits such feelings as apprehension or denial. It tends to fall into the category of those subjects we do not talk about. Yet, suicide is a common occurrence in our day, especially among teenagers. It rates as one of the leading causes of death among teenage youth along with traffic accidents and homicides. It's so common that you are likely to know some acquaintance who has died as a result of suicide. It's important to realize that whether you have considered suicide or you are trying to help someone with suicidal thoughts, you are not alone.

Experts have many theories as to the causes of suicide. Most of them are based on the inability of kids to cope with what appears to be insurmountable stress. The stage of adolescence itself carries many anxieties initiated by such things as emotional mood swings, self-doubts, the search for identity, and the need for peer acceptance.

Pressures may arise from the family. The lack of quality time spent with family members may lead to feelings of isolation, alienation, or rejection on the part of the teenager. Lack of rules or restraints can leave a child feeling as if his parents don't care for him. Divorce can cause anxiety and leave him feeling responsible for the split between Mom and Dad. Remarriage and the joining together of two or more families can leave a child feeling lost among a group of strangers.

Competitive pressures can arise from one's failure to reach perceived expectations. The need to get good grades to please parents or peers, or perhaps the initiation into a job market that has no more room, can leave a teenager feeling useless and lost in a society that has gone on without him.

Another possible cause for suicide is one's need to feel powerful or in control. A suicide attempt may be a means of gaining the attention of someone who has previously ignored him. On the other hand, it may serve as a means for punishing someone who is in a position of authority, akin to a small child holding his breath.

Whatever the cause, the outcome will be the same. The individual slips into depression, feeling hapless, helpless, and hopeless. There appears to be no way out of the depressing situation other than suicide.

Those people who contemplate suicide unconsciously cry out for help by exhibiting behavior that is uncommon to them. Some of these warning signs are fatigue, loss of sleep, sudden loss of appetite, mood changes, a significant decline in schoolwork, heavy smoking, writing lots of letters to friends, or the needless breaking of friendships. Initial use or increased abuse of drugs or alcohol, giving away of prized possessions, the loss of a sense of humor, an increased tendency to cry, the loss of interest in usually enjoyable activities, the loss of self-control or anger, confusion, personal devaluation, and feelings of guilt, sadness, or emptiness are signs of extreme depression, and to the teenager thinking of suicide these will often appear in groups. Unlike the "sad and blue times" everyone experiences, the potential suicides experience these feelings more and more until the intensity makes these kids appear different from what they normally are.

It's important that any potential suicide be treated as a serious threat. That means dealing with it immediately. The following steps will provide you with the means to help someone in this situation.

1. *Talk openly and frankly about the person's problems.* Often a compassionate, listening ear can provide healing to one who is overwhelmed by the pressures of life.

2. *Determine the seriousness of the individual's suicidal thoughts.* Has he determined a plan or a time when he will take his life? Often a potential suicide will feel some relief at having planned his action, knowing his problems will soon end. Professional help should immediately be found.

3. *Provide alternatives to his problems other than suicide.* Sometimes one can be so caught up in suicidal thoughts that he fails to see other options open to him. Make suggestions.

4. *Assign him small tasks to keep him busy.* Though this is no solution, it does temporarily take his mind off of himself and his problems.

5. *If problems cannot be resolved after initially confronting the potential suicide, seek professional help.* This may mean contacting a crisis hot line or suicide prevention center, a community mental health program, the juvenile department, the police, or the clergy of a local church. The important thing is to let someone else help in this situation. It's a matter of life and death.

6. *Finally and most importantly, you need to seek help from the Source—God Himself.* He instructs us to cast all our burdens on Him because He alone can handle them. Together with the potential suicide, pray for mercy and guidance in life's problems and trust Him to provide the answer and work things out. Then look into His Word, the Bible, for it

instructs us how we should live our lives and receive the blessings which He has already given us. Then determine to submit yourselves to the authority of Christ Himself as director of your lives.

Only then can true hope and life be found.

Related Article
Chapter 23: Dealing with Death

Learning from Physical Handicaps

DAN SARTIN

I never thought that anyone who had a physical handicap could stand before a group of 1,500 people and thank God in prayer for his problem. But Mike did. He helped restore the distorted vision I had concerning handicaps in life. He helped me see clearly that the true value of a person is found beyond the physical. It is found on the inside.

I remember the first time I heard Mike speak at our youth group club. His loud raspy voice caused me to squint my eyes and strain to understand his words. I could also sense the reaction of the other students in the room as they gazed in confusion and astonishment. When Mike had finished his statement, I had to admit to him with embarrassment that I did not understand what he had said.

To my surprise, I found this experience disrupting. Mike began attending our meetings regularly and I remember thinking, "I hope he doesn't show up tonight." But my heart would not let me live with that statement.

Why? Because each week I stood before my club kids and told them how much I loved them. My heart was willing to accept them whether they believed in Jesus Christ or not, or whether they ever came to another meeting or not. But here, I found my heart struggling to accept someone who was different in another way.

I decided to face the struggle head-on, and began meeting with Mike once a week. As I got to know him, I discovered that he was no less of a person than anyone else, and I had much to gain from his life experiences.

Mike taught me the difference between being handicapped and being crippled. I discovered that all of us have handicaps, whether they are mental, physical, social, or spiritual. "The danger," Mike would say, "is when the handicap becomes a crippling factor in your life." He said, "My handicap has made life more difficult for me and others around me. But I cannot let my handicap cripple my attitude and outlook on life."

His words have run deeply through my thoughts and heart over the years. Meanwhile, our friendship has strengthened and our love for one another has grown. He has taught me many valuable lessons.

The many experiences which I have had with Mike remind me of the Bible story where Jesus healed a blind man in the city of Bethsaida (Mark 8:22-26). This is the only time in Scripture where Jesus performed what I would call a "double-healing."

In verse 23, Jesus spit on the blind man's eyes, laid his hands on him, and asked, "Do you see anything?" As the man looked up he said, "I see men, but they look like trees walking about." Again Jesus laid his hands on the man's eyes. The blind man looked intently at Jesus and his sight was fully restored. He began to see everything clearly.

Many questions popped through my mind when I read that account, the most important one being, "Did Jesus not have the power to heal this man on His first try?" And my answer was, "Of course He did." Then why did He heal the man's eyes only in a distorted way first, and then to clarity when the blind man looked intently at Him? I think the reason can be found in the verses that follow.

Immediately after this event, Jesus and His disciples were walking up a mountain. Jesus turned to them and said, "Who do people say I am?" It is here that Peter, for the first time, said, "You are the Christ." For quite some time Jesus had been trying to get His disciples to look at Him intently. Only then would they discover that He was the Christ.

The point is that the disciples didn't see Jesus clearly. They saw Him in a distorted way, through eyes that were unclear as to His real mission and purpose. They couldn't see who He really was.

When I think of physical handicaps, I often think of the way the disciples looked at Jesus. When we look at handicapped people, we're not really seeing the true persons. Our vision becomes distorted by the visible inadequacies that we presume to understand in their lives.

Mike once told me, "There are people in this room who are more handicapped than I. But their handicap is not as visible because it is emotional or social." Mike

HANDICAPPED, BUT COMPLETE

One of the most difficult "growth" combinations is trying to form one's identity while having a physical handicap. Answering "Who am I?" is an important task for the young person throughout adolescence and well into his twenties.

One "resolution" of this problem is to deny the handicap and to try to work on identity apart from it. Unfortunately, this results in confusion. And whenever someone tries to help this person by asking, "Can I assist you?" he is usually met with defensiveness or abrupt rejection.

Of course, the handicapped person has good and bad days, and the amount of help accepted and the attitudes expressed can vary dramatically. People tend to generalize about handicapped persons because of an isolated experience or two. They may say, "I tried to help a blind person once, and he refused!" Therefore they become reluctant to reach out and help another blind person, as if they were all the same! We should respect each person individually and try to get to know his needs. And we shouldn't be afraid to ask first how we can help. It is also important to respect the independence of others and not be an "overbearing" helper—listen to what the person needs. We can help there (and only there).

People who have accepted their handicaps usually can ask for what they need. They are the easiest to respond to.

Personally, I have a visual handicap, and the issue of control is very important. Losing control of driving, planning to go places, seeing people and walking up to greet them, and 100 other small things are lost. Helping the handicapped person maintain as much individual control over situations as possible allows him to feel like a fully functional, complete person.

Tom Perski

helped me see how all of us have some sort of handicap. And though some may be more obvious than others, it does not mean they are more crippling. In fact, those of us who cannot face our problems are more crippled than those who will never walk, but have learned to accept it.

Now I look intently at each person I meet. I try to look beyond what might appear to be a handicap and into the true heart and real person that lies within.

Struggling with a Weight Problem

BYRON EMMERT

When you're a fat kid, you nearly die of embarrassment on your first day of seventh-grade gym class, because there's always some thin kids who believe their mission in life is to provide a play-by-play commentary of your getting dressed and undressed.

When you're a fat kid, you try to get out of going to family reunions so you don't have to listen to relatives joke about how you've grown—out rather than up!

When you're a fat kid, you hate going swimming with the opposite sex, because you know their looks and laughs will destine you to life in a monastery as a celibate, whatever that is.

When you're a fat kid, you can look forward to being a fat adult, because the world seems to excuse his rolly pounds, or at least it doesn't pick on old fat people like it picks on you.

When you're a fat kid, you hurt more on the inside than you do on the outside.

You see, I'm an "expert" on this subject, because I was a fat kid. In fact, I remember most of my youth being referred to as "that fat kid!" Besides my own personal experience, I've worked with many overweight teens during my ten years in youth ministry. I'm convinced that few things in life feel more traumatic than being a fat teenager.

Did I survive? Yes, thanks to my parents! If you have a son or daughter with a weight problem, please read on. My parents did some of the right things and so can you. Here are some suggestions on how you can help your overweight teen:

1. *Understand the physical reasons for obesity.* "When an overweight condition is caused by excessive deposits of fat in the body, it is defined as obesity. A person is obese when body weight is twenty percent above the recommended weight for age and height. Obesity has two causes: faulty metabolism, which fails to process food into the basic elements the body can use for energy and growth (this accounts for less than three percent of obesity problems); and unrestrained eating. If you take in more calories than you burn up by expending energy, your body stores the extra calories as fat. One pound of stored fat equals approximately 3,500 calories. Every calorie (a unit of heat) consumed in food is either burned or stored. The more calories we store the more fat we accumulate and the more obese we become" (Virginia Rohrer, "How to Eat Right and Feel Great," *Group* magazine, February 1980, p. 31).

2. *Understand the psychological reasons for obesity.* Not all psychologists agree on why people get fat. Some possible clues, however, are found in Eric Berne's book, *Transactional Analysis,* in which the psychologist talks about the three psychological persons that we all

are: the "Child," the "Parent," and the "Adult."

The "Child" in us keeps some of our irrational thinking as we grow to maturity. *Food represents security, warmth, comfort,* and helps the Child to overcome anxieties and other uncomfortable feelings. Often we continue to use food as a symbol of security and gratification.

As a result, many overweight youth blame their parents for their plight. Psychologists point out that this reasoning is a person's irrational self (the Child) trying to say that he or she is merely a victim of circumstances. This attitude of helplessness stimulates the impulse to eat when facing emotional trauma. The more we eat, the more we gain; the more we gain, the worse we feel, the worse we feel, the more we eat . . .

The "Parent" in us is the mental conditioning that we received from our parents while growing up. It was important that we ate everything on our plate and when we did, our parents beamed!

This is using *the pleasure-pain principle*—rewarding us for eating, withholding approval for not eating. "No vegetable? Then no dessert." The "Child" in us responded by associating eating with reward.

The "Adult" in us evaluates all the facts and does not go by feelings, as the "Child" and "Parent" attitudes do.

An overweight condition may affect a person psychologically. The "Child" in a person may want to solve all problems by eating. The result is cyclical and worsens health. On the other hand, an "Adult" perspective would say, "No one made me fat, and no one can make me thin—but me" (Henry C. Pucek, *Group* magazine, February 1980, p. 36).

3. *Affirm your teenager with your love and acceptance.* As a youth, I remember a family that was visiting our church one Sunday. The father introduced his two thin children by name only, but when he came to his overweight junior higher, he said, "This is our little fatty, Bill. There's lots of him to love!"

Being an overweight junior higher myself, my heart ached for him as I watched him die a slow death of embarrassment. The quiet look in his eyes shouted out his doubt about his dad's love and acceptance for him.

It made me so thankful for parents who never ever put me down because of my weight, either publicly or privately. In fact, they complimented me in front of others and alone. I can't tell you how many times my parents told me that they loved me, accepted me just the way I was, and would always be proud of me. Believe me, this created the atmosphere in which I could begin to deal with my weight problem.

4. *Affirm your teenager with God's love and acceptance.* Because I trusted my parents, I began talking with them about my weight problem. Their love and acceptance helped me realize that God made me special, that I was indeed "fearfully and wonderfully made" (Ps. 139:14). I started accepting the things about myself that could not be changed and I began believing that God would give me the courage to change the things that could be changed, like my weight! This was a major breakthrough for this eighth-grader who was five-foot-three and weighed 162 pounds at the time.

5. *Let the child own the weight reducing plan.* You may try to force your teenager to go on a diet, but effective results will come only if he or she wants to change. I owned my decision to lose weight and willingly gave my parents the opportunity to help and encourage me. I knew they would encourage me for my sake and not for theirs.

6. *Encourage and encourage some more.* Your overweight teenager knows about his or her problem without being reminded or reprimanded like a training coach shaping someone up. As parents, you can encourage in a variety of ways:
• Arrange for a checkup with your doctor for a well-devised, *safe* reducing plan.

• If your teen's weight problem is severe, look into professional counseling or weight loss camps. Check with your doctor or the American Camping Association.

• Private and appropriate public compliments and praises are worth millions in motivation. If there is a temporary setback, like a few pounds gained back over the holidays, remind your teen that he hasn't failed. Help him focus on the progress and the future rather than on one tough weekend.

• Set some short- and long-term goals with rewards along the way. It's amazing how some new clothes or a special trip can help keep incentive high.

• Special coded support messages in the form of smiles, winks, and hugs can ward off the worst ice cream attacks. A little team spirit helps keep the goal within reach and maintains good results.

So does any of this help? You're probably wondering if I lost any weight in the eighth grade? Well, with the encouragement of my family, I started dieting and lifting weights. Seven months later I had lost thirty-three pounds and had grown three inches. Wow! My self-image and outlook on life really changed! I seriously doubt that I could have done that without loving and supportive parents. Best of all, the lessons learned were more valuable than the weight loss.

Now as an adult, I must remember some of those lessons as once again I struggle with my weight. But you know what? My parents helped me learn how to deal with it and you can do the same for your kids.

Coping with Adoption

COULSON DAYTON

The first piece of advice for both the teen being adopted and the adoptive parent is, "Don't look for a miracle panacea." There aren't any! I know from personal experience, because a few years ago, my wife and I adopted an older boy. Even before you meet your future son or daughter, spend much time in prayer. Remember that this youngster is coming from an unwanted background and has gone through traumatic experiences. Read Mark 11:24, 1 John 5:14-15, and Jeremiah 33:3, and claim them as yours.

I remember our son, Peter Philip, telling us, "I love you as my parents, but I can't trust you yet." He said this because for eleven years of his life he had bounced among foster families, orphanages, and children's hospitals. He had no roots, was never able to become attached to anyone, and looked at everybody with distrust. He had been abused along the way, as well. Today he is still struggling, but the trust has come.

When the young person comes, don't push too fast or too hard. Give him time to adjust, to explore, and to get used to the new surroundings. Without smothering with hugs, let him know you care and that you love him. Allow God's love to flow through you consistently, steadily, and quietly. Sooner or later, your love will be reciprocated when the youngster realizes, "Hey, these people love me."

Accept your adopted child as he is. What a joy it was when Peter accepted Christ as his personal Saviour. He was drawn to Christ when he realized that the love my wife and I had for him was unusual. It was a supernatural, *agape* love that could come only from Jesus

Christ. It took a year and a half for our son to decide for Christ. We didn't push him or constantly "preach" at him, but we *did* include him in our family devotions each night after dinner.

That first year and a half was quite an experience! Peter really put us through it. More than once I had to go find him and physically bring him home. He started hanging out with the type of kids he had known in his old neighborhood and at some of his foster homes. He was smoking behind our backs, came home drunk more than once, and was into marijuana. I prayed but never "preached" to him. I punished him, but not with a "religious" piety about it. Even then, I could see love and trust growing between us.

Spend time with your child. Find out what he likes to do, and do things together. Encourage a hobby and don't let TV become the "drug" with which you keep your new member of the family occupied.

Right away, sit down and discuss the rules of the home including curfew and family duties. We gave Peter three jobs: sweep the kitchen floor each day, take in the empty garbage pails twice a week, and feed the dog. These were "free" simply because he was a part of the family. Then we told him of the other duties which would be expected of him. These included shoveling snow and cutting grass, and in each case he would be paid for his work (a fair wage). It is important not to take advantage of the adopted child. That is, if you pay him for any chores, be fair and pay him whatever other kids receive for the same jobs.

Also, teach your adopted son or daughter about discipline. I informed Peter that I believed in and would use corporal punishment. He got spanked a few times by both my wife and me. I didn't "beat" him to the point of abusing him, but he knew he had been spanked. If he cried before I finished, I would stop. He soon caught on to that; and once, after one whack, he bawled for all he was worth. I put down the "spoon," and turned to look at him. He was mischievously smiling at me, and I knew I'd been had! We both had a good laugh, and the matter was dropped. For parents of an adopted child to be able to discipline, they must obey Proverbs 20:7 and watch how they live. Set the example; let God's love flow through you to your child, and be consistent with your discipline and home rules. But do not be a tyrant either.

There will be tough times, but don't give up or give in. Our son is by no means out of the woods, and he still has problems coping. Some of these times are stormy, but there is progress. At times we have no recourse but to turn to the One who created Peter Philip and pour out our souls to Him. Romans 8:24-25 and James 1:5-7 give us hope. God will work through us as *He* builds these young lives.

Related Article

Chapter 21: The Challenge of Being a Stepparent

When to Seek Professional Help

GARY D. BENNETT

Numerous public and private agencies exist which provide services to adolescents and their families. Each one has its special and unique contributions; however, only one "agency" in existence today has the capability of meeting all needs. Only through the resources of the church of Jesus Christ can an individual's social, physical, mental, and spiritual needs be met fully. Other agencies concentrate on one or two aspects, but the church should be utilized for a balanced and complete approach.

In other words, it is important to first seek help from the minister of a local church. If the needs of your adolescent and/or family are beyond his expertise, an appropriate agency in the community is the next step. Ask your pastor to assist in making such a referral and to remain involved in a supportive role.

When should you ask for help with your teenager? Whenever the teenager requests or indicates in other ways that he needs help, whenever you feel you can no longer handle the situation, or whenever the teenager's behavior may have harmful long-term consequences. For example, chronic unhappiness, behavior problems (e.g., lying, stealing, running away), feelings of worthlessness, and continuing depression or loneliness may be reasons for referral. Often a few counseling sessions with a professional will be all that is needed.

Besides the church, here are some community resources which can be contacted for help with:

Discipline:	Family service agencies
	Juvenile court
	School counselor
Drugs:	Counselor on alcoholism
	Drug crisis or treatment centers
	Police department
Runaways:	Police department
	Runaway centers
	Social services and family service agencies
Sexual misconduct:	Family service agencies
	Planned Parenthood

How do you encourage your teenager to take advantage of these community resources?

1. Make your teenager aware of the availability of specific resources.

2. Share the responsibility for making and keeping appointments.

3. Help your teenager understand that seeking help doesn't mean he is sick, crazy, or "psycho."

4. Emphasize the educational nature of many resources, and that appropriate help will usually broaden the individual's freedom of choice by providing more options.

5. Convey the attitude that seeking help and using appropriate services are signs of maturity.

6. Point out that going to an agency does not give the agency control over the teen's life, and that he will retain the right to continue or discontinue using its services.

7. Find out as much as possible about the agency's procedures, and then explain in detail to your child what will happen, how he will be received, what questions will be asked, etc.

What about other alternative living arrangements? The basic reason for placing a child in an alternative living arrangement is to provide a period of separation to work out personal problems. Separation from the family provides the teen the opportunity to take a close look at himself and his behavior. Separation also provides the parents the opportunity to make needed family changes to facilitate a more meaningful relationship when the child returns.

Foster care is the most common alternative to home care, providing a home for adolescents when their parents are unable or unwilling to provide for their well-being. Foster care is usually a temporary, short-term arrangement. Being raised by "temporary" parents can be traumatic. Though a good substitute, foster care should never be considered permanent.

For more intense problems and seriously disturbed teenagers, "residential treatment" facilities are available. Usually these are group homes where staff provide treatment and supervision of youngsters in residence. Their goal is to return and reunite the adolescents with their families. Residential care is only necessary when it can provide specialized treatment not available in the community.

One final thought: Seeking outside professional help is not an admission of parental failure. It is simply recognizing the need for help.

WHEN THE FAMILY RUNS INTO THE LAW

- Why do teens get in trouble with the law?
- What to do if your teen gets arrested
- Could you turn your own teenager over to the authorities?
- Dealing with stealing
- Can the church or community help the troubled teen?
- What rights do parents have with wayward minor children?
- Can you still treat your outlaw teen as a son or daughter?

The heart of delinquency is the heart of the delinquent. To help solve his problems, we have to work from the inside out.

Often juvenile delinquency is simply an extreme reaction by an adolescent, unprepared for life, who comes in contact with a hostile and negative society. In too many cases delinquency is a parental problem.

In a good family, the father will come to his son's side in a moment of need and help him through the tough period. In the case of many delinquent young people, there is no one there to help. The juvenile justice system does its best, but it is too impersonal to provide the kind of help a family can give. Occasionally Christian children get caught in this web. Understanding parents can help them through.

What to Do When Your Teenager Gets in Trouble with the Law

JOHN W. WHITEHEAD

Crime is a learned activity. As such, no one is immune to its influence. We live in a fallen world, and even children from "good, Christian homes" have a tendency to sin.

Teenagers can get messed up for different reasons, but I think two major causes for their involvement in crime are: (1) too much leniency on the part of the parents, and (2) peer pressure. Peer pressure is probably the most dangerous problem children face in the public school system today. Young children have an intense desire to be liked by their peers, especially during their teenage years. This craving for acceptance often leads them into experimentation with drugs, sex, alcohol, and crime.

A strong Christian background is the best remedy for destructive peer pressure. The child needs the positive influences of church and family to counteract what he experiences at school. Parents must love and care about their child enough to maintain communication with him no matter what. When the child comes home and says, "Hey, the kids at school are smoking marijuana," parents should be honest enough to say, "I don't think it is right."

But sometimes problems do arise and parents are forced to face the fact that their child has become involved in some illegal activity. The situation is often as much a trauma for the parents as it is for the teen. If the teen has become involved in a crime with adults, like burglary, the chances are good that he will be tried as an adult. For smaller crimes like petty theft or vandalism, the teen is likely to face a juvenile judge who will call the parents to come down to juvenile court.

If the parents cannot be contacted or if there is any indication of parental neglect, the teen will probably by held in a detention center until the court makes some kind of disposition of the case. Often in a juvenile situation, social workers will meet with the parents, conduct what is called a home study, and propose sentence alternatives. In other words, they can recommend whether a child be placed on probation and sent back to his parents or put in a juvenile center for a while to be counseled. Either way, the parents can be in for quite a shock.

The first concern for a lot of parents is worry about their reputation in the community and what other people will think. But they should forget all that and worry about what is going to happen to their child who has committed a crime. I believe that there are many kids in prisons today who wouldn't be there if their parents had shown more compassion at the time of the crime. If parents need help in coping with the situation, I urge them to seek it.

Parents should work with pastors and, if possible, social workers. The pastor should be involved in the entire process, not condemning the teen, but helping just by showing he cares. Social workers are occasionally hard to work with—some are humanistic and even antiparent. But usually they will call the parents, try to get the child released into parental custody, and make themselves available for counseling.

Of course, the child himself can refuse to return home with his parents. Usually this occurs if he is alleging child abuse. In such cases the judge recommends what should be done. The teen will probably then be placed in a home detention center or foster home.

I'm still speaking of treatment of less serious crimes. As a whole, the courts are more lenient on juveniles. But if juveniles are involved in a violent crime like murder, they are treated just like adults. The basic difference in the treatment of adults and juveniles is that the parents have more input in juvenile cases. The whole disposition in juvenile courts seems to be whatever is best for the child.

Teenagers need to be taught a healthy respect for the law, preferably before they begin to engage in criminal activities. Many teens have the attitude that policemen are their enemies. I think the church could greatly reduce the tension between teenagers and the law. (Unfortunately, there is much antagonism between some churches and the state as a whole, including the police.) But I think that whenever churches have picnics or sports activities, the local police should be invited. Policemen could even be invited to speak at church meetings about community programs, activities, fun fairs, and so forth, so that teenagers will begin to see them in a more positive way.

Such interaction could even benefit many of the policemen I know. Some of them have developed a cold attitude toward the public in general. By bringing teenagers and the law together, each side can become more sensitive to the other. Teenagers need to see policemen as more than just men in uniform—to realize that many of them are parents, and that they all have distinct personalities and problems. As teens begin to see law enforcement officers as real people, perhaps they can develop the confidence to walk up to a policeman and say, "Hey, I've been involved in something that might get me in trouble. Can you help?"

Respect for the law is important even if the teenager has already committed an offense. The family must pull together to support the child. The Scriptures should

---

YOUR TEEN'S RIGHTS UNDER THE LAW

Many parents have a nagging fear that one day the phone will ring and a police officer will tell them that their teenager is in custody down at the station. And by the time you hang up that telephone, it may be too late for your teenager if he doesn't know his rights under the law.

As parents, you should never condone your teenager's wrongdoing. And you should never side with your child when you know the authorities are fair and just. However, teenagers have rights under the law just as adults do. As parents, it is our responsibility to tell our children exactly what they should and should not do when picked up by a law enforcement officer.

Right #1. Teenagers have the right to remain silent. If they are juveniles, they must notify their parents.

Right #2. Teenagers have the right to consult an attorney before answering any questions. If they cannot afford an attorney, they have the right to have one appointed for them.

Right #3. Teenagers should know that when a law enforcement officer advises them of their legal rights, that officer is technically making an accusation of guilt. Anything they say after those rights are read can be used against them in court.

Make sure to tell your children that if they are ever advised of their rights by a law enforcement officer, or if they are ever accused of a violation, they should say *nothing* except their name and address. There is plenty of time to tell law enforcement officials what happened *after* the parents have learned the facts and received the advice and presence of competent legal counsel. The attorney will tell you *when* and *if* making a statement to the authorities is the right thing to do and in your child's best interest.

Teenagers also need to be alerted not only to the obvious abuses of police power (brutality, threats), but to the more subtle dangers of perceived friendliness ("OK, Son, I understand. I'm your friend. Just tell me what happened."). While most law enforcement officials can be trusted, many cannot. Protect your teenager from these possible abuses of the intent of the law.

As parents, you must tell your children these things—don't let them find out the hard way, and don't assume that the school will map it our clearly. Remember that moral guilt and legal responsibility are not the same thing. Always insist that your child face his wrongdoing in his own mind. But he has no obligation under our laws to incriminate himself to authorities or in the courts.

Gordon McLean

---

be taught. The pastor ought to counsel. Even a good local policeman could come in to talk with the teen. By working together, you can show him where he is headed if he continues in crime. Give some examples of people who began by committing small crimes who are now in the state penitentiary for life, having lost all their freedom.

Parents should be sterner with children who repeat their offenses. The punishment should depend on the teen, but I often hear probation officers say that if a child is involved in several crimes, it might be a good idea to let him sit in jail for a few days. That way he will get a fair indication of where he is headed if he doesn't shape up. A couple of nights spent in a jail cell with criminals has a sobering effect—even on adults.

Parents should prepare for the worst, so that if they ever have to confront a teenager who is involved in a scrape with the law they will be able to say, "How can I help you?" instead of, "What are you trying to do to me?" In the meantime, parents should take practical steps to prevent their child from becoming involved with criminal activity.

It is important for parents to be involved in a strong local church so their children will associate with other Christian families. It is especially important for teenagers to take part in church activities. Wise parents will exercise control over who their child can associate with and try to reduce negative peer pressure whenever they can. As the entire family learns to yield to the power of the Holy Spirit, they will seek better models to imitate and crime will not be a problem.

Related Articles

Why Your Teenager Gets in Trouble with the Law

GREGORY MONACO

Delinquency, or departure from the accepted norms of behavior, is an individualized problem whose causes vary from person to person. I know, because I've worked with hundreds of delinquent young people, and no two have problems alike. There are some clues, though, to how the process begins, so let's look at these.

Two things happen as children grow. First, they learn from their experiences at home, in school, on the streets, in church, on TV, wherever they go. They are amassing files and files of information on how to act, who they are, and what they believe. At this point they are simply *storing* input from the world around them.

Second, at some future point they begin a process of *owning* that input. All children put aside the values they have gathered thus far in life and evaluate them, subconsciously asking questions like: "Do they fit with my experience?"

"Are they true?" "Do they work?" Remember, not all kids step as far back from their values or stand away from them for as long as their peers might, but all young people go through this process.

The average young person with a stable home, consistent modeling of values, and a sufficient dose of love and self-worth, makes it through this period with a minimum of rebellion or moving away from his family's values.

Occasionally though, a traumatic event occurs in an otherwise average young person's life—the death of a loved one, divorce, an experience of personal failure—that can trigger a deeper questioning and doubt of those family values. Often this leads to a rejection of a value or set of values and in extreme cases, a headlong plunge into a countervalue. Thankfully, this does not usually last long; as Proverbs 22:6 says, "Train up a child in the way he should go, and when he is old he will not depart from it" (NASB).

But then there is the young person who never had a consistent experience while growing up. He saw parents, peers, circumstances, and his environment constantly giving strong but conflicting messages. Maybe Mom was an alcoholic; the family often went hungry while surrounded by TV's messages of affluence; peer influence was often aimless or even destructive.

What does that inconsistency mean to the young person? First, it leaves him without a foundation as he enters this crucial period of value examination. Contrary to the "normal" teen who is rebelling or testing learned values, this teen has no system of values to test. It creates a time of turmoil and fear, of questioning his very existence. "What is this world all about?" "What am I about?" he asks.

Second, this young person is in a "Catch 22" situation. Without a base on which to build, he needs all that much more support, love, and direction than the child who comes from a more stable home. But, the lack of these things is the very reason the young person has no value system in the first place.

This is the source of deepest delinquency. The child from a stable, loving home has the tools to grow through this period of testing. The child with no consistent home, peer, and community base finds himself without values and thus without identity. Delinquency is merely acting out this experience of confusion and aimlessness.

The causes of delinquency are varied and complex. Test your own home situation with these simple questions. First ask, "Does the child have a strong foundation for testing values?" Then ask, "Has any trauma brought about a temporary and serious questioning of values?" And ask finally, "Are resources available for the young person to fall back on—the love, consistency, and direction it takes to formulate a healthy self-concept and value system?"

Related Articles

THE INS AND OUTS OF THE JUVENILE JUSTICE PROCESS

The following tabular presentation shows some of the key decision points in the formal processing of an accused or dependent juvenile. The process varies widely from one state to the next, but the general pattern is similar to that in this simplified series of ways in and ways out of the system.

Arrest

The juvenile justice process often begins with an investigation by a police officer either because he or she observes a law violation or because a violation is reported to the police.

The police officer may decide to release the child to his or her parents with a warning or reprimand, or on condition that the juvenile enroll in a community diversion program.

Or the officer may take the juvenile into custody and refer the matter to the juvenile court's intake officer for further processing.

Intake

The intake officer is responsible for determining whether or not a case should move ahead for further court processing.

The intake officer may decide to release the juvenile to the parents with a warning or reprimand, or may release the child on condition that the child enroll in a community diversion program or submit to informal probation (supervision) by a juvenile court officer.

If not, the intake officer will recommend that a petition be filed, equivalent to filing a charge, and will refer the case to the juvenile court prosecutor. The intake officer also makes the initial decision as to whether the child shall be detained pending further court action or released to the parents pending a hearing. If the juvenile is detained, the decision is received by a judge or a court administrator at a juvenile court detention hearing.

Petition

The juvenile court prosecutor reviews the recommendation of the intake officer that a petition be filed. The petition, if filed by the prosecutor, is a formal document that initiates the court adjudication process.

The prosecutor may dismiss the case or, in contrast, find the allegations so serious that he recommends the juvenile be waived to adult court for trial as an adult.

Adjudication

The juvenile court judge must review all the evidence presented at a hearing and determine whether to sustain or reject the allegations made on the petition.

> The juvenile court judge may reject the allegations made in the petition; then the juvenile is released. In some cases the judge may believe that the allegations are true but withhold adjudication on condition the child agrees to enroll in a community program that the court feels will help resolve the problem.

If the allegations in the petition are sustained, the child is adjudicated delinquent, dependent, or in need of supervision. From here the case moves to disposition.

Disposition

At a hearing, the juvenile court judge reviews the recommendations of all concerned parties as to what should happen to the child.

> Even now, the judge may decide that a severe form of treatment is not to the advantage of the youth or the community. In this case, the disposition may be probation, a warning or reprimand, some form of community service, a fine, or "home detention," in which the juvenile continues to live at home but receives rigorous daily counseling.

Other dispositions are more stringent. They may be such nonsecure custodial treatment as foster care or group home placement—but they may range up to incarceration in a secure juvenile correctional facility. The judge's disposition will depend on the seriousness of the offense and the child's previous court history.

Aftercare

> Whatever disposition is made of the case, the court may make the termination of that disposition contingent on the juvenile's acceptance of aftercare—probation, counseling, enrollment in a community program, or any of a number of other forms of treatment designed to lessen the chance that the youth will get in trouble again.

From *Facts about Youth and Delinquency*, prepared by the National Juvenile Justice Clearinghouse, U.S. Dept. of Justice. Used by permission.

"He's Done Something Wrong. . . . What Do We Do Now?"

GORDON McLEAN

The parents were shocked. They had just confronted their daughter with some merchandise Mom had found in the girl's room while cleaning. Things that were stolen from a nearby store. What were they going to do?

We put this situation in the form of a question to a group of inner-city gang youth, young people still in their teens, to whom stealing is, in many instances, as normal as breathing. Their response may be surprising.

They were unanimous in agreeing the worst thing that can happen to a kid is to do wrong and get away with it. But they felt the correct response was important too. Most of them had been beaten by angry and drunken fathers for their actions and all that did was add to their bitterness and daring next time around.

These street kids suggested the parents should go to the store with their child but let the child handle the situation. The merchandise should be returned or paid for. The directness and humiliation of such a response should certainly serve as a deterrent of future misconduct. They also noted the merchant may not want to let the police know the goods were returned so he can end up with both his merchandise back *and* money from the insurance company. These kids don't trust anybody.

But the situation may be more serious, such as a fight where someone was severely hurt and the police are involved. Our youthful experts, again veterans of such situations, considered a number of alternatives before suggesting this: The parents should immediately contact a private attorney. They stressed a private attorney because their confidence in court-appointed public defenders is very limited and often for good reason.

They suggested that the parents and child should tell the attorney exactly what happened and then have the lawyer go with the young person to the police station.

Going alone to the police without benefit of an attorney is not a good idea. The police are primarily interested in clearing cases and getting convictions. That is not to say there are not some very concerned police officers who want to help and do all they can to redirect a young offender. There are. But there are too many of the other kind around who want to clear a case and lock up an offender for as long as possible. And, sad to say, there are some who are not above fabricating evidence as well as physically and mentally abusing a naive youth. Thus the advice: To admit you've done something wrong to a police officer is like bleeding in front of a shark. A good attorney can advise on when and what to say to the authorities.

Certainly the advice that a suspect has a right to remain silent and have an attorney present for any questioning should be taken seriously. A youth should not be swayed by harshness or even kindness on the part of officers, nor should he think that a minor doesn't need or can't have a lawyer. A young person should never be abusive or disrespectful to an officer, nor should he lie to one. The minor should give his name, address, and phone number and ask that his parents and an attorney be notified if he is held.

Just as you would call a doctor if your child were sick, a legal problem calls for the best professional help available: a good lawyer to guide a concerned family through trying and unfamiliar waters in the criminal justice system.

Your concern is to right the wrong, to see your young person learn from a mistake, and to make sure that proper restitution is made. The justice system does not always have those same goals.

But above all don't miss turning a crisis or a mistake your young person may make into a corrective, positive learning experience. Even young veterans of the streets wish their parents had done that.

Related Articles

Facing Up to the Consequences
HARVEY HOOK

How can the parents of a delinquent teen help their son or daughter once an offense has been committed? Several questions must be answered in order to provide the most appropriate aid.

Is this a first offense or is this part of a continuing cycle of problematic behavior? With an increase in frequency and severity of crime it becomes imperative to move to a more formal intervention with greater external controls. Such controls range from parental intervention, counseling, and specialized programs to juvenile court, probation, and institutionalization.

What type of offense has been committed? Is it a *"victimless" crime,* such as alcohol or drug abuse? If so, seek specialized counseling; courts and other juvenile authorities are more concerned that a teen be helped than that he be punished for such wrongdoing. The schools, juvenile court, and some churches will have a list of programs where help can be provided.

One of the greatest influences on a teen is the peer group. Quite often a teen's friends support his alcohol or drug use. It is important to break the current circle of friends and seek an alternative support group that does not reinforce such behavior. In extreme cases it may require moving the child to a new school, removing him from the home, or moving the entire family.

Is it a *misdemeanor,* such as a theft from an acquaintance, a minor item shoplifted, or a traffic offense? When possible, handle immediately and informally with a specific consequence. Have the teen face the victim, agree to restitution in terms of cash or work, and then follow through until completion. Also try to involve him in an ongoing youth program.

Is it a *felony,* such as an auto theft, burglary, robbery, or aggravated assault? The seriousness of the offense indicates a more serious emotional problem and mandates formal intervention with a greater number of restrictions. Fewer options remain available at this point. Parents should contact the juvenile court or the police and follow their direction. Following any formal action, a support group should be provided to work with both the family and the child.

In summary, several guidelines can be followed that will assure the most immediate and complete consequences for the teen's behavior, while giving the greatest consideration to his needs.

First and foremost, parents should seek guidance and counsel from a minister, church elder, teacher, counselor, or trusted friend. This additional perspective will help to maintain their objectivity while providing greater resources in looking at the options available. Second, parents should communicate their awareness of the crime, their deep hurt, and yet their unchanging love in spite of such behavior. Third, parents are encouraged to seek options that bring the teen into contact with the victim. This can be handled informally and bring an immediate consequence to the teen's action. Last, it is imperative that parents follow through to the conclusion with the established consequences.

Dealing with Stealing

GARY D. BENNETT

Some teenagers steal exclusively from family members; others steal only from people outside the family; still others steal from both. Some steal food; some steal insignificant articles; and others steal items of great value (or any combination of the above).

Children are motivated to steal for a number of reasons:

1. *They are needy.* They haven't had enough or don't have their "fair share" of food or possessions. Some teenagers steal because they want things and have no other way to obtain them.

2. *They replace.* Young people with great emotional hunger will often steal things to help them feel better. (How can someone steal an emotion?)

3. *They want attention.* It is better to have someone angry with you than to have everyone ignore you. Negative attention is better than no attention at all. Stealing may be a signal that teens are not getting enough attention from the family.

4. *They want to demonstrate anger or aggression.* Stealing is a way to "get back" at people.

5. *They seek recognition.* Stealing will startle or get the attention of their friends.

6. *They are responding to peer pressure.* Stealing will help them be part of the group; especially if stealing is considered the status symbol for being "macho."

7. *They are copying others.* "Important" adults have provided poor models. They have been seen stealing from the company or office or simply borrowing things from the neighbor and "forgetting" to return them.

It is important to try to figure out and understand why your teenager is stealing. What are his motives? What pulls the trigger? What are your feelings when this happens? (Is this a clue to their motives?) Are there certain situations that lead to stealing?

Next, try to change the situation so the teenager is less likely to steal.

1. *Establish property rights.* Give the teenager a place to keep his things free from disturbance, and don't borrow or use his things without first asking.

2. *Teach how to borrow and return.* This also involves asking for permission and handling disappointment when permission is denied.

3. *Insist on restitution for stealing.*

4. *Provide legitimate sources of income.* Give the teen opportunities to earn money, as well as, perhaps, an allowance, which will enable him to purchase things he desires.

5. *Remove temptation.*

6. *Help the teenager to feel good about himself.* A child who feels inadequate, insecure, and unaccepted may simply be expressing his feelings by stealing from others.

7. *Listen carefully.* Try to understand his feelings regarding his needs.

8. *Demonstrate your honesty by sharing honest feelings of embarrassment and disappointment.* Make sure he knows your feelings are about his behavior and not directed at him personally.

9. *Establish clear, specific rules.* Make sure that these rules are enforceable, that

DEAR MISTER ROBBER

It is now 12:15 A.M. and I have just wiped the late evening tears from my daughter's eyes and promised her that I won't go to bed until she is asleep.

Sleep comes with difficulty since you robbed our home one warm autumn afternoon not long ago. Before that day she always saw the good in people, experienced little fear, enjoyed bouncing upstairs at bedtime and the chance to gaze at the ceiling fan while anticipating the joys of the next day.

All that has changed now. Her world has caved in. Ceilings now reveal strange and horrifying shadows, night sounds cause her heart to race. We talk; we pray; we read comforting Scriptures. All of this keeps her from a sense of hopelessness. But you stole more than a few material goods that day.

She got off the bus, skipped up to the front door, and saw her house with rooms turned upside down, a window broken out, expensive items hastily left behind lying on the floor, and the kitchen garbage emptied in the middle of the room so the sack could carry that which you thought so valuable. You never got to my daughter's room, but what she lost was far more precious than replaceable goods covered by homeowner's insurance.

If you are ever caught and brought before a court of law, I ask not that they judge you for stolen jewelry and cameras—they are ultimately so meaningless. But may your conscience have a tender crack where you will be condemned and sentenced to feel that no stranger can be trusted. May you beg for sleep to come quickly on frightened nights. May peace of mind be sought after more diligently than anything that can be hawked at a pawn shop. For if you could feel just for a moment these same haunting emotions my daughter feels each sleepless night, repentance would likely be very near.

Larry Kreider

they are understood, that they have specific consequences, and that the consequences follow the behavior.

Shoplifting is quite common among children between the ages of ten and twelve. A couple episodes of shoplifting with a child do not mean that there is a serious underlying problem. Meeting this behavior with parental disapproval and insisting that the child return or pay for the merchandise will usually "nip it in the bud." Usually more drastic measures are necessary when a teenager shoplifts frequently. When this happens, parents need to give the clear message, "We know this is a problem, and we are going to work together to make it easier for you not to be tempted to take things." One mother approached the problem with, "It will be easier for us both if you show me a receipt for everything you bring into this house. That way I won't unjustly accuse you if you really did buy something. It will be easier for me to trust you, and for you to trust me."

For a teen with a history of stealing, prohibiting him from keeping things which have been "found, borrowed, or received as gifts" helps avoid many hassles. The responsibility should be placed on the teen for proving that he has acquired things honestly, rather than on the parents to make sure that he is not lying.

Related Articles
Chapter 23: "Why My Teenager?"
Chapter 23: When to Seek Professional Help
Chapter 24: What to Do When Your Teenager Gets in Trouble with the Law

Can the Church Help the Troubled Teen?

GREGORY MONACO

The troubled teen basically lacks one thing that *only* the church can provide—a positive, affirming relationship with a person who knows *who* he is and *why* he is here, a relationship with a Christian.

In examining all the treatment plans, corrective programs, and books about troubled people, you will find a common thread woven in the methodology—the need for healthy relationships. But these cannot be just any relationships. They must be those which serve without asking in return and which provide unconditional love. They must involve people who are at peace with themselves and the world around them, with people who understand what life is about—Christians.

The church is not a building, or a denomination; the church is people. If ten people from every local church committed themselves to reaching out to one troubled teen each, our nation would experience unbelievable change.

Unfortunately, troubled young people probably won't enter churches on Sunday mornings to seek out those relationships. The church must become aggressive and reach out. Then, after relationships have been formed, these teenagers will see the church not as a religious building, but as a group of people like Joe and Mary, their friends, who really love each other—and them!

How can this happen? It is not possible for every church to hire a full-time social worker to coordinate an outreach. But many churches have a social worker, counselor, or youth worker within their congregations who can volunteer time to the project. Maybe the church down the street or around the corner can help. In addition there are excellent "secular" programs like Big Brothers or Police Boys' Clubs which will provide training and supervision for your volunteers. The Youth Guidance Department of Youth for Christ is dedicated to enabling church people to reach out and has materials to help you, as do Volunteers in Probation and Partners (both evangelical organizations).

The church provides the only answer for troubled teens, a personal relationship with their Creator. Only *personal* communication through a *personal* relationship with a child of that Creator will introduce them to the Answer.

Youth for Christ
P.O. Box 419
Wheaton, Illinois 60189

Volunteers in Probation
200 Washington Square Plaza
Royal Oak, Michigan 48067

Partners
1260 West Bayaud
Denver, Colorado 80223

Related Articles
Chapter 16: Can the Church Solve My Teen's Problems?
Chapter 16: What Can the Church Do?
Chapter 24: Can the Community Help the Troubled Teen?

Can the Community Help the Troubled Teen?

JOHN PERKINS

I believe the community truly desires to help the troubled teen through a variety of structured programs. Unfortunately, in many cases those structured programs remove people from the community instead of helping them to learn to function within it.

Because a teenager can be greatly affected by the people who live in his community, a secure and healthy environment needs to be created on a neighborhood level. The community has to engage people to create programs designed specifically for its particular needs. It needs to ask, "How can this program affect the block in which I live?"

We ask the wrong questions when we ask other people to tell us what we should be learning ourselves at the commuity level. Of course, we need *some* direction about what should be done, but the specific methods should be up to each city or town. The general principles are the same for each community. The community needs a park. There must be a place where kids can play, where drugs are not acceptable, a place where they can enjoy life. But detailed manuals aren't going to help in the long run because each community has a different starting point.

Parents must be especially sensitive to the felt needs of the kids within the community. Then they must do what is necessary to show love to those kids by meeting those felt needs. Just remember, the felt needs are going to vary from community to community.

Starting right in our own homes, we need to create an environment where neighborhood kids know they are welcomed and encouraged to come for help. In fact, we should try to make our homes a place where people of all ages can feel comfortable and experience Christian love in action.

We are substituting institutions and programs for people. Programs only facilitate. They are the means, not the goal. As good as a program can be, it doesn't take the place of personal contact. We get people to volunteer for half a day down at the mental health center, but that is not equal to what they can do right in their own neighborhood.

Related Articles
Chapter 23: When to Seek Professional Help
Chapter 24: Can the Church Help the Troubled Teen?

Your Teenager's Day in Court
DWIGHT SPOTTS

The laws relating to parents' rights and liabilities are written by individual states. Often these laws are enforced differently depending on the jurisdiction and on the interpretation by the county-based juvenile courts. These courts basically are geared to protect, not punish children, and juvenile proceedings are civil, not criminal, in nature. Therefore, the parents' "legal liabilities" are seen in light of the child's needs as determined by the court. Specific questions can be answered by local juvenile court personnel, listed under "County Government" in the phone book. Usually, similar legal "rules of thumb" apply, regardless of jurisdiction.

The family unit continues to be the fundamental institution for working with children. Most states try to keep children with their families to solve their problems in the home. A child will be taken out of the home only when it is necessary for the protection of the child, other family members, or society at large. While many legal decisions seem to infringe on the fundamental framework of families, in reality most juvenile courts only intervene as a last resort. Parents remain legally responsible for the adequate care and supervision of their children.

According to the Uniform Juvenile Court Act of 1968, parental rights can only be terminated when a child is "deprived of proper care or control, subsistence, education as required by law, or other care or control necessary for his physical, mental, or emotional health or morals, and the deprivation is not due primarily to lack of financial means." Many states hold parents financially accountable for a child's maintenance even after their rights have been terminated.

This is not necessarily true for a "delinquent" (one who has committed a "delinquent act" [i.e., an offense applicable to adults, and requiring treatment or rehabilitation]) or an "unruly child," one who:

• While attending school is habitually and without justification truant
• Is habitually disobedient of the reasonable and lawful commands of his

parents, guardian, or other custodian and is ungovernable
- Has committed an offense applicable only to a child (i.e., truancy, running away, drinking underage)
- Is in need of treatment or rehabilitation.

In summary, juvenile courts have jurisdiction over matters pertaining to children and parents. Juvenile courts treat similar cases differently from county to county. Parents are legally responsible for the reasonable care and supervision of their children. If the court determines that parents are at fault, they may require them to pay for a child's mainte-nance once the child has been placed elsewhere.

Most courts will try to help rather than punish parents of willfully unruly children so that the family unit will remain intact. If you believe that a juvenile court is not considering your parental rights/needs, consider the selection of legal counsel that will represent your interests.

Related Articles

Chapter 24: What to Do When Your Teen-ager Gets in Trouble with the Law
Chapter 24: Why Your Teenager Gets in Trouble with the Law

Should a Young Person Be Locked Up?

GORDON McLEAN

Chris Peterman's parents, unaware of the risks involved, let their seventeen-year-old son spend a weekend in the Ada County Jail, Boise, Idaho in hopes he would learn a lesson in personal responsibility. Chris had failed to pay $60 in traffic fines.

Sadly, the lesson he learned was not the one his parents intended. He learned that behind bars human life is not worth much. After several hours of beating and torture inflicted by his youthful cell-mates, Chris was dead. Only a week before, another juvenile, Rick Yallen, had been beaten so severely in that same cell he required hospital attention.

These incidents happened in Boise, certainly not considered a violent community. And they happened in a county jail where all too many young people are held. Only one in three counties in this country, generally in larger population centers, even have juvenile facilities and not all of them are safe or suitable for housing young people. In a growing number of states young people in their midteens and older will be turned away from juvenile centers to be confined only in county jails with adults.

Not all young people who are locked up have committed criminal acts. In many places minors can and will be confined at the request of their parents for status offenses, violations that are not considered illegal for an adult—disobedience, skipping school, staying out late, or running away from home. Well-intentioned parents may think a beyond-control youth will benefit from such confinement and learn a much needed lesson. But few good lessons are apt to be absorbed in a penal setting rife with violence, illicit drugs, sexual assaults, hostility, and gang rivalries carried over from dangerous streets.

Children of the rich may not suffer such indignities, but may be hauled off in handcuffs on private planes—without benefit of charges, trial, or court order— to private rehabilitation facilities. In total disregard of their rights as citizens, they will be held in secure and expensive facilities and placed in an intensive training program designed "for their own good."

No one should be confined without having committed a clear criminal offense which was determined at a fair trial where the accused was represented by competent counsel. Pure motives and good intentions are no excuse for unwarranted detention.

Even more important, parents should not allow their hurt, frustration, and disappointment at youthful irresponsibility to keep them from dealing with the underlying problem faced by the youth in their home. "I'll show you" may offer some temporary respite and satisfaction to angry parents but it is no long-range solution.

Here is where the family needs the skills of the most competent professional counselor available, hopefully a Christian, who can help both parents and children to sort through mixed feelings, hurt attitudes, peer pressure, and confused values. Sadly, many families will rush to treat a physical illness or a broken bone, as well they should, but leave unattended festering emotional hurts that can be far more crippling and destructive in the long run.

Beyond-control conduct, rebellion, and a pattern of law violations are symptoms of moral vacuum, spiritual disarray, lack of self-respect, and emotional hurt. Such behavior calls for a response of patience, firmness, and intelligent caring that knows when to go outside the home for competent professional help.

Confinement can delay dealing with the problem, but it certainly won't solve it. And, as the Boise experience reminds us, the result may be a tragedy no one wants.

Related Articles

Healing a Relationship with a Troubled Teen

WAYNE GEORGE

In order for parents to enter into a positive, healing relationship with their troubled son or daughter they must first face two facts. One, "Our child is troubled and we have contributed to his present condition." Two, "All teenagers are troubled to some degree, some more than others." Accepting these facts will give you a healthy perspective from which to initiate a new relationship. You are not accepting total responsibility for your child's troubles nor are you projecting total responsibility on your child. Together, you and your teenager must accept mutual ownership of the problems as well as the solutions which follow.

As parents you need to make the first move by reaching out to your teen with unconditional love and acceptance. Demonstrate through your words and actions that "I love you and accept you as you are—period," not "I will love and accept you if you meet the following conditions."

Nothing can substitute for an investment of your time in your child's life. Spend time with your teenager. It is popular today to say that it is not the quantity but the quality of time that is important. This may sound good but it's garbage. You cannot have a real quality relationship with anyone without investing a good quantity of time. This is especially true in the parent-child relationship. Don't give your teenager the scraps. Plan specific and special times to spend with your child.

Teenagers don't always need advice. Often they just need to be heard, to be listened to, to be understood. Listen to what is said, what is *not* said, and what is said between the lines. Demonstrate a genuine interest in trying to understand your teenager—his fears, desires, frustrations, needs, and interests.

Avoid talking "down" to your teen and don't substitute lecturing for talking. Recognize that your teenager is no longer a child, that he is growing and maturing, that he is capable of independent thinking and reasoning. You must adjust the way you communicate to your child as he grows older. What may have been appropriate a year or two ago might no longer apply.

Allow your teenager to express his own unique individuality and identity. Respect honest differences of opinion, preferences, and tastes. Don't insist that your teenager always give in or conform to your preferences in minor, inconsequential situations. This only produces needless and senseless arguments. Save confrontations for truly important issues, so your teenager will realize that you reserve your veto powers for matters of real significance. When you say no, you are not merely exercising your parental power or being unreasonably argumentative. Simply stated, don't major on the minors.

Be an adult. Don't try to relate to your teenager as "one of the gang." He doesn't need another buddy; he needs a parental role model. Set reasonable rules and guidelines. Teenagers expect and need this from their parents. But be prepared to answer the question, "Why?" Be firm; be fair.

Finally, be human. If you don't have an answer to your teen's question, admit it, but tell him you will help find the answer. Admit when you are wrong and ask forgiveness. Your child will respect you even more. Always encourage growth and independence, but never without support. Develop the habit of praying for your troubled teen, and soon you will see signs of change and growth in both of you.

Related Articles

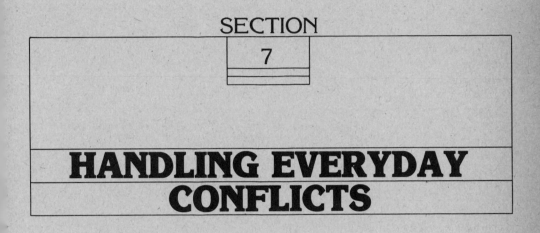

SECTION

7

HANDLING EVERYDAY CONFLICTS

TEENAGERS
AT HOME

- What is the parents' role in refereeing family conflicts and arguments?
- Why there are no perfect families
- In what ways are parents unfair with their kids?
- What if you don't like your teen's friends?
- Are you parent or chauffeur?
- Why is television such a source of contention?
- The battle over the telephone
- Locking horns over music
- Parents need privacy too!

If, as we believe, God designed the family to be the basic unit of society, then it should come as no surprise to us that the enemy of souls attacks us at the family level. To say this is not to accept "Flip Wilson theology"—"The devil made me do it"—nor does it do away with human responsibility. But we must recognize that selfishness, avarice, unconcern, stubbornness—the characteristics that weaken and destroy families—are spiritual problems with an evil source whose purpose is to undermine human happiness. Yes, family conflicts are normal, but they should be dealt with in a positive and Christian manner that leaves no foothold for the devil.

Refereeing Family Arguments

BILL BRIGHT

If parents want their children to live peacefully with each other, they have to be models of that kind of behavior. They should apply the kind of love described in 1 Corinthians 13 to all family relationships. Of course, conflicts between father and mother should be resolved apart from the children. But if parents have had a conflict in front of the children, then they should, in front of the children, confess their sins to God and ask the children to forgive them for failing to be good models.

When parents have had a conflict with the children, they also need to ask the children for forgiveness. There have been times when I have had to say to our sons, "Your father was not a good example. I have asked the Lord to forgive me, and I want you to forgive me too." That is not easy to do, but it gains credibility with the children. Some parents don't want to admit that they are human and make mistakes, but their children already know they do. So it is hypocritical not to acknowledge our sins against the Lord and each other.

What do parents do if children have conflicts with each other? First, you sit down with them and express love to both of them. Even if you know one child is right and one is wrong, you need to maintain objectivity so that one child doesn't feel you are siding with the other one. Your goal is not to resolve the differences between them, but to be sure

WHOSE TABOOS?

Compromise is a dirty word—at least according to many families. Inevitably parents run into conflicts with their teenagers. Before these conflicts blow into major wars, think through the areas of conflict. Are they over timeless values or negotiable values? (Have some negotiables become your "laws" over time?)

Many family taboos or prohibitions bring shame or guilt feelings if we violate them. It helps to decide for each taboo whether it is an *opinion* (a feeling I have formed without necessary input from anyone else), a *bias* (an attitude or conclusion based on teaching of the group—society, family, church—which may or may not be sound) or a *conviction* (God's attitude as taught by the Holy Spirit from Scripture). Use the accompanying chart to help you.

Taboo—a behavior, attitude, or activity I have been taught is wrong (be specific).	Is this an *opinion*—a conclusion based on my own feelings or attitudes?	Is this a *bias*—a conclusion based on a teaching, a prejudice or attitude of the group?	Is this a *conviction*—God's attitude as revealed in Scripture, the character of Christ, or suggested by the Holy Spirit?

So when you talk with your teen about what you can consider negotiables:

1. Let your teen summarize what he or she wants.
2. Summarize what you want.
3. Propose alternatives (after discussing points 1 and 2).
4. Work out a compromise.

Don't hang onto your taboos—and don't make compromise a dirty word in your home.

YFC Editors

that both children are being obedient to God. When that happens, they will work out their differences.

Second, before bringing up the problem at hand, talk about their relationship with the Lord. "Susie, do you feel that your life is fully surrendered to the Lord?" "John, do you know that you're filled with the Spirit?" It is foolish to try to resolve the conflict between the children if their relationship with the Lord is not right, so start there. And once they are right with the Lord, they won't have any problem embracing and saying, "I'm sorry. I know I was wrong. Please forgive me."

Bring Christ into all these experiences. Show your children how attractive He is and how exciting it is to "walk in the light, as He is in the light" (1 John 1:7, KJV). I like the passage in Psalm 32 where King David, after committing adultery and murder, confesses his sins to God, and God restores to him the joy of his salvation. We read about it again in Psalm 51. Our children need to realize that they will be miserable until they confess their sins to God and then reconcile with each other.

Third, restitution may be necessary. Restitution, as well as confession, is important so that the child will come to understand the law of sowing and reaping (Gal. 6:7). If teenagers deliberately disobey God, the consequences are going to be tragic. In a moment of belligerence toward God or toward family, they can get involved in all kinds of things that can destroy their lives forever. So they need to know that it is dangerous to disobey God. What you sow, you reap.

Be a mediator, never a dictator. "Thou shalt" or "Thou shalt not" only turns off the children and destroys their relationship with their parents. A dictator is out of fellowship with the Lord. He is very demanding, arrogant, and overbearing. Though firmness is important, it should always wear the velvet gloves of love.

The most important thing parents can do in maintaining the peace is to make sure they are good models of the kind of behavior they seek in their children. Parents must have no unconfessed sins in their own lives. They must be filled with the Spirit, applying the kind of love described in 1 Corinthians 13 in all they do. This goal is not beyond the reach of the average parent. God has commanded us to live in this loving way, and He never commands us to do anything He doesn't give us the ability to do if we trust and obey Him.

Family fights can be devastating when they happen, and parents may not always handle them wisely. But God is a specialist at turning tragedy into triumph, heartache and sorrow into joy and rejoicing. James 1:1-4 gives insight into the blessings that can come from problems if we cast them on the Lord. God can take our weaknesses and turn them into strengths.

Related Articles

Family Fights Don't Mean Failure

HAROLD MYRA

Every family has conflicts. Each person has an ego, needs to establish self-identity, and wants things to go his way. That naturally is going to cause friction. Add the fact that parents and children have different sets of priorities, and things are inevitably going to heat up.

Wise parents know conflict is normal. Unfortunately, too many try desperately to pretend it doesn't exist. Somewhere they've picked up a golden picture of the way families should be—an image of tranquility, of calm cohabitation. When reality doesn't match their peaceful ideal, they're ashamed. They avoid the conflict, refusing to admit there are problems.

The Christian life, however, is one of facing truth even when the dark side is showing. How we handle conflict is one of the greatest teaching opportunities we have for training our children. The example we provide will likely affect for a lifetime their ability to cope with disagreement.

Unless it's handled right, conflict will have a polarizing effect. If a child sees Mom and Dad fighting, he will feel insecure, in many cases guilty. He may go through life dreading conflict, withdrawing at the first signs of hostility.

In our house, we try to make clear that conflicts are OK, and they don't mean we don't love one another. We try to joke, "Get ready, Mom and Dad are going to start arguing—they haven't had a good fight in a couple weeks." And we try to publicize the fact when a squabble is over. When I lose my temper, I try to apologize—even though that's mighty difficult for me.

Through all this, we demonstrate that even though we have some angry, high-decibel, knock-down-drag-out, er, "discussions," it's not the end of the world. Maybe Mom and Dad are having words, or Mom and child are mad at each other, but it's a passing thing. Pretty soon it will all settle back to normal.

Related Articles

Are You Unfair to Your Children?

BRUCE B. BARTON

Most parents don't like to admit it. Many people resist giving up the hope for it. Yet the dream of the "perfect" family is more a fantasy than a reality. In everyday usage, *perfect* means "flawless." In biblical usage, *perfection* means "completion, maturity, or fulfillment." There are no flawless families. Conflicts

550

are normal. Conflicts occur throughout biblical history, and at least one can be found in every book in the Bible.

While conflict is ever present and even desirable for building character, much conflict in the home is undesirable and destructive. Many parents deal with interpersonal conflict with their teenagers by using unfair tactics. When tension mounts over policies, goals, or even territory between parents and teenagers, parents overuse power and control.

Four Ways Parents Are Unfair

1. *Ignoring the teenager*. One way to face conflict is to ignore it. Overusing this approach can escalate from ignoring the problem to ignoring the teenager as a person. Examples include:

• Not acknowledging communication. When your son or daughter speaks, do you respond? If you don't, your kids feel ignored. Dead silence or "um . . . yeah" never works. Try repeating back to them what was said every now and then. It conveys, "I'm listening."

• Hiding financial and other problems. Teenagers learn values from your example. How will they learn to solve their financial problems if they never hear about yours? What are you facing? How are you solving it? What have you tried? Why did or didn't it work?

• Overlooking improvement. When extra effort or improvement is made on a task or problem, do you pass over it? When a job well done receives no reinforcement by encouragement, the quality may decline next time around. To say: "I expect it to be done right; what's the big deal?" is to ignore the feelings of the teenager.

• Not setting limits or expectations. Having no expectations for the young person does not convey love. In fact, it says just the opposite. A teen, deep inside, feels, "If you care for me, you will believe in me, have high hopes for me, and be clear about what you want from me." When there are no expectations, he feels of little worth.

• Not regarding friends. Teenagers invest themselves in peer relationships. If you ignore their investments they feel anxious and alone.

In summary, ignoring your teen overuses power because you maintain control and withdraw from the relationship.

2. *Isolating the teenager*. By making your child feel alone and isolated, you increase his or her feelings of weakness and loss of influence. Many times we isolate without even realizing it by:

• Comparing with others. When you compare and contrast your teen with other teens, both siblings and peers, you put him in the defendant's chair. A person is never so alone as when he is on trial. Comparisons degenerate to criticisms and are rarely helpful.

• Removing affection. When appropriate physical touch is absent, teens feel isolated from and insulted by their parents. A hug or pat on the back reverses isolation and enhances communication.

• Setting expectations too high. While no expectations at all convey: "I'm ignoring you," expectations that are too high isolate the teenager by drawing a circle of potential failure around him. Built-in failure and self-fulfilling prophecies of doom set in when success is defined in such a way as to be unobtainable.

• Not checking up. When you don't follow through to see if your instructions have been carried out, you are leaving your child all alone to succeed or fail. When you follow through, you are showing a teenager how to follow up for himself. Also, when checking up, you can find opportunity for praise, for correction, and for taking a break just to talk.

3. *Dominating the teenager*. By far the most obvious overuse of parental power is domination. The three elements of domination are: "Do it! . . . my way! . . . or else!" Consider some ways parents dominate their teens.

• Preaching, blaming, and criticizing. When we preach, overtalk, or place the blame on the teen, we are dominating the conversation and the relationship. Guilt paralyzes the teenager and produces inaction rather than action. Studies have shown that it will take four positive affirmations to offset the sting of one negative criticism.

• Not regarding their agenda, goals, or values. Believe it or not, all teenagers think! They have goals, values, and dreams. They have an agenda for the day or the evening. If you sweep it away without looking into it, you are dominating the situation.

• Making all policies too limiting. If the rules and regulations are made without individual consideration for the teenager, they can stifle his growth. When dominat-

---

WILD HORSES, WILD DONKEYS

In the early days out West, many horses and donkeys strayed from pioneer caravans and grew wild on the prairie. Their main enemies were wolves, which would attack in packs. The horses' and donkeys' differing responses to these attacks provide an interesting illustration.

When an attack would come, the horses would gather into a tight group and watch the wolves. As the wolves came closer to the group, the horses instinctively would begin to kick in self-defense; but, because they were backed together watching the wolves, they succeeded mostly in kicking each other. Donkeys had the opposite reaction. When wolves attacked, the donkeys came together, face-to-face, and presented the enemy with a circle of sharp hooves.

How does your family react when the pressure is on? How does your family react when tough problems "attack"?

---

ed, young people cease to want to communicate. Check to see if your policies allow for slow learners or hard times.

• Not giving the plan time to work. If you set up a program for your teenager to clean up her room, give the plan time to work. The first breakdown may not necessarily signify lack of follow-through or defiance. Allow time for self-learning and self-correction.

• Seeing all issues cut and dried. Most adults resent meetings where all the decisions are made before the meeting starts. Teens resent cut and dried issues as well. Allow time for discussion. In spiritual or religious issues, don't lead with the dogmatic answer; instead, share why you believe as you do. Give insight into the life situations that brought you to your convictions.

4. *Waging cold war.* You have all seen the strategies of two countries involved in cold war. Both sides use cold-war tactics to stall for time until new alliances can be made and new opportunities for power or territory can be seized. Worse than no parents at all or hostile parents are indifferent parents. While there may be no open war, a second look reveals lack of love. How do we wage cold war?

• Broken promises. Do you promise them anything to get them out of your hair? When you break a promise, you leave your teen stranded with no hope but to retreat or retaliate. It can be overt and aggressive or hidden away in emotional withdrawal. Both sides lose.

• Double messages. Double messages confuse opponents. Likewise, teenagers don't know how to behave if they hear one message and see another lived out by their parents. If father and mother give different messages on the same issue, confusion sets in. The inconsistent message stifles action.

• Nonspecific instructions. To say, "I want all your homework done" may get an "I'll do it" response. You may mean "before supper." They may have agreed to "by Friday." Unclear instructions prepare fertile soil for the weeds of conflict to grow.

There are many ways to be unfair in dealing with teenagers. To be sure, teens know how to use many of these same devices with parents. What's to be done? You can either withdraw toward two opposing battlefronts or you can seek ways to negotiate conflicts fairly.

To find success in building family relationships, use compromise, communication, and coordination. Most Americans conclude that compromise portrays weakness. They would rather control the high ground that reach out in love. If you seek to win and to come out on top, it may be at the sacrifice of intimacy. You must give up some of your power, be willing to change, and, above all, listen. One way to negotiate when facing a conflict is to find a solution that allows both parents and teenagers to win.

1. *Listen to what is being said both in fact and in feeling.*

"I want the car Saturday." (I have an important date.)
"You always want the car." (And you never seem to enjoy being home.)

2. *Make sure parents and teenagers understand what is being said.*

"You don't want to mess up this great date."
"You feel I don't spend enough time with you."

3. *Find a solution that meets the need for both parents and teenagers.*

"How would it work if we spend time together at home on Friday and you use the car on Saturday?"

Related Articles

Rules for the Right Reasons

GLANDION CARNEY

Parents are only human. Sometimes they can be unfair in their assessment of a problem with their teenagers, and the subsequent response and punishment.

Unfairness can result from an archaic, seemingly irrelevant, rule system. Or parents can be paranoid about their teens getting in trouble, and set outlandishly rigid rules that lead the kids to rebel and get in trouble. And of course, there are the parents who set no rules at all. The middle ground is to dialogue with your teenager, expressing the rules you feel are important, and letting him respond to them.

A husband and wife need to talk with each other about what they feel the rules should be. Parents are individuals with differing opinions. For example, my rules might be stricter and more chauvanistic for my daughters than for my son. My rules might tend to be a bit archaic and prudish, while my wife might be much more flexible and modern in her approach to discipline.

If parents haven't talked previously about what they expect from their children and what the rules are, when the time comes to punish a child, they may disagree. Worse, the parents might confront one another about their opinions of a rule in front of the child. Teens can see the missing communication link between parents and play on the opportunity.

The husband and wife *must* come together and agree on certain rules. Perhaps they may even write them out, with corresponding consequences for violations clearly defined.

Teenagers need to know that a rule can be appealed. Just as the Supreme Court hears appeals without prejudice, on occasion teens will want to appeal a decision. Then the parents need to hear the teen's case, weigh it with as little prejudice as possible, and make a decision they can agree on.

In practice, of course, the parents must work at implementing their discipline system. It's hard not to be emotionally involved. But rules are good, healthy, and necessary. We live in a society full of rules.

However, parents shouldn't get "rule happy." Rules are not intended to be fences to hem children in, but guidelines and suggestions to help them make the right decisions.

Even though, on occasion, teens will still not make the right decisions, hopefully the carefully planned punishment and discipline will teach them valuable lessons they can apply in future situations.

Related Articles

"I Don't Like His Choice of Friends!"

GORDON McLEAN

"That new boyfriend my daughter goes out with. He looks like a creep . . . talks like a creep . . . acts like a creep. He is a creep! But what can I do about it?"

Many parents have that reaction to a friend or group of friends their son or daughter suddenly finds attractive. And it can be disconcerting to think all the good manners, careful speech, and sense of values that you have worked so hard to instill are apparently being casually tossed aside in the process.

Screaming is not the answer to this problem (or most others). If you have done a good job teaching values, respect, and convictions to your child, don't worry. The problem will probably eventually solve itself. In fact, if your patience can endure—and the situation is not overly threatening—it is better left alone. How much better for your child himself to reach the conclusion that a certain friend or group of friends is not desirable and to decide to drop out of that circle. The alternative is to back your child into a corner, in which case he usually comes to the defense of his friend, the ties become stronger to that person, and the problem gets deeper. There is no more important area for a teen reaching out to show his growing independence than in the area of selecting friends.

What should the response of caring parents be? First, allow your young person to openly communicate how he feels about his friends. Listen without being overly critical.

Second, encourage your child to bring his friends into your home. Get to know them. You may be in for some surprises, both good and bad. Tell your daughter's boyfriend what you expect in terms of conduct and curfew and ask his cooperation. Include your child's friends in family outings, fun events, and even church activities when possible. Treat them with respect and you just might get some back. You may be their first contact with a caring home and a positive Christian witness.

But suppose your openness is rejected, your standards ignored, and your values insulted? Your child will see this, be offended by it, and likely extract himself from that relationship—if he is given the freedom to make that choice.

Still there are times a youth from a good home is strongly attracted to an undesirable crowd over a long period of time. This pattern indicates your child has a problem with self-worth and communication at home. The crowd he chooses is only symptomatic of personal emptiness and frustration. Perhaps some advice from your pastor or a Christian family counselor can help bridge those gaps.

Most important, remember you cannot save your child from every bad decision and rough knock in life, and friends are the key to many of those situations. But you can guide your child right, pray for him, then trust he will learn from experience how to make right and mature decisions.

_____

Related Articles

You, Your Teen, and His Friends

Learning to Get Along

CLAYTON BAUMANN

My oldest daughter jokes about becoming pregnant. "The wedding is so far away," she complains, "and I'm tired of working. I want to start my family now."

"Let's practice your part of the ceremony and rehearsal dinner," I quickly respond. "You can practice the honeymoon after the wedding."

This is an example of how I try to cope with the possibility of my daughter's rebellion and association with people at work whose standards and values are vastly different from her own. I don't have much choice in accepting my daughter's friends, but that doesn't mean I must accept their actions or lifestyles. After letting her know that I disapprove of her friends, I give her my reasoning. Occasionally my wife and I have said, "We're not comfortable with one of your friends. We feel that this person is going to have an unhealthy, long-term effect on you. We also feel this relationship may lead to activities that are inconsistent with the values we have tried to develop in you. As

555

a result, you're probably going to be as unhappy as we are if you continue in this friendship."

I then try to give the responsibility of the decision back to my daughter. Instead of spiritualizing, I confront the issue on an adult level with her. Many people assume that confrontation is negative and are unable to confront their own kids in love. In my experience, confrontation has usually meant progress and growth in relationships.

By confrontation I don't mean a direct assault on a teen's identity. Never say, "You're a bad kid because you've got bad friends." Instead, try to set expectations about your teen's values and morality.

In dealing with your teenager's friends, the old saying, "An ounce of prevention is worth a pound of cure," is appropriate. The home should be a place where teens can find security, acceptance, and love. Having your teen's friends in your home may seem an inconvenience at times— our bedroom is right next to the family room! However, the advantages of knowing where your child is and what he is doing are well worth the inconveniences.

For example, it is not uncommon to have six to eight kids bounce into our house at 11 P.M. to eat pizza, play Atari games, or watch TV. Those six to eight kids could have gone to any of their own homes and had that same experience. Instead of using our homes for grounding or restrictive measures, we have worked with these other parents to make our homes fun places.

I've never had to deal with the problem of having my daughters associate with people who were heavily into drugs or criminal activities. However, I would make several suggestions. First, parents need to determine to whom or what their teen is reacting. Have the parents disciplined improperly? Have they been too lenient, allowing their child to do anything he wishes? A lenient home can create an atmosphere of insecurity where the teen is starving for affirmation.

Second, parents need to verbalize their fears and seek counsel. They should open up to other families as well as to their child. At this point in parenthood they need all the support they can get.

I know a woman whose teens were involved in the drug scene. In this mother's case, she never gave up praying or seeking advice. She refrained from lashing out at her children, and as a result, those young adults have begun their own Christian homes. You can just see the radiance of the Lord emerging in their lives.

Finally, parents should try to live by the standard of unconditional love. Though they disagree with their teens, the parents should keep encouraging them. Openness and honesty will go a long way.

Related Articles

When Schedules Clash

Creating Harmony out of Chaos

DAVID VEERMAN

Schedule conflicts are the norm in the average American home. A husband and wife have enough problems synchronizing their appointments. Throw in a few children (including a teenager or two) and there can be chaos.

Schedule conflicts may be summarized in four categories:

1. A child wants to do something. The parent(s) want(s) him/her to do something else at the same time (e.g., family vacation, studying vs. playing, etc.)
2. The parent(s) is (are) scheduled for one activity. The child wants him/her/them to do something else at the same time.
3. The child has "double-booked" himself/herself.
4. The parent wants to relax or to run errands. The child needs a ride.

There are no easy answers to these situations, but a few suggestions should help:

1. *Communication.* Make a family calendar and record all the major events. This will help you talk through potential problems beforehand.
2. *Compromise.* Be willing to give up an activity for the sake of another family member. Make sure the family understands that everyone will have to compromise from time to time. It may mean changing a routine to accommodate another person or going late to or leaving early from an event.
3. *Creativity.* As a family, brainstorm new ways to work out solutions and consolidate transportation. Make it a challenge, even a game.
4. *Care.* Realize that your children will soon be gone. Value your time together, even if it is just chauffeuring. Driving the kids to their activities can be a great opportunity for building relationships and for one-on-one discussion. Too often parents push their kids into having their own cars to save a few minutes.
5. *Curriculum.* Teach your children how to manage their time by using a "to do" list and prioritizing on a daily basis. They need to learn how to handle responsibilities and to discipline themselves to get things done.

Related Articles

Living without Television

DAVID & KAREN MAINS

Raising our children without television started quite by accident. We were living in Oak Park, a close-in Chicago suburb, while we were pastoring an inner-city church. We didn't have much money, so when the television broke we decided not to get it fixed for a while. As time passed, we began to think that it was nice not having it around. It was a relief not to have to hassle about it.

Later, after moving to Wheaton, we bought another TV so that we could watch the Olympics, though we weren't at all sure how we felt about having one again. But an amazing thing happened; someone broke into our home and stole the TV. We thought maybe the Lord was telling us to continue our "experiment" a bit longer.

Now we've reached the point where we've found that in many ways we are better off without a TV. And one of the good side effects has been for our kids to see that, as Christians, we do things differently than people who don't believe in Jesus. It's not that we are putting down other people, but the kids have come to realize that following Christ may mean making different choices. And the decision not to have a TV symbolizes this difference to them.

We don't leave the kids in a void. We substitute by developing their individual interests. We try to pick up on the clues our kids give and develop the gifts that God has given them. For instance, Randy is an excellent ornithologist. Since his time was not taken up watching TV, he became interested in birds. So we got him a small pair of binoculars and a guidebook. Then he began watching birds more seriously. He's also interested in photography and stamp collecting. In fact, he has a lot of different talents that might never have been discovered if he had spent his time watching television.

It's not as though, by choosing not to own a television, we have forbidden ourselves from ever watching it again. It's just that we make conscious choices about what we do watch. For example, if we want to watch the World Series, we ask friends if we can watch it with them; or we go over to Granddad's home and watch it with him. In fact, if it's really important, we might even rent a TV.

What's interesting is that all four of our kids feel positive about not having a television. (In fact, we would be more prone to buy one again than they would!) They feel this way because all their friends seem to talk about is what TV programs they've seen. But because our kids think critically about what they see, they know that a lot of what's on television isn't worth seeing.

The kids' critical eye was illustrated when we were asked to rate a TV program as part of a course we were doing for a Christian publishing company. As a family we watched and rated a popular nighttime TV show, which none of us had seen before. When we finished, we asked the kids what they thought of the show. They said that the characterizations were good, that the story flowed together pretty well, and that it was entertaining (but not always true to life). However, the profanity really bothered them, and they did not like the "bed scenes" because they presented sex in negative ways. At the end of the experiment, each family member decided he'd prefer not to watch the program again despite its popularity.

It proved that our kids do not have a herd mentality. They will not watch something just because everyone else is doing it.

Of course, when we first started this process, it was hard for the kids. It wasn't that they really wanted to watch TV, but that their friends would ask them what they saw the night before. But now that's no longer an issue unless someone new joins their friendship groups.

If a family wants to give up TV, we'd give this advice: experiment first. Talk about it as a family. Then decide to put the TV away in a closet for a certain period of time (the longer the better; it's hard to see results in a short period of time). If in the middle of the time period, someone is dying to see a particular show, take it out and let him watch it. Then put the TV back in the closet. After the time period, evaluate. Discuss the pros and cons of not having a TV.

Of course, you have to fill the TV time vacuum with other things. Try to work at developing your children's gifts. If you do, you may find that TV is something you can live without.

Solving Problems at Home

Chores and Other Sticky Issues

DAVID VEERMAN

Divide the family chores into *assigned* (and required) responsibilities and *bonus* jobs. The expected and assigned tasks would include keeping one's room clean, taking care of one's belongings, cutting the grass and shoveling snow, and helping in the kitchen. Bonus chores could include cleaning the house, washing the car, helping younger siblings with homework, and baby-sitting.

At a family meeting, discuss the chores, making assignments and laying down the ground rules (when certain chores are expected to be completed, etc.). Use a point system with rewards for reaching specific totals. Assigned tasks could be rated 1-5 points depending on the quality of the work. Failure to fulfill certain responsibilities could result in negative points, and bonus jobs would be worth extra ones. Rewards would be decided beforehand, and could include special privileges, concert tickets, money, or use of the car.

Television

The use of the television is a difficult problem for most families. Each person has his or her own needs and TV agenda so *more* people lead to multiple scheduling conflicts. Since it would be a waste (and a cop-out) to buy a set for each person, here are a few suggestions to help minimize them.

As parents, decide on the basic ground rules for TV use—then discuss them with the rest of the family (be open to their suggestions and ready to adapt). The ground rules should include priorities (studies, piano practice, etc. before TV);

maximum number of viewing hours each night; your right to censor objectionable shows; sensitivity to younger viewers; and the priority of shows required by teachers. Also, discuss alternatives to television viewing, like family activities or reading books.

The key to avoiding conflicts after the ground rules have been reviewed and decided on is to *talk through the schedule on each Sunday for the rest of the week.* Emphasize the necessity for compromise and the reality of reruns. Remember also that your example will speak volumes.

Telephone

If overuse of the phone has been a problem, identify the peak use periods (this would be a great assignment for a teen), and limit the length of calls at those times. Also, designate certain hours as off-limits, reserved for studies, meals, family devotions, and other special events. Set a maximum limit for all calls at any time and special limits at other times. Make this "fun" by fining rule breakers a quarter a minute and a dime for every *incoming* call during "no phone" time. Save the fines, and spend them on pizza or other family treats. And remember, you must abide by the rules too!

Curfew

Curfew is one of the touchiest areas with teenagers. They want an increasing amount of freedom, and comparisons with their friends' restrictions (or lack of them) are inevitable. There's no absolute bewitching hour for every age—your decision will take careful consideration, and should involve your teens in the process. Here are some variables to consider:
• School nights or weekend
• Special events and activities
• Age
• "Behavior" record
Whatever is decided, be sure to insist that they call whenever making a curfew is a problem.

Food, Diets, and Sleep

Adolescents' bodies are growing rapidly —they need nourishment and rest. Unfortunately, they feed themselves a steady diet of junk food, and their youthful energy keeps them running without sleep. As responsible parents, it is important to take action without food bans and other counterproductive responses. Here are positive steps to take:
• Insist on a decent bedtime—if studies keep them up, make sure they begin studying earlier.
• Begin each day with a good breakfast.
• Discourage fad diets—if they want to

MIXING STUDIES AND MUSIC

Current research has found that some children learn better in total quiet, while others learn better with some background noise. Ironically, your teen's studies may actually benefit from listening to background music, *as long as it is not loud enough to break their concentration.* However, TV is a no-no.

If you let your teen listen to music while studying, carefully monitor his grades from the time you let him begin listening. If the grades remain the same or improve, you need not worry. If the grades fall, your teen may be one of those who learns better in quiet.

It is interesting that most parents don't complain about the mixture of music and studying as much as they complain about the *type* of music their children listen to while studying. *They* couldn't tolerate that music while studying, so they think their teens won't be able to either.

YFC Editors

go on a diet, design a reasonable one and do it together.
- Study nutrition together.
- Make creative, nutritional snacks.
- Exercise together.

Studies

Here are some suggestions for helping with conflicts over studies:
- Explain why education is important— help them get a broader perspective.
- Set *realistic* goals for grades.
- Set aside a place for studying.
- Insist on the principle of concentration (do one thing at a time)—eliminate TV and other distractions during study hours.

- Design a manageable schedule.
- Make sure they cover *every* subject, every day (even if there is no assignment due).

WHAT ABOUT ROCK?

For many families, rock music is an insurmountable barrier between the generations and a constant source of conflict. Undoubtedly, rock music greatly influences our kids; they pick up many values through it.

Kids need to be confronted by parents who are willing to confront lovingly, objectively, *and with knowledge.* You might say, "I would like to know something about rock music. What records do you recommend for me? I want to know what your music is saying."

Listen to the music alone, not with your teen. Then come back and be very honest. You could say, "Hey, look. I'm not sure I buy into any of the stuff that's coming across in this music."

Don't react in ignorance. It's OK to react negatively, but make sure you know what you are talking about and are able to discuss things, not just deliver edicts.

I listened to some records my daughter had and gave her my opinion. She agreed that I was right on some issues and thought I was wrong on others. We listened to each other with understanding and mutual respect. And we both learned some things about rock music from each other. That too can be your experience.

Anthony Campolo, Jr.

Deciding to Solve Conflict

CLAYTON BAUMANN

"**A**re you forbidding me to go to the dance?" probed my daughter.

"No, I'm not forbidding you to go," I said hesitantly. "You can make your own decision, but I want you to look at the issues. My recommendation is that you stay home."

So she went.

When she came home, she excitedly told me, "Dad, you would have loved it. There was no liquor or making out in the corner. The parents were in the thick of it the whole time. We didn't even dance; we just had a good old time."

If I hadn't given my daughter the freedom to make her own decision and she had heard the next day's report on the party, this conflict could have hurt our relationship. This is just one example of conflict where I've had to stop and analyze my own beliefs and values—to determine what actions honestly deserve approval or disapproval.

Dealing with conflict is not a time to blow your cool. It is a time to sit down and rationally discuss problems. The most important aspect in dealing with conflict is to create a climate where dialogue and communication are increased, not decreased. For example, one of my teens came home from school and disclosed that she had copied someone's homework. Immediately, I was ready to reprimand her with a discussion on honesty. Instead, I decided to listen. As she explained her reasons I saw that the copied homework wasn't as big a deal as I had first thought. When she finished explaining, however, I was able to calmly tell her that this action troubled me, and that it did seem to smack of dishonesty. I

also told her that I appreciated her sharing this with me, but I suggested we take honesty as a standard.

Temperaments and moods can greatly influence the effectiveness of an open climate at home. If a teen appears hostile to discussing problems, reconvene your meeting another time. In an effort to keep an open climate, I try to discuss problems with my children when they're in a good mood. For example, if I have to drive my daughter to school or a friend's house, I use that opportunity to bring up such issues as, "What would you do if you went to a party and got in over your head?"

Sometimes I ask my teens to put themselves in my place as a parent. I discuss my problems, and in return they give me good advice. In some cases, I find that my concerns about them are unwarranted or that I am overreacting.

Conflicts and decision-making are closely related; in fact, conflicts often result from poor decision-making processes. Sometimes it's harder working through a conflict with your teen than it is just to say no.

I believe there are four major facets to good decision-making. The first facet is to help your teen learn to develop his own thinking process. Teens need to be challenged to analyze and evaluate their decisions. Often I have teenagers ask me what they should do, what decision to make, etc. I respond by refusing to give them answers. Instead, I begin asking the teenagers questions like: What conclusions have you come to? How did you arrive at those conclusions? What Scriptures relate to these issues? Have you prayed about these issues?

For example, not long ago I asked a young man, "You really don't have any standards, do you?"

He responded, "What?"

"You really don't know how far to go on a date and why, do you?" I questioned.

He said, "Sure I do."

I said, "OK, how far? Where would you draw the line? At what point would you feel you were taking chances, or do you care if you take chances?" Our conversation became very serious and personal at that point.

The issue was not what *I* believed about dating. Ten years from now when this young man is married, Clayton Baumann's values won't mean a hill of beans to him. The important element is for him to reach his own conclusions.

The second facet in helping your teen become a better decision-maker is to assist him in developing personal standards and values. When a teen knows his own standards and values, he can easily decide not to participate in activities that conflict with those values.

My kids and I have a deal. They know their standards and if anything goes on at a party or on a date that conflicts with those standards, they can call me and I'll go pick them up. If they're in over their heads, they are not trapped because I refuse to go get them. No questions are asked. My oldest daughter went to a party once with some non-Christians. After getting a good scare, she resolved to never again date a non-Christian. As parents help their child in moral development, the child is able to make wise decisions based on his Christian values and standards.

The third facet in good decision-making is examining issues as dealt with in Scripture. When I work with a teen, I direct him to Scripture passages that relate to the issue with which he is concerned. A small Bible study group can help keep communication lines open as well as developing basic principles for decision-making.

The fourth facet in good decision-making is using available resources. Resources such as books, older adults, other kids, and personal experiences can help a teenager examine the implications of a situation.

To decrease conflict and reinforce good decision-making, parents must provide an environment that rewards decision-making. The first step in creating this environment is to take an interest in your teen's decision. Begin treating your child as a human being, not as a piece of livestock. If a guy on the job comes to his employer and shares something meaningful in his life, the employer has the common courtesy to listen. Yet a teen can come home from school, share a meaningful decision, and the parents say, "Later kid. We're busy eating supper."

Listening to and encouraging teenagers as they share their decisions is vitally important. If the teenager made a semi-bad decision but used a good decision-making approach, the parents should not put down the conclusion. The process is more important.

Limiting a Teen's Social Activities

Is It Necessary?

GLANDION CARNEY

Setting limits on a teen's social activities is a common area of conflict in many families. Though many parents today seem to be afraid to set limits, it's part of the duty of being a parent—it's part of the package.

The question of setting limits on a teen's social activities boils down to: Do you *not* set limits because you want to be loved and appreciated by your child? Or do you set them *regardless* of how you think your child feels about the limits because you love and respect him and have to do what is right?

Parents who argue "no limitations" say they want their children to be able to be individuals and to grow up making free choices. When children come of age, (about their senior year in high school, in my opinion), that philosophy is helpful because they will eventually have to make their own decisions about social activities, and they need to learn profitable lessons along the way.

But until then parents who don't set limits for their teenager are parents who really have a problem being parents. It's part of the whole area of being liked and disliked. Sometimes a child will run to his room, slam the door, and say, "I hate this rule and I hate you!" As parents, you have to be strong and not allow your ego to be jeopardized or your security threatened. It's OK to respond to a teen, "Fine, if that's the way you feel about it. But the rule sticks."

Setting limits applies to many areas of life. People need to know the limits related to normal activity and society, and the corresponding punishments for

violating those principles. If I want to go out and rob a bank, I need to know that I'm violating a social limit or boundary, and that when I do, I'm going to pay for it. Rules and boundaries are necessities.

When dealing with children, keep in mind that kids are individuals. I set entirely different limits for my eleven-year-old than for my fifteen-year-old.

Limits are necessary for different reasons. Some limits are set for normal everyday activities, while others are a result of the punishment process. To be most effective, punishment limits shouldn't dictate limits for everyday activities.

For example, a child might violate the curfew hour. As parents, you might say, "From now on, you have to be home by 4:00 in the afternoon. That's the limit." Two or three months later, the child is still coming home by 4:00 in the afternoon, and the parents have completely forgotten about the rule. When Dad comes home and sees that everyone is home for dinner, and no one is running out the door, he may decide that he likes that limit. From that day forth, the limit will always be in existence—it is decreed. Yet the limit was set in response to a problem, as punishment. That limit may not be necessary for the average everyday activity. But it becomes comfortable because we see limits as controlling factors. It might be better to alter the limit.

Besides curfew, there are rules and boundaries for hygiene, finances, diet, homework, and many other areas (phone calls, chores, etc.) where discipline is deemed necessary. Concerning personal hygiene, teenagers need to maintain cleanliness in their appearance, as well as in their rooms and living spaces. In monetary matters, teenagers need to learn to budget their resources to reserve money for phone calls or special occasions. Those teens with weight problems need certain rules related to their diet to teach them discipline. Many families have a "no television until the homework is completed" rule.

It may seem like there are too many rules, but I don't think so. In some ways, teenagers are like wild horses. While we can't aim to "break" them, because that implies breaking their spirits, they do need to be controlled. In my eight years of counseling in a school system, I've seen many parents who were afraid to establish rules because they wanted to be liked or appreciated. The irony is that the "buddy, buddy" system usually caused all kinds of commotion. It simply backfires. Often the parents and teens in these situations end up becoming alienated.

Of course, there are times when parents have to be flexible with rules and limitations. When parents feel that maybe they could lighten up on a rule for a little bit, or not be so tight about it, it's usually a good indication that they should be flexible. It depends on how the child handles responsibility when the rules are relaxed.

Let the teenager be a part of the rule-making process. Offer to sit down and talk with your teen about what rules you feel are important, and get his input. Suggest guidelines and get feedback. Often teens set harder boundaries and punishment on themselves than what the parents would. Make a point of working out guidelines that work for you and your teen.

Related Articles

Watch Out! Teens Can Talk You into Almost Anything

DAVID RAHN

Kids learn very quickly how to get what they want. If the daughter of the family discovers that Mom's no can turn into Dad's yes with the right amount of lip protruding, you can bet that this tactic will become used often to get her way. Parents who already experience pain in disciplining a misbehaving teen may find themselves held emotionally hostage as the young person runs to his room, his screams of hate echoing in the halls. Manipulation leaves traces of bitterness and resentment on its victims, breaking down relationships.

For any person, the process of choosing manipulative persuasion is quite simple: "If it works to get what I want, I'll do it." The easiest way to change this pattern is to render ineffective all "unfair" tactics. Manipulations may be overt ("If you really loved me, you'd let me . . .") or subtle with hidden implications ("Susie's parents are super. They let her stay out two hours later than you let me.") In either case, parents should ignore the hidden statements and respond only to what actually was said. After a while, kids will learn to speak straightforwardly and honestly if they want a response.

In addition, parents should reward a teen's attempts at fair persuasion by listening attentively and by trying to understand their son's or daughter's responses. It should not be threatening to parents for a young person to want to know "why" a certain thing is as it is, provided that he is not belligerent. To dismiss an honest inquiry with a sharp "Because I said so" tends to send the teen away thinking that it doesn't pay to be upfront and honest.

On the other hand, parents should

FIGHTS OVER LOOKS

"Button up that blouse!" "Must you wear all that makeup?" "You march right back up those stairs and change your outfit. No child of mine will be seen running around in that thing."

Does this sound familiar? Battles over your teen's physical appearance are quite common. But who's really right and who's wrong? Are parents too conservative or are teens trying too hard to "fit in"?

Of course, every family is different, but here are some guidelines you might want to follow.

In mapping out a strategy in the battle over physical appearance, parents must weigh three things: *modesty* vs. *motives* vs. *morality*.

Of course, if teens are blatantly immodest, they should cover up. But what about those gray areas where parents would like to see a little less skin but teens don't see what the problem is all about? And what about those tight pants and crazy styles? These cases are extremely difficult for parents and must be dealt with on an individual basis. Be careful, however, not to stereotype clothing or styles. No, you may not have worn those kinds of clothes when you were a teenager, but styles change. Be sensitive to what is in style and don't force your kids to be out of it. Is their clothing rational, or are you just embarrassed to see your teens dressed that way?

Next, ask yourself, "Is this a moral issue?" This is possibly the key question. Don't hit on morality if your teenager is simply trying to be in style. For example, some parents think that anyone who wears a denim vest is part of the "wrong crowd." This simply is not true. And if you hold a stereotype like this, be prepared to have your teen ask why. You'd better have a more solid reason than, "Because I said so," or "It's just not right."

Last, examine your teens' motives. Are they wearing these styles just to "catch" a boyfriend or girlfriend? Or are they wearing these things so everyone will think they are "cool"? These are probably not the best motives. However, if they are wearing these styles in order to "fit in," that is not such a bad motive in this case, because feeling like you belong is a very important aspect in the development of self-esteem.

In summary, it might be more beneficial to spend a little less time haggling over specific articles of clothing, and a little more time helping your teens look their best within the framework of their style.

YFC Editors

beware that a new resolve on their part not to give in to unfair tactics may provoke the teen to use the worst of his manipulative arsenal. But maintaining a firm, loving, and fair posture should improve a teen's behavior as the new parental pattern becomes consistent and dependable. This is a hard assignment, but it will bring considerable family rewards.

Parents Need Privacy Too!

ART & LOIS DEYO

How many parents of teenagers have heard the exclamation, "Stay out of my room!" Many teenagers crave privacy, but they often give little thought to the privacy of others. We have always tried to have an open-door policy with our two teenagers, and we are grateful for the openness they have shown in discussing their concerns. But sometimes we are literally bombarded with a plethora of questions, comments, and just plain trivia as we are relaxing with a book or a newspaper just before bedtime. The truth is, parents need privacy too!

For many parents, children demand so much attention that there is no time to develop a relationship with one's spouse. This often happens in situations where the mother develops the stronger relationship with the children because the father has such a heavy work schedule. Or even when both parents work, the children may dominate the parents' entire evening so that they have no time alone or with each other.

There is only one thing more important than our children, and that is our relationship to each other—our marriage relationship. Our children will leave home, but we plan to remain together long after that.

We have found that we need personal time each day alone and with the Lord as well as with each other. We need time for communication so we can understand the other's goals and aspirations. We need planning time for family activities as well as determining guidelines for the children. This creates a greater respect between us in the crunch of on-the-spot decision-making and even discipline of our teenagers. Also, getting away from our children has helped us be more objective about how they are doing in light of feedback given by those who cared for them.

Parenting is not easy and demands much giving. Thus, we need time away from our children to "take in" and replenish ourselves physically, mentally, emotionally, and spiritually. It all began when Deanna and Jeff were very young.

Art would come home from the office, eat with the family, play with the children a short time, and then put them to bed. They were in bed by 6:30 or 7:00 P.M. every night. We had the entire evening to ourselves. We could talk and share together; Art could study for seminary; and Lois could pursue her professional sewing duties. Or we could hire a baby-sitter to come in shortly before the kids' bedtime so that we might attend a church or Youth for Christ (our ministry) function or enjoy our weekly date night.

We have observed so many parents whose children literally control them.

They can't seem to get anything done as long as their children are awake. We have visited in homes where young children are always the center of attention because they are allowed to stay up as late as the adults.

Training small children to accept baby-sitters is not easy, but firmness and persistency is the key. Mothers who breast-feed their babies should occasionally bottle-feed them so that they can be left with sitters for a longer period of time. A nonworking mother should plan her day around her preschooler's naps and playtimes so she can get things done.

Don't just take the children to the grandparents' home for baby-sitting, but try to vary the sitters from time to time so that the children get used to responding to different caring people in their lives. Because Deanna and Jeff learned early discipline, we found success in taking them with us to the home of friends whom we were visiting. At their appropriate bedtime we put them to bed in their sleeping bags, on the floor of our friends' bedroom until we were ready to go home.

Now that our children are teenagers, they often stay up as late as or later than we do. They, of course, have their own interests, homework, music lessons, and household chores to keep them busy, but they still find time to interact with us. However, we still have to plan for times of communication and times of privacy. Admittedly, this is sometimes more difficult now that Lois is teaching full-time.

Because we have encouraged it from their first day in kindergarten, Deanna, seventeen, and Jeff, fourteen, want to talk about their day when they arrive home. Earlier, Lois would set aside ten to fifteen minutes immediately after school to talk, but now sports and music activities often keep them at school until the dinner hour. Now dinner hour is a sacred time of family communication. We often have to bite our lips to wait until the kids are finished before we share our day.

Sometimes we call a family conference, or one of us will take Deanna or Jeff to lunch for other times of communication. Privacy is obtained now through walks around the block, discussions while driving, a night out (with no need for a baby-sitter!) or just plain locking the bedroom door. We have literally counted twelve trips into our bedroom by Deanna some nights during a twenty-minute period "to tell you something else." We are pleased that she wants to talk, but have had to ask her not to bother us any more on a given night.

We hope that it need not be said that parents should try to have a separate bedroom from the children. Sex in front of them, even at the youngest of ages, is quite inappropriate. As they grow older, the lock on the bedroom door becomes more valuable. We have discussed sex, even our own times of sexual enjoyment with our children, and this helps them understand this important aspect of our lives. They seem to know when those nights arrive, for then it's not at all difficult to get them to clear our bedroom. They likewise would agree that "parents need privacy too!"

Related Articles

Home: A Restricted Area?

CLAYTON BAUMANN

I once attended a secular rock concert with my daughters. I had my doubts before we went—I knew this music wasn't too severe, but I thought that money spent on a secular concert would be a big waste. Then when we got there, our seats were behind the stage. All we could see was the guy's back and his microphone.

My daughters loved it, but they never went to another secular rock concert after that. Their curiosity was appeased. I've begun to realize that it is important to allow my teens the freedom to go through with certain acts that allow them to show their independence. And rather than saying, "No, you can't go," I just go with them.

Communication and openness in the parent-teen relationship is more important than the parents and teens having to agree on every issue. I would rather make certain concessions to my children than create barriers that don't have to exist. I didn't particularly want to go to the concert, and I didn't like it when we got there, but my being there was a positive factor in my relationship with my daughters.

Some parents try to set limits on how much time is spent away from home. I don't, as long as certain conditions are met. The real issue is not how many nights a week a teen is away from home. More important considerations are: What is healthy? What gives the family time to interact? Is homework getting done? Are my children with the right kinds of friends at the right kinds of activities? Are my kids on the go all the time just because of pressure from other teens?

If a healthy kid is involved in positive activities every night of the week, good for him. If it's my kid, I'll take him where he wants to go. But at the same time I realize that not all teens are alike.

I told my fifteen-year-old daughter that she was old enough to use her head, and that she would slow down a little when she finally got mono. "You would let me get mono?" she asked. I replied, "I'm going to let you burn off all that energy. If you're dumb enough to catch mono, it's not my fault." We had a good talk after that. She began to realize that because I was allowing her the freedom to go out so much, she, in turn, was going to have to make some wise decisions on her own.

One of the major arguments against so much teenager activity outside the home is that families don't have time together. I don't agree; the only reason families don't have time together is that they don't make time together. Some families set aside one night a week as family night, but our family tries to make sure every week is family week.

Most days contain many hours when the parents and kids come into contact with each other, but often parents don't use that time. Driving your kids to school is a wonderful time to talk together. Or hang around a few minutes when you go in to tell them good night. Each day contains several such opportunities.

The other night one of my kids was watching a TV show that I thought was a dumb program she didn't need to see. But I kept my mouth shut, got a book, plopped down, and had a delightful time reading. Some people would disagree, but I think the two hours we spent there in silence was quality time together. Any time spent together is quality time. Lecture and dialogue are not necessarily requirements.

I consider it an honor when my kids want to sit in my presence and do something else. If they want to lay around on the sofa talking, laughing, disrupting me, making fools of themselves, and making their fifteenth call of the evening, I am pleased. As far as I'm concerned, that's all quality time. By doing all those crazy things in my presence, they are treating me as someone they trust.

I wouldn't want my teens to get a call and have to say, "I can't talk to you now. My folks are here. I'm going up to my room." Our daughter takes her calls wherever we happen to be as long as our twenty-foot cord will reach—beside us, at the kitchen table, in the family room. The cord gets wrapped around furniture and things get knocked off tables, but how can I complain? She reveals the secrets of her world to me by discussing them with someone else in my presence.

Sometimes I'm a little tempted to get on her case for some of the things she says, but I try to restrain myself. I'm thrilled she feels free enough to be so open in front of me, so I try not to use her conversations against her.

I should again emphasize that the freedom we give our children is based largely on our knowledge of who their friends are. If they want to go to a Christian concert with kids we know and a driver we trust, I don't care if they come home at 4:00 in the morning (as long as they call around midnight to let me know they're coming in late). Of course, if they want to go to a questionable activity with people we don't know or trust, all of a sudden the curfew becomes 9 P.M.

We let our teens know if they are getting into areas we don't like. We also let them know what we *do* like, and we do everything we can to encourage those positive activities. They like to stay out late, so they are usually influenced by our opinions.

If a teenager has a mental image of home as a place of restriction and parents as enemies, he will not have the freedom to be the person he wants and needs to be. As parents begin to understand, accept, and involve themselves with their teen, their home will become a much less threatening place for their teenager to spend some time.

Expect Conflict and Learn from It
DAVID RAHN

"Conflict" is a terrible word for many people. When used in a word association game, the responses may include "hurt," "anger," "frustration," "fighting." These are negative words, but conflict is not necessarily bad or good; it just *is.* Wherever humans are together and the issues are sensitive, conflict can be expected. The family, especially one with a teen who's beginning to think independently, is, therefore, a natural setting for conflict.

To accept conflict and even expect it as a natural process helps to lower the

570

"terror" level when it comes, and as long as conflict does not succeed in blotting out hope, it can be viewed naturally.

A good family exercise would be to try to discover which of the five basic styles of responding to conflict is characteristic of each family member.

Style #1. *The Avoider.* There are those who are convinced that nothing good ever comes from conflict, that it is always wrong, and, therefore should be avoided at all costs. When conflict begins, the avoider withdraws.

Style #2. *The Appeaser.* This is the person for whom no issue is worth the strain on a relationship, so when conflict brews, he gives in to "keep everyone happy." Sometimes important values will be sacrificed on the altar of peace-keeping.

Style #3. *The Winner.* This person views each conflict as a win or loss situation, so winning is his goal. Where issues and values should not be compromised, this may be a helpful style, but in most conflicts it tends to run over people and to devalue them.

Style #4. *The Compromiser.* For this participant, the answer is that everybody gives a little and everybody gets a little. Here no one is a clear winner, but no one goes away empty-handed either. The difficulty lies when values are held so deeply that compromise may not be truly possible. This style is most effective when a person's attachment to an issue is not very deep.

Style #5. *The Problem-solver.* This person wants everyone to come out of conflict a real winner. In many conflicts it is very possible for people to emerge more tightly bonded together because a creative problem-solver focused attention on the common needs, goals, and desires. A conflict management style which is positive and hopeful can help all parties "win."

In any family, any combination of styles may produce certain continuing patterns of conflict. Two "winners" in a family may argue continuously. If you add an "avoider," he will most certainly head for the protection of his room when disagreement starts. Trying to identify personal style tendencies and reviewing some recent conflicts together may add insight.

The next news is good news. No one is slave to his primary conflict style, but knowing one's tendencies in conflict is the first step toward choosing a response. There are many helpful books on the market to aid in identifying conflict styles and in choosing appropriate responses for specific situations.

Most important, learn to fight "fairly" with one another. Accusations and personal attacks usually serve only to raise tempers. Instead, statements should be phrased in a way which accepts responsibility for one's *own* feelings and attitudes. For example, the phrase, "You make me so mad . . ." is much more inflammatory than, "I feel very angry when. . . ." Above all, if those in disagreement know that they are loved and cared for, a climate of hope can persevere in the midst of conflict. Best friends are often those friends with whom we feel free to disagree, knowing that differing opinions will not threaten the relationship.

Related Articles

TEENAGERS AND TEMPTATION

How to Evaluate Outside Influences

- Is the family really open to more attack than in the past?
- Should parents try to protect their children from negative influences?
- How much does the media really affect parent-child relationships?
- Could your teen become involved with the cults?
- How to deal with authorities who have a say with your kids
- What are some positive influences for teens?
- What to do when your children's friends are bad influences

Someone has observed that choices would not be difficult if they were just between bad and good. But they are often between good, better, and best. Some things that happen in a democracy are the result of thousands of concessions, accommodations, and compromises in an effort to come up with something acceptable to everybody.

Once while my father was listening to church members discussing the color the church ought to be, he suggested that everyone bring a gallon of paint, put it in a big barrel, and mix it together. Of course, we'd have had to learn to like a khaki-colored church. Society is often khaki as well as black and white.

Part of our Christian responsibility is helping our kids find the best. And the best must take into consideration not only the history of civilization and human learning, but also the revelation given to us by God in Scripture. Only God can give us the very best.

Society's Assault on the Family

Are You Equipped for the Attack?

JOHN W. WHITEHEAD

The family, a once revered institution in our country, is under tremendous attack today. During the past forty years, we have seen a significant decline in what we call the traditional family, and I believe much of the problem is of a spiritual nature. Some Christian counselors tell me that fifty percent of the Christian marriages in their areas end in divorce. As a result, many children are now living in single-parent homes, foster homes, state centers, and orphanages.

However, I believe the trends of the past couple of years indicate a resurgence of the Christian family. People are having more children, and I think families are going to get stronger. But there are still a number of influences in our society that are having a negative effect on today's families.

The strong *feminist movement* is one

negative influence on the family. In many ways, this movement tends to be anti-family, primarily due to its pro-abortion attitude.

Another influence with which the family has to contend is the *media.* Television presents a one-sided view of the family—mostly bad. Almost all of the programs are aimed at singles; there are very few family shows. Even a lot of the early TV shows were centered on one-parent families—"Andy Griffith" and "Lassie," for example. Other programs are excessively violent or just plain anti-Christian.

I'll probably get criticized for including this third negative family influence on my list, but I think that *excessive church activities* can often be so demanding that parents don't have time to spend with their children. Churches should encourage families to get together at nighttime and have devotionals or do something as a group. But I've seen many churches plan so many activities for parents and children that they are rarely together at home.

Parents who don't spend time with their children miss a very special relationship. Yet some people tend to think it's more spiritual to spend every spare minute plugged into a church activity than to lay around on the carpet at home and play with their children. Strong family relationships just can't be developed if part of the family is *always* at church for one reason or another.

If you want to develop better relationships with your children, it's always good to identify any negative influences of society you see in your family situation. But it isn't enough to identify them—you must do something about them.

For instance, if TV is a major problem, turn it off. We have very limited viewing in our family. We watch only what we feel to be wholesome shows, and we either watch them *with* our children or *before* we allow them to watch.

TV can be used in an educational way.

What we do with our children is tell them what is happening in the world (such topics as abortion or evolution) and then watch shows and read books that deal with those issues. By the time my son was in the third grade, I had taught him the basic catch words for evolutionary thinking, and he could watch a show and tell me if it was promoting evolution even if the word *evolution* was never used. He could tell that a discussion on "adaptation," for example, was actually on evolution and went against the creationist beliefs he had been taught. If you take the time to educate your children about other world views, they will filter out a lot of television programs through their "Christian screen" without any further instructions on your part.

It is good to help your teens practice using their Christian screen. After a TV show or movie, my teenager and I frequently sit down together and discuss what we have just seen from a Christian world view. What was the message of the

---

THE DEVIL MADE ME DO IT

The devil does not know the hearts of men, but he may feel their pulses, know their tempers, and so accordingly can apply himself. Just as the farmer knows the proper seed for the proper soil, so Satan, finding out the temper, knows which temptation is proper to plant in one's heart. That way the tide of man's constitution runs, that way the wind of temptation blows. Satan tempts the ambitious man with a crown, the sanguine man with beauty, the covetous man with a wedge of gold. He provides delicious meat to suit the sinner's taste.

The Biblical Treasury

program? What moral problems were raised on the show? How would you resolve them? Was the main character's method of resolution a good one to imitate?

This type of education must be taught in the homes by the parents, not in the schools. As the parents work with their teens to develop a Christian world view, many of society's negative influences can be overcome. You probably won't get rid of all of them, but you will start your children in the right direction.

Another example I can use from my own experience is rock music. I'm not saying all rock is bad, but few will argue that some rock music is a very bad influence. Our thirteen-year-old began about four or five years ago to learn classical guitar, and he became familiar with classical music. Sometimes we will put on a rock record, listen to it, and discuss it. Many times he will say, "I don't want to listen to that song because it isn't orderly. It doesn't fit in with the scheme of music." If you expose your children to the right influences, they will soon begin to filter out a lot of the wrong ones by themselves.

Our nation is facing a horrible moral crisis today. If we are to have revival, reformation, or whatever you want to call it, the reform must come through two channels. The main burden is on the church, though I think the church has failed in our country in recent years. The other avenue for reform is the family, the basic institution of society. When America had strong families, America was strong morally. Religion is a product of the family. If a child is not taught religion in his home, he probably will not be religious.

The church where we are members is a place we go to worship with other Christians. But we are taught there that the primary worship center is the home. Christians today have a false idea of what worship is all about. Worship involves more than attending church or handing out tracts. It means doing the best you can at whatever you are doing, and being the best person you can be. We are commanded to let our lights shine before men, and there are many ways we can do that.

Parents should make sure their lights shine at home. Family Bible reading is a good place to start. By the time my oldest son was eleven, he had already read the King James Bible from cover to cover with us. By the time a child is able to read, he should be encouraged to participate in family devotions.

Our family also uses devotional books. We particularly like one called *Timeless Insights,* put out by the International Christian Graduate University. But we emphasize Bible reading. I have found that most Christians haven't read the Bible cover to cover, and that's a problem that can be dealt with in the homes.

Of course, you're going to have some problems with your children. We don't live in a fairyland. Society's assault on the family is real. But as parents begin to recognize and attend to the problems their children are facing, they can successfully counteract the negative influences their teens encounter every day.

Related Articles

Should Parents Protect Their Children from Negative Influences?

DONALD COLE

Some people say that you cannot protect your teenagers from negative influences. To a certain extent that is true. You can't protect them from all negative influences, but you certainly can protect them from many and you should, even when they are teenagers.

A typical teenager is not prepared to cope with many of the temptations that come his way. Temptations don't simply sneak up on you in this modern world. They come vacuum-packed, under great pressure. A teenager who is not given support may succumb, when, under better circumstances, he might stand firm.

I'm not saying that you should keep your kids isolated from the realities of the world. They should be prepared for what they will face. But part of that preparation is protection from assault before they are equipped to meet it.

I try to keep my kids from seeing pornography because I do not believe that any person can be exposed to pornography without having his mind permanently affected.

The same holds true for dirty books. Anything that is degrading should be kept away from children. The lie of the devil is that experience will make you wiser. The fact is that experience may destroy you if you are not mature enough to handle it. The devil says that sexual experimentation is OK because once you've done it, somehow you've matured. But it doesn't work that way.

I also think that kids should not be allowed to watch X-rated movies. My responsibility as a parent is to protect them. The yardstick is: Would I expose my fourteen- or fifteen-year-old daughter to a thirty-year-old man whom I suspected of wanting to seduce her? No, I'd protect her from that. I'd also protect her from seeing that in a movie.

I would also do my best to keep comic books out of their hands. The reason is quite simple: I want them to learn to appreciate literature. Once they have developed a taste for literature, they are not going to read junk.

As for teen music, some of the words and music are plain rotten. You may not be able to prevent your kids from listening to it somewhere, but you can keep it out of your home. I do not think that a Christian has to be so tolerant and liberal that he has it in his home.

A record that has suggestive lyrics will not find a place in my home. You may cultivate in your children a certain amount of resentment, but that will resolve itself and do less damage than the potential effects of some of the music.

I know that kids have to learn to make choices about what they see and read and do, and I'm realistic enough to know that I'm not the only one to have a part in bringing up my children. But they don't have to learn by bitter experience. They start off making choices when they are very small. Our job is to inculcate in them moral values. They should be protected from bad influences until they are sufficiently mature to cope with them.

Teens can also be exposed to negative spiritual influences, with cults and gurus.

This can be especially harmful because in the teen years, conversions are made. It's the age when untempered idealism reigns; when, in spite of their sophisticated talk, teens are extremely naive.

A teenager exposed to negative spiritual influence is in great danger unless he knows God and is firmly grounded in the truth. There are teens like that. But for the others, I would use whatever influence I had with the teenager and say, "I'd rather you didn't go there and these are the reasons: we believe this is a very bad spiritual influence; it is not of God, and I don't want you exposed to it." If he objects and protests, you may not be able to stop him, but at least you will have made an attempt. I believe that we will fail in many things we try to do, but our responsibility is to make the attempt and leave the results with God.

Related Articles

Making Faith Work in a Media World

DAVID & KAREN MAINS

A huge shift has taken place in our society. It is a different kind of world than the one in which we were raised. When we were children, we didn't go to movies and they had little effect on our world. But now the media, television especially, affects everything that happens.

Because the school of the world has shifted, we feel it is almost impossible to make a list of do's and don'ts for our children to follow. That's because much of what happens in our culture isn't directly spoken about in Scripture.

Of course, there are direct scriptural prohibitions, and our family is obedient to those prohibitions. But most of these ethical, moral, Christian rules are brought to bear on areas where there are no direct scriptural injunctions. The Bible doesn't say anything about television, theater, magazines, or a whole list of other things which some Christians include on their lists of do's and don'ts.

Thus, we have found that a number of the do's and don'ts that we grew up with don't help our children decide what Christian morals and ethics apply to this media-affected culture.

This creates a problem in some families because family members aren't comfortable talking about issues where faith and the lives of their children meet head-on. This results in two things: parents become dogmatic and young people get their backs up. Those things in turn lead to continuous arguments or refusing to discuss certain subjects altogether.

This has a direct effect on the lives of many Christian teens. Some become insulated against or isolated from society. Others develop a dual standard. For instance, they think it is wrong to go to a movie but have no dilemma about watching that same movie on TV or on a video viewer. Such duplicity keeps kids from developing a critical viewing standard whereby they can measure each media piece on its own merit.

Developing a critical viewing standard is something that we've worked very hard at in our family. We've helped our children develop evaluative tools and methods whereby they apply those tools and methods to everything they see, hear, or read.

Here's how it works. First we use a rating game to get the ball rolling; then we ask questions from a Christian viewpoint about what we've rated.

Step 1: The Rating Game

If someone in our family reads a book or sees a movie, it is customary for us to say, "OK, on a scale of one to ten, what did you think of it?" (ten—high, one—low) By doing this, we are inviting the young people to share their opinions.

This helps the conversation begin without direct spiritual overtones. Instead, it begins with a personal opinion. This helps us hear where the other person is coming from, and means that we listen noncritically. We don't say such things as, "How in the world could you give that crummy thing a nine?"

We might say, "Oh, that's interesting. You gave it a six and I gave it an eight. Why did you give it the rating you did?"

At that point, the children have learned to say, "Well, technically it was terrific camera work." Or, "The way the book was written was great, but I had problems with the content." They've learned to back up their ratings with a critical evaluation of what they have seen or read.

Often we make our evaluations in a family setting. For instance, coming home from church we might talk about what we thought of the sermon.

This can be fascinating because our evaluations might be radically different. For instance, since we have been Christians a long time, we might rate a sermon we've heard time after time rather low. Yet, our eleven-year-old may rate it a nine because he found tremendous value in it. What's more, it might be a topic we've never discussed with him because it was old hat to us.

When we do the evaluating, we let the kids go first. When they share things like, "I gave it a nine because it hit right where I am," we learn things about the needs of family members.

Step 2: A Christian World View

Once we've done this rating, we move on to the second step, asking questions that help the children come to grips with what they have seen and how it relates to their faith in God.

There are scores of questions that could be asked, including: "What was real about what you saw? What was unreal? Were there Christian themes? Anti-Christian themes?" If it was fiction, "Can you just watch it for amusement or does it say something about our world?" If sexual themes were presented, we ask questions such as: "Was the presentation honest? Do the people we know who have had affairs find the kind of happiness the film portrays? Do you know any Scriptures related to these areas?"

Let's see how this works out in our lives. Say our subscription to *Time* magazine runs out. Instead of automa-

tically renewing, we ask every family member questions about the magazine. Thus, each person evaluates *Time* magazine's effect on their life and on their faith.

Step 3: Personal Ownership

This is a continuing process which leads our kids to a point where they have ownership of their Christian values. They are not dependent on Daddy or the church's list of do's and don'ts. They act from the base of values they themselves have developed.

To get them to this point of ownership, we generally end by asking such questions as: "How do you feel about it? Was it worth your time? Would you do it again?"

We believe that this process is part of the transformation by the renewing of the mind talked about in Romans 12:1. It makes our kids think for themselves, which makes them less dependent on peer pressure or the values promoted in the general society.

For instance, if the entire sophomore class thinks a film is great, most freshmen will immediately agree. But, Joel, our freshman son, will be able to say what he thinks of the movie and why. His ability to think critically about what he has seen will be more important than what his classmates think.

It's the same for our daughter, Melissa. She's a little shy, but that doesn't stop her from talking to station managers and theater managers about previews of films that were rated "G," but really aren't for general viewing. Her critical thinking gives her tremendous strength to do what she knows is right.

Our critical thinking also affects our family operations. For instance, our family has decided not to have a television set. For the past thirteen years we've lived without one. This is not something we've pushed on the kids. In fact, we've offered the kids a TV. But they have chosen not to have it. They have come to the place where they say it's an influence they would just as soon not have to contend with all the time. Instead of television, we've tried to expose the children to a wide variety of the best culture the world has to offer.

Sometimes it's hard for us to decide what to see or not see. If that's the case, we use these guidelines: What do people whom we trust think of it? What is it rated? Is it the kind of thing we want to spend our time seeing or doing?

Of course, even with the best guidelines, we sometimes make mistakes. But that has a place too. It helps our kids see that there are some things that are not edifying and that they should avoid seeing in the future. It also gives us chances to discuss some of the topics that were in the show.

This happened a few summers ago when Melissa went to see a popular film while she was visiting at a friend's home. Most kids her age were going wild about the film, but when we asked Melissa, she rated it a five and a half. She then gave us her reasons for her rating. The funny thing was that same week *Time* magazine pointed out the same flaws in the movie that Melissa had observed.

TELEVISION: MOLDER AND SHAPER OF LIVES

Most television programming is awful! According to Dr. Gerald Looney, University of Arizona, by the time the average preschool child reaches fourteen years of age, he will have witnessed 18,000 murders on TV, and countless hours of related violence, nonsense, and unadulterated drivel! Dr. Saul Kapel states, furthermore, that the most time-consuming activity in the life of a child is neither school nor family interaction. It is television, absorbing 14,000 valuable hours during the course of childhood! That is equivalent to sitting before the tube eight hours a day, continuously for 4.9 years!

There are other aspects of television which demand its regulation and control. For one thing, it is an enemy of communication within the family. How can we talk to each other when a million-dollar production in living color is always beckoning our attention? I am also concerned about the current fashion whereby program directors are compelled to include all the avant-garde ideas, go a little farther, use a little more profanity, discuss the undiscussable, assault the public concept of good taste and decency. In so doing, they are hacking away at the foundations of the family and all that represents the Christian ethic. In recent seasons, for example, we were offered hilariously funny episodes about abortion, divorce, extramarital relationships, rape, and the ever-popular theme, "Father is an idiot." If this is "social relevance," then I am sick unto death of the messages I have been fed.

Television, with its unparalleled capacity for teaching and edifying, has occasionally demonstrated the potential it carries. "Little House on the Prairie" was for years the best program available for young children. I would not, therefore, recommend smashing the television set in despair. Rather, we must learn to control it instead of becoming its slave. *James Dobson*

From *Dr. Dobson Answers Your Questions*, by James Dobson, Tyndale House Publishers, Inc. © 1982. Used by permission.

The neat thing is that this critical thinking process has helped us have a tremendous amount of trust in our children. And, in turn, they can talk about almost anything with us. For instance, the movie Melissa saw contained a sex scene. But she didn't hesitate to talk with us about it. Then we could ask such questions as: "Should you have left the theater when the scene came on? Did the scene bother you? Does it flash back into your mind?"

This process with Melissa ended with a discussion on the need to protect our minds from some of the things that non-Christians have no problem observ-ing. That, in turn, made Melissa stronger and better able to apply her faith in Christ to her life.

And, that is the goal of this whole process: to enable our kids to critically evaluate everything they go through and to see how their faith in God applies in the different situations.

How the Media Affects the Family

ANTHONY CAMPOLO, JR.

The media has an overpowering impact on teenagers today, due primarily to its fast-paced format and the sheer amount of time kids spend watching TV. Its impact has three main effects, in my opinion:

• *TV often causes teenagers to become bored with life.* The special effects and relentless image blitz of TV make other things in life seem dull by comparison. Family, school activities, and reading become boring. There are no fast camera cuts, music and image blitzes, or special effects to dazzle and rivet their minds to these concerns. There are no quick solutions to life's problems. On TV most problems, even the tough ones, get solved in thirty or sixty minutes! So parents are constantly confronted with a kid who is bored and who almost defies them to entertain him or her. Parents are driven up a wall, trying to figure out how to rescue their teenagers from the apathy and boredom that have become so very much a part of their lives.

• *The child's vision of what parents ought to be is largely determined by the media.* For the first time fathers and mothers have to realize that they are being measured against an ideal type. And the ideal type has come across from TV programs such as "The Waltons," "The Partridge Family," and "Little House on the Prairie," that show ideal-type fathers (like Michael Landon as Charles Ingalls) who never get angry, who are so understanding, and who are never out of touch with the real needs of their kids.

The parents portrayed in these TV programs are so idealized that parents can't possibly measure up to them. Consequently, today's real parents come off looking like failures because they compare so poorly with the ideal parents depicted by the media.

• *The media has become a primary communicator of values.* The peer group (which we often stress when talking about teenagers) is simply intermediary. In fact, the peer group's primary responsibility is to see that the values communicated by the media are communicated to the individual teenager. If the teenager doesn't comply with those values, the peer group will apply pressure to keep that individual in line.

Unfortunately, the parents' values often stand in diametrical opposition to media values, and parents come off looking somewhat socially unacceptable to their children.

How bad has the situation become? A group of students at Columbia University ran a study on teenagers from the general population. They asked: "If you had a choice of turning in your parents for new ones, would you do it?" Over forty percent of the teenagers interviewed said yes. When asked who they would trade them in for, Burt Reynolds was selected as the ideal father, with Cheryl Tiegs being the top pick for mother!

What advice do I have for parents who are concerned about their relationship with their teenager?

I think that parents must, I repeat, *must* be aware of the competition. Parents have two basic choices, it seems to me. Turn off the TV, or in some way *buy into* the positive values that can be found now and then on TV. Take a good look at how idealized parents on TV behave. Then try to pattern or model the positive qualities depicted in their lives. That sounds pretty far out, I know. But you say, "What if the media values don't conform to Christian values?" Let me respond that some of the "positive" programs *do* conform, as a whole, to basic Christian values. However, in some respects they don't. For example, in very few situations other than on "The Waltons" or on "Little House on the Prairie" does going to church come across as a normative part of the family life.

How do I reconcile this as a Christian? In most respects the parents on these programs come across as very decent. Much about them should be emulated by Christian parents. Other things, like the absence of regular church attendance and worship, can be noted and discussed.

TV: ZING . . . ZAP . . . POW!

Current TV commercials flash up to 120 images on the screen in thirty seconds. With special effects and rapid-fire images, TV has managed to blunt the interest of today's teenagers in other important areas of their lives. Books, newspapers, radio, school activities, and family just don't cut it anymore.

Teenagers are being conditioned to pay attention only when information or events come packaged in the fast-footage format. *Star Wars* and similar space movies are examples of how this technique is used. The message or content becomes unimportant. If you really look closely at the story line in *Star Wars* and similar sagas, you will find them very superficial. Without the special effects, frenetic music, and image blitz, the TV program or movie would be boring!

So when parents take teenagers on a vacation they find them bored by what they see or by what is happening around them. Stand them at the edge of the awesome Grand Canyon, for example. The kids look up and down the canyon once (twice, if you're lucky) and that's it! What you get is a king-sized yawn and an urgent plea to get back to the motel to watch TV. Because to today's TV-conditioned teenager, reality isn't nearly as interesting as the artifical world that TV communicates with such zing . . . zap . . . and pow!

Anthony Campolo, Jr.

Some people might say, "Tony, I never see them have devotions. I never see them talking about Jesus. They never quote Bible verses." That's true. And what they *don't* do is very important. But, what they *do* do is often positive and valuable. I think most of us, including me, have a very wary attitude toward anything that comes across the media. And it just may be that there is more good coming across than we are ready to accept at first. When one takes into consideration what is absent, one *can* get alarmed: the absence of church, the absence of devotions, the absence of prayer. But when one looks not at what is *absent* but at what is *present,* one would have to say that there were some very positive things to be said about Charles Ingalls as a father and about the recent "Little House on the Prairie" series as a whole. Here you had "lifelike" people seeking to come across in very real ways. Parents could say, "I *can* learn much from the values and attitudes they depict on the program."

I have a suggestion for parents on how to make TV viewing more meaningful. It is important for parents to spend enough time watching the programs their teenagers watch so that the parents can evaluate and discuss the situations, the realism, and the values that are depicted and imparted on those programs. That's basic. Within that context, Christian parents can ask, "To what degree does that family really represent the kind of family values and ideals that Jesus Christ would like adopted in our family?"

If I did not want my teenagers to watch a seamy nighttime soap opera, I would not permit them to do so. You ask, "What if that breaks the relationship with your kids? What do you do then?" I think that *whenever* you discipline children, relationships are *temporarily* blunted or broken. If you can't risk temporarily breaking a relationship (which is what discipline implies) then you can't discipline at all.

How to Evaluate Media Today

• I think that one should ask first, *"What is the attitude of the media toward sex outside marriage?"* It seems to me that the media approves of it. Christian parents should pass negative judgments on such behavior.

• Next, *"What is the attitude toward wealth or material things on TV?"* We need to evaluate *lifestyle.* Is the lifestyle of the family depicted as so affluent that it orients the viewer into a consumption lifestyle contrary to Christian principles? I think that becomes very important. That's why I think "Little House on the Prairie" and "The Waltons" had some very positive and constructive points to make about lifestyle. They weren't about particularly affluent families. But love, loyalty to one another, consideration for others, a sense of responsibility for one's actions, and contentment with the "basics" came across clearly.

• Another thing to note would be *the degree to which the teenage lifestyle depicted on TV is one that seeks happiness through conformity to the dominant values of their peer group.* Also observe the degree to which the family stands as a countervailing force, at times setting the teenager against negative peer group pressure.

Some ask, "Who decides what programs to watch, or not watch? Mom, or Dad? I think we have moved beyond that kind of question. What *is* important is for families to accept a more democratic model in which there are long discussions and in which a family consensus is reached through discussion. The parents should guide, inform, and stimulate the discussion. This is the sort of thing that should be talked about around the dinner table.

James H. S. Bossard, a very prominent authority in the field of teenage development, points out that long dinner conversations are the primary way values are communicated in an informal manner. The fact that parents are eating on the run, kids are coming and going, and that there is no stated time (of at least forty-five minutes) to sit around the dinner table so parents and teens can talk, means that the major instrument of values communication from parents to teenagers has evaporated.

I want to emphasize that *the family that eats together, stays together!* This is very crucial. What parents often try to do is to be didactic, to communicate values in a very teachy, and sometimes preachy fashion. The advantage of the dinner table is that, without calling a family conference, discussions at mealtime can, in fact, help teenagers evaluate all kinds of things—including the media, politics, the church, and the meaning of Christianity.

Let me illustrate this.

One evening, years ago, my family was having a pleasant time around the dinner table. In the course of conversation, my son, Bart, who was then ten years old, mentioned that there was a new boy in his class at school. I asked, "What's his name?" My son didn't know his name.

I asked, "What's he like?"

Bart said, "Well, I didn't talk to him and neither did anybody else."

I said, "Why?"

Bart replied, "Well, he came into the class before recess and when recess started he thought he could just come out and be on one of the teams, *just like that!*"

At that point I asked him, "If Jesus were a member of your class, how do you think He would have tried to make the new boy feel? What would He have said to him?" And suddenly my son became very sensitive to how Christianity related to the context of the school situation he had just experienced. This is the kind of informal discussion that communicates values more than an abstract lecture on the subject.

***

Related Articles

Who's Watching Your Kids?

JOHN W. WHITEHEAD

Your children have many authority figures over them, but the basic foundational authority belongs to you, the parents. All other authority is delegated. When a child goes to school, authority should be delegated to the teachers. Or after school, a coach might be responsible to act in place of the parents. The legal term (in Latin) for "in place of the parent" is *in loco parentis.*

Public schools used to be viewed as *in loco parentis,* but they have lost some of their authority lately. Some courts have upheld the requests of certain parents to prevent the teachers from having any real authority over their children. When parents refuse to delegate authority, they limit the ability of another person to regulate the activities of their kids.

But parents have a responsibility to delegate authority wisely. I even suggest that parents who have unmarried children in college encourage them to live at home while they go to school. College puts a lot of pressure on students—much of it anti-Christian. If they can come home to their parents and go to church with them, they will do much better in school. It was not uncommon in the Old Testament for children to live with their parents until they got married.

On a high school level, parents can

take a personal interest in the people who share the authority over their teenager. In doing so, they may run into problems, but it is still well worth the effort to insure that their child gets the best training he can.

One common problem for Christian students is having to deal with a teacher who is not a Christian. If so, the parents need to explain to the teacher that their child is a Christian, has certain biblical beliefs, and may possibly have to disagree with some of the material that is taught in the school. If the parents explain in a nice way, the teacher will usually try to respect the child's beliefs. I know of some recent instances where students refused to answer certain questions on a test about evolution because the "correct" answers went against their religious beliefs. I think teachers should respect the wishes of students not to answer in such circumstances.

Another occasional problem at school is the coach. Some coaches are so determined to win that they become overbearing and yell at the kids. If your child's coach gets out of hand, you need to have a talk with him. If he doesn't respond, you should take your teenager off the team. (And if your teen is a good athlete, the coach will sober up real fast.)

Again, the key is how you approach the coach. You need to explain that you are a Christian family, and you think there are better ways to motivate young people than yelling at them excessively. Try not to be defiant, or you will destroy your witness. Just tell him that your Christian

QUESTIONABLE IDOLS

Our star-conscious society parades a smorgasbord of celebrities for our children to idolize. Of course, it's not wrong to look up to older "models"—we've all had our heroes. The problem is when these modern facsimiles espouse or encourage immoral and un-Christian ideas and lifestyles. It makes us nervous to imagine our children becoming like them.

These are legitimate fears, but first we should analyze the situation, and think through which values are being perpetuated. We should also look at the larger picture. The fact is that kids have idols because they are going through a time of role confusion and role sampling. In trying to find their identity, they emulate different people. Also, sometimes parents get too involved in underlying facts. For example, a rock star may have been married and divorced several times. Our kids may not even know that or care—they just like the music. We shouldn't assume that they believe in several remarriages.

The most helpful antidote is to spend time talking over this whole area with our kids. We should encourage them to evaluate the idol and to identify what they really want to emulate. (Is there a legitimate conflict of values?) In love, we can also help them see the logical conclusion of following a certain star and examine the subculture that he or she represents. When all is said and done, we need to be willing to accept a *modification* of the "hero-worship" and not a total rejection. Perhaps our greatest achievement will be to help them begin to think beyond "looks" and "sounds" to the deeper issues of values and lifestyles.

YFC Editors

principles teach you that people are created in the image of God, and you just can't go along with using abuse—verbal or otherwise—to win games. I've coached teams, so I find it easy to talk to coaches. But anyone can do it with a proper attitude.

Schools aren't the only places where parents need to be cautious about who has authority over their children. Sometimes, problems even arise at church where a pastor or youth minister is setting an example for your teen that goes against your family's values. What I have done in similar situations is to have the pastor over for dinner or tea and just talk to him. I also like to give him books that I think could help him in the area where we disagree.

Since the pastor is such an authority figure, it is important to approach him slowly and with respect if you feel he is doing something nonbiblical. Don't walk up to him and say, "Listen, I think you're a rotten sinner and you need to repent right away." Wise parents will preface their comments with a lot of positive remarks before they confront the pastor with a point of disagreement.

Probably the most serious problems with authority over teenagers arise when one parent is a Christian and the other is not. It is one thing for two Christian parents to agree to take some action with a teacher, coach, or pastor who influences their child. But when one parent is in conflict with the other within the family, the problem is not so easily settled.

I've had Christian wives come to me whose non-Christian husbands were abusing them—some physically and others only verbally (about their religion). No woman should allow her husband to beat her up, but verbal abuse is another matter. According to 1 Corinthians 7:14, an unbelieving husband can be sanctified through his wife. A Christian parent should go out of his (or her) way to be a positive influence to his spouse and to their teen.

I know a very good Christian lady who was having problems with her non-Christian husband. She had a job and he didn't, so she was expecting him to do some of the household chores while she was working. He thought it was her duty to clean the house, so they were fighting a lot. I advised her to stop confronting her husband, and to just come home, hug him, and show him that she loved him. She tried it, and their relationship grew a lot stronger. The basic thing to remember if you are a Christian married to a non-Christian is to be the best parent and spouse you can possibly be. You may have to draw the line at how much you will give in to the other, but you should let your Christian light shine within your household whenever you can.

In all your relationships with other people who have authority over your child(ren), you must be open about your Christian feelings and beliefs. But above all, you must be compassionate. The burden is on you to be the most excellent parents you can be and so impress any other people who are over your teenagers so that they will listen to what you have to say.

Related Articles

When Your Teen Has Permissive Friends

CLAYTON BAUMANN

Sometimes a teen's values and morals are developed through peer pressure. My daughter, Kim, came in one afternoon and said, "I'm going to see a movie with some of the kids at school." After hearing the film was rated PG, I gave my approval. When Kim arrived at the theater, she discovered that the rest of the group had decided to see an explicit R-rated film. Though Kim is not usually an assertive individualist, she responded "My father won't allow me to see this film. I came to see this PG film so I'll meet you when it's over."

My daughter bought herself a great deal of freedom when she came home and shared this situation with me. Over the years, my wife and I have tried to express our own values and make our demands reasonable enough that our children would absorb and gain ownership of those same morals. Now, when someone challenges Kim, saying, "Your folks are too strict," we are thankful that she is able to defend those values and standards as her own.

To facilitate moral development in their teens, parents should concentrate on several key areas while their children are very young. These areas include discipline, climate, and decision-making. Often parents decide to develop these areas too late.

My wife and I were very strict with our children when they were small. We never allowed our youngsters to throw temper tantrums or show any form of disrespect toward us. Physical discipline was a must. My daughter can recall the "Double Whammy," where her mother first disciplined her, followed by a second spanking when her father came home.

As our children grew older, we began to get their input in regard to the form our discipline should take. We'd ask our teens, "What form of discipline would be consistent with your disobedient actions?" Eventually, our teens didn't want to suggest anything. They were afraid the discipline they chose would be harsher than our choice. As a result, we found ourselves laughing amidst a pretty tight situation.

In regard to climate, we have tried to create an openness in our family. This openness has allowed our teens to choose standards that are very similar to our own. We've helped our teens experience a happy home where parents aren't afraid to express love, fears, and frustrations to each other. We have refused to lie to our children, and, in return, we expect them not to lie to us. They might avoid telling us something, but eventually it comes out.

Imagine this scenario. Jill Jones, the pretty high school freshman, was in a predicament. Her boyfriend's parents had just confronted her parents. "Are you aware that our son kissed your daughter?" they asked. "No, we weren't," the Joneses replied. At the time, dating was a new experience for Jill and she obviously wasn't comfortable sharing this with her parents. In fact, she was embarrassed by the whole situation.

Rather than making this a moral issue, as the other parents had, the Joneses tried not to overreact. Mrs. Jones said to Jill, "When a boy kisses you, I want to hear about it. That sounds pretty neat!" Suddenly, Jill didn't feel like lying or avoiding the topic. Her mom actually wanted to hear about her dates!

The third and final area of consideration in moral development is decision-making. Children see morality in their parents' decisions as well as through openly discussing morality. I began making decisions for my daughter when she was small. As she grew older, I gave her more and more freedom to make her own decisions. In this way, she developed her own identity, character, and values while still under my roof. Though the church and friends contribute toward the moral development of a teen, the parents have the most influence and give the most direction in regard to their teen's values and standards.

Related Articles
Chapter 13: Communicating Values to Our Children
Chapter 14: How to Help Your Teen Choose Good Friends
Chapter 26: Should Parents Protect Their Children from Negative Influences?

PORNOGRAPHY

What should parents do when they catch their teen with dirty magazines or other pornographic material? Confrontation in a caring manner is the best method. Perhaps it would be helpful to share from your own experience and emotions the sexual drive and temptations you had as a teenager. This will put you in a more vulnerable position, but by being more honest with your teenager, chances are you will be more effective. Your teen will see that you can identify with him, and as a result he may consider your point of view important and may not want to disappoint you.

Explain that it is normal to have sexual desires, and these desires are especially pronounced in the teen years. This drive is God-given and natural, but it needs to be channeled in the right direction so that his or her sex life in marriage can be more meaningful and free from the emotional and physical consequences that come from misuse of sex. Talk about sublimation— alternative activities such as exercise, social gatherings, crafts projects, and a myriad of other constructive ways to divert sexual energy.

Talk about pornography and its effects. When discussing this, talk about the value of human beings—that people are not objects, but individuals of worth and dignity. Talk about how God intended sex to be something beautiful, not something dirty. Those mental images are hard to erase and lustful thoughts are only promoted when these materials are in your teenager's hands.

Galen Dolby

Why Your Teenager Could Get Involved in the Cults

LARRY KREIDER

Harold L. Bussell in his book, *Unholy Devotion,* makes an alarming statement that children raised in evangelical churches are increasingly being lured into the cults.

It's hard to admit that we can and are losing teenagers to the seduction of alien dogma and practices. How can it happen? The answer lies somewhere between the all-out onslaught of Satan and his kingdom and an ignorant Christian church.

The following seven reasons for many falling away from mainline orthodoxy are not exhaustive, but they are primary. All of us should evaluate our own churches to see if the ground is fertile for foreign seed.

1. *Insufficient biblical grounding.* Two problems must be faced by every church in relation to its ministry of education. The first is the problem of overfamiliarity, where a child has had a cranium full of Bible stories and Scripture memorization without the motivation for it to make a difference in his life. The second is a lack of providing a sound strategy for presenting the basics of the faith, where learning is exciting and contagious, and the subtle differences of sects or cults can be detected by well-trained minds. The key is a well-conceived plan for reaching clearly defined goals for young people at various age-levels.

2. *Uninspiring leadership.* No minister plans how he can best be dull in the pulpit each Sunday or how he can recruit ill-trained and boring Sunday School teachers. In fact, the responsibility of selecting inspiring leadership really lies on the shoulders of the laity. If parents are in tune with their young people, they know who is effective and who is not.

To prevent a witch hunt for someone who happened to present a flat lesson, it's important that there is a system within every church where honest concerns and evaluations can be brought to the attention of the church leadership.

Often there is an unwillingness to replace a leader with someone who is more gifted because of the disruption and pain it might cause. If the elders or deacons are sensitive to using people in the areas of their greatest gifts, they can actually help solve everyone's problem by honestly and gently placing and replacing people in the areas of their strengths.

3. *Departmentalization without integration.* There are advantages to having nurseries, preschools, Sunday School classes based on age, youth group meetings and services. Young people enjoy being with their peers; learning is accelerated, and it's easier to be honest without adults hearing their conversation. But there are also dangers. A kind of elitism can develop from a constant attention and preoccupation with their own problems without developing a sense of caring and responsibility to all ages.

Churches need to plan some events where all ages are integrated. Young people who participate in the worship service can expand their horizons beyond their own ego-centered needs. Family picnics, athletic events, camps, and retreats are all excellent ways for everyone to come together. When a young person develops a social relationship with an adult, it's more difficult to hurt that adult by deserting the church for a cult.

4. *Cold orthodoxy.* Actually, the phrase "cold orthodoxy" is a technical contradiction. The orthodox faith embraces *all of the Scriptures,* which by God's very nature and intent prevent it from being cold. True Christianity is warm and caring as well as theologically accurate.

Unfortunately, the caring side of our faith is seen as unessential. Everyone needs someone. The insecurities of adolescence make teens susceptible to persons who show love and concern. There are many ways of expressing this love, but the two most critical are physical contact and trying to solve a real problem that is a primary concern to the young person.

A pat on the back, a hug, or some other nonsexual gesture should not be left to the hired youth worker. Caring attention from many adults provides the kind of gratification that many teens find in the warm circles of cult members.

5. *Pluralism.* Freedom provides its citizens with many choices. Countless options are available to young people in every area of life. There are racks full of fashionable clothes, entertainment smorgasbords, numerous colleges competing for their attention, and career opportunities unlimited. There is also a wide variety of religious beliefs to choose from. Such pluralism creates two problems; one is that there is a tendency to look at religion and faith as similar to trying on a pair of jeans. Wear them until they either wear out or no longer fit. Second, the unlimited choices create confusion. Without some foundation for measuring truth, teenagers are left to their senses and desires to make the right choice. Sometimes pluralism leads to paralysis, and no choices can be made.

6. *No outlet for service.* A church trying to be true to the Gospel preaches the necessity of a humanitarian approach to the world. Young people are challenged to help the poor, create a better world, make necessary sacrifices to save society.

Being motivated, they leave the sanctuary to . . . go back to the routine of life without an outlet for the compassion that has been aroused within them.

If the desire is strong enough, a teen will either find a legitimate outlet within Christianity to express his zeal for service, or he may be attracted to a cult where such opportunities are ample.

7. *Insecurity.* We've already said that adolescent insecurity can be partially helped through the warm hands of caring adults. Yet, insecurity has its source in areas not solved by legitimate affection.

The possibilities of unemployment, nuclear war, crime, permissiveness of parents, confusion over beliefs, inconsistencies of friendships all lead to a desire for someone to tell a teenager what to do and when to do it.

Though teens often reject authority, there is a deep-seated desire to have life made simple. A "thus saith the Lord" once in a while and an accurate presentation of legitimate biblical absolutes can prevent them from seeking a cult where thinking is done for them.

Fortunately, it's never too late to start making changes. In fact, a church which starts making positive moves has the opportunity for just as powerful influence on its young people as those which have been consistently doing things right all along.

Culture Shock

Returning Home from the Mission Field

DONALD & NAOMI COLE

Our kids had quite a few adjustments to make when we returned home from the mission field. Life is different here in the United States from what it is in another culture.

Our oldest came home before we did to spend her last year of high school in an American school. She lived with relatives who had four teenagers, and it should have been an ideal situation. But she never felt part of the family and it was quite painful for her.

They tried too hard to make her feel comfortable. She was always the star guest instead of a member of the family. It was not the host family's fault. They simply didn't understand her needs. Any family that tries to assimilate a teenager into their home for a year faces a difficult task.

Our two boys were fourteen and twelve when we came home. One of the most obvious problems for them was the way they talked. They both spoke with a Rhodesian accent, which embarrassed them. Neither of them knew American slang either. So whenever they opened their mouths, they felt alien to the American culture.

They did not know how to play basketball, which is an American sport, or American football. They had an added problem in that we lived in a rural area on the mission field and they went to a small mission school. When we left Africa, we came to a big city, Chicago, and the boys were dropped into a school of 3,000.

The Christian teens they met thought that missionary children were superspiri-tual. If anybody was needed to pray, the Cole kids were called on. They were avoided by fellow Christian teens who thought they lived on a higher spiritual plane because they were "MKs." One son overcompensated by tending to seek out kids inclined to misbehave. The other son retreated into himself.

We read about a missionary couple who sent their teenage daughter to charm school when they got home. She learned how to dress, how to use makeup, how to do the things her peers were doing. That is a terrific idea. It's important for teens to be a part of their peer group and whatever missionary parents can do to make the teen feel more at home is good.

One mistake we made was not getting involved in any of the school activities. We went to two or three PTA meetings, but just as onlookers. As a result, we didn't know what was going on at school. It never really occurred to us to go. We needed somebody to sit down and say, "These are the kinds of things you should be doing with and for your children here."

You should join a fairly big church so that your teens can belong to a good youth group. It is not helpful for missionaries coming home to associate themselves with little churches. For the sake of their teenagers, they should belong to a big, active church.

You also need to create special family times. You need togetherness. For a few years after we returned to the States we didn't take vacations. They seemed other-worldly and horribly expensive. But we should have gone away; it would have been good for us. You may think that you can't afford to take a vacation, but really it is the other way around. You can't afford not to.

There should be some way to get missionary kids together for a rap session with an objective third party who could lead them in a discussion of issues that concern them. When you return from the field you go to a dentist; you have a physical checkup; you get new clothes; so why not have a rap session to deal with the emotions and feelings of returning to the States?

Read, read, read, and then read some more. There are many good books available on raising children. Yet often missionaries don't read when they come home. Or they read but then put the ideas out of their minds. If you don't implement what you read, it doesn't do any good.

The Positive Influence of Christian Camping

DAVID HOWARD

A couple of years ago, my wife and I asked our oldest son, David, "As you look back over your life, where would your roots be?" We weren't sure where he thought his roots were because he had lived in a number of places. For five years he had lived in Costa Rica, then ten years in Colombia. After that, we came back to the States and lived in Illinois. From there he went to college.

Without any hesitation he said, "Deerfoot." I was amazed that Deerfoot, a Christian camp in New York, had given him such a sense of continuity that as an adult he felt his roots were there.

He first started going to Deerfoot when he was nine, while we were home on furlough. During subsequent furloughs he went back. He later returned for six or seven summers as a counselor.

A number of things were built into him at Deerfoot that helped give him that sense of continuity. One was an appreciation for Scripture. He was getting that input from other places too, but it was reinforced at Deerfoot. Another was appreciation for God's handiwork in nature.

Perhaps the most important thing was the sense of discipline—of setting goals and then reaching them. Deerfoot has an achievement program which David plunged right into from his first year there. He kept at it and by the time he was seventeen, he had reached what they call the Lone Eagle achievement (like the Boy Scout Eagle badge), which took a great deal of hard work.

As he worked on the Lone Eagle award, he learned discipline. He later told me that getting the Lone Eagle was more significant to him than graduating from high school or college.

The Christian camping experience also showed both our older sons they had gifts for working with people. Being counselors let them see that they could relate to boys and really build character into their lives on a deeper level.

Our daughter also became a counselor—at Tapawingo, a girls' camp near Deerfoot. I think that being a counselor taught her the importance of being a good example and motivated her to examine her own life. She realized that if she was going to be an example, she would have to work strongly on her own relationship to the Lord.

The friends a teen makes while at camp can also be a significant part of his or her life. Tapawingo gave our daughter some good friends with whom she still keeps in touch, though she spent only a few summers with them. I think that's great.

The Positive Influence of the Parachurch

DAVID VEERMAN

"**P**arachurch" is an interesting word. Literally it means "alongside the church," and refers to Christian organizations, each with a narrow ministry focus and each supplementing the work of the local church. "Parachurch organizations" include, among others: hospitals, schools, mission boards, publishing houses, social service agencies, and youth movements.

In this vast spectrum, parachurch *youth* organizations have come under the most scrutiny because they work closer to the local church and have a direct impact on Christian families. It's not surprising, therefore, that questions have arisen about their value, purpose, and possible competition with the church. The largest and most well-known of these groups are Campus Crusade for Christ, Fellowship of Christian Athletes, Inter-Varsity Christian Fellowship, Navigators, Young Life, and Youth for Christ (Campus Life).

As parents who care about our children, it is important to check out any youth group seeking to influence them. Assuming this has been done, here are some of the benefits which a responsible, evangelical, parachurch youth organization can offer.

1. *Outstanding programs*. These groups sponsor trips, special events, concerts, and challenging speakers, all of which are available to "members."

2. *Caring staff*. The principle of "concentration" is at work. For example, if the organization's goal is to minister to high school students, its staff will be well-trained for that purpose, and job descriptions will be designed around spending time with kids, cultivating friendships, and counseling.

3. *Fresh perspective*. Often when a young person grows up in the church, he or she "takes for granted" basic theology, slipping into a cliché lifestyle. Hearing the Gospel and its implications from a different angle can open one's eyes to its powerful, life-changing truths.

4. *New friends*. Students from a variety of churches, backgrounds, and neighborhoods are involved in a specific "club," giving our sons and daughters expanded friendship possibilities.

5. *Interdenominational dynamic*. An exciting atmosphere exists when young people from a cross section of community churches study the Bible together. No one can anticipate the answer of another, and each person brings fresh insight to the Word.

6. *Outreach opportunities*. Christian students can use special evangelistic programs and emphases to reach their friends for Christ.

Remember, parachurch organizations were created to minister *alongside* local churches, not to replace them. Our children will gain most from active involvement in both.

WHAT OTHERS HAVE TO OFFER

In an effort to protect their children from negative outside influences, parents will often prohibit them from joining any "secular" organizations. This sheltering is unnecessary and even harmful. Our children need to learn how to live in the real world; and besides, many of these groups offer excellent counsel and education (for example: Junior Achievement, Girl Scouts, Boy Scouts, Campfire, Outward Bound, dance, aerobics, YMCA, YWCA, swim clubs, Key Club, and others). In reality, all truth is God's truth, regardless of the source. Conversely, just because an organization is labeled "Christian" doesn't make it good. Whatever the group, however, it is important to learn about those who would influence our children. Here are some guidelines.

1. Find out the nature of the organization; do a little research and write for information (endorsements from well-known local people are helpful).

2. Look for who is behind the group, the group's ultimate objectives, and its sources of funds.

3. Take the child to the organization, observe it together, and meet the leadership.

4. Volunteer to help the organization.

5. Ask the leaders if they are reinforcing Christian perspectives even though the organization is secular.

6. Don't be afraid to let secular organizations supplement church and home.

YFC Editors

27

TEENAGERS AND MONEY

- Do parents have a say in teens' finances?
- Should teens be given an allowance?
- Parents on a tight budget—how do they handle teen needs and wants?
- Tips on developing a savings program before you need one
- Car insurance and expenses—who pays?

It's important that our children learn to handle money early in life. They should receive some sort of reward for effort expended; they should learn when they're young what it means to run out of money. Some young people raised in affluent homes do not know what zero is. Many parents confess, "My kids have never asked for anything that they didn't eventually get." Such children will be at a real disadvantage when, as adults, they face the world of credit and debt. Wiser is the father who allowed his young teenagers to run the family checkbook for a month at a time. Learning where the paycheck goes is a great way to prepare for adult life.

Some people erroneously feel that it is spiritually wrong to tie money in any way to human effort or activity. But the Bible talks about reward "pressed down, and shaken together, and running over" (Luke 6:38, KJV). It speaks of prosperity for the diligent rather than for those who are not (Prov. 13:11). Handling money well is part of our stewardship of all of life. We must teach our children to handle it in a spiritual manner.

Should Teens Get an Allowance?

ART & LOIS DEYO

While driving past an ice-cream store, our son asked, "How about some ice cream, Dad?" But he wasn't nearly as interested when he heard Art answer, "I'll be glad to stop, if you buy, Jeff!"

By giving our children an allowance, we can teach them the value of money (beginning at an early age). Of course, sometimes we do stop for ice cream, but because we sometimes don't, they appreciate it more. And they learn not to spend their *own* money frivolously.

An allowance is a mini-salary to help young people pay for their needs and wants. Our children are required to set aside portions for tithe and savings. An allowance with specific guidelines and restrictions will help children plan for adulthood when they are on their own financially. It can prevent a constant "gimme" attitude, and we believe that it is better than paying for each chore done. We require certain set job responsibilities around the house each week in return for a regular allowance. Thus, they can count on a certain amount of money twice each month (on the days Art gets paid). Of course, there must also be accountability.

We began giving Deanna and Jeff an allowance when they started school. It was at that time that they needed milk or lunch money and had to begin making their own transactions. We started them on twenty-five cents semi-monthly and increased that amount as they showed they could handle it. We got them a bank and a billfold or purse. They set aside ten percent tithe to take to church and twenty percent savings to put in the bank. The rest they could spend as they wished (within certain guidelines).

In a few years, when their math skills were better developed, Art taught them how to keep a ledger of income and expenses, so they could keep an accurate record of their finances.

After accumulating a tidy sum in the "bank," we opened savings accounts for each of them at a real bank. Soon they were able to watch the balance in their savings books grow regularly. Later when sufficient money had accumulated, we placed their money in a money market fund where it drew much more than the minimal passbook interest.

We have been very pleased with the results of our children's savings program. It has taught them a good habit which many adults never learn. It teaches them to plan ahead, to be patient, and accept delayed gratification. They have truly learned not to sacrifice the permanent on

TEACHING YOUR CHILD THE VALUE OF MONEY

One good technique is to give him [your teen] enough cash to meet a particular need, and then let him manage it. You can begin by offering a weekly food allowance to be spent in school. If he squanders the total on a weekend date, then it becomes his responsibility to either work for his lunches or go hungry. This is the cold reality he will face in later life, and it will not harm him to experience the lesson while still an adolescent.

I should indicate that this principle has been known to backfire occasionally. A physician friend of mine has four daughters and he provides each one with an annual clothing allowance when they turn twelve years of age. It then becomes the girls' responsibility to budget their money for the garments that will be needed throughout the year. The last child to turn twelve, however, was not quite mature enough to handle this assignment. She celebrated her twelfth birthday by buying an expensive coat, which cut deeply into her available capital. The following spring, she exhausted her funds totally and wore shredded stockings, holey panties, and frayed dresses for the last three months of the year. It was difficult for her parents not to intervene, but they had the courage to let her learn this valuable lesson about money management.

Anything in abundant supply becomes rather valueless. I would suggest that you restrict the pipeline and maximize the responsibility required in all expenditures.

James Dobson

From *Dr. Dobson Answers Your Questions*, by James Dobson, Tyndale House Publishers, Inc., © 1982. Used by permission.

the altar of the immediate. Recently, our daughter helped with a large share of the purchase of a very fine flute which she plans to use as a flute major in college.

Today our fourteen-year-old son, Jeff, gets $10 twice-monthly and our seventeen-year-old, Deanna, gets $15 each time. Of course, parents must determine what is right for their own children. We also give our teens lunch money for three lunches each month. The rest of the time they make their own lunches at home. Because Deanna and Jeff know we have tried to treat them fairly, they have rarely complained.

As they grew older we insisted, however, that they spend some money on clothes. We still buy the necessary items for their wardrobes, but require them to buy any "extras." We also require that if

WHOSE MONEY IS IT, ANYWAY?

Perhaps one of the most difficult areas and yet one of the most potentially positive is the use of money. Teens are notorious for spending it like "water," and family expenses can hit the ceiling during adolescence. Instead of responding with yelling, nagging, and threatening, we can use these economic tensions as opportunities to learn about managing personal finances (a lesson many *adults* need).

Here are some principles to follow:

1. *Be a good example* of how to handle money, not wasting it or haggling over its use.

2. *Be open and honest* about family finances. Too often parents give the impression that money is no problem, and they can afford anything. Instead, give a realistic picture to the kids. This means sharing financial struggles and letting them help decide what can be cut out to save money. Also, when you can't afford something, explain that it is because of your spending *priorities*, not lack of money. (You *choose* not to buy the VCR unit because the money will be used for. . . .)

3. *Begin early* to teach budgeting and financial responsibility. With the fifty-cent allowance and the "payment" for household chores, discuss how their cash will be spent, letting them know that money, dialogue, and advice can go together.

4. *Allow them to experience the consequences* of spending money and living with their purchases, teaching what a good purchase is. (Work up to this—don't suddenly announce that they're responsible.) Explain the function of money and set spending priorities.

5. *Set general guidelines* (and principles), not specifics, for saving and spending money (especially when a part-time job is involved). Suggest that they tithe ten percent, save twenty-five percent, and use the rest (or save more if a special purchase is desired). Help them begin a savings account and teach them how to budget and use a ledger.

6. *Refuse to designate "their money" and "our money."* As a family, all the resources should be "pooled." Certain family members have authority in specific areas, but everyone's in it together. This concept, of course, will necessitate cooperation and communication, but it will teach volumes.

YFC Editors

they want jeans with name designer labels, that they pay the difference over "plain-pockets" jeans. Recently, Jeff wanted two pairs of brand name tennis shoes which cost $10 per pair more than the usual shoes. He paid the extra $20.

About two years ago, Jeff purchased a very nice twenty-inch dirt bike with his own money. Though we warned him not to leave the bike unattended in front of our house, he did, and it was stolen. It was summertime, and he knew summer would be over before he could accumulate enough money to purchase another bike. We agreed to loan him the money at ten percent interest. Art showed him how to figure the principle, interest, and balance each time he paid us. Since he didn't like paying the interest, he made every effort to pay the bike off as soon as possible—in just a few short months. Rest assured that he looks after *this* bicycle *very* carefully.

Related Articles
Chapter 19: When Can We Trust Our Teenagers?
Chapter 27: Helping Teens Use Money Wisely

Helping Teens Use Money Wisely
BRUCE B. BARTON

As in so many of the principles for guiding teenagers, financial planning concepts should be taught to children at all ages. However, many basic principles about money that you have taught your children can be refined and upgraded in the teenage years.

Guiding your children about money offers you as parents the opportunity to teach them an increased sense of responsibility and self-reliance. It provides tremendous opportunity for teenagers to learn how to make good choices. Teenagers can put money in its proper perspective as a resource for life-management and not an end in itself. First Timothy 3:3 teaches that we should be free from the "love of money."

1. *What is money management?* Money management is "planning and using money to obtain what you need and want." There's nothing uniquely Christian about having and using money; however, Christians bring an additional attitude to their finances—stewardship. We are instructed in Scripture to be responsible stewards of the gifts given to us. Trouble starts when "stewards" begin to act like "owners." A good steward manages his resources well, knowing ultimately they belong to Someone else and must be used for a greater purpose. On the other hand, an owner has complete control. He may choose to hoard or to waste his resources. As Christians, we do not have the sole ownership of our resources.

2. *Developing a spending record.* Young people can develop a tracking system to record where money comes and goes. The best way to begin a time-management plan is to write down how time is spent every half hour throughout the day for a three-week period. The same thing is true in developing a spending record. Write down how money is spent for an entire month, noting every expense and every income item. At the end of the month, review it to see what can be learned from that record. You can set up the three-column monthly journal to record income, expenses, and balance.

As you can see from the example, a sheet can be developed on notebook

MONTHLY JOURNAL

Month_____

Opening Balance $47.50

Date	Description	Income	Expense	Balance
1/13	Allowance	3.00		50.50
1/15	Baby-sitting	5.00		55.50
1/16	Pizza after game		3.00	52.50
1/17	Folders for class		2.00	50.50
1/20	Allowance	3.00		53.50
1/21	Deposit to savings account		45.00	8.50
Closing Balance $8.50				

paper or you can purchase a three-column monthly journal from a stationery store. The month and the opening balance, all the money the young person has in his possession at home, is listed at the top. A description of the item, whether income or expense, is listed with the date. For each entry on the page, an amount is written either in the income or expense column, and a running balance is listed in the far-right column. At the end of the month, the closing balance is written at the bottom of the page. This will be the opening balance for the next month. After a one-month period has passed, the young person should review his *expenses* and categorize according to the following:

• Tithing
• Savings—future education, trips
• School—activities, lunches, carfare, books
• Personal—grooming, cosmetics, jewelry, clothing, sports equipment, repairs of sports equipment
• Gifts
• Entertainment—dates, movies, sports events, records, food

When the expenses are categorized, the teenager will have a very clear idea where the money is currently being spent.

3. *Set up a system for budgeting.* Once you determine where the money is going, then you can determine a plan for where it ought to go. This can be done by allocating percentages of income to the established categories. For example, once the monthly income is established, the young person could say, "I am going to allocate ten percent of my income for tithing, fifteen percent of my money will go for savings, twenty-five percent for entertainment, twenty-five percent for personal, twenty percent for school, five percent for gifts." That kind of a very basic budget can be set, then can be reviewed for several months to see whether or not these percentages are realistic.

4. *Establish goals for saving.* One of the main reasons young people don't save is that they fail to establish goals for their savings plan. If a person does not have a goal for his savings program, all he is doing is accumulating money. Young people will save more if the money is to be used for future education, for a special trip, or for some special sports equipment. Have your teen establish a savings account, and make a practice of depositing his money in the bank whenever enough has been accumulated that it is no longer wise to keep it at home. Many teenagers establish monthly savings

deposit plans. If your teen is employed, he should be encouraged to deposit some portion of his check into a savings account each time he is paid.

5. *Teach the principle, "Never overspend."* A main principle of financial planning is never to spend more than you make. Sounds simple, but think how many people spend more than their incomes. By keeping track of where money goes and by establishing a basic budget system, the young person can learn not to overspend. Parents may have

---

HOW IMPORTANT IS MONEY?

It is interesting to me that Jesus had more to say in the Bible about money than any other subject, which emphasizes the importance of this topic for my family and yours. He made it clear that there is a direct relationship between great riches and spiritual poverty, as we are witnessing in America today. Accordingly, it is my belief that excessive materialism in parents has the power to inflict enormous spiritual damage on our sons and daughters. If they see that we care more about things than people . . . if they perceive that we have sought to buy their love as a guilt-reducer . . . if they recognize the hollowness of our Christian testimony when it is accompanied by stinginess with God . . . the result is often cynicism and disbelief. And more important, when they observe Dad working fifteen hours a day to capture ever more of this world's goods, they know where his treasure is. Seeing is believing.

James Dobson

From *Dr. Dobson Answers Your Questions,* by James Dobson, Tyndale House Publishers, Inc., © 1982. Used by permission.

---

to pitch in and help when there is an unusual expense, a repair, or some unanticipated item that neither his allowance nor his income can handle. For example, if your teen is playing football and accidentally breaks a window, the cost of repairing it might be greater than he can stand. You may want to help out. Parents need to be realistic and flexible to help teens through rough times.

6. *Reward your teenager for staying on a budget.* You may want to begin by reviewing his budget with him on a monthly basis. If the teenager stays on budget for that month, then give him permission to spend some portion of the money he has accumulated. Your options are to reward him with praise or with some extra income. Allow him to live with the natural consequences of his spending —when he runs out of money he has nothing more to spend.

7. *Correct impulsive buying.* If your teenager is an impulse buyer, here are some suggestions you might make:

• Before the teenager can purchase an item that he wants, he must get three separate prices from three separate stores.

• Make an impulsive buying list. To use an impulsive buying list, all the items desired for purchase must be written down. Then have the teenager list them in order of priority. In order for an item to be purchased, it must stay in the number one spot for thirty days. If, for example, she wants to buy a pair of jeans, the jeans must be number one on the list for thirty days. If halfway through the thirty-day period, she decides she'd like a new hairdryer; then that hairdryer must stay number one on the impulse list for thirty days before it can be purchased. This will help spread out impulsive purchases. This would primarily apply to items that are not normally budgeted and are not routine purchases.

As you work with your teenager on his financial plan, a good approach to take is to suggest and guide rather than to direct and boss. If you can function as his financial adviser, he can learn good principles. The results will be rewarding.

Your Teen Needs a Bank Account
Developing Savings and Insurance Plans

GORDON McLEAN

We sometimes are so excited about our son or daughter getting that all-important first job that we neglect a very vital follow-up—counsel on how to wisely use the money he or she will now be getting. Habits learned at an early age about handling money, whether good or bad, can often last a lifetime.

The Christian principles about money are simple and basic: earn it honestly, spend it carefully, invest it wisely, give it generously, and enjoy it heartily.

How can those principles be applied in a practical way?

First, a young person should have a bank account with his own checkbook and learn how to manage that account.

Second, he should learn about giving to the work of the Lord, not only by teaching but by family example.

Next, he should learn about savings.

Even a young person can and should have an Individual Retirement Account (IRA). And if he puts into such a tax-free account even a portion of the legal amount he is allowed each year, in later life he will have built a very substantial nest egg. That is learning to be a good steward.

Such accounts can be opened at a bank or even through a no-load, commission-free, mutual fund. The financial section of the public library can provide data on the success of such funds as well as the addresses of where to write for a prospec-

tus. (Note: Readers can obtain a list of no-load mutual funds by sending $1 and asking for No-Load Directory to: No-Load Mutual Fund Association, 11 Penn Plaza, Suite 2204, New York, N.Y. 10001.)

A young person may also want to consider life insurance. The younger the age at which it is purchased, the cheaper it is. But be sure to get the right kind of policy. Too many people buy the wrong policy, from the wrong person, for the wrong reason, at the wrong price!

There is only one kind of insurance to buy: *a term policy, guaranteed renewable.* Of course, agents, who are often old family friends, like to sell whole or permanent life policies with savings features called cash values. The return on such policies is minimal and the cost high, though they do have the advantage of paying good commissions to agents who sell them!

Variations of such policies are offered in plans called *universal life,* an alternative that pays money market fund interest rates, but only on the not-too-generous cash values.

While term policies do provide good protection, they are poor places to build savings for the future. A term policy coupled with a good savings plan in mutual funds, or even the more secure bank certificates of deposit, is much more profitable for the customer.

As soon as a young person is dependent on his income or supporting a family, he should also buy disability income insurance. This is not to be confused with a medical plan that pays hospital bills, but rather is insurance to see that his salary continues should he be unable to work for a long period due to sickness or injury. Of course, any automobile he owns should be covered with a liability policy that will protect him from damages sought by passengers in his car or another with which he may have an accident.

The important thing about insurance, after understanding what kind to buy, is to shop around for it just like you would any other major purchase. An independent agency representing a number of companies is generally your best source for all insurance information and prices.

An accountant or tax attorney can work with the family in suggesting ways parents can help their children through (1) employing them in a family business; (2) the Uniform Gifts to Minors Act; and (3) trusts and annuities. All of these offer tax advantages and thus more money for the intended help.

Money can be a useful servant or a terrifying master. Young people need to learn to handle it well, to respect but not worship it, and to be good stewards of it even in their youngest years.

Related Articles
Chapter 27: Should Teens Get an Allowance?

Chapter 27: Helping Teens Use Money Wisely

FINANCIALLY INDEPENDENT

Our oldest son tells me how I really demonstrated to him that he was on his own financially. It was right after he graduated from college. We were in Pennsylvania with the family car, and I was going to let him have it to visit a friend while I took the train home.

Just before we parted, he made a comment about buying gas. I hadn't thought this through but I said, "Well, I'm assuming that since you're using the car, you'll take care of that." Up to that point, we had been helping him through college.

Though I hadn't really meant to convey the message, my son suddenly realized that he was now on his own financially.

Years later he told me that was a real crossroads for him, and clarified his financial independence.

David Howard

Raising Teens on a Tight Budget

ART & LOIS DEYO

When our children were born, I recall being shocked at how much it cost for the laundry, diapers, bassinette, baby clothes, toys, and baby-sitters. We somehow developed the notion that expenses would lessen the older they got.

How wrong we were!

When teens reach high school age, you can look forward to additional school fees and supplies, more expensive clothes, and more activities such as ball games, plays, concerts, and movies. You will also need to make decisions about furniture, athletic gear, music lessons, cars, class rings, senior pictures, yearbooks, graduation announcements, parties, dates, camps, retreats, college, and possibly even marriage.

Whether or not you have a tight budget, it is good to teach your children how to live on a budget and be frugal with what they have. From the start, you must distinguish between their needs and their desires. The less you cater to their desires and wants when they are younger, the easier it will be when they reach adolescence. "Treats" should be more the parents' idea than the children's.

Training in this area should begin when the children are infants. Work toward helping them have a simple lifestyle and a nonmaterialistic attitude. Don't give in to their begging or they will expect you to do so consistently.

When our children, Deanna and Jeff, were young, they often went to the grocery store with us. It wasn't long before they learned to point to their wants and desires. It is our belief that our resistance to their pleas many years ago coupled with the positive teaching which we gave them about money was responsible for the present healthy attitude which they have toward financial matters in their teenage years.

From the beginning, we encouraged them to bring their friends to our home, rather than playing at theirs. This kept them more satisfied with their own toys rather than coveting so much after possessions of their friends. This also kept them more under our supervision instead of under the control of other parents with different values.

Among the values we taught were that good times don't have to cost much. We played games and went on family outings, picnics, nature hikes, drives to the country or the park, visits to relatives, and had long talks. We might spend an entire evening playing "hide and seek" or reading a book or playing a board game.

The overriding philosophy here is to emphasize "experiences rather than things." We spent our money on trips rather than new cars or the latest appliance or gadget or piece of furniture.

We taught them the common sense of waiting to receive something good by anticipating an activity and imagining how much fun it would be once the time finally arrived. We often took pictures of our activities so that we could look back on them with fond memories.

We invested our money in "growth activities" rather than wasting it on instant gratification. This included church, youth group activities, concerts, museums, and meetings. We attempted to expose them to as many people with our values as possible. As they have grown older, we have taught them to resist some peer pressure. For example, Deanna, who is a high school senior, has often gone with her friends to a fast food restaurant near her school. After we pointed out to her how much she was likely to spend in a month's time, she began drinking water—even though her friends ordered substantial amounts of food and drink. After all, she was paying for what she ordered.

Gifts at Christmas and on birthdays should be kept inexpensive but meaningful. In the early years, we especially relished all the homemade gifts, cards, and notes Deanna and Jeff would give us. They knew and we knew it was the thought that counted. Don't make the mistake when the kids are young of setting a precedent that you can't live up to once they become aware of how much things cost.

When our children were young, we bought them good used furniture for their rooms. We upgraded it as they grew older. Lois is very handy with the sewing machine and was able to remake many hand-me-downs and make most of the clothes for the family, including Art's dress pants and sport jackets. Since she started working outside the home three years ago, she no longer has time to sew extensively, but she's still the best bargain hunter in town. We taught our children discrimination in shopping. We buy irregulars or a defective piece of clothing for half price, and Lois repairs it so you can never see the defect.

Lois also has a knack for keeping the food budget way below average—even with two teenagers and lots of entertaining. We don't buy junk food, and we regulate *what* can be eaten *when*. From the beginning, we taught Deanna and Jeff to like a variety of foods to the point that today they have only two or three foods that they dislike. Furthermore, we didn't overfeed them when they were young, so they now seek to maintain the proper weight. Lois has taught them to cook from scratch so that they can prepare good, balanced meals for themselves. They have also prepared their own school lunches for years—looking forward to the "treat" of buying their lunches at school three times each month.

When our children were small, we avoided eating out in restaurants more than once a month. When we traveled, we always packed a cooler with food which lasted a day and a half rather than eat in restaurants.

We have given our children an allowance since the time they started school. Art has taught them budgeting, and we had a requirement that they should tithe ten percent, save twenty percent, and spend the rest with certain guidelines. Our policy was that we bought

CAR EXPENSES—WHO PAYS?

Perhaps the greatest drain on finances by a teenager (before college) involves the family car. With each new driver (especially a young one), insurance rates skyrocket, and fuel and maintenance costs take a dramatic leap.

Many parents "solve" this dilemma by encouraging their son or daughter to buy his or her own car. This may ease the pressure on Mom's and Dad's wallets and schedules, but will breed other problems. The next step becomes obtaining a job to pay for the car, gas, and upkeep (thus missing out on many high school activities). The "instant distance and freedom" offered is frightening, especially when combined with the attitude, "It's *my* car!"

Instead, the parents and teen should come to an understanding of the use of the car(s) the family already owns. This will involve communication and compromise (on both sides). Priorities will have to be outlined, schedules adjusted, and guidelines for use discussed. It would be helpful to put these in writing as a sort of contract, signed by all the parties involved.

Expenses should also be a part of the agreement and should include insurance, maintenance, and gas. The amount borne by the young person could be based on a straight percentage, mileage, or a combination. Other mitigating factors to consider would include the family *advantages* of another driver (e.g., chauffeuring younger children), the responsible care of the car, and the amount of his or her income.

In all of this we must keep in mind our goals: to be able, as a family, to afford the car(s); to provide transportation for the teen without shortchanging his or her high school experience; to teach the real economics of automobile ownership; and to move the teen toward independence.

YFC Editors

their necessities and they took care of their wants, gifts, etc.

We tried to avoid coming across to our children as a bank—always doling out money as if there were an endless supply. When Deanna and Jeff were old enough to understand, we explained our own income sources and household budget to them. This is invaluable because they appreciate so much more why you can't buy them a car or a stereo or a computer, etc.

In addition, our children stay so busy with music lessons, school, church and Youth for Christ activities, homework, and household responsibilities that they have very little time to shop or browse in stores. Staying out of stores keeps temptation to a minimum for all of us.

In family meetings we have deliberately agreed in advance who would pay for gas, dates, parties, outings, camps, and conferences. We have often helped our children find ways to earn their way to certain functions by selling candy, coupon books, and magazines, or through baby-sitting, paper routes, or doing odd jobs. We prepared them well in advance for the fact that they shouldn't expect to have everything their peers have, such as a car at age sixteen, or a drum set, or a synthesizer, etc. They both want to attend a Christian college, and that's reason enough to pinch every penny we can.

As with discipline, if you lovingly but firmly control the purse strings while your children are young, you will remain in the driver's seat during their teenage years.

Related Articles

TEENAGERS AND SEX

- How do you talk to teens about sex?
- What does the Bible say about sex?
- How should you react to your teen's steady boyfriend or girlfriend?

- Ways to develop quality relationships with the opposite sex
- Helping teens through the dating years
- How to prepare your teenager for marriage

Sex was God's idea. Satan cannot create anything. He can only pervert and twist and bend. Our society is twisted, fallen, bent, and often broken. It is important to educate young people to understand that sexuality is God's gift and that it has high and noble purposes both for procreation and for relational richness.

Sex is often a difficult topic for parents to approach because it has been so shrouded in secrecy and perversion. But when sexuality is understood in the context of human experience and God's relationship with us, it affords beautiful opportunities for growth, unavailable in any other area.

How Do I Talk to My Teen about Sex?

RONALD P. HUTCHCRAFT

The *first* of four essential steps when discussing sex is to give teens the correct information. Call intercourse "intercourse." Call the parts of the body by their right names. Don't be too cute; teens don't appreciate halfway answers to their questions. They know that babies are not left by storks.

Second, give them co-ed information. By that I mean that both Mom and Dad need to be involved in educating teens about sex. I am convinced that no woman fully understands male sexuality, and no man has a complete understanding of female sexuality.

For example, a man is the best person to explain to a daughter how men are stimulated more by sight than by touch. A mother can explain this, but because she hasn't actually experienced male sexuality, she can only convey what someone else has told her. Likewise, a mother is the best person to explain to her son about how a woman is stimulated more by touch than by sight. A father can't explain this as well. Neither can he do as meaningful a job telling how a woman looks for leadership qualities in a man and how she would rather have a moral leader than someone who wants to play a cat-and-mouse game of "How far does he want me to go tonight?"

Third, take the initiative to talk about sex more than just once in a while, and let teens know you're comfortable with the subject. Try to get away from the idea of one or two "big talks." I've learned to bring the subject up as often as is comfortable, and recently I saw the value in that.

One day my son said to me, "Dad, when are we going to have *the* talk? You know, the one about sex and stuff." So we started to talk, and in a few minutes he said, "Oh, is that all?" "Yes," I said, "we've been having this talk all along."

One of the best ways to take the initiative in talking to your teens about sex is to bring up your courtship. Kids like to hear about it, and you can tell it to them with both humor and seriousness. Another way is to tell them about certain television programs that you're not going to watch. Why aren't you going to watch them? Then talk to your teens about some of the sexual values communicated by those programs. Or, one other way is to ask your kids what their friends are saying about certain subjects. The point is, it's up to you—the parents—to initiate these talks; you have to locate and isolate the teachable moments.

Fourth, it is your responsibility to create a model of healthy sexuality. If my wife and I are consistently telling our teens to wait for marriage before having sex, then we'd better show them a marriage that's worth waiting for. If they don't see Mom and Dad affectionately touching and hugging each other, then the marriage looks boring and dull. Obviously you don't want to show them moments of deep intimacy, but there is nothing wrong with displaying kisses and hugs of affection.

When our youngest son was a baby sitting in his high chair, Karen and I would be hugging and soon we'd hear him banging his cereal bowl on the tray. We would quickly turn around to see little Brad watching us, clapping his hands, and laughing. It was an infant's appreciation of his mom's and dad's affection for each other; in his own way he was telling us to go for it.

Another parental responsibility—and certainly the most important—is to communicate God's standards on sex. God made sex something special; keep it special. His requirement of sex only in

TOO EMBARRASSED TO TALK

A lot of times communication breaks down in the teen years because parents do not understand the teen world. It is easy to think we have always been as mature as we are now. We forget our own struggles. But no matter where we grew up, we were not faced with the choices about drugs and sex that our kids today have to make at an early age.

With our parents, it was normal for a girl to reach puberty at about age thirteen to fifteen, sometimes as late as sixteen or seventeen. Now it is not uncommon to find girls who are nine or ten starting their first menstrual cycle. Kids have so few years to get ready for this new sexual identity, and it consequently puts more stress on their teen years. Yet, though there is more sexual freedom, we are no better prepared to handle it.

Instead of being uptight about sex, we as parents need to be aware of our permissive culture and our children's premature adolescence, and consider what practical steps we can take to keep ahead of the times. For one, we can talk about sex with our children much earlier than we think it needs to be discussed.

Jim & Sally Conway

marriage is a pathway to sex at its best.

Be positive yet realistic. Don't be embarrassed to tell your teens that God invented sex, its beauty and pleasure when tied to the bonds of total marital commitment. "Rejoice with the wife of your youth . . . be thou ravished always with her love" (Prov. 5:18-19, KJV). That's pretty explicit, but that's the Inventor talking.

God says, when you're married, go for it. But save it for that one special man or woman He has saved for you. Keep sex special, and you will have sex at its best. Don't settle for anything less by taking sex out of marriage.

Stress to teens that when God created sex, He put a fence around it called marriage. When you take sex outside the fence, people end up hurt and lonely. For a couple in marriage, sex brings them closer together; for a couple outside of marriage, sex drives them farther apart. When they break up, it's like ripping their hearts out, because people weren't made to break up with the person they have sex with. It was designed to be with one person in a forever commitment. And when it's not, it's like tearing apart two pieces of paper which have been glued together.

God's standard is not only right, it's smart; there's something in it for us.

_____

Related Articles

SEX EDUCATION AT SCHOOL

Sex education is one of the most controversial issues in modern education. And there are many valid points to be made on both sides of the question.

There is no doubt that sex education should be in the home, but in many families it just doesn't happen. As a result, there are young adults with unbelievable misconceptions about sex. They are, in fact, sexually illiterate.

Schools have responded by making sex a part of the curriculum. These classes provide helpful information, but they can teach unbiblical values (implicit or explicit moral statements depend on the teacher).

As responsible parents, we should not assume that our job is done because it's taught at school. Instead, when our kids come home and discuss these things, we should take advantage of the opportunity to follow up, passing on our wisdom, experience, and values.

We should not be afraid to discuss sex, openly and honestly. If anyone has that right, responsibility, and privilege, we do. The story is told of a mother who never told her daughter about menstruation. For two years, the daughter thought she was bleeding to death every time she had her period. Finally she told her mom, who blurted out, "Why didn't you tell me?" To which the daughter responded, "Why didn't *you* tell *me*!" To open doors later, we must discuss puberty and other important sexual facts during early adolescence.

We should also realize how free and open the conversations at school really are. We may not feel like we're experts, but we can tell our kids what we know about alternate lifestyles and values. We should give spiritual insights, taking the information they receive and adding the morals to it.

YFC Editors

What the Bible Says about Sex

NORMAN WRIGHT

Scripture has a great deal to say about human sexuality. Some topics such as fornication and homosexuality are discussed specifically there, while others including kissing, petting, and masturbation meet with silence. Still we can draw inferences on most subjects, finding principles to guide our teens.

I believe that parents should have the first shot at sex education. The church should also be involved, preparing the parents to fulfill their responsibility. But like it or not, children receive facts, values, and misinformation at school—not only in sex education classes, but from their friends. Movies and TV also provide a sort of silent curriculum.

The best defense and offense for parents is to give their children a positive, healthy view of sex that is grounded on a Christian value system. Start when the child is four or five, providing information appropriate for the age group. But be sure to prepare yourself first, making sure you understand both biblical principles and the physiology of sexual response. I find many couples who are quite unaware of the latter.

It's also important to help your child develop a healthy self-image. A teen with low self-esteem may become sexually active because he or she feels affirmed by it. As with depression and anger, sexual behavior can be a symptom of something else—in this case, a desire for approval. A teenager who already feels loved and cared for by family may be less likely to look for such affirmation elsewhere.

Most kids in Christian families have already heard that the Bible says to flee youthful lusts, to shun fornication. They want to know, "But what *can* I do?"

A good way to deal with this is to sit down with your teen shortly before he or she starts dating, to help develop a standard of sexual expression. Where will he or she draw limits? For example, there are many levels of physically expressing affection: (1) simply touching, (2) holding hands, (3) holding hands as if they were glued together, (4) various types of kissing, (5) fondling of the breasts or sexual organs, and (6) sexual intercourse. Ask your adolescent which are proper for someone who's newly dating, someone who's going steady, someone who's engaged, or someone who's married. It's far better to think about it beforehand than to make the decision in the back seat of a car.

Once your teen has determined which standards he'll uphold, ask how he'll maintain that standard when the pressure is on. How will your daughter, for instance, respond when her boyfriend hands her certain "lines"? How will your son react when a peer tries to break down his defenses?

You might want to try a "dating covenant" as we did with our daughter. This signed agreement included the time by which she'd get home, a promise to call us if she'd be late, places she would go, and a pledge to follow the standard of sexual expression she'd developed and discussed with us. The document also stated that her mother and I would have to meet the guys who took her out—not so that we could give him the "third degree," but so that he'd know we had an interest in the boys our daughter dated.

What if your adolescent doesn't care

about biblical principles? Can you still help him or her to treat sex responsibly? There are limits to the influence you can have over any teenager, short of locking him or her in a room with bars on the windows, but talking openly about feelings will earn you a hearing.

If your teen reveals that he or she is sexually active and doesn't care what Scripture has to say, there are three things you can ask him or her to consider:

1. What is the purpose of the sexual involvement? To gain approval or attention? To express love?

2. If it's to express love, what would the relationship be like without sex? Would there be enough to form a marriage with the person? In a marriage, other types of love are more essential than the erotic.

3. The more a young person sleeps around today, the greater the chance that he or she will end up with a venereal disease. It's almost to the point, it seems, where those without herpes will be a minority. And once a person has it, it's there to stay.

The subject of teen sexuality is a massive one. There are many good resources available, including Tim Stafford's *A Love Story: Questions and Answers on Sex* and John White's *Eros Defiled: The Christian and Sexual Sin* (both mainly for teens), and Letha Scanzoni's *Sex Is a Parent Affair*. This is one area of parenting in which such written references can be especially helpful.

Related Articles

Helping Your Teen through the Dating Game

JOSH McDOWELL

By the time teenagers begin dating, much of the preparation their parents can give them has already been done. Their attitudes toward the opposite sex began forming when they were in the cradle. The way their father treats their mother—the respect, admiration, and love he shows for her—becomes a model for good relationships with the opposite sex. If the parents get angry with each other or take each other for granted, that also is a model for the children. That is why it is important that they see their parents apologize to each other and ask forgiveness.

Being a good role model is the most effective way to prepare children for dating, but what parents say is also important. Even small children notice the way their father talks about women, for example. And children need information about dating that is best given by the parents. Rules and guidelines are important, because teenagers do not have the experience to know how to act in all situations. Education is passing on experiences and knowledge so another person doesn't have to make the same mistakes.

One general guideline I would give my children is to be careful not to arouse the sexual feelings and emotions of their dates. Kids need to watch where they go and what they do there. If a couple watches a sexually explicit R-rated movie from the back seat of a car in a drive-in theater, only supernatural intervention could keep their sexual feelings under control.

Another general guideline is always to treat the other person with respect. I'd tell my son to treat his date the way he would want his friends to treat his sister. An important guideline for all human relations, and not just dating, is to pay attention to the other person's enjoyment.

In addition to general guidelines, parents should make some specific dating rules. A boy, when he picks up his date, should ask her parents what time she should be home. Then if for some reason he cannot make the curfew, he should call her parents. He owes them that much; he is taking out a precious part of their family.

For the most part, single dating should not begin until the junior or senior year of high school. Group dating or double dating may be OK earlier than that, depending on the young person's emotional maturity and spiritual insight. A person shouldn't date until he or she is able to say no, for instance to sexual advances. A young person's level of maturity has a lot to do with the kind of relationship he has with his parents. If there is a lot of love at home, a lot of hugging and kissing, children usually won't seek that abroad. They are much better equipped to control their emotions when they are with other teenagers if they can let them out at home.

I would advise my children not to kiss on the first date. A kiss is something meaningful, an expression of intimacy, a communication of deep feeling. Most people do not have that intimacy after only one date. I wouldn't try to turn my good advice into a dating rule, however. That wouldn't do any good.

Sometimes a teenager gets too deeply involved with a boyfriend or girlfriend. It helps if the parents already have a strong relationship with the teen. They then may be able to get him or her to talk the situation through with them.

Parents may have to put down some pretty strict guidelines about seeing the boyfriend or girlfriend. A friend of mine did just that. He sat down with his tenth-grade daughter and said, "I think that right now you should be nothing more than friends. It has gone a little too far." The girl later told me that she

CAN YOU TRUST YOUR TEEN ON A DATE?

The biblical perspective on sex is a minority view today in our society. The average American teenager has probably watched 15,000 to 20,000 hours of TV, which means he or she has stored up a lot of unbiblical input. Add to that the pressure exerted by other kids, and you have some of the reasons why a majority of adolescents—even Christian ones—are most likely sexually active.

As the child grows, you can help him or her to understand in stages what sex is all about. You can explain what Scripture says about sex, and help the young person to develop a sound standard of sexual expression. You can let him or her know how others will try to use pressure to bend that standard.

Beyond that, however, all you can do is trust your teen and pray. Your trust may be broken. But as Christian parents, you can offer real help if and when the teen slips up and falls into sin. You can help your adolescent to realize that forgiveness is available through Christ, and that his life can go on from there.

Norman Wright

backed off from the relationship with her boyfriend because she had such deep respect for her family.

It's good for teenagers to date. The purpose of dating is not only to select a mate; it's also to have fun, to learn to feel comfortable around people of the opposite sex. Still, some teens aren't interested in dating, and parents should not force them or even encourage them too strongly. Any time you try to force a teenager to do anything, you're going to get reaction, rebellion. Kids have to set their own pace.

Some teens have the opposite problem. They want to date, but nobody wants to go out with them. The mother and father should talk together about what may be keeping the child from dating. Does she turn people off? Is he obnoxious or unfriendly? Does she dress or wear her hair in a way that is unacceptable to the other kids? If the parents find one or two problems that can be corrected, they can then concentrate on helping the teen overcome these. Parents don't need to tell the child why they are trying to help; telling him could make him too self-conscious to make the improvements.

Some teens are better looking than others. Some are not good looking at all. But even if people are really ugly, according to the accepted standards of beauty, they will still be invited out if they develop a healthy self-esteem, show an interest in other people, and are fun to be around. Parents who pressure their teen to do something about his or her appearance may end up accentuating the problem. The teen develops a negative attitude and is no longer fun to be around.

Unattractive people can improve their appearance by the way they dress or do their hair, but more important is their ability to relate to other people. When I directed Campus Crusade on one campus, I met a girl who was unattractive and obese but very popular. Everyone wanted her at their parties because she was so much fun. She was friendly and interested in what others were doing, and people just wanted to be around her. Good looks don't last long, but children who are self-assured and interested in others have

THE COST OF DATING

Without blinking, a hundred dollars or more can be spent on a date. Concert tickets, dinners, transportation, and other miscellaneous expenses add up quickly.

As parents, we should be concerned about what our kids do on their dates and how much is spent. At the same time, however, we want to trust them and move them toward independence.

Communication is the key. Hopefully we will have a strong enough relationship with our teenagers to be able to discuss dating openly and honestly. We should let them know that they have freedom to design their dates and that they have our trust. (Of course, we always will have the right to "veto.") But we should also encourage them to be *creative* in dating. The best dates are not necessarily the most expensive (contrary to popular opinion), and many inexpensive or free activities offer great opportunities for fun and getting to know the other person. These could include hiking, tennis, community service, parlor games, zoo visits, parades, "fast food" or "specialty" progressive dinners, scavenger or treasure hunts, ball games, frisbee tossing, wading, fishing, and a myriad of others.

Dating, like automobile use and other expenses, should be a part of the budget—we should encourage this and teach through it.

YFC Editors

an asset that will last a lifetime.

THINK BEFORE YOU DATE

As your teen enters his dating years, try to be aware of his thoughts. It is normal for teenagers to be insecure during this time, and to have a low degree of self-esteem. Help point out that God places a much higher value on him than he puts on himself. The chart below is to help you begin to understand what your teen might be going through on the inside, and what you can say to help build self-confidence.

WHAT YOUR TEEN THINKS	WHAT GOD THINKS
(If your teen is dating): How does dating this person make me look in the eyes of other people?	Have you considered how I feel about your dating this person?
What do I *want* to do?	What *should* you do?
How will this date affect me?	How will this date affect the other person and your relationship with Me?
(If your teen is not yet dating): I'm a nobody unless I'm dating someone.	Your self-worth should be based on how *I* feel about you—not someone else.
My life is being wasted.	Use this time to become a godly person.
I need to work harder to get dates.	You need to work harder to become the person I want you to be.

Barry St. Clair

612

How to Relate to the Opposite Sex

BARRY ST. CLAIR

A friend and I have conducted several seminars for high school students across the country on the topics of dating, love, sex, and marriage. I see a real need for these subjects to be dealt with in a specific way, and I think that the training must begin with the parents.

It is important to stress to teens that their purpose in life should be to glorify God. "Glorify the Lord with me; let us exalt His name together" (Ps. 34:3, NIV). Teens should be taught that their worship of God should permeate every area of their lives—including dating.

One passage that can help them glorify God in a practical way is 2 Corinthians 6:14—7:1 (NIV):

"Do not be yoked together with un-believers. For what do righteousness and wickedness have in common? Or what fellowship can light have with darkness? What harmony is there between Christ and Belial? What does a believer have in common with an unbeliever? What agreement is there between the temple of God and idols? For we are the temple of the living God. As God has said: 'I will live with them and walk among them, and I will be their God, and they will be My people. Therefore come out from them and be separate,' says the Lord. 'Touch no unclean thing, and I will receive you. I will be a Father to you, and you will be My sons and daughters,' says the Lord Almighty. Since we have these promises, dear friends, let us purify ourselves from

---

"DON'T SACRIFICE YOUR FUTURE"

Parents don't have to apologize for being more experienced than their kids. It's good for kids to know they live in a world where some people know more than they do. Of course, you can't treat the kids like dummies, either.

One of the secrets is helping kids project themselves into the future.

In our congregation a few years ago, for instance, were a young man and young woman who enjoyed one another as friends. Nothing romantic, but they enjoyed tennis together and seeing one another regularly.

The young man began considering marriage to another woman, but said, "Why do I have to cut off my relationship with Sue? Why can't we still play tennis? There's nothing sinful. We're still just friends."

This man's father was an elder in our church, so I said, "Well, let's say I enjoy surfing and your mother enjoys surfing. My wife doesn't like the beach at all, and neither does your dad. How about next Saturday your mom and I go surfing, and my wife and your dad go for a drive?"

Right away he felt that wasn't right. He could see in that situation it wouldn't wash, but in his own situation he hadn't been able to see the problem. I was able to expand his vision without patronizing.

Larry Christenson

everything that contaminates body and spirit, perfecting holiness out of reverence for God."

The point that is stressed over and over in this passage is that Christians and non-Christians can never reach complete unity. We are light, righteousness, and have the Spirit of God; they are darkness, lawlessness, and of the flesh. Because our purposes in life are different, we can never achieve partnership and harmony.

In spite of this biblical warning, many teens still desire to date non-Christians. You have probably heard some of the common excuses:

• "Christians don't know how to have a good time."
• "Christians don't date very much."
• "This is just a date. I'm not going to marry him!"
• "But he's such a nice person."
• "I don't know any Christians."
• "Don't worry. I'm going to lead him to Christ."

In spite of their good intentions, teens are seldom able to handle the situation as well as they expected. Once they begin to become emotionally involved, the other person starts to take control of the relationship. It's a logical process: (1) emotions get out of control; (2) the teen makes excuses, gives in, and begins to date the non-Christian; (3) the Christian falls in love with the non-Christian; and (4) the Christian eventually has to choose between God and the person he loves. If a marriage takes place at this point, there tends to be a rapid spiritual decline and the person is miserable.

It is important to understand these reasons why dating relationships sometimes don't work. Second Corinthians 6:17 tells us to "come out . . . and be separate." If your teens are to come *out,*

STEPS TO A POSITIVE RELATIONSHIP

Following are some general guidelines for your high school teens as they begin to develop relationships. Some of them deal with relationships with the opposite sex, but most apply in any kind of friendship.

1. Make sure your motives are pure.
2. The objectives of the relationship need to be defined upfront.
3. Openness and good communication are necessary.
4. Honesty must be stressed.
5. Set a proper atmosphere. Don't let yourself be caught in an awkward situation.
6. Don't become trapped by the relationship. Do things with other people.
7. Strive to build up one another in Christ.
8. Don't touch.
9. Don't start to get romantically involved.
10. Pray for the relationship.
11. Be holy and righteous. Let Christ be in control at all times.
12. Set your mind on the purpose of the relationship—in prayer and in the Word.
13. After being aware of all these things, if a friendship still turns into a romantic relationship, don't be in a hurry. Remember that God has a plan and He calls us to be patient.

Barry St. Clair

they need to understand how they got *in* to begin with. Were they naive? unsure? rebellious? No matter how they got into the situation, they need to repent and change their behavior.

The next step is to gracefully break the relationship. If a teen blames God for having to break up with someone, the non-Christian will develop a negative attitude toward God. Instead, the teen might say, "We just aren't going in the same direction." Then the other person can see the purpose behind the need to break up. Give the non-Christian time to change *after* breaking up—not while still dating. If he is really sincere about wanting to become a Christian, he will change.

The best way to avoid being bound together with a nonbeliever is to seek God's direction *before* becoming involved with someone. When a teen is seeking guidance concerning a relationship with the opposite sex, there are three things he or she should consider: (1) God's peace (Col. 3:15), (2) God's Word (Col. 3:16), and (3) advice from his parents (Col. 3:20). These three factors will help determine if a teen is really interested in someone, if the other person is interested in him or her, and if it is OK to date that person.

When teens begin to date, one verse parents should have handy is Psalm 27:14, (NIV): "Wait for the Lord; be strong and take heart and wait for the Lord." Then when your teen hits you with, "I'm afraid he is going to get away if I don't make a commitment," you can encour-age your child to postpone a hasty decision that would probably do more harm than good. *Impatience* is a major deterrent to God's will for teens.

Another big deterrent is *infatuation*—an emotional impulse of love based on supposed knowledge, untested by time or circumstances. Infatuation strikes when a teen pretends or daydreams that he has "fallen in love." When this happens, encourage him to think of the other person not as someone he is in love with, but as a brother or sister. Help him discover the meaning of genuine love. It is a teen's responsibility to consider the feelings of others as well as his own feelings (see Phil. 2:3-4). The emphasis should be on relationships rather than romance and on a spiritual level instead of a physical one.

Don't let your teen settle for any relationship that just happens to develop. Strive for *quality* relationships. The time you spend giving guidance and direction at this stage of your child's life will return great dividends later. By learning to develop strong relationships during his teenage years, your child is much more prepared to acquire friends that you can trust, a spouse that he will always love and respect, and a lifestyle that will glorify God.

Related Articles

At What Age Should Teens Date?

DAVID VEERMAN

Perhaps one of the most perplexing questions faced by parents is what age their children should be allowed to date. And there are probably as many different answers as there are families. It is a difficult issue because dating itself is so complex. A unique teenage ritual, dating approximates "cruel and unusual punishment." The variables seem infinite. Consider a few:

- The age and maturity of the child
- The age and maturity of the "date"
- The dating activity
- Double-, single-, or group-dating
- The use of a car
- "Going steady"
- The expectations of peers
- The expectations of the date
- Sexual pressure
- Setting a precedent for younger brothers and sisters

Let me offer a few principles on dating, and then suggest some guidelines.

Principles

1. Make your family "rules" solid enough to be understood and obeyed by *all* children in the family.

2. Be flexible with the specifics, remembering individual differences in personality, maturity, and other important areas.

3. Let everyone know the rules well before "the dating game" begins, so there are few surprises.

4. Keep the communication lines open and enforce the rules with love and understanding.

Guidelines

1. There is no magic formula or Bible verse for this, but sixteen has proven to be a good age for permitting a daughter *or son* to begin normal dating. (Sixteen is when most young people are learning to

THE FIRST DATE

I think parents should set an age limit on dating. However, I wouldn't want to say, "Thirteen, that's the age." Character qualities, trust, dependability, and open communication are the major factors in determining what age a teen should begin dating.

A guiding Scripture that I've used is 1 Timothy 4:12: "Let no one look down on your youthfulness, but rather in speech, conduct, love, faith, and purity, show yourself an example of those who believe" (NASB). When a teen is mature enough to set an example for other believers, then he's old enough to begin considering dating. If parents look down on the teen as too young, the teen is probably acting immaturely.

I believe that dating should gradually be allowed over a period of time. You don't just say, "OK, yesterday you couldn't date since you were fifteen, but today's your sixteenth birthday so now you can date." Parents can permit group dating at first, followed by double dating. In this way, the teen will be prepared for single couple dating at a later time.

Barry St. Clair

be responsible drivers, and they are upperclassmen in high school.) "Normal" dates are those where a boy and girl go to an event (activity) together without a chaperone. This doesn't mean that there is total freedom. The boy should pick up the girl, meet her parents, and obey the parents' curfew. The evening's activity should also be approved. Freedom can expand as the teen matures and proves to be responsible.

2. Before that sixteenth birthday, you may want to allow occasional, special kinds of dates. Once again, these would depend on the specific person's maturity and other considerations. "Special dates" could include extra-special events (like homecoming or a church banquet), group

READY TO DATE?

A problem faced by most parents is deciding when their child is old enough (or mature enough) to begin dating. When that time comes for you, I think the first thing you should do is sit down with your child and define some specific dating standards. (These should be worked through together. If you try to dictate your standards to your child without his input, they will only be wasted words to him.)

The next step is helping your child determine to follow those dating standards in the future, no matter what it might cost him. Emphasize that his desire (or lack of desire) to follow his predetermined dating standards will affect four areas of his life:

• His worship of God (Isa. 59:1-2)
• His self-image (Ps. 16: 1-11)
• His witness to others around him (1 Peter 3:15-16)
• His wedding (Song 2:16)

Teach your teen that if he discovers the importance of established dating standards and puts them into practice while he is young, he will see long-range positive effects in his life. Otherwise, he will see long-range negative effects. As the old saying goes, "You reap what you sow. You reap more than you sow. You reap later than you sow."

When setting dating standards, he should ask questions like:

• How old should I be?
• What do I want my dating relationships to be like?
• What qualities do I want to see in the person I date?
• How will I treat my dates?

After your teen writes down questions from every possible area of dating life that he can think of, use the Bible to discover God's answers to those questions. Make sure the standards are specific. And after your teen decides in his heart that he will not compromise those standards, have him show them to his dates when he begins to go out.

Perhaps all these steps seem like a lot to go through just to begin dating. But remember at all times—and make sure your child understands this—that our goal is to please God and not ourselves. When a teen can glorify God in his dating relationships, the other areas of his life are likely to shape up as well.

Barry St. Clair

"dates," and meeting the person at the activity.

3. Work at building an open *and* trusting relationship with your teen. Let him or her know that you understand the pressure to date and the games that are played.

One final note: Your son or daughter may not be asked (or have the courage to ask) for a date. This can be a devastating experience, heightened by peer pressure. Give acceptance and encouragement by sharing your own experiences and by assuring him or her of the reality of God's love and perfect timing.

Is It Love or Just Infatuation?

HOWARD G. HENDRICKS

Is it possible to distinguish between love and mere infatuation, especially in our fuzzy-valued society? The answer is yes.

Infatuation is more than a passing fancy for a person, but because it is emotionally oriented, it does not stand the test of love or time. Love, on the other hand, is meant to last. Here are ten yardsticks for love, which provide an objective way to measure a relationship.

1. Are you in love with the body or are you in love with the person? True love involves being attracted to the total person, not just his or her physical attributes.

2. Do you have, along with a feeling of pleasure, a feeling of reverence? In true love, a sacredness of the relationship develops. A partner won't ask the other to do something that will cause loss of respect. The man will not say, "If you love me, you will give me everything."

3. Do you care more about the other person than you do for yourself? True love is self-giving. Its primary purpose is not to exploit but to enrich. Many people are only in love with themselves. But in true love, you think more of your partner's happiness than your own.

4. Are you willing to take responsibility and accept it joyfully? Responsibility in love calls for commitment—to each other and to Jesus Christ. True love does not consider divorce a live option.

5. Do you enjoy being with each other so much that it hurts to be separated for a long time? True love is marked by pain in separation. You cannot be away from your partner for long without feeling that something is missing. A mature relationship can sustain separation even though it hates it.

6. Do you enjoy each other without a constant need of physical expression? If you cannot be together without always petting, you do not have the maturity needed for marriage. In true love, you can enjoy each other without physical expression.

7. Do you have a protective attitude toward your partner? True love desires to shield the partner from anything detrimental. You magnify your partner's strengths and avoid focusing on his weaknesses.

8. Do you feel you belong to each other? The person in love always thinks of himself in relationship to the other person. You really aren't two—you just happen to be located in different places. You want to share and identify with each other.

9. Do you understand each other? True love has a feeling that you understand each other unusually well. You feel the same way about important issues because your minds are fused with understanding.

10. Is your love maturing? True love is dynamic in its growth. Centered in Christ, your love begins to take on the characteristics of Christ. It begins to resemble the love described by the Apostle Paul in 1 Corinthians 13.

Related Articles

Chapter 28: How Do I Talk to My Teen about Sex?

Chapter 28: How to Relate to the Opposite Sex

Chapter 28: Boyfriends and Girlfriends

YOUNG LOVE

Glassy stares into space, endless phone conversations, excruciating clothing choices, and marathon mirror sessions—these are all symptoms of young love. This teenage phenomenon carries them to the heights of ecstacy and to the depths of depression . . . and parents are taken along for the ride.

Our first reaction is usually condescension, minimizing the reality of their feelings and calling it "puppy love." This response is counterproductive—we must resist putting them down.

Instead we should realize that "being in love" is very important to them—it's probably the most exciting thing that has happened in a long time. We may be rightly concerned about the "seriousness" of their feelings, but making light of or ignoring the situation won't make it go away.

When the opportunity arises, we should discuss the relationship *at their pace*. We shouldn't pry, but when they are ready, drop everything and listen. By spending time listening and empathizing, we will "win the right to be heard," so that later we will be able to share our mature, adult perspective, insight, and counsel.

If we don't like the boyfriend/girlfriend, we should follow the same guidelines while asking very caring and thought-provoking questions (e.g., "Do you both have the same values?").

YFC Editors

Boyfriends and Girlfriends

JACK CRABTREE

"We don't like Sharon's boyfriend," said the voice from the telephone. "He dominates her life. It seems he is taking her away from our family. He's not the kind of boy we would like Sharon to marry. We've tried to discourage the relationship, but it has only caused conflicts with Sharon."

Rarely do teenagers date a boyfriend or girlfriend that meets the expectations of their parents. Frequently, parents allow personal preferences to cloud their minds from being fair and open. They realize the importance of healthy dating, and it is not unusual that they frequently disagree with their teenager on the criteria for evaluating what is proper and acceptable.

It is often disheartening to parents to see the boy or girl to whom their teenager is attracted. It is natural for the negative traits of that boy or girl to be quickly observed by the parents. Meanwhile, their teenager is apparently oblivious to these "glaring flaws." All this can lead to a great deal of misunderstanding and hurt for everyone.

How should parents react to their teenager's boyfriend or girlfriend? Here are a few suggestions:

1. *Be involved and interested regardless of your opinion of them.* It is common for parents only to give attention to a relationship when they are unhappy. Such a stance casts a strong negative atmosphere in the parent-teen relationship. It also raises the possibility that a teenager, desiring increased attention from his parents, will seek it through a relationship that they disapprove. The parents' interest and involvement needs credibility to be an effective force of guidance and counsel.

2. *Seek to build friendships with the teenagers who date your son or daughter.* As family systems continue to disintegrate, more teenagers need adult friends. Building a friendship with a teenager is not unlike building a friendship with any other age-group. Be friendly. Show interest. Share time and experiences together. Ask nonjudgmental questions. Verbalize concern.

It is natural to fear the unknown. The lack of interaction with your teenager's boyfriend or girlfriend enhances these fears, and the lack of friendship or interest forces your teen to pursue romantic interests outside the home. It creates a tug-of-war struggle—"Are you going to be with *us* or *him?*"

Lack of contact also allows the concerns of the parents to be misrepresented by their teenager. A developing friendship opens the door to positive confrontation should any problem arise. In addition, such a friendship can outlast the teenager's romantic interests and give opportunity for guidance and witness.

3. *Help your teenager learn to make good decisions about his romantic life.* The goal of parents is to teach their teenager how to make good decisions in all areas of life. It is a mistake to think that parents can make decisions for their teenager without negative ramifications. Develop your child's potential for decision-making, offering fair and realistic guidelines.

Dating is a time of constant evaluation and self-awareness. The parents' role is to be supportive, loving, and available. The greatest challenge to parents is to allow time for their teenager to exercise the judgment he has been taught.

4. *Clearly define expectations and boundaries for dating.* Conflict between parents, teenagers, and their boyfriends or girlfriends can be reduced if there are clear standards and boundaries. Many parent-teen conflicts about dating center on curfew, destination, and the activity. All these categories are legitimate concerns for parents. Arguments arise when these decisions are discussed at the last minute when plans are already made and the teenager feels pressured by both peers and parents.

Teenagers enjoy being spontaneous. Activities planned on short notice often bring the most pleasure. However, the teenager needs some clearly stated guidelines from his parents that help decide whether it is appropriate for him to participate. Together, he and his parents should compose a brief list that clearly states a policy on the most important items (i.e., curfew times, notifying parents, acceptable activities). Any variance to these guidelines must be discussed before plans are made. This simple procedure can help avoid arguments in time-pressure situations and can build a responsible decision-making process. The purpose of this system is not to stifle a teenager's dating life, but rather to provide a growing freedom within the

IS BIRTH CONTROL AN ALTERNATIVE?

"My daughter's on the pill! What should I do?"

This anxious cry of a desperate mother strikes an empathetic emotional chord in the hearts of most parents. We wonder, "How would I respond if I made this discovery?" (or one similar with a son) The possibilities range from a Pollyanna-ish overlooking of the situation to judgmental insults.

First of all, however, it would be imperative to deal with our own feelings of failure, anger, distrust, hurt, and/or shock. We would feel quite irrational, and it would not be the best time to confront the teen (who would feel trapped and defensive).

The initial step should be to talk it over with our spouse and to come to a unified and realistic analysis and strategy.

Next, it would be important to choose the right time to talk to our son or daughter. We should be "pre-prayered" and focus on the person, letting him or her know that our love is unconditional. The discussion should be open, honest, and relaxed—not an opportunity to accuse or punish. We can begin by retracing what we've taught about premarital sex and then help him or her understand the real consequences (i.e., baby) and that birth control doesn't always work.

Many teenagers do not connect pregnancy with sex and are oblivious to the health hazards. They indulge for "fun" and as a way of expressing strong feelings toward another. Our discussion, therefore, should focus on the potential damage to oneself, the partner, and the child. We should then talk through how far to go and when to draw the line.

The discovery of birth control devices will be a shock, but it is also a symptom . . . of curiosity, experimentation, or lifestyle. It's a neon sign that says *help!* Our children need our moral guidance, perspective, love, and insight—it takes more than sex to go "all the way."

YFC Editors

boundaries of responsibility.

5. *Beware of provoking a desperate action.* Resist giving ultimatums or making unbending statements. Always leave room for possible change of heart or mind.

"Your mother and I have decided that we don't want you to see Steve anymore," the father said sternly. "No contact at all."

"But I love Steve! We want to get married when he finishes college," his daughter replied.

"We don't want you getting married so young. You've hardly dated anyone else. Steve is not the guy for you," the father barked. "He's immature. He can't take care of you."

"When he finishes school and gets a job, will you change your mind?" the daughter pleaded.

"No! He's not the guy for you, period," retorted the father. "Nothing will change our minds."

The daughter is faced with a big decision. She is being forced to choose between two sources of love. Regardless of her choice, she will be hurt.

The ultimatum that forces teenagers to choose between parents and boyfriend or girlfriend can damage relationships and people for a lifetime. This daughter is being provoked into an angry, desperate act. Perhaps if she and Steve "consummate their relationship" or she becomes pregnant, it will force her parents' hand to allow the marriage to avoid public disgrace.

She could also run away and cut her ties to home. Or she could obey her parents' ultimatum, with the strong possibility that bitter resentment might grow inside her that will eventually affect all her relationships.

What are parents supposed to do when their teenager seems determined to make bad choices in his or her romantic relationships? Should they stand idly by?

There are appropriate actions to take.

Follow the admonition of Scripture and pray without ceasing about every situation. Cast the cares and concerns on God because He cares. Ask God to intervene in the teenager's heart and mind. Ask God to give you special wisdom and love to handle things. Sometimes, if all else fails, and—within a reasonable, reversible situation—the hardest thing parents will have to do is allow the teenager to experience the pain of a wrong decision.

Parents need to take time to listen to their teenager. It is appropriate for parents to express their care and concern and to raise the important questions and issues. These matters should be discussed in an adult manner. The teenager's opinions can be respected while parental experience is shared in a gentle spirit. In later years, this same youngster, now a mature adult, often will recall gratefully his parents' stand during those turbulent times.

The teenager needs to hear a loud, clear message of the parents' unconditional love. Regardless of their teen's choices, parents must show their commitment to stand by him, ready to forgive and support. Avoid at all costs the urge to say, "I told you so." Most of all, parents must always be there, ready to talk and listen. With all the fluctuations of young love, the teenager can know that his parents' love is stable and secure.

When parents and teenagers go through deep water together, the parents usually come out the winners. They win, not because they get their way (many times they don't), but by gaining a new understanding of their own relationship with God. For, as parents love and guide their child, so God deals with every person.

Related Articles

Preparing Your Teen for Marriage

HOWARD G. HENDRICKS

Dr. James Peterson, professor of sociology at the University of Southern California, thoroughly researched the question, "Why do marriages fail?" He came up with three reasons. The first is an improper choice. People get married without enough exposure to their mate. They treat finding a partner like Russian roulette, without real understanding.

The two other reasons why marriages fail, according to Dr. Peterson's study, are because of unrealistic expectations and inadequate preparation. These last two are areas where parents can make a difference.

Parents can do several things to help their teen prepare for marriage. The first is to master the biblical objectives for marriage by reading passages like Genesis 1—2 and Ephesians 5. In Genesis 2:24, for example, it talks about leaving, cleaving, and becoming one flesh. That's what you are preparing your child for. You're preparing him to leave; you're preparing him to cleave; and you're preparing him to be one flesh.

Some parents don't do a good job in preparing kids to leave. Though we have at least eighteen years to prepare them for this, some kids *still* don't feel emotionally free after they've left home.

Cleaving means commitment—the fact that marriage is one man and one woman *for life.* Today the attitude is, "If it doesn't work out, we can always bail out." People get a divorce on the basis of fifteen percent of the marriage being troubled. They are throwing away eighty-five percent of a good marriage because they didn't learn the importance of cleaving.

The second thing we need to do is to begin early. We have a utopian system of marriage but it makes one fundamental blunder—that is the failure to realize that marriage begins in infancy. That doesn't mean that parents can't start preparing their teens for marriage, but it does mean that an awful lot has happened already to prepare the child for marriage that the parents might not have been aware of.

In the bonding process of early life, as parents relate to their child, the child grows up with a feeling of being loved or rejected. He develops an opinion of whether the world is essentially a good place or a hostile place. All of these are basic components that determine what kind of marriage partner he'll be.

Most of the problems that we have in marriage are the problems that we've never solved in childhood or adolescence. They are not the problems of marriage, but the unsolved problems of youth.

Third, both parents need to cultivate healthy relationships with their children so that they are free to ask questions and to give and receive love. In a single-parent family, children are obviously missing one model. This is an area where the church might help by matching single adults with the children of single parents in a big-brother, big-sister kind of arrangement.

The fourth way parents can prepare their child for marriage is to communicate their love for him. If you ask a parent, "Do you love your child?" he'll reply, "Of course I love my child." But the question is: How does the child know that? He can know it, first of all, by the time you spend with him, both the amount and the quality.

Then you can listen. That's the greatest compliment you can ever give to a person. You can love your child by being interested in what interests him. Often parents of teens don't even know what their teens are interested in.

You communicate love to your child by what is called "presence." That means when you are there, you are all there, not emotionally detached. You don't watch the football game or read a book while your son or daughter is trying to explain something to you.

And you can love your child by affirming him. Be on your teen's team. Tell him that he is doing a good job and you're proud of him, that your greatest claim to fame is that you are his father or mother.

A fifth way to prepare a young person for marriage is to feed his responsibility. I was at Yellowstone Park one summer watching the people feed the bears, even though they are warned not to. I talked to a ranger about it and he said, "That's bad, but in the winter these bears die by the side of the road waiting for tourists to give them a handout. They have lost the ability to fend for themselves."

I think parents often do the same thing with their teens. Every time you do something for your child that the child is capable of doing, you are making him a marital cripple. One way you can help your teen with responsibility is to encourage him in the decision-making process, such as determining where he wants to go to college. Another way to teach responsibility is by giving him the freedom to make mistakes. We all fail but that does not mean we are all failures.

The sixth preparatory step is to help your child develop a healthy appreciation for his own sex and a respect for the opposite sex. Men and women need to be complementary instead of competitive. We need to magnify the role of the man and the role of the woman, and respect each other's distinctive qualities. Sex is not something that we do; it is something that we are.

MARRIAGE CAN BE A MIRAGE

Many people act as if they believe marriage is the chief end of life, the final solution to loneliness, unhappiness, and boredom. But Christians believe that to be complete in Christ is the chief end in life. Happiness and joy are by-products of that relationship.

Many people marry only to find it doesn't live up to their expectations. Married people face some of the same problems single people do: loneliness, sexual temptation, lack of sexual fulfillment. Marriages can be cannibalistic if two people destroy each other by expecting the other to satisfy his or her needs, dreams, and desires.

It is more important for you to be the right kind of person than it is to find the right kind of person. What steps are you taking to grow to be the person you want to be?

You really can't find love until you find yourself. If you struggle to fulfill your romantic ideal in marriage, you may miss what life is all about. First experience God's love and complete acceptance. Develop your love relationship with other brothers and sisters in Christ. Grow and develop in Christ. Realize that all Christians do not have to be married to be joyful. Reexamine your expectations of marriage. Then relax, and let love come to you.

Bruce B. Barton

624

Seventh, provide a good role model in your own marriage, or through the marriages of others. If you are happily married, the greatest thing you can do for your child is to love the child's mother or father. For the single parent, you can invite couples into your home to be models for your children. Jeanne and I regularly open our home to students just so they might learn what a Christian husband looks like, what he is supposed to do, what a Christian wife does.

Finally, commit your child to the will of God. We get so uptight over whether the child is going to find the right mate. But that is a function of our faith. We have to trust God for that.

Looking back, our children have agreed that the most helpful of these preparations was the quality of our marriage. I didn't have many positive models of a marriage. But I knew what I didn't want.

About the only thing Jeanne and I had going for us was a total commitment to Christ and a total commitment to each other. Our children have always said, "If we don't marry right, it won't be your fault, because we certainly had a wonderful model to go by."

Having a good relationship was also very important. We were very open and free to discuss all aspects of dating. The children would come home and share with us what was going on with their dates, who they were thinking about, etc. Developing a healthy relationship with both parents is extremely important.

What Kind of Marriage Are You Modeling?

RONALD P. HUTCHCRAFT

This is a worthy subject because all of your life up to marriage is but a prologue to your marriage. It is preparation. If you think you start getting ready for marriage when you get or give a diamond, you're in big trouble.

Modeling Marriage
Marriage is under greater pressure today than it's ever been. Parents need to understand that they have a lifetime responsibility to model a good marriage. Perhaps the best way to do this is to remember this: When it comes to marriage, the *media* is the *message*.

Chances are, children will replicate the marriage they observed while growing up.

What I'm about to say is valid only if it is *modeled* in Mom and Dad.

1. *Commitment.* First, I think our kids need to understand three key words that make a marriage *biblical.* The first word is *commitment.* Mark 10:7-9 speaks of a permanent commitment—one man, one woman, united by God in a relationship where there is no parting.

To many today, marriage is more like an *experiment* than a *commitment.* You just try it on like a new suit. If it fits you, fine! If it doesn't, you just take it off and try another one.

When Karen and I got married, three important words were part of the ceremony: *forsaking all others.* That's the essence of commitment. Commitment means that, as long as we both are alive, I'm going to be married to you.

Commitment means that I close the door to all other possibilities. Not knowing what possibilities may come later, I commit myself wholly and exclusively to my spouse.

Our kids need to learn about commitment on small levels too. We need to tell them, "If you *say* you'll do something, we're going to see that you *do* it because commitment closes the door, even if something better comes along." We need to help our kids see how important it is to think about commitments before making them. So at a very early age we must prepare our children by helping them understand what commitment means. And when it comes to marriage, we need to teach our children that divorce is not an option. It's not a multiple choice situation. Commitment is fundamental. There is no back door on the house called marriage. There are not fifty ways to leave your lover; there's not even one.

2. *Love.* The second key word to teach our kids the meaning of is *love.* First John 4:19 (KJV) says, "We love Him, because He first loved us." God's love for us is a *decision* He made, not just a feeling He has about us. There is nothing about us that would make us lovable to God. He loves us because He has *chosen* to love us.

Christian love is a choice; it is a decision, not just a feeling. Our kids grow up with this kind of ooey-gooey feeling about romantic love. Married people know that the romantic feelings ebb and flow, come and go.

Love needs to be seen in practice in

GOING ALL THE WAY ISN'T FAR ENOUGH

Because it takes more than intercourse to make a relationship, God has given directives for the expression of sex in the Bible. Sex is such a high powered expression of you as a person that it cannot be treated as other aspects of yourself. It is easy to give in to the feelings produced by sexual attraction and fall in love before a mature relationship can be founded. Getting involved in intercourse is easier than building a relationship, a family, or a home.

The biblical perspective on intercourse is that it is reserved for marriage and until marriage (Mark 10:7-9; Gen. 2:24). A good way to understand marriage is to see it as a unique combination of *commitment* and *romance*. The commitment of the wills of two people to the social and legal bonds of marriage provides the foundation, the limits, and the responsibility to protect the romance.

Commitment without romance is a burden, a paper contract. Romance is symbolic of God's creative activity in the world. This intense blending of heart, mind, and body gives passion to the relationship. On the other hand, romance without commitment can lead to delusion.

Many arguments have been given for not having intercourse until marriage. But experience has shown that creative minds can think of counter arguments for every reason given or verse quoted. However, going all the way before marriage is a poor substitute for sharing the newness of intercourse with the one person you love and plan to spend your life with. It's worth choosing the time and setting of the experience with clarity and conviction so that you are honoring God in your relationship.

Bruce B. Barton

family relationships before kids have a family of their own. And they need to learn that they can decide to love even when they don't feel like it. Sometimes it is a feeling, but it is much more than that.

3. *Unselfishness.* The third key word to teach our kids the meaning of is *unselfishness.* These days the attitude toward marriage is, "When you don't make me happy anymore, then I'll go my way." We've got to demonstrate to our kids what Jesus said, "For whoever wants to save his life will lose it, but whoever loses his life for Me will find it" (Matt. 16:25, NIV). Unselfishness pays off. "Give, and it will be given to you. . . . For with the measure you use, it will be measured to you" (Luke 6:38, NIV).

Unselfishness is saying, "What can I do for you?" And when I take that approach, I actually end up doing the most for myself.

Steps to a Happy Marriage
To lay the groundwork for a happy marriage, I suggest several steps:

1. *The best romances were first good friendships.* We need to help our kids realize that the way to have the most secure relationships is to make a *friendship* and then let God make it a *romance.*

Marriage is not ultimately just a sexual or legal commitment. It is the ultimate friendship. Your ability to be happily married will depend on how much you know about being a friend to someone of the opposite sex. We need to really fan the flame of friendship.

We need to encourage our kids to experience group dating, non-romantic relationships, and good friendships with the opposite sex. One of the things that compromises this concept is that the sooner a person becomes physically involved with another person, the less chance there will be of being his friend.

Sexual involvement preceding the friendship will result, chances are, in the friendship never developing. With teenage glands being what they are, as soon as "the physical" gets involved, the talking stops. And you never get to really know the person.

2. *The best choices are made by those who shop around.* "Don't try to see how quickly you can narrow your friendships to one partner. You're going to have one partner for the rest of your life!

"So shop around. The people who make the best purchases don't buy the first thing they see. You've got to develop your romantic radar through variety."

3. *Be what you want to be married to.* "Basically, the American myth is that you find a partner by hunting for one. Actually, a good way to find the right partner is to make a list of all the qualities you would like to have in the person you want to live with for the rest of your life. Then start to be that person—because the bait attracts the catch.

"If you want a gentle, respectful, affectionate, godly person, then be gentle, respectful, affectionate, and godly. You will tend to attract what you want."

4. *Don't make a long-term commitment for a temporary reason.* Marriage is a forever commitment, and many kids make that commitment just to fill a temporary need in their lives; for example, to escape from a bad situation, to legalize sex, to get revenge on a parent, or to deal with loneliness. That probably guarantees that the forever commitment will turn out to be only temporary.

Whatever you call it, if it's not forever love, it won't be a forever relationship, and you'll have forever scars.

———————
Related Articles

TEENAGERS AT SCHOOL

- Helping teens survive spiritually at school
- Competing with the powerful force of peer pressure
- Public vs. private education
- The battle over grades: Does anyone come out a winner?
- When teachers teach something you don't believe in: Is there anything you can do?
- The rights of Christian students in the public school system
- Why so much competition?
- Identifying and responding to learning disabilities
- How to help the school help your teenager

Most American teenagers go to public school; only thirteen percent go to parochial schools, either Catholic or Protestant. A great deal of teenage life takes place in school—not only learning information, but also interacting socially with peers.

Yet more important than what happens at school is what a young person brings to the school. We parents cannot abdicate our responsibility to the school system. Properly understood, the family and the school form a partnership. Schools become bad or less good when parents are not involved. A proper relationship between teachers and parents is vastly important.

Teachers are nearly always positive people who are interested in teenagers. They may not share all of the parents' values, but parents who take the time to understand the teachers' situations usually find allies in them. Sometimes this is not true, and then strong corrective measures have to be taken. But in most cases, good communication between parents and teachers can greatly help family life.

The Power of Peer Pressure

BARRY ST. CLAIR

The number one reason teens give in to peer pressure is a bad self-image. A teen who has low self-esteem feels a strong need to have others agree with him. To him, this means that he's made a good decision. But this need often causes a teen to be unable to respect or accept others as they are. Therefore, he is more susceptible to negative peer pressure.

The effect of giving in to peer pressure is what sociologist David Reisman calls an "other-directed personality." The teen develops a sixth sense which enables him to feel out what others expect of him and then act accordingly. In other words, a teen will compromise his own identity in order to be accepted by his peers.

The second major cause for giving in to peer pressure is fear. Fear keeps teenagers from being their own unique selves and usually expresses itself in several ways. A teen may fear what his friends will think of him. As a result, most teenagers try to build relationships and their reputations without offending anyone.

Fear also expresses itself when a teenager is scared that choosing to follow God won't be any fun.

And lastly, in what I call the "Chameleon Process," a teen, afraid of losing friendships, will develop the knack of blending in when he's with his friends because he's too self-conscious to stand up for what he believes. Proverbs 18:24 says, "A man of many friends comes to ruin, but there is a friend who sticks closer than a brother" (NASB). Second Timothy 1:7 also speaks to the issue of fear: "For God has not given us a spirit of timidity, but of power and love and discipline" (NASB).

Parents need to respond to the powerful force of peer pressure in several ways. First, they must realize the depth of the problem. During the teen years, the most important area in their child's life is that of acceptance. Risking rejection by his friends (which could involve being badly hurt) is a daily danger for a teenager.

WHEN YOUNG PEOPLE "KEEP UP WITH THE JONESES"

In a recent television program, a group of teenagers was asked, "What do you see as the greatest problem facing teens today?" Overwhelmingly, the response was, "Peer pressure."

Peer pressure affects all teenagers in some way. And it isn't all bad. Peer pressure causes us to behave according to standards set by a group. These standards may be good, poor, or self-destructive.

We tend to think of peer pressure only as a negative force for children and teenagers. But many young people have been challenged to excel in schoolwork or in sports because of healthy competition. Often a young person learns the value of money when he must save his allowance to buy something that "everyone" has.

Peer pressure is not a problem experienced just by teenagers. As adults, we call it "keeping up with the Joneses." We are still conforming to standards set by someone else. But maturity allows us to be less influenced by others.

Being accepted by others—our family, classmates, or co-workers—helps us develop positive self-images. That, in turn, gives us the character to withstand temporary failure, rejection, or loneliness. Being part of a group provides affirmation. And when the group has healthy standards, the peer pressure is a positive force.

But as parents, we often see young people influenced by negative peer pressure. Following the crowd has led many teens into drugs, sexual experimentation, cheating, etc. Teens and preteens are too often wrongly influenced by others before they've established their own standards and values.

How can we help?

First, *accept peer pressure as normal.* Everyone experiences it—young children, teens, and adults. It's a necessary part of society, since some conformity to rules and guidelines is vital if we're to survive. (Imagine if we all drove as fast as we wanted!)

Second, *give positive support.* Praise young people when they achieve. Don't wait until your teen earns straight A's, hits three home runs in one game, or plays like a concert pianist. Encouragement strengthens identity.

Third, *examine yourself.* Are you the kind of example your teen should follow? The old adage, "Do as I say, not as I do," seldom works with teens. As they are stretching, trying to find their own limits, teenagers need to see examples of mature adults with healthy values and Christian lifestyles.

Finally, *give teens as much choice as they can handle, within clearly defined guidelines.* For example, "John, today I'd like you to mow the lawn. You can do it anytime, as long as it's done by suppertime." As a young person gets more practice making decisions—and facing the consequences of his decision-making—he becomes more confident of taking control. A young person who has planned his own schedule for doing homework will be more confident when he must decide whether or not he should join the group for an after-school snack.

The secret is giving up control gradually. Never releasing control forces teens to rebel. And, dropping all controls overnight is like putting a ship in the middle of the ocean without a rudder, map, or compass.

Though it often seems children (and especially teenagers) don't want to receive guidance and rules from adults, that isn't true. The controls and guidelines tell a child that someone cares. While they may not like all the rules, interviews with young people show that they'd rather have too many rules than none at all.

We must pass our traditions, wisdom, beliefs, and convictions on to our children. Teens need positive models for growth—emotionally, physically, and spiritually. Values deeply planted in our children help them resist the quick cure—drugs, drinking, sex—for too much negative peer pressure.

YFC Editors

Second, parents need to understand the fact that being accepted by friends is more important to their teen than being accepted by parents. Most teenagers do *not* want to conform to the lifestyles and actions of their peers. They want to stand on their own, but in most cases they lack the self-respect and confidence to resist peer pressure.

The parents' primary responsibility in helping their teen deal with negative peer pressure is to provide an atmosphere, such as a church youth group, where their teen can find acceptance with Christian peers. Though they can't totally remedy the situation, parents *can* express concern and keep the lines of communication open. Sharing their own experiences and frustrations with peer pressure can be an encouragement to a struggling son or daughter.

By developing their child's self-image and convictions, parents can help him better cope with peer pressure.

Self-image

God expects His children to have a good self-image as seen in Mark 12:31, Christ's commandment "to love your neighbor as yourself." In Psalm 139:13-16, we are told that no one else is like us—that we are fearfully and wonderfully made. God created your child for a unique purpose and He intends to fulfill that purpose.

Parents need to develop their teen's self-image in three areas: mentally, physically, and spiritually. In the mental and physical realms, they can encourage their teenager to accept his capabilities, such as athletic ability, natural intelligence, and inborn musical talents, right where they are—while working to improve those areas that show promise. Don't allow a teen to limit his self-image to physical appearance or abilities. Though compliments on looks and achievements are very important to a teenager, 1 Samuel 16:7 assures us that God looks on the heart. He is more concerned with inner beauty than He is with what we look like on the outside.

Spiritually, a teen needs to realize that his relationship to God has potential for change and growth. He also needs to know that he can rely on his parents to always be there in his time of need. That's God's way of loving kids! Parents should encourage their teen and pray specifically for him and his friends.

Convictions

Developing positive convictions in a teen can help him deal with negative peer pressure. A teenager who has no convictions will fit in with any group of people. That's a sign of real immaturity. On the other hand, a teen who can stand up and say, "Hey, I'm doing that for these reasons . . ." shows a real maturity.

Convictions must come from the teen's own experiences and study—not from another person. The only solid convictions come from the Word of God. I like to use the comparison between a thermometer and a thermostat. The thermometer is an instrument that is *controlled* by the environment; the thermostat is an instrument that *controls* the environment. In their ability to develop convictions, teens can be either thermometers or thermostats.

Standing up for convictions will result in conflict, not conformity. Teens must be aware that they are going to run into conflict with their friends as they develop convictions. Yet by having convictions, teens are rewarded by developing self-respect and maturity.

The first step toward helping your teen develop convictions is to help him analyze his relationships with others. Are his friends really interested in him? Is God really interested in him? What are his friends' responses when he crosses

---

PARENTS, PEERS, PARTNERS

Parents sometimes wonder, "How come peer influence is so strong in a teenager?" "Why are friends so influential?" When kids reach their teens, they don't seem to listen to what their parents have to say. Instead they listen to their friends who do not have their parents' wisdom and life experience. Parents need not worry. Such is the normal pattern.

The development process of all people can roughly be grouped into three time periods: childhood, adolescence, and adulthood. During childhood, the *parents* are the most important influence in developing and shaping values. During adolescence, the *peers* become the most important influence. As teens struggle with their own identities, they look to others their own age who are going through this same struggle for clues as to how to respond. Later as adults, the *partners* or spouses become most influential in shaping values.

Teenagers who successfully become independent of their parents and learn to deal appropriately with the influence of their peers are becoming well-prepared for a lifetime together with their partners and the establishment of a strong Christian home.

James C. Galvin

631

them?

The second step is to help your teen choose to go God's way. First John 2:15-17 talks about the importance of remaining in God's will. Your teen needs to learn that it takes a conscious decision to walk God's way.

The third step is to encourage your teen to allow God to overcome fear. Perfect love casts out fear of rejection.

A final step is to help your teen *verbally* identify with Jesus Christ. To say, "Well, because my mom won't let me," or "I'm not going to buy a six-pack because I'm not thirsty" is a cop-out. I suggest using the statement, "Because I belong to Jesus Christ, I can do this or I can't do that. . . ." That kind of statement clarifies where he stands.

Of course, the most significant way to deal with peer pressure is to remedy the situation while your child is still young. If parents wait until their child is sixteen to start developing convictions or building up his self-image, it's possibly too late. By helping their child develop solid convictions and overcome the fear of rejection, parents can be confident that their teenager will grow into a "thermostat" in control of his environment.

IN THE RIGHT MOLD

Parents worry a lot about peer pressure. It seems that whenever we think of it, we think only of the negative. But Proverbs 13:20 says, "He that walketh with wise men shall be wise" (KJV). God uses other children to mold our children, and with the right type of children, peer pressure is beautiful. I go out of my way to expose my children to outstanding Christian college students and Youth for Christ and Campus Crusade staff members. I want my children to be around them because they look up to them. God uses these young men and women to help me mold my children.

Josh McDowell

Related Articles

Helping Teens Survive Spiritually at School

WARREN W. WIERSBE

We need to prepare our teenagers for the various stages of life. Too often, we see them only in the stage they're in now, and we don't prepare them for what's coming.

When our children first started school—public school—we warned them that they could probably find just about anything there, so to live a Christian life, they would have to be strong. We offered our support, but they had to fight the daily battles. We tried to brief them on what was coming.

We also tried to use the Word of God in discipline. Sometimes applying a Bible verse has stronger impact than a spanking or taking away privileges. It has a way of getting into their hearts.

When our children reached their early teens, I gave each of them a copy of my book, *Be Challenged,* which discusses six Bible teenagers and how God worked in their lives. This was a bit of curriculum to help prepare them for the teenage years.

Throughout their growing-up years, I always tried to be accessible to my kids. When I was home, I made it a policy that whenever one of them wanted to see me, I'd drop what I was doing.

The one time I didn't, I still remember. Judy came in while I was pounding on the typewriter trying to meet a deadline. She stood there silently until I said, "Can I see you after while?"

"I want to see you now," she said.

"I'm awfully busy."

"You took time to *have* me. Why don't

SPIRITUAL HOMEWORK

Many parents worry about the bad effect school may have on their children's spiritual life. I would advise concerned parents to do the following things and then send their children to school in faith and trust:

1. Give your children unqualified acceptance.
2. Demonstrate unconditional love for them at all times.
3. Maintain a trusting spirit toward God and toward your children.
4. Be firm.
5. Insist that your children maintain high biblical standards. Present these standards in a thoughtful, reasonable way.
6. Memorize Scripture along with your children.
7. Encourage them to become involved in a Bible study, prayer group, or witnessing group on campus.
8. Encourage them to take a stand for Christ openly, so that they are not just "Secret Service" believers.

Bill Bright

you take time to *listen* to me?"

She had me there. So I stopped.

Even now, my secretary at Back to the Bible knows that any time the kids call, if they ask to interrupt me, I'll come to the phone. I always want to be available because they learn about their heavenly Father from their earthly father.

If you want your teens to apply their faith to life, however, the most crucial thing is for you to examine your own life. With few exceptions, kids follow the patterns of their parents.

Take the scriptural example of a three-generation pattern of sin: Abraham lied about his wife, Sarah (Genesis 20). Isaac lied about his wife, Rebekah (Genesis 26). And Jacob lied about almost everything. We pick up these things.

To help teens live their faith at school, we have to be living it at home.

Related Articles

Chapter 13: Instilling Values That Will Last a Lifetime
Chapter 15: Helping Teens Live Their Faith
Chapter 29: The Hardest Test at School
Chapter 29: The Rights of Christian Students in Public Schools

The Hardest Test at School

When Your Teen's Values Are Challenged

LARRY RICHARDS

High school presents all sorts of pressures that challenge a teen's values and faith. Most children are brought up thinking everyone is like them, more or less. Their childhood friends are selected from a closed neighborhood group that has the same values. The adults they know are chosen by their parents through association at church or other groups. Though they may be exposed to people with different values, their everyday life takes place among a homogeneous group that has a similar outlook on the world.

But when they get to high school, teens are confronted with a very different culture. Suddenly the teen's values are challenged. He meets kids from other neighborhoods. He sees teens who like to have fun in ways that are unacceptable to the Christian. He sees the Playboy philosophy at work. He becomes aware that there are other adults whom he respects, namely teachers, who have different values than his parents.

In light of these pressures and challenges, parents can expect young people to question their faith. Some parents think that questioning is a negative behavior, but it's not. Questioning and doubting are very natural and positive experiences. Developing personal convictions is part of the growth process, and one way to do that is by questioning.

In fact, if a young person doesn't question, he's likely to have more problems later on. He should question practices and beliefs that he took for granted when he was younger. He should wrestle with the basic foundation of his faith as well as the superficial issues of Christianity.

An Open Atmosphere

To facilitate this, a teen needs an atmosphere at home where doubts and questions can be talked about; where he is free to raise issues without his parents assuming that his faith is on the verge of being destroyed. Providing that atmosphere is one key way parents can help a teen survive the pressures put on his spiritual life at school.

It's important, though, for parents to be careful not to contribute to the strain by putting pressure on the teen in the form of negative expectations. This can happen when parents communicate a lack of trust in the teen's ability to work through

BRINGING CHRIST INTO THE CLASSROOM

Teenagers who want to be Christian witnesses in their schools must realize upfront that if the principal or the school system is antagonistic toward Christianity, they are likely to get into trouble. Some teens must be ready to face persecution. But for those who are willing to stand up for their Christian faith, there are three effective ways to witness.

1. *Tracts.* A tract ministry is a simple way to witness to other school students. Teenagers should be sure to conduct this kind of ministry in their spare time—not in the classroom or during other school activities. As long as they don't interfere with regular school functions, teens have the right to pass out tracts without running into trouble.

2. *Student newspapers.* A number of Christian students are starting student newspapers, and several courts have upheld their right to distribute them on campus. The only restrictions they face are time, place, and manner of distribution. Newspapers are excellent tools for witness because they are so versatile. A lot of school newspapers are rather bland, and if Christian students publish a quality newspaper, it will be noticed and read by other students.

Editorials, reports on current school events, and features on Christian personalities will usually be well-received by public school students. A number of big athletes and top stars today are Christians, but many people don't realize it. The media portrays Christians as second-class citizens and clowns, so student newspapers can show Christianity in a much more positive light.

3. *Personal excellence.* The most effective witness any Christian student can have is to be excellent in whatever he does. Some of the greatest witnesses for Christ today are men like Julius Erving. "Dr. J." demonstrates his excellence as a basketball player on the court, and often stays after the games to witness to the crowd. The people listen to him because he has proven himself an expert in what he does.

Christian students should set a good example academically. They should excel in extracurricular activities—sports, music, or whatever. If anyone should set an example for excellence, it should be the Christian high school student.

Paul's witness to the Gentiles usually had the greatest impact in the midst of crisis and confrontation. Similarly, Christian high school students can have a great influence on non-Christians in the public schools if they take the initiative in witnessing for Christ and determine to continue in spite of any opposition they might face. As parents, encourage them to begin this needed ministry on their campuses and support them during the times they do face conflict.

John W. Whitehead

questions and make good choices. Panicky reactions like, "I'm scared to death you're going to go wrong" cause the teen to feel guilty and to wonder, "Am I trustworthy? Maybe I'm not."

A teen may come to his father and say, "Dad, today a couple of guys sitting outside school lit up a joint and asked me to do it, but I said no." If Dad becomes alarmed and flies off the handle, his son may decide it's not worth the risk to tell him the next time something like that happens. What's more, the boy may begin to doubt his ability to make a good choice.

Instead, parents need to respond and deal with their teen on the assumption that he is going to make the right decision. Parents can help him work through tough situations by asking questions like, "How did you react to that?" "What did you think?" "How are you going to handle that in the future?" By doing so, they're providing support that will help strengthen their teen's confidence in decision-making.

That's why I decided to send my oldest son to public high school. Up until then, he had gone to a Christian school. But I wanted him to face the kinds of choices a young person has to make, while he was still at home so I could help him. I didn't want him to face those issues later when I wasn't around to listen and help.

Important Support Systems

Teens also need support relationships with their peer group. This doesn't have to be a group of eighty kids; just one or two other teens who share his values is enough to give the teen encouragement and strength in handling the pressures.

Youth for Christ, Young Life, and Campus Crusade have significant ministries with kids in this area because they give teens a chance to meet other Christians at their school. This is especially important if the teen goes to a church where kids come from a large geographic area and don't go to the same high school.

My teenagers were fortunate to have close relationships with a few kids who shared their values while in high school. They had grown up in a certain value context and felt comfortable with others who shared those values. If I had jumped on their backs all the time at home, they might have not felt comfortable, and made different choices for friends as a reaction. But, while they did some crazy things, they never got into immoral or harmful kinds of behavior.

A relationship with an older person with whom to talk through his doubts and questions also bolsters a teen's faith. This doesn't have to be a parent; in fact it may be even better if he or she is a youth adviser, family friend, or Sunday School teacher—any adult with whom the teen feels comfortable and who can help explore troublesome issues in a nonjudgmental way.

Parents can't be at school with their teen to help him with all the challenges to his faith. But they can develop a healthy relationship and have good communication. They can provide an atmosphere where the teen is free to question. They can help him sort through his responses to tough situations and they can let their teen know they have confidence that he will make good decisions.

The Good and Bad of the Public Schools

D. BRUCE LOCKERBIE

I was once a guest on the "700 Club," hosted by Pat Robertson. The camera's red light came on, and he said, "Tell me, Bruce, what is wrong with the public schools in America?" I said, "Well, Pat, I would like to begin by saying what is *right* with the public schools in America." It was a point I felt needed to be made.

Only in America has there been an attempt to educate an entire populace without regard for class, social status, or ability to pay. In no other nation in the world is this true. No, the success rate is not as high as we would like it to be and, yes, there are unpleasant influences in the schools. But what too few of us seem to realize is that the schools are not an autonomous institution unrelated to the rest of society. Schools are only a mirror of the society that sponsors them. If there is rebellion, insolence, or shoddiness in the school, they are only reflections of these same elements in the home.

No parent can be believed when he says, "My child never talks to me that way." The child is talking to *someone* that way before he tries it out on a teacher—maybe not Dad, but certainly Mom, Grandmother, or younger sister. Any outrageous behavior he exhibits in school is a reflection of what is going on in his home, housing development, community, or possibly what he is seeing on the television that his parents bring indiscriminately into their living room.

My wife is an elementary school teacher. She tells me that vulgar language that occasionally used to come out of the mouths of sixth-graders now is frequently heard in third grade. A couple of years ago, some first-graders went to her classroom all upset because they said a boy and girl had been "making it" on line in the corridor. My wife wasn't altogether certain that all those kids knew what they were talking about, but some of them did.

A Christian child in the public school system will eventually face iniquitous influences of which he is not aware. We hear a lot of talk these days about *peer pressure,* and the context is almost always negative. But I think parents can encourage and help to provide *positive* peer pressure to help their children combat the sinful influences they are bound to come up against.

Our children went to public elementary schools through the sixth grade, but we found ways to expose them to other Christians. Every year we sent them to a superb summer camp that promoted a rugged, rigorous kind of Christianity—nothing wimpy or pious. The kids had a good time, met young people from similar kinds of homes, and even made their first professions of faith in that environment.

Another source of positive peer pressure came through church programs such as Pioneer Girls, Christian Service Brigade, and choir. We looked outside the home for paralleling influences that would complement the kinds of things we were teaching in the home. There were also several Christian families in our community where our kids could see other good models.

With our children receiving those

positive influences on a regular basis, we did not prevent them from playing with kids whose parents were not believers. They were exposed to the playground experiences of anger, bad language, and occasional fighting, but they were able to see the contrast of that lifestyle with the one that was being modeled by their Christian contacts. When a child comes up against his first experience with drinking, smoking, and parking-lot sex, he has to have a certain kind of inner confidence that tells him he doesn't need to get involved with that stuff.

I'm not one of those traditional Christian educators who teach that Christian parents who don't send their children to Christian schools are neglecting their welfare. I believe Christian schools are right for a lot of families. But I also believe there is a special kind of blessing for those parents who do the increasingly risky thing today and send their children into an environment where the influences are largely hostile. And the hostility in public schools is going to increase.

A recent document I received from the State Board of Regents of New York began, "The education of children is the primary responsibility of the State." I don't agree. Parents *should* have the responsibility of educating their children, but too many of them have passed on that obligation to the school system. The problem intensifies because a typical teacher's contract prohibits the teacher from exerting any authority or responsibility outside of his own area of teaching.

One section of the school that is nobody's area of responsibility is the parking lot. Driving through the typical high school lot, the evidence of drinking parties—discarded and broken bottles, crushed cans—leads one to wonder how much longer school authorities can persist in turning their heads, as though such behavior on school premises weren't a fact. But parents in a community must also accept their responsibility: the high school parking lot, like everything else paid for by our taxes, belongs to us, not to the teenagers who trash it and drive away to risk their own and other people's lives on the roads. We are all responsible for upgrading the tone, the moral environment. Many parents want to do so. But we've got to convince teachers of our support; otherwise, they'll say, "It's not my affair. I'm just here to teach English grammar."

Our public school system has a lot going for it that is good. But Christian parents must beware the great secular lie which says that knowledge can be acquired regardless of behavior. A teenager can apply knowledge until he has the aptitude of a Nobel Prize-winner. But unless his parents have supplemented what he has received through the school system, both intellectually and spiritually, his personal life is likely to fall short of the quality needed to be truly successful.

Related Articles

What Do They Mean by a "Christian" School?

KENNETH O. GANGEL

A Christian school is an institution of learning committed to the lordship of Jesus Christ. It is a place where the educational process moves forward with a calculated commitment to the Scriptures and to the development of the spiritual and mental dimensions of the student.

This description encompasses a wide range of Christian schools, but parents can choose the best school for their children by selecting one that is accredited and based on a Christ-centered philosophy.

Academic quality is often indicated by accreditation. Accredited schools are required to meet specific standards set either by a region or an organization, such as the Association of Christian Schools International (ACSI). The faculty credentials, library books, physical facilities, and other details have been examined by the accrediting organization, and this guarantees that the school has met at least minimum criteria.

After limiting your choices to specific certified institutions, check to see if the school's philosophical statement—purpose and goals—is really being practiced. Do teachers integrate faith and learning? Is every class God-centered and Bible-based?

You will find that different Christian schools have contrasting philosophies of faith, and this is reflected in the student enrollment. Some schools admit only applicants who profess to have a personal relationship with Christ; other institutions are more evangelistic and accept non-Christian students with hopes that they will trust Christ through the school's influence.

The school that our children attended had a policy that at least one parent had to be a believer even if the student was not. This ensured some contact with Christianity in the home. Some schools set a limit on the admission of non-Christian students so that the Christian atmosphere can be maintained.

If a school begins accepting more non-Christians than Christians, it is in danger of losing its distinction as a God-centered institution. Interesting, isn't it, that public schools in some highly conservative religious communities could have a higher percentage of Christians enrolled than a Christian school with liberal admission policies? When Christians are in the minority in a Christian school, the school's distinctives are in danger of dilution.

Catalogs and brochures can help you determine if the schools you are interested in have a distinctly Christian philosophy. Check the accreditation and church affiliation, and talk to other parents who have children attending the school. Interview faculty members, talking to them about their faith and seeing how they relate classroom tasks to Christian living.

The choice of elementary schools for your children may narrow down to an inferior Christian school or a superior public school. I would choose the Christian school because of its philosophy, even though it may mean compromising academics for a time. Sometimes the choices are pleasant. When we were selecting a high school, for example, there were six possible schools to choose from, and we selected one with well-rounded athletic, music, art, and extracurricular programs. My wife and I feel we chose good elementary and secondary schools for our children and have never regretted our decisions.

But while we were making our decisions, it was important to examine *why* we wanted our children to attend a Christian school—what was our motivation? Some parents want their children to go to a Christian school so they won't be involved in drugs. But even Christian schools have drug problems. Or they might want their children to be exposed to prayer and Bible reading. But that's a lot of money to pay for five minutes of devotions that your child could just as easily be doing at home. They may want their children to think just like they do about life, but no school, secular or Christian, can always guarantee that.

So there are wrong reasons for wanting your child to get a Christian education. The right reason is a focus on God-centered, Bible-based curriculum and teaching which relates everything to the lordship of Jesus Christ.

Of course, there are times when it is necessary to send your child to public school. Our children had to attend public school for three years when we had no other choice.

Sometimes, the only available Christian school may be a hotbed of theological or political irresponsibility. In that case, I would choose a public school. But in most instances, the benefits of Christian schools outweigh the drawbacks.

After all, if all truth can be ultimately traced back to God, then any educational system that rejects God automatically rejects truth. This is what public education is doing. The whole system is out of the truth pattern—occasionally it will stumble on truth here and there, but most of the time, it is out of God's plan.

Public education also encourages students to model themselves after a secular lifestyle of drug use, homosexuality, and broken families. Teachers often exemplify a lack of morals instead of godliness. And the student's peer group has a negative, not positive, influence on character.

I want my children in an educational system that fits into God's truth-seeking pattern, where the teacher is constantly relating his subject matter to the Word of God. After all, they will spend twelve years of their lives in school—why not make them years of Christian influence?

Related Articles

Public School vs. Private School

Which Is Right for Your Child?

D. BRUCE LOCKERBIE

Before parents can begin to select the proper school for their child, they must accept the fact that they are responsible for the education of all of the children God has given them. If one child is gifted and excels academically, and another one doesn't, there is no reason to send them to the same school and expect the same result. We should look for the right school for each member of the family. The "right" school might be the same school, the same school with a different program, a different school in the same community, or even a different school some distance away. As parents examine all available educational opportunities, they may decide they want their child to receive supplementary exposure to Christian principles that will augment what they are teaching at home.

Christian schools have several positive advantages. The beneficial influence of Christian teachers and an early exposure to the Scriptures are two of the major ones. And if the school is worth anything (some are not), it will provide an understanding that all truth is God's truth. Then when the students study biology, astronomy, literature, and physical education, they can see those subjects as elements of the revelation of God's truth in nature and in human nature that can help them learn more about Him.

Some Christian schools no longer restrict admission to Christian students. My own children attended such a school. There an evangelist's son, a missionary's daughter, or a college president's child could end up with a roommate who was a nonbeliever. Some people argue with us and say, "My goodness, how can you have a Christian environment when you have unbelieving students?" We tell them that the Christian environment begins with the adults, and that all of the teachers are Christians. The school administration gives priority to the lordship of Christ and the study of Scripture, and our Christian students thrive in a "real" environment. The school is not a cocoon or a greenhouse that keeps the Christian students removed from the rest of the world.

Any parent who wants to seriously evaluate the strengths and weaknesses of public and private schools must take an active interest in local school government. If parents do not wish to take leadership roles, they can at least participate in the PTA and the selection of curriculum. Some professional educators are smug and patronizing to parents, but are still required by law to open the board of education meetings to the public when school policies are being discussed. If policies are being made that are hostile to Christianity, the parents can act accordingly.

One of my wife's two elementary school principals is so personally against any kind of religion that he allows neither Hanukah nor Christmas songs at the December music concerts. He won't permit a menorah, a manger scene, or even a Christmas tree.

If I were a parent with a child in his school, I would first appeal to the local board of education and say, "There are five elementary schools in this district. Mr. So-and-so's hostility to any kind of religious observance is so reprehensible to me that I want my child to attend a different school." The permission will be granted, but you have to make the effort. You have to motivate yourself to stand up for what you believe. If the school district turns you down for some reason, and you still feel strongly about the issue, then look for another alternative.

I want to issue a warning at this point. It is not enough to examine the pros of Christian schools against the cons of public schools. In some instances, a seemingly bad public school situation is no worse than what you might find in a shoddy Christian school. Some Christian schools strive for docility in students by suppressing questions and enforcing long periods of total silence. They say the procedure is part of teaching a child submission, when actually it is a brutal approach that is not in the least Christ-like. I expect any school that purports to be operated in the name of Jesus Christ to be better than a public school. But if I see that it isn't, I'd rather my child took his chances in the public school.

Parents also need to help their teenage children make wise decisions when considering a "Christian" university. One may look good at first, but turn out to be a segregationist school. It may turn out to be a school that distorts the truth in favor of a particular dogma. I have an English handbook from one of the prominent fundamentalist Christian universities. It cites a poem by Gerard Manley Hopkins, but I was horrified to read in the next sentence that "because Hopkins was Catholic, he lacked a Christian vision."

Textbooks can tell you a lot about a school too. I have seen books used to teach European history that say that everything before the Reformation was satanic deception. They also say that Michelangelo's famous statue of David denies scriptural truth because it represents David as a muscular young man (and therefore suggests that it must have been his own strength—not the power of God—that killed Goliath).

So when it comes time to choose a school for your child or teenager, try to consider all the factors. Don't select an institution just because it is labeled "Christian," and don't rule one out just because it is secular. Keep searching until you find one that can meet your child's needs, both academically and spiritually.

(For further reading on this subject, see my book, *Who Educates Your Child?* [Zondervan, 1981].)

Related Articles

How to Help the School Help Your Child

BRUCE B. BARTON

If you believe education is solely the responsibility of the school, you may find yourself saying, "I pay taxes; they'd better do a good job!" You may nurture negative attitudes toward the system by saying, "Well, teachers have it easy . . . they have the whole summer off," or "The whole school system is run by non-Christians, so why get involved?" Consciously or unconsciously, many people harbor negative attitudes toward the school system. As a result, they forfeit the right to help the school help their child.

School Is Not the Enemy

The school system is made up of very human beings with dreams, goals, concerns, and feelings like all human beings. The school is filled with professionals who have dedicated themselves to furthering the development of children. Since parents share this goal with teachers, perhaps parents can take steps to build bridges rather than barriers. Here are some bridge-building steps you can take:

1. Don't assume that "no news is good news." Take time to check up and find out what's going on with your teenager in school.

2. Read everything that comes from the school.

3. Get involved in the school's orientation and registration procedure for your teen.

4. Get to know your teen's teachers and guidance counselor by name.

5. Volunteer for school activities so you can see teenagers in their own setting. This will: show school personnel that you care; enable you to get to know your child's friends; help you see how eccentric and difficult the social system at school really is; show your child that you understand that school life involves more than studies.

6. Don't be put off by your teen's complaints when you get involved. After a while, his embarrassment will fade.

7. Be realistic about part-time jobs. Don't let jobs destroy homework. Many parents think that jobs teach dependability and skills that will help teens in the future. In reality, most jobs don't teach anything at all; they just provide teenagers with a "premature affluence" that is unrealistic when compared with later life. When they really do face responsibility on their own, they will not have this extra income to spend any way they want.

Teachers Are Your Colleagues

As you get to know teachers, assume the best about them. You'll go farther to help the school help you if you take the approach that teachers try their best. Say thank you for jobs well-done by teachers. Help the teachers by supporting what goes on in the classroom and by reinforcing assignments at home.

Keep in mind that teachers have feelings too. You know that you have deep feelings of hurt when you hear negative comments about your child. You may even avoid the school because it evokes feelings of deep disappointment and pain. Teachers feel a sense of failure too. They don't always know how to cope with the problems in the classroom. They need to be reassured that you think that they're doing a good job. Don't overload negative criticism on teachers. Many times the only contact parents have with teachers is when they criticize. The best way to approach teachers is face-to-face. Don't write a letter; don't phone. Make an appointment and visit them. When you do, be sure both you and your spouse go.

As Christians, you have a deep responsibility not to bear false witness against your neighbor. Often, statements about the school include gossip and lies about teachers. By simply agreeing with your teenager when he says a certain teacher is a "jerk," you may be fostering a bad attitude in him.

How to Make the Most of Your School Interview

For years, schools have been stressing that fathers should go along to school interviews. However, in the past ten years there has been no appreciable increase in the number of fathers who visit. One drawback to Dad's staying home is that Mom has to convince Dad of everything she's heard; therefore, she has to relay the information secondhand. In the school interview, you need to reiterate the love relationship that you have with your child. This will create the proper climate of mutual concern as you face the interview. Here are more specific tips to improve your interview:

1. Listen carefully. Be sure to take notes.

2. Try not to make any demands on the teacher who is already very busy.

3. Since the material that you're going to be dealing with may be difficult, you may want to practice beforehand what you'll need to say.

4. Feedback helps. Repeat what you heard the teacher say. Ask the teacher, "Could you tell me what you heard me say?"

5. Remember that every situation has both facts and feelings. Relate the facts and also talk about your feelings.

6. Be sure to involve the teen in any agreement that you establish with the teacher.

7. Talk about the home situation first. Explain what is going on there that leads you to feel there may be a problem at school.

8. Correct the home situation first. The responsibility for a teenager's education begins first at home, not at school. When the home situation improves, take the initiative to contact the teacher.

9. Follow up on what you decide together. Be sure to be honest about your responsibilities. If you have no intention of doing homework with your child, don't volunteer. If you know that you do not do a good job teaching math, see about a tutor. Be honest about your follow-up.

10. Set up a communication system between you and the teacher. Your job should be to make sure that the teacher knows what responsibilities will be carried out at home. You should check up with your teenager to monitor how he is doing. It is the student's responsibility not only to do the work that's required, but also to communicate the progress to the teacher.

Here are some questions you can prepare ahead of time for the interview. You may want to ask the teacher:
• Does my teen participate in classroom activities?
• Does he join in discussions or make suggestions?
• Does my teenager show self-control in school situations?
• How does my teen get along with classmates?
• Does he relate well to the teacher and other adults?
• Can my teen handle the subject matter?
• What does he do during his spare time in class?

- Can he express his thoughts and ideas clearly?
- How is his written communication?

You may want to tell the teacher:
- Which school activities your teen talks about at home
- What responsibilities the teen handles at home
- If anything has happened lately at home that might affect your teen's performance at school
- Your teen's favorite activities outside of school
- How you discipline your teenager at home
- What his strengths and weaknesses are

When You Feel the School Is Wrong
Keep in mind that the school is not only made up of human beings, but it is also an institution. Schools make mistakes. You should not be intimidated when you feel that something is wrong. Initiate contact to make sure that the problem is resolved. Make every effort through the school first.

Remember that there is a chain of command that needs to be observed when contacting the school:

1. Speak to the teenager first to make sure that you both have done everything possible.

2. Speak to the teacher, following the principles for good school interviews.

3. Speak to the guidance counselor, if at all possible with the teacher and the child present. Do not threaten the teacher or guidance counselor. Contact the guidance counselor or principal only after you have talked to the teacher.

4. Finally, contact the principal if a resolution cannot be reached.

When the plan goes wrong, check to insure that proper diet, sleep, and study habits are being followed at home. Ask Christian educators or youth directors at church for feedback on your teenager. Give the plan time to work.

Remember that learning styles are different in different children. Your own personal learning style may not be the same as your child's. Some learn best by reading up on a problem; others learn by asking questions; some learn by exploring the reasons why something is true; others learn by observing a model or a demonstration; and some learn by hands-on experience. All are valid. None is superior to the others.

You may find a teacher who does indeed have a prejudice against your child. Children can learn perseverance from facing hard situations. Life is tough and isn't always fair. There may be a real lesson learned by sticking out a class with a teacher who "has it in" for your child. However, if you run up against teachers who are cruel, punitive, or destructive to the total learning process for your child, you may want to seek intervention from the guidance counselor.

Solving problems is hard work. Real progress can be made by showing the school that you care and are willing to cooperate.

Related Articles

The Battle over Grades

DAVID L. McKENNA

One of the biggest hassles between parents and teens is the issue of grades. Often, parents desire their teens to have exceptional grades, while many teens have a nonchalant attitude about them.

When a teen doesn't seem to care what grades he gets, parents must creatively motivate him to take an interest in school. Studies show there is *no single pattern* by which a teen can be motivated, so parents must use their own discretion in learning what would best motivate their child.

Think about motivating, rather than "pushing" a teen to learn. If a teacher gives a B- to a B student to push him to try harder, he might indeed be challenged.

But if he's a teen with an aggressive personality, he'll probably just give up, feeling he has been punished.

Especially well-educated parents tend to push their children even harder for good grades much as a frustrated jock expects a daughter or son to excel in sports.

Sit down with your teen and set reachable goals. Get his feedback. What career is your teen aiming for? What courses must he concentrate on? Ralph Waldo Emerson once said that when he was in school there were certain subjects he didn't mind getting a C in because he *had* to take them. But he really bore down

---

DROPOUTS

Preventing your teenager from dropping out of school doesn't begin during his sophomore year when the first failing grade comes in. It doesn't begin when the truant officer comes to the door and says your child has missed the past thirty days. It starts the day he enters kindergarten.

Parents should take the time to set up a quiet, undisturbed place for their child to study, and then observe him from time to time to make sure the work is getting done. Monitor the use of television. Turn it off, restrict its use, and throw it out if necessary. But throwing it out should be a last resort. The child is better able to learn discipline if the parents are able to say, "No, you can't turn on the TV until you finish all your work." Even then, it should be watched selectively.

Of course, children and teenagers are not always going to be happy when parents try to enforce these rules. But it all comes down to whether parents really care to be parents. If they take their responsibility seriously, they will oversee their child's learning process from the beginning, regardless of any resistance they might face. But their efforts will be rewarded during the child's high school years after he has acquired proper study habits. By then, the possibility of dropping out will be much less likely.

D. Bruce Lockerbie

in subjects that had a bearing on his future.

Children are individuals. The same family can have a devoted bookworm and one who hates school. Incidentally, comparing children is not only unfair, it is an invalid motivator.

Rating Your Teen's Report Card

D. BRUCE LOCKERBIE

I have three children, now all in their mid-twenties. My oldest son was a real "quick study" who could coast through the subjects he wasn't interested in, and who really applied himself to the things he enjoyed. Academic honors were easy for him. My second son thought of himself as being less capable, and studying was a grind for him. But we never had to tell him to do his homework. He would go up to his room, shut the door, and work hard. My daughter is truly an academic. She is probably going to be *the* member of the family to get a Ph.D. Yet each of our children won an athletic grant-in-aid as a runner, each was involved in music and participated in theater.

Perhaps they had an advantage because they grew up on the campus of a college preparatory school where academic rigor is a significant part of life. But I also believe their successes as students were partially a result of my not making a big deal about whether or not they made straight A's. I think there is more to intellectual development than just quadratic equations and periodic tables.

When both of our sons were competing in sports as well as participating in the production of *Death of a Salesman* (where

rehearsals went until 11 P.M.), we assumed that their grades were going to suffer. There is no such thing as the nonsense you hear about giving 110 percent. All a student can give is 100 percent, and if he chooses to participate in other kinds of school activities, something else has to give.

Parents of teenagers need to be wise enough to recognize that a child's intellectual development relates to playing a clarinet or twirling a baton as much as it does to sitting in a classroom. Physical exercise should be encouraged by the parents, because it benefits the circulatory system which feeds the brain which helps us think better.

I have known parents who would see one poor report card, pull their child out of volleyball or wrestling or whatever, and say, "OK, that's it. You're out of sports. From now on you'll come home and study from 4 o'clock till supper and then from 7 till 9." Rarely will such drastic action have positive results. A teenager, like anyone else, needs some sort of diversion. He will work harder when there is joy in his life. When he begins to see other teens less qualified than himself make the varsity team, he is robbed of the joy he could have felt. Consequently, he will often begin to resent the academic

647

world that deprives him of such joy and can eventually become resentful of his parents.

Wiser parents will encourage each of their children, recognizing that they are not equally gifted academically. One child might achieve with ease something that another would really have to work for. So parents need to say, "Your brother, Johnny, has problems in math, so if he gets a C in math we'll be very happy. But if you get a C, we'll be annoyed because we'll know you aren't trying hard enough." And then to keep Johnny from feeling inferior, the parents should focus on the areas in which he excels and hold up high standards for him.

Learning involves more than making good grades. It is complete only when the teenager is able to integrate the joy of accomplishment, the discipline of managing his life, and the beneficial experiences of activities he can only discover outside the classroom.

Related Articles

Identifying Learning Disabilities
Maybe Your Child's Not as Dumb as You Think

CHRISTIE STONECIPHER

Parents suspecting that their child may have some type of learning problem or a learning disability need not be discouraged. Resources are now abundant for helping parents determine specifically the problem their child is having, and exactly how they can intervene.

It is important, however, to make a necessary distinction between learning problems and learning disabilities. Learning problems relate to poor initial teaching, problems of mother-child separation in the early years of life, emotional tensions, broken homes, abuses of different sorts, and a multitude of other socioeconomic factors.

Learning disabilities, on the other hand, refer directly to perceptual processing deficits which have some sort of neurophysiological base. Though these children do not have problems with their vision, they will have difficulty in translating what they see into an appropriate motor function. While demonstrating no problem with their hearing, they will have problems translating auditory stimuli into socially expected communication systems. As research has clearly demonstrated, the key word to understand these children is "processing." Learning disabled children are unable to correctly process visual and auditory stimuli.

There are five basic characteristics of children with learning disabilities. A child may possess one, two, or several of these. For further clarification, a child's level of intelligence is unimportant when describing the boundaries of the problem. Children of all intellectual levels (normal, slow-learning, mentally retarded) can possess a learning disability. The degree or severity will differ from child to child.

The first characteristic is *hyperactivity,* either sensory or motor. Sensory hyperactivity refers to the child responding to unessential or irrelevant stimuli. Movement, smell, color, and sound may easily distract the child from attending to a specific task. Motor hyperactivity, on the other hand, occurs when the child is unable to refrain from responding to stimuli that produce or prompt a motor response. Anything within the bounds of a child's vision will be touched, bent, twisted, pulled, or turned over.

A second observable characteristic is *disassociation,* the inability to see things as a whole, as a totality. A child will see part of a picture, but not the whole thing, and therefore does not necessarily see things as forming a meaningful unit.

A third character is *figure-ground reversal.* For example, when a child reads a page in a book, he may see the background more distinctly than he sees the foreground.

Perseveration, the fourth characteristic, is the child's inability to change from one activity to another with ease. He is unable to move quickly from one mental idea to the next.

The last characteristic is *poor motor skill,* and can be witnessed in a child's difficulty in learning to ride a bicycle or his inability to maneuver smoothly and accurately through a series of obstacles. He may have a general fear and insecurity about his coordination. Learning to swim may prove quite difficult.

When parents identify one or more of these problems in their child, they have several avenues to pursue. First, they should insist that their school district provide an education evaluation. A general pediatric examination would also be completed at this time, after which parents would be wise to pursue the following diagnostic services: ophthalmological and optometric examination, pediatric clinical psychological examina-

tion, pediatric neurological examination, pediatric psychiatric examination, social history questionnaire, speech and hearing examination, and a psychological evaluation. The list is staggering. But each test is important and has a specific purpose. Accurate diagnosis is critical. When a child's learning disability is clearly identified, the parents, child, and school will know how to specifically intervene and assist.

Though learning problems and learning disabilities have been defined as two separate spheres, parents of a learning disabled child should still be keenly attuned to their child's self-esteem. Because the child has continually met with frustrations, failure, and/or negative feedback from adults, he may demonstrate various types of behavioral problems (i.e., rebellious attitude, lack of attention, apathy, fighting, depression, etc.). Parents' emotional support and understanding is crucial.

Often due to the problems this type of child encounters, it is difficult for him to be included in a regular group or classroom. Thus, parents need to be strongly advised and encouraged to seek out the proper diagnostic help and educational assistance available to their child.

Children with learning disabilities need not feel that they have little hope for a normal, productive school career and adult life. In fact, they have every reason to have hope!

(For further reading, see *Learning Disabilities in Home, School, and Community,* by William M. Cruickshank [Syracuse University Press, 1977].)

Related Articles

The Big Business of Athletics

BYRON EMMERT

"**D**addy, when I grow up, I want to be a football star!" My four-year-old, Benji, had the command of a quarterback's voice as he shared his dream with me. The spark in his eyes ignited the flame in his daddy's heart! Not only did he want to play football, but he wanted to be the star!

But wait a minute! How did he come up with this dream? Was it his idea or had he absorbed mine?

Suddenly, my fatherly insight was tackled for a loss by a blitzing question! Would I contribute to the pressure that athletics could put on my son, or would I be a release valve against it?

During my ten years in youth work, I've seen too many parents place athletic demands and expectations on their children that are absolutely devastating to the kids' development. On the other hand, I've seen and experienced parents who have placed athletics in proper perspective.

Sports can be a terrific tool in a teenager's maturing process. So I share these thoughts for my kids' sake and maybe for yours too. Hopefully we can all help our kids deal with the pressures that athletics can place on them.

1. *Understand the pressures that high school sports place on youth.* To both male and female athletes, sometimes verbally and sometimes not, the message is loud and clear: "You do well for us, and we'll do well for you."

In the community: High school athletics is big business even in little schools. A championship team can put a small, obscure town on the state map, and can mean adulation and praise for the kid who is the star. With all the applause, media coverage, and community prestige available, it's no wonder that a teenager feels the pressure to succeed. It's pretty hard for a sixteen-year-old to survive all this without having an exaggerated concept of who he or she is.

In the school: My high school football coach was also my English teacher. If you were a football player, you automatically received a B on all book reports. If not, your work needed to be exceptional. You can imagine how this coach was obsessed with winning. After one loss, in which we blocked and tackled poorly, our coach suited up and took us all on, one at a time! His philosophy was simply, "You'd better be an athlete and you'd better win!"

Unfortunately, such an atmosphere exists in many high schools because the community applies the pressure for success. Consequently, many schools hire coaches first and teachers second.

Fortunately for our community and school, a new football coach arrived my senior year. His priority was to help all students develop their abilities and learn from the experience, regardless of the outcome. Hooray!

Socially: There was something special about game day! You'd wear your jersey and the cheerleaders would put neat little good luck charms on your locker. You'd get patted on the back, receive more food at lunch, and be cheered at the pep rally. It did wonders for your self-image! In fact, I only asked girls for dates on game days!

In most schools, kids are socially in if they're athletes, especially if they're good. The pressure is for kids to perform well so they can be someone and feel good about who they are. They learn this from the media, society, and the community. Are we teaching them the same thing at home?

2. *Let your teen decide about athletics.* Because the pressures already mentioned are nothing new, it's no wonder many parents decide that their sons and daughters will be involved in athletics and that they will be "good." These parents are usually trying to relive their own glory days, or find some, through the lives of their children.

My father was an all-state football player in high school. That makes me proud! But I'm even prouder and more thankful that he let me choose sports for myself and not for himself.

He played ball with me as a youngster, but my interest in sports developed naturally. My parents never forced me to go out for sports, but they encouraged me and supported me when I did. Best of all, my dad remained my father and never played coach unless I asked him to.

3. *Love your child regardless of performance.* It was a beautiful October Saturday during my sophomore year in high school. My dad was harvesting corn and I was plowing in the same field. As I drove the tractor, I was feeling sorry for myself. Not playing in the previous night's football game made me realize that I would never be a football star like my dad had been. Sure, I'd eventually be a starter, but I'd never be great!

Just then my dad came over to see how I was doing. He could tell that the plowing was all right, but I wasn't. So we talked. When I started telling him that I thought I was letting him down, he cut my pity party short.

"Byron, if you play football, that's fine. But if you don't, please know that I love you very much and that I'll always be proud of you!"

"You will? Why?"

"Because you're mine."

Of course that brought on a few tears, a great hug, and some good conversation! That day my dad pointed out my creativity and ability to speak. I haven't played a lot of football these past fifteen years, but I sure do a lot of talking!

Parents, tell your teenagers you love and accept them regardless of how they perform. Help them discover their special God-given talents and abilities, whether or not they're athletic. They'll show you their gratitude in their lives of tomorrow.

4. *Model a healthy perspective on competition.* We're all familiar with Vince Lombardi's famous quote, "Winning isn't everything; it's the only thing." Nothing personal against Mr. Lombardi, but that kind of philosophy warps young minds. I've seen families who "love" each other if the kids win their games, but practice domestic abuse during times of defeat. Interestingly enough, they also seem to trust God when life is sweet, but rebuke Him when seasons are tough.

If only we could help our kids realize that the winner is the one who gives it everything he has, and not necessarily the one who comes in first. Our youth will see this if we applaud their involvement and progress and not just the winning score. They'll believe it if we show them that it's OK to fail. They'll live it if we model the motivation to serve God and become what He wants us to be rather than what man wants us to be. "Whatever you do, work at it with all your heart, as working for the Lord, not for men" (Col. 3:23, NIV).

You know something? That makes sense. I need to talk about this with my kids. You can't start too early, you know.

Related Articles

Of Competition and Apple Pie

DAVID VEERMAN

Christ's defeat on the cross was His greatest victory. He taught us that in His kingdom the "first will be last; and the last, first" (Matt. 19:30, NASB). "God has chosen the foolish things of the world to confound the wise" (1 Cor. 1:27, KJV).

We need to examine our lives and motives by these standards because competition is deeply rooted in our culture. Proof?

- "How did you do on the test?" the father asks.

  "I got the best grade in the class," the daughter replies.
- Mark gets cut from the football squad. He's just not big enough.
- The cheerleaders chant, "We're number one! We're number one!"
- At the Letterman's Club dinner, the coach paraphrases Vince Lombardi: "Winning isn't the most important thing. It's everything!"

From friendly neighborhood games and school contests to "keeping up with the Joneses" and contemporary advertising, being first is where it's at.

Consider our insatiable hunger for professional sports.

Consider the TV craze for awards shows—Oscars, Emmies, Grammies, Miss America, Miss Universe. We want to know, "Who is the fairest of them all?" as well as who is the richest, the most powerful, the strongest, the fastest.

Competition is as American as apple pie (made with only the choicest apples, of course).

It's in our economics, our education, our politics.

It's in our blood.

Proponents of competition point to its effects:

- The "will to win" leads to greatness.
- Take the "will to win" away and the individual is lethargic, unproductive.
- Competition in free enterprise has made America great.

But some voice opposition. Professional and collegiate athletes speak of the dehumanization of sports when the object is to "win at all costs."

We learn competition from our earliest years. A *Chicago Tribune* article quotes Dr. Thomas Tutko, a San Jose State University professor of psychology: "Too many American fathers think they're Vince Lombardis and wind up abusing their children—physically and psychologically—through sports. Many parents live their lives through their children. When a child wins, the parent thinks he's a winner. When a child fails, he interprets it as meaning he's not a success."

Christian parents are also caught in this whirlpool. We certainly want our children to achieve, but we ought not pressure them too much. Even our churches seem to be encouraging the "winning is everything" syndrome ... Bible drills, quizzing, Scripture memorization, athletic leagues, and boasts about the largest Sunday School or membership.

As parents, we must first realize that winning isn't everything. Competition does not necessarily motivate a person to achieve. Winning means doing better than the competitor, not necessarily doing well yourself. Because this is true, many spend their efforts putting down others rather than doing their best. Or perhaps cheating becomes the route to follow. If winning is all there is, how one wins doesn't seem too important.

Second, we must motivate our young people by intrinsic means rather than an easy substitute. For example, we must teach the value of study to improve one's mind and to use one's God-given mental abilities, not to be first in the class. Physical exercise is good because we need to keep in shape and in good health, not to beat the other team. The Bible should be read and memorized because it is God's Word, not so our church can win the quiz.

Third, competition can become an excellent opportunity for parents to relate lovingly to their children. What could be more helpful and meaningful than a loving hug or arm around the shoulders after a disappointing loss. Our daughter might not win, but she is not a loser.

"What is the ideal of competition?" former soccer star Kyle Rote, Jr. asks. "If it's merely to label a person a winner and another a loser, I think it is wrong. I don't think competition is right unless both sides are evaluated on how well they did with what they had."

Fourth, we need to ask ourselves, "Whose needs am I meeting?" When we push children to perform in a certain endeavor, is it what they need or what we need? Do we need to win to feel good about ourselves? "I want *my* son to be on first string." Or, "*My* girl is homecoming queen." Or, "Straight A's, that's *my* boy." We dare not force these needs on our children.

Fifth, we must always remember that for every winner there is at least one loser. Are we concerned about his or her

PUTTING THE PRESSURE ON

Our children are under more pressure than ever today. They need the support and affirmation of the family, not additional or unnecessary pressure from within the family. Parents can help their children strike a balance between striving to reach God-given potential and striving to reach unrealistic expectations.

As parents, *look at your own expectations for your children.* Why do you want your child to get A's? Is it because it looks good for you, or so they can go to a socially elite school? Or is it because they are able to do "A" work and need encouragement to apply themselves toward a reasonable goal? Is your love for them *agape* love or *performance-based* love? Parents need to encourage their children to reach their potential, but not go beyond that encouragement to the point of pressure.

Keep a balanced life in perspective. Don't withhold good influences from your children (church, youth groups, music lessons) because you want them only to study. Pressure in one area tends to send down the others.

Have mutually acceptable objectives. Explain to your children why they should work up to their potential and why good grades are important; don't just spend time nagging them. Work with them to plan and reach toward goals that are meaningful to them.

Help them learn discipline at an early age. Don't let them drift without defined limits until they are in high school and then impose a new set of rules. At home, as well as in school, they will remember the principles that will enable them to deal with pressures and live effectively.

YFC Editors

feelings? How did you feel when you were chosen last for baseball or didn't measure up by some other standard?

Finally, we must be good examples for our young people. Do they observe mature responses to losing, personal drive for excellence, sensitive caring for our contemporaries? Or do they observe frustration in front of TV football, yelling at referees, rationalizations, and shortcuts to success? Do they see Jesus in our "washing feet" and dying to self? Let's reexamine our lives by Christ's standards.

Adapted from an article first published in *Moody Monthly* magazine.

Related Articles
Chapter 12: Kids Aren't Carbon Copies
Chapter 29: Rating Your Teen's Report Card
Chapter 29: The Big Business of Athletics
Chapter 29: The Trauma of Tryouts

The Importance of Education
D. BRUCE LOCKERBIE

I once met an English professor at the University of North Carolina at Chapel Hill who teaches a course in the medical school there. The course is called "Doctors in Literature" and is sponsored by the Department of Ethics in Medicine. The university officials have recognized that, for the most part, the students in their medical school have an insufficient number of courses in the humanities. They also know that if they are going to have ethical practitioners of medicine, their students must understand human values—not just human anatomy, but the value of the human anatomy.

I'm on the road two dozen times a year, mostly in Christian colleges and seminaries, and I am appalled at the materialistic attitude of most of the students I speak to. We are currently in a career-oriented, job-conscious society. One of the ways Christian families ought to stand apart from the materialism of our age is to promote the higher value of education. Parents should teach their children to consider more than, "What kind of job will this education get me?"

Even in evangelical colleges, many of the students have come out of an environment where college had not been a part of the family experience prior to their generation. Some of them feel that college will be their ticket to financial success. I think such an attitude is a satanic delusion.

Being created in God's image, we have inherited the ability to think, reason, and express ourselves. Those are not gifts to be taken lightly. Yet many students today are saying, "All I want is a good job. I'll grind through accounting and data processing, get a business degree, and take as little as possible of history, literature, philosophy, and those other subjects that I don't really need."

Fortunately, all pendulums swing back to the center, given time. Secular education is beginning to recognize the shortcomings of a purely career-oriented learning experience. So some schools, like the University of North Carolina, are beginning to take first steps to provide a better balance of studies for its students.

Education is not just a means to an end. Education is its own means—the means to a life of the mind and a life of the spirit. If education teaches us only how to put a nut on a bolt or how to access a computer, it isn't really education. It's no more than a kind of dog obedience school in which we learn how to sit up and bark.

True education prepares students by inspiration. The life of the instructor should reflect the value of what he is teaching. If a teacher has no sense of his role as example, scholar, thinker, human being, or—in the case of Christian universities—follower of Jesus Christ, all he can do is transmit information. A good instructor will do much more. Let me give you an example.

A recent program on the Public Broadcasting System showed the return of Maya Angelou, a successful black poet and actress, to her birthplace in Stamps, Arkansas. As she stood there, a cosmopolitan woman within a hovel of a schoolhouse, the little black children looked up at her as if she were a creature from another planet. But she helped them see the value of what she was trying to teach them with these words: "When I look at you, I see who I was. When you look at me, I hope you see what you can become."

American Telephone and Telegraph used to advertise that it was in the "knowledge business." As an educator, I'm not at all interested in the knowledge business. I *am* interested in the wisdom business. Suppose your Christian life were based on the mere acquisition of facts and data. You would miss most of what God had in store for you. Similarly, any education that is not an abundant, overwhelming experience is not the education it should be.

WHEN TEENS AND SCHOOL JUST DON'T MIX

When teens just don't seem to fit in at school academically, perhaps it is time for the parents to seek another alternative. Don't get me wrong—there is never a healthy alternative to learning. But the environment in which the learning takes place may need to be changed.

Confront the child with the facts: "You don't study; you don't do the work that is assigned; you don't advance; and we need to find a way for you to become more motivated." Perhaps the teen is much more interested in lawn mower engines, car repair, or food preparation than in purely academic things. If so, perhaps a trade school should be considered.

Perhaps the child should be given a chance to work at some kind of minimum wage job—pumping gas, or something similar—to see if that is all the ambition he has. Once he sees others around him advancing because of what they know or skills they have acquired, he might decide to go back to night school, trade school, or pursue some other form of education.

One other option is military service, but I hate to think of our armed forces full of people who can't even read the artillery handbook. If your teen is seriously interested in a branch of the service, it might be the right alternative for him, but I don't agree with sloughing off all our high school dropouts into an illiterate military.

D. Bruce Lockerbie

The Bible As the Key to Education

JOHN PERKINS

My son worked at a boys' club one summer. Out of that experience he told me he saw a crying need for the Ten Commandments to be reestablished in our society. There are no moral parameters from which morality and discipline can come. There are no principles. We have to go back to the "Thou shalts" and the "Thou shalt nots."

Special times are needed to teach the Word of God in the family, especially when the kids are small. While the kids are younger, you can do it at bedtime. When they get older and busier, you might have to look for another time slot and hew it out of the family schedule. At one point, our family spent time in the Word each morning before school. I would lead the study, then my wife would lead it. Eventually we began to let our kids lead the study and affirmed them in that.

Another thing we felt was important was that each child have his own Bible. At special times throughout their lives, the kids would get new ones. The Bibles my wife and I bought for them became very precious.

Teens can use the Bible to evaluate what they learn in school, but to have them do that we need to go beyond teaching the Bible for the Bible's sake. We evangelicals tend to deify the Bible. But the Bible is the means, not the end. The Bible reflects God. The Bible is a production manual.

My kids were always taught to identify Christianity with excellence. Young people tend to identify religion with stupidity and emotion. Our kids identified the Bible with wisdom, and that was helpful.

Related Articles
Chapter 15: Helping Teens Live Their Faith
Chapter 15: What Teens Should Know about the Bible
Chapter 15: Bringing the Word to Life
Chapter 29: Helping Teens Survive Spiritually at School

The Rights of Christian Students in Public Schools

JOHN W. WHITEHEAD

A public school in Lubbock, Texas was once taken to court because of a policy it had that allowed students to meet a half hour before classes started to discuss religion, ethical, or moral problems. The court ruled that such a policy was a violation of the First Amendment. The decision was upheld on appeal, and the Supreme Court refused to hear the case.

I'm currently involved in a case in Lake Worth, Florida where a public school principal reacted strongly to a page he saw in the yearbook. The picture was of a Bible club that had been on campus for twenty-five years. But the principal was so opposed to its presence at school that he kicked the club off campus and called in his staff of teachers to cut the pictures out of the yearbooks with razor blades. The principal's reaction was so spontaneous that he didn't even look to see what was on the other side of the page. As a result, the school had to reprint pictures of the Spanish Club as inserts.

Christians should be treated equally under the law, but that doesn't seem to be the case in many instances today. The apparent attitude in schools these days is that everybody is equal except religious people—especially Christians. We need to stress that we *do* have the same rights to have a club on campus as any other club in school. If it is within the law to have a Charles Darwin club, or whatever, it should also be legal to have Christian organizations on campus. And if it is OK to talk about popular sports figures over lunch, why should religious discussions be banned?

Yet some schools even prohibit teens from praying over their lunches. A lot depends on the attitude of the principal. Many are under pressure from non-Christian groups, such as the American Civil Liberties Union. So Christians must be aware of their rights. Let me review a few of them.

One right is what I call *accommodating neutrality,* and is based on the First Amendment. The idea is that the government should accommodate or assist religion whenever it can. If it doesn't *assist* religion, it becomes *hostile toward* religion. The latter would definitely seem the case for Christians who can no longer pray over lunch hour, talk about God on a public school campus, or have a Christian club. Therefore, we are not being treated fairly—accommodated—

by the state. Such treatment is a violation of the First Amendment right to freedom of religion.

A 1969 Supreme Court decision ruled that high school students have the same rights as adults in public schools, with two conditions: (1) they cannot disrupt the orderly operation of the school, and (2) they cannot invade or violate the rights of others. As long as those two criteria are met, any Christian student has a right to say what he wants to say in the area of free speech.

The test case that led to the decision was a result of students wearing black arm bands to protest the Vietnam War. They refused to take them off at the principal's request, so he suspended them. The case went to court and the students won. The Supreme Court ruled that the arm bands were so closely related to free speech that the students must be allowed to wear them.

The same principle would apply, for instance, if a Christian student has a cross around his neck. He has a right to wear that cross as long as he doesn't violate the two conditions mentioned previously. He has a right to freedom of speech in public schools. He has a right to associate with his peers as anyone else would. The freedom of association guaranteed by the First Amendment applies to the Christian student every bit as much as to non-Christian students.

Students have the right to free speech, but they also have the right to hear. Let me explain. One hypothetical case people use is that citizens of the Soviet Union have a right to free speech, but only in the areas where nobody else can hear what they have to say. If students don't have the right to hear, they don't truly have free speech.

I have suggested that students start Christian clubs, Bible clubs, C. S. Lewis clubs, or the like, and then demand their constitutional right to hear the information that will be presented at these meetings. The Fourteenth Amendment says that everybody should be treated equally under the law, no matter if they are religious or not.

A myth has been perpetrated since the 1940s that anything religious on public property is automatically unconstitutional. A lot of courts and judges seem to have started believing this myth. But our founding fathers didn't believe it. No one believed it until recently, so I think the trend is just starting to turn the other way. With all the new books coming out and the rise of Christian lawyers who are arguing cases, I think we're going to see a turnaround on some of the injustices Christian students are facing on public school campuses.

Every person—including every Christian—has equal protection under the Constitution. That protection includes freedom of religion, freedom of speech, freedom of association, the right to hear, and the right to be treated equally under the law.

Related Articles

When Teachers Teach Something You Don't Believe In

JOHN W. WHITEHEAD

Christian teenagers in public schools are going to hear a lot of non-Christian values and ideas coming from some of their teachers. Parents should anticipate this problem and prepare their children to face it. The best way to prevent this problem from becoming serious is to begin teaching your child at an early age the basic presuppositions of Christianity and some of the basic presuppositions of the humanistic world in which we live today. If the child can begin to differentiate between the two at an early age, he will be prepared to handle a problem situation as a teen.

Sometimes when I speak to teens, they tell me that one of their teachers is promoting certain non-Christian teachings, but they don't know what to say in response. I tell them to educate themselves in the areas of conflicting beliefs. They can read basic Christian books, see films, and so forth.

After they have accumulated some knowledge on the controversial subject, they should question the teacher the next time he brings it up. They shouldn't be disrespectful, but they can respond with phrases like, "I just read a book that said . . ." or, "Do you realize that recent information goes against what you are saying?" or something similar that would open the topic for discussion.

Some teachers are likely to get upset and defensive, but if a student shows proper respect and interest, a good teacher will listen to what he has to say. "The way of a fool seems right to him, but a wise man listens to advice" (Prov. 12:15, NIV). If a teenager is hesitant to go against something his teacher has said, the parents should encourage the child to speak up on matters he feels are not right—especially about the Bible.

For example, I have run into several instances where a teacher has told his class that the Bible is a myth. Christian students should object immediately. They should raise their hands and say, "That is contrary to what I believe, and you shouldn't say that." If a teenager is too shy to say anything, he should at least let his parents know what the teacher said so the parents can talk to the teacher.

Parents, develop a relationship with each of your teenagers so he feels free to tell you everything that is going on at school. And also try to know your child's teachers. Stay in contact with them. Then any time a teacher expresses vocal anti-Christian ideas, you will have a line of communication open to both your teen and his teacher.

Wise Christian parents, however, will go one step further in dealing with teachers. No teacher likes to be approached only when the parents feel there is some kind of problem. It's a good idea to call each of your child's teachers once in a while just to say, "I appreciate your hard work. My teenager is learning a lot." Another way parents can support the teacher is to attend all school functions with their children as a family.

Your children will face non-Christian influences throughout their lives. By starting their training while they are young, and by helping them to deal with teachers who may promote non-Christian values, you will do your teens a valuable service as they grow into adulthood.

WHEN A TEACHER DOES NOT LIKE YOUR TEENAGER: THE FOUR Rs

1. *R*emain neutral: Don't take your child's side every time he or she resists authority.

2. *R*einforce the authority image, as well as the child's responsibility to go to the teacher and try to deal with the situation.

3. *R*esolve: If the child can't work out the difficulty, the parents may need to investigate what is happening and what has caused the conflict. Your child may very well have a legitimate complaint.

4. *R*ealize that everyone gets some less capable or competent teachers. It's a good learning experience for you and your child to deal positively with these situations.

YFC Editors

The Trauma of Tryouts

DAVID VEERMAN

Self-worth, popularity, identity, and a bundle of emotions are all involved in the decision "to try out" for a team, a play, or the chorus. Our high schoolers, immersed in the search for themselves, want to belong, to be noticed, and to succeed; and sports, music, drama, and other extracurricular activities offer abundant opportunities. But there is also the risk of failure—the chance of being "cut" for not being "good enough." Our teenagers live between these poles of success and failure.

As parents, we can empathize with this internal "tug of war." No one likes to fail. At the same time, however, we have learned the value of trying and taking risks. We also know how helpful these activities can be, offering experiences of performance, teamwork, and accomplishment, and teaching practical lessons unavailable in classes. And, when kids are busy practicing for a sport or a performance, they don't have time to get in trouble.

It is good, then, to encourage our teens' participation in a variety of activities. We must be careful, however, not to push them in order to bolster our *own* self-esteem. In other words, we must not *meet our needs* through our kids. All too common examples are the father who wants his lightweight son to be a football star and the mom who wants a beauty queen for a daughter. At the same time, we shouldn't rely totally on the way they feel at the moment. They need our perspective, enthusiasm, and encouragement. Here's what we can do:

• Take an honest and objective analysis of our young person's strengths, abilities, and interests.
• Check with school officials about the activities available (and requirements for acceptance)—these will include publica-tions, sports, music, drama, dance, cheerleading, and clubs representing all sorts of interests (languages, computers, chess, service, etc.).
• Look for other options in the community—including parachurch and church youth groups, Junior Achievement, and 4-H.
• Talk over the situation with our teen, emphasizing the priority of grades, the advantages of involvement, and the value of trying. Then lay out the options.
• If he is cut from the team or doesn't make the grade, assure him of *our* acceptance, love, and understanding, and encourage him to try again.

One more note: There is extra pressure on guys to achieve in sports, so our sons will need careful attention. Not everyone is built to be a football player. Look for other sports options. Running, tennis, and racquetball have gained popularity; bowling takes neither size nor speed; and hunting and fishing are great outdoor experiences.

The Matter of Moving

GLANDION CARNEY

In today's transient society it is not at all uncommon for families to make several moves. Yet often teens are reluctant to move, preferring to stay behind to finish their schooling at familiar schools with longtime friends.

When we learned that we would proba-bly be moving out of town, we had a conversation one night at dinner. We sat down and said, "OK, if you kids had to stay here and finish school, who would you want to stay with?" As we had anticipated, all three of them wanted to stay. They had thought, planned, and given a lot of consideration to the matter. One even sat down and wrote a letter listing families she would like to stay with and stating that the new family would have the right to punish her if she violated any of their agreements.

While we knew it would be impossible, we were at least giving our teens the freedom to think about and discuss the options. We didn't say no right away, but rather that we would look into their suggestions. Later we told the girls that while their suggestions were good, and helpful, we had decided that the *entire* family would be moving anyway. We told them we appreciated their input. Because it would be difficult to get back to see the girls and because we'd miss seeing them, we said we thought they should come with us.

It is amazing how talking and letting the kids believe they had the chance for input can help in the adjustment period. I strongly believe you should take a family vacation prior or en route to the new destination. Driving breaks up the emotional trauma of change. When your company transfers you, ask for this time.

The company will have you the rest of your working days, but an adequate adjustment by your family is crucial to your happiness. Request a week or two for the move—to plan it, take a vacation, and avoid having to rush. This time allows the family to let their separation feelings mend.

Another thing I recommend is giving your teens responsibilities to keep them preoccupied so they won't dwell on the negatives of the moving experience. For example, ask teens to pack their own belongings. Let the teens know that they are partners with you in the move.

If a teen *really* wants to stay behind, parents might consider the options of finding a support group, responsible adult, or relative for him to stay with until the term or school year is finished. It is usually easier to make friends *during* the school year, however, since other teens will naturally be interacting with your teen. In the summer months, your teen will have to take more initiative in finding peers to pal around with. As parents, keep your eyes open for likely friends for your teen. Though leaving a teen behind is probably the least desirable option, it all depends on the teen, the distance of the move, and your individual situation.

When a teen is vehemently opposed to moving and he doesn't have the option to stay behind, try empathizing and sharing your feelings about the move with your teen. Say, "Hey, moving is just as hard on me emotionally as it is on you. I understand. I'm leaving my friends and the people I love too." Let your teen see you with your friends. Let him see how you handle your separation from the people you love. Don't hide your hurt or sadness for pride's sake. That example, along with your understanding of his hurts, will help your teen deal with the situation.

We've just made a second major move to California, and our kids were really great about it. We sent off to the school for information so the kids could register for classes. We talked about the high points of the move—the activities in the community, being able to vacation and see our old friends. Dwelling on the positive aspects seemed to help.

Because children are individuals, they may respond differently to the move. Stress the good points and spend time individually with your children, as well as spending time together as a family. Rather than imposing your sovereign will on them in dictator fashion, let your teenagers be a part of the move, and the adjustment will be much smoother.

CHAPTER

30

TEENAGERS AT WORK

- How to instill the value of work in teens
- Should your teenager have a job in high school?
- How do parents guide their teen in choosing a career?

- Helping your teen compete in the world
- Facing an unethical employer
- Responsibilities and chores for teenagers: How much is too much?

From the end of World War II until the early 1970s, opportunities for young people were almost unlimited. Society cried out for more youth, better trained, to fit into various areas of opportunity in the professions, trades, or services.

We have now entered a much more difficult time. Society is changing over to a different base—one based on data, technology, and services. The raw resource of humanity is not needed as it once was, and young people are struggling with these realities. In fact, no question except the nuclear one provides anywhere near the anxiety for young people that the economic one does. Many fear they will not make it at all. Teenagers' fear of having to face the world of work is indeed a new challenge, with a good deal of uncharted water.

Why Work?

Helping Teens See Its Value

JAY KESLER

In our world, there is a strong connection between work and reward. It is no favor to young people to give them everything. We will do them far more good if we teach them to earn their way.

I saw an example of this kind of teaching at a college in the South. The student body is made up of young people from all walks of life, some very rich and some from ordinary or poor families. But whether rich or poor, every young person there is required to earn at least half his tuition. This institution believes that

young people appreciate what they work for.

Early childhood is not too soon to begin teaching young people the value of work. First, a warning: we should never put a price on love. That is, we should never withhold our love from a child because of poor performance. But material rewards —bicycles or sleds or ice skates or sweaters or designer jeans—are another matter. They should have some sort of effort connected with them.

It's the parents' duty to help young people make this connection. One way to do this is to hire the children to do certain household chores, not the normal routines of daily life which they should be expected to do anyway, but larger tasks —window-washing, oven-cleaning, wall-

662

paper-stripping. Expect them to be punctual, careful, and thorough; and pay them for a job well done, either in cash or with the item they've been wanting. By helping them make the connection between work and reward, we will be teaching them something that will be useful to them all their lives.

It is appalling to see how many young people graduate from college and have never entered the world of work. They have never understood that one has to arrive on time, stay until the work day is over, finish what one starts. They don't fully realize that if you don't do it, you don't get paid; and if you don't get paid, you don't have money to live on.

To keep this knowledge from a young person is about as cruel a thing as parents can possibly do. But some parents don't want their children to learn about work for two reasons. Some think, "If my children work, it will reflect badly on me. It will look like I haven't provided adequately for them. I want my friends to know I can afford to give them anything they want."

Other parents just find it too hard to enforce a work program, to supervise, to nag, or whatever it takes to keep the children working. All parents know that it's harder to teach children to pick up their socks than to pick the socks up for them. This is true of almost any job we ask our children to do, at least at first. But to do everything for them is to teach them to be irresponsible. It is to prepare them for disaster in adult life.

Children must be taught to work if they are going to achieve in life. I cannot encourage parents enough to teach their children, when they are very young: how to work responsibly, the value of money, the connection between work and rewards. In fact, it is wise to let seventh- or eighth-graders balance the family checkbook for a few weeks at a time, so they learn both how it's done and understand that there's an end to the money supply, that it has to be made to go around.

Zero is a real number. In a credit society, however, zero seems virtually nonexistent to many people. Young people have to learn about it. The best way to learn is to have a paying job and certain financial responsibilities. If there are no jobs available to children outside the home, then jobs need to be provided in

"STICK WITH IT"

Hot July days arrive . . . and suddenly your teenager wants to quit that summer job. "It's so-o-o boring," "I hate my boss," "They don't pay me enough for the hard work they make me do!" You realize it's a question of commitment—of completing what is started. What can you do?

First, teaching commitment starts when they are children. You must teach them to complete the jobs they are asked to do around the house. Second, they need to see commitment to a job as valuable and fulfilling. If Dad complains about his job every night during dinner, the kids will enter the working world thinking jobs are nothing but hassles. But parents can help teens see that jobs can move from being *needs* to fill immediate desires (like money for college) to *opportunities* that can bring future results. From your own experience, you can point out good reasons to stick with a job, if only for the summer: something can always be learned; it's a stepping-stone of good experience; it will look good on a resume.

By offering this kind of motivation, you can help them "sweat out" those hot summer days.

YFC Editors

the home. The system of reward and payment needs to be strict and unbending and rigid, because that's the way the world outside the home works.

Some parents fear that this will make their children materialistic. It will not. Instead, it will give them a strong sense of responsibility. I've observed many thousands of young people, and I've learned that those raised to know the value of work tend to be more responsible in all areas than those raised without this knowledge.

Chores and Responsibilities

Determining Reasonable Expectations

ART & LOIS DEYO

Work! Work! Work! It seems as if it's never ending around our house. Have you ever felt like all you ever do is clean up after your family members? And what about all that ingratitude from the kids? Does it seem like they never appreciate the things you do for them?

Any household has a myriad of routine jobs that must get done. It's best for all concerned that these responsibilities be spread out as much as possible among capable family members.

Even preschool children are able to help in a limited way, but teenagers are especially well-qualified to take the load of chores off the shoulders of Mom and Dad.

Teenagers need to be prepared for the responsibilities which they will carry as adults. In the past twenty years, many parents have been guilty of handing everything material to their children without requiring anything in return. As a result, many adolescents grow into adulthood thinking that the world owes them a living. The Bible says, "If anyone will not work, neither let him eat" (2 Thes. 3:10b, NASB).

Work has taught our children self-discipline and orderliness in their lives. It has helped produce in them the proper values, motives, and priorities. Setting a standard and the expectation that that standard be met will build character in your teens. Ours have learned patience, a servant spirit, time management, and delayed gratification as they have sought to complete a task before recreation or entertainment.

Work allows teens a time to think about some of the deep questions of life. Some of our best family discussions have followed the Saturday mornings when our two teenagers cleaned the house. When we studied under Francis Schaeffer at L'Abri, Switzerland we would study four hours and then work four hours. As we worked along with other students, we were to discuss with them what we had previously studied. Work time is good think time.

Another reason to give teens responsibilities is to keep them out of mischief. As the saying goes, "Idle hands are the devil's workshop." Without chores or homework to keep them occupied, many

664

teens become bored and set out in search of excitement—only to discover it too often in premarital sex, drugs, booze, shoplifting, vandalism, and the like.

Teens ages thirteen to fifteen should be given more chores because teens sixteen to nineteen usually have more school activities, homework, or even work outside the home. Be sure they work by the job rather than for a certain number of hours. On weekdays, tasks should take no longer than one-half to one hour. On weekends, they might work one to five hours, depending on the project.

Always begin their work schedule at a young age—gradually adding to their responsibilities as they get older. Divide the chores as equally as possible between all the children, but do not allow discussions of comparison in which one feels that he or she is not being treated fairly.

There may be times when the schedule of one or more children will not permit time for the necessary work to be done. If so, that person's work may need to be divided among the others, or perhaps the parents should pitch in to help. This can teach an attitude of servanthood.

Determine a list of regular weekly or daily household duties such as dishes, cleaning and straightening, emptying and taking out the trash, laundry, yard-mowing and trimming, pet care, making lunches for school, etc. You might want to add music lesson practice, homework, and a daily quiet time. Establish how these will be divided up and a basic time when they are to be completed. It is best to establish guidelines that will encourage the work to be done promptly and correctly. This might include making sure these responsibilities are taken care of

GETTING TEENS TO CARRY THEIR WEIGHT

My parents had a management approach to family jobs that has greatly influenced my own approach to personnel management on-the-job in my vocation as an adult. My brother, sister, and I had specific responsibilities ever since I can remember; my parents didn't wait until we were teens, then dump on us all the chores they didn't like. Each of us knew what we had to do and when it had to be done, though we could share jobs, trade jobs, or take on bigger responsibilities as appropriate. My parents also did their part, and they tried to create a balance between what was enjoyable for each child and what had to be done.

As much as possible, our work periods were arranged at the same time, so that work was the activity to be accomplished. That same time period also gave us a chance to take fun breaks together.

When the work was finished, we knew there would be some type of reward for our efforts. The reward was not always tangible, but sometimes included such things as a special privilege or a choice for a family activity or the granting of a request we had made.

My parents also had realistic goals and expectations for us as workers. We knew there was an *end* to work toward, rather than an endless list of chores for us on a Saturday morning. Maybe my parents just knew us children well enough to know what we could do, what we enjoyed doing, what motivated us, and how to make work a productive-yet-pleasant activity. The people I manage on-the-job seem to think that this is a good approach too.

Marty Grasley

before recreation, TV watching, etc.

We strongly recommend that you *not* pay by the job. Give a regular weekly allowance which they can count on, but expect regular duties to be done cheerfully and with a good spirit—as part of carrying their own weight within the family. If you pay for chores, they will lose that servant attitude and begin to expect something for everything they do.

Occasionally, your teens will ask for extra jobs to make money. You should pay extra for such jobs as leaf-raking, window-washing, cleaning out the basement or garage, etc.

Be careful of possible work overload with any one teen. Expect consistency, and follow through with proper discipline if the work isn't done. You might want to encourage them with a nice surprise or reward after a given work period in which they do an especially good job.

Following these guidelines, your teens will develop a healthy attitude toward the work that is a necessary part of life.

Related Articles
Introduction: What Do You Really Want from Your Teenager?
Chapter 30: Why Work?

Should Teenagers Have a Job?

DAVID VEERMAN

I had been in Ted's home many times. It was in the best section of town and beautifully decorated and landscaped. In addition, the family owned a place on the lake, two cars, and the latest home entertainment equipment. Every spring they traveled to some resort.

That's why Ted surprised me when he said, "I can't come to Campus Life anymore. I got a job."

"Why do you have to work?" I responded.

"To earn money for college," he said. "Besides, I want to get a car."

And Ted is typical. The American work force is burgeoning with high school students. Employers appreciate the lower wages they can pay, and parents enjoy the additional family income.

In many situations, teenage employment is a necessity because of poverty, illness, single-parent families, and so on. But in Ted's case (and many similar ones), it is difficult to understand why he *had* to get a job.

The usual parental response is that it is good for kids to work because they learn how to handle money. Parents don't have to give up luxuries or change their lifestyle to pay high school costs (car expenses, spending money, etc.). In addition, the teens can contribute to the family's financial pool. And in these days of economic hard times, it all helps.

In reality, however, our young people learn to waste money. They feel this income is theirs to spend at will for concerts, records, clothes, a car, junk food, and other indulgences.

Because of heavy work schedules, students must curtail or miss extracurricular activities at school and programs at church. Family times suffer too when employment hours conflict with mealtimes, vacations, and church. High schoolers also can develop an insatiable desire for more.

The Bible has much to say about love of money, worries about financial security, where our treasure should be, and stewardship of resources (see especially Matt. 6:19-34 and 25:14-46). Jesus must

666

be Lord of our wallets.

The solution begins with a family commitment. It is not enough to tell the children what they should do; we need to discuss money and pray together about it. It does not hurt to be honest about the family's real financial situation.

In addition, we should exemplify stewardship, tithing, sensitivity to the poor, and nonmaterialism in our lives. Our children catch our attitudes. Praying, saving, and giving together make a real impact.

Compromise is an important word also. We need to give up some adult toys and be willing to be inconvenienced. Use of the family automobile would be a good place to start. Instead of our son or daughter getting a job to support his own car, we can work out creative alternatives (scheduling car usage, raising the allowance, keeping the work to a minimum during the school year).

If he does choose to work, then bring the teenager's money into the family financial pool. Decide how it will be spent and keep a budget. Instead of a problem, this can be an exciting opportunity to apply God's Word to real life.

But do encourage your teen's involvement in church and school activities. Make a job the last resort.

Adapted from an article first published in *Moody Monthly* magazine.

HELPING TEENS FIND A SUMMER JOB

Summer again! And your teenager wants (or needs) a summer job. Teens who can walk back into previous jobs are lucky—the road is rougher for the novice job-hunter.

Motivations will vary: extra spending money; saving for college; saving for a car (or other large item); experience for the future; or simply to relieve boredom.

Your encouragement will be vital to the novice job-hunter who may not know where to begin. Don't pressure him to "find a job this week or else." Jobs *aren't* easy to come by. You can offer resources. These may be names of people to contact; suggestions concerning newspaper ads; someone to help in writing a resume; tips on how to dress; maybe a practice, "dry run" interview. However, *don't find a job for your teenager*. Don't make phone calls or do the footwork. Though job-hunting is difficult (you may remember the pain of rejection after rejection and want to spare him), once the job is secured the teen will have the satisfaction of having done it alone and will have grown through the experience.

That, in itself, is valuable to every teen.

YFC Editors

When Your Teen Runs into a Dishonest Boss

GORDON McLEAN

Through her work experience class in high school, Marilyn got a good job in a fashionable women's clothing store in a northern California city. She was excited but soon encountered some practices she hadn't counted on.

"I was quickly introduced to the way things were done by my supervisor. Employees stole items they wanted from each other's department and blamed the shortage on shoplifters. No matter how much the manager tried to tighten security on customers, the losses continued," Marilyn explained to her class and me during a discussion on ethics.

When some of the students expressed amazement at the situation, Marilyn calmly replied, "Don't you know one out of every three customers who come into a store will steal what three out of four employees haven't already taken." And she did indeed have a point—employee thefts are far more costly to businesses than thefts by customers.

Fred, another student in the class, worked at a service station. All the young employees filled their own cars with gas and thought nothing of it. "The boss was no saint. He did a lot of expensive auto repair work in his shop and asked for payments in cash so he wouldn't have to pay taxes. He was also in a barter club and did repair work in exchange for merchandise he wanted. Do you think he declared the value of those goods on his taxes? Forget it!"

It was easy to see how students, perhaps none too firm in their own moral values starting out in the business world, could all too easily go along with dishon-est practices they saw owners and managers condoning. None of these young people discussed the problem with their parents—they didn't consider it a problem. They figured that is the way things are done. When thievery is so blatant, the only suggestion I could make was to leave the firm and get another job, no easy task for a young person.

But there was another side to the story I heard in that classroom: the situation where the management was not dishonest, yet an individual supervisor or employee was. What should the working student do then?

"After all," complained one young lady, "nobody likes a snitch. If I told on my supervisor, he might get fired and all his friends I work with would give me the cold shoulder. Or if they decided to give him another chance, he could really make life miserable working there. I don't want those kinds of problems. I'll just keep quiet."

Go along with employee thefts, report them, keep quiet, or quit the job—those were the choices the students faced. None were really easy. But we did agree the right decision could be made if the students talked frankly with a trusted counselor or their parents about what was happening.

"I sure don't have to do things wrong on the job just because other people do," one student suggested. That was the key to turning the situation around, the group agreed.

Sometimes a young person has to go against the tide, face criticism, misunderstanding, and even lose a job for doing what's right. The stand he takes will depend on his own values. But it will be greatly helped by the understanding and support he gets at home and from friends, beginning with the openness to discuss the problem and standing with him when the pressure comes to drop the matter or take the easy way out.

Business dishonesty costs everybody, not "just some big insurance company," as one student described it. And its biggest toll may be in the damage it does to young employees caught up in it, a value not measured in dollars alone. A firm stand for what is right is much more apt to be taken when there are some sympathetic adults close by to listen and lend support to a youth facing the dilemma.

Related Articles
Chapter 10: Honesty Is the Only Policy
Chapter 13: Dealing with Value Conflicts

"We're All in This Together"
Teens Need Our Support
DAVID HOWARD

As parents, we need to be open with our teens, sharing with them, letting them know where we are hurting, what our needs are. It's a great help to teens to know that we are not perfect, but struggling just as they are. If they can see that we have good qualities, in spite of our failures, they are encouraged. It gives them hope that the same can be true about their lives.

By being vulnerable with our teens, by communicating that we are one with them, we identify with them. We are accepting them where they are. We are not up on some pedestal, but we are slugging it out alongside them.

Of course, there are some areas where parents shouldn't be vulnerable. In the case of a private sin, it may be just as well for us to deal with it by ourselves, particularly if the sin doesn't affect someone else.

I had sins of my thought life which I did not share with my teens. Now as our sons have grown up into their twenties and thirties, I have talked with them frankly about the problems of my thought life. They can deal with that now and it's good for them to know that I've had these problems. But it probably wouldn't have been wise for me to open up on that level when they were teens because it would have been difficult for them to integrate it.

Helping Your Teens Compete
We need to be totally supportive of our teens, especially in competitive areas—academic, athletic, or social.

I remember when our son, Mike, went to the state wrestling tournament. He was expected to do well and he did. He advanced to the quarterfinals where he lost by a point, and then went on to place high and win a medal. After the tournament, his coach came to him and said, "Mike, I really thought you were going to be my first state champion." Later on Mike said to me, "Why didn't he tell me that before? If he had told me that, I probably would have been."

The coach had enough confidence to believe that Mike could be the state champion, but Mike didn't believe it because the coach didn't tell him. Mike didn't think he would make it that far.

There are two ways to look at what happened with Mike. Some people would say that if a teen sets his goals too high and then doesn't make them, he will be disappointed. They would say that a coach telling Mike he could be the state champion would put him under too much pressure.

They may be right. My feeling is to let a teen set high goals and if he makes them fine; if not, then deal with the disappointment. I think if the coach had told Mike he could be the state champion, it would have given him the little bit extra needed to carry him over.

We need to be totally supportive when our teens compete. We need to let them know that they can do it so they will have the confidence to try. My feeling is we should encourage our children to set high standards and try to reach them. But if our teens don't achieve their goals, we should say, "That's OK. You've done your best."

Guiding Your Teen to the Right Career

DAVID L. McKENNA

Parents usually wonder what they can do to help their teen make good, solid decisions regarding a career.

Begin by the simple process of *noting your child's gifts.* When we do career counseling, we first ask if students want to work with things, numbers, or people. Usually this interest can be ascertained early in a child's development. Each of these areas is valuable, so don't force a "numbers" child to work with people. Begin to encourage your teen in the area which he feels comfortable. Praise any evidence of success in that field.

For example, my assistant has an eleven-year-old son who has an uncanny ability within the field of math. On Thursday afternoons he is enrolled in a course in model rocketry at the University of Kentucky, as an adjunct to his regular schooling. You can almost see a career line developing from the gift of the boy coupled with his parents' funding of the opportunity.

My son, on the other hand, is a "people person." I saw this developing when he became the assistant director for our church's Vacation Bible School. Little kids in town flocked to him. He is learning to develop his gift.

A second suggestion is the *need for counseling in the school system.* Parents need to meet their teen's teachers and sit down with them to discuss natural abilities. Look at standardized test scores and see where your child scores highest and lowest. This will give a sense of direction.

Above all, *encourage your teen to keep his options open and build a strong base.* Then he will be adequately prepared when the time and opportunity come along.

Develop and maintain a genuine inter-

670

est in the total development of each of your children. Your model for them is important; your influence, indispensable. It's wrong, though, to expect that young people will follow in the career path of their parents. Dynasties seldom pass from one generation to another.

Don't push your child into a career. But help him determine, with God's guidance, what his gifts and abilities are. Then encourage him to develop them.

TEENAGERS AT COLLEGE

- Preparing teens to survive at college
- Which college is right?
- Your teen doesn't want to go to

college—what are the alternatives?
- The high cost of a college education—who pays?

The values that young people establish at college and the friendships that they make there will be among the strongest in their whole lives. The choice of a college will mark a person forever. He or she will never be the same again after a particular college experience. This can be true in a positive sense as well as a negative one. Because of the strong influence for good or for ill of the college experience, it is vitally important that we and our children choose carefully the colleges they will attend.

Preparing Your Teenager for College

BRUCE B. BARTON

Recent statistics reveal that eighty percent of the young people who drop out of college do not drop out because of academic problems. Most drop out of college because of failure in "life-management" skills. They do not know how to manage their time and personal lives in such a way as to complete the academic program. What can you as parents do to help prepare your teenager for college?

Though there is a lot your teenager can do in preparing clothes, books, and desk articles needed for college, probably the most important preparation can be done together. Here are some suggestions of what both parents *and* teenagers can do as they're preparing for college.

1. Obtain the October issue of *Campus Life* magazine. Every October, *Campus Life* runs a "Guide to Christian Colleges" which contains information on the top Christian colleges across the country. It's also loaded with tips for survival in the college atmosphere. Buy a subscription for your teen. All the articles are helpful in dealing with both the Christian and non-Christian world.

2. Parents should keep in close contact with the teen's high school guidance counselor, who can advise students as to what coursework will be needed to prepare for college. Teenagers should not wait until their junior or senior year to nail down prerequisites that are needed.

3. Parents and teenagers can attend college nights at the high school.

4. Students should talk to the college representatives visiting the high school. Most high school guidance departments have notices of when college representatives are going to visit. Parents, encourage your teenager to make appointments.

5. Teenagers can find out the admis-

sion requirements for each school. What are the required tests and when do they have to be taken?

6. Parents and teenagers should visit colleges before a decision is made. See if you can arrange to have your teen stay in the dorm. Discuss impressions of dorm life with him. See if the high school has checklists of what to look for in a college and what to take with you.

7. Contact the financial aid departments of the colleges your teen is interested in. Your local high school may have free publications on organizations that sponsor grants or scholarships. Take a look at what financial aid is available.

8. Spend time talking with your teenager to decide the one result he wants from college. Years ago, many college students would say they attended college to get a well-rounded education. Today, most students consider they're at college to get a job. If your child knows what he is looking for from a college education, he is more likely to get it.

Developing Life-Management Skills

You've all met the high school student who made you wonder, "Does he have enough sense to come in out of the rain?" Some of them may not! Many families have produced children who live in a "never-never land" of deferred responsibility. As a result, when they face the great challenges of the freedom and independence of college life, they do not know how to make appropriate choices. They can't manage their lives in such a way to survive the rigorous college schedule. Parents can get a running start on preparing their children for college by withdrawing most rules during their senior year of high school. This will provide a laboratory to see how they will react without rules. You might try to arrange for your child to work at a summer camp or take a summer job in another town while living with a relative to see how he will do when he is in an environment without your control.

Here are some of the main areas that cause teens to drop out of college:

1. *Poor sleep habits.* Many high school seniors think they will stay up all night when they find no curfew or parents standing over them to make them come home. In many cases, students stay up late to finish school work and visit with friends. If it becomes a pattern to stay up late every night and begin their studies around 11 P.M., to sleep-in the next morning, and to often take naps, they may be headed toward poor health and skipped classes. Observe your teen over the summers and vacation periods. What are his sleep habits when he has more freedom to sleep-in? Sit down with him and discuss the consequences of not observing a regular sleep schedule.

2. *Mismanagement of money.* Failure to manage their money wisely leads many college students into trouble. The most important thing to do would be to establish a budget with them early in their high school years so they have some practice managing money on their own.

3. *Lack of good diet.* Many college students sleep-in, skip breakfast and other meals, and resort to junk food. They overuse caffeine and sugar. They don't get enough fruit and vegetables into their diets. The results of poor diet do not show up immediately since most young people are energetic and strong, but improper eating habits can lead to more serious maladies later on if not corrected. If you sense that your teenager is having a problem in this area, make sure he knows how to cook and let him plan some fast but inexpensive and nutritious meals.

4. *No priority management.* Many people talk about time-management problems. In most cases, they are priority-management problems. Teach your children the importance of setting daily, weekly, and monthly priorities. Have them arrange their priorities as to A, B, and C. "A" are those priorities that must be done and must be done today; "B" are those priorities that can be done after all

the "A"s are done. "C" are those priorities that are least pressing and may have to be put off until another day.

College-bound students need to know how to plan a balance of work and relaxation. They need to plan some time for exercise every other day. Students would do well to plan a regular routine for their work week. By planning a work week of sixty hours, most students could not only survive college, but do it extremely well. Many adults in the education and management fields have to work sixty hours every week of their lives. Most college students are in class only fifteen hours each week, though it may vary according to their academic program. If the student worked 8 A.M. to 10 P.M. every day, Monday through Friday, allowing three hours for meals and relaxation, if they worked five hours on Saturday, and did not work at all on Sunday; then they would have put in a sixty-hour week with no late nights. This, of course, would have to be modified if a job or athletic schedule is also involved.

Students can manage their time and work regularly. If they do, they're going to get as much as three hours of study time for every hour of class. Problems for many students are that they take breaks between classes to read magazines, check the mail, watch television, or goof off with their friends. As a result, precious time slips by and they don't feel the pressure to start studying until late at night.

5. *Underdeveloped study skills*. Students need to develop good study habits. If there are opportunities for seminars or clinics in your school, encourage your teenager to take part in them. There are special tips on how to read a book effectively, how to take proper notes, and how to outline. Encourage your teen to participate in a speed-reading course. Remind him that repeated practice over a long period of time is better for his studies than cramming the night before. Encourage him to make initial contact with his professors, get to know them by name, and make sure the professors know him by name. Perhaps you can give your teen an experiment. Ask him to go to the civic library to find information that you need, perhaps a comparison in a consumer's guide on refrigerators or information on carburetors. See how well he can function in the library to know if he is going to be able to survive academically at college.

Tips for Maintaining Spiritual Life

Many times the Christian life declines at college because of failure to observe good life-management skills. Some spiritual problems could be solved by eight hours of good sleep. Poor diet and lack of exercise can also lead to a depressed outlook on life. In general, some tips for maintaining a vital spiritual life would include:

* Encouraging regular times for reading the Bible and prayer
* Becoming involved in an active church
* Getting into a small group for support and prayer
* Contacting Inter-Varsity, Navigators, Campus Crusade, Youth for Christ, or Young Life, and finding out whether they have groups active on campus
* Getting a catalog from InterVarsity Press, and purchasing books that might be appropriate to the needs they feel.

Preparing for college includes preparing every phase of life for new responsibility. Begin by helping your teenager develop good habits in high school that will insure a successful college experience.

Related Articles

Should Your Teen Go to College?

DAVID L. McKENNA

We must face the reality of a society that has been called the "Information Age." People growing up today must be committed to lifelong learning. College is becoming less of an option and more of a necessity.

Unless God calls a teen otherwise, I think he should plan on attending college. God has given each of us unique gifts and it is our responsibility to develop those talents to their fullest potential. Proper education is a part of that commitment to become all God intended us to be.

For example, I have a son-in-law who is doing his graduate study at the University of Arizona in exercise physiology. His brother is brilliant and his father is a nuclear physicist. At first, his family wasn't sure that he had what it took to go to college. But he became a Christian and decided to attend a Christian college. He graduated from college with a strong B average, decided to apply to graduate school, and is now on his way to his doctorate. Though he'll never be first in his class, he has gifts of motivation and persistence.

I believe we're in an age when God expects us to develop our gifts to the maximum. Even if a teen is an average student, he must develop himself to the fullest. We make a false assumption that there is only one kind of intellect.

There are many dislocated workers today who have nothing to fall back on. They worked on developing skills for a lifetime, only to be displaced in the work force.

College may not be for everyone, but there are so many alternatives within the

---

SHOULD YOU PRESSURE TEENS TO ATTEND COLLEGE?

Many parents struggle with deciding how much pressure to put on their teens to attend college. Rather than force decisions, I like to ask my children, "What are your options?" Of course, a trust relationship and open communication are essential prerequisites for parents and teens to come to the right decision for each child.

The question invariably arises, "What about staying out of college to work for a year?" A general principle can't be mass-marketed for individual teens. But generally speaking, in my experience with colleges, I've found that it's usually more difficult for those students who wait a year to come back to school. Many never come back at all, and a large percentage of those who do eventually drop out.

I encourage teens to get as broad and solid an educational base as possible so God can use them for options in the future. Otherwise, it's easy to dead-end early in the race.

David L. McKenna

college setting, that if you look hard enough, there is probably one to suit your teen's needs.

Besides job security, college is important as a grounding base for Christian citizenship. I think a teen should attend a Christian college for at least a year or two. Faith and learning are integrated through biblical studies, the humanities, and the social sciences.

If a teen chooses a narrow vocational track, consider the support systems through the home or church whereby he can come to grips with what's outside the narrow definition of his vocation. Teens need to grapple with moral and ethical issues and learn to make decisions in a society which has an overload of information. As someone has said, we may be producing a generation of technical giants and moral dwarfs.

Related Article
 Chapter 31: Preparing Your Teenager for College

How to Choose the Right College
KENNETH O. GANGEL

Assuming that most Christian parents take an active role in helping their teens select a college, here are eight options to consider before making a choice.

1. *Size:* How large or small are different colleges, and what size of school does your teen prefer?

2. *Location:* Is a distant location preferable to a school that is close to home?

3. *Cost:* How much money will be spent for tuition, books, living accommodations, etc.?

4. *Programs of study:* Which schools offer the program your teen is interested in?

5. *Types of students:* What kinds of people are attracted to which schools? What kinds of people does your teen want to have as friends? Does he wish to be part of a Christian student body? Or is evangelism in a non-Christian setting a personal goal?

6. *Faculty:* Which schools attract a quality faculty?

7. *Accreditation:* Which schools are accredited by a recognized and legitimate agency?

8. *Philosophy:* Which schools have the educational and religious philosophy that best suits your teen's needs?

I believe parents and teens need to constantly seek God's will through personal and corporate prayer regarding college. If family devotions are possible, one of the best times for them is when your teen is in high school. Seek God together about what the next few years hold.

I also recommend that you write away for as many college catalogs as you need to guide your decisions about college. I am overwhelmed at how rarely students read catalogs before choosing a school. They come to campus with ideas and notions totally alien to what the catalog and student handbook say.

There are a number of books that help in choosing a college. The best, in my opinion, is *How to Choose a Christian College* by Webber. But before you buy one of these books, be sure that it's been updated with current information.

Money, of course, can be a discouragement when trying to select a private school. I'm appalled at college costs, and many schools are on the verge of pricing themselves out of the market. This is an area which demands seeking God and His best purposes; spending money for education must be between each individual and the Lord. Perhaps your teen wants preparation for missionary service, but you do not have the money. God may want you to channel some of what you give to foreign missions into your child's education. But decisions such as this must be led by the Lord.

I also recommend visiting campuses. Sometimes catalog pictures mislead students into thinking a campus is beautiful when in reality it is not. Pictorially, college brochures and catalogs tend to put their best foot forward. You need to check them out personally. I know Christian parents who have taken two weeks in the summer to visit six or seven college campuses with their teenagers. They have arranged ahead of time for their kids to talk with department chairpersons, admissions officers, etc.

Above all, I believe Christian parents should take an active role. In my daughter's case, for example, I recommended she go to a college I had suggested, based on our ability to afford the school. She had chosen another college— one that was totally out of reach financially—and I said, "Well, you don't have to go to the school I selected, but you know we can't handle the finances on your preference. Now what are you going to do?"

She agreed to at least look at the first college. So we visited the campus and her final decision was to attend. In her second year, she had the opportunity to transfer to her first choice but she chose not to.

A MAJOR DECISION

Suzie is a sophomore at ESU (Enormous State University). So far she has done quite well in all of her subjects, and now it's time to declare a major, narrowing her field of study. Suzie chooses "Art Literature." When she shares her plans with Mom and Dad, however, they are less than pleased, demanding, "What kind of job can you get with that?"

This is the classic confrontation between an idealistic nineteen- or twenty-year old and her practical parents. Suzie wants to study what she enjoys, but her mother and father are concerned about "marketability." Other confrontations may involve career choice (e.g., the son wants to be a youth minister, but Dad wonders about the job security and earning power of that profession), a decision to extend education (or cut it out), or a number of other possibilities. The question is whether parents should push a particular field of study or vocation.

Certainly Mom and Dad know their sons and daughters better than anyone else. From changing diapers and watching their first steps to sharing decisions, wiping tears, and teaching about the "birds and bees," they have lovingly reared their children. They want the very best for the kids, and they have a good idea where they will succeed and what will bring them happiness. Mix this in with a healthy dose of adult pragmatism (a perspective learned by experience), and speeches pour forth.

Our children, however, are quickly learning what it means to be "grown-up" and independent from Mom and Dad. They are testing *their* wings and making *their* decisions about *their* lives. And, with a perspective limited by age and experience, it is difficult for them to understand the conflict.

The answer to the dilemma rests in these short verbs: let go, love, and lead.

Let go. First, as loving and responsible parents, we must allow our college-aged children to be adults and make their own choices. They will also be the ones who will have to live with the consequences. This doesn't mean walking away from their lives; in fact, we should let them know years before that this freedom of choice will be theirs and what it will involve. We should also share some guidelines for their decisions and insights into the lessons we learned by *our* mistakes. Obviously, if we see a disastrous decision on the horizon, we can take corrective action, but this will be the exception.

Love. The entire process must be bathed in love. This means total and unconditional acceptance of them as persons and as our sons and daughters, whatever they choose. We may disagree with the choices, but still we love them.

Lead. Carefully and lovingly, we can and should share our insights, explaining how we feel about them, what we know about their personalities, gifts, and interests, and what we have learned about the "real" world (e.g., someone has to pay the bills; what normal living experiences include; where marriage and family fit in; etc.). Hopefully, we will have led by example and our values have been caught (perhaps that's the source of their idealism, and we should see it as a compliment).

We have so much to offer our kids—let's not close their ears. And they can teach us—let's listen!

YFC Editors

Paying for Your Teen's College Education

It's Still Affordable

JAMES C. GALVIN

For a few parents, paying for their teenager's college education is a matter of long-range planning and writing checks from the savings account. For most, however, the full implications do not hit until their teenager has selected a college. They sit down with an estimate of the tuition, room, board, and travel expenses. They multiply this by four and reality comes crashing in. "Our house didn't cost this much. It took us twenty-five years to pay for this house. How are we ever going to pay for college?"

Fortunately, we live in a nation where

any person who truly desires a college education can afford one, thanks to generous financial aid policies. We also live in a country with a strong history of private higher education. We have many outstanding Christian colleges from which to choose. Though a college education may appear impossible to fund for those who have not saved, you can afford a college education for your teenager through: (1) careful selection of an appropriate school to reach the academic goal, and (2) using a variety of means to reach the financial goal.

You may find it helpful to think about schools as being in three categories: (1) community colleges, (2) state universities, and (3) private schools.

Community colleges have been designed to bring higher education to the people. In general, they are very low-cost and allow for students to live at home for the first two years and take classes on a part-time or evening basis, if needed. This is the lowest cost of the three categories.

State universities are neavily subsidized by the state and federal governments to allow young people to attain a college education. These tend to be the medium-priced alternatives. While tuition is relatively low, room, board and travel expenses do add up if you live far away. Crossing state boundaries also adds to the expense of the tuition.

The United States has a strong tradition of private schools in higher education. In fact, in most states there are more private schools than public schools. But because most of them lack government subsidies, tuition and other expenses are normally higher at the private schools. In many cases, however, support from alumni and church denominations has kept the cost of tuition competitive.

Each of these three alternatives has unique advantages which may be viewed as more or less valuable by you and your teenager. The school your teen selects depends on his academic goals and values about the setting. Some parents ask, "Since money is such an important factor, and state universities also lead to a degree, how can we afford to send our teenager to a private school?" Other parents respond, "How can you afford not to? These four years are important in shaping the heart and mind of your teenager. Should you trust these years to an institution where so many are antagonistic toward a Christian world view?"

Christian parents should not automatically send their teenagers to a Christian school. Instead this should be a reasoned and informed decision. Some students will grow better spiritually on a Christian campus and other students will grow better spiritually on a secular campus where their faith is constantly being tested. It is important to give strong consideration to your teenager's desires on this matter. Career goals will also have an important influence here. A student wanting to pursue a career in architecture or solar engineering, for example, will find very few Christian schools with any type of program in these fields. In order to make a wise decision, get together with your teenager and, given all the options, make a list of every school that would be a realistic possibility. Use your high school or community library to get more information on nearby schools. Write to distant schools to obtain catalogs or brochures with more information. As your list narrows, try to visit the campuses together with your son or daughter. This will greatly diminish wrong impressions and give you ample opportunity to search out what your teenager is looking for in a school.

How Do the Bills Get Paid?

If you are approaching this situation without a savings plan, the first step is to decrease expenses by selecting the lowest cost school which will be adequate for the academic goals and values of you and your teenager. The second step is to find ways to increase income. There are at least four ways to reach your financial goal.

The most common way is for both the teenager and the parents to chip in to a common pot to cover expenses. They then use the school bill as the goal to accomplish this together. Often this is split. For example, the parents might cover tuition, room, and board, while the teenager is responsible to cover travel and all incidental expenses. A division like this helps a teenager to become more responsible for a part of the bill. Questions often arise as to whether a student should work while in school or concentrate on studies. This depends on the academic load of the student, his degree of involvement in extracurriculur activities, and the availability of employment during breaks and summer vacations.

Some parents feel strongly that their teenagers should work while they are at school to help cover expenses, and others feel strongly that while at school they should spend their time studying, rather than wasting time with a low-paying job. They feel that they can put in their share of work during vacations and after they graduate. Another problem arises when a teenager can not secure a job over vacation. As some parents have faced this, they have encouraged their teenagers to make a job, such as baby-sitting, mowing grass, and washing and waxing cars, as opposed to sitting and watching TV all day or standing in line filling out job applications all summer. Though the hourly pay for odd jobs may be lower, it does encourage resourcefulness.

A second method is for the family to begin a new side business to help pay for college educations. These are often seasonal businesses where only summer help is needed. Some parents have begun landscaping companies and others have started stores that would only be open during the summers. This becomes a project to pull family relationships closer, as well as a true educational experience. Evaluate your family's resources. Per-haps you can make small wooden toys and sell them at shopping centers, or start a mobile tune-up service where the mechanic goes to the car rather than bringing the car to the mechanic. Look for unmet needs in your immediate neighborhood and see if you can find a way to fill them.

A third option is to make your teenager completely responsible for covering the cost of his college education. This can be handled through part-time work, part-time school, and financial aid. A mature teenager can handle this responsibility if he is self-disciplined and goal-oriented. Occasionally, he may be able to secure a job with an employer who has educational benefits and would cover the entire tuition for a college education. However, these types of educational fringe benefits may not be available through corporations in your area.

The fourth option is to rely on loans or scholarships to meet your financial goal. Student loans, especially those financed by state and local governments, are a good deal. Often there is little or no interest to be paid while the student is in school full-time. On graduation, the repayment plans do not place a great monthly burden on the student. If there are interest points, parents sometimes cover the interest charges while the student is in school and pass them on along with the bill after graduation.

What about Scholarships?

True scholarships are few and far between. Those that are based on athletic or musical ability are rare and competitively sought after. Scholarships based on financial need are accessible to everyone who is in financial need and takes the time to complete the financial aid form. Even if you are independently employed, and need to hire an accountant to complete the financial aid form, this is well worth the effort if you think you may qualify for a grant. If turned down for financial aid in one school, complete forms for other schools. The criteria for selection and amount of available funds often differ between schools.

Scholarships can also be used as a recruitment method. One school may charge $5,000 tuition yet have limited financial aid and scholarship packages. A comparable school, however, may charge $7,000 tuition but offer your teenager a $1,000 scholarship based on academic or athletic ability. This is often successful in recruiting students because some people do not examine closely the total yearly cost for attending schools. They also enjoy the prestige in having their teenager receive a scholarship. Similarly, some schools offer very low or free tuition but charge very high rates for room and board. So examine total costs closely before accepting scholarships.

Besides opportunities for scholarships and financial aid, all of the expenses for a year, including travel, need to be taken into careful consideration. After an academic goal is set, the least expensive school that is appropriate should be selected. Totaling all the expenses will help you establish a financial goal to reach with a combination of summer work, loans, and scholarships. If the costs seem unattainable or unrealistic, the options of two years at a community college and student loans should be explored again. Both of these programs have been instituted by federal and state governments to make higher education affordable. The introductory classes taught at community colleges are often of higher quality than those at state universities. The interest rates and repayment schedules for student loans are very reasonable. Going in debt for an education may not appear very attractive, but it makes more sense than going in debt for an automobile.

The preceding guidelines are helpful if your teenager is finishing high school and you have not been able to save for college expenses. If your child is just beginning his teenage years, however, start saving now. This is best done with tax-deferred savings plans which are available through banks and investment counselors. If you start saving now for this expense, your child's choice of schools will not be limited by finances. If your teenager should decide not to attend college, the money can always be used for covering the costs of a wedding or helping with a down payment on his first home. Start saving now and you won't need to study this article in a few years.

Related Article
Chapter 31: How to Choose the Right College

INDEX

690

692